Date Due

When Television Was Young: Primetime Canada 1952–1967

A decade after the first Canadian telecasts in September 1952, TV had conquered the country. Why was the little screen so enthusiastically welcomed by Canadians? Was television in its early years more innovative, less commercial, and more Canadian than current offerings? In this study of what is often called the 'golden age' of television, Paul Rutherford sets out to dispel some cherished myths and resurrect the memory of a noble experiment in the making of Canadian culture.

He focuses on three key aspects of the story. The first is the development of the national service. He examines the critical acclaim won by Radio-Canada, the struggles of the CBC's English service to provide mass entertainment that could compete with the Hollywood product, and the effective challenge of private television to the whole dream of public broadcasting.

The second deals with the wealth of made-in-Canada programming available to please and inform viewers – even commercials received close attention. Altogether, Rutherford argues, Canadian programming reflected as well as enhanced the prevailing values and assumptions of the mainstream.

The final focus is on Marshall McLuhan's question: What happens to society when a new medium of communication enters the picture? Rutherford's findings cast doubt upon the common presumptions about the awesome power of television.

Television in Canada, Rutherford concludes, amounts to a failed revolution. It never realized the ambitions of its masters or the fears of its critics. Its course was shaped not only by the will of the government, the power of commerce, and the empire of Hollywood, but also by the desires and habits of the viewers.

PAUL RUTHERFORD is Professor of History at the University of Toronto. He is author of *The Making of the Canadian Media* and *A Victorian Authority: The Daily Press in Late Nineteenth Century Canada*. He is also editor of *Saving the Canadian City: The First Phase 1880–1920*.

PAUL RUTHERFORD

When Television Was Young:
Primetime Canada 1952–1967

UNIVERSITY OF TORONTO PRESS
Toronto Buffalo London

© University of Toronto Press 1990
Toronto Buffalo London
Printed in Canada

ISBN 0-8020-5830-2 (cloth)
ISBN 0-8020-6647-X (paper)

Printed on acid-free paper

Canadian Cataloguing in Publication Data

Rutherford, Paul, 1944–
  When television was young

  ISBN 0-8020-5830-2 (bound) ISBN 0-8020-6647-X (pbk.)

  1. Television broadcasting – Canada – History.
  2. Television programs – Canada – History.
  I. Title.

  PN1992.3.C3R87 1990   791.45'0971   C90-093148-5

This book has been published with the help of a grant from the Canadian
Federation for the Humanities, using funds provided by the Social Sciences
and Humanities Research Council of Canada, and with the assistance of the
Canada Council and the Ontario Arts Council under their block grant
programs. Publication has also been assisted by a generous grant from the
University of Toronto Women's Association.

To Stephanie & Jennifer
Two of TV's Children

Contents

Graphics

Charts

Figures

Frames

Tables

Acknowledgments

The progress of this project from conception through to completed manuscript has depended upon the goodwill and support of many people. Two deans of Arts and Science at the University of Toronto were generous enough to grant me an allotment of monies in each of my five years as chairman of the Department of History to support my research efforts, a sum that was supplemented on occasion by modest grants from the university's Research Board. The Ontario Arts Council, the research branch of the Canadian Radio-Television and Telecommunications Commission, and the Social Science and Humanities Research Council of Canada provided additional sums to support aspects of the project. The University of Toronto allowed me an administrative leave in 1987/8, which enabled me to complete the manuscript. The Canadian Federation for the Humanities supplied funding to cover some of the costs the University of Toronto Press had to face in publishing the manuscript.

Much of the research money went into hiring a bevy of research assistants. I was fortunate: only one of the people I hired proved inadequate to the job I assigned. Listed here are the talented souls who worked hard to uncover research material of one kind or another: Stephen Baker, Lyne Gascon, Brigid Higgins, Phillipe Landreville, Nancy Lee, Margaret McCallum, Stephen Strople, Jocelyn Thompson, and Diane Way. Two of these people deserve special thanks: Stephen Baker, then a psychology student, organized and completed all of the viewing analysis of Radio-Canada programming in Montreal; Stephen Strople, at the time a doctoral student at York University, did the same thing with CBC programming in Toronto, and prepared (sometimes along with Brigid Higgins) superb analyses of all kinds of shows that provided me with more information than I had any right to expect.

Researching television requires access to records held by a variety of different bodies, not all of which are geared to meeting the peculiar needs of the scholar. Even so, very few of my requests were turned down. I mention here the people and the institutions that went out of their way to assist the project: Ward Cornell, Frank Peers, and Johnny Wayne agreed to interviews; Professor Ross Eamon of Carleton University gave me access to interviews he and his team of assistants had collected for the CBC Oral History Project; Ernie Dick, Andres Kestseris, Sylvie Robitaille, and Jana Vosikovska, of the Moving Image and Sound Archives, as well as Ghislain Mallette, of the Federal Archives Division, guided me through the extensive broadcasting records held by the National Archives of Canada in Ottawa; John Coleman, then a CTV vice-president, gave me a lunch as well as some documents and some leads; the Bureau of Broadcast Measurement and A.C. Neilsen Company of Canada allowed me to utilize their data held by the networks and the Moving Image and Sound Archives; Françoise Icart of the CRTC's Research Branch directed me to some material in the commission's library; Bill Ross shepherded me through CBC headquarters in Ottawa, and Arthur Laird, Director of Research there, graciously allowed me to cart away extra copies of documents, photocopy many others, and even supplied a machine and operator so that I could copy these more rapidly; Elsie Butkovsky and Victoria Wilcox of Audience Services at CBC-Toronto helped my assistants collect information on schedules, and Elizabeth Jenner, the reference librarian at CBC-Toronto, opened up her invaluable files of program data; Bernard Normand (Montreal) and Martin von Mirbach (Toronto) arranged the viewing sessions for my assistants. I am especially grateful to Richard Wright, once an archivist and administrator with CBC in Toronto, who has since moved into the production game: over the years he helped me in all kinds of ways to contact people and to obtain important records, including copies of CBC programs, for the purposes of private research. We also shared thoughts over beers and lunches during the years of research and writing.

Unfortunately, there aren't too many people in academe interested in television history. So, I've worked largely in isolation from other scholars. Still, I did correspond with Professor Gérard Laurence of Laval, who has produced a massive CRTC report on the first years of TV at Radio-Canada. I shared findings and opinions with Professor Mary Jane Miller of Brock who was well into her study of CBC-TV drama even before I began. I've tried out a number of conclusions on fellow members in the Association for the Study of Canadian Radio and Television; on audiences at the University of Western Ontario in the School of Journalism, at a popular-culture conference organized by professors David Flaherty and Frank Manning in April 1988, at talks to the McLuhan centre and the Southam Fellows at the University of Toronto, as well as on my own students and colleagues. And I wish to thank the anonymous appraisers for the Press and the CFH for the time they took to read the manuscript–I've incorporated a number of their suggestions in the book.

I gratefully acknowledge the permission given by BBM, Nielsen, and the CBC to include their material in this book.

Finally, I'd like to express my thanks to three special people. Virgil Duff, my editor, was involved with the project from its inception as something quite different; he stayed with the book during the years of delay and change, always willing to give me wise counsel and comfort to ensure it would indeed be completed. Eva Hollander, a good friend, was my secretary when I was chairman of the Department of History, and she arranged things to allow me additional time for research and typed up an assortment of documents to speed the project–losing her services was one of the few things I regretted about retiring from the chair. Margarita Orszag, my companion, has lived with this project, occasionally helped out with viewing programs, and always listened (if not always respectfully) to my views on one finding or another. Her deep suspicion of TV and her commitment to the arts were an invaluable foil to my enthusiasm for the ephemeral products of popular culture. I've been very lucky to have the benefits of her critical intelligence.

PAUL RUTHERFORD
April 1989

WHEN TELEVISION WAS YOUNG

Introduction:
A Personal Journey

My family first got a television set in May 1958, in Calgary, when I was at the ripe old age of fourteen. That was a bit late, at least from my point of view. I'd been introduced to television back in England, by a kind neighbour who'd invited me over to watch children's programs on her tiny set. Even then I felt miffed that we didn't have our own TV, putting it down to the poverty of my parents. Much later, in Canada, I told them I was deprived, since more and more of the kids I knew had access to a TV. I recall one instance of acute suffering. While playing with some chums, I was asked what I thought of Elvis Presley who'd just appeared on 'The Ed Sullivan Show' to the acclaim (or horror) of millions: I had to admit, much to my chagrin, that I didn't have the foggiest notion of who he was. What embarrassment to have to show ignorance of the newest star in the land. My parents, who were unimpressed by TV and looked upon it with some suspicion, weren't moved by my chagrin.

Their attitude changed when my father had to undergo a lengthy period of convalescence as a result of an operation. Friends of theirs, a couple with two TV sets, lent us one for a month. The marvellous gift was installed on a dressing-table in the bedroom. I was allowed to join my parents on the bed to watch the new array of entertainment. The next month we rented a set, and in October, after a move to Edmonton, purchased our own nineteen-inch portable, which went into the living-room. We even began to eat in front of it. Another family had fallen under the spell of the tube. Never again would I suffer the ignominy of being TV-less.

I wasn't one of those children addicted to the 'idiot box,' not at first anyway. Watching television didn't interfere with homework, reading, or playing. My parents found no need to regulate what I watched, perhaps because they usually sent me to bed soon after 8:00 PM on weeknights. I do remember sampling the assorted delights scheduled by the Canadian Broadcasting Corporation, such as 'Cross-Canada Hit Parade,' 'Wayne and Shuster,' and CBC teleplays, since my parents had a liking for the Canadian style of one-shot drama. What I never quite realized, of course, was that many of my favourites were in fact American imports. I was a great fan of 'Howdy Doody' (though I don't recall whether this was the Canadian or the American version) and later 'The Mickey Mouse Club.' I was allowed to watch 'Ed Sullivan' on a Sunday night with my parents. But what really caught my fancy were the assorted dramatic series: I gained my first impression of Latins, for instance, from viewing 'The Cisco Kid,' a stereotype that was later confirmed by 'Zorro.' This growing fascination, first with a host of westerns, then with crime shows, and eventually with professional sagas about doctors and action shows about war and spies, turned me into an addict, mostly of made-in-Hollywood television. There seemed nothing surprising about this, to me or to my friends, which in itself is a statement about the perception of things Canadian among young people growing up in the late 1950s and early 1960s.

I wasn't aware that something momentous had entered my life when my parents finally acquired a TV set. Television had so swiftly become a fixture in the home that I thought no more about its significance than I did of the importance of the toaster or the toilet. Even when the name Marshall McLuhan began to be bandied about at university in the mid-1960s, I took little notice – he seemed just another of that crew of crackpot theorists who flourished at the time, unusual simply because he was Canadian (but hardly as interesting or important as George Grant, whose *Lament for a Nation* was a hot topic of student discussion). Yet, at this time I was approaching the end of one of those 'big stories' of the era that often seem outside the ken of contemporaries and are intelligible only to a later generation. That story, of course, was the rise of television and its emergence as the most potent source of mass culture in modern society. By the mid-1960s television had taken on a definite shape and had already begun to work its magic on the rest of our lives. It is this story that I intend to tell here, one that began in 1952 and concluded in 1967, a decade and a half later – the period of black-and-white television, which, in some respects, was a different kind of visual medium from the one that supplanted it after the spread of colour and cable. Still, the cut-off date is a trifle arbitrary: readers will find that at times my account of a particular event or issue concludes before 1967 or extends into the early 1970s, to suit the idiosyncrasies of history.

The story is, in fact, an amalgam of three distinct subjects. The first of these, of course, is the career of the noble experiment of a national television service (francophone and anglophone, public and private) that strove to supply viewers with a made-in-Canada brand of entertainment, news, and views. Right from the beginning, the television scene was in an almost continuous state of upheaval, first because of TV's expansion across the country and later because of the competition between the CBC and the CTV networks. The record of achievement was certainly mixed. Canada did have one of the most extensive and sophisticated systems of delivery in the world by the end of the 1960s. The francophone service was something of a triumph, because Radio-Canada (the French-Canadian version of the CBC) proved able to produce a lot of programming that critics praised because it expressed the 'soul' of French Canada, and with only limited resources. But the anglophone service fell victim to the 'villain' of the story, Hollywood, which after the late 1950s was the centre of a programming empire extending throughout the continent and across the world. Only in the area of news and public affairs was the CBC really able to claim much of a victory. If English-Canadian television was 'sold out,' as Herschel Hardin has charged in *Closed Circuits*, that happened before the massive spread of cable television in the 1970s, which his book treats.[1]

The second subject grows out of a vague if widespread nostalgia for the so-called golden age of television, the era before the arrival of colour and cable. Indeed, as early as 1961, intellectuals and journalists began to talk as though television had passed through its moment of glory. How strange that seems. Doesn't a 'golden age' usually come towards the end, and not the beginning, of the career of a cultural enterprise? Well, in the case of television, novelty apparently begat a brief era of experimentation and fostered an innovative art-form that was soon snuffed out (or was it perverted?) by the dominion of commerce. Formula and convention came to reign over the production process, thus ensuring mediocrity as well as high profits. This book will explore the 'art' of television (in itself a contentious phrase), broadly defined to include both the styles and the messages programmers and producers offered viewers. I will touch on the virtues and the defects of the 'highbrow' critique of television as a source of cultural decay. Along the way, I will also consider the arguments of Morris Wolfe (among others) in *Jolts*, an extended essay on television that celebrates what he sees as a special Canadian tradition of documentary realism. But

I'm most intrigued by what was on the air, rather than its relative quality, and why the nature of this early programming changed over the years. Reflections on 'the golden age' usually smack too much of the personal tastes of the observer.[2]

The third task is to answer what I call McLuhan's Question (with a little help from Harold Innis): what happens to society when a new medium of communications enters the picture? McLuhan may not have been the first to ask the question, but his book *Understanding Media* certainly brought it to the attention of people inside, and especially outside, academe. This question was the one I missed when I lived through the era. My answers owe very little to Marshall McLuhan. I do recognize the imaginative genius of the man, and I relish his puckish wit, but I find his technological determinism and his mysticism off-putting. My mentors come from the realms of sociology and semiotics, where hosts of scholars have been at work to uncover the dynamics and the import of communications. Here my main interest is in television in Canada, rather than just in Canadian television, since viewers watched an enormous amount of imported programming. What most intrigues me is that old theme of change and continuity. How did individuals, groups, and institutions in Canada respond to the arrival of television? What new rituals of life emerged, and which of them died away in the process? Did any change in the patterns of authority or the exercise of power in Canada result from television? My answers cast doubt on the exaggerated, and all-too-common, assumptions about the revolutionary effects or awesome powers of television: TV has had a greater impact on the private or personal spheres of life than on the public arena, where its chief role has been as a usurper, taking over tasks once accomplished by other means, often other media. This is more a story of adjustment than revolution.[3]

The book is styled as 'a viewer's history,' meaning that I'm especially interested in what people saw in the way of home-grown shows when they turned on the TV set. This subject has received surprisingly little attention from scholars in Canada, except for the pioneering work of Gérard Laurence on the first five years of francophone television and the equally original study by Mary Jane Miller on CBC-TV drama in English. That's why seven of the chapters here (grouped as 'Part Two: Genres') deal with the content of television, specifically with the major varieties of made-in-Canada programming, and why each contains one close reading of a particular broadcast. The sequence of chapters is roughly chronological, looking at each genre as it attained prominence (and sometimes waned) to conclude with the last major experiment in the mid-1960s in the field of public-affairs programming. Early on, I decided it was best to concentrate on only a limited number of samples of the various genres prominent on the small screen, a fortunate decision since a lot of what was aired in the 1950s and 1960s hasn't been saved, either in Canada or in the United States. Much of television is constructed according to a relatively small set of designs (meaning when you've seen one sitcom, you've seen them all). Besides, the broad nature of my study required information about the culture of television rather than all of the varieties of, say, horse operas or talk shows. Watching thousands of hours of programming just wasn't necessary. The handling of the samples, by the way, didn't replicate how we ordinarily look at TV. It wouldn't do to sit in front of a television set and watch one show after another, as do the infamous 'couch potatoes.' The readings are based upon a particular technique of viewing analysis, derived from semiotics, which requires breaking down the broadcast into some of its smallest components of meaning, or signs, and then using these to re-create the ever-larger sets of meaning, the mythologies and ideology. This book includes two appendices, on the schemes of content and viewing analysis, for those readers interested in how I approached the study of TV's offerings.[4]

Still, even 'a viewer's history' requires some discussion of the economics, institutions, and personnel of television if the reader is to understand what happened. (The existence of Frank Peers's *The Public Eye*, the definitive account of the politics of television, allowed me to avoid much discussion of the role of government.) That accounts for the three chapters on the building and the character of a Canadian system of TV (grouped as 'Part One: Structures'): these chapters treat the rise and fall of the networks, the American presence, battles between managers and artists in the CBC, how a schedule was made, the maturing audience, the responses of outsiders, and the like. There is an amazing wealth of material in periodicals, government reports, and above all the CBC archives at both the National Archives of Canada and the Ottawa headquarters of the Corporation. (Sometimes I had the impression that the CBC produced as much paper as it did broadcasts.) These findings have been supplemented with the results of a number of interviews with people active in television during the events discussed.[5]

The rest of the book delves into the effects of television. The first chapter, 'Expectations,' considers what people in the immediate post-war decade thought television might be and do, as well as the career and views of the most outstanding Canadian media theorist, Marshall McLuhan, which extends the account into the 1960s. This chapter amounts to an essay in intellectual history of a sort, using material from magazines and books of the time. The final chapter, entitled 'On Viewing,' deals with the habits of television's audiences and the impact of television on people. These findings are based on an enormous collection of ratings data and audience surveys prepared to serve advertising agencies and programmers, a host of anecdotes by contemporaries who paused to reflect on their experiences, and a wide assortment of mostly non-Canadian studies of the audience response to TV. It attempts to lay bare what television, as a rule, meant to and for individuals, and why it was so successful. The brief afterword puts the Canadian story in the wider context of the history of television elsewhere, and after 1967. There I've sought to come to grips with the overall nature and significance of TV.[6]

Much of the argument in this book focuses upon two aspects of the 'big story.' First of all, the book is chiefly concerned with what was on during the evening hours, and most especially primetime (7:00–11:00) when viewing totals reached a peak. By 1960, primetime viewing had become the single most common cultural experience of Canadians, a fact that often caused distress among social critics. Good or bad, the power of television derived from the extent of primetime viewing. A lot of research time for this book went into collecting and analysing records of the continuous evening schedules, and the program data, of the CBC flagship stations in Toronto and Montreal, the CTV outlet in Toronto, and the three American networks. Second, the largest amount of space here is spent on CBC programming, both French and English but with greater emphasis on the troubles of the English service, which strikes me as the more interesting of the two tales. Not only was the CBC the dominant network throughout the era, in some places the only service available, but it was the main source of made-in-Canada programming, even after the arrival of independent television. Less attention has been paid to the American invaders (whose story is well covered in the existing literature) and 'their' local network, CTV, even though both were crucial to the qualified failure of Canadian television in English Canada. What we need to know most about is home-grown programming, if we wish to assess the cultural import of the medium.[7]

Readers will detect my sympathy for the CBC, especially the English service, which struggled to meet an impossible mandate as well as to satisfy public demands. I didn't begin with that view – but the evidence was convincing: while the CBC made mistakes, its stubborn persistence and efforts in the realm of programming were impressive. Besides, whatever the promises of private television, the independent stations and CTV produced little in the way of memorable entertainment and their record in news and public affairs wasn't especially exciting in the 1960s. It used to be a sad joke that the only unique dramatic series the private network offered was the kids' show 'The Littlest Hobo.' Even so, the CTV schedule proved immensely popular with viewers because it did bring them a lot of American hits. My own viewing in the 1960s was more often of the private stations, first in Ottawa and later in Toronto, than the CBC outlets. People like me were the main reason that CTV was overtaking the CBC as the major network in Canada's cities by the end of the decade.

My feelings about television may not be so obvious. I trust that I've avoided the dangers of nostalgia, even if this book has the taint of a personal journey through my own past. There's definitely a particular kind of pleasure, rare for a historian, in being able to talk about one's own experiences. I don't claim to be especially pro or anti television. My addiction, born in the late 1950s, died away about twenty years later. Most of what appeared on the screen in the 1970s, and what is offered up nowadays strikes me as pretty boring stuff. It can hardly be counted among the glories of our way of life. Nor do I subscribe to any demon theory of television. I don't sympathize, by and large, with the typical views of highbrows or cultural nationalists, then or now, about the baneful influences of TV. I can find evidence that it fostered social or moral decay, at least as defined by an earlier generation, as well as proof that it buttressed the existing order, especially the Canadian versions of capitalism and democracy, either of which (always depending on one's perspective, of course) could be an object of blame. Neither offends my bourgeois sensibilities. The rise of television was an enormously important phenomenon: the new medium did work to express and to shape our culture. The lost opportunities and the controversies are now in our past, even if we still live with the consequences. It is possible to distance oneself from these events, and to enjoy a fascinating story. That's what I've tried to do.

1

Expectations

The trouble with television is that it's hard to lie about it fast enough to keep up with the truth.

Fergus Mutrie, 1950[?][1]

The coming of television wasn't really a surprise. During the war journalists and admen throughout North America had predicted the happy event when celebrating what was often called the 'world of tomorrow,' an imminent millennium of abundance and comfort that science would create to enhance the lives of ordinary people. In September 1943, Creighton Peet entertained readers of *Maclean's* with a wild story about a typical home of 1955 – full of such wonders as 'movable walls,' an 'electric-eye burglar alarm,' a new 'blanket-rolling device,' a 'facsimile newspaper printer,' a dishwasher, a temperature-control unit, and, of course, a television set. A month later, he followed with a tale extolling 'television's promise for the future': 'a front-row seat in your home for theatre, movies, sports and news events.' It was the prospect of 'a new pageant of entertainment' brought 'right into your home,' in the words of a Canadian General Electric ad of 1945, that made the notion of owning a television set so attractive to the millions.[2]

The Setting

There's no doubt that television arrived at the right moment. Post-war Canada was enjoying good times, after all those years of depression and war. The economy was booming, employment rates were high, real wages were increasing, and people were on a spending spree. The 1951 census told the happy tale of a rising Canadian standard of living by comparing the current situation with that of a decade earlier: half of Canadian households now had an electric or gas stove (up from 40 per cent), about the same number of refrigerator (up from 21 per cent), two-fifths a vacuum cleaner (up from 24 per cent), three-fifths a telephone (up from 40 per cent), and a whopping three-quarters a 'powered washing machine.' The most spectacular gains were registered in the rural parts of the country, where prosperity and electrification allowed farm families to play catch-up with their city cousins. The material conditions of life would improve even more for most Canadians during the 1950s and 1960s.

The press, movies, and radio were also enjoying their own touch of affluence in those halcyon days before the advent of television. Advertising expenditures had risen appreciably, keeping pace with the Gross National Product, from almost $10 per capita in 1946 to nearly $19 in 1952. Newspapers and magazines still picked off by far the largest share of that money, some $157 million or 57 per cent of the $274 million of net advertising expenditures. Daily newspapers were riding especially high, both as the premier news medium and as profit-makers. By 1951 the 95 dailies had a combined circulation (3.6 million) slightly greater than the total number of households (3.3 million). That was striking evidence of their mass appeal, an appeal that had grown since the end of the war. While some newspapers were upscale, such as the Montreal *Gazette* and the Toronto *Globe and Mail*, most others were definitely middlebrow, perhaps with a bit of sensationalism as in the case of the biggest dailies, *The Toronto Daily Star* and Montreal's *La Presse*. The typical Canadian daily was a specialist in local and regional news, and offered as well national coverage created mostly by the news agency Canadian Press and international stories originated by foreign, especially American, agencies, plus a number of features (such as comics), also thanks to American syndicates. It was a formula that worked very well.[3]

Magazines couldn't claim such great success. One contemporary source listed around 650 Canadian periodicals with a total circulation of 10.6 million in 1951. The most popular (at 3.9 million) were the consumer magazines, such as *Maclean's* and *Liberty*, though not far behind (2.5 million) was an assortment of rural publications for farm and town readers, focusing on the interests of an older Canada then beginning to pass away. What troubled all magazines was the competition from enterprises based south of the border, including *Life, The Saturday Evening Post*, and even *Time Canada*. Indeed, American magazines seemed to dominate the market, overflowing news-stands, popular with all kinds of readers, and setting the standards and style that their Canadian rivals had to emulate. Even so, Canadian magazine publishers could earn enough to keep going, if not always to prosper as did their brethren in the daily press.

There wasn't any Canadian movie industry to speak of. That had been a casualty of Hollywood competition back in the early 1920s. The National Film Board had a reputation as an educator but never as an entertainer. Not that the ordinary Canadian seemed especially bothered: he or she paid to attend the movies 256 million times in 1952, generating a revenue of more than $100 million, which worked out to an annual rate of 17 visits for every man, woman, and child. In fact 'going out to the movies' was then at the peak of its popularity: never before, and never again, would it be so common a ritual of Canadian life for people of all kinds. What they saw on the screens, of course, was mostly the Hollywood product in all its vulgar and enchanting splendour, perhaps minus a few scenes clipped out by the provincial censors.[4]

Last, but hardly least, came radio. It too was extraordinarily popular: the census discovered that nine out of every ten households in Canada had a radio set in 1951. Indeed, radio was enjoying what later would be called its 'golden age,' offering listeners an enormous range of program that made it the most diverse of all the mass media. True, it was the grand music box of the nation – a study conducted by Charles Siepmann in 1949 found that roughly half of the output of Canadian radio was musical – but the music was 'serious' as well as 'light,' and then there were newscasts, talk shows, plays, drama series and serials, comedies, and so on (the most mixed programming occurred at night when audience numbers peaked). Radio had become the cheapest form of mass entertainment for the family. Primetime, in fact, was a radio phenomenon that television would only later bring to its climax.[5]

How Canadian was radio? The government's intention back in the 1930s when the Canadian Broadcasting Corporation was organized had been to ensure that radio would be not only Canadian but a powerful agent of national unity and expression as well. And the CBC had created three networks, using public and private stations to deliver two complete services, one French (usually called Radio-Canada) and the other English (the Trans-Canada network), plus an evening-only service (the Dominion network). The CBC programmed for both the general public and minorities, offering a mixed fare that included some choice American shows – from the Sunday 'Metropolitan Opera Broadcasts' (French and English networks) to such hits as 'Lux Radio Theatre' and 'Fibber McGee and Molly.' Yet the

CBC faced increasing competition for the attention of the ordinary listener from private radio stations, and notably from the independent community and local stations in the country's big cities. These made use of a lot of recorded and transcribed material (mostly American in origin), averaging nearly three-quarters of broadcast hours in 1949, supplemented by local live programming, which was geared to the presumed mass taste. According to tallies of numbers of listeners, at least in English Canada, the top bands and songs and drama shows were nearly exclusively American. So the answer to the question wasn't clear at all.[6]

A couple of features stand out in the brief survey. First, Canadians were already well-served by a series of mature mass media supplying all kinds of material to fill leisure hours and even to make working more pleasant. Second, many of the messages offered people were either imported from the United States or modelled on American originals. Third, what was variously called 'mass' or 'popular' culture, the culture of bubble gum and baseball and Hollywood, was everywhere. This last had recently become a cause of considerable worry among the highbrows living in Canada's ivory towers.

The March of Culture

Among the novelties of the post-war era was something that Ron Poulton, the 'See-Hear' columnist of the Toronto *Telegram*, once (9 September 1952) in passing called 'culture with a capital cultch.' In the previous decade or so, the country's intelligentsia had been seized by an urge to associate, whether for mutual admiration or for protection: witness the birth of La Société des Écrivains Canadiens (1936), Les Amis de l'Art (1942), the Canadian Writers' Foundation and the Canadian Arts Council (1945), the Canadian Music Council (1946), and the Canadian Humanities Association (1948). The first sign that a lobby was at work came near the end of the war when representatives of the arts and letters presented a brief to the Turgeon Committee, a parliamentary group formed to investigate the shape of post-war Canada, the wisdom of government action on behalf of Culture. A few years later, that leading sophisticate Vincent Massey published his tract for the times, *On Being Canadian*, which proclaimed the need for the Canadian people to recognize the claims of Culture and for the Canadian state to sponsor the growth of Culture. Then, in 1949, the government established the Royal Commission on National Development in the Arts, Letters and Sciences to study the problems of cultural progress, the universities, and broadcasting. The commission was headed by none other than Massey, and he was joined by three academics (plus one lonely engineer) – the ivory tower was in charge. All manner of educational, arts, literary, and musical associations submitted briefs in support of their particular causes to this 'culture probe.' The commission's report, both lengthy (517 pages) and literate (opening with a quote from St Augustine), became the new bible for the apologists of Culture.[7]

One of the causes of the crusade was a sense of grievance. That found expression in some of the passages of the Massey Report, notably the chapters entitled 'The Scholar and the Scientist' and 'The Artist and the Writer,' where Canadians were told how scholars were underpaid, painters laboured on without proper recognition of their dignity or worth, and writers suffered the most extraordinary loneliness. The whine was amplified in the more blatant kinds of special pleading. So La Société des Écrivains Canadiens lamented that writing was treated 'as a luxury, therefore useless, and the writer himself as a kind of parasite or dreamer incapable of aiding the real progress of the nation.' Perhaps a bit wryly, the noted liberal gadfly Frank Underhill commented that there was 'no other country in the world where intellectuals suffer from such low repute as in Canada.' Underlying the litany of complaint, of course, was a demand for recognition, for a place in the sun.[8]

The intelligentsia had taken up the task of civilizing Canada. The drive to build a bigger and richer Canada had left a 'cultural vacuum': Hilda Neatby, historian and Massey commissioner, thought that a survey of the Canadian scene could suggest only that the country was 'a nation of barbarians.' Where were all the museums, art galleries, theatres, and concert halls that must humanize life? Too many Canadians valued only mines, factories, and the range of goods they produced. 'Material things become ends in themselves,' warned Arthur Lower, another historian, 'and the opium of the people turns out to be, not religion, but mechanical appliances.' Enthusiasts even employed the rhetoric of the Cold War to support their case, arguing that an appreciation of 'the finer things in life' was vital in any battle for men's minds.[9]

The emphasis was very much on 'the finer things,' meaning the traditional and the folk arts, serious music, sophisticated thought, the pure sciences, and, for some people, the avant-garde movement. The Massey Commission's definition was especially enlightening: 'Culture is that part of education which enriches the mind and refines the taste.' That led to a brand of chauvinism which was both élitist and Canadian: a celebration of painting, literature, music, sculpture, philosophy, and scholarship, all made in Canada, reflecting the experience of the country as well as meeting the high standards set in the international world of culture. The mission of civilizing the country was to be accomplished with money: by building museums and cultural centres, subsidizing arts groups, paying better academic salaries, funding university research, and on and on. Here the state had to lead, crafting a policy that would encourage a general awakening of Culture across the land. Such dreams did win a measure of support, at least among some newspaper editors and politicians, although there persisted worries about the rise of cultural socialism and a feeling that 'the finer things' were really frills.[10]

The champions of Culture were often upset by the increasing power of 'mass communications' and the subsequent spread of something more and more frequently called 'mass culture.' Both terms had recently entered the lexicon of the times as a result of studies of the social and personal effects of cinema and broadcasting. In a special report for the Massey Commission, B.K. Sandwell, editor of *Saturday Night*, made much of the way in which the machine now ruled over the human mind: it was the printing press, the movie camera, and the radio microphone that effectively controlled 'the diffusion of ideas and ideals' and the 'transmission of culture.' The brief introductory section, 'Mass Media,' in the Massey Report lamented the passing of traditional ways and folk arts, from the popularity of organ music in village and urban churches to the death of the feisty, old-time country newspaper, as a result of the concentrated impact of mass communication. These passages were suggestive of a particular mood, a feeling of nostalgia for a world that was now lost as well as a kind of fear about the new world created by the telephone, the gramophone, the movies, and radio.[11]

The man most exercised by the impact of mass communications was Harold Adams Innis, a professor of political economy at the University of Toronto. During the war years, after a distinguished career as an economic historian, Innis had suddenly 'revealed,' so to speak, the central importance of communications in the making and unmaking of civilizations. He drafted a huge manuscript, incomplete even at a thousand pages, on the history of communications, out of which he took material for papers and eventually for a series of books that appeared just before his death in 1952: *Empire and Communications* (1950), *The Bias of Communication* (1951), and *Changing Concepts of Time* (1952). There, he elaborated a series of complicated arguments about how the inherent bias of media, whether towards preservation over time (like stone) or towards proliferation across space (like paper), fostered distinct social systems. He saw a contrast between the oral tradition and the written tradition, favouring the oral tradition (which he felt the university should embody) because it fostered a more humane approach to life than print, which fostered excess in everything, including cruelty. Indeed, in some of his essays, notably 'A Critical Review,' he displayed an absolute horror of mechanized communication as the source of myriad cultural ills, and he believed that the United States was, by the mid-twentieth century, the chief centre of this technology. One minor theme in Innis's grand version of human history was the plight of Canada: he feared that the massed power of the American media virtually doomed Canada to live out a life designed in New York, Washington, and Hollywood. It's difficult to gauge just how influential Innis's ideas were in those days, although his impact on Marshall McLuhan is well-known. There's no obvious evidence that he had any major impact on people outside the university. Even so, his pessimism wasn't at all uncommon among highbrows, although most were much more fearful of the content than the mode of communications.[12]

What frightened was the swelling amount of readily available trash, be that comic books, Mickey Spillane novels, soap operas, Hollywood movies, or pop music: such material could well drive out taste and quality, defeat Culture, and debase the public mind. Here the crusade blended with the assault by American highbrows, such as Dwight Macdonald, on the social consequences of modernity. This 'root cultural problem' led the continentalist Frank Underhill to urge an alliance between Canadian and American highbrows in defence of excellence. But his fellows were too concerned with the prospect of losing their souls to place any faith in such an alliance. Mass culture appeared to be an essential ingredient of an American civilization, noted French-Canadian historian Michel Brunet, and its presence in the dominion had virtually converted English Canada into a satellite of Hollywood and New York. The answer, or so the Massey Report had outlined, was a made-in-Canada culture. That would insulate, better yet inoculate, the Canadian people against the perils of vulgarization *à la* America. It was a line of argument that managed to sway even such a doubting thomas as Walter Dinsdale, a prairie Conservative member of Parliament worried more about morality than about culture.[13]

Who was the enemy? In 1951 Marshall McLuhan published *The Mechanical Bride*, a sprightly monograph analysing the images and stereotypes manufactured by the advertising, magazine, and publishing industries in North America. The book better fitted the American highbrow tradition than it did any particular brand of Canadian nationalism – it had nothing to say about Canada as a country. Ironically, given his later fame as the guru of the television age, McLuhan largely ignored the electronic media and bitterly attacked popular culture. *The Mechanical Bride* was actually a collection of probes that tried to chart the extent of cultural decay that had resulted from the cheapening of taste, tradition, and life by the media. A zeal for profit had led the media masters to exploit the basest instincts of man: lust, greed, envy, power-seeking, and a fascination with death. The consequences were the rise of the alienated, passive man; the increasing power of conformity; the dominance of a gospel of consumption; the degradation of the human experience. Commerce and technology were the chief villains in this conspiracy, a view that gave McLuhan's critique a distinctly anti-modernist slant. At the same time he upheld the vision of the artist as a social prophet who must lead a hapless and helpless industrial man out of the wasteland of depravity. That smacked of a kind of intellectual snobbery which was all too evident among highbrows. While McLuhan's approach may have been striking, and his views were certainly extreme, the substance of his message was already clichéd.

The highbrows were eager to blame 'commercialism' for a good portion of the cultural sins of the age. That line of argument won them the sympathetic ear of an assortment of other groups, from labour leaders to consumer activists and Marxists, to moralists, who might have other reasons for distrusting the ways and power of the capitalist. It seemed that the devout materialism of so many Canadians for so long had allowed business too much freedom to determine the country's character. 'Nothing is sacred to the man who is trying to turn a penny,' asserted an angry Arthur Lower. Such a person would give the people whatever they wanted, no matter how rubbishy, to earn a buck. Little wonder that Hilda Neaby found much of the opposition to the Massey Report in English Canada had its roots in a 'barbarism' cultivated by commercial interests. (Neatby, by the way, was engaged in a related dispute, through the publication of *So Little for the Mind* [1953] and *A Temperate Dispute* [1954], over the nature of modern values and their impact on education, for the trends of the times threatened to undo the wholesome influence of the humanities on young minds and so upon society.)[14]

This sort of vitriol reflected the élitism and the alienation of many a highbrow. They took on airs: they thought themselves better than most people, certainly than most business types – or so it appeared. 'Democracy is not to be equated to the dominance of the mass,' warned Lower. A brief to the Massey Commission by the Public Affairs Institute of Vancouver spoke of that segment of the population 'which includes the best brains, the leaders of thought and culture, the people who are advancing civilization or even dragging it forward in spite of itself.' From this standpoint the high-brows were locked in a struggle for power, endeavouring to challenge the authority the business class exercised over the Canadian character.[15]

The most significant of the prizes was undoubtedly broadcasting. One view of history held that the creation of a national broadcasting system, and in particular of the CBC in 1936, had been a triumph of Culture over Commerce. That victory had to be protected against the increasing power of private radio as well as the escalating campaign for 'free radio' launched by the Canadian Association of Broadcasters, the instrument of private enterprise. *Canadian Forum*, very much a highbrow organ, kept a close watch on the radio scene throughout the 1940s, alert to any sign that private radio was making gains or that the CBC's pre-eminence was threatened. The intelligentsia looked upon private radio as little more than a conduit for commercials, popular music, and American imports. The CBC, by contrast, offered food for the mind and the soul: the inauguration of 'CBC Wednesday Night' late in 1947 on the Trans-Canada network gave highbrows a three-hour block of commercial-free time from 8:00 to 11:00 PM – modelled on the British Broadcasting Corporation's celebrated 'Third Programme' – where all their delights could be showcased. True, as the Massey Report indicated, there remained room for improvement. There were complaints in the briefs submitted to the commission about the mediocrity of some of the CBC's popular programming. Yet it shouldn't surprise that the CBC had earned a reputation as a vital agency of cultural progress and a crucial defence against Americanization. Nor was it hard for the highbrow to believe that the CBC could sponsor, or already had promoted, 'a general upgrading in taste' among the populace.[16]

So it was quite possible to see the government's television policy as another highbrow triumph. By the end of the 1940s, the Liberals had come under increasing pressure from the press, the CBC, private radio, and the public to do something about television. There was a distinct sense that, with the Americans rushing ahead to develop a nation-wide service, Canada was being left behind: by the end of the decade, there were actually four U.S. networks offering primetime TV to American homes. On 28 March 1949, J.J. McCann, the minister of national revenue, announced that the CBC was authorized to commence national television services in French and English, using public and eventually private stations. The obvious purpose was to still the public clamour for television now. But McCann also emphasized that the aim, as it had been in the case of radio, was to ensure Canadians would shortly begin to receive made-in-Canada program-ming. Two years later, the Massey Commission would be even more emphatic in its declaration that television must be under the command of the CBC. By this time, of course, the imminent prospect of a Canadian television had given rise to a wide-ranging discussion of the pros and cons, the nature and significance, as well as the purposes of the new mass medium.

Looking at Television

The first Canadian debate over television began right after the war, extended into the early years of television broadcasting, and ended in the mid-1950s, when a new royal commission, set up to investigate the broadcasting scene in Canada (the Fowler Commission), reported to Parliament in 1957. The debate was carried on largely in popular and quality magazines by both journalists and academics as well as in the briefs submitted by voluntary associations to the Massey Commission and Fowler I (so named because a second Fowler Committee looked at broadcasting in the mid-1960s). It was informed by what were taken to be the lessons of experience outside Canada, most especially in the United States. But it remained highly speculative since people weren't constrained by much actual knowledge of the new medium. 'We didn't really understand what television was all about, most of us,' admitted Finlay Payne, a CBC official, when interviewed much later about those early days. 'It was a case of the blind leading the blind really.'

What radio could do, couldn't television do even better? Hyperbole was a hallmark of the speculation about television. One writer after another proclaimed that television was the greatest invention in the field of communications since the discovery of the printing press. It quickly became commonplace to repeat, as did Frank Chamberlain in *Saturday Night* (18 November 1944), the widespread assumption that 'television and facsimile will one day revolutionize culture, the arts, education, communication and industry.' The language of awe was liberally employed to describe the new innovation: 'electronic miracle,' 'miracle medium,' 'home marvel,' 'cette merveille technique,' 'the ultimate instrument of mass communication.' The Montreal *Gazette* (7 September 1952) greeted the launching of Canadian television with the editorial headline 'REVOLUTIONS IN EVERYDAY LIFE' – though what 'revolutions' television would bring, it couldn't specify.

Much of the early commentary focused on the hardware of television, partly to explain to readers how the marvel worked. But that also evidenced a fascination with video as one of those frontiers of science where the technology was constantly evolving. The new 'expert' would move swiftly from a note about, for instance, the mysteries of coaxial cable and micro-wave to a discussion of pay and colour television, UHF, or occasionally that precursor of satellite TV called 'stratovision.' Nor did this sort of musing ever die away completely. In 1956, for example, *Maclean's* published a breathless article called 'The Next Ten Years of TV' by Barbara Moon that surveyed a new range of technological improvements, including colour television, designed to bring more pleasure to North Americans. This theme in the contemporary literature suggests how widespread was the worship of technology in the post-war world.[17]

Yet attention had soon shifted to a discussion of the exact nature of television. What had to be explained was the almost unbelievable appeal of TV in North America: consumers were purchasing sets like crazy. Lorne Greene, at the time one of Canada's radio celebrities, noted how people tended to describe television in the light of their own experience. Was it 'a new branch of motion pictures,' 'an extension of Broadway,' 'a better way to sell soap,' or a form of radiovision? The answer was yes – to all questions. Television seemed able to handle anything and everything: news and views, ads, music, drama, sports, education. Its capabilities were restrained only by the limits of the imagination and the problem of expenses, for it was estimated that a TV program cost from five to ten times as much to produce as a radio program. That versatility led Alphonse Ouimet, then the CBC's general manager, to argue that television could bring to the home most everything that 'radio, the cinema, the stage, the arena, the billboard, the display window' had brought to people in times past. What television did, suggested one brief to the Fowler Commission, was to amplify the impact of whatever it purveyed, most especially when it focused on personalities, and to cloak all content in 'un réalisme merveil-leux.' Television was the acme of broadcasting.[18]

People often exaggerated just how gripping it was to watch television. In truth writers popularized the myth of the helpless viewer. It all came back to that old saying, 'seeing is believing': the fact that people saw, and did not just hear, a broadcast had to give it extra impact. One early discussion meant for housewives pointed out that whatever the imperfections of the medium or the programs, 'television fascinates. A good evening of it completely takes over your household.' By 1956 Gérard Pelletier used the analogy of the prison experience to explain the nature and impact of viewing. The typical viewer was held captive in his own home by the dancing images on the small screen. The viewer was 'désarmé, passif, livré sans défense á ceux qui ont capté son attention.' The brief submitted by the Confédération des Travailleurs Catholiques du Canada to the Fowler Commission (written by Pelletier?) contained the same analogy, this time with a comment that television commanded a viewer's total attention and that it consumed an enormous slice of a viewer's daily time, so its messages could easily penetrate into his or her mind. A group of doctors observed that TV's impact on the eye and ear was 'arresting, authoritative, and personally intimate' and that its psychological effect had been described 'as bordering on "hypnotic" '[19]

These assumptions produced ambivalence as well as awe. Witness the comment by Fergus Mutrie, in 1950 the CBC's director of television for Toronto. 'Someone has said that the topics most talked about today are the atom bomb and television – the difference between the two being that we know how to use the bomb.' That kind of observation reflected the other side of the worship of technology, a worry about the effects of the new marvels. The trouble was that no one, not even those who disdained television, could escape its influence, a conclusion Alphonse Ouimet highlighted when he called upon the 'cultural and intellectual elite' to control this new powerhouse. Nearly everyone who wrote on the subject repeated in some form or other the cliché that television must be an agent of change, and perhaps of revolution, that it seemed to have a social momentum all of its own. Many would have agreed with the extraordinary claim of CBCer Neil Morrison that 'no other single factor will be so influential in shaping the future life of this country as television.' Both Gérard Pelletier and his fellow journalist André Laurendeau, for example, saw television as the instrument of a modernity that challenged the very fundamentals of French-Canadian society. Pelletier emphasized how the onset of television meant the end of isolation, the constant and unstoppable invasion by the outside world of the home, the countryside, Quebec, and Canada. It all sounds a bit like the arrival of what McLuhan would later call the 'global village.'[20]

The Massey Report worried about the 'unpredictability' of television. That was the rub. Another cliché of the times, repeated ad nauseam, was the claim that television had as much potential for good as for evil: it was 'neither depraved nor divine' and thus it could be either 'un facteur de progrés ou de recul culturel.' It all depended upon the actual use made of television. For a time Canadians suffered a mild case of the jitters, caused more by imported fears than by any hard knowledge of television's effects. That wasn't just because foreign publications brought horror stories into the country. Americans also came up to explain the challenge of television: one, radio producer Norman Corwin, gave a talk on the Trans-Canada network entitled 'What NOT to Do with TV,' and another, writer Gilbert

Seldes, warned 'Television Will Get You' even if you never own a set. Besides, Canadian commentators looked outside, especially down south, to see what television was doing, and they repeated the worries of Americans about the changes wrought by the video revolution.[21]

There was quite a selection of ills that had to be avoided. Number one on the highbrow's list was the threat of further cultural decay. It was essential to prevent 'la dictature du goût de la masse,' or television would drive out Culture. Indeed tasteless programming would foster immaturity, immorality, and conformity. There were certainly enough examples of silly and even dangerous shows on the air in the United States. Did we really need a Canadian version of Milton Berle's video vaudeville? Then there was the peril of 'cultural annexation' should television become merely a conduit for the programs of New York and Hollywood. A prophetic article written in 1949 by Jean Tweed for *Saturday Night* worried that what had happened with radio transcriptions might well happen with telefilms: Canadian television producers would be unable to compete in the same market with the polished but cheap imports of American studios. That would leave Canadian television with 'about as much originality as a mimeograph machine.' A variation on this theme was the French-Canadian concern that television might strengthen the forces of anglicization in Canada.[22]

One of the chief actors in the drama, private radio, was not especially interested in trying to avoid the peril of Americanization. Rather it was attracted by the notion of delivering television to an eager public, as was clear at the outset of the debate. The key question was not what kind of television, decided a writer in *Canadian Business* in 1949, but when television would come. Business spokesmen saw television as another industry that should be ruled by the ways of the marketplace. What intrigued F.R. Deakins, president of RCA Victor Co., was the hope that delivering television to the Canadian people would make for a business bonanza in which broadcasters, electronics manufacturers, advertisers, and artists would share. What exasperated Canadian Marconi Co. was the needless delay occasioned by the government's unwillingness to set private radio free to bring Canadians the benefits of television. It seemed a sin against nature: the delay had caused 'serious loss to Canada' and threatened to kill 'initiative' – 'we cannot make our contribution to the country's welfare.' The result of freeing the 'showmen' of private radio, according to Jack Kent Cooke, president of Toronto Broadcasting Co., would be television suited to the tastes of the public. Had these showmen not 'brought AM radio to its full, successful flowering'? Cooke even went so far as to urge the wisdom of a free trade in cultural products. 'If we are ever to have a

Canadian culture,' he argued, 'it will come only as the result of full exposure to what is undoubtedly the fastest rising culture in the world today – that of the U.S.A.' Private enterprise would make television into a new source of entertainment, catering to a mass audience and giving that audience 'what it wants': a lot of diversion, made in Canada or imported from the United States.[23]

The possibility that commercial interests would gain control of television sent shudders up the spine of an admitted 'academic "highbrow" ' such as Arthur Lower. His 1953 diatribe 'The Question of Private TV' simply updated the old charges against private radio to warn against any surrender to business demands. First of all, he foresaw a new wave of commercialism as a result of private television: after all, should he own a station, he 'would obviously go in for sex, liquor advertisements, the soul-stirring battle cries of perfervid religious groups denouncing their opponents, undertakers' advertisements, and all that sort of thing.' Second, he predicted that viewers would be offered only 'vapidity': 'No political talk, no discussion of anything controversial, no modern music, certainly no good music – that would bore those who buy the advertised soaps.' Lastly, the dominance of private television could only mean 'the Americanization of the new medium.' This view, with variations, was widely held among nearly all the intellectual, cultural, labour, and farm spokesmen who debated the issue. Little that was good could be expected of private television.[24]

Ralph Allen drove that point home with humour in his 1954 satire on broadcasting entitled *The Chartered Libertine*. Towards the end of the novel, when the CBC had been sold off to private interests, he showed his two Toronto highbrows searching desperately through the newspaper for something to hear or see that was worthwhile. All that radio offered were various combinations of Bob Hope, Bing Crosby, and Danny Kaye brought to Canadians courtesy of recorded programs made in the United States.

'What about television?' Hilary inquired weakly.
    'Channel Eight: I Love Lucy. Channel Four: I Married Joan. Channel Twelve: I Wed Wanda.'
    'Oh.'
    Bertram sat forward. 'Here's a new one on Channel Ten, though.'
    'What?'
    'I Adore Adele.'

So, instead, they went off to a baseball game.[25]
    More novel was the worry about the viewing habit itself, especially

common before the arrival of Canadian television in 1952, a worry that originated in a concern over the well-being of the family. T.S. Eliot's fear that watching television was in itself a threat to the mental, moral, and physical health of people, especially the young (an anxiety resulting from a trip he'd taken to the United States), had wide currency. In 1951 J.B. McGeachy, associate editor of *The Globe and Mail*, suggested that television 'may destroy conversation and could even make thinking obsolete.' The same year, Don Magill noted in *Maclean's* that 'daily doses' of television might turn children into a generation of 'televidiots.' And Nancy Cleaver in *Saturday Night* speculated that television could be a 'home-breaker,' upsetting the harmony and routine of domestic life, unless parents took care to regulate its use. By the time of the Fowler Commission, experience had refashioned these doubts about the new family ritual into a concern over 'the danger of spectatoritis.' The very ease of watching television, warned the brief from the University of Toronto, encouraged 'passivity of mind.' Implicit here was the fear of a programmed public: the viewer would become a sort of sponge who would soak up any message deemed desirable by television's masters.[26]

In fact such fears and doubts were overshadowed by an optimism that was based upon a firm and widespread belief in the promise of television. Brief after brief submitted to the Fowler Commission made the case that television could serve to realize some useful purpose. The YMCA thought television should aid international understanding by bringing 'the rest of the world into our living rooms.' A group of children's librarians believed that both radio and television could 'arouse' and 'stimulate' the curiosity of children, awakening them to the virtues of reading and knowledge. Religious and moral associations thought television must work to bolster the old Victorian imprint on Canadian life now imperilled by the ethics of affluence. One French Catholic group proclaimed that television program- ming had to protect the family and exalt 'la puissance du foyer, ses joies et ses beautés.' Likewise, a group of Anglo-Protestant women reasoned that programming must 'uphold the conceptions of wholesome family life; of co-operation rather than self-interest, of honesty rather than deceit, of amity rather than hatred.' The promise of such 'good television,' of course, was not just a healthy family but a moral nation.[27]

Even the members of the Fowler Commission persuaded themselves that television-viewing and radio-listening might rejuvenate family life eroded by industrial change. Television could create 'a headquarters, a gathering place,' where young and old came 'to see a play, to enjoy a variety show or to listen to a concert or a lecture.' Wouldn't the unity of the family be enhanced by this ability 'to encounter life together' in the home? Wouldn't the social and moral fabric of the country be strengthened as a result? This hope reflected not only the propaganda of the television industry in the United States but the prevalence of the cult of togetherness that had spread throughout North America during the 1950s.[28]

But the promise of television shone brightest in the eyes of highbrows. One great difficulty in Canada, so it seemed, was that few people outside of the major cities had the opportunity to enjoy the pleasures of Culture. Television's reach could fill the gap. Neil Morrison rhapsodized over the fact that television had produced huge audiences for ballet, concerts, Kafka's plays, and the like. The same medium had provided a vehicle for the expression of the Canadian spirit by carrying adaptations of the works of W.O. Mitchell and L.M. Montgomery. 'They said in effect to an audience of hundreds of thousands from coast to coast, this is the kind of people we are, this is the way we behave, these are some of the things we believe.' A similar glee and the same hope were evident in the assortment of briefs to the Fowler Commission authored by literary, musical, and artistic groups across the country. The day of Culture had dawned.[29]

Then there was the cause of sophistication. 'The average citizen,' warned the Fredericton branch of the Humanities Association of Canada, 'grows less and less competent to deal with the great mass of issues on which he is required to pass judgement.' Yet the flexibility and appeal of television gave it an enormous potential as a tool of adult education. The dramatist Mavor Moore, at the time chief producer for Toronto TV, was captivated by the thought that television could do 'the biggest and best job yet of giving us a fuller glimpse into life around us, of taking us into ourselves, and out of ourselves.' And not just highbrows were impressed: The Confédération des Travailleurs Catholiques du Canada saw television as 'le principal espoir de la culture populaire' that could improve the level of knowledge among a working class kept in ignorance by a lack of education. More generally, the Fédération des Sociétés Saint-Jean-Baptiste du Québec claimed that television might augment the sense of civic responsibility as well as enhance the status of politics. So exuberant was the rhetoric of hope that one would have thought television was a panacea for all the troubles of democracy.[30]

Finally, of course, there was the dream that television would be a grand nation-builder. The YMCA foresaw a cross-country network promoting 'a sense of Canadianism' from coast to coast. The Fowler Commission placed its imprimatur on such notions by proclaiming that 'radio and television may be able to perform unifying and cohesive functions for our society.' A medium that could work for Canadian unity might also sponsor cultural sovereignty. André Laurendeau believed that 'la télévision canadienne-française' could be a powerful agent of renewal and growth in Quebec's culture. The Canadian Radio and Television League dreamed that public broadcasting would become 'a method that enables us to recapture some portion of our cultural and spiritual life: a method that will help make us masters in our own house.' Arthur Lower added that radio and television might be 'our last chance' to resist 'the weight of this American mass culture.'[31]

What is especially intriguing about all this comment, notably from the highbrows, was the advocacy of a strategy of capture. These writers wanted to take over television to realize their own special dreams of good and glory. Here was a mass medium that could undo the harm to morals, values, Canada itself, done by past innovations, if only the right people were in command. The naïvety and the optimism speak volumes about the way in which even the intelligentsia of the day had been captivated by the fetish of technology.

'McLunacy'?

In retrospect the arguments of Marshall McLuhan can be seen as a strange conclusion to the first debate over television, even if his fame at the end of the next decade was very much a consequence of the craziness that afflicted the North American mind then.[32]

The work of Marshall McLuhan caused an extraordinary flap in America's intellectual circles during the mid and late 1960s. To admirers he was 'a brilliant socio-cultural theorist' (Neil Compton), close to being a 'seminal' thinker (Richard Schickel), and 'an enormously exciting icono-clast' (George Steiner). His work was praised as 'stimulating,' 'insightful,' 'novel,' bound to shake things up. But to critics McLuhan was something of a fraud; maybe an intelligent man, mused Arthur Schlesinger, though someone a bit perverse who preferred to play the role of the charlatan. His work?: 'the latest of the illusions of progress' (Northrop Frye); 'cut-rate salvation' (Anthony Quinton); 'a novel and bizarre form of obscurantism' (Sidney Finkelstein); and respectively 'impure,' 'pretentious,' or 'arrant' 'nonsense' (Dwight Macdonald, Theodore Roszak, and Louis Dudek). Jonathan Miller, who'd become one of his most severe critics, wondered whether the man had actually set out to stimulate inquiry by erecting 'a gigantic system of lies' – a comment to which McLuhan naturally took great exception. Just who was this 'oracle of the New Communications,' and why was he causing so much fuss?[33]

One of the minor mysteries of McLuhan was that he came not from New York City or from Harvard or some other heavyweight centre of American academe, but from the University of Toronto. You can detect the note of astonishment in Richard Schickel's description of McLuhan as 'Canada's intellectual comet' in his *Harper's* essay of November 1965. It's tempting to ascribe some special importance to the influence of place, especially given the fact that the university was also home to Harold Adams Innis and Northrop Frye, two other professors with radical ideas about communications and culture. The university was a lively intellectual community, plugged into the wider world of Anglo-American thought and scholarship. Perhaps the very fact that it was on the margins made it possible to experiment more freely with received ideas. McLuhan himself later on found cause to highlight the significance of the Canadian location: he was wont to describe Canada as an 'anti-environment' for the United States, a country that lived the American experience yet managed to remain detached from the mainstream, so that its leading thinkers (like Innis, he argued) could understand the true nature of America. Indeed, McLuhan even foresaw a special mission for Canada as a 'distant early warning' system of the changes occurring in American society and culture (that, of course, was a play on words, since Canada was already the site for a radar defence system called the DEW line).[34]

McLuhan had started to break away from the older highbrow tradition even before *The Mechanical Bride* was published. He told Ezra Pound in a letter written early in January 1951 that he was now convinced technology determined modes of thinking in America; and eighteen months later McLuhan outlined, also to Pound, what would be the main themes of *The Gutenberg Galaxy*. His new approach to media and culture wasn't really his own discovery: later, McLuhan made abundantly clear how he owed a great intellectual debt to Innis whose works had set him on the right course, even describing *The Gutenberg Galaxy* as a kind of footnote to Innis. It was from Innis that McLuhan had 'learned' that the particular characteristics of the media, not content, as the highbrow tradition dictated, determined the contours of culture. (In a letter to William Kuhns in December 1971, however, he claimed that Innis's greatest problem was his lack of knowledge of the arts.)

This influence shouldn't be exaggerated: Innis died in 1952, and McLuhan was soon embarked on his own unique journey that took him far away from the kinds of issues that had troubled his supposed mentor. In 1953 a two-year Ford Foundation grant of $44,250 to probe the effects of the electronic media enabled McLuhan to establish his special seminar on culture and communication at Toronto. Also in 1953, he and his group of like-minded souls drawn from other disciplines launched a journal under the general title *Explorations: Studies in Culture and Communications*, which went on until 1959. All the while McLuhan was working through mounds of literature to produce *The Gutenberg Galaxy*, a book about the rise and fall of print culture that was finally published in 1962. Meanwhile, in 1959, he was commissioned by the National Association of Educational Broadcasters, another American group, to prepare an approach and syllabus for teaching about the media in secondary schools. Out of this experience came a report that formed the prototype for *Understanding Media*, a book on the present-day scene, which appeared in 1964. These two works, roughly fifteen years in the making, were the foundation of the fame McLuhan would shortly enjoy.

The McLuhan who'd emerged after all this study and work was very much an eccentric, the product of a lot of different influences. His Roman Catholicism played some part in determining his notions of the ideal life. He'd remained rooted in the arts and humanities, his first love. He drew ideas and inspiration from novelists, poets, and short-story writers (such as James Joyce, T.S. Eliot, and Edgar Allan Poe); an assortment of literary and cultural critics (such as G.K. Chesterton, F.R. Leavis, and Wyndham Lewis); art historians (such as Heinrich Wölfflin and Siegfried Giedon); the occasional classicist and historian (such as Eric Havelock and Johan Huizinga); and even a medieval philosopher (Thomas Aquinas). But he'd also branched out into sociology (David Riesman), linguistics (Benjamin Whorf), physics (Werner Heisenberg), anthropology (Edward T. Hall), and psychology (Hans Selye). Not that his scope was universal: he took little notice of either Marx or Weber; he had only a smattering of knowledge about Freud and Jung and little respect for Noam Chomsky's seminal work in linguistics or Claude Lévi-Strauss's equally important study of mythology; and he never mentioned Roland Barthes (until the late 1970s) whose work would be so important to the birth of modern semiotics. Indeed, McLuhan wasn't especially interested in economics (no matter what the influence of Innis), sociology, or even much of psychology. He was, in short, very selective: he'd ransacked a particular collection of writers to find the raw material to inspire and buttress his opinions.[35]

Nor did McLuhan ever carry out extensive testing of his own theories. True, in a letter of 4 March 1965, he outlined to Claude Bissell, the president of the University of Toronto, a madcap scheme to develop what he called 'a sensory typology' for a number of different populations, perhaps starting with Greece, which hadn't yet got television. Apparently that research would eventually enable him to make accurate predictions about what would happen to cultures under the impact of electronic media. But, again, McLuhan did borrow from the results of other researchers. In *The Gutenberg Galaxy*, for example, he used the experiments John Wilson had carried out on the African response to films to illuminate how non-literate people had a quite different approach to the world. His letters in 1970 and 1971 reveal that he was especially excited by the findings of Herbert Krugman at General Electric, whose team carried out a series of brain-wave measurements to show how people's minds responded to the messages of different media. These experiments added a nice touch of scientific credibility to his theories, or so it seemed.

The prose style of McLuhan's books was rightly notorious among intellectuals and laymen alike. It seemed ironic to contemporaries that a man who hoped to explain the significance of communications should write in a way that confused and irritated readers. (Pity the poor businessman John Snyder, the target of a McLuhan letter in 1963, who asked McLuhan politely if he could express his ideas in a fashion that an ordinary mortal might understand.) But the fact was that McLuhan consciously set out, as Jonathan Miller once put it, to write 'in a way which outrages elementary laws of literary aesthetics.' That style embodied McLuhan's desire to break through the constraints of literary convention, what he called 'Mandarin prose,' to devise a new mode of presentation more in accord with the times. He didn't like regular, sequential discourse. Instead he tried to fashion mosaics: juxtaposing different examples drawn from, say, the sciences or the arts, using metaphor (money as 'the poor man's credit card') and pun ('Now all the world's a sage'), employing contraries (East and West, 'hot' and 'cool,' the typographical and the electric ages) and paradox (how play was taking over work just as work was taking over play), above all hyperbole ('The effect of radio is visual, the effect of the photo is auditory') – all to craft a new kind of 'multi-level prose' which he considered 'a serious art form.' That was carried even farther in *The Medium Is the Massage* (1967) where McLuhan's insights were illustrated by graphic designer Quentin Fiore through different typefaces, geometric designs, cartoons, photographs (many altered for effect), and the like. Here, apparently, was the new-style book: *Publishers Weekly* remarked on the novelty of the production techniques used, plus the fact that the printer had checked on a number of occasions to see whether some of the effects weren't errors.[36]

McLuhan was equally unrepentant about his unusual views. He argued, time and again, that what he presented were probes, rather than final opinions, which he was willing to discard if necessary. But what McLuhan really did was to add to his corpus of concepts, allowing some once salient terms (such as 'hot' and 'cool' in *Understanding Media*) to recede into the background when they didn't seem to work well any longer. He didn't really reject any of his probes. In reality his views were impervious to criticism, as they were to disproof of any kind, because they were less a system and more a gospel, or as Tom Nairn put it 'a kind of contemporary *mythmaking*.' While McLuhan's work was full of insights, its most striking flaw resulted from his determination to cut through the complexities of human endeavour: his reductionism, his zeal to simplify and to exaggerate, might make 'McLuhanism' seem a powerful tool of explanation, but it also brought his gospel within the domain of metaphysics. As a matter of fact, in a letter written to reviewer J.G. Keogh, in 1970, he proudly affirmed that he was a metaphysician, certainly not a sociologist or any other kind of classifier.[37]

What follows is a highly abbreviated summary of McLuhan's views, based chiefly on *The Gutenberg Galaxy, Understanding Media*, and *The Medium Is the Massage*. The focus is on his approach to television, and I've supplemented the summary with comment (in italics) on where McLuhan's findings were problematic.

1 *The medium is the message*: McLuhan simply meant that the particular medium, be that print or radio or television, shaped the attitudes, institutions, patterns of behavior, and modes of thinking predominant at any moment in history. It didn't really matter whether TV carried trashy drama or a lot of ads or educational features since what moulded the minds of the viewer were the special attributes of the medium. Each medium became an art-form in its own right. The observation allowed McLuhan to dispense with the detailed analysis of content that so absorbed the time and energies of most researchers and critics – indeed McLuhan had a certain contempt for these drudges who thought content was so important.

   The strength of this approach was that it focused attention on the attributes of the media as unique channels of information. The difficulty was that it exaggerated the import of these media and neglected the greater significance of content, clashing with the dictates of common sense and the findings of research. He never admitted that a particular form of expression, such as storytelling, might fulfil similar roles and have a similar kind of effect irrespective of the medium involved.

2 *The extensions of man*: A human being was a bundle of different senses and organs that had a natural equilibrium or ratio. Each medium was an extension (sometimes he also claimed a 'self-amputation') of a human faculty, which allowed him to argue, for instance, that clothing was an extension of the skin. Certain media were hot, for example, radio or movies, which extended one single sense in high definition and provided a lot of data that made the individual into a passive consumer. Other media, such as the telegraph, were cool, providing little data, and requiring the consumer to participate to understand. The psychic effect of a new medium was to alter the natural ratio, and so the way in which individuals understood the world and organized their lives.

McLuhan had reduced the human mind to a relatively simple mechanism that was subject to intense pressures from man's own inventions. That presumption was the basis of the charge of technological determinism. The trouble was that McLuhan never really explained how the mind operated or what was the natural ratio of senses. Besides, he failed to recognize how the ways in which people used the media, whether for relaxation or excitement or education, counted to determine whether a message was hot or cold, or what its impact might be.

3 *Print*: Print was the great villain in McLuhan's picture of things (although he often claimed he was wedded to literate values personally). Print was an extension of the eye and a hot medium: it fostered a fixed point of view, linear and sequential thinking, the fragmentation of knowledge, individualism and nationalism. The people of a print-dominated society, and both Britain and the United States were once such societies, were abstracted from the reality around them, cut off from the richness of experience, regimented by their approach to life – it was print, above all, that had fostered the split between head and heart.

McLuhan had confused a mode of perception (visual) and a technique of thinking (logic). He had wrongly assumed that people approached a text in one single fashion. And he'd assigned to print the chief cause for such phenomena as individualism and nationalism, which had their origins in a wide diversity of influences.

4 *Television:* Television became the hero in the human drama. TV was, above all, an extension of the sense of touch, which resulted in the best possible interaction of all the various senses. It was also a cool medium: the scanning finger produced a flat, two-dimensional image (not at all like the hot medium of movies) more like an icon or sculpture than a photograph, which required that the individual participate to fill in the missing information. Its effect, along with radio, was to retribalize man,

to return him to the primitive state that reigned prior to the invention of the alphabet. Television fostered an awareness of experience in depth and a yearning for wholeness. Altogether, the electronic media amounted to an extension of man's central nervous system.

If television was an extension of any sense, then that was the visual not the tactile. In fact the television image was perceived by people as little different from that of movies. And the medium itself has been emphatically controlled by people who were disciplined in the conventions of logic and literacy: television is very much a scripted medium. Whether television involved or relaxed the individual depended on the nature of the programming and the mood of the viewer.

5 *The age of anxiety:* McLuhan argued that the multimedia situation bred a kind of civil war among the media and thus among our senses. The roots of the troubles of the 1960s, then, lay in the revolutionary impact of radio and especially television. TV was actually dissolving the fabric of life because it undermined the ground-rules based on the dominance of print. That, for instance, was the root cause of the generation gap: adults were products of print, youth the result of radio and television. In fact McLuhan was able to explain all manner of phenomena, from the declining popularity of Detroit's cars to the prospect of race war in the United States, by assessing the effects of the various competing media.

This was a monocausal explanation of affairs that didn't take into consideration the import of the baby boom (demography), affluence (economics), the bureaucratic revolution (politics), 1960s liberalism (ideology), and so on. Put another way, it mystified rather than explained what, and why, something had happened: McLuhan asked his fans to accept on faith what he said was the cause of the changes occurring in America and elsewhere.

6 *The global village:* This was the utopia (or was it a distopia?) towards which the electronic media were driving people, a world of total involvement that would realize the Christian ideal of a single, spiritual community. The boundaries between individuals, between peoples, between ages and classes and sexes, would disappear. It would be possible to regulate the life of this village via the selective use of the various media, to heat up or cool down a populace, depending upon what was desirable.

This concept highlighted the dangers of analogy. McLuhan's claim that the electronic media, in particular, had worked to conquer distance and cut across boundaries was a valuable insight. But that didn't mean civilization was returning to some mythical village of the pre-literate past. Nor was it ever easy to discover just what life would be like in this global village. Did it signify the victory of the irrational and the emotional? Was it the end of democracy, the triumph of totalitarianism? In fact this was the kind of concept that just about anyone with a modicum of imagination could fill with a special meaning.

McLuhan always claimed that he'd eschewed moral judgments after the publication of *The Mechanical Bride*. He denied any intention to establish either a cult or a school. He told Gerald Stearn that he would never be numbered among any collection of 'McLuhanites,' that he saw disciples only as a bother since they would likely restrict his cherished freedom to explore what he wished. And he added that he derived no particular joy from announcing so bluntly the disruptive effects of the media. Rather he was a disinterested observer, without any point of view, who tried to discover how the media operated on man's psyche and society. The analogy of Edgar Allan Poe's mariner who saved himself from drowning in the whirlpool through a kind of detachment, by studying the vortex and co-operating with its actions, was highlighted in both *The Mechanical Bride* and *The Medium Is the Massage* as a strategy for comprehending what was happening. He did hope to educate the public, to overcome its 'numbness' to the reality that their lives were controlled by the technologies they embraced. So the aim of *Understanding Media* was to bring the media 'into orderly service': *The Medium Is the Massage* emphasized that education should be a form of 'civil defence' against the impact of technology, or as he put it 'media fall-out'. McLuhan had wrapped himself up in the garb of the value-free social scientist, committed to the ideals of inquiry and objectivity, devoted to explaining rather than lecturing or cajoling.

But there was more to McLuhan's purpose than he disclosed. He had always honoured the artist as the one person who could explain to a waiting public just what was in store. McLuhan's artist was no ivory-tower figure: he was a social actor who strove to expound his insights to the masses. That notion had been present in *The Mechanical Bride*; it was still evident in *Understanding Media*. McLuhan clearly believed that he was such a far-sighted artist. His letters, especially from the mid-1950s, reveal a person who lacked a sense of humility, who was unwilling to listen to critics, who wanted to tell his acquaintances what was true rather than to exchange views to reach that truth. Beginning in 1959, he sent out occasional 'Media Logs' to close friends, or prepared one letter for a number of correspondents, full of his questions, his opinions, and his instructions. At the end of the 1960s he edited *The Dew-Line Newsletter* to bring to subscribers the latest version of the truth. The adman Howard Gossage, one of his strongest fans, admitted that McLuhan just didn't listen when others talked. A journalist claimed that in one graduate seminar he visited the person who spoke was nearly always McLuhan, leaving the students dazed if not intimidated by his constant stream of words. All in all, McLuhan showed every sign of becoming a messiah who wanted the unthinking support, if not the adulation, of colleagues, leaders, and the public.

A messiah has to be something of a promoter, willing to sell himself and his ideas, and McLuhan proved an expert at this task. Much later, Bob Fulford recalled that McLuhan was an inveterate 'publicity hound' who was wont to call up a journalist to 'demand coverage of some half-baked idea he had just concocted.' A letter in May 1959 indicates he'd just given a talk to the Winnipeg Ad and Sales Club about the rules of business in the electronic age. He made contact with assorted business people, from Edward Morgan (the assistant editor of *Marketing*) to John Snyder (chairman of the board of u.s. Industries) – he showed none of the animus towards the men of commerce that afflicted his fellow highbrows. He cultivated friendships with university officials, such as Claude Bissell: the institution wisely moved to recognize his stature by creating for McLuhan the graduate Centre for Culture and Technology in 1963. He worked in cahoots with CBC producers to create a documentary on teenagers, the new tribe shaped by the electronic media. His 1962 article on television for *Canadian Art* was later summarized in *Marketing* for the edification of admen. By the spring of 1963 his 'name' was sufficient to elicit an invitation to the first Delos symposium: a collection of experts (including Margaret Mead and R. Buckminster Fuller) who gathered on a ship to sail the Aegean for a week and talk about human settlements.

But what made McLuhan into a star, into 'the world's first Pop philosopher' in the words of *The New Yorker*, was the amazing response of intellectuals and other literary figures, primarily in New York, to *Understanding Media*. The great critic of 'masscult,' Dwight Macdonald, denounced the book at length, a sign to all and sundry that it should be taken seriously. Likewise *Time* told readers the book might have 'just the right combination of intelligence, arrogance and pseudo science' to make it a summer fad. A new cheap edition of *Understanding Media*, out in 1965, sold well on college campuses and apparently in drugstores. That year the McLuhan phenomenon took off: there were reviews of articles in *The New Yorker, The New York Review of Books, Commonweal, The Nation, The New Statesmen, The Times Literary Supplement, Harper's*, and so on. Tom Wolfe wrote a witty piece in the New York *Herald Tribune* asking the key question 'What If He Is Right?' (rightness would make him the most important thinker since

Newton, Darwin, Freud, Einstein, and Pavlov). Another observer of the pop scene, Susan Sontag, looked with favour on McLuhan in a *Mademoiselle* article, later republished in her book *Against Interpretation*. Thereafter, he would be celebrated by a cartoon in *The New Yorker*, his face would appear on the cover of *Newsweek* and *The Saturday Review* (though he didn't make the cover of *Time*), and his ideas would be popularized by an hour-long NBC documentary that coincided with the publication of *The Medium Is the Massage*. The TV appearance wasn't a great success, though: ironically, McLuhan rarely worked well on television where his one-liners and puns and paradoxes served to confuse more than to educate.[38]

No matter. The McLuhan bandwagon was unstoppable. Michael Arlen, the famed TV critic for *The New Yorker*, noted just after the NBC telecast that McLuhan was the most sought-after dinner guest in New York. One observer counted eight articles on McLuhan (as against only four for John Kenneth Galbraith) in American periodicals in a three-month period early in 1967. *The New York Times* alone carried twenty-seven items about McLuhan during that same year. Over the next five years or so, he was honoured by the publication in the United States, Canada, and Europe of collections of essays plus some substantial books, popular and scholarly, all about his work. His own books were translated into a variety of languages and seemed to cause a great deal of interest in France and Italy – it was in France that the term 'mcluhanisme' was coined.[39]

What fed this interest among journalists, scholars, and publishers was the public response to McLuhan himself. He'd become one of the most available and popular lecturers of the day, able to appeal to businessmen as well as college students. He was flown in to talk to people from Bell, General Motors, and IBM. The San Francisco admen Howard Gossage and his partner Gerry Feigan sponsored his appearances on the west and east coasts of the United States. A story in December 1966 in *The Nation* noted that Container Corporation was underwriting a McLuhan speaking tour. All this attention must have been lucrative: in 1969 he told J.A. Bailey of Eastman Kodak that his fees for a seminar were $5,000 and for ordinary talks $2,000, although in practice he often gave lectures for an honorarium of less than $500. The extraordinary college response was evidenced first by a special 'McLuhan Festival' organized at the University of British Columbia in 1965: it was a maze of huge plastic sheets, slides projected at random intervals all over the place, musicians making odd noises, dancers whirling about, even a girl behind a screen whom people were supposed to touch. *Understanding Media*, according to *Newsweek* (6 March 1967), was the best-selling non-fiction work at Harvard and at Ann Arbor. The article quoted a woman at Columbia who compared reading McLuhan to taking the wonder drug of the day, LSD – 'it can turn you on.' But McLuhan was popular with college authorities as well: he received the first Albert Schweitzer chair awarded at Fordham University (through a friend, John Culkin), a twelve-month appointment at $100,000 for himself and staff that commenced in August 1967. Town and gown apparently agreed on the merit of McLuhan.

Explaining McLuhan's success isn't difficult. First of all, he was an academic with all the proper credentials, which lent credence, even authority, to his books and sayings. It was striking how often articles in popular and quality periodicals referred to his scholarly reputation and his professional environment. Why, he even graded papers, asserted an astounded fan. The fact that McLuhan often dressed up his ideas in the jargon of pseudo-science ('sensorium,' 'servomechanisms,' 'autoamputation,' 'counter-irritant,' 'synesthetic force') and that he focused attention on the importance of hardware suited the bias of the age, especially the fetish of technology.

Second, he was adept at exploiting the myth of the avant-garde, which enabled him to appear as an anti-establishment figure, someone who was 'with it.' He was part of an age when Andy Warhol was a name to conjure with, when Timothy Leary was still Mr LSD, when the New Left was up in arms, when the Beatles were in full flower. McLuhan took great pleasure in posing as an iconoclast, unhindered by the normal rules that afflicted ordinary men. He was quite ready to take on experts of any sort, claiming they were trapped by their own training. So his ideas conveyed legitimacy on admen, media people, pop artists, and some unconventional scholars, all in need of respectability, sufficient to win him a collection of sympathetic fans in or near the centres of intellectual power in America and Europe. Some admen (those suffering a sense of guilt?) were particularly taken by the notion that their product wasn't in itself debauching the public's mind but rather was part of a general revolution in human consciousness. Likewise his implicit identification of youth as the first citizens of the new electronic age stroked the collective ego of university students who were flexing their muscles on and off campus in an effort to challenge the powers that be.

Finally, McLuhan was dealing with the Big Picture, with questions of man and technology and the future that troubled all kinds of people, and he was offering easy answers that enough readers and listeners felt they could understand. There was an important element of optimism in McLuhan's romanticized version of the global village, which could give hope to the businessman, housewife, and student that things would work out in the end. All of which is another way of saying that McLuhan came along at the right time with the right message, and the media made him, in the words of Benjamin De Mott, almost 'Everyman's Favorite Brain.'

His fame and his influence soon waned, of course. He expressed bafflement in a letter to one acquaintance over a London *Times* story in April 1971, which proclaimed that the vogue for McLuhan, plus an assortment of other 1960s heroes, was rapidly ending. Part of the trouble was that more and more of the academic and literary community, including some one-time admirers, such as Jonathan Miller, decided that 'the emperor had no clothes': McLuhan's gospel was too flawed to deserve favour. His letters show he never understood why, putting down his opposition as a sign of nineteenth-century thinking or some such similar failing. Perhaps more important, though, students and the fashion-minded public just got bored with a person whose insights, however outrageous, were no longer novel. He suffered, in short, the fate that awaits any pop star whose image becomes too stereotyped in the mind of the fickle audience.

There was a McLuhan legacy of sorts. He left behind a couple of catchphrases, notably 'the medium is the message' and the 'global village.' He was identified in the hazy memory of the public as the Cassandra who proclaimed the death of print culture and, paradoxically, as the prophet who celebrated the ways of the electronic age. In university circles he's sometimes remembered as a highly imaginative, if undisciplined, explorer who helped to stretch people's minds. There's been occasional talk of a 'Canadian communications theory,' though normally its fans have looked much more to the arguments of Harold Innis than to the insights of Marshall McLuhan. Only a few writers have continued to take his work seriously, and most have developed their own brand of eccentricity rather than followed in his footsteps. Certainly the discipline of communications studies has moved very far away from his naîve belief in the omnipotence of technology. So, in the end McLuhan's lasting importance is as a historical figure, a pop philosopher whose rise and fall was intimately connected with the operations of the mass media he endeavoured to understand.

Whatever its novelty, 'McLuhanism' was in many ways an extension of some of the ideas and approaches that were commonly expressed by Canadian observers about culture and media during the late 1940s and early 1950s. Yes, McLuhan had split away from the highbrow tradition, with its focus on content and its critique of mass culture. But his works did carry a certain moral freight, an implicit assumption that television was making for the progress of mankind towards some better state in the future. That reflected the same kind of vague optimism that a lot of writers had purveyed in the early days of TV. Likewise McLuhan's fascination with hardware, his belief in TV's power to captivate the viewer, and his claim that TV would work a revolution were all commonplace back then. Even his hyperbole was dated. And his argument that the artist should guide how people used, and how much they used of, a particular medium was a bizarre twist on the old strategy of capture. Experience with television hadn't disillusioned him. The greatest irony of all was that McLuhan had never come to grips with the reality of television in the 1950s and 1960s.[40]

Part One: Structures

2

Enter CBC-TV

'*Canadian* TV Is Worth It!'

Alphonse Ouimet, 1957[1]

Such was the title of an ebullient speech by the CBC's general manager, J. Alphonse Ouimet, delivered to the Montreal Rotary Club in October 1957. He was in an aggressive mood: he adopted an upbeat tone to answer queries about the supposedly high cost of CBC-TV, and he used the occasion to celebrate what had been achieved since television broadcasting began in Canada in September 1952. It amounted to a story of triumph, over doubt and over adversity. Much that he had to say was at least arguably correct – the launching of CBC-TV had been a remarkably successful endeavour.

The Story of Growth

Something often forgotten is that the coming of television reconfirmed the basic structure of Canadian broadcasting. That was a bit ironic, given all the noise made in the press about the revolutionary impact of TV. Canada readily, and inevitably, opted for the transmission and receiving standards of the United States, since any other course would have erected 'a television curtain' (in the words of Alphonse Ouimet) against American signals and swiftly outraged the viewing public. The decision, of course, ensured that the television scene, like the radio scene before it, would be full of American messages.[2]

None of the challengers of the CBC's dominance succeeded. The effort of the National Film Board to take control of early television didn't get anywhere with a government that seemed to look upon the agency as an expensive liability. While there were assorted experiments designed to develop a viable kind of subscriber or toll TV, notably the Rediffusion service started in Montreal in 1951, pay television never amounted to more than a novelty during the 1950s. That remained true even when Famous Players Canada showed some interest because cable could be a way of getting movies into homes. An independent television-production industry, occasionally heralded in the press, just didn't materialize. The much more considerable pressure for independent, private television was blocked by government policy until the end of the decade. Right from the beginning TV was seen as an extension of radio, and logic decreed that it be placed under the control of the country's premier broadcasting institution, the CBC. This was the same kind of logic that reigned in Britain and the United States, where existing broadcasting institutions took command of television. Whatever the disruptive potential of television, it was constrained when the new medium was housed in an institution built by radio. That said, television soon had an extraordinary impact on the size and the expenditures of the Corporation, and so upon its very nature.

The CBC in the days of just plain radio was a modest institution, if judged by the standards that would prevail in the video age. Back in March 1949, long before the inauguration of the television service, the Corporation employed some 1,200 people. Its operating expenditures (excluding the International Service) for the fiscal year 1949/50 amounted to a mere $8.2 million, much of this covered by the revenue accruing from listeners' licence fees (set at $2.50 a year) and a modicum of commercial broadcasting. That was sufficient to run the three networks as well as to supervise the overall radio scene.[3]

By law the policy of the CBC was determined by the board of governors, a collection of part-time members representing the public interest who were appointed by the government and headed by a permanent chairman. The ten part-timers in 1952, in typical Canadian fashion, had been selected from all parts of the country, from Charlottetown, on the east coast, to Victoria, on the west coast. But otherwise they were representative only of a very narrow definition of the Canadian public: nine men and one woman, five from business, three from academe plus one from education, and a single labour spokesman. Not that it seemed to matter very much, since the board of governors wasn't really a legislative or an executive body. It met only five or six times a year and found much of its energy consumed by the task of issuing new or revising old broadcast licences for private radio interests. Members lacked the time or the knowledge to do much more than modify or approve the initiatives of the Corporation's real bosses – the chairman, A. Davidson Dunton, and his two top administrators, J. Alphonse Ouimet and E.L. Bushnell.[4]

Dunton was once listed among the Corporation's 'bright young boys,' something of an idea-man or even a 'professor.' Fortune had smiled on his career: he'd graduated from the élite Lower Canada College in Montreal, enjoyed the time to study at universities in Europe, won the patronage of John McConnell (one of Canada's biggest businessmen) who made him editor of the Montreal *Standard*, and joined the Wartime Information Board, where he soon became general manager. It was from this job that Prime Minister Mackenzie King plucked a thirty-three-year-old Dunton in 1945 to head the CBC. He swiftly proved himself an amazingly effective chairman, perhaps because he moved so easily in the corridors of power (including the Rideau Club, where he was a member), because he was so well-connected, because he was so charming. He was the best kind of Liberal mandarin, unflappable and conciliatory, and his ability to win friends, to earn respect, inside the Corporation and on Parliament Hill, became the stuff of legend. No less important were his intellectual skills: Dunton had a mind that enabled him to grasp the significance of television and to articulate his vision convincingly to a wide variety of audiences. Looking back, it's no wonder he appears as the most successful of the CBC's many leaders.[5]

Still, if anyone deserves the title 'the father of Canadian television,' it is Alphonse Ouimet, not Davidson Dunton. Ouimet belonged very much to the technical camp among the CBCers. Born, raised, and educated in Montreal, he'd completed studies as an electrical engineer at McGill University by 1932. For the next two years he was involved in some experiments with television broadcasting before joining public radio (then called the Canadian Radio Broadcasting Commission) as an engineer. He nurtured his early passion, and in 1946 (when he'd become assistant chief engineer) he was assigned the task of producing a report surveying television throughout the world. That report proved a masterful, and sometimes witty, account of all things great and small, from cameras to programs, and later was credited with guiding the CBC's own plans for the new marvel. In 1949, Ouimet was appointed to the new post of co-ordinator of television, at the same time as he became the Corporation's chief engineer; in January 1953, he was promoted to general manager of the CBC, which made him the chief operating officer of the Corporation during the 1950s when it pioneered

Canadian television. What captured his imagination was the miracle of television itself: once, speaking at his alma mater, he waxed poetic about the marvels of television past and future, the way it could link cities, a country, eventually the globe, into one community. That bespoke the romanticism, the grand vision, of the engineer.[6]

Ernie Bushnell ranked among 'the old song-and-dance men' in the Corporation. Oldest of the three, Bushnell began his career during the 1920s in private radio in Toronto. He joined public broadcasting almost by default, since for a time it seemed there might be no other game in town. Bushnell worked in the program department where he earned a reputation as a showman – a person who believed that radio must entertain its listeners, whatever else it did. That made him something of an outsider among the cadre of top administrators, and may well have limited his influence on CBC policy. He was passed over for the post of general manager on a number of occasions. But, when Ouimet was promoted, Bushnell became his assistant, as well as the new co-ordinator of television. Although Bushnell had been impressed by BBC-TV (he had visited London on CBC business to learn about television), his instincts drew him towards the philosophy of mass entertainment that guided the makers of American television. That philosophy, however, was not much in favour among the rest of the Corporation's managers.[7]

During the late 1949s the CBC had begun to lay down the fundamentals of a plan for what it thought would be a unique television service suited to Canadian needs. This design the Corporation sold first to a hesitant government early in 1949 and later to a sympathetic Massey Commission. More difficult was the task of getting the Canadian public to buy the package, an effort that Scott Young in a *Maclean's* article would date from the summer of 1952. It required a combination of talents: Dunton was joined by other executives, such as Ouimet and Mavor Moore, Toronto's chief producer, to give interviews, make speeches, and even write articles. Along the way the policy attained the status of Holy Writ. Indeed the gospel of CBC television had become hackneyed, and certainly a bit boring, by the time that it was preached to the Fowler Commission in 1956.[8]

There was something for nearly everyone in the CBC design. That shouldn't surprise. The gospel reflected the Corporation's experience with radio, tempered somewhat by the concerns and the moods of the times. The influence of highbrow views, for instance, was especially striking. Implicit was a good deal of admiration for what the BBC was doing, and an equal amount of distaste for the vulgarity of so much of American television. But CBC television was fashioned to meet the problems arising from Canada's dilemma. 'Canada is an anomaly,' said Dunton: geography, demography, and economics conspired against its independence. The 'ordinary commercial arithmetic' would dictate a television service that simply conveyed imported New York and Hollywood entertainment to the big cities across Canada. What was necessary was a different kind of calculation, an arithmetic of patriotism perhaps, which recognized that the public must pay to protect its identity and its community. So CBC television was a national service designed to please as wide a spectrum as possible of the Canadian people, whether they lived in Toronto or Rivière-du-Loup, with programming that would reflect and enrich the soul of the country.

The distances involved, the sparseness of the population, above all what Ouimet called television's 'apparently insatiable appetite' for money, meant that the task couldn't be carried out by either public enterprise (the British model) or private enterprise (the American model) working alone. Instead the country had to rely upon the co-operation of public and private development, 'a typical Canadian compromise' that Dunton once argued combined 'the best advantages of both systems.' This compromise enabled CBCers to appropriate the language of growth so fashionable among business apologists. Thus, early in 1953, Ouimet told a McGill audience 'television today is Canada's fastest growing postwar industry,' and listed off a series of statistics on television sales to back up his claim. Some years later, in 1955, *Business Quarterly* published an article by Dunton that celebrated what he termed the 'big role played by Canadian business' through the manufacture of equipment and the construction of stations. One of the Corporation's briefs to the Fowler Commission dwelt on the contribution of advertising to the expanding volume of Canadian programming. All of which was a clever ploy to associate the CBC with the cause of private enterprise much favoured during the 1950s.

Even so, the Corporation was adamant in its belief that television was more than a simple industry – Moore called CBC television 'a public trust.' That imperative was made abundantly clear in the CBC's conception of the purposes of telecasting. 'It must aim to serve Canadians in all walks of life, old and young; to bring broadcasting of pleasure and value to them; to meet in fair proportion their varying interests and tastes,' argued a Corporation brief to the Fowler Commission; and 'in doing so to use the vivid power of television to communicate many things that people want – varied entertainment, information, ideas, opinions, pictures and reflections of many doings and developments, of many aspects of life; to offer plenty that is diverting and relaxing, and also to offer things of beauty, of significance.' Whatever the source of funding then, uppermost was the priority of public service.

At bottom, the justification for CBC television had to rest upon a particular ideal of social utility. Its apologists had swallowed the clichés about the 'tremendous power' and 'ever present impact' (to use Ouimet's words) of television. According to Dunton, Canada's national and social future in the next thirty years or so would depend 'to quite a considerable degree' on television. Consequently television 'should communicate an array of programming that, on the whole, would have a useful effect on society.' But what did that mean? One can glean some answers from the Corporation's briefs to the Fowler Commission: the CBC's networks would strive to stimulate the nation's life, to reflect diverse regional and ethnic traditions, to bolster or better yet teach democracy, to strengthen the home and educate the child, even to enhance the efficiency and productivity of the economy. Put another way, CBC television promised to act as an agent of nationalism *and* regionalism, of democracy *and* the popular arts, and always of the forces of decency and propriety. Above all, CBC television would work to prevent the 'Stars and Stripes' from capturing the hearts and minds of future generations. It was a tall order: there was a naîve sense of limitless possibilities implicit in the CBC's gospel of television that later events would prove took little account of the realities of the Canadian situation.

None the less the Corporation had acted slowly to bring TV broadcasting to Canada. The preliminary expenses for television listed on the CBC's balance sheet were a mere $55,571 in 1949/50 (or less than 1 per cent of total operating expenditures), rising only to $369,225 by 1951/2 (or about 3 per cent). As late as March 1951, only 19 of 1,454 employees were officially assigned to television. Dunton and the top brass were determined not to undermine the existing radio networks, still considered the 'senior' service, and not to rush into television thoughtlessly, a recipe for error and waste. Thus, Nathan Cohen, writing in *Saturday Night* (26 June 1951), could readily declare, 'TV will creep in on soft-soled shoes.' Soon after, *The Financial Post* (7 July 1951) announced that a steel shortage, plus the failure of a British company to deliver equipment on schedule, had delayed the opening of Canadian television until the fall of 1952. Roughly three and one-half years after the government gave its approval, back in March 1949, CBC-TV finally arrived: CBFT-Montreal began broadcasting on 6 September 1952, CBLT-Toronto two days later.[9]

The event led radio's businessmen to argue vigorously that the time had come to authorize private television. The government was ready to listen.

It didn't want to finance any grand scheme of CBC expansion. Early in 1952, the Corporation had asked its Liberal masters to approve the construction of seven more CBC stations in central and western Canada, which, together with the almost operational stations in Montreal and Toronto, would enable the CBC to reach half of the population and secure more ad revenues. During the summer the government decided for the moment to approve only the construction of the proposed Ottawa station, though a lot of noisy outrage from the west coast soon brought the promise of a Vancouver station as well. In November and December the government came forward with a compromise that gave the CBC new stations in Winnipeg and Halifax, instructed the Corporation to consider licences for private stations in non-CBC centres, dictated that all stations must carry the basic national service, and prohibited any competitive service in Canadian cities. The compromise buttressed CBC pre-eminence, leaving it the task of co-ordinating development and controlling network broadcasting, but without the promise that the CBC could develop a large array of 'owned and operated' outlets across the land. The compromise also ensured that private television would have a marvellous opportunity to flourish, though not in Canada's major metropolitan centres, where the CBC was in charge. The 'single station' policy determined that public and private investment would work together to bring television to as many different places in Canada as possible, avoiding any concentration of television services in Montreal, Toronto, or Vancouver.

That laid the foundation for television's first boom. In March 1953 only a quarter of the Canadian population was served by Canadian television; seven years later, 94 per cent of Canadian homes were within range of Canadian stations. Over a span of three years the government pumped $16.25 million in the form of special loans into the CBC for the construction of new stations and facilities, which, together with the money already authorized, amounted to a total expenditure of $24.25 million between 1949 and 1955. Quickly the CBC opened its promised stations in Halifax, Ottawa, Winnipeg, and Vancouver, plus a second station (English-language) in Montreal and a second station (French-language) in Ottawa. But this was modest compared to the expansion of private television. During the spring of 1953 the CBC governors dutifully granted seven licences for private stations, just the beginning of a long list. The first to open was CKSO-Sudbury in October 1953, followed by CFPL-London in November. The numbers jumped from four stations at the end of March 1954, to nineteen a year later, and to thirty-six in the same month of 1958. Private television served large cities, such as Hamilton, London, Regina, and Saint

John, as well as smaller places, such as Swift Current, North Bay, Rimouski, and Charlottetown. By 1961 business had invested some $51,748,000 in plant and equipment for television.[10]

No less impressive was the successful effort to knit all these stations into two connected networks, one English and the other French. By the summer of 1953 CBC people were meeting with the winners in the private-television sweepstakes to arrange a network service. The service was at first supplied via kinescope recordings: 'kines' were shows filmed off a high-quality television monitor – the results often were not very pleasing to the eye. That was only a stopgap measure, though, to await the completion of a national microwave relay system (at a cost of around $50 million) by Bell Telephone and other members of the Trans-Canada Telephone System. Ironically, the first stretch completed linked Toronto and Buffalo, in January 1953, thus allowing the direct transmission of American shows. But the following May, Toronto, Ottawa, and Montreal were linked, by December London joined, and in July 1954 so did Quebec City – though Winnipeg, the first city outside central Canada to be privileged, had to wait until September 1956. The grand engineering feat was considered completed on Dominion Day, 1 July 1958, when the CBC broadcast live from coast to coast a 'Memo to Champlain' to mark the opening of the world's longest network. By comparison the opening of the Calgary Relay Centre in June had gone almost unnoticed: yet the centre's seven videotape-recorders enabled the CBC to save network programs for delayed broadcast at times more convenient to western viewers. The network was not really finished until the next year, when St John's, Newfoundland, was reached by microwave.

Just as much effort had to be put into programming. The CBC had initially promised 10 1/2 hours a week of network shows for the private affiliates. By March 1957 the English service had extended to 48 hours. At first the corporation tried to make do with two television studios each in Montreal and Toronto, but in the next five years or so it was forced to build or buy up to seven additional studios for each city. So desperate, and poor, was the CBC, claimed Alex Barris much later, that it acquired a former automobile showroom that it tried with only limited success to transform into Toronto's Studio Four. But more important than the studio problem was the fact that the CBC was compelled to hire lots of people to assist in the making of the shows. Witness what happened at Radio-Canada in Montreal: the costume and make-up department grew from four people in September 1952 to nearly forty by March 1956, the number of announcers increased from one to twenty by the end of 1957, and while fifteen producers might have

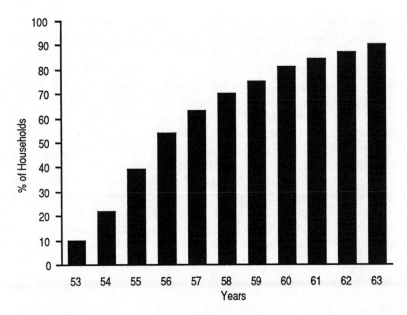

Chart 2.1 The growth of Canadian television households
Note: The yearly figures represent different counts at different times: 1950 and
1951, January; 1953–6, September; 1957–63, May. Information from Canada,
Dominion Bureau of Statistics, 'Household Facilities and Equipment,' *Bulletin:
64–202* and International Surveys Ltd, *Seasonal Listening and Viewing Habits in
Canada and Its Three Major Markets, 1958–59*, 79.

sufficed in January 1953, seventy-five were deemed necessary by July 1957.
Overall, by March 1959, the Corporation employed 7,000 people – the staff
was about six times greater than it had been a decade earlier, much of this
expansion taking place between 1952 and 1957. By the end of fiscal year
1959/60, the annual operating expenses and capital expenditures of the
CBC would finally top $100 million, ten times that of a decade earlier.[11]
    There wasn't any doubt that Canadians wanted this service, even if
people did sometimes grumble about the cost. Television had conquered
the homes of Canada very quickly indeed (see chart 2.1). Television caught
on more quickly in Ontario and Quebec than in the rest of the country, in
the big cities, and (by a slight edge) with French Canadians. As early as 30
April 1950, around 13,500 Canadians, mostly in southern Ontario and the
Vancouver area, where an outside antenna could often pick up American

signals, had bought TV sets. The arrival of CBC-TV sparked a sales boom, first in central Canada but soon across the country, as more and more stations began broadcasting. Although initially television may have suited better the pocket-books of the well-off – the average cost of a set in December 1952 was $425.20 (the average annual income of a male wage-earner in the manufacturing industries in 1952 was $2,915) – it wasn't long before middle- and low-income Canadians were rushing to the stores. An International Surveys Ltd report in 1953 found that purchases in Montreal were concentrated among homes in the third and fourth income quartiles. It proved increasingly difficult for retailers to keep up with the buying spree. The promised broadcast of the Coronation of Queen Elizabeth II in 1953, for example, inspired a lot more people than anyone expected to acquire sets. In September 1954 alone, Canadians bought 82,000 sets, for a total list value of $28 million (domestic set production that month was only 64,000). According to a report in *Canadian Broadcaster & Telescreen* (2 March 1955), demand in the Rimouski area was so high that one dealer tried to satisfy the clamour of his snow-bound customers by using a snow-mobile to make deliveries. This buying spree slowed down only in 1958, when the first great demand had been satisfied – in May 81 per cent of Ontario households and 79 per cent of Quebec households had television; the prairies lagged behind at 49 per cent. By January 1959, International Surveys Ltd estimated that some 90 per cent of urban households (cities with more than 100,000 people) had acquired a set. The census of 1961 revealed that more households had TV sets (82.5 per cent or 3,757,476) than had their own baths or showers, flush toilets, furnace heating, or cars.[12]

So, in 1959 the poor souls in what some researchers called 'Radiotown' (Quesnel, British Columbia, which then lacked access to a decent television signal) were well aware that they lived in 'a world of television.' Apparently one eager family had not only a set but an antenna as well. Usually they tried the set every night, even though in practice weather conditions were such that they only managed to get reception two or three nights a year. And reception meant either sound or pictures, seldom both. Being without television service was already something of a stigma.[13]

Which didn't mean that having access to CBC-TV made people satisfied. If there was one desire common among viewers everywhere, it was a yearning for greater choice. Viewers didn't want to be 'captives' of the CBC; they wanted more and more channels, whether Canadian or American. According to a front-page story in *Marketing* (6 February 1956), for example, the TV Owners' Association in Toronto got mighty upset over the possibility that CBLT's proposed channel switch from 9 to 6 on the dial would interfere with the reception from stations in Rochester and Buffalo. What made captivity seem all the more unfair was that many Canadians could view an American station: a CBC report for October 1956 estimated that just under a quarter of the Canadian population and under a third of the urban population were within reach of good reception of American stations. This boon was very unevenly distributed: New Brunswick, Manitoba, and Saskatchewan had no American service at all, whereas four out of five city-dwellers in British Columbia could get American channels. The desire for choice explained the loud demands for second stations in Winnipeg (a 'captive' market) and Vancouver (a 'competitive' market), even during the hearings of the Fowler Commission in 1956. Why should the deprived Winnipeg viewer have to watch such CBC offerings as 'The Plouffe Family' or 'Concert Hour' when his Toronto compatriot could sample the delights of the NBC or CBS schedules? The desire also explained the popularity of outside antennae in areas lucky enough to be close to the border. Thus, as of February 1959, just under half of Montreal's TV homes, three-quarters of those in Vancouver-Victoria, and a whopping 88 per cent of those in Toronto-Hamilton were apparently equipped with the necessary means to secure better television. And the same impulse underlay the surprising amount of interest that the press showed in the feeble experiments to establish pay television in various parts of Canada. Television was welcome; the CBC monopoly wasn't.[14]

The roller-coaster had at last begun to slow down by the close of the 1950s. The basic 'plant' of Canadian television was already in place. A new Conservative government, led by John Diefenbaker, had quickly passed an act in 1958 that overhauled broadcasting policy. The government had also announced its intention to license new, independent private stations in existing CBC markets, thus ending the CBC monopoly. Davidson Dunton, so very much a Liberal, had taken the opportunity to leave the CBC to take up the presidency of Carleton University, just after the Dominion Day festivities of 1958. It was almost inevitable that his replacement would be Alphonse Ouimet, who was identified with television and was one of the few prominent francophones in the service of Ottawa. (The top position was now president, not chairman – Bushnell became the new vice-president.) And in his first 'President's Message' in the *Annual Report* of 1959/60, Ouimet correctly called the past twelve months 'the first "plateau" year since the start of Canadian television.'

A Managerial Revolution?

The spectacular growth killed off the old CBC. Some years later, Ernie Bushnell would talk about how television had transformed 'a comparatively small family' into 'a vast impersonal corporation' during the course of the 1950s. Not that that was in itself surprising. Events had propelled the Corporation's masters to impose ever-greater doses of bureaucracy upon the CBC to ensure the proper administration of affairs. What resulted was not just a more efficient organization (though the degree of efficiency always remained a matter of dispute), but the rise of a new managerial élite and the emergence of a species of 'class warfare.' The will to power, even more the routines and priorities of this breed of administrators, increasingly upset many of the artists – producers, writers, performers, even journalists – who made the CBC's programming.[15]

There's no doubt that the CBC did face problems resulting from the arrival of television, specifically how to manage effectively the sizeable resources in manpower and money involved in mounting a national service. Whatever routines might have existed to control radio programming didn't survive very well in the new era. Don Hudson, a Toronto producer, later mused that things were pleasantly informal in the early days of television: once he was told about the budget for his show, 'The Big Revue,' in the men's washroom by Stuart Griffiths, the chief programmer. Guy Parent, a Montreal producer, remembered the early days as a good deal more cha-otic: he recounted how people without much training (like himself!) were hired and put on jobs without much forethought, shows were abruptly conceived and sometimes just as abruptly cancelled, schedules and times were altered at the last moment, and so on. It's hard to believe that any management could live very long with this kind of confusion.[16]

Then there was the problem of the unions. The growth and militancy of the new trade unions made outdated any notion that the CBC was a family. Bushnell believed that the rise of the unions was a result of the widespread hiring of Americans who had caught the union habit in the wild and woolly world of commercial television. But Finlay Payne, one of the early unionists, pointed out that 'the old paternalism just didn't work anymore' in the new television age: employees felt short-changed on salaries, overtime, and working conditions, believing management was much more interested in building up the system. (The first major union, the National Association of Broadcast Employees and Technicians or NABET, came about, Payne claimed, because of a huge 'overtime debit' owed the technicians, which the Corporation could never have paid off.) As early as March 1954 most non-supervisory personnel were in one bargaining unit or another: various kinds of news people, the radio and television technicians, clerical staff, and an assortment of skilled employees such as carpenters and film editors. In 1956 the CBC estimated that around 3,500 of its 5,000 employees were represented by seven labour organizations. This harsh reality forced upon management the need to order labour relations according to collective agreements and generally accepted codes of behavior. Ironically, the CBC soon earned a reputation as one of the most spineless of employers, unable to fire delinquent staff or resist exorbitant wage demands.[17]

But just as important was the problem of high visibility. Management might well be excused for believing that it lived in a fish-bowl. It had to satisfy two royal commissions, the Massey Commission in 1949 and the Fowler Commission in 1956. The special House of Commons broadcasting committee met in 1950, 1951, 1953, 1955, and 1959 to investigate various aspects of CBC behavior. Nor was that the end of the politicians' fascination with the Corporation: opposition leader George Drew and finance critic Donald Fleming in the Liberal years of the early and mid-1950s were ever ready to expose or denounce any signs of CBC waste or immorality. They could expect to win applause from the many champions of the private-broadcasting industry as well as a lot of writers in the press, for whom CBC-bashing had become almost a tradition. Indeed television was so very much a public concern that the CBC knew its activities would always excite a degree of controversy. Such a working environment was conducive to caution – to a bureaucracy that could police the Corporation.

No one person was the architect of this bureaucracy. E. Austin Weir dated its beginnings from the creation in 1944 of the Personnel and Administration division, often called 'Pest and Aggravation.' That division eventually arranged a new scheme of job classification and salary structure and, after fierce internal battles, imposed its own vision of order, wrapped up in a lot of red tape, upon corporate life. But Alphonse Ouimet was clearly the grand master of the managerial revolution that overcame the CBC in the 1950s. And, to listen to his critics, he was also the man most responsible for the administrative woes that troubled the Corporation during the 1950s and beyond. Ironically, Ouimet had caught 'the management bug' back when he became a chief engineer, according to Bushnell, and pursued his obsession by constantly tinkering with the CBC organization to match some textbook model of proper management. Judy LaMarsh, another harsh critic, noted that Ouimet had 'a positive passion for organization charts, and none at all for people they represented.' But it's only fair to add the comment of Ron Fraser, one of Ouimet's fans, who not only counted 'Al'

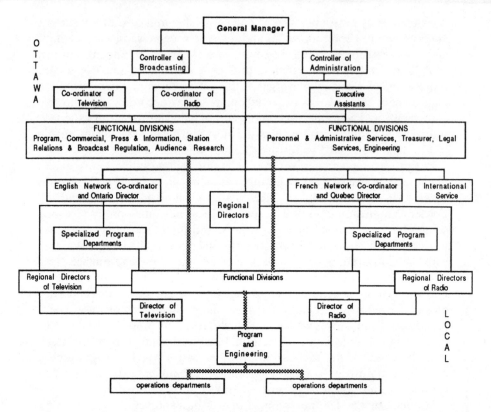

Figure 2.1 Abbreviated organizational chart of the CBC, 1956.
Note: The heavy lines indicate the connections among functional divisions. The figure is based upon information contained in one of the CBC submissions to Fowler I, 'Organization, Functions and Management' for 1956.

a 'good administrator, excellent,' but someone with 'a very good conception of how a large corporation should work.' Anyway, the post of general manager in a time of novelty and expansion allowed Ouimet the freedom to indulge himself.[18]

What critics forgot was that the Corporation was in desperate need of some kind of reorganization. Perhaps things would have been better had Ouimet been able to remake totally the organization of the CBC. The CBC brief to the Fowler Commission outlining the management of the corporation showed that it was a terrible patchwork of the old and the new (see figure 2.1). The model that comes to mind is less that of the modern, streamlined corporation than of the medieval kingdom: duties overlapped and authority was shared among a welter of competing units. There was, of course, a proliferation of titles: chief producer or chief engineer, an assortment of supervisors, directors galore, various co-ordinators and controllers and their assistants, plus the general manager and his assistant. Two principles of organization, the one territorial and the other functional, vied for supremacy, and each of the resulting units was further divided into special departments. The regions in English Canada, claimed the long-time CBCer Marce Munro, reported directly to Ottawa, not to Toronto, which in reality gave them a good deal of the autonomy that they jealously guarded. A distinct television service had been added on at the local and regional levels, only to be integrated in the offices of the respective English and French networks. The separation of these networks, by the way, dated back to 1938, and had left the CBC with two major program centres, one in Montreal and the other in Toronto, which symbolized the power of the 'two solitudes' in the cultural affairs of the country. Davidson Dunton admitted much later that the 'distance' between the two centres actually 'widened' in the television age.[19]

Ouimet had hoped to overcome this separation of the English and French services by strengthening the hitherto puny headquarters staff in Ottawa. It wasn't only rationality, efficiency, and economy that Ouimet planned to achieve. In addition, according to Bushnell again, Ouimet hoped his brand of centralized direction would eventually convert the CBC into more of a single, pan-Canadian agency. After some struggle, since people were reluctant to leave Montreal and Toronto, Ouimet had compelled a series of executives, now called directors, to move to Ottawa from each production centre, commencing in 1953. The 1956 organization chart indicates that he also had a number of titled assistants tied directly to the general manager's office to assist his endeavours. The task of this new team was to supervise operations and to plan for the future. They were supposed to exercise control through the receipt of a regular (in some cases weekly) series of reports from the regions and the divisions, a cumbersome network of committee meetings (often in Ottawa) to handle policy and practice, as well as an increasing variety of rule books on how to act, announce, produce, write, and so on. They were supposed to command the budget-making process, the key to any organization chart, because regional and functional directors were expected to submit competing estimates. My impression from reading a lot of memos written during the late 1950s is that the enlarged central office did, in fact, exercise an increasing degree of control over what happened in the two program centres. There is, however, no evidence that Ottawa's new importance bridged the gap between the French and English, except perhaps to create in the minds of some program people a common enemy.

The inflation of the top brass and the spread of its brand of bureaucratic rule had soon fostered a 'them and us' mentality in the CBC. That might seem a trifle strange, given the background and views of the managers. Many had come up through the ranks, albeit in the days of radio. They too could justly claim a devotion to what Charles Jennings (the controller of broadcasting) once called 'the sense of vocation' that must imbue every employee. But these managers were increasingly divorced from the actual task of programming, even though their wishes might determine what did and did not go on the air. That was the rub. The people who became the most cynical about the turn of events were the very artists so vital to the CBC's 'public service.' The animus towards managers could become truly extraordinary: Harry Boyle recalled that they were virtually a new species, driven by goals and moods different from those of the creative worker because they were engaged in a 'rat race,' presumably to satisfy personal ambition, that made them indifferent to the content of either radio or television. Producers began to ask, or so Don MacPherson remembered, 'What right do they [the managers] have to make those goddamned decisions?' That mood was strengthened among TV workers by the belief that most of the managers were really radio people, 'scared silly of television,' in Len Lauk's words, and therefore ill-equipped to decide the fate of CBC-TV.[20]

A special meeting of management called in September 1958 lamented 'the serious lack of loyalty' among the staff. How prophetic. The mood of dissension climaxed in two rebellions in the ranks in 1959, when administrators and artists, first in Montreal and shortly thereafter in Toronto, locked horns over issues of authority and autonomy. And in one of those sad ironies of history, the official who would suffer most was Ernie Bushnell, the vice-president who had never sympathized with Ouimet's reforms.

The lengthy, bitter producers' strike in Montreal came as a shock to the Ottawa managers. It began on 29 December 1958 and ended on 9 March 1959: not only did the strike cripple local French television, but it excited the nationalist juices of many a French Canadian. Brewing since the fall of 1955 when supervisory staff had started to usurp the prerogatives of producers, the dispute heated up in the fall of 1958 after local management proved not only unwilling to listen to producers' grievances but cavalier in its assignment of tasks, a kind of treatment that bruised the rather tender egos of these artists. The upshot was that the producers formed a new association, authorized to seek incorporation as a professional syndicate, and struck when management refused to admit their right to union affiliation or collective bargaining. The CBC team was eventually led by Bushnell, after a heart attack took Ouimet out of the fray, and for a time the Corporation tried to hang tough on the issue of managerial rights. The Ottawa officials were 'mystified' by the whole business, asserted Finlay Payne, since they looked upon the producer as a sort of manager who, by definition, shouldn't become part of a union. Although the rebels never won the sympathy of their Toronto compatriots or even in the end some national and international unions run by Anglos, the producers did receive the support of leading performers and writers in Quebec, notably René Lévesque (the star journalist) and Roger Lemelin (the famed author of *La famille Plouffe*), as well as the Confédération des Travailleurs Catholiques du Canada, which saw the strike as a precedent-setting event that would open up the white-collar and professional work-force to unionization.

The Corporation did eventually settle, on instructions from cabinet, according to Ouimet. What the strikers wanted was job security, respect, and something *Maclean's* called 'creative freedom,' meaning a near-sovereign power to command resources when entrusted with a production. What they got was the right to bargain collectively, though not to affiliate with any other union. The manager on the scene, André Ouimet (brother of Alphonse), who'd been the director of television at Montreal since 1953, became the scapegoat, kicked upstairs to a staff position from which he soon resigned. H.D. Woods, the arbitrator chosen to settle the unresolved issues, found cause for alarm in the attitudes of both parties: management because it had real difficulties accepting the legitimacy of the strike or the producers' grievances, and the producers because their 'occupational nearsightedness' made them distrust management and blinded them to the Corporation's problems. In any case the strike soon became part of the legend of the Quiet Revolution, emerging as an uprising of French-Canadian artists against Anglo authority.[21]

Just when the CBC was trying to get off the front page, the second clash broke out over the precipitous cancellation of the radio talk show 'Preview Commentary,' late in June 1959. Perhaps because of political pressure, perhaps because he was just plain tired and scared by continued controversy, Bushnell himself killed the show that had earned notoriety in Conservative circles for its criticism of Diefenbaker. What was so surprising was that the acting president moved without talking to the programmers involved. His explanations to others left the impression that he was submitting to some outside dictum. Frank Peers, the supervisor of the Talks and

Public Affairs department, and his three deputies resigned, after failing to get the decision rescinded. About thirty radio and television producers in Toronto also walked out, with other resignations in the offing. The spread of this whirlwind (even Dunton would shortly speak out against the cancellation) convinced the CBC board of directors to reconsider and reinstate 'Preview Commentary.' That decision was linked to a special leave for Bushnell, who had a drinking problem and was clearly expected to retire from the Corporation once the commotion subsided. Bushnell resigned in November, a man embittered by events that had shown he lacked the skills and the will to run the CBC properly. Once again the workers had challenged management, this time in defence of the CBC's integrity, and once again management was bloodied.[22]

Yet nothing changed to undo the effects of the managerial revolution. When Ouimet returned, he immediately regained control of a board of directors that had shown a bit too much independence in the confused days of Bushnell's acting presidency. He shortly carried out a major revamping of the headquarters team, creating three new general managers (for the English networks, the French networks, and regional broadcasting) plus five new vice-presidents, one of whom was responsible for programming (and for sales). In fact, before long, rumour had it that E.S. Hallman, the new vice-president of programming, enjoyed a big title but little authority.

A few years later, the Glassco Commission, investigating government organization, agreed, finding that neither Hallman nor the general managers had much control over the networks: 'effective management of broadcasting remained where it had always been – in Montreal and Toronto.' Indeed its report made the astonishing charge that programming was treated as 'an ancillary function' in Ottawa. Nor was that the end of the indictment. The commission lamented the fact that the board of directors was so much under the president's thumb, which meant that 'Corporation policy is largely dictated by management.' It attacked the continued pattern of shared and overlapping duties, the 'profusion of committees,' the lack of an 'effective central authority,' 'an over-zealous control of secondary activities,' and the general 'incoherence of the organization.' All that had been achieved, so it seemed, was to add new layers of management on top of the old.[23]

This wasn't news to the producers and performers, of course. They now assumed that the managers lived in a different world. At some point the Toronto folk had come to call the CBC executive offices on Jarvis Street 'the Kremlin.' What separated the Kremlin and the CBC's studios, decided

Barris, was 'a parking lot and a few million light years.' Administrators and artists marched to quite different drummers.[24]

Issues of Control

Management faced challenges to its authority from outside the institution as well. True, the independence of the CBC was guaranteed by the Broadcasting Act and by tradition. Yet television was too tempting a prize not to attract attention – indeed, at one point, the CBC's top brass found that it had to resist pressure from the Corporation's own part-time directors.

Only a few of these challenges came from government itself. By and large, government leaders respected the independence of the CBC. On occasion, though, a minister did wish to muzzle CBC news and public affairs. So, in 1954 an over-wrought C.D. Howe, the Liberal's super-minister, threatened to fire everyone, including Dunton, should the CBC air a proposed television documentary on unemployment. Quickly Howe realized how silly, and dangerous, was such a threat; instead, he expressed his annoyance and his desire for a postponement – in fact the show aired at the scheduled time. In 1956 Prime Minister Louis St Laurent wrote a letter – as a private citizen he said later – objecting to the critical tone of one guest speaker's comments on Canadian foreign policy. Tom Earle, a CBC Ottawa reporter, noted an occasion when Prime Minister Diefenbaker actually told him not to pose a particular question on Britain, Canada, and the Common Market (then a highly contentious issue) to Harold Macmillan, the visiting British prime minister. The to-do was overheard by some print reporters, and Diefenbaker's ban caused a bit of flap in the press, embarrassing both Earle and the prime minister. Much the most serious case arose out of the brief cancellation of 'Preview Commentary' in 1959 because of suspected 'clandestine political influence.' But in fact the show was swiftly reinstated and a parliamentary investigation discovered no evidence of such direct influence. The CBC was reasonably safe as long as it adhered to its policies of impartiality and balance. That was one very good reason why the Talks and Public Affairs department kept lists to prove that the topics selected and the speakers invited conformed to the rule of balance.[25]

Relations with the business community were a good deal more complicated, of course. What might have been the most serious adversary was the Canadian Association of Broadcasters (CAB), which represented the interests of the private radio and television industry. Toronto's Jack Kent

Cooke, owner of the radio station CKEY, would have been delighted to sheer the CBC of its stations and networks, leaving the Corporation only the task of making programs for private distribution. Early in 1953 he did use his newly acquired journal, *Saturday Night*, to question the virtues and even the legitimacy of CBC television, publishing first a remarkable critique by Joseph Sedgwick, the long-time counsel of the CAB, followed by an articulate plea for a private service written by one 'Woodman Lamb,' thought to be Hugh Garner. Theirs was a plea for a cultural democracy, in which no élite, however sophisticated, could prevent the public from getting what it wanted. It was also, of course, a plea for American-style TV. Rarely was the case for private television put so well. Still the same kind of notion justified the pioneers of private TV, such as Ken Soble of CHCH-Hamilton who proclaimed (according to a profile in *Maclean's*) his 'very average tastes' and his determination to supply 'what the people want.' It was a viewpoint that found support from politicians of all stripes during the 1950s – whether a Conservative such as George Drew or a CCFer such as Clarence Gillis or even a Liberal such as Jack St John.[26]

But what the CAB eventually told the Fowler Commission was merely that an independent board should take over the task of broadcast regulation, and that the single-station policy should give way to competitive television. What Dunton replied was that the CBC could live with both suggestions, since neither threatened to undo its responsibility for national broadcasting. Likely the CBC's willingness to surrender its privileges was a politic move to avoid the perils of a head-on clash with private interests. The agreement was embodied in the Fowler I as well as in the Broadcasting Act of 1958, passed by the Conservatives. The assault on public television and the CBC feared by such apologists as Arthur Lower or Ralph Allen simply did not materialize during the 1950s.

One reason was that the CBC had bought off much of its potential opposition. It had proved an exceedingly lenient, and generous, master of private television. Right from the beginning the CBC's board of governors seemed happy to grant licences to people in the radio and newspaper businesses, even if this meant strengthening 'local information monopolies.' That action stilled any lingering fears among radio men that television might be turned over to newcomers to broadcasting.[27]

The Corporation also worked hard to assure its affiliates that they were allies in a common enterprise. So the Station Relations and Broadcast Regulation division tried to keep the private affiliates happy, careful that network needs and the assorted rules didn't step hard on the toes of the private owners. Its success can be measured by the public's complaints to the Fowler Commission that the CBC didn't enforce its own regulations on private television with sufficient rigour. Even so, there were some signs of unhappiness among affiliates: a Maritime broadcaster once took out a newspaper ad to apologize for bringing the highbrow 'Folio' to irate viewers – 'Blame CBC,' he declared.[28]

Most important the CBC's network service supplied the affiliates with a much-needed wealth of programming free of charge. By May 1955, for example, CFPL-London relied on the network for forty-four hours, or 51 per cent of its schedule, and the next year the Fowler Commission would find that this was very common. Besides the CBC paid, and paid well, for the privilege of using the affiliates. Yearly it forwarded a share of the consequent advertising revenues – the private stations received $5.2 million in fiscal year 1960/1 – which only highlighted the most obvious cause of satisfaction: after a few rocky years, private television had proved to be a very profitable business. A front-page story in *The Financial Post* (17 December 1955) noted that station owners were 'riding the crest of a prosperity wave' because the demand for air time by advertisers was apparently insatiable. The Canadian Bank of Commerce Letter of 6 June 1960 ranked broadcasting the third-best profit-maker among 140 industries in 1957.[29]

Dealings with advertising agencies also proved happy – eventually. The creed of public broadcasting required that the CBC carefully avoid any taint of commercialism. That assumption explains the sensitivity of the Corporation's executives to the issue of advertising. Certain kinds of broadcasts, such as news, public affairs, and religion, were considered inappropriate as vehicles for any commercial messages. The content of commercials was vetted by CBC personnel to ensure it wouldn't offend. Yet the CBC relied upon advertising revenues to generate the extra monies necessary to support its made-in-Canada programming. Indeed the CBC's monopoly position allowed it to impose a special burden on national advertisers. They were required to sponsor some made-in-Canada programming if they wished to sponsor an American import, which wasn't a popular move because Canadian shows rarely got the ratings to justify the expenditure of much of the adman's dollar.

A special difficulty was that in the beginning the agencies wanted a say in the programs that carried their client's names, just as in the days of radio. That the CBC refused. 'They were used to paying the money and calling the piper,' Dunton was later quoted as saying. 'We said, you pay the money, and we'll call the piper.' The American networks didn't achieve a comparable control over their own schedules and programming until the end of the 1950s. Novelty had its costs: again according to Dunton, some big companies, such as Proctor and Gamble and Lever Brothers, initially refused to buy any time.[30]

Sooner or later, though, a modus vivendi was worked out. The CBC admitted to the Fowler Commission that it consulted advertisers about the shape and content of Canadian shows, trying where reasonable to meet their wishes. Leonard Starmer, a supervisor of variety, recalled later how he was 'always prepared to listen,' tried to find a 'compromise' when necessary, and wouldn't do something to 'conflict with a client.' The record suggests that sometimes the CBC went a bit farther. At one time, argued Alex Barris, the agency for General Motors objected to so many script proposals for 'General Motors Presents' that the play anthology earned the title 'General Motors Prevents.' Then there was the case of the variety extravaganza 'Showtime': the dissatisfaction of Canadian General Electric with Norman Jewison, then one of the English network's top producers of variety, led the CBC to replace him. Scott Young claimed there was an instance in which General Motors actually vetoed the production of a spoof of big business, even after the play was scheduled and cast. Two specific examples of sponsor pressure came before the 8th program committee of the CBC board of directors in January 1960. When General Motors decided to disassociate itself from *Shadow of a Pale Horse*, the CBC went ahead anyway with the taping and the airing of the play as a sustaining (non-commercial) show. Not so with *Point of Departure*, a play planned for 'Ford Startime': after the agency raised questions about the script, the CBC did complete the taping, only to kill the show after a special viewing. In fact the CBC record shows nothing approaching a horror story comparable to the quiz scandals that blackened the reputation of the American networks during the 1950s. In those days, at least, the CBC did manage to keep the demon of commercialism at bay.[31]

The toughest problem of them all, ironically, was how best to deal with the public. In the radio age the CBC had benefited from the presence of a substantial public-broadcasting lobby made up of academics and artists, organized labour and organized religion, women's and consumer groups, farm associations, and so on. They had proved their worth during the deliberations of the Massey Commission by sending in a host of pro-CBC briefs. But the proceedings of the Fowler Commission demonstrated that this loyalty was on the wane. Even though many of the briefs submitted by voluntary associations continued to support the CBC, they also criticized a lot of the details of CBC programming.

More serious, a fair number of submissions wanted to compel the CBC to take account of their particular views. So the idea of program advisory committees found favour with such diverse groups as the YMCA, the Nova Scotia Federation of Home and School, the Canadian Arts Council and the Canadian Council of Artists and Authors, the CTCC and the Labour-Progressives (Communists), and La Fédération des Sociétés Saint-Jean-Baptiste du Québec. The Société Saint-Jean-Baptiste de Montréal wished that the board of governors was made up of representatives of the universities, trade unions, and other voluntary associations. It was particularly interested in the increased representation of French Canadians. By comparison the Canadian Association of Consumers desired the appointment of at least 'one representative woman' to the board, in order to offset the unease about the lack of citizen input. All of these suggestions were part of a strategy of capture on the part of the voluntary associations. Television seemed to provide a golden opportunity to aid their causes, be they popularizing opera or psychiatry, protecting morals, or advancing labour, and the dreamers wanted to command the medium.

That wish the CBC could never grant. The Corporation didn't rule out the notion of consulting with outsiders. The Talks and Public Affairs department tried to maintain a close contact with academics, journalists, and assorted experts to ensure a full and fair coverage of affairs. 'Citizen's Forum' and 'Les idées en marche' were produced in co-operation with adult educators. The English network relied on a national religious advisory council to assist the Corporation in allocating time, producing shows, and even buying imports. Indeed, during the first half of 1959, Bushnell and his beleaguered assistants actually gave tentative approval to the proposal of an advisory committee for the French networks to stem the tide of criticism over programming. That initiative was scotched by the directors – the historian and director W.L. Morton thought that the committee would amount to 'an abdication of the CBC's responsibility' to control 'its own output.' Besides, a surrender here would constitute a precedent for surrender everywhere to any clamour raised by any special interest. Program appraisals through ratings and letters were okay, as was some variant of the special panels then employed in Britain to reflect viewers' opinions. Anything more substantial, though, could only lead to chaos.[32]

Two years earlier, the Fowler Commission had argued that advisory committees could only 'usurp' the role of the board of governors – 'to represent the people of Canada.' That raised the question of the make-up and the activities of the board. The nine part-time directors appointed by the Conservative government differed little in type from the earlier governors: there were two women and seven men, representing the spread of regions, four of whom were from the business world, two from academe, one from a farm association, and another active in community affairs. The one unusual director was Kate Aitken, an experienced broadcaster most closely associated with the private Toronto radio station CFRB. The directors' minutes show that she came to the board with a particular mission in mind, namely to represent the middlebrow tastes of the mainstream of society (in her words the 'middle-income-and-education group'). Aitken was convinced that the CBC didn't serve this mainstream nearly as well as it looked after both highbrows and lowbrows. She had conducted a survey of opinion from among a range of English-Canadian voluntary associations. She regarded the board's program committee as the tool of reform where she could question corporate executives, propose changes, and push for innovative programs. At the committee's second meeting, for example, she told Jennings (the controller of broadcasting) that the CBC's afternoon programming for women was poorly scheduled to suit the viewing needs of 'four and a half million Canadian housewives.' Some of the other directors, notably the two academics, C.B. Lumsden and W.L. Morton, were also willing to air their own particular concerns. And Raymond Dupuis, the sole Quebec representative, actually criticized the CBC's tolerance of minority views, wanting instead a celebration of traditional beliefs about life and society.[33]

Whatever the promise implicit in this obstreperousness, neither survived the return of Ouimet to the CBC's helm. He moved swiftly to discipline the program committee by subjecting the directors to a tight agenda, a lot of executive reports, and a series of motions endorsing aspects of the status quo. He neutralized Aitken by accepting the notion of a national survey of listener/viewer opinions about CBC programming – a survey that, in the end, produced little more than a mass of idiosyncratic data that corporate executives claimed was unrepresentative. And at the ninth meeting, in April 1960, he got the program committee to endorse management's draft of a document entitled 'The Future Role of the CBC.' The program committee might be effective as a complaint bureau, a place where directors could express their grievances about this or that program, but once more management had staved off a challenge to its authority.

Ouimet's success was a Pyrrhic victory though. Even management recognized by 1960 that the CBC had lost 'the active support' of the old public-broadcasting lobby. That loss it put down to a growing perception of CBC-TV as merely 'a commercial operation.' What management apparently didn't consider was that its insistence on control might well have alienated one-time friends. Could they any longer believe that the CBC was open to public suggestion?[34]

Money Troubles

The most persistent difficulty, and sometimes the most critical problem faced by the CBC, was money. Two kinds of money were required. First came capital funds to acquire land, build and equip studios, construct new stations, and expand administrative facilities. If initially the need for such funds had been great, it had tailed off after the middle of the decade – by fiscal year 1959/60, the CBC was down to a parliamentary grant of $6.3 million for capital expenditures. Not so the need for the second type of money, operating funds. The CBC required larger and larger sums to operate the rapidly expanding television networks as well as to maintain its radio service. Between 1953/4 and 1958/9 the overall operating expenses were jumping upward by more than $10 million a year. That increase was explained by television. In 1952/3 it cost the CBC roughly $2.9 million to operate its fledgling television service; by 1959/60 it was costing $65.6 million gross (or $39.5 million net for the total cost of the TV service) for what the Corporation considered the 'production and distribution' of a mature service.[35]

By far the largest chunk of the TV dollar, some $46.3 million, went to pay for programming, almost all of the funds consumed by domestic production though with a little left over for imported telefilms (see chart 2.2). That demonstrated both the commitment of the CBC and the expense of the effort. Next came the delivery charges, only $1.7 million for station transmission but $7 million for network distribution, a financial burden that resulted, of course, from the attempt to span the country. Then there was the payment to the private affiliates of $5.2 million for the use of their time and schedules for sponsored network shows. The final costs of $5.3 million in commission fees went mostly to advertising agencies, with something in the neighbourhood of $1.7 million going to U.S. networks for live feeds of sponsored programs.[36]

The CBC had known from the beginning that operating a television service would be expensive. Back in the late 1940s, Ouimet's report on television had made clear that the public must contribute $10 and later $15 a year for each television set to keep the service healthy. That was the origin of the famous '1952 plan' explained to the Fowler Commission in 1956, namely a plan for providing a service with 'a reasonable proportion

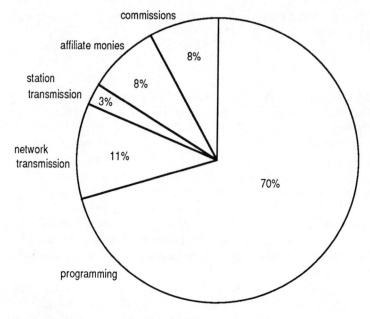

commissions

affiliate monies

station
transmission

network
transmission

programming

8%

8%

3%

11%

70%

Chart 2.2 The television dollar, 1959/60
Source: Based on data in Fowler II, 331

of Canadian programming in two languages' to 'about 75 per cent of the population from coast to coast' at a cost of $15 per television home per year, 'together with commercial support.' The plan had been brought to the government's attention early in 1952.[37]

Thus broadcasters and politicians knew that the public would supply a lot of the money necessary to finance CBC television (see chart 2.3). The key questions were how much and by what method. The Corporation had at first expected to receive its public funds for television through the proceeds of a yearly licence fee, as in the case of radio. The prospect encouraged the comforting thought that in time CBC television would be self-sustaining, its operating needs covered by the revenues from licence fees and from advertising. What dashed such dreams was the government's decision to do away with the licence fee because of its unpopularity with a public that believed broadcasting should be 'free' as it was in the United States. The public had always resisted paying the $2.50 radio licence fee. That sometimes choked the courts with spring business, or so Pierre Berton claimed, and he recounted how an irate Mr John T. Schmidt sent in his

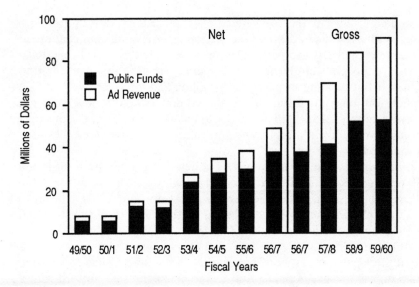

Chart 2.3 CBC operating revenues, 1950s
Note: The figures on television revenues are first 'Net' and later 'Gross' as a
result of a change in the way the Corporation counted the monies earned from
advertising – the change-over had no effect on the size of the public funds.
Data from CBC *Annual Reports.*

summons, fee, and even radio set to the Kitchener police. The Massey
Report observed that the existing licence fee should have yielded 'over
eight and a half millions a year ... instead of something over five million,'
which suggested how extensive was the evasion of the payment of this 'tax.'
One writer later stated that collection costs were about an eighth of the
gross proceeds. Such experiences convinced the government that the task
of collecting a $15 television licence fee would be too costly, in money and
goodwill. This was an unfortunate decision, and one the Corporation clearly
regretted, because the existence of the licence fee strengthened the appearance of independence so important to the morale and mission of the CBC.[38]

The government had already begun to move away from the licence fee
before the advent of television. The Massey Report had recommended a
statutory grant in lieu of an increase in the radio licence fee, and in the
fall of 1951 the government had authorized an extra $6.25 million annually
for five years. Then the government delayed announcing the expected
licence fee for television. Finally, in February 1953, the government did

away completely with the licence-fee policy, replacing it with an ingenious scheme whereby the CBC would receive the returns of a 15 per cent excise tax on television sets and parts. That produced a feast in 1953/4 and 1954/5 because people were buying TV sets so eagerly: the first year the CBC managed an operating surplus of $6.5 million and the second year of $4.3 million. But once the buying boom slowed down, the CBC was faced not just with deficits (of $1.3 million in 1955/6) but with starvation. The prospect was one compelling reason for the government's decision to establish the Fowler Commission.[39]

Little wonder that the make-up of the new royal commission suggested a business bias quite different from the highbrow cast of mind of the Massey Commission. Robert Fowler was a lawyer whose career in business and the public service had been shaped by that alliance of the state and the corporations fashioned in the Liberal years during and after the Second World War. Unquestionably Fowler and his compatriots were worried about the escalating costs of Canadian television, and wished to limit the drain on the taxpayer's purse. Still the commission came forward with a report that recommended leaving the receipts of the excise tax for capital expenditures and establishing a new system of statutory grants for operating funds that would be fixed for, say, a five-year period. The latter would have guaranteed the CBC some security from the vagaries of government and the moods of Parliament.[40]

That proposal died when Diefenbaker and the Tories came to power. They had been fierce critics of the fiscal record of the CBC: Diefenbaker himself, in 1956, denounced the Corporation's 'hog-wild expenditures.' Their Broadcasting Act of 1958 laid down that the Corporation's capital and operating needs would be financed through annual parliamentary grants. The yearly exercise ensured that the CBC's performance could be closely watched by government. The exercise also closed the distance between the CBC and Parliament, which had offered some protection against political pressures in times past. Did the change threaten the independence of the CBC? Frank Peers, the Toronto supervisor of Talks and Public Affairs, apparently thought that was one lesson of the 'Preview Commentary' fiasco. But the change, in government and in the act, didn't seem to make much difference to the public funds of the Corporation, for operating funds actually jumped $10 million in 1958/9, though the total levelled off at $52.3 million the next year.[41]

What was especially remarkable about this funding was that its size fitted well the old estimates made by Ouimet some ten years earlier. By the end of the decade the public cost of television was around $16 or $17 per television set per year, very close to the planned $15 (and recall that the coverage was much greater than the planned 75 per cent). CBC briefs and executives often boasted that television only cost about four cents a day per family, one cent per individual each day, or even one cent an hour. It was so marvellously cheap.[42]

It wasn't cheap enough for the CBC's political masters, however, who hoped that the Corporation would generate more and more of its operating revenues from advertising. That view was sanctioned first by the Fowler Commission report, and given added force by a recommendation of the parliamentary committee on broadcasting in 1959. In fact the CBC had recognized the need to secure supplemental advertising revenue from the beginning. Management knew that it couldn't afford as many sustaining shows on television as it had on radio. Whereas in 1950/1 around one-fifth of the CBC's radio schedules had advertising, early in 1957 about one-third of the programming on French television was sponsored, as was almost half of the English programming. The individual television stations were expected to drum up local advertising business as well. The result was that CBC television did begin to earn a larger and larger share of its keep. The change-over from 'net' to 'gross' financial data makes comparisons tricky before and after 1957, although it appears that commercial revenue began to swell rapidly from the mid-1950s (see chart 2.3). By 1959/60 advertising generated a sufficient sum to cover 41 per cent of the total corporate expenses. Television had produced $36.3 million, or well over half the cost of running the two television networks. The contract with General Motors alone was worth roughly $2.25 million. It was a banner year for the CBC's sales division. Never again would commercial revenues cover so large a portion of the general expenses of television or of the Corporation.[43]

This degree of success hadn't come easy. One problem the Corporation had was the lack of local CBC stations. Such stations were the real money-makers. Running a network and producing a lot of live programming were the most costly and the least profitable aspects of a television service. Yet the CBC couldn't persuade either the Liberal government or the Fowler Commission of the wisdom of increasing the roster of public stations across the country. That hobbled any commercial strategy.

Nor could the CBC charge sponsors the full cost of made-in-Canada programming. Ironically, the CBC could easily make money out of the broadcast of American network shows or syndicated telefilms. But the costs of television production were just too high and the Canadian market too small to try to compel sponsors to pay the whole shot for live programming. It seemed wiser to get as much as possible from advertisers to cover the expenses involved in producing the sports and light entertainment that had to be a big feature of any CBC schedule. So the CBC devised a formula that involved a charge for direct costs, an estimate for indirect costs, a series of special discounts and the like, which might result in a return of only half of the money invested. This practice was later criticized as a subsidy for advertisers, though the CBC correctly responded that it was one way to stretch the public's dollar farther in an effort to produce more made-in-Canada entertainment. In 1956, for example, Aylmer Food Products and Nabisco Foods shared 60 per cent of the costs of the country music show 'Holiday Ranch,' leaving the CBC the other 40 per cent. The financial adviser for the Fowler Commission discovered that the Corporation recovered 55 per cent of its costs for commercial shows aired during the week 15–21 January 1956: $116,155 from sponsors for programs costing $211,942. Even more striking was the admission, much later, that the CBC had managed to lose money on sports. According to Bushnell, after paying for the broadcast rights, production costs, and distribution charges, the CBC had lost about $300,000 on football in 1959. He did offer the consolation, though, that the Corporation made money on hockey broadcasts.[44]

There was one other avenue that promised to yield the CBC additional revenues – exports. The CBC was among the world pioneers of television, and its success might well allow it to find markets in countries where the medium was just starting up. There was much hope that the CBC could become a global producer of television drama, especially of the teleplays that were among the most expensive offerings of CBC television. A report in *The Financial Post* (29 June 1957) enthusiastically proclaimed that Canada was 'the world's third TV producer' and talked of sales to Britain and Australia plus nibbles from France, Germany, Sweden, Finland, and even Japan. Indeed one teleplay had proved a smash hit in Britain and in the United States: Arthur Hailey's *Flight into Danger*, though in the end this had a much more lasting impact on the author's career than on the CBC's export policy. Much later, in February 1960, Granada Television, a British firm, purchased over $200,000 worth of CBC-produced material, including a science program 'Web of Life,' segments of 'The Friendly Giant' (a kids' series) and 'The Unforeseen' (half-hour dramas of the occult and unexpected), plus a lot of teleplays from 'General Motors Presents.' In addition, the CBC was part of a co-production effort with the independent Crawley Films and the BBC to produce 'RCMP,' a filmed crime drama, for broadcast at home and abroad. American syndication rights had gone to a California firm, showing rights were sold to the Australian Broadcasting

Commission, and the 'first foreign sales' were to Lebanon and the Philippines. It seemed a promise of great things to come.

The promise wasn't fulfilled. The few foreign sales that the CBC secured never amounted to much in terms of its production costs. Indeed the worldwide spread of Hollywood's empire had already doomed whatever chance the CBC may have had to earn money from outside Canada. The American product was so much more polished than any Canadian competition, and that was because Hollywood producers had lavish budgets by comparison with those of their Toronto or Montreal compatriots. So the Corporation's failure highlighted what was otherwise hidden in all this description of grants and expenses. The government may have seemed generous in its willingness to fund the expansion of CBC-TV, and advertisers may have contributed millions to the benefit of made-in-Canada programming, but all this money was only sufficient for a basic service. The fact was that Canadian television was undernourished by North American and British standards: the target figure of $15 per TV home on which CBCers had based their hopes was too meagre.

3

What's on Tonight?

There has never been any doubt, there is no doubt now, about the CBC's job. It is to offer the whole of Canada everything that broadcasting has to give.

J.B. McGeachy, 1959[1]

J.B. McGeachy had taken up the cudgel for the CBC at a time of crisis, following the Montreal producers' strike and the 'Preview Commentary' fiasco, when an array of critics were condemning the Corporation for just about everything, including its philosophy of programming. McGeachy was responding to the people who thought that the Corporation 'ought to provide only Bach, Ibsen, folk music and lectures on existentialism.' His declaration merely summarized what the CBC had been preaching to Parliament, the press, and the public throughout the 1950s. Understandably the Corporation was dead-set against arguments that its service should be limited to minority programming or even to Canadian productions. That fate would have made the CBC something much less than the BBC or the American networks, and would have consigned CBC-TV to the fringes of Canadian culture. Only a complete schedule, full of all kinds of delights, could hope to realize the CBC's goals and satisfy public tastes.

The Programmer's Task

Half seriously, Roy Shields once told readers of *The Toronto Daily Star* (27 September 1962) that they could blame a largely unknown Michael Sadlier for the failings of the CBC's nightly schedule. Sadlier was a network program director and so had the biggest say in the selection of shows for the English network, reasoned Shields. This 'logic' was at the heart of what would soon become an enduring myth in North American television: the notion that the 'programmer' was all-powerful. At times that soul was seen to be invested with the power to make or break new shows, to determine network profits, even to start public trends, all because he enjoyed the chief responsibility for creating a schedule. In this way, the programmer became a kind of tyrant whose eccentric will shaped the viewing experience of millions of individuals. The virtue of this myth lay in the fact that its focus on personality simplified a mystery of life that, however mundane, was none the less of key importance to many, many people. The reality was much more complex.[2]

The actions of Sadlier and his cohorts were in large measure predetermined. The making of a schedule is a kind of artistry conditioned by the ways of television as well as by the needs of the local setting. Any schedule had to adjust to certain basic facts, all of which developed over the course of the 1950s. First, while special events, such as the opening of Parliament or a play-off game, and the occasional spectacular, such as the performance of *Peter Pan*, might disturb things, nearly the whole of the weekly schedule was made up of episodes of regular shows suited to the viewing habits of the millions. Second, the television year was actually composed of three fairly distinct seasons. Increasingly, the fall season, September through December, was the time when new titles were introduced; the spring season, January through April, saw only slight changes in the mix, usually because some new series had obviously failed to please viewers; and the summer season, May through August, was a one of confusion, when old shows completed their runs, trial replacements tested their luck, and reruns or movies and films filled time. (The CBC did use July, though, to introduce some new shows that would continue throughout the fall.) Third, what shows the programmer chose to place on the schedule reflected the wisdom that prevailed among the networks. It was here that the story of primetime began to take on the dimensions of a drama in its own right.

It's necessary at this point to consider briefly the ingredients of a primetime schedule. Television entertainment meant borrowed entertainment: borrowed, that is, from radio, the cinema and the stage, the novel and the short story, the world of sports, and vaudeville and night-clubs. Television news relied heavily for its standards and values on the norms of newspaper journalism. But TV rarely offered up any of this material unchanged. The networks imposed their own ways of doing things, as a result of the bias of the technology and their desire to serve everyman and everywoman. The particular difficulty posed by television was and remains its continuous stream of images and sounds that doesn't allow the viewer (as print does the reader) much time to reflect or reconsider. It's a situation ready-made for misunderstanding, especially if the showman doesn't take care to encode his message in ways that suit the occasion. Thus, when the CBC first offered American football in the early 1960s, the broadcast had to include elaborate explanations by an American of the rules and the plays so that viewers versed in the Canadian game weren't confused by what was happening on the screen.[3]

Experience led producers to develop shows that would speak in an idiom common to all kinds of viewers, shows that would command the understanding of the audience, even if it comprised the most casual or indifferent of viewers, to ensure that the intended meaning of any message would be conveyed. The priority fostered a liking for gimmicks (a pretty face, stirring music, lively dancing, etc.) to grab and hold the attention of the viewer. It encouraged simplicity; an effort was made to reduce any message to those bare essentials that could be easily and swiftly conveyed via the repetition of a series of overlapping images, sounds, or words. It led to a heavy emphasis on formula, on a limited range of character types, on the myths and moods and even gestures and habits general throughout society, both in the design and in the execution of a show. Television shows are, by and large, products of convention: each usually belongs to a particular genre, although many shows may succeed only when they vary the formula slightly to capture the eye of the viewer. That's why most of what appeared on television eventually became very predictable.[4]

For the sake of convenience, I've adopted a simple brand of content analysis, which identifies a number of distinct TV forms that are themselves collections of more specific genres of programming. 'Information' incorporates newscasts, panel discussions and press conferences, features and documentaries, talk shows and human-interest shows, and instructional programs, all of which purport to provide the viewer with data about reality useful to his or her life. 'Display' refers in particular to variety shows of all kinds, from country music to comedy, plus performances of opera, ballet, and dance, where the participants offer the public demonstrations of their talent. 'Contests' covers sportscasts, games, and quizzes, where the participants are expected to perform in some kind of arena according to a set of rules to win victory or a prize. 'Storytelling,' which became the dominant form of programming on television, refers to all kinds of fictional drama: plays and movies, situation comedies, action/adventure series such as westerns or spy shows, mysteries, and professional sagas and soap operas. 'Advertisements,' while not usually considered programming, none the less constitute a form of television defined by its purpose, namely to sell a good or service, as well as its eclectic character, since commercials borrow conventions from all of the genres of fact and fiction. These, then, are the building-blocks out of which programmers must construct a primetime schedule.[5]

Fowler I boasted a meaty chapter entitled 'The Programme Fare' that was replete with facts and figures about the shows available here and in the United States. The chapter also embodied the ideal of 'balance' that had swiftly attained a hallowed status among champions of better broadcasting. Apparently any schedule that deserved to be called good had to offer viewers a choice among different forms of programming, thus serving to inform, to enlighten, to entertain, and to sell goods. 'A broadcaster who provides his audience with nothing but XVIth century music and Ibsenish dramas is no better than the broadcaster who never moves out of tin-pan alley and the cops-and-robbers theatre.' What surprised and pleased the commission was the fact that statistics demonstrated CBC television had a very good record here, better than American television.[6]

The conclusion, however, only hinted at some of the striking contrasts characterizing the assorted brands of primetime television and the clashing philosophies of programming that determined the shape of the evening schedules. The priority of profit-making plus the fact of competition led the American networks to endorse the logic of mass communication, striving to craft schedules that would reach the largest number of viewers and generate the largest amount of advertising revenue. The ideal of 'balance' enjoyed little clout in a world where the language of ratings and money prevailed. There was room for innovation, especially at first, though as primetime programming matured the fall seasons became better known for imitation than novelty. So the American brand of primetime displayed an inevitable sameness: not only did the networks come to offer much the same mix of programs, but over time this mix became more heavily weighted towards specific forms of television (see chart 3.1).

Put another way, viewer choice extended little beyond an opportunity to select among similar shows from a restricted series of genres popular with the mass audience. In the fall of 1951, for example, American networks offered an extraordinary number of variety shows (well over one-third of the total schedule), from Ed Sullivan's showcase 'Toast of the Town' to Milton Berle's 'Texaco Star Theater'; but by the fall of 1959, these networks had filled nearly half of the schedule with action/adventure drama, particu-

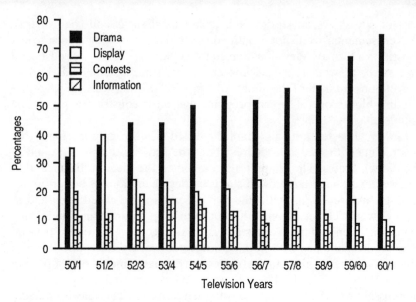

Chart 3.1 American primetime
Note: The chart is based on network schedules for the fall and spring seasons
chiefly. Sources are Tim Brooks and Earle Marsh, *The Complete Directory to
Prime Time Network TV Shows 1946–Present*, 2nd ed. (New York: Ballantine
1981); Alex McNeil, *Total Television: A Comprehensive Guide to Programming
from 1948 to 1980* (New York: Penguin 1980); and Harry Castleman and Walter
J. Podrazik, *Watching TV: Four Decades of American Television* (New York:
McGraw-Hill 1982).

larly westerns such as 'Gunsmoke' and crime dramas such as 'The Untouchables.' Even viewers lucky enough to receive all three networks would often
find themselves with little choice but to watch one kind of story or another.
The American networks were the happy prisoners of fads and fashions,
ready to embrace any genre that promised to capture for the moment the
public's fancy. The programming philosophy prevalent in the United States
appeared to suit the maxim of 'giving the people what they wanted.'[7]

That maxim was anathema to the masters of the CBC who were imbued
with the ethos of public service. 'If everybody pays,' Ouimet told an interviewer, 'everybody should get something back.' Right from the beginning,
the Corporation (like its mentor, the BBC) had denied the existence of a
mass audience. 'There is no "typical Canadian listener", no uniform Canadian "public", which has one taste,' went the argument presented to Fowler

1. 'The Canadian public is made up of a great many individuals, each with personal tastes in broadcasting. There are actually a number of different "publics", whose memberships greatly overlap.' It followed that 'part of our responsibility to the Canadian people is to cater to many different tastes,' asserted Mavor Moore, 'and not to reduce everything to the lowest common denominator.' The CBC's perception of the audience dictated a weekly schedule containing 'a good mixture' and 'a pretty wide choice of fare,' in Davidson Dunton's words, a view that resulted in schedules far different from what prevailed south of the border (see chart 3.2). People should be able to find 'lots of things that are simply entertaining, that pass the time in an amusing way.' But, in addition, they should also find 'there is a good deal of material that adds a touch of beauty, new insight, perhaps a bit better understanding of things that go on in Canada, a glimpse of what big minds in other places and other times have created.'[8]

Back in 1950, Pierre Berton had neatly labelled the CBC's radio fare a 'curious brew of corn, culture and Canadianism,' flavoured with borrowings from both the British and the American styles of broadcasting. That same description would have been equally appropriate for CBC-TV five years or even ten years later. The primetime schedules of both the English and the French networks were much more diverse than those of their American counterparts. That's why the occasional American critic who looked at CBC-TV got the feeling that he had travelled back into the past: primetime Canada still retained the design of an earlier era when programmers and producers were trying out all manner of programming.[9]

But there were definite constraints on just how far the CBC could go to realize its philosophy of programming. One of the biggest was the fact that it had only one channel to serve each of the language groups. Much of its programming had to be aimed at the widest possible audience available at any one time, although the CBC did try to reserve a chunk of time for the needs of children, especially in the late-afternoon time-slot before 6:00 PM, and another chunk for adults, male and female, in the late evening (see chart 3.3). Ouimet admitted later that the corporation couldn't do 'a proper job of serving everyone with one channel.' The effort led to particular difficulties with the Montreal audience in the 1950s, he recalled, when Radio-Canada served up wrestling one night for the lowbrows and the next night a concert hour for music lovers, resulting in complaints from both. His lament?: 'Everybody says "you're neglecting me." '

Besides, the CBC, especially in English Canada, never had full control of its own schedule. Some portion of primetime was always filled with foreign imports. The Corporation never spelled out exactly how much Canadian

A. CBLT-Toronto

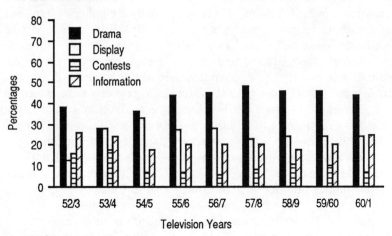

B. CBFT-Montreal

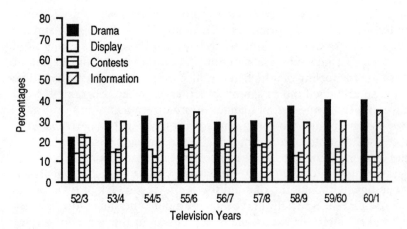

Chart 3.2 Canadian primetime (1950s)
Note: This chart depicts the whole year and is based on published schedules of
regular programming. It does not have the accuracy of a count based on actual
data. Data taken from weekly program listings in the CBC Times and La
Semaine à Radio-Canada.

A. French Network

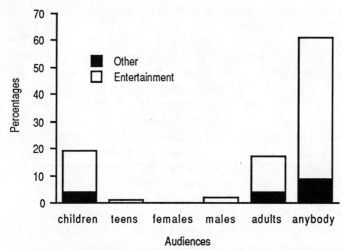

A. English Network

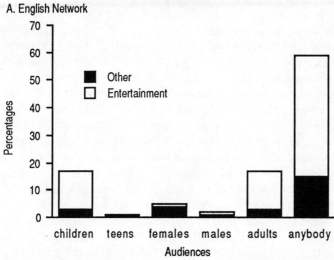

Chart 3.3 Target audiences
Note: 'Anybody' means literally 'anybody who would listen.' 'Females' and 'Males' refer to adults only. 'Other' refers to all non-entertainment programming. Data from CBC, Audience Research Division, 'Program Statistical Analysis Report,' Winter 1957–8, 39

content it was reasonable to expect. The French service was largely dependent upon its own resources, and its people enjoyed the freedom to place shows roughly where they pleased on the schedule. Even when imported drama such as 'Histoire d'amour' and 'Télépolicier' from France or 'Théâtre Colgate' (the French version of 'Foreign Intrigue') and 'Le Théâtre des étoiles' from the United States began to make their appearance, the French-Canadian shows remained predominant. Radio-Canada produced around three-quarters of its own programming: that achievement was the result of both a lack of French-language alternatives available from elsewhere in the world and the existence of a distinct sense of identity that could feed, and boost, an indigenous programming. In fact French Canada already had its own brand of popular culture, its own myths, heroes and villains, and traditions, that diverged from North American norms.

But in English Canada the proportion of foreign, especially American, programming remained very high, necessary to please audiences and to earn monies. Dallas Smythe, the researcher for the Fowler Commission, noted that only a third of the entertainment broadcast by English stations during his sample week in 1956 was Canadian. It might cost no more than $25, $50, or $100 for an individual station to run the cheap drama or wrestling shows offered by American syndicates. Country-wide rights were going for $2,000 a half-hour in the late 1950s. When the Board of Broadcast Governors announced late in 1959 that made-in-Canada programming must reach a minimum of 55 per cent of the schedule, that actually reflected about the limit of what the CBC's English service could achieve.[10]

One of a CBC programmer's most important jobs, reporter Roy Shields claimed, was to travel down to Hollywood in April to view the pilot films of new television series so as to prepare a wish-list of possible purchases for the fall. When at work in British Columbia, Marce Munro received prospective schedules from the network office with times blocked out for as yet unspecified American 'hits.' The imports often took over the peak viewing times: so the spring schedule in 1955 boasted such variety favourites as Ed Sullivan (Sunday), Sid Caesar (Monday), Milton Berle and others (Tuesday), and Jackie Gleason (Saturday), all running from 8:00 to 9:00. Made-in-Canada variety such as 'Showtime' (Sunday, 9:30–10:00), 'Pick the Stars' (Tuesday, 9:00–9:30), 'On Stage' (Wednesday, 9:30–10:00), and 'Holiday Ranch' (Saturday, 7:30–8:00) appeared before or after the imported highlights. But the CBC did retain the power of choice: it was loath to fill its schedules with large doses of jeopardy and violence, for example. (The top-ranking 'Gunsmoke' didn't appear on CBLT-TV until the fall 1960, and then it was aired on Friday night at 11:30.) In short, the CBC held firm to the ideal of balance, resisting the full effects of any programming craze that might overcome the commercial networks to the south.

The fate of made-in-Canada shows depended as much on office politics as it did on personal whim. American programmers had eventually gained the freedom to purchase and schedule shows to maximize profits, once ad agencies lost control of programming and Hollywood production companies became the makers of entertainment. By contrast no one programmer at the CBC could determine exactly what shows would be scheduled when. By the mid-1950s the Corporation's program division was divided into a congeries of specialized departments: Talks and Public Affairs, News, Drama, Music, Variety, Farm and Fisheries, Outside Broadcasts, and so on. Each of these had a claim, which it jealously guarded, for some time on the schedule to offer its particular wares – as, in English Canada, did each of the regions. The schedule was concocted at weekly meetings of department heads, recalled Alphonse Ouimet; the current schedule was used to fashion the future. It was in these departments, on the whole, that ideas were generated for new programs: Variety, because of its commercial thrust, seems to have worked in close concert with advertisers, whereas Talks and Public Affairs, widely considered the most arrogant department, relied more heavily on its own thinking. The result was reported up the line for approval and, when Ouimet became president, received some discussion in the program committee of the board of directors. The process might lead over the years to some important changes: Ouimet cited the cut-back in the amount of time given to farm broadcasts, as a result of the decline in the farm population, to make room for other kinds of programming. More important, the process ensured a struggle among little fiefdoms to protect or enlarge their share of the schedule. Presumably this resulted in compromise, if not consensus. It certainly did prevent any one person playing god.

The fate of a show, a producer, or a performer might also depend on some 'significant outsider.' By the end of the 1950s American networks were already notorious for their submission to the tyranny of the ratings. The life-span of a program that didn't do well in these sweepstakes was likely to be short, simply because the network wouldn't be able to sell time at a high enough rate to admen. The tyranny made some inroads into CBC television as well. A series of commercial rating services, most of which had sprung up in the radio age, now endeavoured to probe the extent of viewing, using a variety of different techniques. The oldest company, Elliott-Haynes Ltd, employed the coincidental telephone method, phoning people during the course of a show to discover who was watching. A newer rival, International Surveys Ltd, used the diary method, whereby a national panel of homes filled out a log of their viewing and their preferences. Much the same technique was adopted by the Bureau of Broadcast Measurement (BBM), a creation of the broadcasting industry itself, and by McDonald Research, a firm that eventually managed the BBM surveys as well as sold its own special brand of ratings. One newcomer, Pulse Inc. of New York, experimented for a brief time with a personal-interview system in which employees actually questioned people in their homes. But the eventual winner in this competition was the A.C. Nielsen Co. Ltd, the big American ratings service, which was encouraged by the CBC to bring its expertise to Canada at the end of the 1950s. Nielsen used the diary method, supplemented (at least in 1960) by the 'recordimeter,' a device attached to the television set to monitor the amount of tuning.

Each of the firms employed some kind of sample, wherein the practices or preferences of a very few people were taken as representative of the masses. The focus of attention was the home, rather than the individual, although some services supplied information on the age and sex of viewers. All of these services provided statistics on the amount of viewing, the character of the audience, the reach of various stations, and above all what programs the television homes watched.

In 1960 the CBC carried out a detailed appraisal of the worth of the commercial services. The review committee decided that none of the ratings was reliable according to the canons of statistics. Samples were too small, suffered from a bias because of the design or the selection process, and often masked a very high amount of 'non-response' from people who refused to participate. Yet the committee also discovered that program ratings were regarded as a vital 'index of popularity' by the advertising and broadcasting industries, regardless of their reliability. Private stations needed statistics to aid in the business of selling spots. Likewise the commercial department of the CBC believed the corporation should take the results of all ratings services since these were so vital in dealing with ad agencies. These agencies were naturally keen on definite figures that could be used to persuade clients of the virtues of buying time. In fact, account executives rarely worried about the limitations of ratings, often using them to rationalize decisions made on the basis of hunches or personal likes and dislikes. But what struck the review committee as a trifle peculiar was the fact that some of the program departments in the CBC were also eager to acquire all the ratings they could. Both Religious Broadcasts and Talks and Public Affairs claimed that they used ratings for the planning and scheduling of shows. Sports and Variety were even more enthusiastic, no doubt because of the commercial nature of their programming. Overall, the ratings seemed to meet 'a psychological need for a "Box Office" ': the department heads apparently treated the ratings as if they were 'some tangible measure of success for the show, the producer, the supervising producer and even the department itself.'[11]

(The findings of the CBC review committee about the reliability of the TV ratings weren't at all unusual. American studies were also quite critical, then and later. But the fact remains that the ratings are very useful to the historian. There's no other source of information that is so comprehensive or so complete. The ratings can tell a lot about the appeal of particular programs, especially hit shows, as well as audience habits and viewer preferences. In succeeding chapters I will employ the ratings to investigate the success or failure of assorted forms and genres of television. Readers should recognize that the figures quoted, and the calculations made from them, do not carry the seal of scientific accuracy – they are well-informed estimates.)

In fact the CBC (just like the BBC) had its own Audience Research division, which had been set up in 1954 as a result of a special report by E. Austin Weir, a one-time commercial manager of the Corporation, as well as the personal initiative of Ouimet who wanted reliable data to guide the Corporation's activities. While its origins may have been in commerce, the division almost immediately found its true home in the social sciences, and it launched special studies of all sorts – notably an investigation of the response to television in Halifax and Dartmouth, before and after the advent of telecasting – which produced some fascinating material on the nature of the viewing habit and the audience. But its greater importance to the day-to-day operations of the Corporation grew out of its focus on programming. According to its first director, Neil Morrison, the division treated the results of the commercial ratings services as raw data for the purposes of analysis. These findings it circulated throughout the Corporation. It commissioned special test-audience surveys of CBC programs by two American firms, the Schwerin Research Corporation and Millard Research Associates, in the late 1950s, out of which, Morrison recalled, came the fact that Robert Goulet had a lot of potential as a star singer. Its francophone branch investigated the response of the Montreal audience to the strike-bound schedule offered by Radio-Canada early in 1959, and discovered that many viewers were actually pleased by the programming of so many movies to replace regular series. By 1965 the division had a network audience panel of 2,000 respondents in English Canada who were to measure the intensity of the viewing experience, which produced the CBC's 'index of enjoyment' that was used to counter the simple 'index of popularity' offered by the commercial services. It remains unclear exactly what impact all these data had on programming, though apparently the assorted reports did inform the activities of the program departments and affect scheduling.[12]

It's even more difficult to assign weight to the role of newspaper and magazine critics. The trade of television criticism wasn't held in high regard by most journalists. Writing about the dearth of 'intelligent criticism' in 1962, Sandra Gwyn found quantity but little quality in the newspapers and neither in magazines: she exempted from complaint only a few critics, notably Pat Pearce of the Montreal *Star* and Robert Fulford who had written about TV in a variety of publications. Whether out of spite or disdain (for television was, after all, a rival medium), a couple of newspapers, including the Toronto *Globe and Mail* and the Halifax dailies, hadn't bothered to review television. But most did employ one television critic. The trouble was, as Gwyn put it, that all too often 'the television beat is regarded as a kind of graveyard, somewhere between the obituary column and the service clubs.' Reviewing television was typically treated as 'pretty easy stuff,' requiring little thought or feeling, and soon became a chore rather than a joy. The critic came to see himself as a 'paid viewer,' in the words of Jon Ruddy (Toronto *Telegram*, 2 August 1961), who believed he had a perfect right to voice his own prejudices against this or that performer, program, or genre. Ruddy and his compatriot Bob Blackburn went a step farther, for their criticisms revealed a definite bias against the CBC network, reflecting, perhaps, the fact that John Bassett owned both the rival CFTO-TV and *The Telegram*. In general the critic proved to be a smug middlebrow, sometimes jaded, sometimes angry, attuned much more to the norms of American television than to the aspirations of the CBC, which continually produced shows that either didn't match the standards of New York or Hollywood or were suspiciously highbrow and cultured. Only when *The Globe and Mail* a bit later employed Dennis Braithwaite (previously at *The Toronto Daily Star*) to write a regular column on television did Toronto get a critic who would consistently bring some deeper sensitivity, and in his case a very traditional cast of mind, to the job.[13]

Magazines of all kinds, from *Points de Vue* to *Relations* in Quebec and *Liberty* to *Maclean's* in English Canada, had all given space to occasional comments on television during the 1950s and into the 1960s. But only a very few regularly offered a column of television criticism during that first decade, notably *Saturday Night* and *Canadian Forum* in English Canada. Gwyn claimed in her 1962 article that both *Canadian Commentator* and

Chatelaine had dropped earlier columns. The picture improved a little afterwards: both the French and English versions of *Maclean's*, for instance, would shortly offer regular reviews of television. And the popular excitement fostered by public-affairs programming, in particular by 'This Hour Has Seven Days,' would compel all kinds of journals to focus on TV.

Because he didn't face the task of making immediate comment on an evening's or a week's offerings, the magazine critic could adopt the pose of social analyst, free to find in the popularity of a genre or the appeal of a performer evidence of the trend of the times or the mood of the populace. Catholic critics in francophone periodicals, such as *Culture* or *L'Action Nationale*, assumed a definite moral stand, which meant that they often frowned at the lifestyles depicted on the small screen. A highbrow such as Miriam Waddington, who wrote in *Canadian Forum*, was also censorious, though in her case because the content of television too often seemed a debasement of Culture. Her replacement, a youthful Bob Fulford, was consistently more perceptive, more thoughtful, for he tried harder to understand the structure of shows than did any of his fellow highbrows. Critics such as Hugh Garner and Mary Lowrey Ross in *Saturday Night* were bemused by what was on, seeing in, say, the character of talk shows an indication of how people now viewed celebrity.

Reflecting on television seemed particularly hard on the sensitive mind: the tedium of the craft often led to an outburst against dismal programming. Miriam Waddington finally declared (*Canadian Forum*, August 1958), 'I have lost my faith in television,' contending that it was 'corrupt, crazy, and no good.' TV was just too ephemeral, too middlebrow to attract and hold the interest of people in the way the High Arts or even movies did. That, by the way, was true in the United States as well, though during the 1950s Jack Gould of *The New York Times* was a justly renowned critic and from the mid-1960s Michael Arlen at *The New Yorker* would emerge as one of the most brilliant TV critics anywhere.

But did any of this comment have much effect on programming? Johnny Wayne told me that he had relatively little respect for the opinions of the Toronto critics. The producers Sandra Gwyn talked to claimed that newspaper criticism was of 'very little help.' Even so, they did read 'avidly' what was said about their work in the press. The CBC Reference Library in Toronto kept large program files full of newspaper and magazine comment, although how that resource was used isn't clear. The views of critics were occasionally summarized in internal CBC documents for circulation to interested parties and even appeared in the minutes of the directors' program committee. At the 19th meeting, in February 1962, Kate Aitken raised the issue of the critics' response to the controversial play *Crawling Arnold*, which had just be shown on the avant-garde anthology 'Quest': she wished further evidence that the play was suitable for the Sunday-night schedule. The meagre evidence available suggests that the critics were treated as surrogates for the audience whose opinions might inform the discussion of a performer or a program, even a genre, but rarely played the same role as did the personal views of colleagues or the meaning of the ratings.

The Production Game

The CBC produced nearly all network shows made in Canada during the 1950s. A mere 2 per cent of the shows telecast on its networks during one week in February 1958 came from 'Other Canadian Sources.' Who could compete? There wasn't a Hollywood North, and the CBC was hardly ready to encourage such, although it did work with private film companies to produce a bit of series drama at the end of the decade. Nor did the National Film Board, that other government agency of Canadian culture, ever realize an ambition to play a significant role in Canadian television: Donald Mulholland, head of production, did make overtures to the CBC for some sort of an alliance, but the NFB wasn't structured to turn out product in the volume and at a speed suited to the CBC. After the first year or so, when films were needed as cheap filler, the contribution of the NFB (whose funding and staff had been severely cut back) was kept to a minimum.[14]

The private stations concentrated on local production, happy to leave the expensive evening shows to the CBC. Even here, costs limited the amount and quality of their output. So, in the spring of 1956 CFPL-TV London programmed seventeen hours of local live shows and twenty-five hours of film in an eighty-six-hour schedule. Two years later, CKNX-TV Wingham ('the world's smallest town with its own TV station') aired a kind of neighbourly television for rural viewers with shows in which 'housewives demonstrate cooking and sewing; farmers discuss marketing and feeding programs; local doctors and nurses advise on health matters.' Such offerings were apparently welcomed, or so Fowler I discovered. But they may not have been necessary for success. Graham Spry told the story of one private station that didn't bother to unpack its two cameras 'for nearly 18 months,' finding that it could quite profitably fill the non-network time with 'elderly and cheap American film, and advertising.' People watched anyway.[15]

All this suited a Corporation that thought its mission necessitated a monopoly. The CBC's mandate was to express and promote 'a separate Canadian consciousness and sense of identity.' That presumed there was already a Canadian culture. Defining that culture didn't cause too much difficulty. True, the Massey Commission was clearly suspicious of the pleasures of the masses and much happier to equate culture with the High Arts. But the Fowler Commission set the record straight: 'our distinctively Canadian culture' apparently embraced 'everything from hockey and lacrosse to the Group of Seven and Andrew Allan's radio drama,' and included sports announcers, ice skaters, poets, musicians, in short all who contributed to 'the whole way of life of the Canadian people.' That grab-bag definition avoided tackling such thorny questions as the issue of quality so important in the world of the High Arts or the issue of Americanization so obvious in the case of English Canada. It didn't matter much, because the very vagueness and generality of the definition suited the CBC's purposes. Some years later, President Ouimet could blithely declare that 'Canadian culture embraces everything from sled-dog races to symphony orchestras, from comedy to opera, from good talks to jazz.' Whatever was Canadian, so it seemed, was worthwhile.[16]

Made-in-Canada programming had to cover the range of television's forms, including not only news and views but Culture and above all fun. An optimistic Moore thought that television provided 'a rare chance to do something freshly Canadian' for all the world to see. Indeed the Corporation once admitted that 'a broadcasting organization is a mechanism for enabling persons with lively minds and artistic flair to reach the public.' And it believed that Canadians could develop 'something distinctive in the entertainment field,' a national brand of the popular arts. Implicit was the hope that television might lessen Canada's dependence on the cultural products of New York and Hollywood.[17]

There were, however, restrictions on what the CBC could and couldn't do. The American achievement always conditioned the Corporation's activities. Simply filling up time became one priority (sanctioned by Fowler I) to wean Canadian viewers away from a dependence on American stations, and that task grew increasingly more difficult as broadcasting consumed first the evening hours and then expanded into the afternoon. (Not that either the CBC or the private stations could match the American example: when Fowler II looked at television in 1965, it discovered the average Canadian schedule ran around 100 hours a week while the American was up to 140 or more.) Nor was the CBC really able to set its own standards. The CBC told the Fowler Commission that 'exposure to American programming tends to give Canadians expensive tastes in television programs' that weren't reduced by 'the economic arithmetic of their own country.' Anything the CBC did would be compared to the efforts of New York and

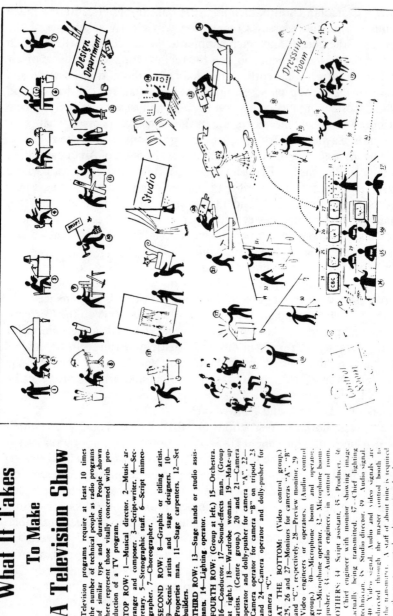

What It Takes
To Make
A Television Show

Television programs require at least 10 times the number of technical people as radio programs of similar type and duration. People shown here represent those vitally concerned with production of a TV program.

TOP ROW: 1—Musical director. 2—Music arranger and composer. 3—Script-writer. 4—Secretary. 5—Stenographic staff. 6—Script mimeographer. 7—Choreographer.

SECOND ROW: 8—Graphic or titling artist. 9—Scenic artists and stage designers. 10—Properties man. 11—Stage carpenters. 12—Set builders.

THIRD ROW: 13—Stage hands or studio assistants. 14—Lighting operator.

FOURTH ROW: (Group at left.) 15—Orchestra. 16—Conductor. 17—Sound-effects man. (Group at right.) 18—Wardrobe woman. 19—Make-up artists. (Centre group.) 20 and 21—Camera operator and dolly-pusher for camera "A". 22—Camera operator for camera "B" on tripod. 23 and 24—Camera operator and dolly-pusher for camera "C".

AT THE BOTTOM: (Video control group.) 25, 26 and 27—Monitors for cameras "A", "B" and "C", respectively. 28—Preview monitor. 29 Video engineers or operators. (Audio control group.) 30—Microphone boom and operator. 31—Microphone operator. 32—Microphone boom-pusher. 33—Audio engineer, in control room.

OTHERS: 34 Script assistant. 35 Producer. 36 Chief engineer with monitor showing image actually being transmitted. 37—Chief lighting technician. 38 Studio director. 39 Audio signal. 40 Video signal. Audio and video signals are directed through the master control booth to the transmitter. A staff of about nine is required in the master control and transmitter booths.

Figure 3.1
Source: *CBC Times*, 14–20 March 1952

Hollywood. Yet Canadian programming had to be in two languages, a costly proposition that led inevitably to a concentration of production facilities in Montreal and Toronto. While local and regional shows were produced in other CBC cities, the expense of any significant decentralization of programming struck the Corporation and the Fowler Commission as too great to be worthwhile, even though concentration upset parochial sensibilities.[18]

Ever present was this problem of money. CBC production had to be done on the cheap, especially as compared to American programs. Indeed every extra half-hour of programming was an additional drain on resources, reducing the amount of money available to any single made-in-Canada production. Thus in 1953, when Milton Berle had around $68,000 for each show and the teleplay series 'Studio One' cost roughly $30,000 an episode, the CBC budgeted each week $10,800 for its top variety showcase 'The Big Revue' and $10,200 for 'CBC Television Theatre.' Perhaps that explains why 'The Big Revue' was singled out for special abuse by the critics as the worst variety show offered Canadians. In 1959 Allan Manings, a comedy writer, noted wryly that the funds set aside for writers on some New York shows were greater than the total budget allowed a Canadian production. That had a particular effect on the production values of the CBC product: Roger Lee Jackson, who investigated CBC drama in the mid-1960s, pointed out that the Corporation simply lacked the means to either pay or equip their technical and support crews 'on the Hollywood scale.'[19]

There seemed to be a contradiction at the heart of the production game. Making television shows was very much a team effort (see figure 3.1). In a review of the television scene, published by *Points de Vue* in April 1957, Jacques Landry, then a CBC programmer, called television 'un art collectif, un art "industriel" ' because it involved so many different kinds of experts. Indeed, during the 1950s, both the *CBC Times* and *La Semaine á Radio-Canada* featured stories on designers, the wardrobe and make-up departments, sound and camera men, writers, as well as a bevy of hopeful stars of variety and drama and even news. But what was particularly striking were the number of stories and interviews that dealt with producers. The *cognoscenti* believed that the producers, if anyone, had the commanding role in making television, that they were the true artists of video. 'We were the fascinating guys of this new medium,' reminisced Guy Parent, one of the first francophone producers.[20]

At the beginning the CBC wasn't especially discriminating in its selection of producers. Rumour had it that both Dunton and Ouimet kept top radio people out of television to preserve the quality of the radio service. The rules were changed so that television producers went on yearly contracts, which meant that radio men who were staff producers would have to give up their tenure to shift into the new medium. Ouimet, in particular, believed that it was necessary to get new and vigorous people, not tied so closely to radio's past. Experience proved his reasoning had merit: some established radio-drama producers, such as Andrew Allan and even Esse Ljungh, didn't excel on television; likewise, Nathan Cohen claimed much later that the most successful people were 'TV babies' such as Eric Till or Ted Kotcheff.[21]

The policy opened up a golden opportunity for newcomers, mostly young men (and very, very few women) who had apprenticed in radio, the movies, the stage, a few even in television. Radio-Canada drew a number of its first producers from the ranks of people once active at the National Film Board: Pierre Petel, Roger Racine, Jean-Yves Bigras, Guy Parent, and Jean-Paul Ladouceur who came to television in May 1952 to produce children's shows. Toronto picked up such talents as Mavor Moore and Henry Kaplan from the stage; David Greene, an English actor who had worked in television; Ronald Weyman, who apprenticed at the NFB, and Sydney Newman, previously at the NFB and NBC-TV; and Norman Jewison, who'd been in all kinds of show business. There really wasn't too much training, although the CBC did bring Rudy Bretz, an American expert on live television, up to Toronto and Montreal to instruct its hopeful producers. However, Len Starmer, hired by the Variety department in 1953, with a background in the live stage, recalled jumping into directing immediately.[22]

What attracted these souls was the opportunity to do something novel and exciting, perhaps significant as well. Robert Allen, who became one of the most accomplished of the CBC's drama producers, recalled that as a radio producer in Vancouver he used to stop after work in front of a store featuring a TV set showing American stuff from Bellingham: he'd stand there, in the rain, his nose pressed against the window, repeating 'I can do that, I can do that.' Harvey Hart was captivated by the 'spontaneity,' 'directness,' and 'force' of television. Henry Kaplan enjoyed the freedom to try out new techniques – 'the more you experiment with cameras, scripts and acting, the more you learn. And the more fun you have too.' David Greene hoped that his television work would contribute to the fostering of 'what may one day be called the Canadian style of acting.' He added that he couldn't escape the conviction that 'television is art.' That was the key. In his memoirs Guy Parent recalled the extraordinary enthusiasm in 1954 when he and his colleagues in Montreal lived and breathed television from nine in the morning to midnight. A few years later Roger Rolland, program director for Quebec, spoke of CBFT-TV as a miracle-maker that showed how television could bridge that gap between art and the people. The first producers thought they were pioneers, testing the limits and showing the power of a new art-form.[23]

The Canadian producer, as a rule, enjoyed more responsibility and even control over a show than his American counterpart, since lack of money usually forced the producer to act also as a director (and occasionally as a writer). Early on, the CBC Times gave readers a glimpse of the producer's life with a run-down of the making of 'Stopwatch and Listen,' a satirical show designed by Ross McLean (and shortly to prove a flop): six weeks ahead of broadcast time, McLean selected the show theme, contacting a series of writers to prepare sketches, out of which he created 'a shooting script'; during the last two weeks he called a production meeting, arranged costumes and props and rehearsal times, assigned roles to his actors, and finally managed the rehearsals as well as the live broadcast. This kind of authority reigned even where the producer wasn't the show's creator. 'For a long time,' Nathan Cohen who was also a story editor for 'General Motors Presents,' admitted, 'we would not buy a play unless a producer would agree to do it.' A bit ruefully, Alex Barris recounted how his first producer on 'The Barris Beat,' Len Casey, constantly and often successfully tried to impose his own vision of the show upon Barris, the writer and host. Perhaps more common, certainly more fruitful, was Parent's early involvement with 'C'est la loi,' where he and the creators worked together to produce a show to popularize the law. His memoirs are replete with anecdotes that illustrate the routine power of the producer. That could have some unfortunate long-term results: 'We have given our producers so much freedom in the development of their own likes and dislikes,' recognized John Barnes, a production manager, 'that we are sometimes caught in this sticky business of being on the air with a schedule over-balanced with the experimental type show.'[24]

Yet, in the end, a disillusioned Parent condemned the CBC for restricting the creative freedom of the producers. In reality the fault lay more with television than with the rise of the bureaucrat. True, from above, supervisors set budgets, assigned jobs, and sometimes imposed actors on the producer. Parent told how on 'Cartes postales' he was forced to take a particular singer, even though she wasn't up to the task. And La Semaine à Radio-Canada explained how each program was subjected to the discipline of a budget that itemized the costs of each aspect of a production even before work began. Further, no matter how competent, the producer had to rely on the expertise of many others if his efforts were to succeed.

That was one reason why Henry Kaplan claimed he'd got more personal satisfaction out of theatre than television. But Kaplan thought the most serious constraint was 'so little time to do so much.' Producers found themselves on a treadmill, forced to make an unending series of shows without much time to pause or ponder. Parent noted that he completed 214 productions between January 1954 and August 1958 (in one hectic eight-day period he juggled four different shows). The tension of live broadcasts was so great, recalled Weyman, that ten seconds before he went on the air, one of his colleagues was usually in the washroom, throwing up. This kind of story lay behind the comment in a writer's magazine that producers could work for only about five years, after which they either switched professions or suffered a nervous breakdown and had their ulcers removed. The making of a program demanded speed, efficiency, and stamina as much as it did artistry.[25]

Perhaps that's why so many of the first programs seem more like 'radiovision' than television. Producers in a hurry naturally turned to existing broadcasting lore in search of guides and inspiration. The tendency was more pronounced in Canada, because the CBC was the only game in the country, but it applied in the United States as well, before Hollywood took command. Shows, stars, and formats proved on radio were exported to television to fill out the expanding schedules. That meant the first viewers were treated to a lot of talking heads. Even more striking, though, was the fact that newscasts, public-affairs shows, quizzes, variety, and dramas were often sound productions supplemented with pictures. Hugh Kemp, a writer in the early days, remembered how he and his compatriots would write a radio play and then ask themselves, 'What pictures should go in here or there?' Charles Israel, another writer, was actually told just to worry about the dialogue in his scripts, leaving the producer and his crew to put in the action. Almost all of the action in an episode of a 1953 science-fiction series, the CBC's 'Space Command' for children, was in fact dialogue among a crew of three in their spaceship's control room. What passed for special effects, later a feature of scifi shows, was pitiful: occasionally, for example, a picture of a model spaceship against a backdrop of a starry night appeared on the screen, the image enlivened with a jet's 'woosh' to suggest motion. This was an adventure series? At first, a viewer could have turned off the video and still enjoyed much of the evening's entertainment without a great sense of loss.[26]

The grip of radio's legacy slackened as producers attempted to exploit the visual dimension of television. There was a collective mood of excitement that made people experiment and share the results with colleagues,

Robert Allen recalled. What excited them most was the potential of the camera, even though TV cameras then were large, cumbersome instruments that weren't easily adapted to the needs of inspiration. Parent, for example, claimed that nothing was impossible with the camera, and tried to demonstrate the new axiom by producing a sketch on capital punishment where the camera, not a performer, was the main character. Norman Jewison strove to use the camera to 'paint' a scene in his variety shows, convinced that instrumental music could be watched. Sydney Newman emphasized how the television camera via close-ups could focus on the small, on the individual, to create a mood or cause a sensation. 'The most natural subject for a TV picture is the expressive face of an actor in a drama, of a close-up of a crying child in a documentary.' By contrast, Leo Orenstein, another drama producer, explained how television excelled in displaying movement, likening the interplay of camera work and staging and acting to 'the choreography of a ballet.' So, over time, producers learned how important were camera angles, different kinds of shots, timing and transitions, as well as costume, lighting, graphics, and make-up, in getting their messages across.[27]

This enthusiasm for video blended into another of the emerging rules of the game, namely the belief that all programs should use the techniques of 'show-biz' to capture the viewer's attention. Early on, even before Canadian TV began, Mavor Moore, writing as Toronto's chief producer, emphasized that what had to be avoided was 'the dull program.' In particular he disputed the prevailing wisdom that entertainment and education existed in two separate realms. American experience had shown that the purely educational program simply failed to reach the masses, that people learned much from what was labelled entertainment. 'Wisdom often comes from clowns, and where can you find a deeper comment on life than in the dance?' The CBC, Moore insisted, would explore the 'middle-ground,' striving to educate and entertain.[28]

That goal swiftly became gospel in CBC circles, and the fact troubled adult educators who worried about show business dominating television. In one interview, Alphonse Ouimet tried to present himself as a 'showman' who recognized that 'the great sin was to be dull.' Network programmer Peter McDonald added that the CBC must 'use *all* the fundamental values of showmanship – humor, lightness of touch, human communication.' Parent was always striving to make his shows lively. Once he overdid it: his production of a modern ballet in the series 'Divertissements' turned American star Liza Hamilton into something of a vamp, eliciting from his Montreal supervisor the exclamation 'Wow.' And one public-affairs producer, Ross McLean, made a name for himself as the man who brought 'the flair of show-biz to the often-dull realm of televised talks and public affairs,' notably with 'Tabloid' and then 'Close-Up.'[29]

But in fact programmers and producers were well aware that their ability to experiment was limited by the prevailing notions of what was and wasn't proper. Reginald Boisvert, a leading French-Canadian producer, claimed that broadcasters must submit to a degree of social control, that they must avoid the urge to shock the public with sensational ploys or novel themes. Sex might win viewers, especially male viewers, but it also offended – Parent's ballet did provoke an outcry. There was a general ban on the use of profanity 'for effect' in all television programs, claimed J. Frank Willis. This worry over good taste did lead to a more crippling kind of self-censorship. Management turned down a suggestion from Kate Aitken for a 'Human Relations Forum' à la Norway because it would clearly upset the sensibilities of many Canadians. Quebec authorities cancelled the broadcast of an interview with Simone de Beauvoir in the series 'Premier plan' because they were sure her views on moral issues would give offence. No wonder one TV writer noted that there were all kinds of taboos in Canadian television.[30]

Much was achieved during those years of trial and error. In Montreal and Toronto, boasted Ouimet, the CBC produced more programming than any other organization, including CBS and NBC, and at just over 'one-tenth of what they spend for their service.' This volume certainly provided an outlet for Canadian talent – in 1959, claimed Barbara Moon, the CBC employed 2,000 (mostly Canadian) actors to fill some 18,000 roles in network drama. Occasionally, observers recognized the Toronto achievement: so Frank Rasky, writing in Liberty early in 1959, discovered that Anglo programming was 'alive and kicking' (American programming, by contrast, was 'comatose'), the result of the 'most energetic spurt of professionalism yet.' Time and again the vitality and variety of Radio-Canada's programming, and especially its brand of drama, was celebrated – even a slightly envious Maclean's, the national magazine of English Canada, recognized this triumph when it published 'The Wonderful World of French-Canadian TV.' Above all, the polish and the quality of the corporation's prestige and specialized series improved with experience. That explained the acclaim CBC-TV earned outside Canada. In 1959 English-Canadian entries won six of the seven Ohio Awards (the documentary and drama anthology 'Explorations' alone received three of these) given for network programming by an American association of educational broadcasting. Likewise, three years later, Les Reed noted that French-language programming had secured 'a large number of awards at European festivals.' By the end of the decade, in short, CBC-TV could be justly praised as a powerful cultural agency contributing 'towards a Canadian identity in the mid-twentieth century.'[31]

Yet this achievement had definite limits, which critics in English Canada were all too eager to highlight. What had happened wasn't quite what enthusiasts had hoped for. In the spring of 1956, *Maclean's* printed the transcript of a round-table discussion among thirteen 'TV personalities' that reflected the main themes of complaint during the decade. The discussion was chaired by Ralph Allen, the magazine's editor. The participants included two people from private broadcasting, Joel Aldred and Roy Ward Dickson; five outsiders once or currently involved with the CBC: Nathan Cohen (theatre critic), J.B. McGeachy, Mavor Moore (then 'free-lance writer and actor'), Gordon Sinclair (journalist), and Lister Sinclair (playwright); and six CBC performers: Cal Jackson (jazz musician), Jane Mallett (actress), Pat Patterson (actress, writer, announcer), Toby Robins (actress), Frank Shuster, and Johnny Wayne. While hardly one-sided, the debate centred mostly on the defects of CBC-TV's programming (only the English version, though). Both Mavor Moore and Johnny Wayne, for example, thought that the CBC was too much of a copy-cat, trying to imitate hit shows from south of the border. Yet Gordon Sinclair and Roy Ward Dickson found CBC television lacking in that quality of 'showmanship' that seemed to characterize Hollywood's series. Lister Sinclair lamented the lack of respect for the individual artist, what would become known as the CBC's 'no-star policy.' Pat Patterson called for an end to the producer-director who faced a nearly impossible task – and, others would add, exercised a power that stifled performers and so rendered CBC's entertainment less appealing. In fact there was much truth to all these charges. That's why the CBC had only delivered on *some* of its promise.[32]

No one fully understood, however, that the CBC's achievement was already becoming dated. The era of live television was fast passing away. The tele-recording, at the time telefilms, was 'the wave of the future,' and most especially in the field of drama. That had been recognized by Eric Hutton in *Maclean's* in 1957 where he commented on the way films were taking over the primetime schedule in the United States. Film eliminated the hazards of miscues, flubbed lines, equipment failures, and so on, generally making for a much more polished performance. What really engrossed the viewers of live drama, as Nathan Cohen explained much later (*The Toronto Daily Star*, 21 May 1966), 'was whether the actors would get through without drying up on their lines or mixing up cues; which of the props would collapse on camera; and how often we'd see the microphones and crewmen in a scene.' Film gave producers a lot more freedom, releasing them from the tyranny of time and the studio, even allowing them to produce the kind of spectaculars and offer the sorts of action scenes movies were famous for. Altogether, film techniques emphasized the visual dimension of television, a fact that gave Hollywood a victory against New York in the struggle to control television entertainment.[33]

The trouble was that the CBC lacked either the will or the means to respond to the new thrust. The Corporation was leary of going into competition with private film producers in Canada, however small their industry, because the CBC was subsidized by government, or so Hugh Gauntlett, then an assistant program director, said in 1964. Nowhere in the country was there any vigorous tradition of movie-making on which to build. The studio facilities in Montreal and Toronto weren't really equal to the task of making, regularly, shows whose production values matched American standards. The wages paid producers, hosts, and above all performers weren't sufficient to support a pool of experienced professionals. Equipment and production expenses were much higher for film than for live television. Although there was a steady shift towards the videotaping of shows, the Corporation still celebrated the famed spontaneity and immediacy of live television. As late as the 1960/1 season, nearly 95 per cent of the made-in-Canada programming on the English network service was live (to air or on tape).[34]

The prospects for future glory, then, weren't quite as exciting as Ouimet and his cohorts liked to proclaim. This fact may well have contributed to the sense of frustration out of which came the producers' strike of 1959 in Montreal. But French-Canadian talent really had nowhere else to go. That wasn't the case in Toronto. Almost from the beginning, Anglo talent realized there were golden opportunities in Britain and the United States. Fowler I thought the luring of talent to 'greener pastures' down south was part of an international phenomenon that shouldn't cause much worry. John Barnes saw nothing wrong in the CBC acting as 'a training ground' for somebody else. By 1959, though, the producer Harry Rasky, writing in *Saturday Night*, correctly called the talent haemorrhage 'our national blessing and shame,' proof that however great the progress of Canadian television something was going badly wrong.[35]

Rasky was able to list a series of Canadian-born or Canadian-made performers who'd trekked off to 'greener passages.' The attractions weren't only monetary, as Wayne and Shuster told one reporter: 'In New York, they tell us, "We're surprised you're never nervous before you go on a show." We tell them, "Why should we? It's like coming from a cafeteria to a deluxe French restaurant. Here 12 people follow us around, just worrying for us. We have our own costume valet and our own prop men. We have 800 people in the audience ready to laugh, instead of 150 who can't see us through the CBC equipment in a tiny studio. When we step off the stage, a guy is waiting for us with a glass of water. We don't expect the drink of water, but it's so nice to be pampered for a change." '

Among the stars of light entertainment who left were such women as Elaine Grand, for fame in London, and Gisele MacKenzie (once 'fired' by the CBC), to win plaudits in the United States. Similarly, the hit male singers Paul Anka and later Robert Goulet migrated to the American scene in search of richer rewards. Then there were the actors, once active in Toronto, such as the Englishman Patrick Macnee, who would shortly gain international fame as a star of the British spy thriller 'The Avengers,' and the native Lorne Greene, who would become a superstar as the grand patriarch on the western 'Bonanza.' True, others such as Christopher Plummer, Barry Morse, and even William Shatner (soon to win lasting fame on 'Star Trek') didn't altogether disappear from Canadian screens. But staying in Canada permanently, as Wayne and Shuster fully recognized, required the performer also restrain his ambition permanently, whether for fame or money or pampering.[36]

Far more serious was the export of top producers. Norman Jewison went first to New York to produce variety series, such as 'Your Hit Parade,' though he became a superstar only when he shifted to Hollywood and movies. The list of exiles in the variety field, according to Alex Barris, would grow to include Stan Harris, Bill Davis, Norman Sedawie, Harvey Hart, Stan Jacobsen, and Mark Warren. The situation seemed worse in the case of drama. Henry Kaplan initially began to commute to New York from Toronto and eventually went to England. Silvio Narrizzano made his name at Granada Television as a major director (and found there programmer Stuart Griffiths, who had helped start CBLT-TV). In 1958 Sydney Newman went off to even greater fame to take over 'Armchair Theatre' at ABC Television, also in England, where he sponsored a renaissance in television drama. Later, he moved on to become head of BBC Drama. The United States took its share of talent as well. David Greene became a leading teleplay director, first at CBS's 'Playhouse 90,' while Arthur Hiller learned the joys of producing the Hollywood western 'Gunsmoke,' also for CBS. The loss extended into journalism. Reuven Frank joined NBC in New York, for a time engaged in producing the highbrow series 'Kaleidoscope,' until he found his true métier in the news and documentary field. And he was eventually joined by Harry Rasky himself. Both would shortly win Emmys for documentaries.

The draining away of this kind of talent in such a 'producer's medium' as television was crippling. It meant that Toronto had no hope of competing effectively with the swelling tide of telefilms from abroad. Where could it find the experienced masters able to produce a style of entertainment that could counter the challenge? In fact only a massive infusion of new money or a dramatic cut-back in the level of production could have released sufficient funds to enable CBC-TV to hold its own in the new era. Even then, perhaps, the Canadian scene might well have proved too restricted to prevent the loss of television's 'artists.'

The 'Golden Age' of Television?

'There was a time, seven or eight years ago, when TV in Canada reached its "Golden Age." ' That statement opened a capsule history of television in North America written by Hugh Garner, one-time TV critic and frequent TV viewer, for *Star Weekly* (23 December 1961), then one of English Canada's largest weekend magazines. Much of the piece was an exercise in nostalgia, celebrating a series of mostly American shows from the early 1950s, from the comedy extravaganza 'The Jackie Gleason Show' to the famous dramatic anthology 'Playhouse 90.' But its publication was also part of a wave of comment on television that had been launched by a stunning speech Newton Minow had delivered in May. Indeed Garner's closing remarks contained a long quotation from this new document of the TV age.[37]

Minow was the newly appointed chairman of the Federal Communications Commission in the United States. He was also a Kennedy man, a reform-minded critic of the establishment. Along with President Kennedy, he'd been invited to address the annual meeting of the National Association of Broadcasters, the main industry body, which included network executives and station owners. In his address, he had suddenly and unexpectedly lashed out against the TV industry, condemning it for making a schedule that amounted to a dreary 'procession' of sitcoms, game shows, violence, and endless commercials, presumably all in the pursuit of greater profits. Here it was that Minow coined the marvellous phrase 'a vast wasteland' when describing the culture of television, a phrase embraced by legions of television critics, journalists, and highbrows across the land. Somehow its message seemed so right, embodying their sense of malaise over what TV had become. Newspapermen, naturally, loved to tag their rival with the label 'wasteland.' Next May the CBC would air a documentary entitled 'Report from the Wasteland,' which took a 'hard look,' a requirement of a good 1960s documentary, at the sad state of American television under the thumb of Hollywood, the ratings agencies, and the adman. All in all, outside the industry, there seemed a consensus among commentators that TV had, in Garner's words, reached 'its nadir.' The promise of the new medium had been betrayed.

Along with this storm of TV-bashing, though, came the notion of a past 'golden age' of television when things had been far better. The notion soon hardened into a lasting myth that has informed the popular understanding of television ever since. In 1976 Max Wilk, present at TV's infancy, actually used the term to entitle his so-called valentine to the past about 1950s television. Newspaper critics have time and again talked about a golden age of drama, of live television, of comedy, that ended in the late 1950s. It has taken on a special meaning for some Anglo-Canadians: 'The cliché is right,' observed Finlay Payne, because the 1950s did seem a time when the CBC really had created 'the nucleus' of a great Canadian television. 'It was incredible,' exclaimed Ronald Weyman, speaking particularly about drama. 'What was done, what was achieved, and what was attempted, indeed it was golden.' Was it really?[38]

No doubt the character of primetime television was different, especially in the early 1950s. This was, after all, the high point of live television. All live TV meant was that the camera and the microphone broadcast the actual performance as it happened. Yet there remained a certain mystique about the whole experience. In retrospect live television did present more of an actual record of what happened, rather than the made-up version of reality created by delayed shootings, film and tape editing, and technical wizardry that would prevail in later years. Garner praised early TV because it made 'the viewer feel a part and parcel of the great wonderful world of show-business.' The makers of shows could be equally enthusiastic: the whole crew was bound together in a joint enterprise to put out a show at one moment in time, Don MacPherson mused, which made for an enormous sense of accomplishment. 'Every television production was opening night,' recalled Tom Nutt, a lighting man in the 1950s, where the audience numbered in the hundreds of thousands, not a mere five hundred or six hundred people in a theatre. There was an immediacy, a spontaneity, a reality to live television that set it apart from anything else – it might be related to film or the stage, but it was 'its own creature,' according to Ronald Weyman. Counted among the most exciting of TV's offerings were the live contests, whether a Grey Cup game or an election broadcast, where the outcome might remain unsure until the end. But the fact is that most live entertainment was carefully scripted and rehearsed, as the playwright Charles Israel pointed out, which casts doubt on any claim to spontaneity. And the quality of most TV products was improved when the use of tape and film became common, because they allowed the producer-director to edit the broadcast into a more polished performance. Most viewers couldn't really tell the difference among live, live to tape, and edited tape or filmed production, except that live was usually the least appealing to the eye.[39]

A more compelling argument for a 'golden age' was that the programming of early TV was a good deal more diverse, innovative, 'fresh.' That was because producers and programmers were experimenting with all kinds of formats and formulas to find something that would work. Viewers were treated to a range of sports presentations, including roller derby and ladies' softball, hour-long musical game shows and highbrow quizzes, an assortment of historical docudramas, the famous teleplays, a bit of concert music, serious panel discussions, and the like. The first hit telefilms were enjoyable, in part, because they were novel: sitcoms such as 'I Married Joan' and 'The Life of Riley' or crime shows such as 'Dragnet' had seemed 'alive and exciting' back in the early 1950s, when they were first introduced, wrote Garner. 'I began writing TV plays myself,' he admitted, 'finding in the medium the wide-open range of the spectrum that covered everything we call realism and true-to-life drama.'

That ended. By 1960, whatever the particular mix of programs, whether ABC decided to emphasize violence and CBS comedy or Radio-Canada touted social drama while the English service struggled on with variety, the primetime schedules of all networks were made up of representatives of a narrow range of television's forms and genres. In August 1957, Eric Hutton in *Maclean's* indulged in what would shortly be an annual rite of the dying summer, namely identifying the genres – then westerns and musical variety – that would be 'in' at the opening of the new television year in September and October. Freshness seemed an increasingly rare commodity. New titles certainly appeared: in the fall of 1958, nearly a quarter of CBLT's primetime offerings were 'new,' and the next year the proportion rose to 40 per cent. But often it seemed little more than replacing an old tweedle-dum with a new tweedle-dee. In particular, TV play-writing was 'as dead as the sonnet as an artistic medium.' The plots and the characters of the prevailing dramatic series were now 'boring and banal,' asserted Garner: there were all too many wimpy husbands and bratty children in the sitcoms; 'The Untouchables' had become 'a cliche-ridden bore;' and 'The Naked City,' however realistic its plots, was 'a weekly yawn.' 'All television isn't bad,' he recognized, 'but too much of it is the same thing packed in varying formats.' What had been lost was the urge to experiment.

At bottom the myth of the 'golden age' was rooted in nostalgia, of course. The arrival of television had been so sudden and so common an experience throughout North America that millions of people were affected in much the same way. In the beginning there was a sense of wonder, a fascination with all the things that little box in the living-room offered people for their nightly pleasure (such a sense of wonder, by the way, had been present in the infancy of movies and radio). 'It was a time, remember,' asserted Garner, 'when the gang at the office or the boys from the shipping room gathered at the water-cooler and exchanged quips about such shows as Sid Caesar, *Playhouse 90, Mr. Peepers, Your Hit Parade*, and a hundred others, depending on their taste, interest and inclination.' What ended 'that feeling of mass interest and mass involvement' was simply the fact that television soon lost its novelty. The passage of time turned the TV set into a familiar appliance, and viewing into a nightly ritual. So people came to recall those years when TV had first enthralled them with that kind of vague, warm feeling often reserved for memories of first love and childhood glee. (One of my American-born colleagues at the university, for example, looks back on the antics of Sid Caesar and Imogene Coca in 'Your Show of Shows' and of Jackie Gleason in 'The Honeymooners' with fond memory, even though he is nowadays indifferent to most of what appears on the small screen.) This nostalgia gained added force because it was a shared sentiment among so many different kinds of people.

The myth hasn't much validity as a way of describing or explaining the overall history of television. It's very much a matter of personal experience: my own golden age would extend from the late 1950s to the mid-1960s, the years when I first began to watch TV intensively. It includes recollections of some live television, namely the hockey broadcasts and the Kennedy funeral. But, even more, I recall fondly the filmed dramas of Hollywood such as 'Have Gun, Will Travel,' 'The Twilight Zone,' 'Dr. Kildare,' 'I Spy,' and 'Star Trek.' While I have personal favourites from later years, still it is by and large the first samples of the various genres that stand out in my memory. That's to be expected. Their successors just can't have the same freshness because the viewer has already been introduced to the conventions and style of the genres. But that's no justification for arguing that TV reached its artistic peak in those years.

There is, however, a sense in which the term 'golden age' has some merit. During the 1950s, and even into the 1960s, it seemed possible that the CBC just might produce a made-in-Canada TV that would serve the two languages and the many tastes and needs of the public. Over the years the evening schedules on the two networks did boast newscasts and news magazines, features and documentaries, talk and interview shows, a lot of variety, games and quizzes and sportscasts, play anthologies and drama series, much Culture, all of which were produced at home, usually in Montreal or Toronto, and some of which won either a substantial audience or critical acclaim (occasionally both). The achievement was the high point of Canadian television. And it amounted to one important chapter in the history of popular culture in Canada.

4

Enter CTV

You know, it's just like having a licence to print your own money!
Roy Thomson, 1957[1]

The only thing that really matters in broadcasting is program content; all
the rest is housekeeping.
Fowler II, 1965[2]

These two aphorisms were forever on the lips of contemporaries inside
and outside the television industry during the 1960s. Not that observers
necessarily agreed with either. Rather these statements spoke to two of
the chief concerns of television people of all kinds, namely profits and
programming, as they struggled to come to grips with what was happening
around them.[3]

All of a sudden, the Canadian television system seemed in a state of
upheaval because of the activities of a new regulatory authority, the Board
of Broadcast Governors, (BBG), the boom of private TV sponsored by that
agency, and above all the elimination of the CBC's network monopoly and
the rise of an independent Anglo network, called CTV. The effort to build
upon the grand success of CBC-TV in the 1950s had somehow got horribly
confused. No wonder that, for a decade after the passage of the Broadcasting Act of 1958, television was nearly always an item of some importance
on the public agenda: politicians, journalists, bureaucrats, CBCers, and
businessmen tried to sort out its fate in a series of hearings and rulings by
the BBG, investigations by parliamentary committees, innumerable articles

and studies in the press, special probes by the Glassco Commission on Government Organization (1963), by the 'Troika' (in 1963 and 1964), and by Fowler II (1965), books such as Albert Shea's *Broadcasting: The Canadian Way* (1963) and Don Jamieson's *The Troubled Air* (1966), a white paper on broadcasting in 1966, and finally the debate over a new act in the winter of 1967/8. The terrible irony is that much of this discussion and worry was wasted. Novel ideas were forgotten in the rush to find some kind of consensus satisfactory to all the assorted players in the television game. The Broadcasting Act of 1968 really marked the failure of efforts to build a rational Canadian television system. The best that could be said was that a humbled CBC was left whole.[4]

So the 1960s was very much a time of lost opportunities in broadcasting. Its legacy wasn't just an unimaginative and out-of-date piece of legislation but, even more serious, a sense among succeeding politicians that broadcasting had somehow been 'dealt with,' certainly that it was both boring and intractable and as a result ought to be left off the public agenda. Indeed the whole exercise was proof that too much debate can be a costly sin in a political democracy.

The BBG's Revolution?

There wasn't much doubt at the end of the 1950s that the structure of Canadian television was soon going to be transformed. Fowler I had recognized that it was time to unleash the tiger, to establish an independent, competitive, private television service in major centres across the land to meet the self-evident demand of the public for more channels. The real question was just how far the changes would go.[5]

The Broadcasting Act of 1958 was a hastily produced, rather prosaic document that avoided giving much general definition to the purposes of television in Canada. It re-established the CBC, complete with its own board of directors responsible to Parliament and compelled to seek parliamentary approval each year to secure an annual operating grant. That ensured the Conservative majority could keep an eye on the Corporation. It established the Board of Broadcast Governors, a separate body whose task it was to advise on who should get new TV licences and to regulate the industry, including the CBC, in order to provide 'a varied and comprehensive broadcasting service of a high standard that is basically Canadian in content and character,' whatever that meant. The innovation would satisfy private interests who wanted an impartial agency of control. According to one reading of the act, the BBG was given a lot of leeway to determine the character of television broadcasting, to 'provide for the final determination of all matters and questions in relation' to the purposes and activities of broadcasting. According to another reading, though, its authority was circumscribed by a list of specified powers that suggested it was to regulate practices rather than to supervise operations. What was clear is that its life would be burdened with considerable routine business.[6]

The person appointed to become the new czar – or was he just the referee? – of Canadian broadcasting was Dr Andrew Stewart, an agricultural economist, a university administrator (he was president of the University of Alberta), and an experienced government servant (he was also chairman of the Royal Commission on Price Spreads), who would serve as chairman of the board throughout the decade. In fact he was a peculiar choice as an architect of the new system, the role circumstances thrust upon him, since he was noted more for his 'gentle humour and kindliness and good manners,' according to Judy LaMarsh, than for any gift for getting his own way. In the long run he proved more congenial acting as a referee: he preferred to guide rather than direct, to avoid taking a aggressive stand, to find a consensus that would maintain at least minimum standards. Stewart didn't want the discretionary authority the government had apparently given to the BBG, and before long he asked the politicians to offer direction or revise the act to make clear Parliament's will about broadcasting – to little avail, of course. He was assisted by two other full-time members, Conservatives Roger Duhamel and Carlyle Allison, both newspapermen, and twelve part-time members, who ran the gamut from a person snidely referred to as 'John Diefenbaker's dentist' to the always redoubtable and very independent Eugene Forsey. None of these people had significant experience in broadcasting, and only two were businessmen. Furthermore, the BBG was expected to operate with only a modest support staff, under fifty people until the late 1960s, a surprisingly small number given its duties. The confusion about the scope of the BBG's authority, the lack of experience of its members, and the limited resources it had at its disposal explain in part why it would seem all too inactive, even a failure, to critics (including Fowler II) at a later date.[7]

The first crucial task before the BBG was to establish some basic rules before licensing new private stations, which meant dealing with the fact that TV was already so American in content and character as to make a mockery of the rubric stipulating that any service should be 'basically Canadian.' True, the act did specify that new licences for stations or networks should be held only by Canadian citizens or by a corporation largely owned by Canadians. But Dean Walker pointed out in a *Saturday*

Night article that, in the competitive market of Toronto, American stations had captured roughly two-thirds of the audience. There were stations in the United States, such as KVOS-TV Bellingham, that really earned their ad monies by winning Canadian viewers, in this case in the Vancouver region; indeed the Federal Communications Commission in the United States had recently approved a new Pembina, North Dakota, station whose extraordinary 1,450-foot tower – 'If it toppled, it would fall into Canada,' complained one broadcaster – would shoot signals into Winnipeg. (That action led to a sharp rebuke from the BBG in its first report to Parliament in 1960.) Indeed, overall, Walker estimated that close to three-quarters of the viewing time in English Canada was devoted to American programs, whether found on the CBC network, in the schedules of local stations, or on offer by American channels. In a similar vein, Graham Spry (who'd played such an important role back in the 1930s in the establishment of public broadcasting) now concluded that the Canadian system, excepting the non-commercial offerings of the CBC, was 'essentially an imitation or replica of the American system,' notably in primetime when it was used first and foremost 'to sell goods, most of them American goods.'[8]

What the board eventually came up with was the notorious Canadian-content regulations, which established the minimum amount of material designated 'Canadian' that a station must air during a specified period of time. The amount was eventually pegged at 55 per cent during the broadcast day and, in a later amendment, 40 per cent in the evening hours, phased in over a number of years and defined according to specific clauses. Quotas weren't unusual. Britain allowed a maximum of 14 per cent of imported programming on its airwaves. But it was a sign of just how serious the problem was that the quota was put on Canadian programming, not on foreign shows. Private stations, especially the new ones, would simply fill their schedules with cheap imports to secure the ad revenue necessary to survive and prosper. 'It is estimated that the cost of an American program to a Canadian station is generally no more than 5% to 8% of the cost of production,' Fowler II later declared. 'Left to operate freely, economic factors would quickly tend to make Canadian private television stations mere extensions of American networks.'[9]

The idea wasn't to compel Canadians to watch home-grown television, as Stewart was careful to point out in an interview with Pierre Berton on 'Close-Up.' 'If there isn't sufficient appeal in the Canadian programs,' he admitted, 'I don't suppose the people will watch them.' He was under no illusions about the contrariness of the Canadian mind. People didn't necessarily behave in a manner consistent with their public views. 'I think collectively that there is a great deal of support for the wish to make broadcasting Canadian,' he told Berton, 'but whether the individuals will come through on this or not is another question.' The BBG's aim was simply to ensure that the option of 'watching Canadian' remained alive.[10]

Before very long, however, people began to notice that the Canadian-content regulations were something of an exercise in illusion. Dean Walker, for example, pointed out that once there were more competitive stations around, the viewer would easily be able to avoid made-in-Canada programs and to find 'slick "nonthink" shows' made in Hollywood, aired at home or across the border. Others discovered that 'Canadian' didn't always mean made in Canada. Robert Fulford got mighty upset because special exemptions for Commonwealth and French programs gave them a certain amount of Canadian credit, proving that Canadian content was little more than a brand of anti-Americanism, 'the nastiest aspect of the Canadian character.' Indeed the assortment of exemptions and special clauses led the Winnipeg *Tribune* (24 November 1962) to point out that both baseball's World Series and an address by President Kennedy would be ruled Canadian (since they were of general interest to the public), that the British historical thriller 'Ivanhoe' would come under the Commonwealth clause, and that a Brigitte Bardot movie made in France would get a half-credit, as long as it was aired in French. The most serious flaw, however, was that the regulations pertained to the quantity of programming, not the quality. Broadcasters weren't being compelled to make good shows, just Canadian shows, no matter how cheap and unappealing. A half-hour game show followed by a half-hour interview would count just as much as an elaborate, hour-long drama. But the BBG was unwilling to go beyond establishing minimum stands, never mind to create some complicated mechanism that could determine the worth or quality of a show.[11]

The stage was now set for the 1960 hearings into the licensing of second stations in eight major cities, the choicest markets in the country: Halifax, Montreal, Ottawa, Toronto, Winnipeg, Edmonton, Calgary, and Vancouver. The easy assumption ruled that the advertisers' demand for air time was so great that the second stations would soon turn a big profit. The vistas of new wealth attracted a drove of business types, mostly allied in a series of competing companies. Roy Thomson himself had his eye on the Toronto licence, until told by Stewart that the likelihood of the board's awarding the second station to the owner of such a chain of newspapers was very, very slight. Among the hopefuls were foreign interests such as Britain's Granada TV for Toronto and America's Twentieth Century Theaters for Ottawa, the head of Woodwards department stores and the president of Macmillan-Bloedel (lumber) in Vancouver, the Richardson family (grain merchants) in Winnipeg, press magnates such as the Siftons in Winnipeg and the Southams in Vancouver, and radio people such as Canadian Marconi in Montreal and Jack Kent Cooke's CKEY in Toronto.

As things turned out, though, the most important applicant was John Bassett, a prominent Conservative, the owner of the Toronto *Telegram*, who would become the second of the architects of Canada's TV system. Bassett was a brash, dynamic, and innovative capitalist, who exuded a kind of charm that was very unusual among his fellows. He loved to make money, he loved challenges, and television offered him both. Bassett was allied with the Eaton family (via 'Baton'), Ted Rogers of CFRB, and Joel Aldred, perhaps the most prominent radio announcer in the private business and a loud champion of free enterprise. It was apparently Aldred who designed the grandiose plans to make CFTO a major production centre with excellent studio facilities that would ensure it became a master force in private TV. It was Bassett, though, who had majority control on the joint board.[12]

Greed wasn't the only motivation behind the excitement of business. Private television was finally going to be given a chance to show its stuff, something the CBC monopoly had made impossible (it was argued) during the 1950s. Certainly all kinds of lavish promises were aired at each of the hearings, and some writers assumed that a promise was 'a binding commitment.' The key promise was that the private stations would offer an alternate, and at least by implication, a much more popular service to viewers. The applicants didn't adopt an anti-CBC line in their written briefs, but optimists in the industry were telling journalists that finally the viewer would be 'courted and coaxed, his preferences given as much consideration and weight as the whims of a feudal monarch.' In competitive markets such as Toronto and Vancouver the lusty newcomers would soon lure Canadian viewers back from American stations. The Baton Aldred Rogers brief in Toronto, for example, promised to commence immediately what it called 'the Battle of Buffalo.'[13]

How were they going to woo the viewer? The applicants admitted that they would schedule a lot of the Hollywood product, as well as some British imports, just as the CBC was doing. The Vantel application for Vancouver told the board that CHAN-TV would offer an assortment of syndicated series, including 'The Donna Reed Show,' 'Father Knows Best,' 'Have Gun, Will Travel,' and 'Peter Gunn.' The Misener application in Winnipeg promised many late-night movies from Great Britain. But this was hardly what the briefs emphasized, since the BBG was clearly much more interested in how the second stations would boost made-in-Canada television.

One common theme in the briefs was a promise of local service, the argument that each of the newcomers would strive to be a community station. Baton Aldred Rogers wouldn't build 'a carbon copy' of the Buffalo channels but rather a station with 'a strong emphasis on local events' to win over the Toronto viewer – and the ad dollar of the Toronto merchant. Vantel planned 'CHAN-O-Rama' at noon and 'VAN-O-Rama' around the dinner hour to provide Vancouver's audience with 'informative, educational, and entertaining' interviews, features, and news pertinent to their community. The successful CFTM brief for Montreal contained a number of service programs, such as 'Je Suis Disponible!,' a kind of television employment office for ordinary folk.

Even more exciting, though, was the second theme, the promise of a made-in-Canada PopCult. The Bushnell application promised over two-thirds Canadian content during the evening hours between 7:00 and 11:00. Applicants talked about locally produced drama workshops and specials (CFTM, a new ninety-minute original Canadian play each month), sports coverage, talent and variety programs, country music, games and quizzes, and talk shows. A *Saturday Night* story emphasized how a fledgling private television production industry was gearing up to produce women's programs, musical variety, and panel game shows for what one person estimated as a $2 million demand in the first year. In fact, much of what was promised sounded like radiovision, lots of talking and performing heads, the very kind of programming that the CBC had pushed in the fields of mass entertainment and popular facts for eight years, not always with a great deal of success. The applications didn't say too much about plans to schedule large quantities of made-in-Canada popular drama, even though by this time storytelling was clearly the most successful genre on North American television in the primetime hours.[14]

None the less the BBG managed to pick and choose among the applicants (there were nine alone for the last free VHF channel in Toronto). Eight licences went to private interests, two in Montreal to serve the French and the English, and one to the CBC in Edmonton, which turned the existing private station into a free agent. It wasn't always easy to see, on the basis of the awards made, exactly why the board favoured one application over another. Apparently the governors were interested in financial backing, experience, innovation, and energy, qualities that might be displayed in different degrees by the applicants in each competition. So while a youthful Art Jones secured the Vancouver licence, supposedly on the basis of his imaginative proposals, the experienced foreign radio broadcaster Canadian Marconi got the Montreal English licence. Naturally there were charges of political favouritism, especially in the case of Toronto where the fix seemed to be in when rumours circulated that Bassett had boasted that he was assured of victory before the BBG made its decision in his favour. Neither this, nor other suggestions about the awards to the ex-CBCer Ernie Bushell (Ottawa) and Finlay MacDonald (Halifax), friends of George Nowlan, the minister responsible for broadcasting, were ever proved.

Already the board had begun to wonder about a network service for the newcomers. This hadn't seemed in the cards at the time of Fowler I, or even as late as November 1959, when Stewart spoke to Berton on 'Close-Up,' because the costs of operating a private network looked too great. But there was clearly room for some kind of joint hook-up to ensure each new station did have a modicum of enriched programming that their individual resources couldn't fund. That was the rationale for the Independent Television Organization (ITO), set up in mid-summer 1960 by the newcomers: it would facilitate the buying of imports as well as the exchange of Canadian shows. Enter Spencer Caldwell, who'd handled syndicated films for television and the like in the 1950s and had been one of the unsuccessful applicants for the Toronto licence. He saw in the idea of a private network another way to become an architect of the emerging TV system. Stewart was interested. The board eventually came forward with guide-lines for a private network that specifically prohibited a station co-operative because that could turn the network over to the new CFTO-TV in Toronto. The second stations weren't pleased – neither was Joel Aldred of CFTO who'd hoped to organize his own network in time – since they didn't see much need to share any profits with a new private company. Even so the BBG went ahead in December 1960, giving Caldwell permission to seek affiliates. He succeeded only in winning the reluctant support of the newcomers because of John Bassett, who wanted a vehicle to deliver the broadcasts for the 'Big Four' football games that he'd purchased for the next two seasons for the princely sum of $750,000. The upshot was that the BBG gave its approval in the spring for CTV to begin operations in October 1961.

CTV was a funny kind of network. It couldn't claim any 'owned and operated' ('O&O') stations, which had proved to be the source of so much profit to the American networks. It didn't have any of its own production facilities, and consequently was dependent for made-in-Canada programs on affiliates or outside production companies. Its eight affiliates weren't altogether happy with the association, never picking up anywhere near the 49 per cent share of ownership offered them. Caldwell had been forced to grant them the lion's share of ad revenues accruing from the network programming, which promised financial troubles in the future.

What CTV had going for it was the BBG's blessing, microwave facilities (extended coast to coast by mid-1963), and Caldwell's super-confidence. 'We intend to prove that private enterprise can provide better entertainment than the government,' enthused Caldwell in conversation with a reporter for *The Financial Post* (6 May 1961), and 'without costing the taxpayer a cent.' His program director, Michael Hind-Smith, recently from CBLT, went even farther in a Toronto *Telegram* (23 August 1961) interview, promising 'a very genuine alternative to CBC viewers.' Not only would CTV offer 'a much more popular schedule,' it would 'emphasize commercial Canadian content' (since 'at CBC, they're hot-shots at grabbing American shows'), eventually challenging the public network in the realm of current affairs with 'lighter, easier to watch,' and sponsored fare. The implication was that CTV would become a major distributor of made-in-Canada programming.

A worried CBC watched all these developments closely. In charge was Alphonse Ouimet, who would prove the last of the architects of the new TV system. The decision to appoint him president has often been judged a mistake, at least in the press. Ouimet's reputation suffered very badly during the 1960s, especially because of the 'Seven Days' affair. In the opinion of his most public enemy, Judy LaMarsh, 'he was tragically miscast by temperament to be the President of the Corporation.' She cited his cold-blooded fascination with management techniques, his lack of social skills, his arrogance and imperiousness, his inability to empathize with producers or to understand the programming imperative of the CBC. There's a bit of truth behind these charges. No doubt some of his difficulties with politicians and producers were of his own making. But LaMarsh never fully understood the man's extraordinary competence, his capacity for hard work, and his devotion to public broadcasting. Nor did her charges take into account the increasingly serious situation the Corporation faced during the 1960s, which would have strained the energies of any person, including another Davidson Dunton. The Corporation was fortunate to have such a strong-willed leader as Ouimet at a time when its future was constantly at stake.[15]

The immediate problem the Corporation faced was to protect its autonomy against the BBG and its integrity in the so-called single, mixed system that was emerging. There was no doubt that the Broadcasting Act had 'reduced the stature of the Corporation,' as Stewart bluntly informed the

CBC's board of directors. Robert Fowler, for one, had urged on Stewart the wisdom of taking command of broadcasting. No doubt many Conservatives would have favoured such a move. But Ouimet and his managers were able to persuade the directors to resist any efforts to subordinate or humiliate the Corporation. The aim was to assert the pre-eminence of the CBC as the chief agency of national broadcasting in Canada, ensuring that private TV remained a secondary, supplemental service. Neither Dunton before, nor Ouimet now, opposed the idea of second stations or the creation of a private network. But Ouimet did declare that it was the BBG's responsibility to establish carefully the duties of these new elements – he wasn't at all sure that CTV (termed 'a creature of the BBG' in one CBC document) could be considered a proper network by any reasonable definition. And he made abundantly clear that the CBC was the programming body, the BBG merely a regulatory agency, according to the laws of the land.[16]

There were bound to be clashes. In 1960, for example, the BBG formally conveyed its opinion on the unsuitability of the import 'Johnny Staccato' (a crime drama, noted for its graphic violence, which as I recall was one of my favourites at the time). Early in 1962 the BBG asked the CBC to respond to charges made by CTV and its affiliates that the Corporation was engaged in unfair commercial practices. A few months later the agency threatened the CBC with legal action because of an inadvertent breach of the election regulations prohibiting the broadcast of partisan material forty-eight hours prior to election day. And, although it had granted the CBC an Edmonton licence, the BBG delayed approval of a Quebec City licence for the Corporation in 1962, largely because of political pressure, an action that led to the resignation of Eugene Forsey and another governor.

But by far the most serious threat was over what came to be called 'cross-programming' and 'network-splitting.' The BBG wished to be able to exercise some control over network schedules in order to realize its view of national broadcasting. In December 1961, after CTV was on the air, the BBG actually put out a statement declaring how desirable it was for affiliates of one network to carry programs of another, in those hours outside reserved time. That Ouimet vigorously opposed, since its real effect would be to allow CTV to extend its audience by using CBC affiliates. The issue came to a head over the strange Grey Cup fiasco of 1962 when the BBG tried to force the public service to carry CTV's broadcast of the football finale, commercials and all. The Corporation simply refused, and secured an opinion from the Department of Justice to back up its stand. 'If our affiliates were shared by another network, CBC would lose its identity, its cohesiveness and its control,' noted a spokesman. 'While we may entertain two-way seduction, we refuse to be raped.' By that time a compromise had been worked out, which allowed the joint broadcast of what came to be called the 'Fog Bowl,' when bad weather rolled in from the lake to cover the Toronto stadium and obscure much of the action. The fact was the Corporation had not only defeated the BBG but won a good deal of public support to boot. Behind the whole business, Ralph Allen declared a bit later, was the desire of Caldwell and Bassett to invade the public network, 'either borrowing, seducing or kidnapping the key stations,' in the pursuit of more profit. The BBG had acted as an instrument of private TV, according to this argument. No wonder the experience convinced Ouimet it was time for another royal commission, presumably to buttress the role of the CBC as the chief agent of national television.[17]

The experience had likewise convinced Stewart not to mess with the Corporation. Some years later, Fowler II grumpily complained that 'the BBG seems to have tried to avoid conflict with the determined and at times belligerent Management and Board of the CBC.' That, it presumed, had defeated the intent of the Broadcasting Act. LaMarsh personalized the whole dispute: 'Had Stewart or Ouimet been different men, the 1958 Broadcasting Act might well have worked, but in every contest with the B.B.G., the C.B.C. had won.' These regrets were evidence of a fundamental misunderstanding of the gravity of the situation. What saved the CBC from permanent and crippling damage at the hands of the BBG was the 'belligerence' of Ouimet and his colleagues.[18]

The Booming Business of Private TV

The BBG's grand design for private TV began to unravel almost as soon as it was in place. The key problem was money, of course: start-up and operations proved very costly, more than were expected in some cases, and ad revenue was not as lucrative as optimists had hoped. The eight CTV affiliates reported a loss of over $5 million in 1961 and $1.6 million in 1962. The losses were spread unevenly, since the independent stations in markets away from American competition didn't do too badly. Bushnell's CJOH-TV in Ottawa, for example, registered an operating profit after only a few months, although the expenses of becoming a CTV affiliate plus the acquisition of the failing CJSS-TV in Cornwall as a satellite prevented any dividend to shareholders. The greatest difficulties were in the more cluttered markets of Montreal, Vancouver, and Toronto, where as a result there were changes in the ownership and plans of each of the newcomers. It shouldn't surprise that late in 1962 the BBG announced a freeze on the addition of new second stations (though not necessarily new CBC 'O&O' stations), because it feared ad revenues just weren't sufficient to justify more competition and so expansion might jeopardize achievement in the realm of Canadian programming. Events would prove that last presumption rested on a widely unrealistic view of what could be expected of private TV.[19]

By far the most newsworthy story of troubles occurred in Toronto. The local press had a field-day covering what happened to CFTO-TV. That station had opened with great fanfare on New Year's Day, 1961, boasting studio facilities and equipment and staff that were sufficient to make it a major producer of programs for sale in Canada, indeed in North America. But the elaborate establishment proved much too expensive to maintain – according to a report in *The Toronto Daily Star* (30 August 1961), CFTO had lost around $1.1 million in seven months of operation. The result was a series of cut-backs in plans and in staff, commencing in the early spring, which station brass referred to as 'streamlining.' At the same time there was a struggle for control of the company itself between the 'visionary' Joel Aldred and the 'capitalist' John Bassett. By mid-summer Bassett arranged for ABC-Paramount to buy out Aldred's share and provide a new infusion of capital. That deal the BBG, at a September meeting, refused to sanction, although only after considerable public and private pressure forced the governors to alter an earlier, tentative decision in favour of the stock transfer. The champions of national broadcasting were concerned lest this transfer signify a forthcoming American take-over of private TV in Canada, where foreign interests already had too much of a share in television ownership and management. The wily Bassett got around the obstacle, though: the directors rearranged the ownership of the shares anyway, which removed Aldred's interest, and accepted a loan agreement with ABC (for around $2.5 million) that allowed it representation on the company's board as well as a say in management. That agreement, however distressing to some BBG members, worked to secure the future of CFTO.[20]

The struggle to make a buck doomed any prospect that the second stations would really deliver on their promises. These promises had never been made conditions of licence, so they weren't legally enforceable by the BBG. Anything original had to be done on the cheap. The local programs awarded annual accolades by *Liberty* sounded very amateurish, a lot of talking and singing heads, who might just as well have been on radio. ACTRA, the artists' union, complained in 1964 that none of the second stations had produced 'a single drama' in the past three years. The entrepreneurs replied to complaints with the comment that sponsors were most reluctant 'to underwrite almost any kind of Canadian production.' Stations met the legal minimum of Canadian content by dumping this programming in the less-profitable morning and afternoon hours, leaving primetime for the imports that generated healthy revenues. Recall CJOH-TV in Ottawa, which had promised two-thirds Canadian content in peak viewing hours? In July, August, and September 1964 it actually ran only 14 per cent, about the same amount of British imports, and filled the rest of its time with American shows. It was this kind of behaviour that led cynics in the press to conclude that the second-station hearings had amounted to a gigantic exercise in hypocrisy. The assorted briefs, observed Nathan Cohen in 1963, were 'hilarious fantasies to everyone except the members of the Board of Broadcast Governors.'[21]

The most important victim of financial troubles turned out to be Caldwell's CTV, although the axe didn't fall until 1966, long after the profit picture in private TV was rosy. CTV was able to expand its network service from eight hours a week at the beginning to roughly twenty-two hours in 1962/3. It did acquire three new affiliates in the years up to the end of 1964. It was able to secure an increasing volume of advertising revenue, though Caldwell's claim to *The Financial Post* (30 November 1963) that he intended to make CTV 'Canada's biggest advertising medium' still sounded excessive.

CTV managed to cause a few waves with its sponsored news, talk, and public-affairs programming. It endeavoured to develop a more lively, 'personality-oriented' newscast modelled on American practice, and even scheduled (for a time) that newscast earlier in the evening than the CBC's famous 'National News.' With some modest success, too: a Bureau of Broadcast Measurement (BBM) report for the middle of March 1963 found that CTV news (10:30–10:45) on nine stations reached a weekly average of 320,000 households a night, while the total for the rival's news (11:00–11:15) on forty-four stations was 707,000 households. A little later when the broadcast moved to 11:00, a youthful Peter Jennings made his debut as one of four anchors, paired off in two teams: Jennings soon left for a career (as anchor, then reporter, finally anchor again) at ABC, although the Huntley-Brinkley arrangement continued on CTV's newscasts for a few more years. Then there was CTV's 'Telepoll,' singled out for brief mention in Fowler II, which sampled Canadian opinion about assorted public questions; yet it appeared in the evening only in one season and thereafter was sent off to the Sunday-afternoon schedule. Likewise the most novel offering, the syndicated 'Pierre Berton Show' (sometimes 'Hour') was aired late in the evening during weekdays, after 11:00 or 11:30, when it couldn't gather a very large audience. This interview program consistently earned praise because Berton was able to establish a rapport with many of his guests that often made for revealing discussions.[22]

But what success the network had wasn't a result of any triumphs in the realm of made-in-Canada entertainment. In its first year CTV earned the nickname 'the Roy Ward Dickson network' because its most successful offerings were cheap game shows of a kind associated with the name of this famed quiz-master. Indeed the game show remained a staple of CTV's Canadian programming in later years. The variety format proved more troublesome. The second-season, late-night variety extravaganza entitled 'Network' lasted only a few months before it was canned. The next fall, a comedy-variety show hosted by the old American star Jerry Lester was even more short-lived. All that survived were country-music shows. And Canadian stories hardly appeared at all. A modest flurry of rumours about forthcoming drama series didn't pan out, until the debut of 'The Little Hobo' in Fall '63, a show produced in Canada by an American firm with its eyes on the U.S. market. It was aired on CFTO's primetime schedule Tuesday nights, from 7:00 to 7:30, until Spring '66, where it was the only made-in-Canada melodrama. Of course it wasn't particularly 'Canadian,' except by accident of location: this kids' adventure story about a wandering German shepherd who helped people out was (however charming it might be to its many fans) just a variation on a formula made famous by 'Lassie' and 'Rin Tin Tin' back in the mid 1950s. That wasn't what people had hoped CTV would offer in the way of Canadian PopCult.[23]

CTV had only limited control of its own programming, even shows that earned it some fame. 'The Pierre Berton Show' was produced by Screen Gems and sold separately to the CTV affiliates. The national newscast came from the Ottawa studios of CJOH-TV, funded on a tiny budget compared to that of its CBC competitor, managed by station personnel, and there were complaints the station subsidized its own local newsroom with network monies. According to *The Financial Post* (30 November 1963), CTV had less control over scheduling than 'any other TV network in the world,' since a decision of two-thirds of the affiliates could govern its programming. They even employed the Independent Television Organization to war against CTV management, or so Fowler II claimed. In fact the affiliates compelled the network to reduce its weekly feed from fifteen hours in primetime to eleven hours, thus boosting their ad revenues at the network's expense.[24]

CTV just didn't have the funds to cover the expense of any major innovations, unless these products found a good market south of the border. The affiliates claimed too much of the advertising dollar that did come to the network: the financial report on CTV in Fowler II found that the network had to pay back to affiliates $2.6 million of the $7.2 million it earned from network sales and billings to sponsors, which left it in the red on operating expenses by $227,000 that year. Producers could only spend around $2,500 to $3,000 per half-hour program, according to Michael Hind-Smith, a paltry sum that 'wouldn't have bought the coffee on an American network production.' The amount of money CTV's eight original affiliates, its major producing units, expended on talent fees actually declined from over $1 million in 1961 to $662,000 two years later. No wonder it was hard to attract audiences to watch, and advertisers to pay for, the results of such 'enterprise.' A CBC report in 1962 claimed CTV had to cancel a musical show because its cost of $3,500 a week wouldn't be covered by the sponsors.[25]

Was there any way out of this bind? There were occasional stories in the press about the wisdom of some sort of public subsidy to assist CTV in mounting a richer, made-in-Canada fare. That would have been very ironic, given the claims CTV wasn't going to cost taxpayers a cent. The BBG fiddled with the Canadian-content rules, establishing a slightly higher amount of commercial time on sponsored Canadian shows than on imports. CTV tried to get all advertisers buying time on American shows to buy time on a Canadian product, at a special, discounted price. Caldwell bent his energies to finding more affiliates to extend the network's coverage, ultimately to 80 per cent or more of the Canadian population, which would generate larger ad revenues, and to securing some television outlets of its own, which would ensure CTV benefited much more from the advertising bonanza that the affiliates shared. The network acquired an interest in CJCH-TV Halifax, but a bid to take over CJOH-TV Ottawa (purportedly involving monies from Maclean-Hunter, Southam, and Sifton) failed. Fowler II was sufficiently concerned that it recommended compelling the affiliates to carry a proper amount of network programming, and, failing all else, that the BBG or its successor actually run the network as a trustee for the public. What Fowler II felt had to be avoided was a take-over by the affiliates, which hadn't demonstrated the necessary competence or responsibility to carry out a network function.

What actually happened was that early in 1966 CTV itself made application to the BBG to allow a transfer of shares and debts to the affiliates, a move that the BBG approved on condition no station owner have shares in another affiliate. The fact of the matter was, of course, that John Bassett became the strongest force in the new co-operative: his personality, CFTO's audience and weight, and the importance of his production company Glen-Warren ensured he would have a more than equal say in the councils of CTV. That he demonstrated when the network newscast was moved to

CFTO's studios in Toronto. Rumour had it he was also the cause of assorted resignations and dismissals in the next couple of years, including those of Peter Reilly (who served a brief time as news and public-affairs chief), Michael Hind-Smith, and the network president Gordon Keeble. Keeble later claimed his leave-taking in 1969 resulted because Bassett and the rest just weren't ready to endorse his view that CTV should put more money into producing a greater quantity of Canadian programming than was the legal minimum.[26]

They certainly could have afforded that course. By this time the private industry (meaning CBC affiliates, CTV affiliates, and independents) was doing very well indeed. At the end of the decade, the Davey Committee used a variety of measures to show just how profitable the business had become. There had been a major shift of ad revenues away from the CBC to the private sector, which was willing to offer advertisers many more popular vehicles, flexible placement rules, special discounts, and sometimes better demographics. Network and national advertising dollars in the private sector had nearly doubled between 1963 and 1968, and overall CTV and the TV stations had earned 80 per cent more in that last year or a total of $88.6 million dollars in advertising. The Hopkins, Hedlin report on the economics of the mass media, specially prepared for the Davey Committee, was struck by the fact that TV stations (operated by companies with no radio stations) had a before-tax return on equity of 64.4 per cent in 1965 and 42.3 per cent the next year, compared with 18.9 per cent and 16.9 per cent for the manufacturing industries in general. The profit levels were significantly higher for the private stations in major centres, notably in Toronto and Montreal, where there was considerable demand for advertising time: Hopkins, Hedlin found that eight of the largest stations earned a whopping $12.1 million after expenses in 1968. Most of their commercial revenue came from primetime advertising, between 60 and 70 per cent by one estimate.[27]

Private television hadn't earned this money by doing very much that was imaginative in the way of original programming, though. Yes, they had by and large complied with the Canadian-content regulations. And they did offer a certain amount of local news and service programming, though not much in the evening hours. But the proportion of total costs going to pay talent had dropped in the past seven years, whereas the proportion for the purchase of films and tapes had risen. All too many stations had simply been willing to take CBC, CTV, and syndicated material to fill primetime – content to 'sit at the end of the pipe and suck,' thought the disgusted Davey Committee.[28]

The committee noted that CFTM-TV Montreal was a bit of an exception. Popularly known as 'Le 10,' the newcomer had been forced to produce a certain amount of original programming to fill its schedule as well as to buttress the claim that this was French Canada's station for the ordinary people. True, the independent had made use of foreign movies and translated American drama to win a lot of attention. It also carried many game shows, as well as the hockey broadcasts, which francophones seemed to like even more than did other Canadians: indeed the CBC may have been correct in its complaint of 1967 to the BBG that CFTM had bought audiences by mounting give-away quiz shows offering prizes to viewers. But CFTM did program popular talk and variety shows, and eventually a farcical drama, 'Cré Basile,' which proved a phenomenal hit. At one time this half-hour was considered must viewing for the vast majority of TV households – according to an anecdote, even the patrons in an otherwise noisy tavern were kept quiet, and unserved, to allow full attention to the screen during its run. The upshot was that CFTM stole the audience away from Radio-Canada's flagship, CBFT: 'Le 10' apparently had twenty-three of the top twenty-five shows in its market in March 1966, according to the Nielsen Broadcast Index. By this time, CFTM's programs were being distributed by private stations in Chicoutimi, Matane, Quebec, Rimouski, Rouyn, Sherbrooke, and Trois-Rivières, making it a kind of Quebec super-station.[29]

The CTV affiliates didn't have to program so much original material to win audiences in English Canada. The result was that the planned network schedule of CTV in the 1966/7 season, that is after the affiliate take-over, was shaped like an American schedule, emphasizing entertainment and particularly drama, and dominated by American programming, especially between 7:00 and 11:00 (see figure 4.1). Almost the only kinds of stories available were American. The actual Fall '66 schedule of CFTO-TV had a few changes in times and shows, replacing one American series with another, as well as three more instances of American drama, namely 'Peyton Place,' 'Family Affair,' and 'The Pruitts of Southampton' to fill the local time-slots. During much of the evening, then, CTV was only an over-the-air cable system for Hollywood's products. And it worked. A CBC survey of evening audience levels in major markets during the decade proved that: by 1967 CTV affiliates were running neck-and-neck and sometimes well ahead (CJON-TV, St John's, and CFRN-TV, Edmonton, were each around twenty points ahead) of their CBC rivals, except in the case of Vancouver, where CBUT and KVOS were slightly more popular.[30]

In a retrospective, published in 1987, Robert Fulford railed against the 'great accomplishment' of John Bassett and his cohorts. It wasn't just that

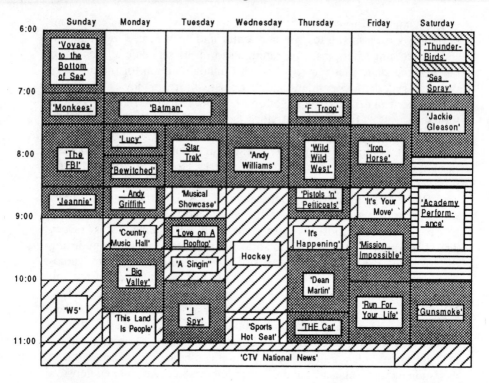

	Sunday	Monday	Tuesday	Wednesday	Thursday	Friday	Saturday
6:00	'Voyage to the Bottom of Sea'						'Thunder-Birds'
							'Sea Spray'
7:00	'Monkees'	'Batman'			'F Troop'		'Jackie Gleason'
		'Lucy'	'Star Trek'	'Andy Williams'	'Wild Wild West'	'Iron Horse'	
8:00	'The FBI'	'Bewitched'					
	'Jeannie'	' Andy Griffith'	'Musical Showcase'		'Pistols 'n' Petticoats'	'It's Your Move'	'Academy Perform-ance'
9:00		'Country Music Hall'	'Love on A Rooftop'	Hockey	'It's Happening'	'Mission Impossible'	
		' Big Valley'	'A Singin''		'Dean Martin'		
10:00	'W5'		'1 Spy'			'Run For Your Life'	'Gunsmoke'
		'This Land Is People'		'Sports Hot Seat'	'THE Cat'		
11:00			'CTV National News'				

Underlined

Titles Drama   Commonwealth

     American   Local programs

//// Canadian   Assorted origins

Figure 4.1 CTV evening program schedule, 1966–7
Note: This was a proposed schedule used for promotional and selling purposes,
supplied courtesy of the CTV network.

they'd made and broken promises, thereby beginning what would become a ritual of licence hearings before both the BBG and its successor, the CRTC. They'd also redefined the actual meaning of network, designing 'a kind of non-network, or anti-network, in the main a distributor of programmes from elsewhere,' which set the pattern for private television in English Canada forever after. There's much evidence to justify that harsh judgment. The record of CTV and its affiliates was and remains unusual in the annals of private television. The commercial program-makers in Britain produced a wealth of popular drama, some of which, including the cult favorite 'The Avengers' from ABC Television, turned up on Canadian screens because of the Commonwealth credit. Although the Australian private stations first made their name running American imports, they eventually aired locally produced hit dramas, such as the police series 'Homicide,' which proved there was a popular hunger for home-grown settings, heroes, and themes. After 1971 the independent TVA network, created by CFTM-TV, programmed assorted téléromans, as did Radio-Canada, to meet the fascination the Québécois had with their own social life. The striking fact is that CTV just didn't really try very hard to achieve any similar success throughout the 1960s and the 1970s, until pressure from the CRTC in the 1980s compelled a reluctant effort to find and air made-in-Canada drama.[31]

The newcomers had succeeded by giving a lot of viewers roughly what they wanted, otherwise the stations never would have been able to generate the kinds of profits that apparently signified their betrayal of the purposes of Canadian broadcasting. Most English Canadians wanted to watch the Hollywood product. In a 1963 interview, Spencer Caldwell pointed out what that meant in practice, although he admitted there were a few exceptions, for example, hockey, some game shows such as Roy Ward Dickson's 'Take a Chance,' and CBC's 'Don Messer's Jubilee': 'We've found that when we put an American show up against a CBC-produced show, we get the audience; when they put an American show against one of our Canadians shows, they get the audience,' according to Caldwell. 'When we put Canadian shows up against each other, viewers who can turn to American stations.' Commercial programmers in Britain and private stations in Australia didn't have to meet the increasing threat of direct American broadcasts that would steal away their audiences. Bringing in 'I Spy' or 'Jackie Gleason' would please audiences and advertisers, cost little, and generate a lot of income. Producing a Canadian crime drama or sitcom was a chancy business at best, and likely to be costly. There weren't any entrepreneurs willing to risk these odds, especially when CBC's ventures in the field hadn't usually been very successful.[32]

The BBG felt it lacked the authority to compel CTV to pour money into the production of made-in-Canada entertainment sufficient to develop a product comparable to the American imports. By and large it had continued the tradition of lenient regulation begun by the CBC board of governors in the post-war years. Nor was the BBG induced to pursue that will-o'-the-wisp, the use of individual performance standards as a condition of licence, that had enticed both Fowler I and Fowler II. Such a mechanism could have gone far to force private TV to live up to its claims, although it might well have resulted in a bureaucratic nightmare and probably wouldn't have pleased the viewing public, never mind the industry. The reluctance of the BBG to impose its will was the reason the regulatory authority was cherished by private broadcasters and why nationalists thought it was a captive of the private sector. What a pity that the BBG didn't recognize the fallacy of Canadian content and urge the politicians free private TV to do what it did best, supply American entertainment and sell time. The one industry group that seemed to have a compelling self-interest in the maintenance of the rules was the artists' union ACTRA, for whom Canadian content spelled jobs for the boys and girls – but that wasn't a very good reason for keeping alive a failure. The whole experience, in any case, should have put to rest the long-standing notion that private broadcasters could do what the CBC had been unable to do. The irony was that later regulators never seemed to learn the lesson.[33]

The Embattled CBC

Early in 1960 a slightly bemused Alphonse Ouimet told an audience at the Canadian Club of Toronto that no other organization, other than the government, was 'so often talked about, written about, editorialized on, for and against, damned, slurred, supported, inquired into, ignored, blamed, upheld, detested, liked, criticized or praised, as the CBC – and often by the same people.' Nor did this controversy lessen during the decade. The Corporation was the focus of much of the debate that swirled around the issue of broadcasting in the press and in Parliament. The CBC seemed to be caught up in an escalating series of crises that were linked to the changed broadcasting environment brought on by the sudden rise of private TV.[34]

Its troubles weren't a result of any ground swell of disenchantment with public broadcasting among Canadians. Management was encouraged by the findings of a special survey of public opinion carried out in 1962 that showed people overwhelmingly supported the objectives of the CBC and, on the whole, were satisfied with its general performance. A Gallup report of 24 April 1965 found that half of the respondents thought the Corporation was doing a 'good job' and a further group, nearly a quarter, thought it was doing a 'fair job.' Support was strongest in Quebec, dissatisfaction greatest in the West. The overall rating was slightly higher than the Corporation had achieved in a similar survey in 1949.[35]

The Corporation had only a few declared enemies, mostly in the ranks of private broadcasting. The creation of the BBG and the freeing of private TV hadn't quelled the desire to get the CBC out of the broadcasting business altogether and re-establish the Corporation as a program-maker that would supply, perhaps free of charge, the necessary Canadian shows to private networks. That was a line of argument Richard Lewis of *Canadian Broadcaster* had pursued for years – sell off all the CBC's 'hardware,' its studios and stations and transmitters, and turn it into something like the National Film Board. Even Caldwell dreamed about such a happy solution to the television tangle, since that would remove a major competitor for the ad dollars CTV so desperately needed, as well as relieve the network of the responsibility to produce a lot of Canadian material. At the end of the decade, the Canadian Association of Broadcasters told the Davey Committee much the same thing. (These views weren't held by all private broadcasters – Donald Jamieson, ex-president of the CAB and then a Liberal MP, was always ready to champion the legitimacy of public broadcasting.) But there were only a few yahoos in the press or Parliament who were willing to take up the cudgel to do battle for such a self-serving vision of broadcasting.

Much more serious was the steady stream of criticism directed against the Corporation. 'Sniping at the CBC,' observed the Davey Committee, had become something of 'a national pastime that ranks with watching National Hockey League games and thinking deeply about the reform of the Senate.' This had a demoralizing impact upon the top brass of the Corporation. There was an ever-present atmosphere of insecurity at Ottawa headquarters. What seemed at stake was the reputation of the CBC. Friends of the CBC observed that the constant battle to defend its conduct so absorbed the time of its executives that they were unable to deal effectively with the quality of its service. 'We're so busy defending our honor,' admitted a senior official in 1963, 'there's no time left to defend our virtue.'[36]

One target of this sniping was the institution itself. There was a widespread belief that the Corporation was too expensive, too inefficient, and too bureaucratic. The CBC's 1962 survey found that over two-thirds of Canadians believed the annual cost of bringing radio and television to the public was $35 or more per home; indeed many thought it was fully $200 (when in fact it was about $23). Although usually more knowledgeable about the actual costs, politicians none the less grumbled at the annual increases in funds requested by a Corporation, which seemed to rely too heavily on the taxpayers' dollar, and that explains the constant pressure on the CBC to increase, or at least maintain, its share of the advertisers' dollar.[37]

Then there were the questions of economy and efficiency. Glassco and Fowler II found plenty of evidence that the CBC could cut expenses and save monies in clerical staff and production techniques. Indeed Fowler II believed the CBC could do far better if it farmed out more of its production of Canadian programming, which would simplify administration and benefit private enterprise now inhibited by the Corporation's monopoly. Judy LaMarsh claimed that she was privy to all kinds of stories of waste and extravagance: excessive payments for American films, people sitting around in offices doing nothing, reporters assigned and paid to cover the Arab-Israeli War who didn't even go overseas, the air-conditioning of two floors of a Winnipeg building to house staff covering the Pan-Am games when athletes and fans sweltered in the heat wave, and such like slanders, all a bit petty. The impression was left that the CBC was one of the most profligate crown corporations around.

Finally there was the criticism of management. Recall that the Glassco Commission had decided the Corporation was in a terrible mess because of a confused and overly elaborate structure of organization. Fowler II concurred, emphasizing that a top-heavy administrative group was unable to control effectively the operations of its Montreal and Toronto production centres. Its report added that there was an appalling lack of understanding between administrators and producers that worked against the goal of improved service. Both Ralph Allen and Robert Fulford argued that the bureaucrats had taken over, strangling the creative energies of CBC producers in a sea of red tape. 'The CBC, to put it briefly,' decided an angry Fulford in 1965, 'is no place for heroes.' Much of this disarray and decay was laid at the door of Ouimet, of course.[38]

The second object of complaint was the CBC's programming. All kinds of special interests took issue with what the Corporation decided, or didn't decide, to put on the air. Bob Blackburn, television critic of the Toronto *Telegram*, spoke for many people when he argued that the CBC ought to confine itself to handling 'public affairs' and guarding 'the cultural heritage,' leaving popular entertainment to the people who knew how to do this best, the private broadcasters. Réal Caouette was disturbed, as were some Quebec Liberals, by evidence that the news and commentary of

Radio-Canada had a separatist bias. An assortment of Anglo Conservatives and Social Crediters believed that the CBC was too sympathetic to communist or socialist or anti-American views. All kinds of traditionalists felt that CBC programming was undermining the nation's morality: a petition entitled 'The Declaration by Canadian Women' circulated in 1964 among women's and church groups condemned the CBC because it was spreading 'propaganda for perversion, pornography, free love, blasphemy, dope, violence and crime.'[39]

That might be expected. But what was much more depressing was the increasing evidence that the CBC had begun to alienate its highbrow constituency. Thus in 1962 author Stephen Vizinczey, writing in *Canadian Art*, condemned the CBC from a Vancouver perspective as an excessively commercial entity, much like private networks, that broadcast 'the attitudes, problems, predicaments and, mainly, the illusions of the least distinctively Canadian part of the country, its industrial heartland.' A few years later, Robert Fulford (who'd once admitted that he'd never been a great fan of CBC-TV) damned the Corporation for its apparent unwillingness to serve the higher mind of Canadians, to look after the interests of Culture. And he cited a meeting of the Canadian Conference of the Arts where the CBC was roundly condemned for 'its failure to use properly the dramatic, literary and musical talents of Canada' as proof that it had lost the intelligentsia. The CBC was no longer counted 'a stronghold of civilization' as it had been in the days of radio.[40]

How did the Corporation respond to this litany of complaint? Much of the answer was determined by Ouimet himself. Ouimet maintained very close control over the activities of his Ottawa staff, too close if we are to believe the Glassco report, which argued that Ouimet was both the chief operating officer and the chief executive officer. He was usually able to get his own way with the directors as well, much to the chagrin of Judy LaMarsh who would have liked to use the board to interfere in CBC affairs. She was especially upset when the board stood by Ouimet during the two major crises of the mid-1960s, the 'Seven Days' affair in 1966 and the furore over LaMarsh's charge of 'rotten management' the next year. Ouimet listened to the politicians, just as he read the opinions of critics and the public. But he was never ready to accord these opinions much import, simply because he didn't believe any outsider could really tell the Corporation what it should be or do. One can imagine how unsympathetic he was to LaMarsh's rather silly suggestion that some well-known foreigner, such as the American Fred Friendly or the Australian J.R. Darling, be hired to tell the

CBC how it might improve its administration. Ouimet's usual response to criticism was to defend the record of his regime and his producers, even in the face of considerable public or political outcry.

Ouimet had been well aware that the setting free of private television was bound to affect the fate of the Corporation. So, right from the beginning of his presidency, he'd launched a reconsideration of the role and purpose of public broadcasting, in effect an exercise in self-definition whereby the CBC would decide what its mandate was. The result amounted to an updating of the gospel of television articulated by CBC spokesmen back in the early and mid 1950s. Ouimet's 1960 speech at Toronto's Canadian Club was really an extended discussion of the principles that must guide the national service: it had to be 'complete,' and balanced, offering something for everyone; it had to 'link all parts of the country' together; it must be 'predominantly Canadian in content and character'; and it had to 'serve equitably' French and English Canada and the needs of the regions. Note that Ouimet was adamant about the pre-eminence of the CBC: he would never accept any claim that private television would become the main service, leaving to the CBC the task of looking after Culture and the minorities. Similarly, an internal document, 'The Future Role of the CBC," argued that the Corporation must establish the 'national standard,' the essential 'yardstick of excellence' for private TV. Above all, Ouimet wrapped the CBC up in the Canadian flag. He emphasized that these principles would ensure the CBC remained 'a unifying force in Canada' that would work to develop 'a sense of national unity.' As before, this mandate ran counter to the logic of North American television, with its emphasis upon serving up entertainment for the mass audience. Thus 'The Future Role of the CBC' warned that the Corporation must avoid any surrender to commercialism, which would make it like other networks. It was as much a tall order then as it had been in 1952. It was also, unfortunately, much less realistic.[41]

The abiding problem was, as always, money. The Corporation needed a lot: increased capital funds to establish broadcasting centres at Montreal and Toronto that were adequate to meet the demands of production, extra money to cover the costs of building new stations and eventually the expense of colour broadcasting, and above all greater operating funds to improve the quality of programming. It just wasn't there. The returns from television advertising stagnated because of the vigorous competition of private TV (see chart 4.1). CBC-TV generated gross ad revenues of over $36 million in 1959/60, fell back to $28,150,000 by 1962/3, and only recovered to its previous level in 1967/8. So the CBC's share of net TV ad revenues, nearly 52 per cent in 1960, was more than halved by 1967, and the amount

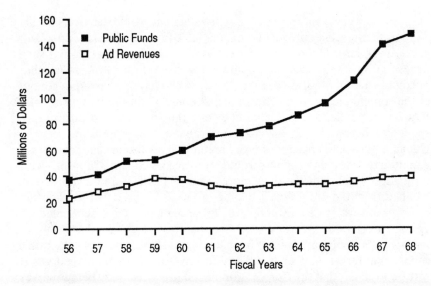

Chart 4.1 CBC ad revenues versus public funds, 1960s
Note: Fiscal years commenced in April. Data taken from CBC *Annual Reports*,
Fowler II, v. 2 of the Davey Report, and the *Canada Year Book*.

of operating expenses for television covered by advertising fell dramatically,
from close to 40 per cent to below 25 per cent. Governments, even in the
Conservative years, did reluctantly come up with increasing grants to cover
the shortfall. They weren't willing to find the extra millions necessary to
enrich the CBC service, however: by 1966, the CBC thought it needed
between $30 and $35 per television home, which would have resulted in
additional funds of $30 million to over $50 million in 1966/7. The fact
that the CBC none the less managed to produce an enormous range of
programming, in French and English, greater by far than most other broadcasting agencies, and much more cheaply than in the United States or
Britain, as Ouimet told a broadcasting committee in 1966, was a source of
pride, and evidence that the charges of extravagance were exaggerated.
But the boast also suggested that the CBC was doing far too much, with too
little money, which resulted only in a Canadian product that could rarely
approach the production values of the Hollywood import.[42]

Even though the relative importance of ad money as a source of overall
funding was on the wane, the Corporation found itself compelled to seek
this revenue more vigorously than in times past. Fowler II even lectured
the CBC on the virtues of commercial programming, which supposedly

ensured a livelier, more popular schedule than would be likely if the
Corporation carried only sustaining, and all too often esoteric and avant-
garde, programs. Ouimet and his colleagues, among others, found such
pressure disturbing because it threatened to turn the CBC into 'just another
obedient child of Madison Avenue.' They would have preferred to get out
of the commercial business altogether, although Ouimet never went quite
that far in public, for they couldn't deny that the need to please gave
sponsors a degree of influence over programming and scheduling. Eugene
Hallman, the vice-president of programming (then also in charge of sales),
admitted that CBC entertainers would try to accommodate a sponsor's wish
for a guest artist to give a show more appeal. 'The Nature of Things' was
bumped from the primetime schedule in 1963/4 because its time-slot had
to be given over to sponsored fare. Programmers once rescheduled an
episode of 'Quentin Durgens, M.P.,' about auto safety, to avoid a clash with
its sponsor's (General Motors) introduction of some new cars. The CBC's
commercial thrust, of course, displeased private TV, which charged, often
with good cause, that the Corporation priced its air time well below market
value to attract commercials. And that thrust disturbed such highbrows as
Bernard Trotter who noted that primetime CBC was 75 per cent commercial, unlike the days of radio when it was only around 35 per cent commercial. He was all too correct: although the CBC managed to place a lot of
sustaining or unsponsored shows in the morning and afternoon schedules,
that was only at the cost of selling the peak viewing hours in the evening
to a horde of advertisers. CBC in the evening was almost as much a vehicle
of commercialism as was CTV or the American networks.[43]

The problem of organization was no more amenable to an easy solution.
A good dose of bureaucracy was inevitable in an institution of the size and
scope of the CBC (there were slightly over 8,000 employees by 31 March
1965). Ouimet's personal style of management had resulted in a cumbersome, and probably excessive, headquarters' staff divorced from the life of
the production centres in Montreal and Toronto. A modest reshuffle of
offices and responsibilities late in 1964, in response to criticism from the
Glassco Commission as well as a special internal study, didn't effect any
obvious remedy. Yet charges of an uncaring top brass were patently unfair.
The minutes of the director's program meetings show that management
was constantly at work worrying about programming, even about individual
cases. Management was surprisingly tolerant of the escapades of Patrick
Watson and Douglas Leiterman during most of the run of 'Seven Days.'
Among Ouimet's last acts as president was his defence of the public-affairs

show 'Sunday' against a bevy of angry senators who thought the program had, in the words of one, 'a flavour of perversion.'[44]

The sporadic civil war between managers and producers that culminated in the 'Seven Days' affair was actually rooted in a fundamental difference of opinion within the working community. Managers were still wedded to the older concept of public service, with all that entailed in ensuring programming never became too controversial or outlandish to undo the grand purposes of educating and enlightening and serving the public. But producers defined themselves more as professionals than as public servants. Their disenchantment with management rested upon a sense of grievance, as evidenced in the brief of the Toronto producers to Fowler II, the belief that management hadn't recognized the authority conveyed upon the producers by their specialized knowledge. Such arguments were sufficiently persuasive to win the endorsement of Fowler II, which urged that the producer 'be given a reasonably free hand'![45]

The new credo of professionalism wasn't usually articulated with any clarity. Yet it led believers to emphasize a mastery of technique, the joys of innovation, and a commitment to occupational values (such as the adversary journalism of 'Seven Days') that could easily clash with the official values (such as balance and neutrality) of the institution. All that was made abundantly clear in the debate over 'Seven Days' carried on by two outsiders, of a sort, from the French network: Marc Thibault, general supervisor of public-affairs programs, who argued forcefully the need for producer autonomy, and Marcel Ouimet, vice-president and general manager, who stoutly defended the exercise of managerial prerogatives. This split afflicted other public-broadcasting entities during the 1960s, both the BBC and Australia's ABC, and reflected the mood of those heady times. The dictates of 'best practice,' in the words of Lord Windlesham, threatened the declining ideal of public service. Ouimet lacked the personal finesse of a Sir Hugh Greene, the highly successful director-general of the BBC, who was able first to nurture and later to kill 'That Was the Week That Was' without provoking any explosion comparable to the 'Seven Days' affair. But the malaise afflicting CBC wasn't the fault of Ouimet.[46]

An added strain on the Corporation was the compulsion to compete with the new private stations, especially with CTV. Management was desperately afraid of falling behind, almost to the point of paranoia. In May 1961 Ouimet announced that the CBC would have to commence morning telecasts to meet U.S. competition in the border areas. But even more important was the aim of offering Canadians a 'truly alternative service' of public and private television. Throughout the 1960s Ouimet made the case time and again for an increase in CBC 'O&Os,' supplemented by rebroadcasting outlets, to ensure each community would receive the total national package. It seemed particularly important to have 'a CBC "presence"' in each province. Besides, in private, CBC officials found their reliance on affiliates limiting: the extreme reluctance of affiliates apparently blocked efforts to reschedule 'The National' at 10:00 or 10:30 in English Canada, although Radio-Canada's 'Téléjournal' made the switch to 10:30 in July 1962. The notion of extension was supported in the reports of the 'Troika,' the review of broadcasting policy carried out by Ouimet, Stewart, and Donald Jamieson (then head of the Canadian Association of Broadcasters) in 1963 and 1964. Indeed the number of public stations had increased from nine in 1956 to sixteen (plus thirty-eight relays) in 1965. But the Liberal government didn't much care for any grand, therefore expensive, extension of the public service, and its concerns were buttressed by Fowler II, which urged a five-year freeze on building more CBC stations to compel management to show 'a more lively concern with program content.' Fowler II likewise suggested the CBC receive funding sufficient for only a partial conversion of its network service to colour. These recommendations provoked Ouimet's ire, and he demanded sufficient resources to allow the Corporation 'freedom to compete' with private and American broadcasters. Not with much success, though: the government refused to fund the construction of CBC outlets in Saskatoon, Brandon, and Moncton (all BBG-approved) and imposed a severe limit of $15 million for the change-over to colour.[47]

The most important area of competition was in programming. In 1962 Ouimet told the directors that the Corporation should maintain an audience level of roughly 50 per cent to avoid the disaster that had almost befallen the BBC when independent television first took off in Britain. Implicit was the belief, as Donald Jamieson put it, that the politicians would only continue public funding at its current scale as long as the CBC retained 'a healthy share of the television audience.'[48]

The urge to compete had a notable impact upon the character of the CBC's made-in-Canada programming. It lay behind the much-touted effort in 1959 and 1960 to give the CBC's 'O&O's' a local look by launching more and better news, affairs, and service shows geared to their cities. More important, it drove programmers to focus resources on improving the CBC's informational programming, at the expense of home-grown entertainment. There, covering the Canadian reality, the CBC had proved it could satisfy the public with programming that the Americans obviously wouldn't supply and private TV lacked the will or funds to provide in any quantity. By 1965 fully half of the CBC's programming dollars were devoted to news and public-affairs, educational and service offerings. Indeed, just over a third of the English television budget went into news and public affairs, whereas just under a third of the French television budget went to farm and fish, religious, feminine, and above all children's and educational programming. The down side of this approach was that it starved the Drama department, which only got 13 per cent of the programming dollars in 1965 (and a mere 10 per cent in 1969). But it did fulfil the CBC's mandate of public service. The quality of the national newscast, the news specials, the range of the documentaries, and the assorted public-affairs and feature programs became the chief source of the CBC's prestige in English Canada.[49]

This image of news excellence was necessary to counter the reliance on Hollywood imports in the peak viewing hours. The priority of competition ensured the Corporation would strive to carry the most appealing kinds of American entertainment to counter the CTV challenge. When CTV acquired the broadcast rights to the Big Four football games, CBC retaliated by carrying the National Football League games from the United States on a Sunday afternoon (which had the added advantage of pleasing sponsors whom the corporation hoped would spend ad money on shows covering Canadian sports). In the January 1965 sweepstakes, CBLT achieved only a bare ratings victory in the evening over CFTO because its Saturday-night line-up backed up the hockey broadcasts with the sitcom 'The Beverly Hillbillies' and the British thriller 'The Saint.' Dennis Braithwaite noted the reports of the bitter rivalry among buyers for CBC and CTV in their yearly struggles to capture the rights to the hit products of Hollywood. Nor did the irony escape him that CBC, like CTV, depended on American imports 'to give their prime-time hours glamour, interest, and drawing power.' So CBC's Fall '66 primetime schedule featured a lot of imported storytelling (see figure 4.2). Indeed, one unnamed 'high CBC official' told Percy Saltzman that 'the greatest single factor in the Americanization of Canada' over the past decade had been the CBC itself.[50]

At the bottom of so many of the Corporation's troubles was politics. The champions of public broadcasting, Ouimet among them, had expected more of the Liberals. The Liberal party, however, was no longer ready to bestow on the CBC the special favour of times past. Lester Pearson claimed a devotion to public broadcasting: his memoirs speak of his view that broadcasting was best seen as a form of education, that 'the emphasis should be on the public system and private broadcasting should be very much a subsidiary.' But he never showed that he was willing to exert himself to give his rhetoric much substance. In fact, according to an angry Bernard

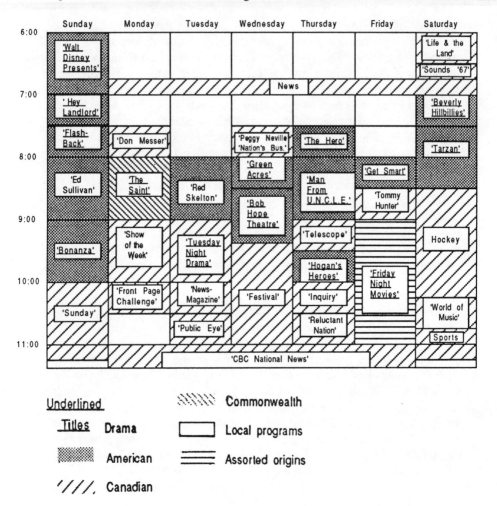

Figure 4.2 CBC evening program schedule, fall 1966
Note: This was called a normal weekly schedule, supplied courtesy of the CBC
headquarters in Ottawa.

Trotter, there was sufficient circumstantial evidence that the Liberals had come to power in 1963 prepared 'to sell out the national system of broadcasting to private interests.'[51]

The first secretary of state, Jack Pickersgill, didn't favour any large increase in public funding, and postponed action by organizing the 'Troika.' That body did more or less agree on a separation of the public and private services, statutory funding for the CBC, and the extension of CBC facilities. Yet, as Ouimet said later, the whole affair became 'an exercise in futility' because by the time the final reports were submitted the government, now through Maurice Lamontagne, announced the establishment of Fowler II. Selecting Robert Fowler to head the advisory committee virtually ensured that the endeavour would be a replay of the earlier royal commission, even though the broadcasting situation had changed dramatically in the intervening decade. Indeed Fowler II adopted a harsh attitude towards the CBC, much harsher than its treatment of private TV, and urged the creation of a one-board system to regulate what it persisted in believing was a single system. (The one-board notion was set aside by the combined opposition of the CBC and the private industry.) Underlying the committee's report was a naïve trust in the efficacy of state action, the regulatory mechanism, which simply didn't jibe with reality, as Donald Jamieson pointed out in his excellent critique *The Troubled Air*. The task of shaping a new piece of legislation was left in theory up to Judy LaMarsh, the third secretary of state, who felt aggrieved by her apparent cabinet demotion and who was increasingly hostile to CBC's management. In any case she had to share her authority with an interfering Pearson and with Jamieson, now emerging as a prominent Liberal. The result was a broadcasting act which largely enshrined the status quo, except that the newly created CRTC was given fuller authority to regulate broadcasting. The CBC didn't even receive the assurance of statutory funding.[52]

It's not difficult to see in retrospect what should have been done. The politicians should have dispensed with the nonsense about a single, mixed system and moved to separate public and private broadcasting, along the lines of the Australian model. In this scheme of things, the CBC would have received the necessary capital funds to create its broadcasting centres in Montreal and Toronto and to broadcast its own national service across the country via its own stations and rebroadcasting outlets. It would have vacated the field of commercial broadcasting, a move bound to please private TV as well as a goodly number of viewers. It would have received a much larger amount of public money, based on some system of statutory funding, perhaps linked to the consumer price index. Maybe private TV could have been persuaded to pay a high licence fee since it would then have had the commercial field to itself. That money could have served to Canadianize the CBC's schedule, especially its evening schedule, and to upgrade the quality of its product. In particular, the CBC should have revitalized its drama, not only acting as a medium of teleplays but of more made-in-Canada stories as well. Finally, planning should have begun to build a CBC-2, distributed via cable and funded through cable subscriptions, to deliver a more specialized service suited particularly to minority tastes.[53]

The point is that the CBC should have become the Canadian showcase of the popular as well as the public arts, of entertainment and of information. Need I add that it's very easy for the historian to dream on? Realizing such a future would have required a kind of political leader who was as committed to public broadcasting as Pearson claimed he was, plus someone with the will to carry out so thoroughgoing a reform. That person wasn't in evidence.

Ouimet finally retired from his exhausting post just before the 1968 act was passed. It wasn't a happy end to the career of a man who more than any other was Canada's 'Mr. Television.' The Corporation he left behind was no longer as important a cultural agency as it had been when he'd taken command a decade earlier. Its finances were insufficient. Its morale still suffered the after-effects of the 'Seven Days' affair. Its public image was tarnished, even among erstwhile friends. It was about to undergo a lengthy identity crisis to discover a more satisfying role, whether as a wholly Canadian service, a non-commercial network, and/or a kind of PBS North. A few years later, Knowlton Nash, then the man in charge of informational programming in English, would pen a nicely provocative memo calling upon the CBC to launch 'a programming revolution' that would make it, at long last, a paragon of quality, and so distinctive in Canada. There would be many other such proposals in the years ahead, all to little avail. The CBC was locked into an illogical structure by an act of Parliament.[54]

The Television System, 1967

Canada's centenary, 1967, was a year of celebration, and a normally restrained populace went a bit wild, indulging in a patriotic binge that cast a rosy hue over all things Canadian. People didn't give much thought to television, even though the networks had just gone over to colour to mark the centennial (as well as to meet American competition) and the CBC had built a $10 million broadcasting complex at the Expo '67 site to show Canadians and the world what was happening. It was too familiar, too much a part of the ordinary routine of life to stand out. None the less the

TABLE 4.1
The audience share of networks and stations, 1967

Channels	English Canada	Quebec	Canada
CBC 'O&O'	16.70	5.69	13.18
CBC affiliate	30.12	1.42	20.96
CBC total	46.82	7.11	34.14
R-C 'O&O'	0.64	19.36	6.61
R-C affiliate	0.81	22.43	7.72
R-C total	1.45	41.79	14.33
CBC/R-C	48.27	48.90	48.47
CTV	23.58	9.03	18.93
Independent Fr.	0.15	38.28	12.32
Independent Eng.	3.72	0.00	2.53
American stations	24.28	3.79	17.74
PRIVATE	51.73	51.10	51.52

Note: Figures in percentages. 'CBC' refers to the English service, 'R-C' to the French service. Data from CRTC, *Special Report on Broadcasting in Canada 1968–1978*, v. 1,28

country's television system was a considerable achievement. Over the past two decades, millions of dollars had been invested by the state, private enterprise, and the people in the purchase and operation of transmitters, microwave relays, studios, TV cameras, television sets, and the like. The result was one of the most complete and modern systems in the world that delivered a rich service, and at a surprisingly cheap cost: the overall expense of television operations that year was roughly $190 million, which worked out to about $38 per television household.[55]

The CBC was still, by far, the largest single entity in the system. The year ending 31 March 1967 the Corporation was on the air just over 100 hours a week at a cost for the production and distribution of programs of $110 million. Television received the lion's share of the public grant of $112.4 million and generated $32.9 million in gross ad revenues (net total was $26.7 million). Its two networks used an estimated 245 'O&O's,' private affiliates, and auxiliary stations to reach approximately 96 per cent of the population. It had an overall audience share of nearly 50 per cent of the total viewing population, in French and English Canada (see table 4.1),

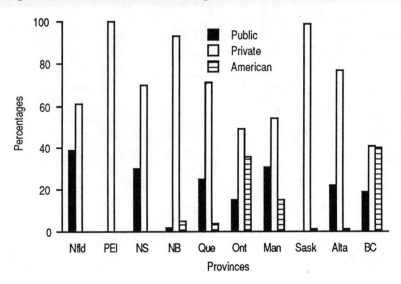

Chart 4.2 Station audience shares (by province), 1967
Source: Data from CRTC, *Special Report on Broadcasting in Canada 1968–1978*,
v. I (Ottawa: Ministry of Supply and Services 1979)

which matched the figure that Ouimet had claimed back in 1962 was necessary to secure the Corporation's future.[56]

But private TV was obviously on the march. Taken together, the network affiliates and the independents had captured over 60 per cent of the audience, and held the lead in every province (see chart 4.2). While only three-quarters of the populace could receive the signals of the new private stations, they had cut deeply into CBC's audience, the CTV affiliates winning nearly a quarter of the Anglo audience and CFTM's unofficial network nearly one-half of the audience for francophone television in Quebec. Some sixty-six stations spent $79.3 million dollars to operate their services and generated $95.1 million in revenue, leaving a tidy operating profit of $15.8 million. The vast majority of private money came from advertising: private TV earned $84.8 million in net advertising revenue in 1967, just over three-quarters of the total. Of course not everyone earned an equal share of this prosperity – not only did Montreal, Toronto, and Vancouver have private stations, but so too did Swift Current and Dawson Creek. Many national advertisers didn't bother buying time in more than ten or twelve major markets, Peter Grant estimated in 1968, leaving stations in the less-favoured cities 'to subsist on the revenue from network affiliation and local car dealers.' He was struck by the 'heterogeneity' of private TV, which, he added, made any kind of regulation most difficult.[57]

Still the lucrative prospects of the television business had been sufficient to attract the attention of a number of big investors. The Davey Report noted that nearly half of the stations by the end of the decade were in the hands of groups, or at least partly owned by groups (though that was much less than the total of nearly two-thirds of daily newspapers). The BBG had accepted media concentration because it believed that larger entities would survive better in the marketplace, an approach that allowed roughly a dozen stations once under local control or influence to get eaten up by the groups. Thus Southam Press, the country's major newspaper chain, had direct or indirect interests, through Selkirk Holdings, in CHEK-Victoria, CHAN-Vancouver, CHBC-Kelowna, CJLH-Lethbridge, CHCT-Calgary, CFPL-London, CHCH-Hamilton, CJCH-Halifax, as well as some assorted cable companies. None of these groups, though, matched the significance of the CBC, or for that matter the co-operative CTV and the independent CFTM.[58]

The statistics on audience share revealed that a very important, though usually unacknowledged, component of the system were the three American networks (see chart 4.3). About half of the Canadian population could receive American signals directly, according to a CRTC survey, and nearly 40 per cent of the people in the English-speaking provinces could receive three U.S. channels. The degree of penetration varied widely by province, or course: it was greatest in Ontario, British Columbia, and Manitoba, considerable in Quebec (about 29 per cent coverage in 1967), and much smaller or negligible elsewhere. The explosive development of cable promised to extend this coverage farther and farther into regions of the country away from the border. A study of the audience levels of CFPL-London showed that the number of homes viewing the station between 7:00 and 10:00 in the evening fell from 55,100 (fall 1961) to 46,200 (fall 1967) as cable spread through the community. A later survey, based on March 1969 data, indicated that the station's audience level among cable subscribers was less than half that among off-air viewers. Cable subscribers split their viewing time among the wide range of American signals piped directly into their homes.[59]

The cable explosion highlighted just how crucial the wishes of the ordinary Canadians had been in the shaping of the television system. Canadians had continued to invest in television equipment during the 1960s, buying first or replacement sets. In May 1960 about 81 per cent of households had a television set; by May 1967 the total had risen to 95 per cent, and only in Atlantic Canada was the figure just below nine out of ten households.

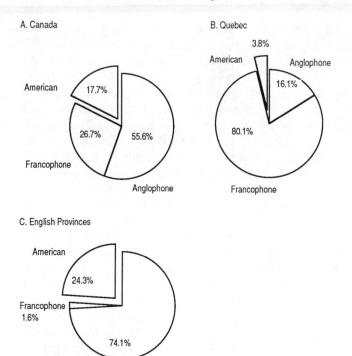

A. Canada

American 17.7%

26.7%   55.6%

Francophone

Anglophone

B. Quebec

3.8%
American

Anglophone

16.1%

80.1%

Francophone

C. English Provinces

American

24.3%

Francophone
1.6%

74.1%

Anglophone

Chart 4.3 Degree of American penetration, 1967
Note: The charts show the overall audience shares of American, Francophone, and Anglo-Canadian signals. Data from CRTC, *Special Report on Broadcasting in Canada, 1968–1978*, v. I

Around 17 per cent of Canadian households (slightly more in Ontario and Quebec) had two or more television sets, a figure that would rise to one-quarter of all households five years later. Only 100,000 households had colour TV, though many people were ready to buy now that Canadian television had gone colour, and five years later one in four households would have switched to colour sets.[60]

What people wanted was more and better television. The viewers who had a lot of choice – over half the population could receive at least four separate channels in 1967 – seemed privileged to those who were captives of the CBC, or deprived of television altogether. During the 1960s individual politicians, as both Judy LaMarsh and Donald Jamieson noted, were forever putting pressure on the government and the BBG and the CBC to extend public and private television service to communities in their ridings. People could become quite disturbed when their viewing 'rights' were threatened. In 1967 the possibility that allowing Barrie's CKVR into the Toronto market would disturb the reception of American signals caused a press and public outcry, which eventually led the cabinet to overturn a BBG decision approving the move of the CKVR antennae. Three years later the CRTC's effort to strengthen made-in-Canada TV by slapping a future minimum of 60 per cent Canadian content on broadcasters, applicable to the evening as well as the daylight hours, resulted in a hue and cry not only from the industry but from angry viewers as well who thought they would be deprived of their favourite Hollywood shows. A Liberal member of Parliament's broadcasting committee told the CRTC chairman, Pierre Juneau, that the mail provoked by the proposal was 'almost unprecedented.' Indeed a Gallup poll suggested that most English Canadians were actually opposed to the 60 per cent rule. Under pressure from politicians and the industry, the commission relaxed the rules considerably.[61]

Cable was the viewer's secret weapon in the battle for better television. In 1967 the Dominion Bureau of Statistics carried out its first survey of cable to reveal what amounted to a new sector of the broadcasting industry, growing at an extraordinary rate: there were already 408,853 individual cable subscribers and 107,631 others, such as apartment buildings, largely concentrated in the southern urban areas of Quebec, Ontario, and British Columbia. By 1970 the figure was more like 900,000, or 17 per cent of TV homes. There were a number of distinct advantages to having cable: it ensured much better reception, important for colour TV, in cities where distance or buildings distorted the signals; it offered subscribers a much greater choice of programs than was possible with off-air pick-up; and, above all, it ensured viewers could get the 'pure' American product from U.S. stations. Cable was a kind of equalizer, making Canadian viewers as privileged as their American cousins, and at a very reasonable cost – estimated at $42.78 per year. The rate of growth of cable was greater in Canada than in any other part of the world.[62]

The Board of Broadcast Governors and the Department of Transport, the two authorities involved in licensing new cable-systems, had put few controls on the spread of cable. The BBG commented unfavourably on only 17 of 173 applications, 1965 through 1967, chiefly because these might disturb plans for a new or second television service. The most important restriction came from Transport, which prevented cable companies from using more than one microwave hop to send signals from the pick-up point to the beginning of the trunk cable. That meant a lot of communities, from Calgary and Saskatoon out west, to Moncton and Halifax in the east, couldn't get American signals. By the time the CRTC decided to get tough with cable the die had already been cast. Its declaration in December 1969 that cable service wouldn't be allowed until communities had a second television service infuriated people in the middle and northern parts of Canada who couldn't see why they were deprived of the range of American programming enjoyed by the folks in Toronto. Its stated intention of April 1970 that cable-systems would be limited to carrying one commercial and one non-commercial U.S. station angered everyone who'd come to accept the full panoply of American signals as a viewing 'right.' After industry lobbying and, apparently, political pressure, the CRTC again backed down, introducing much less restrictive policies, which effectively freed the cable industry to connect new subscribers almost at will. It was just further proof of how ineffective broadcasting regulation was to protect the so-called integrity of the television system. By 1975 about 45 per cent of all homes had cable.[63]

What people meant by choice was in fact very restricted. It didn't really mean alternative service, since all of the major channels were heavily commercial in the evening. When the PBS signal and provincial educational television, such as Ontario TV, became widely available they weren't watched by very much of the audience. It didn't mean diversity, since well over half of the offerings in highly competitive markets were made up of stories of one kind or another. In the happy homes able to get the signals of the three American stations plus CBC and CTV programs early in 1967, a person would find it very hard to avoid watching some action/adventure drama or a sitcom or two during the course of a full evening's viewing (see chart 4.4). It certainly didn't mean a greater wealth of made-in-Canada material, since the more competition there was, even among Canadian channels, the less important home-grown programming figured in the over-all schedule. During the 1967/8 season, for example, the amount of Canadian content scheduled during the peak hours of 8:00 to 10:30 PM was 67.1 per cent by Radio-Canada, 45.7 per cent by CBC English, 38.5 per cent by CFTM, 22.8 per cent by CTV, and 20.0 per cent by the independent CHCH-Hamilton. At bottom, what choice meant, especially in English Canada, was the freedom to select among a wider and wider range of titles of Hollywood entertainment at any given point in the four hours after 7:00 PM.[64]

The striking preference for American entertainment showed up in the statistics on what viewers actually watched in the course of an evening.

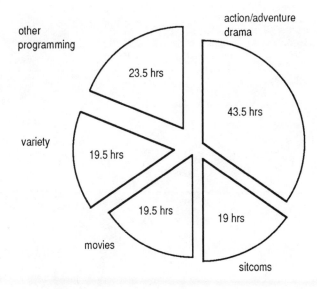

other
programming

action/adventure
drama

23.5 hrs

43.5 hrs

variety

19.5 hrs

19.5 hrs

19 hrs

movies

sitcoms

Chart 4.4 Leading network genres, primetime, Spring '67
Note: This chart counts programs on five networks: CBC, CTV, ABC, CBS, NBC.
Data from CBLT and CFTO schedules plus Harry Castleman and Walter J.
Podrazik, *The Schedule Book: Four Decades of Network Programming from Sign-
on to Sign-off* (New York: McGraw-Hill 1984)

Fowler II learned to its horror that in March 1964 the amount of viewing
of American shows in four anglophone cities ranged from a low of 57 per
cent in Halifax, where people couldn't get direct U.S. signals, to a high of
74 per cent in Toronto, where people could get all the American networks.
What Toronto did today the rest of the country might do tomorrow. Overall,
in 1967, Anglos spent nearly three out of every four hours looking at foreign
shows, while French Canadians spent just over an hour and a half (see
table 4.2). Both groups demonstrated a marked preference for their own
news and current affairs, as well as for Canadian sportscasts. But primetime
television was an entertainment medium first, and here there was a contrast. Viewers of francophone television watched almost as much home-
grown variety and drama as imported material. Viewers of anglophone
television overwhelming watched the foreign stuff, most of which came
from Hollywood. The fact was that after all that had happened during the
previous decade, the Canadian-content regulations, the introduction of
independent private TV, the expansion of both the CBC and CTV, the old

TABLE 4.2
Primetime viewing preferences, 1967

Programming type	Canadian	Foreign	Total
Francophone TV			
News	10.70	0.00	10.70
Current affairs	7.68	0.00	7.68
Other informastion	0.53	0.00	0.53
Sports	6.70	0.00	6.70
Entertainment	32.21	39.05	71.26
Other	0.86	2.27	3.13
Totals	58.69	41.31	
Anglophone TV			
News	7.57	1.18	8.75
Current affairs	4.88	0.32	5.20
Other information	0.07	0.00	0.07
Sports	6.47	0.20	6.68
Entertainment	9.60	68.78	78.38
Other	0.48	0.44	0.93
Totals	29.07	70.93	

Note: Figures in percentages. Data from CRTC, *Special Report on Broadcasting in Canada 1968–1978*, v. 1, 49

dilemma remained: the Broadcasting Act might state television should be 'basically Canadian' but viewers ensured television entertainment was basically American.[65]

Did that mean television in Canada was an agent of Americanization? Well, at times, nationalists sounded as though they really believed that TV was the chief threat to the national soul of the country. That was one major reason for the whoops of joy that greeted the early work of the CRTC when it embarked on its campaign to Canadianize the airwaves in the late 1960s. People didn't know the history of their country.

Recall that about 90 per cent of the information programming English Canadians watched on television was home-grown. The interest in their own affairs wasn't at all new. What has always given special definition to the country is a sense of Canada as a distinct public entity, with its own brand of law, politics and government, and a civic ethic. Even before 1900, and right through the twentieth century, daily newspapers had won large audiences and fat advertising revenues by offering large quantities of local, regional, and national news. Canadian magazines such as *Maclean's* had eked out an existence ever since the Great War by specializing in things Canadian. CBC newscasts on radio had secured the attention of the mass of listeners during the Second World War. The National Film Board had won fame by producing documentaries that tried to mirror the life of the country. Primetime television built upon this foundation. It didn't undermine the fact that a significant proportion of Canadians were eager to learn about their own places and people and country. Rather it catered to the fact that Canadians constitute, in the words of Knowlton Nash, a nation of 'infomaniacs,' just as willing to 'engage' as to 'escape' the day, in the evening hours.[66]

Likewise, a couple of generations of Canadians have been happy consumers of American imports, notably entertainment. At least since the turn of the century, the products of America's culture industries have dominated the market in English Canada and won a lot of favour as an alternative to a more traditional fare in French Canada. American Sunday newspapers and magazines had flooded into Canada before 1914, Hollywood movies were virtually the only kind of popular feature film by the early 1920s, American radio had captured by far the largest audience share by the end of that decade, American comic books were everywhere after 1945, as were American books when the paperback revolution broke a bit later. By and large the ascendancy these 'intruders' achieved early on has lasted; the assorted efforts to promote home-grown competition, notably CBC radio whose most popular kinds of entertainment were usually American imports, had only limited success, especially outside French Canada. There, the arrival of, for example, radioromans and a popular local literature after 1940 indicated a taste for products with a distinctly local flavour. But popular culture in English Canada was emphatically American, long before television came on the scene. The audience totals for Hollywood's storytelling on television shouldn't have caused much surprise.

The country hadn't gone to the dogs as a result, though. Just the opposite. Experience had proved that most Canadians could happily consume American products of all kinds without doubting that they were citizens of a better country, whether that meant more peaceable, more moral, more conservative, whatever. The end of the 1960s found the country caught up in a wave of competing nationalist passions. In Quebec, where two decades of social change had vitiated traditional views and mores and produced a more modern, really a more North American way of life, a so-called new nationalism had captured the fancy of many, many people, especially the young, and sponsored the increasingly popular dream of a separate Quebec nation-state. In English Canada, supposedly drenched by American messages, both economic and cultural nationalism were riding high, and their target was emphatically American power and influence in Canada. The image of the United States as a result of Vietnam and the racial problems was especially tarnished. That hadn't made the English-speaking part of the country any more united, mind you: sectional and provincial loyalties were to play havoc with national affairs during the course of the 1970s. One could well argue that a common acceptance of the virtues of an affluent lifestyle, defined according to American norms and spread by New York's advertising as well as Hollywood's entertainment, was one of the most important social bonds in such a fragmented land.

So television was an agent of Hollywood's popular arts. It had expanded the market for these imports, and extended that market into the far corners of the country. The tradition that Canadian shows were normally poorer in those qualities of excitement and humour, in production values, was firmly established. A lot of viewers wouldn't even look at a new Canadian show unless they had no choice. Events afterwards would simply perpetuate this situation. (Hence this anecdote: in 1987, making small talk while driving, I asked my daughter Stephanie, then thirteen years old, what memorable Canadian shows she'd viewed in the past week. She hadn't watched any. Her response: 'Canadian shows only stink!' She was referring, of course, to entertainment – the made-in-Canada brand couldn't compete with 'Miami Vice' or 'The Cosby Show.') But that didn't make TV the Americanizer nonpareil. Nor, necessarily, was cable, the bogy of the next decade: statistics revealed that in 1978, after the massive expansion of cable, audience totals for the viewing of foreign programming on Canadian TV had fallen slightly to 69.47 per cent for English-speaking stations and risen a bit to 45.80 per cent for French-speaking stations, although the audience share of American stations had increased to nearly one-quarter. Television merely conformed to past patterns, confirmed the reality of American penetration, and buttressed the sense of being Canadian – it may seem contradictory, but, as the saying goes, 'that's television for ya.'[67]

The efforts of Canadian television at home were (and remain) a cause for lamentation only among those people who believed in the impossible: that television really could birth a Canadian PopCult. CBC-TV had a credible record as an agency that maintained a Canadian voice on the airwaves, much like newspapers, magazines, and books have done in the realm of print. But the record was much less respectable when the context changed from Canada to the world at large: made-in-Canada programming won only a domestic audience, never much in the way of an international reputation. Contrast that with the case of the British product that proved able to penetrate the North American market, notably after 1970, or the success of the telenovelas produced by Brazilian TV in the Latin American market. Part of the explanation, of course, lies in the economics of culture: it was very difficult to find the funds to produce any show that could reasonably expect to become an international megahit. The rest of the answer lies in the presumptions of the CBC itself, which rarely set its sights beyond the bounds of Canada. The Corporation, especially its Anglo service, has reflected one of the predominant traits of Canada's cultural industries, namely a hankering for protectionism and a fear of free trade. Indeed its leaders have never recognized that America's popular culture is also Canada's. Rather, at times, they have looked upon the American product as something of an enemy, a view later embodied in the famous 'Touchstone Document' issue by CBC president Al Johnson in 1977: therefore the public network and the government ought to combat the invasion, however paradoxical that stance might seem given the CBC's carriage of American signals. This belief, in turn, has bred a defensive posture, preventing the development of a strategy that might have converted the CBC into a much more aggressive player on the global scene, competing with Hollywood companies for the attention of the TV masses. The fundamental failure of Canadian television, in short, has been in the world-wide cultural marketplace, not at home.[68]

Below, left: The Ottawa-wise chairman: Davidson Dunton, chairman of the CBC's board of directors in the 1950s (Van's Studio Ltd., CBC Collection, MISA, National Archives of Canada: 14659)

Below, right: The successful newcomer: John Bassett, 1972, one of the founders of private television in Canada (CBC Collection, MISA, National Archives of Canada: 14671)

Top, facing: The embattled president: Alphonse Ouimet, the CBC's president in the 1960s (Dominion-Wide Photographs, CBC Collection, MISA, National Archives of Canada: 14657)

The policy-maker: R.M. Fowler, chairman of a royal commission and a special committee on broadcasting (CBC Collection, MISA, National Archives of Canada: 14665)

The public frenzy: a crowd in front of a store window to watch the telecast of the championship boxing fight between Rocky Marciano and Jersey Joe Walcott, 15 May 1953 (Montreal *Gazette*/National Archives of Canada/ PA-77928)

The new household appliance: a television set in 1952 (Montreal *Gazette*/ National Archives of Canada/PA-77934)

A rare breed, the female moderator: Michelle Tisseyre (1954), reputedly the first woman in Montreal television and a famous talk-show host on Radio-Canada in the 1950s and 1960s (Montreal *Gazette*/National Archives of Canada/ PA-77926)

A Canadian charmer (female version): Shirley Harmer, star of 'Showtime'
(CBC Collection, MISA, National Archives of Canada: 14672)

The most famous weatherman of them all: Percy Saltzman of 'Tabloid' fame
(CBC Collection, MISA, National Archives of Canada: 13675)

A Canadian charmer (male version): Robert Goulet, star of 'Showtime'
(McKague Toronto, CBC Collection, MISA, National Archives of Canada: 14668)

Canada's sweetheart: Juliette (Ron Vickers Photography, CBC Collection, MISA, National Archives of Canada: 14662)

Country Canada's favourite trio?: Marg Osburne, Don Messer, and Charlie Chamberlain of 'Don Messer's Jubilee' (CBC Collection, MISA, National Archives of Canada: 13982)

Three comics: Johnny Wayne, Corinne Conley, and Frank Shuster
(CBC Collection, MISA, National Archives of Canada: 12240)

An intellectual on television: André Laurendeau (1963), host of 'Pays et merveilles' and guest on many Radio-Canada panel shows during the 1950s (National Archives of Canada/C75931)

Part Two: Genres

5

Information for Everyone

The ultimate educational responsibility is the development of the individual's equipment to evaluate his society and culture and his own relationship to it, in short the development of his critical perception. This, it seems to me, becomes the legitimate and ... congenial purpose of television as an educational force. The so-called 'mass medium' must become the champion of the individual.

Bernard Trotter, 1960[1]

Bernard Trotter was then the assistant supervisor of Talks and Public Affairs at CBC Toronto. His comments appeared in a most appropriate source, *Food for Thought*, the official journal of the Canadian Association for Adult Education. He was writing near the end of an experiment that had seen CBC-TV emerge as the chief distributor of learning in the country. The ideal of an educated citizenry had conditioned a whole form of prime-time programming during the course of the 1950s. The prominence of this form on both the francophone and the anglophone networks had done much to set the CBC's design for evening television apart from its American rival. The results of that experiment were now cloaked in the rhetoric of achievement: so the Metropolitan Educational Television Association of Toronto called the CBC 'Canada's great university of the air.' It might well have said 'Canada's national art gallery, library, museum, forum, eyewitness, travel guide, or vocational school' as well.[2]

Democracy's School

People, we are told, are curious animals. The problem for governors is how
to satisfy that curiosity in ways that benefit the individual and the society.
Beginning roughly in the years just after the close of the Great War,
idealists and educators worked through a collection of agencies to realize
their dreams of an enlightened populace. Some of the agencies were tied
to existing educational institutions, for example, the assorted departments
of extension created by universities. But equally prominent were voluntary
associations such as the League of Nations Society (1921), the Canadian
Institute of International Affairs (1925), the Canadian Institute of Public
Affairs (1933), or the YMCA and its Canadian Youth Commission (1943),
each intent on spreading a more specialized brand of knowledge. Farm and
labour organizations also joined in, notably the United Farmers movements
and eventually the Canadian Federation of Agriculture (born in 1935 as
the Canadian Chamber of Agriculture) as well as the Canadian Congress
of Labour and the Confédération des Travailleurs Catholiques du Canada,
whose leaders felt a special need to upgrade the skills of their members to
meet the demands of modern living. One especially energetic, if eccentric,
champion was John Grierson, the great advocate of film as propaganda,
who came from England to build the National Film Board (for a time he
ran the Wartime Information Board in addition), and thus was able to use
the war to foster his own vision of an aware citizenry. But the most prominent and active agency was undoubtedly the Canadian Association for
Adult Education (CAAE), founded in 1935, mostly by English Canadians
(though it did acquire a French-Canadian wing), which was led for the next
fifteen years by the veteran educator E.A. Corbett.[3]

There was a terrible earnestness about the rhetoric of adult education.
Knowledge wasn't just its own reward; it was a source of power and progress
as well. Educators and their allies feared that the public lacked sufficient
information to manage their own lives properly as well as to run an increasingly complex democracy. A related worry, at least among highbrows, was
that the prevalence of the popular arts, from comic books to Hollywood
movies, would satisfy the public's curiosity, and relieve its boredom, at
some cost to the cause of Culture. A few activists, in particular Grierson
and Corbett, clearly thought that adult education would give new 'power
to the people' to solve social problems and to shape some future golden
age of general well-being. Other sympathizers, including the Massey commissioners, seemed more concerned with blunting the appeal of 'passive
entertainment,' so that people might use their new leisure time better to

understand themselves, their society, and the civilization of the ages. Adult education could be justified as a method of fostering social reform, reinforcing citizenship, or enriching the individual. As usual, that sort of confusion over purpose actually enhanced the attractiveness of the idea, since people of quite different persuasions could come together to defeat the common peril of mass ignorance.

The idea was bound to influence the way in which the CBC approached its business. Satisfying the needs of 'the whole man' required both education and entertainment. During the Second World War, the CBC, in association with the CAAE, organized first the 'National Farm Radio Forum' (fall 1941) and later 'Citizen's Forum' (fall 1943). Radio-Canada offered its own brand of adult education with such shows as 'Radio-Collège' or 'Les idées en marche' (also in league with adult educators). Both services worked with the mainstream churches to produce religious programming. On their own, the networks scheduled newscasts, talks and lectures, panel discussions, and radio documentaries geared to informing and enlightening listeners.

This thrust carried over into television. The CBC scheduled much larger quantities of informational programming, sometimes up to one-third of the primetime roster in Quebec, than was common in the United States during the 1950s (see chart 5.1). Furthermore, although the CBC did use French, British, and American film material, and for the first few years some American feature series on its anglophone schedules, more and more of this programming was made in Canada. But what became increasingly clear was that the nature of television had fostered a kind of programming that didn't always fit the tenets of adult education, at least not in its classic formulation. Put another way, CBC-TV slowly broke free from the élitist cast of mind and the emphasis upon social utility so obvious in the cause of adult education to fashion an 'information for everyone' that better suited the tastes, if not the needs, of the affluent generation.

A Window on Life

Programming for the higher mind, a matter of keen interest to the universities, was an early victim of television. Not that the CBC didn't try. One of its first offerings, 'Exploring Minds,' was a co-operative venture with the academic world. These half-hours featured lectures by professors from various universities across Canada (at first, mostly the University of Toronto) on topics as disparate as the nature of philosophy and the properties of liquid air. The trouble was that professors were rarely attuned to

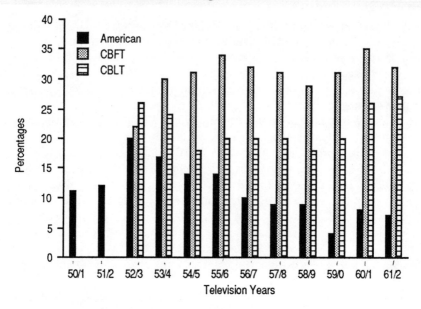

Chart 5.1 Information on the air, 1950s
Note: This chart displays two somewhat different kinds of data, which are not exactly comparable. The Canadian data are for the two flagship stations in Toronto and Montreal, and so include local programming, during the course of a full year (September to the next August). The American data are for network programming only, and reflect largely the fall schedules (from September to December).

the demands of the medium and producers were sometimes too intent on producing an interesting show. In one case a professor planned to illustrate a point about the refraction of light with a diagram. He was overruled by the producer, who substituted a ballet sequence involving twelve children! The result might not be dull – but neither was it intelligible. All too easily the shows could become little more than an exercise in boredom or in triviality, or perhaps both.[4]

Slightly more successful was a CBLT series entitled 'Live and Learn,' also linked to the University of Toronto, which began in the Fall '57 and appeared as late as the Summer '65 on the evening schedule. (The dates indicate when a show was a regular offering on the evening schedule, not when it first came on the air or when it last appeared, unless otherwise specified.) One of its series, the twelve-part 'Focus on Physics,' went national in the Spring '58. The appeal of that program derived in part from its two teachers, professors Patterson Hume and Donald Ivey, who gave practical demonstrations and used diagrams to satisfy those curious about nuclear energy, electricity, motion, gravitation, and assorted other aspects of modern physics. In a similar vein was 'Speaking French' (on Saturdays, 6:00–6:30, Fall '59 to Spring '61, though not in the summer seasons), hosted by Professor Jean-Paul Vinay of the Université de Montréal who, with the aid of an attractive model, Phyllis Clapperton, used sketches and comedy to teach grammar and vocabulary. Vinay acted as both a performer and a teacher and entertained his viewers in order to educate them. It was this light approach, plus the fact that his material was so concrete, even practical, that made the show attractive to viewers. A professorial style and an abstract focus just weren't very suitable to evening television.[5]

Actually 'Speaking French' was something of a hybrid, since it might also be counted among the list of instructional shows that dotted the primetime schedules in the mid-1950s. Budding cooks and handymen, golfers and photographers, children and farmers were told how to improve their skills or their play. All these shows needed, it seemed, was an engaging host able to speak intelligently and pleasantly about something of special interest to a particular kind of viewer. Some hosts became minor celebrities, like Hans Freed, a Toronto restaurateur who specialized in gourmet cooking à la Europe ('Hans in the Kitchen') or, even more famous, Peter Whittall ('Mr. Fix-It') who, for years, told Canadians how to repair or renovate their homes and, on occasion, how to complete such off-beat projects as building a houseboat. Few of these shows required much in the way of money or care, a fact that could only enhance their value to programmers struggling to fill the evening schedule. Yet they could strike a chord among viewers: the CBC Times (21–27 April 1962) once estimated that 'Mr. Fix-It' received about 33,000 letters annually.[6]

Such instruction for living was often blended into a wealth of programs designed, in one way or another, to divert as well as to educate the curious about a whole range of topics, places, and people. In the Summer '54, for instance, CBLT tried to attract men and women with 'Living,' a series on five nights a week that offered all kinds of useful information on handicrafts, homemaking, child-raising, and gardening, much of it in the form of interviews. A series might be modest or elaborate, offering much trivia or some learning, sporting interviews and talks, as well as film and even bits of drama. Producers used sketches to popularize issues in the law on 'C'est la loi' and later 'A Case for the Court,' planned in conjunction with the Canadian Bar Association, perhaps as an antidote to the flood of messages about the American legal system featured in crime drama. The common thread? Each of these shows included an element of human interest. So, an initial blurb for 'Graphic' promised a couple of 'entertaining items of a real-life variety, on the premise that people are always interested in what the other fellow is doing.' In the end 'Graphic' came to focus on interviews with 'the people who make up a nation,' broadly defined to include a Sam Etcheverry (then quarterback of the Montreal Alouettes) as well as a Donald Gordon (president of Canadian National Railways).[7]

On the lighter side were a series of shows that surveyed the worlds of entertainment, recreation, and public affairs. The classic time-waster, the talk show, didn't do very well on the anglophone network, although for a couple of seasons the Montreal-produced 'The Tapp Room' offered up some chat and some acts by assorted guests from the popular-music scene. Contrast that with the success of Michele Tisseyre on Radio-Canada who hosted a talk show, under different titles, that brought in such guests as Montreal's mayor and the finalists in a beauty contest as well as the stars of the popular arts. Both networks, though, did well with sports reviews, from 'Encyclopédie sportive' to 'The Vic Obeck Show,' which offered coverage of the big-time professional sports such as football as well as exotics such as dog-sled racing. Jim Coleman, on after the Friday-night fights, usually with a sports celebrity, became one of Canada's best-known sports journalists. King Whyte won fame as *the* outdoors enthusiast because of his long-lasting series on all kinds of wilderness recreation.[8]

By far the most appealing vehicle of popular facts, however, was a hybrid that combined elements of the talk show, the review, and the news magazine to attract viewers of all ages and types. Indeed in some ways the Toronto production 'Tabloid,' later called 'Seven-O-One,' was representative of 'information for everyone.' The show began in March 1953 and died in September 1963, making it one of the longest-lasting series in the history of early television. It was aired early in the evening, either at 6:30 or 7:00, usually for a half-hour every weekday, though only on the central Canadian network. Much the same kind of show appeared in the other regions, for example, the Maritimes' 'Gazette,' Winnipeg's 'Spotlight,' and Vancouver's 'Almanac' and later its 'Seven O'Clock Show,' which Marce Munro claimed was at one point the top-rated program in the Pacific Northwest, even beating out Seattle's product. Montreal's 'Carrefour' on Radio-Canada had a similar structure, though it was much more serious in tone, perhaps because journalist René Lévesque had initially taken charge of the program.[9]

At its peak, in the late 1950s, 'Tabloid' liked to proclaim its popularity – 'the nightly habit of nearly everyone' was the boast. That was an exaggeration, at least in competitive markets. CBC's Audience Research showed in a survey of ratings during the winter season 1957/8 that the program won an audience share of roughly 11 per cent in Montreal (compared with about 67 per cent for 'Carrefour' and 'Téléjournal') and 15 per cent to 18 per cent in Toronto (compared with 35 per cent to 45 per cent for WBEN's 'Annie Oakley'). But a few years later the CBC Times claimed the show reached on an average winter evening about 250,000 people on CBLT alone. 'Tabloid is a little like a comic strip,' mused Joyce Davidson, one of the show's regulars. 'Read it just occasionally and it doesn't make too much sense. But stick with it and a lot of people seem to get addicted.' Certainly 'Tabloid' did win a collection of loyal fans (who wrote in with their comments) and could claim a fairly wide reach, if that was measured over the course of a week or a month.[10]

'Tabloid' was the brain-child of Ross McLean, the wonderkid of Talks and Public Affairs in Toronto. Youthful, imaginative, arrogant, with a flair for promotion and for getting in trouble, McLean had an instinctive feel for television. He was something of a 'media junky,' impressed by the world of publicity and deeply fascinated by celebrity. His two great successes, first 'Tabloid' and later 'Close-Up,' turned him into a star in his own right, the subject of assorted potted biographies in magazines. McLean didn't much care for working with outsiders, including the adult-education crowd, since that could only make for dull programs. More to the point, he embraced the idea that good television required a 'showbiz' approach: thus he was a champion of news-as-entertainment who believed that his special mission was to make information diverting as well as educational. 'Facts with Fun' was his own motto for 'Tabloid.'[11]

According to McLean, 'Tabloid' first came to the air as 'a bargain basement version of NBC's Today,' a morning show that Pat Weaver (NBC's top programming executive) had designed as a mix of news, interviews, and features to ensure easy viewing for people eating breakfast or preparing for work and school. Thus, in the beginning, 'Tabloid' was an unpredictable pot-pourri of newsreels, interviews, demonstrations, panel discussions, reviews, and so on. Once the news portion was removed, in the Fall '53, the series began to take on its own unique character – 'a kind of spoken-word variety show' – featuring humorous exchanges among the regulars, an extended weather report, and above all guests and interviews. Ted Pope, who took over as producer, claimed that the show's 'business' was 'people,' whether home-grown personalities or, more often, visiting celebrities. By June 1960, the CBC *Times* estimated that 6,500 guests had made their way through the 'Tabloid' studio.[12]

'Tabloid' tried to attract a complete range of guests, although its choice depended in part on just what famous personality was coming to Toronto. There were some serious interviews with such people as Dr Margaret Mead, Nicholas Monsarrat, and Billy Graham. There were also lighter exchanges with Amy Vanderbilt on etiquette and Duncan Hines on what to eat. Once an expert in judo tossed both Percy Saltzman and Dick MacDougal around the studio. At times the show displayed a definite liking for contrasts. Faye Emerson, one of the first sexy women on American television, was paired with two wrestlers, all to recall the pioneer days of TV. Different styles of dance were featured in twin interviews with Samia Gamal (a belly dancer) and Eva Van Genczy (a ballet dancer), different kinds of music with Sir Ernest MacMillan and the last of the local organ-grinders. This was informal education at its best.[13]

The show could be a bit naughty, which did sometimes cause problems. One Dr. E.E. Robbins of Montreal sent in a critical letter, plus a supporting Montreal *Star* review, to Ross McLean early in 1956. Both were read out on air, and then viewers were invited to get in touch with the doctor to 'cheer' him up – his name and address were twice shown on the screen. The result was that Robbins got a lot of unwanted phone calls, received abusive mail, and was the butt of some practical jokes, presumably from 'Tabloid' fans. He sued for damages and was eventually awarded $3,000.[14]

Robbins's distaste for the antics of the 'Tabloid' team wasn't shared by all. Indeed there's little doubt that the regulars were a big reason for the show's success. Viewers' letters indicated that they were welcomed into living-rooms as 'intimate visitors'; people wanted to know a lot about these new friends, from their eating habits to their marital status. The first great star, in fact the first star of English-Canadian television, was, of all people, Percy Saltzman, the 'Tabloid' weatherman. His brash, buoyant way of giving the weather, complete with broad strokes of chalk on a map of Canada and a constant, fast-paced stream of chatter, captured the fancy of viewers almost immediately. On one occasion, the producer actually allowed Saltzman to go on as long as he liked – for twenty minutes. Saltzman's celebrity status demonstrated how the slightly off-beat and colourful character could do so well in a medium that always highlighted personality. Almost equally popular were the 'Tabloid' women, initially Elaine Grand but even more so her replacement, Joyce Davidson, whose presence contributed a touch of glamour. (McLean was later credited with introducing this species of 'talking dolls' to Canadian television.) Davidson added a bit more than blonde good looks once she gained experience: gifted with a natural grace and a quick mind, she not only filled the role of the hostess but won fame as an excellent interviewer. Then there were the assorted emcees, initially Dick MacDougal, whose laid-back style earned him the nickname 'Mr Relaxation,' and later Max Ferguson, the master of radio humour who none the less wasn't able to fit easily into his assigned roles.[15]

A second set of shows offered scenes from the cities and countryside of Canada as well as life in other parts of the world. 'On the Scene,' a local CBLT show, once put a camera on a streetcar to chronicle everything that came along. 'Here and There,' a network show, tried to acquaint people with Canada by showing films on skiing in the Laurentians, on the historic sites of Winnipeg, and on the minting of Canadian coins. 'Four Corners' featured talks by people who had visited other lands, from Ireland to Japan. The most lasting of these travelogues, though, was André Laurendeau's famous 'Pays et merveilles,' which used both guests and film to explore an assortment of countries. One early edition, in February 1953, focused on the Nile, and Laurendeau's guest was Cecile Moussalli, an Egyptian-born Canadian. The camera moved from close-ups of a map (ironically with place-names in English), to the talking heads, to scenes of Egypt (which took up about two-thirds of the program's half-hour), mostly dwelling on the temples and pyramids of the past as well as the traditional way of life still common along the Nile, where primitive styles of farming and fishing persisted. During these film inserts, Laurendeau asked brief questions and Moussalli gave a kind of running commentary. It amounted to a sort of show-and-tell, lacking an explicit viewpoint, though clearly grounded in assumptions about the virtues of modernity and the plight of the impoverished Egyptians. As usual, an account of what life was like in other parts of the globe tended to confirm the superiority of life at home.[16]

The assorted realms of nature, science, and art received some attention, though perhaps not their due. Over the years, Radio-Canada offered a couple of series devoted to painting, literature, and the theatre. At first, the English service relied on American film series, such as 'Kiernan's Kaleidoscope,' to furnish trivia about the wonders of science and nature, in this case for an audience of young people. In the Fall '56, though, the CBC began to air 'Explorations,' an omnibus show that used drama, films, and discussions to delve into society, the economy, and science and technology. One of its series, 'Tomorrow Is Now' (March–April 1959), for instance, surveyed the ways in which the machinery, the medicine, and the pollution of the industrial world were affecting the lives of all people.[17]

The treatment of history and biography amounted to exercises in myth-making. Foreign and domestic accounts of the past were slightly more common on Radio-Canada, a reflection of the fact that a sense of popular history was much more substantial among the populace in Quebec. 'Panoramique' once offered six NFB films that dramatized the recent past of French Canada, since the beginning of the Depression, by highlighting the experiences of a few people – one show, for instance, looked at the effect of the war on a family. Another docudrama, 'Le roman de la science,' focused on major scientific discoveries throughout the ages, linking science to the march of progress. 'Je me souviens/Dateline' tried to present a pleasing bicultural interpretation of such events as the fall of Quebec, the search for the north magnetic pole, and so on. In 1959 'Explorations' used photos, film-clips, and interviews to present a supposedly 'balanced picture' of the Winnipeg General Strike that emphasized its role in advancing the cause of organized labour. In 1960 and 1961 the series aired first 'Durham's Canada' and then the NFB's 'Prelude to Confederation,' two docudramas that tried 'to bring to life the figures' who had made Canadian history. These and other features offered viewers a wide assortment of heroes, or at least acts of heroism, to admire, if not to cherish.[18]

'Two Studies of French Canada', aired on 'Explorations' in March 1958, deserves a bit more attention because it demonstrates well some of the qualities of the early documentary. The miniseries was produced by Radio-Canada personnel, directed by Florent Forget, and hosted by René Lévesque. The shows did have a definite, if unobjectionable, line: their purpose was to explain the true character of Quebec by exploring recent history and dispelling myth. In the first episode, 'Quebec 1939,' for example, an animated, cigarette-smoking Lévesque took up the role of the teacher to lecture Anglos about his province, explaining that the caricature of the simple and simple-minded Jean Baptiste, all too prevalent in English Canada, was woefully inaccurate. His message was underlined by dramatized sketches, written by Reginald Boisvert, to illustrate just what the war did to ordinary Québécois. It was a way of personalizing events, showing in particular how one young man off in Europe came to appreciate the virtues of old Quebec while his fiancée, working at home, was transformed into a 'modern' woman. This was serious stuff, and the whole show seem very earnest, more appropriate to the classroom than to the living-room. The pacing was very slow and the camera work unexciting. The sketches were done in a studio, using simple sets, and looked very staged. The characters were just cardboard figures who existed to express simply and clearly certain views about life. Yet the show had some impact: a few years later, Robert Fulford credited the two-parter with giving him his 'first glimpse of what was happening in Quebec.'[19]

The Anglo network showed more of a preference for screen biographies, notably in the form of such interview series as 'Profile' and 'Graphic,' most of which were best described as acts of celebration. The plan for 'Profile' was that its camera would visit the homes of famous people in Canada and abroad, both Arnold Toynbee and Thérèse Casgrain, Bertrand Russell and Arthur Lismer. The show promised informal interviews: 'the aim is to get at the real person, to let him talk freely and frankly so that he reveals a bit to the audience.' That goal wasn't always realized. On 25 April 1955, for example, the subject was none other than the imposing Cardinal Paul-Emile Léger of Montreal. The interviewer, Murray Ballantyne, was positively reverential, asking brief questions nominally about Léger's career and work that allowed the cardinal to preach his brand of social philosophy. Occasionally Ballantyne added a confirming footnote to the cardinal's message. That way viewers were told about the importance of a happy childhood (and the problem of delinquency), the virtues of the work ethic, the evil of communism and the cure of Christianity, the simplicity and humanity of the Pope ('a virtual prisoner in his Vatican palace'), and the idea of brotherhood (and its Canadian application in the case of Montreal). The interview amounted to an extended, half-hour advertisement for the man and his church. The CBC was paying homage to one of the powers in the land.[20]

The Léger interview wasn't especially interesting television. The few attempts at humour and anecdote were hardly sufficient to relieve the 'heaviness' of the whole production. But the interview did fall within the parameters of adult education, at least the brand that emphasized the goal of education for citizenship. The defining framework was celebration, as much as investigation. Other shows might be more entertaining, less obviously didactic, than 'Profile,' but that framework persisted. Most of the features, reviews, and human-interest shows, at least when they rose above trivia, served to confirm the virtues of the existing order. So an 'Explorations' series of edited interviews with a collection of notable Canadians on the topic of God et al., entitled 'Belief,' highlighted 'the theme of brotherly love,' while a second 'Explorations' series on 'Big Business' turned to the Canadian Chamber of Commerce, the Canadian Manufacturers Association, and business leaders to explain corporate ways and corporate power. Usually viewers were being told how right and proper was the authority of the institutions that guided their lives, how necessary it was to defer to the wisdom of the official ideology that legitimated the way things were. The prevalence of such a rhetoric of conviction shouldn't surprise: the CBC was merely reflecting the conformism that was common during the 1950s.[21]

None of which should be taken as a sneer. CBC-TV could be a marvellous resource for people interested in almost anything, from the beauty of Ireland to the mechanics of American politics, from the art of Matisse to skiing in the Laurentians, from the sublime to the ridiculous. The real-estate agent who wrote the CBC in praise of the physics series on 'Live and Learn,' the children who went to the library to find books on a subject highlighted by television, the 30,000 Canadians requesting a summary of French lessons featured on one program, all were showing that they'd acquired some kind of knowledge from watching television. The point is that these programs did teach, though whom and sometimes what they taught depended upon the viewer and the situation. Put another way, the impact of 'information for everyone' was at bottom the sum total of uncounted effects upon individuals.[22]

Presenting the News

The CBC drew a sharp distinction between news as objective fact and views as opinionated judgment. Perhaps because of the BBC's example, the Corporation proved much more rigid than its American counterparts, where the notion of a single kind of broadcast journalism eventually took hold. Dan McArthur, the man who first shaped the CBC's news, was convinced the service had to be 'an island unto itself': the two brands of programming were actually separated, one, the News Service and the other, Talks and Public Affairs, although the departments did share joint responsibility over certain kinds of stories, such as UN debates, political campaigns, and election coverage at home and in the United States. Both news and views became a source of pride as well as difficulty to CBC management over the course of the 1950s, as television journalism increasingly challenged the primacy of the newspapers and magazines. And both departments suffered the same problems – a lack of resources, not enough trained people and insufficient equipment, at bottom, of course, a shortage of funds, to carry out their tasks effectively. But they were kept apart as in the days of radio.

News amounts to a special kind of discourse, much more concise and stylized than normal conversation, that pertains to the world of affairs. Its supposed function is to provide people with a daily digest of what is happening, especially of significant happenings. It serves as a common topic and source of discussion at all levels of society. Often it may entertain as much as it informs. News has been called 'the exercise of power over the interpretation of reality,' because it strives to determine and transmit what is normal, as well as what is abnormal. Michael Arlen once referred to newscasts as 'these nightly certifications of our shared existence.' In summary, news worked to set the agenda of public concerns, to orient people in a single world of affairs, and to legitimate the patterns of authority in the community.[23]

Although newscasts, especially then, were never as complete as the coverage offered by a normal daily newspaper, television's mix of sound and pictures gave it the ability to deliver a lot of information very effectively. This was obvious to one of the first Canadian observers, Wilfrid Eggleston, then director of the Department of Journalism at Carleton College in Ottawa, who in June 1956 wrote a report for the CBC on its national news:

The old saying about a picture being worth a thousand words may not be mathematically true, but a sequence of pictures can obviously tell some stories in a way no number of words can achieve ... It can be argued that Television is a more concentrated and economical medium in its use of time, because it is possible to address two of the human senses simultaneously. My very first vivid impression of the Television news was how much could be got across within a fifteen minute period. While a film is being shown, accompanied by voice commentary, the eye is registering impressions which illuminate the spoken words, and vice versa. I have no doubt that Television here scores a substantial gain over Radio alone. It is not even as simple as saying that an appeal to two senses simultaneously must give twice the impact of one alone. I suspect that under some circumstances the two sense working simultaneously absorb many times the impression of either one alone, or even experience a result which either working alone does not give at all.[24]

Recently two American political scientists, Shanto Iyengar and Donald R. Kinder, have provided experimental evidence for the power of TV news in their book *News That Matters*. They subjected a series of test audiences, made up of more than one thousand ordinary adults as well as a smaller group of university students, to a series of fourteen different experiments requiring viewing of newscasts that had been altered slightly by the removal or addition of certain stories, plus filling out lengthy questionnaires, sometimes a week after the viewing, to evaluate the results. They found that the frequency and the placement of news stories (lead stories were most influential) did have a measurable impact upon what people believed were the important issues of the day, proof of agenda-setting, in short. They discovered that news stories determined, to some degree, what issues and criteria people employed when reaching a political judgment about a candidate or a policy, a phenomenon they called 'priming.' TV news, they concluded, has the power to command the public's attention and to make aspects of the world of affairs accessible (or forgettable) to that public.[25]

The scope of the CBC news service changed dramatically with the advent of television. The news service had been born back in the war years to offer listeners an account of the conflict and the sounds of battle. Yet even in 1952 it remained largely a collection of editors and supervisors who relied heavily on the copy of outside news agencies to fill each day's radio bulletins. McArthur had cultivated close relations with Canadian Press, the news agency of the daily newspapers, perhaps in part (as Davidson Dunton later mused) because that made it easy for the Corporation to answer complaints by pointing to the fact that the news was actually created by CP. The visual demands of television, though, forced the CBC to become a major player in the business of news-gathering to secure an adequate supply of news film. Besides, W.H. Hogg, the man who replaced McArthur in the early 1950s, was much more interested in actually collecting stories than in just rewriting and disseminating them.[26]

CBC-TV did continue to work with other agencies. Early on, the Corporation began to subscribe to the United Press TV news and Movietone news, and worked out exchange arrangements with the BBC and other broadcasters. At some point Toronto got into the habit of recording both CBS and NBC newscasts for use in its own nightly digests. In 1957 the Corporation was one of the founding members of the British Commonwealth International Newsfilm Agency to furnish news film independent of American sources. But management also found it necessary to employ freelancers and eventually a group of correspondents outside Canada to provide news and film 'in a Canadian context.' By 1958, for instance, 'CBC Newsmagazine' could use the services of Stanley Burke at the UN, James M. Minifie in Washington, Donald Gordon in London, Douglas LaChance in Paris, and William Stevenson in Hong Kong. The next year, Knowlton Nash (a bit reluctantly, because the pay was slight and the work heavy) began to take on news assignments for CBC-TV in Washington, apparently aware that the future of reporting lay in television. At home the CBC expanded its newsroom staffs in the various public stations across the land, worked out a sharing agreement with private stations, and mounted a press-gallery operation in Ottawa. Print reporters weren't always happy about the new competition: no radio or TV men were officially allowed into the Press Gallery until 1959, and the first one, Tom Earle, recalled 'a lot of hostility,' including efforts to sabotage the CBC's tape-recorders to prevent broadcasting from scooping the press. The writing was on the wall, and even then, Earle added, the Conservative leader John Diefenbaker recognized that the most important reporter he spoke to was the CBC's Norman DePoe. Inevitably such rapid growth fostered a crisis, since the news service was only loosely organized under the authority of the chief news editor – by 1960 management faced pressure from Toronto to centralize all aspects of news, and perhaps views as well, in one department.[27]

There was also some confusion over what television news should be. In theory, at least, the abiding principle remained that proclaimed back in January 1941, when the news service first began: to present 'all the significant news of the day's happenings in Canada and abroad factually, without bias or distortion, without tendentious comment, and in a clear and unambiguous style.' Particular emphasis was put upon assuring accuracy and impartiality, which in practice seemed to require a balance between the two sides presumed at odds in any controversy. 'Normal standards of news value,' in Dunton's words, were supposed to determine what was in the national newscast, not the 'availability of film.' News-readers were to avoid an 'over-dramatic style' of delivery. Editors were told to eschew sensationalism: in 1960 W.H. Hogg warned his news people against the routine inclusion of crime, accident, and disaster stories in newscasts, since he doubted whether these added much to 'public enlightenment.' Reporters and cameramen were expect to obey the normal canons of good taste, and that required a ban on offensive language as well as care in dealing with 'physical and mental handicaps or deformities.' Quite clearly, what was accepted as the logic of journalism was supposed to triumph over film logic and the logic of entertainment.[28]

Running counter to these axioms, however, was a dawning recognition that news on television couldn't be quite the same thing as news on radio, never mind in print. The fact that television was pre-eminently a medium of entertainment had to condition the style of news presentation, or so Morley Safer suggested in an interview regarding 'CBC Newsmagazine.' Pictures were of extraordinary importance. A story by the CBC Times on the newly created 'Metro News' in Toronto emphasized how so much effort went into getting and editing the news film necessary to tell a story. Wilfrid Eggleston argued that the real promise of television news lay in its ability to use sound and film to bring actual happenings (at least the illusion of such) to the viewer. All of which meant that news people struggled to find ways of making the news visually exciting, even at the cost of supposed news values.[29]

The news came in a variety of ways. The promise of television, in Eggleston's phrase, was best realized by actuality broadcasts of special events, such as the Coronation, convention or election coverage, and the American space flights, into which the news department threw a lot of resources. The evening showing of the opening of the St Lawrence Seaway by Queen Elizabeth and President Eisenhower on 26 June 1959, for instance, was viewed by an estimated 3 million English Canadians and 750,000 French Canadians. Then there were the reviews, such as 'L'Actualité' and 'CBC Newsmagazine,' modelled at first on the newsreel, which strove to cover the major stories of the week. The most important genre, of course, was the daily newscast, introduced during the 1953/4 television year, which took the shape of special fifteen-minute news bulletins on national and international affairs. These were supplemented at the end of the decade by the arrival of CBLT's 'Metro News' and CBFT's 'Edition métropolitain,' which represented, in part, the Corporation's effort to serve the particular needs of local communities.[30]

The newscasts didn't have the time to do much more than summarize the leading items of the day. The edition of the CBC's national news of 31 March 1960 gave nine and a half minutes to coverage of the just-released Canadian budget, about two minutes to troubles in South Africa, one minute apiece to an airplane explosion over Little Rock, Arkansas, and a visit by Princess Margaret to the site of a fire in Glasgow, a few seconds to Krushchev in France and to a hockey story. Presumably because of the budget, this list of items was smaller than average: Eggleston had found a range of between nine and fourteen items in his 1956 survey. Anchoring the newscast was the 'rock,' Earl Cameron ('as Canadian as wheat,' in the words of one CBC executive), a man who had boasted that sturdy, trustworthy face and that measured, clear pattern of speech necessary to cultivate the impression of neutrality valued by the CBC. Note that Cameron was really a performer, not a journalist: he had no editorial or reportorial duties, and apparently was much more interested in how he said something than in what he said – the role of the anchorman was to give a human face to the news, to provide a link that bridged the gaps between the items, and to render the recital of facts all the more authoritative.[31]

The Royal's visit, even more the air disaster, were included in the newscast because they were filmed stories that would please the eye.

Although the South African piece began with a news update by Cameron, what gave that item its impact was a slightly dated film-clip that showed a society seemingly on the verge of a violent upheaval: it featured scenes of blacks on the march, work boycotts, police and armoured cars, and whites compelled to fend for themselves. The budget coverage consisted of Cameron's thirty-second summary of the highlights ('no tax changes,' 'a modest surplus,' and 'salary increases' for civil servants), a four-and-a-half–minute description by reporter Norman DePoe on Parliament Hill, which explored the economic and human dimensions of the budget, and three interviews with party spokesmen that in effect turned television into a medium of partisan rhetoric. The whole piece was classic radiovision: a lot of talking heads and almost no action.

Even so, the budget item can serve as a good example of what was right and wrong with newscasts. First of all, the report could claim all of the qualities of news: immediacy (the just-completed introduction of the budget), proximity (a national story), prominence (a recognized high point in the political year), and relevance (what did this mean to the taxpayer?). Second, while it contained an element of human interest, and DePoe's comments even made a stab at humour, the budget coverage was definitely a hard-news story, that is, concerned with conflict and change, common themes of network newscasts. Third, the item had been predictable, and so the CBC had been able to plan in advance, the very kind of event that television usually covered best because of the difficulties of filming what was unexpected. Fourth, the coverage could survey only the highlights of the budget: an economic story was always difficult for television to handle because there was so little a visual medium could exploit (though DePoe did use some tables to underline what he was saying). Next morning's front page in the Toronto *Globe and Mail* had a more extensive report supplying a reader with a permanent, comprehensive digest that was, by its very nature, much easier to remember. The CBC news had only furnished the alert viewers with sufficient information to understand the thrust of the new budget, particularly the fact that it was really a stand-pat budget, not especially innovative or exciting.[32]

That very action, however, was an interesting demonstration of the way television news could frame an event. The story had clarified what had happened and what it meant, made 'unambiguous' the budget in ways that confirmed the mainstream perspective on affairs. The drastic abbreviation required by the medium and convention involved not only selectivity but closure: a radical critique of the workings of the capitalist economy or the limits of democracy would have been inappropriate, indeed absurd. The report was mostly a collection of bits and pieces, a fragment of a much larger story of growth that could be understood only by the viewer who followed the news regularly. The journalists had to speak in a fashion that all could understand, and that few would find offensive, which meant not only restraint but also a kind of self-censorship. DePoe employed a familiar repertoire of stereotypes revolving around the theme of economic management through reference to 'the cost of government,' the 'gross national product,' the 'prospects of a surplus,' the 'premium on the Canadian dollar,' and the like. The interviews merely confirmed television's 'partiality' towards official news-makers, in this case an élite of party spokesmen, which kept out of public view opinions of less-predictable types. Donald Fleming, the finance minister, and William Benidickson, the Liberal spokesman, both talked in the language of economic management, even if their messages differed. Only Erhardt Regehr, the CCF financial critic, could mildly suggest an alternative approach, grounded in social democracy, with his references to 'Fleming's few,' 'the days of the hungry Thirties,' a 'union bust,' and the plight of ordinary Canadians. His comments indicated how the Left had acquired a modest niche as source of criticism in the political life of the country. Altogether, the three interviews showed how television dealt with problems of balance and fairness, at least in the political arena – simply by giving equal time to people whose respectability was sanctioned by the party system.[33]

In response to a query about political bias in the news service, CBCer Marcel Ouimet told the fifth meeting of the directors' program committee that the 'CBC does not create news; it reports it. If a political party makes news, it gets into the headlines. Generally, the government always makes more news than the opposition.' (There was one occasion, though, when the CBC did suppress a report by Lévesque that Lester Pearson, then minister of external affairs visiting Russia, had been savaged by Soviet leader Krushchev, because the news reflected badly on the government and on Canada.) This was the classic defence: the CBC always sought protection by touting its objectivity, its neutrality, its devotion to a reportorial rather than an editorial role. The defence missed the point, though. The budget report of March 1960 was not so much biased in favour of the government as the way things were. Here, of course, the newscast was little different from the stories that appeared in the Toronto *Globe and Mail* and *The Toronto Daily Star* the next day. News, as a rule, did serve to assure people about the virtues of the existing order. The lack of detail in television's news only made this more obvious.[34]

Offering Views

The one place where the CBC allowed a much more obvious expression of opinions, and where it began to break away from its path of caution, was in the programming produced by Talks and Public Affairs. That department was imbued with a collective sense of purpose, an esprit de corps, which reflected the fact that the CBC was one of the few sources of information that could reach Canadians across the length and breadth of the country on a daily basis. Its journalists took the task of educating the public very seriously. So, in 1956, René Lévesque told a reporter, what was most important was to sponsor 'high-quality education and honest information' to create an intelligent public and a progressive nation. As late as 1962, Daryl Duke, a CBC producer, would charge that Public Affairs was still hampered by its devotion to the principles of adult education born in the 1930s.[35]

Duke was being unfair. Necessity had forced the CBC to develop its own principles, a process that actually dated back to the war years, based in part on BBC practices. Apparently throughout the 1950s the Toronto department looked especially to Britain for inspiration: according to Frank Peers, one of its directors, there was a feeling that the U.S. networks were doing very little in this realm whereas the BBC was forging ahead, and people read closely the British journals, received reports from Britain, and even made periodic visits. The difficulty with educating people about current affairs was that it could well produce controversy, and such controversy was inherently dangerous to a public corporation. In 1959, for example, Radio-Canada actually cancelled an interview recorded with Simone de Beauvoir made for 'Premier plan' because airing 'her views on moral and religious subjects' could damage 'the image of the CBC' by highlighting opinions offensive to the Catholic ethos of Quebec. The CBC was 'watched very carefully by people of all different shades of opinion because they regarded it as so important,' recalled Dunton. On the one hand the CBC worked to ensure that all opinions deemed respectable were properly aired. On the other hand the CBC wished to prevent its own personnel from becoming actual players in the public arena. Grierson's example, his enthusiasm for propaganda, was something to avoid rather than to emulate. So Talks and Public Affairs was expected to do a kind of balancing act, selecting issues and speakers that would enable the CBC to inform democracy without actually favouring or, even worse, expressing one point of view.[36]

Management seems to have kept a close watch on actual practices.

According to Peers, Davidson Dunton used the phone to get his messages across. Other managers were not quite so informal. In 1958, for example, Charles Jennings, then controller of broadcasting, fired off a memo on the need for good taste as well as a 'fair and honest' presentation of opinion, as a result of the appearance of one Dr Ellis, author of *Sex without Guilt*, on 'Fighting Words,' a quiz show handled by Talks and Public Affairs. What most disturbed Jennings was the fact that no one else on the panel had the expertise to counter Ellis's controversial views. The program had become an unbalanced exercise in sensationalism. By this time, however, management was fighting a losing battle: the rules and regulations appropriate in the age of radio didn't fit the emerging reality of television journalism.[37]

Straight talks were the easiest species of public affairs to control. The CBC had begun offering politicians a regular platform in 1956 when 'The Nation's Business/Les affairs de l'état' and their provincial equivalents began. In the fall of 1957, 'Viewpoint' started, providing an assortment of experts with an opportunity to express their opinions (although the show also used interviews, as did its francophone equivalent 'Commentaires,' which began two years later). More important, that same year CBC-TV had become a vehicle for election broadcasts. But all these talks were hedged in by a lot of restrictions. Supervisors were expected to make sure that no one party, opinion, or group of speakers received too much air time. The ban on dramatized skits and the use of assorted visual aids in election broadcasts, in particular, struck people inside and outside the corporation as much too severe. Adman Frank Flint told a CBC official that the restrictions prevented the CBC from fostering a real political enthusiasm in Canada. After the 1957 election campaign, Michael Hind-Smith, then a producer at CBOT-TV Ottawa, claimed that the CBC's insistence on impartiality, and its timidity, had made for extremely dull broadcasts. A year later, from the Left this time, Ken McNaught told readers of *Canadian Forum* that the CBC had so disciplined the political broadcasts that it had effectively neutralized their potential in election campaigns. Probably such statements didn't much disturb management. As long as talks took the shape of lectures, and so won only a small, knowledgeable audience, they were hardly likely to cause a public uproar.[38]

Yet there was good reason to doubt whether politics television-style was quite as impotent as people had argued. CBC-TV had played virtually no part in the federal election of 1953. The next election in 1957 was quite a different story. Both parties were more attuned to print and radio than to television, although in each case admen were urging their political masters to use the new medium. The Liberals had set up training facilities for politicians back in 1956, complete with equipment and even skilled advisers (no less than René Lévesque for francophone broadcasts). Early in 1957 Dalton Camp, one of the backroom boys in the Conservative party, wrote a memo outlining the virtues of television because of its power to create impressions, and particularly to instil a sense of trust. The high cost of advertising (estimated by Camp at close to $2,500 for a five-minute broadcast on each station) probably limited the use of TV by local candidates, although in the Vancouver area Liberals and Conservatives purchased a lot of time on Bellingham's KVOS-TV to beam spot announcements in the last stages of the campaign. Both sides, and the two minor parties, the CCF and Social Credit, did employ the free-time, fifteen-minute telecasts offered by the CBC to reach national audiences (the Liberal government received eight periods in each language, the Conservatives seven). A CBC post-mortem concluded that approximately 50 per cent of the television owners in seven Canadian cities, and fully 80 per cent of owners where only one channel was available, watched at least one of the forty campaign telecasts. The average audience for a telecast might be small (estimated at 285,000 in English Canada) but that audience was made up of exactly those people who were most likely to vote. Perhaps most interesting, adults with a television rated the new medium higher than newspapers as a source of news about the campaign. Indeed, in Halifax, Toronto, and Edmonton, more than a third of the respondents thought their vote had been 'influenced' by television.[39]

The trouble was that the Liberals weren't at all adept in their use of television. Only one cabinet minister actually employed the TV-training facilities set up by national headquarters to good effect to understand the mysteries of the new medium. St Laurent just didn't like television: he was much more interested in seeing people than in talking to cameras, or so he told a TV reporter at the beginning of the campaign. He looked upon television as a medium of illusion where everything was staged for effect, which meant television could easily be a tool of deceit. He once threatened to tell the audience he was using aids, a TelePrompTer and make-up, to avoid the possibility of creating a false impression. His first campaign appearance was extremely painful: he simply read a text, scarcely glancing at the cameras, and he appeared old and uncomfortable, much too stiff to cultivate an appealing impression. Television, in short, confirmed the opposition charge that St Laurent was a tired man, lacking any sparkle, unable to move Canada in new or imaginative directions. Although he made two more broadcasts to the English audience, the party deemed it wiser to share the remaining time among senior cabinet ministers, such as Lester Pearson and Robert Winters. Despite the fact that a certain amount of money had already been invested in producing films and buying time in Ontario, the party eventually cancelled all its contracts. C.D. Howe, the second man in the government, didn't even bother to purchase time for TV spots on the local Port Arthur station to counter the nightly broadcasts of his CCF opponent, Douglas Fisher. Altogether, then, television turned out to be a disaster for the Liberals – little wonder one Liberal adman would call it 'this difficult and cruel medium.'[40]

Television worked far better for the Conservatives. After the election, Michael Hind-Smith wondered whether the contrast had something to do with the fact that 'the PC's went live, using CBC facilities to the utmost, while the Liberals filmed their programs in advance.' But there was more to the difference than that. First of all, the Conservative party was out to sell its leader to the public, rather than to push a policy or even a creed. The slogan 'It's Time for a Diefenbaker Government!' aptly summed up the attempt to downplay the party label and highlight the new messiah. That was a tactic well suited to television's taste for personality. Second, and much more important, television appealed to the 'ham' in Diefenbaker. Diefenbaker spoke four times to the English audience on the CBC, made five fifty-second TV spot commercials designed to support local candidates, and was usually prepared to find time in his daily campaign itinerary for a television interview. Always something of an actor, he found television a congenial medium, and he took great pains to ensure that his make-up and the staging were perfect for the occasion. He used the national telecasts to blast the Liberal government for its arrogance and élitism, to cultivate his own image as a man of the people, and to convey an impression of both urgency and vigour. His folksy manner, his look of sincerity, and his extravagant rhetoric worked well to fashion the image of a Lincolnesque figure. Under the circumstances, and especially given the fact he was a newcomer with no past to live down, the man's charisma could only be accentuated by such exposure – it helped him connect with his audience. Here was proof that St Laurent's worry about the new medium had some basis in fact. In any case Diefenbaker was the country's first master of the art of politics in the dawning age of television.[41]

It's possible that television was a necessary cause of the Liberal defeat. The election results were very close: the Conservatives secured 112 seats, the Liberals 105, although because of the massive Liberal vote in Quebec the St Laurent government did end up with a slightly higher popular vote than the Diefenbaker forces. Where the opposition had done well was in

English Canada, notably in Ontario; there, the Conservative popular vote had increased from 770,000 (1953) to 1.1 million. A CBC survey of television homes suggested that in Toronto people believed the Conservatives had made the best use of their air time, and the feeling throughout southwestern Ontario was that Diefenbaker had made the most favourable impression. C.D. Howe blamed his personal defeat on the television skills of Douglas Fisher, because it was in the areas of the constituency served by television that Howe found his support had waned badly. Howe added that television just wasn't suited to 'old boys' like himself and his fellow Liberals. That was the point. The Liberals fumbled television, the Conservatives exploited it, and the combination aided in the making of a political upheaval.[42]

Panel discussions could be a trickier form to manage than political talks. Supervisors clearly wished that these shows would submit to the traditional rules of debate, which would ensure that the CBC remained only a forum for the exchange of opinions. But producers were on the look-out for juicy topics and hard-hitting guests, which would make their programs more exciting. Cliff Solway, a producer of 'Background,' once grumbled that he couldn't find enough guests who were sufficiently blunt to give his brand of news commentary some punch. The end result of this conflict was to spawn a collection of programs usually offering a kind of polite and controlled controversy.[43]

One common technique, inherited again from radio, was to work with some reputable outsider, notably the CAAE. The famous 'Citizen's Forum' came to primetime television in Fall '55, opening with a series of discussions of social problems – 'Can prisons reform criminals?' and 'Unemployment: Are we handling it wisely?' – which were debated by a collection of experts, selected because they were known to espouse different views, pro and con, to ensure balance. That show only lasted one season in the evening line-up. Much more successful was its francophone counterpart, 'Les idées en marche,' usually hosted by Gérard Pelletier, which during its six-year run explored quite a range of international and domestic topics, from foreign aid to the quality of education. Among the many guest panelists were such leading intellectuals of the time as André Laurendeau – and of the future as Pierre Elliott Trudeau. The great advantage of these debates, of course, was that the CBC could share the responsibility for engendering controversy, and that offered the Corporation some protection from hostile critics.[44]

The second technique was to rely upon the services of established journalists from the ranks of the press, whom tradition honoured as experts in the field of opinion, which again might serve to distance the CBC from any controversy generated by a panel. This approach was especially common in the long-running series 'Press Conference/Conférence de presse,' which appeared in the first year of Canadian television. A personage of importance, often holding some kind of office, was invited each week: politicians such as Stuart Garson (then minister of justice) or Leon Balcer (a leading Quebec Conservative), foreign dignitaries such as Dag Hammarskjöld (UN secretary-general), labour leader Claude Jodoin, or CNR president Donald Gordon. Naturally the CBC could not be held responsible for their views – although one of the francophone producers, Jacques Landry, admitted he wouldn't invite anyone who might preach a doctrine contrary to public order or morality. The guests were quizzed by a panel of journalists, usually about some matter then topical in the news. At least in the beginning, it may have been common practice for the journalists to submit their questions in advance to prominent guests appearing on 'Conférence de presse.' Later, producers put a higher priority on an unrehearsed and spontaneous discussion. Even so, Lévesque, a moderator in 1955, complained that the show lacked that quality of outspokenness that made the American panel shows effective. And, at least in English Canada, there was some criticism that this and other shows were dominated by the same clique of journalists, especially people at *Maclean's*. The trouble was that such men as Blair Fraser and Pierre Berton proved very impressive on television, unlike all too many of their fellow scribblers who weren't able to shine in the new medium.[45]

Ironically, relying on the journalists could prove embarrassing, at least when most of them seemed to be of one mind. That happened in the summer of 1956 during the infamous pipeline debate that convulsed Parliament and the nation: the CBC found itself acting as a conduit for the anti-government opinions of the Press Gallery on its assorted network shows. The Liberals were not at all amused by what seemed the unfair bias of a public corporation that they had nurtured for two decades.[46]

On a broader scale, there's evidence to suggest that these panel shows did have a special effect on the climate of opinion in Quebec. They seemed to offer a compelling model of a democracy in which leaders were held accountable and people debated public policy. They were one of the few avenues of mass communication not tamed by Maurice Duplessis and his cohorts or bound to a still traditional Catholic church. Indeed many Union Nationale spokesmen boycotted Radio-Canada's programs, and the organizers of 'Conférence de presse' claimed in 1958 that they were unable to persuade any large body of right-wing journalists to participate. The panels gave to critics, the Laurendeaus and the *Cité Libre* people, in Dunton's words, access to a very wide public: journalists from the anti-Duplessis daily *Le Devoir* appeared seventy-two times between 1953 and 1957. The panels made possible, even respectable, 'alternative thinking': in December 1955 Jacques Hébert, for example, caused quite a stink in Catholic circles when he reported on 'Conférence de presse' that a visit to Poland had convinced him there was considerable religious freedom in Eastern Europe. So these forums were one of the first agents of a liberalization that would pave the way for the collapse of the Union Nationale and the forthcoming 'Quiet Revolution.' But it would be an exaggeration to claim much more. The rise of a new liberal mood was all part and parcel of what Gérard Pelletier has called 'a kind of cultural revolution' that occurred in Quebec during and after the 1950s, at the heart of which were television and all its varied shows. Here, then, it becomes impossible to disentangle the import of one genre of programming from all the rest.[47]

Where the CBC unwittingly strayed farthest from the path of rectitude was in its news magazines and news documentaries. That was chiefly because of the passion for interviews. Interviewing was one technique of print journalism that flourished in the age of television, no doubt because it focused attention on personality. The astonishing success of Edward R. Murrow's 'See It Now' on CBS had demonstrated that fact early in the 1950s. The appeal of Toronto's light 'Tabloid' and Montreal's more substantial 'Carrefour' was proof Canadian audiences liked interviews. Then came René Lévesque's own show 'Point de mire' and a new Ross McLean product called 'Close-up' (followed by a francophone equivalent, 'Premier plan'), such programs as 'Viewpoint' and 'Commentaires,' which used interviews, plus, a bit later, 'Inquiry,' hosted by Davidson Dunton who had retired from the CBC's management. These shows, and most especially 'Point de mire' and 'Close-Up,' pleased news lovers. The trouble with interviews, though, was that they enhanced the importance of the journalist as a separate player in the realm of public affairs. He had the power to structure a discussion through his questions, to honour or dishonour a view if he wanted to. He also could establish a connection with the television audience, act as its spokesman, in ways that fostered a kind of news stardom. Interviewing pushed the CBC into a position where its personnel and programs were taking on an editorial role.[48]

The producer could draw upon a bagful of tricks to make his show a success. It was essential to create the illusion of a shared identity between program and audience, somehow to put the journalists on the side of the viewers. Consider the ways in which Patrick Watson attempted to achieve this effect in the first edition of 'Inquiry' on 26 December 1960, which dealt with the topical issue 'Canadian Trade with Cuba,' then a matter of dispute between Canada and the United States. Watson was one of the most accomplished of the younger producers drawn to the CBC in the mid-1950s by the promise of public affairs. He had in Davidson Dunton a man with an established reputation as a public servant who could fulfil the role of a host, able to bridge the gap between the wider world of news and the viewers' more limited world of experience. Dunton introduced the topic, linked together the various segments of the documentary, even questioned Knowlton Nash and a guest, who appeared as experts on American views, and concluded with a brief note on what might happen. Thus he epitomized the role of the journalist as investigator, striving to get to the bottom of things, and he acted as a guide to lead the viewer through the many dimensions of this story. Watson employed the man-in-the-street interview, the so-called vox populi, to explore public opinion. A couple of anonymous New Yorkers were outspoken in their view that Canada was behaving in a very unfriendly fashion towards the United States. Another sample of people, this time drawn from Ottawa's streets, was used to illustrate that some Canadians agreed with this interpretation, while others took a more nationalistic, even anti-American stance. All of which served to authenticate the coverage through its focus on what ordinary people believed as well as to supply a source of identification because it was presumed the selected few spoke as representatives of the general public. Finally, Watson included one no-nonsense interview with the head of the Cuban trade mission to Canada to try to elicit the 'facts' behind the Cuban interest. That way the show could act out the role of a public watch-dog, to discover whether Cuba's Fidel Castro had a hidden agenda that threatened Canadian interests.[49]

There were different ways to interview, of course. Edward R. Murrow was famous for his unobtrusive, even polite style that encouraged guests to speak their minds, and on occasion to reveal themselves. A bit later on, his fellow American Mike Wallace won much notoriety for a hard-hitting, sometimes bullying style that tried to force guests on the defensive so as to elicit new facts or unmask a character. The particular approach depended upon the show, the task, and the subject, as a special article on interviewing in the CBC Times in 1959 made abundantly clear. A straight newsman such as Norman DePoe believed the interviewer's personality ought to remain in the background. Pierre Berton, already emerging as one of the most effective of Canadian interviewers, pointed out that while politicians might be 'fair game,' many other celebrities deserved a gentler treatment to avoid embarrassing the viewer. Douglas Leiterman, then with

'Close-Up,' argued the interviewer ought to play the devil's advocate to foster an interesting exchange of views.[50]

Whatever the particular mode of address, though, any interviewer could use three classic questions to dig out the facts. 'How do you feel ... ?' was the query best offered when the journalist wanted to personalize a story, to probe the emotions surrounding an event, or to recapture that special moment of shock or joy. A 'Close-Up' reporter once asked an unemployed man, 'Does it do anything to your pride to go on relief?,' which apparently worked well to highlight the humiliation suffered by people who had lost their livelihood. This was the kind of question that set some people's teeth on edge, because it amounted to an invasion of privacy. 'Isn't it ... ?' or 'What is ... ?' served well when questioning an expert, leading the subject into a long exposition of his or her views. When, on 'Tabloid' Frank Heron asked of Etienne Decroux, a pantomime artist, 'What is the difference between, say, mime and ordinary movement ... ?' that was the opening for a lengthy description of mime, complete with some illustrative sketches. 'But surely ... ?' was one standard opening for the tough question, forcing the subject to take into account another position. It was particularly useful when the interviewer wished to editorialize. One night on 'Viewpoint,' Clive Baxter of *The Financial Post* threw a series of such questions at Stanley Knowles (a noted left-wing politician) relating to the endorsement of the new-party movement (out of which came the New Democratic party) by a convention of the Canadian Labour Congress. Playing the role of the devil's advocate, Baxter wanted to show that the enthusiasm of the meeting was a trifle phony, that there really was a split within the union movement, that the chances for socialism or social democracy remained dubious. Knowles, by the way, handled the questions very well, using the interview to impose his own interpretation of a fast-rising people's movement upon the events. That example showed how the interview could easily become a contest between journalist and guest over whose views would prevail.[51]

The two masterpieces of the genre were unquestionably 'Point de mire' and 'Close-Up.' Lévesque's half-hour show focused on international stories, though occasionally he would deal with Québécois or Canadian issues. Like Murrow, Lévesque usually avoided editorializing, leaving it up to the viewer to make a judgment on the basis of what was heard and seen. He himself later emphasized that his purpose was to popularize, to teach a viewing public what it needed to know to understand the outside world. That might require around eighty hours of work a week to research the question and then to summarize and simplify. Lévesque would use films, maps and other visual aids, interviews, even a blackboard to illustrate points, and to catch the viewer's eye. But best of all was his own manner: while he might display a range of unlikely habits – his constant smoking, nervous tics, raspy voice, long unwieldy sentences – he seemed able to connect directly with viewers, to involve as well as educate them, which gave his show a common touch. One colleague at Radio-Canada claimed that he had the ability to make his public feel intelligent. According to Gérard Pelletier, Lévesque was able to win the confidence and gratitude of people, a much more useful response than mere admiration.[52]

Look at how Lévesque handled the Algerian question, so worrisome to francophonie in the 1950s. Early in March 1957, he offered a studio interview of Guy Mollet, then prime minister of France, which dealt with France and the world, although much of the questioning concentrated on Algeria. No doubt because of the status of his guest, Lévesque was exceedingly respectful – he didn't grill Mollet but instead tried to make him comfortable (even lighting his cigarette three times), asking a series of brief questions that allowed the politician to state his case at some length. The result was a superb summary of the official French view, although without any attempt at a critique of this view. In October 1958, though, 'Point de mire' offered a news documentary on the Algerian question, made up of a lot of filmed interviews with ordinary Frenchmen and with experts, speeches by de Gaulle and pictures of French settings, plus Lévesque's own summary of the problem. The reports and commentary roamed over questions of empire and colony, race and class, peace and violence, the ideals of equality and freedom and progress. This time the show espoused the idea of 'peace with honour,' the search for a way out of the mess that would satisfy France, the Algerian rebels, and even the French colonists, leaving the distinct impression that de Gaulle might well be the necessary saviour. That message was delivered as a by-product of the process of investigation and clarification, not because Lévesque took any obvious stand. Once again viewers were treated to a thorough account of a complex issue in a fashion that was easy to understand.

What killed 'Point de mire' was the Montreal producers' strike of 1959. The show had attracted a decent audience, averaging 575,000 a week in the winter of 1958/9. But the strike had politicized Lévesque, turning him into a nationalist who was suspicious of Radio-Canada's managers and of what he thought were their anglophone masters. Although the show returned to the air after the settlement, it was cancelled at the end of May because, Lévesque thought, management had decided to punish him for his part in the strike. True or not, the CBC did continue to employ Lévesque on such shows as 'Conférence de presse' and 'Premier plan.' In fact he was now more interested in conquests in a different arena. In spring 1960 Lévesque joined the Liberal team assembled by Jean Lesage to challenge a Union Nationale government shaken by the deaths of Maurice Duplessis and Paul Sauvé.[53]

'Close-Up' was more of a news magazine, offering between two and five segments in a half-hour, with a much broader scope of interest. According to Frank Peers, the show was born out of a suggestion by Dunton that something akin to the BBC's 'Panorama' might be a wise addition to the CBC schedule, a suggestion passed on to Ross McLean. But the result struck one contemporary as a mix of tendencies found in Murrow's 'See It Now' and 'Person to Person,' Mike Wallace's interviews, and even the human-interest show 'This Is Your Life,' which specialized in biography. The point is that McLean again put the focus on people first, using interviews to explore issues of life as well as affairs. He assembled a team that included Patrick Watson (co-producer); J. Frank Willis (an experienced host noted for his objective manner); and Pierre Berton, Jack Webster, Elaine Grand, and Charles Templeton (regular interviewers). During the first year of its run, 'Close-Up' interviewed Norman Vincent Peale and Lucky Luciano, Aldous Huxley and Ann Landers, Joey Smallwood and Peter Ustinov, and as well dealt with Italian communism and San Francisco's beatniks, unwed motherhood and homosexuality, and discipline in the schools. The show tried to offer insights (Templeton asked a convicted murderer if he felt remorse – the answer was no) as well as judgments (a special show on Spanish bullfighting cultivated the impression that it was a barbaric sport, a feudal remnant that would die out with the march of progress). Once 'Close-Up' even staged a bank robbery to dramatize a crime wave in Toronto. All this effort payed off: the program had an average weekly audience of 1.3 million viewers during the winter of 1958/9. Anecdote, moralizing, exposé – all were ingredients of McLean's second great hit.[54]

No wonder 'Close-Up' caused upset. Management got worried right away. Early in January 1958, Marcel Ouimet, the assistant controller of broadcasting, sent off a critical review of the series to the chief programmer in Toronto, for discussion with the producers. The burden of Ouimet's complaint was that the choice of items and the style of treatment were geared to cause contention, if not sensation. Never again, he hoped, would 'Close-Up' 'lose sight of its obligation to present balanced comments.' Ouimet's hope wasn't realized.[55]

People did get excited over what 'Close-Up' said. During that first season, for example, the broadcast of an item from England on homosexuality brought a storm of protest in some places – CKCW-TV in Moncton was forced to cut the program from its schedule, according to one report. In May 1960 'Close-Up' won a lot of notoriety over what came to be called 'the Case of the Shady Lady': it scheduled a lengthy interview with a woman (shown in silhouette) claiming to be a professional 'co-respondent' who helped to stage evidence of adultery in divorce cases. The half-hour interview ran, so McLean wrote later, because it was such a damning indictment of the existing divorce laws. Perhaps so, but shortly afterwards the woman told the press that she was a phony, that the story was just a hoax, which not only caused some huffing and puffing among politicians but left doubts about the wisdom of the show's producers. Nearly a year later, the producers again got into trouble over the Exelby affair. This time, 'Close-Up' was out to show the plight of the unemployed then a topical issue, by focusing on the pain Glen Exelby and his family suffered when he lost his job and couldn't find another. The Conservative government (which was very touchy about the issue) immediately struck back by revealing that Exelby was to some extent the author of his own misfortune, that he'd received pay from the CBC, and that he had actually turned down a job offer. Once more the Corporation had to offer its apologies to political and press critics. Within a few months, McLean himself would sever his links with 'Close-Up' and the CBC to try his luck at CTV.[56]

The advance of television journalism had created a new crop of nationally famous newsmen who regularly spoke to hundreds of thousands of people in a much more intimate fashion than did any print journalist. Such people as Norman DePoe, Blair Fraser, Pierre Berton, J. Frank Willis, and René Lévesque were household names. In 1959 a commentator extolled the role of these specialists who kept open 'our window on power,' in itself an expression of that cult of the journalist which portrayed the newsman as the public's watch-dog. Perhaps it shouldn't surprise that Lévesque and McLean would eventually find themselves at odds with management and leave the ranks of the CBC for greener pastures. Their approaches had one thing in common, the aim of reaching out to as wide a spectrum of viewers as possible. But their success pushed the CBC into the limelight as a newsmaker. That was the rub: television journalism of this kind ill-suited a management worried about the ill effects of controversy. McLean in particular had been a thorn in the side of management. The eventual grand confrontation between management and Public Affairs, though, would not occur until the battle over 'This Hour Has Seven Days' in the mid-1960s.[57]

Judging the impact of this genre of programming upon the minds of viewers is very tricky. Judy LaMarsh's by-election victory in Niagara in 1960 owed something to the impact of a televised mini-debate: during the discussion, she had grabbed a political pamphlet out of an opponent's hands and accused him of not knowing his own party's position. Next day, she learned from meeting constituents that the impulsive action had established her fame as 'an outspoken fighter.' There was one impression conveyed by television that certainly was true to life. Personally, I recall first learning anything substantial about Canada's divorce laws as a result of viewing the episode of 'Close-Up' out of which came 'the Case of the Shady Lady.' But normally panel and interview shows gained only what came to be known as the typical public-affairs audience – older, better educated, and more affluent than the mass of viewers. In competitive markets, in particular, most people normally tuned out much of the information offered them. A ratings survey for the winter of 1957/8 found, for instance, that in Toronto 'Close-Up' ranged between a market share of 7 and 15 points whereas 'The $64,000 Challenge,' its opposition on WBEN, won between 59 and 77. Indeed the most popular of the information shows on Radio-Canada's schedule in 1962 was the light 'Rendez-vous avec Michelle,' reaching almost 1.7 million viewers, or around half the total earned by the leading téléroman. Viewers usually preferred entertainment, and especially when they had a choice.[58]

Bernard Trotter believed that all programming was educational, whether a variety show, a children's program, a panel discussion, or a newscast. That kind of notion was very common in CBC circles, and it seemed to suit the findings of experts in the field of mass communications. Yet, as A.F. Knowles noted, and he was one of those specialists at work in university extension, 'education' and 'learning' lost a lot of their meaning if interpreted too broadly. Educational programming, he thought, had to have intellectual substance, as well as a determination to instruct its audience in some organized fashion about a body of knowledge. What troubled Knowles and his colleagues by the end of the 1950s was the fact that the CBC could neither give education the kind of priority it deserved, nor allow educators a free hand in designing cultural and public-affairs programming. The concern with making information appealing and entertaining was especially troubling. All of which explained why these educators were enthusiastic about the promise of educational television, a new dream that had sprung into sudden prominence south of the border to counter the pap served up by the commercial networks. What ETV meant was the creation of a new, non-commercial service to distribute academic and cultural programming to target audiences. Here was embodied one of the first pleas for 'narrow-casting.' It was also a further instance of that strategy of capture long pursued by highbrows and intellectuals in their search for a television suited to spreading their messages. Its new-found popularity showed just how far the CBC had travelled away from the old ideal of adult education.[59]

Focus: 'Tabloid'

The episode of 31 January 1958 wasn't especially remarkable. Viewers first saw Joyce Davidson, Frank Heron, and John O'Leary seated at a table, engaging in a bit of chat and fun. Percy Saltzman followed with the weather forecast for the country and, in particular, Ontario and Quebec. Then came the two main acts, the interviews, which filled most of the time that was left: the first with Etienne Decroux, a famous mime artist from Paris, questioned by Frank Heron with the aid of a translator, and the second with Dr Paul Dudley White, also famous, but as the heart specialist who treated President Eisenhower, quizzed by the show's 'intellectual,' Percy Saltzman. In the final sequences, the regulars chatted once more, Joyce Davidson promoted the forth-coming episode of 'Close-Up,' and the program ended with a list of credits.

Like any other show, this episode can be 'read' on a number of different levels. First, the regulars went to great pains to demonstrate that 'Tabloid' was a family show, hosted by a team of friendly and ordinary folk who were having a good time (see frame 5.1). That impression was clearly intentional, and probably most obvious to viewers. The opening scene had Joyce Davidson playing with some checkers, which led immediately into a jokey exchange involving a mathematical puzzle, using those same checkers and staged by John O'Leary. The style and the language were casual, humorous, friendly. But the message was really brought home in the closing sequences when Davidson and O'Leary talked with Heron about his return to the

Frame 5.1 The friendly team

warm bosom of his family, a return that was a cause of regret and joy. 'Yes, I didn't think that I would miss them as much as I did, but I did,' claimed Heron, speaking with feeling about his four children. Still, Heron didn't look forward to leaving Toronto, where he'd 'met a lot of old friends, a lot of young old friends.' He was making an obligatory reference to the pleasures of both family and professional life. Then Davidson wished the audience good night, plus a good weekend, and the men waved goodbye to viewers.

The second level of meaning wasn't quite so clear. 'Tabloid' was a night school for adults, dispensing useful bits of information in an easy fashion. That approach was illustrated by the very design of the program as well as by the particular texts. Even the mathematical puzzle amounted to a modest bit of training in arithmetic. More to the point, Percy Saltzman adopted the pose of the teacher: he stood in front of a blackboard map of Canada and used a piece of chalk to fill the map with what was eventually a clutter of weather symbols. Often he faced away from the camera so that he could draw on the map. He spoke rapidly, mixing trivia about today's weather (such as 'minus 25 in the Yukon rising during the afternoon to 0'), some guarded promises about what tomorrow would bring ('most places should have some cloudiness'), and assorted statements on the cause of it all ('three major low-pressure areas, travelling depressions, migratory storms' or 'a strong thrust of warm air scurrying northwards'). He even admitted that 'the science of forecasting isn't that accurate,' a comment that must have been self-evident to his viewers. Weather is one of those marvellously democratic phenomena of nature affecting all, irrespective of age, sex, or status. Perhaps that's why the weather record and forecast have always been so popular with a mass audience: news about where the sun was shining, or the temperature in the Yukon, or the prospect of snow flurries tomorrow is a good basis for ordinary conversation. Television hardly gave birth to this interest – that had been apparent many years before when the pioneers of the mass press made a point of publishing weather statistics – but television did the job better than any other medium and made of the weatherman a special kind of teacher.

The main lessons for the night, though, were in the contrasting mythologies of art and science. The twin interviews with Decroux and White confirmed the common-sense view that art and science were unique worlds of creativity, inhabited by special kinds of people who followed quite distinct routines of work and embraced different perceptions of life.

Etienne Decroux was in town to perform at the Eaton Auditorium. Since he didn't speak English, the questions and his answers had to be translated, which made the whole interview a trifle awkward – and it also underlined how odd was the subject and his talent. Heron didn't stray from his list of prepared questions, though the answers these elicited clearly made him a trifle uneasy. The interview opened with Decroux actually performing, on an empty stage, some basic acts of mine: as a boxer, a weight-lifter, ringing a bell, throwing a discus, and so on. Later on, he again demonstrated his art by showing the audience how mime stylized even such a simple motion as carrying a chair. His movements were highly exaggerated and highly controlled, not at all ordinary. His descriptions of what mime was were esoteric, difficult, not the sort of stuff that would go down very well among viewers who'd just finished supper. Decroux himself appeared almost misshapen: a short, heavy-set, older man with a large head and long hair, dressed in very loose-fitting dark clothes. During the actual interview, camera close-ups confirmed this impression of eccentricity: Decroux had a rough, almost brutal face, with deep-set eyes, yet a

Frame 5.2 The artist

face that could fill with emotion when expressing his opinions. His voice was deep, rich, clear. He exuded self-confidence. His whole bearing said he was a master of his strange art, and of himself (see frame 5.2).

The arrogance, the contempt, Decroux had for his supposed peers and for the general public came across most clearly towards the end of the interview. By this time, in fact, Decroux was clearly becoming annoyed with the whole experience, and seemed less willing to spare Heron or the viewers some harsh truths.

Situation

Three men seated on stools in a bare room, **Decroux** in the middle, flanked by **Frank Heron** and the translator **Mark Epstein. Epstein** a striking contrast to **Decroux**, since **Epstein** young, thin, wears glasses, dressed in a suit, and speaks very rapidly. Camera focus shifts around, including at times the threesome, but usually on **Decroux**. Each question is translated, Epstein gives an answer in fragments, and this is then translated into English.

Video	Audio
— **Decroux** scratches inner ear with finger.	**Heron**: Is the art of mime neglected by actors today, in general?
— Close-up on **Decroux**.	**Translator**: Ah, yes, of course, the mime is neglected and we can go further and say, what doesn't the actor neglect?
— **Decroux** purses his lips.	[**Heron** laughs nervously.] In many dramatic schools, there aren't ah, ah even classes of vocal placing.
— **Decroux** becomes passionate: he frowns, his lips purse, he pushes out his chin, and he moves his head forward.	Sometimes not even diction lessons. And the, er, dramatic student usually will begin by studying a text, ah, which would only be possible to handle at his peak.
— **Decroux** shakes his head and purses his lips. Camera moves back to reveal threesome. **Heron** smiles.	But the theatre goes along very well. Um, all bad things, er, work well. **Heron**: Is the, er, would you say the general public is interested in mime? Do they enjoy an evening of pure mime?
	Translator: No, probably not. He doubts whether any general public likes any art, no matter what it would be.
	Er, he has never seen an enormous crowd breaking down the doors to, er, a painting exhibition.
	Heron [with relief?]: Thank you very, very much.

Art, good art, was only for the *cognoscenti*, apparently.

Dr White, in his own way, also delivered a virtuoso performance. But otherwise, what a contrast. White was in town to launch the Canadian heart-fund campaign, and Saltzman had interviewed him before the luncheon. The interview occurred in what looked like a

Frame 5.3 The scientist

study, both men seated at a table (on which lay some papers), with books on the wall behind the guest. White was dressed in a suit, the typical style of the professional. Where Decroux had looked vigorous, White showed the signs of age: he was thin, lacking hair, delicate. Where Decroux had been mobile, White was calm, generally sitting with his arms and hands resting on a table (see frame 5.3). He spoke well, in a paternalistic fashion, offering detailed answers to Saltzman's questions about the extent of heart disease, the causes and signs of trouble, and what could be done to prevent its onset. It was all very clear and so very rational. White's speech was peppered with references to statistical studies and past case histories. Although he did express his own opinions, he also spoke of 'we,' the medical community, as the great fund of research experience – White was clearly part of a team. And his teachings were full of a sense of past achievement and a promise of future victory.

Eventually, Saltzman offered White an opportunity to deliver his health commercial to the audience. Naturally, he spoke of the need for increased public support, more money to hire more research workers and train them better and build better facilities. Right at the end, he capped off his performance with a message of optimism.

Video

– **Saltzman** and **White** seated at a table. Camera was usually focused on **White** and now moves in for a close-up on his face to give emphasis to his words.

– **White** speaks both to **Saltzman** and off into the distance.

– Camera suddenly moves out from close-up to encompass both men, though **Saltzman** in profile on viewer's left side.

Video

Saltzman: Dr White, from your long experience, er, would you sum up your view as an optimistic or a pessimistic one from the point of view of a possible cure ... ?
White: Oh, I'm very optimistic. At one time it was thought that the, er, infections were God's will and that we were bound, that babies were bound to die of dysentery and that we were bound to have typhoid fever and tuberculosis. This was God's will. But that's, that was the past. So now I think that, er, heart disease is our fault, any kind of heart disease, and that we've got to do something about it and can.
Saltzman: Thank you very much, sir. I've been talking to Dr Paul Dudley White, eminent heart specialist, who as much as any man in the world has his finger on the heartbeat of the people.

At their deepest level, of course, both interviews expressed common presumptions about the world. Each honoured personal accomplishment: the two men were experts and stars, masters of their particular crafts. That fitted into the cult of individualism, one of the dominant mythologies of life in a bourgeois society. And each interview explored an aspect of modernity: artistic expression and cultural sophistication in the case of Decroux, man's control over his world and his ability to solve problems in the case of White. That suggested the idea of progress, also one of those dominant mythologies. In short, this episode of 'Tabloid' had carried the viewer through a wide range of subjects to confirm, and to flesh out, what people should understand about the workings of their world.

In 1960 the name of the show was changed from 'Tabloid' to 'Seven-O-One,' because a drug company that had registered the trademark 'Tabloid' complained to the CBC. The CBC's failure to defend its right to the name of one of its more famous offerings was later taken as the first sign of the decline of the show. Joyce Davidson eventually left for the United States, and her successors never quite caught on with viewers. Producers experimented with different techniques to renew the show's appeal. The highjinks of the past were toned down and the show came to focus more and more on hard-news stories: in-depth coverage of the death of Dag Hammarskjöld, the secretary-general of the United Nations; an interview with Earl Browder, a Communist leader in the United States; or a two-part investigation of the discount-versus-department-store battle. In the summer of 1962, the show came from Montreal with a totally new crew of regulars. On its return to Toronto, in the fall, the only hold-over from the past was Percy Saltzman. During that last season, local Toronto columnists seemed convinced the show was doomed. At the death of 'Seven-O-One,' Percy Saltzman blamed CBC management, by now the common whipping-boy, for imposing an assortment of taboos that destroyed the show's character. Perhaps so, but the more serious problem was that the show had become an anachronism, its approach and format no longer of much appeal to an audience intrigued by the greater visual stimulation of the documentary, the news magazine, and television drama.[60]

6

Variety's Heyday

We are fast becoming a new sort of race – half man and half chesterfield – that sits watching the world's best talent beating its brains out to please us. All we have to do is raise or lower our thumbs as the Roman mob once did at the gladiatorial arena. And, incidentally, most of us know what happened to Rome.

Dr Leslie Bell, 1955[1]

Dr Leslie Bell, a well-known choir leader, was an early victim of the ratings: he'd left a CBC variety extravaganza called 'Showtime,' never to return to TV. Perhaps his *Maclean's* article 'Why I'm out of TV' did seem somewhat like sour grapes. Even so, it was a thoughtful explanation of what was wrong with television entertainment, and in particular with musical programming. TV was a rat-race, he noted, in which even such great stars as Arthur Godfrey and Milton Berle had to worry about their futures. Programmers were too caught up in the need to please sponsors and to pander to a taste for novelty to offer the public something worthwhile and lasting. Why, he wondered, was there such a 'mania for movement' in TV programs? Why were producers bent on showing off their skills with 'fancy sets, trick camera shots and gimmicks'? Didn't anyone realize that good music had to be listened to if it was to be enjoyed? There was more than a grain of truth to that last comment. In retrospect, Bell was railing against the phenomenon of display, so prominent a feature of video entertainment even in these early days of radiovision.[2]

Play and Display

Watching an assortment of talented, and not-so-talented, performers had swiftly become the most common type of play for people of all ages. That cliché requires a bit of explanation. Play helps people cope. For the very young, play is a way of learning about life, acquiring the skills to deal with their environment. For adults, play serves to balance the stresses and pressures of the workaday world. It offers the weary in spirit or body a momentary escape into a different life where the individual can find pleasure, amusement, diversion – where he or she can have some fun. This activity usually occurs only within the strict constraints of a set time and place. It normally reflects the myths and rituals, even the tensions, of the host society. And it should spark some sort of emotional arousal in the players, whatever else it might offer in the way of recuperation or compensation.[3]

Of course entertainment on television differs from the classic forms of play. The actors or dancers or the hockey team are the professionals, working to produce a series of spectacles for the actual 'players,' the audience. The professionals are driven by the logic of their situation to strive to please this audience, a fact that has led true *aficionados* of sport and the stage to worry about whether the result debases their passion. How intense is the experience for the spectator? That all depends on what is being shown, on the spectator's own mood, on the particular moment. Nearly all the time the spectacles serve first to divert the audience, and thus to provide the audience with that bit of fun necessary to any kind of play. Since people identify with the stars of sport or stage, and more often accept the myths they act out, spectators find mirrored or even realized in the performances their own dreams, fantasies, fears, and ideals. Indeed the cult of stardom is itself 'proof' of the pervasive mythology of individualism: doesn't the existence of the star show how the extraordinary person can manage through labour or luck to rise to the top of the social heap?[4]

But recognize that the viewer is not quite like the spectator at a live performance or an actual game. Such a spectator is part of a crowd, able along with fellow fans to express an opinion that may actually have an effect on the action. Not so the viewer. First of all, he or she is usually watching only with members of the family, at home, in their own private space, isolated from the event. It matters not at all to the performance or the game if something on the screen provokes a comment at home. Second, the viewer is unable to appreciate directly the force of the surroundings, the weather, smells, or even the general mood. That's one very good reason why sports fans usually admit that nothing is so exciting as going to a game. Third, the viewer gets panoramic shots of the stage or the arena, close-ups of contestants or performers, and special information from the emcee or the commentator, none of which is usually available to the man or woman in the stands or even the front orchestra. That is why it is often much easier to understand what's being said, or sung, or happening, when watching it on television than when watching it in person. The viewers, in short, both lose and gain because theirs is a mediated, as well as a vicarious, experience.[5]

Nearly all entertainment might seem to be a display of the talent and the magic of television. But there were some shows in which that element of display was uppermost. It served as a particular source of the appeal of much live or event television, a lot of Culture, some talk and interview shows, and above all variety. What these shows lacked was the tension and the excitement generated by a contest or by the structure of drama. Instead they relied upon an exhibition of the skill and the personality of the performers, sometimes of a lavish setting or a clever arrangement, occasionally of the technical virtuosity of the camera as well. Typically the host and the performers adopted a mode of direct address, looking the viewers 'in the eye' and talking 'straight' to them at home. The purpose was to establish a close rapport with the unseen audience.[6]

The effort fostered a special kind of illusion upon which these displays traded. The technique often seemed a reworking of the old theme of hospitality: the clever host insinuated that the viewers were being invited in to watch something interesting and worthwhile. That might pique their sense of curiosity. Recall, for example, how the opening episode of 'Tabloid' (31 January 1958) emphasized the playfulness and friendliness of the regulars who were, it appeared, just waiting around to please their public. Even more, the host tried to involve the audience, to suggest common interests, to build a sense of community. Frank Shuster in an episode of 'The Wayne and Shuster Hour' (11 March 1962) introduced a song with this brief patter: 'About this time of the year, all of us start thinking about the wonderful summer months ahead. And so tonight we're going to bring you a little vacation preview ...' He assumed agreement. The art of the display, one key to the success of any such show, lay in its ability to create a bond between performer and viewer.

The Great Canadian Talent Hunt

Some things never seem to change. In August 1962, CTV's executive producer Peter Macfarlane (who'd apprenticed at the CBC on assorted variety shows) waxed patriotic in a newspaper interview about the future of a planned variety series called 'Network,' initially designed by the great inventor himself, none other than Ross McLean. It was going to rejuvenate light entertainment in the country, to provide a new showcase for Canadian talent. In September 'Network' went on the air, appearing every weekday in a very peculiar time-slot, from 10:55 to 11:20. The show starred Bill Brady and Denyse Angé, a duet who apparently symbolized the balance of the two sexes and the two Canadas. Its intention was to mix talk and music and comedy, to include appearances by celebrities, and to use inserts from affiliated stations, all in an attempt to wean Canadians from their nightly habit of watching Earl Cameron and the CBC's newscast. This was supposed to be achieved at a cost of under $10,000 a week, according to its producer Stan Harris (another former CBCer). The ratings soon proved that it would take more than 'Network' to unseat Earl Cameron. Early in January 1963, the same Macfarlane was explaining to the press that, among other things, there just wasn't sufficient showbiz talent around to keep the dying 'Network' alive by expanding it to an hour. Angé, at least, expressed her disappointment over the show's cancellation because, as she put it, 'a lot of wonderful talent' had been presented in the past months. There was speculation that some of this 'wonderful talent,' notably the Le Garde Twins who specialized in western music, would get their own shows. Very little resulted from either the experience or the speculation.[7]

In fact the whole business was reminiscent of what had been happening at the CBC for roughly a decade, although the record of public television was considerably better (see chart 6.1). Right from the beginning, the Corporation's spokesmen had been telling just about anyone who would listen how television would promote what amounted to a Canadian Pop-Cult. Variety shows were supposed to be the main instrument, perhaps because, as Len Starmer, a supervisor of light entertainment, noted, they were one of the easiest forms to produce in the first years of TV. Variety had grown out of vaudeville and the radio music hall: a variety show promised a collection of performances that could involve music and song, comedy monologues or sketches, dancing, talk, and animal and other novelty acts. It might or might not specialize, say, in a type of music, or a single theme, say, magic. Usually it had one host whose role was vital because that person had to knit the display of talent together.[8]

Finding enough talent to staff all the programming was a continuing problem. At first, producers could count on such veterans of radio as Johnny Wayne or Frank Shuster, Cliff McKay, Juliette Sysak, or Don

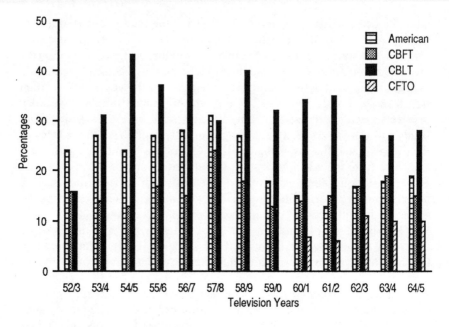

Chart 6.1 Mid-evening variety, 1952–65
Note: This chart documents the amounts of variety programming aired during peak-time viewing, 8:00 to 10:00 PM, by the assorted networks.

Messer. That wasn't enough, though. There was a modest network of theatres and music halls, night-clubs, and eventually coffee-houses to train newcomers. Colette Bónheur, who started in 'Porte ouverte' (Fall '54 to Summer '58), came out of a Montreal cabaret. The CBC itself mounted a couple of primetime talent shows to seek out hopefuls — 'Now's Your Chance' (Fall '52 to Spring '54), 'Pick the Stars' (Fall '54 to Summer '57), and 'La couronne d'or' (Fall '57 to Summer '58). And there certainly were a lot of those people: *Maclean's* Barbara Moon noted late in 1959 that some 7,000 singers and another 1,000 musicians and dancers had tried to break into television the previous year. Some of the hopefuls actually realized their dreams of glory: singers Lorraine Foreman, Paul Anka, Robert Goulet, and the Hames Sisters were all pushed into the national limelight through appearances on 'Pick the Stars.'[9]

Variety, it was hoped, would generate sufficient commercial revenue to cover much of the expense of unprofitable, if more worthy, programming in the arts and public affairs. That meant variety shows were the most susceptible to ratings and sponsor pressure of all the made-in-Canada offerings. Alex Barris became convinced that the sponsor's wishes were often acted upon, whatever the rhetoric to the contrary. He claimed, for example, that Dick MacDougal, the first emcee of 'Pick the Stars,' was told not to wish contestants 'good luck' because it was also the name of a brand of margarine in competition with the show's sponsor. Even more outlandish, the comedian Libby Morris was supposedly banned from further appearances on the long-running 'Holiday Ranch,' sponsored by Aylmer Foods, because her name suggested the rival manufacturer Libby![10]

But a good deal more serious was the fact that the CBC imported a series of hit variety shows from the United States, both to boost its ratings and to enrich commercial revenues. The longest-lasting and most important of these, of course, was that phenomenon of American television. 'The Ed Sullivan Show,' which began offering its incomparable blend of the spectacular and the banal on CBC in September 1953. Just as in the United States, watching Ed Sullivan became a Sunday-night tradition for millions of people in Canada. Perhaps even more striking was the fact that first the CBC and later CTV would schedule a succession of more specialized shows featuring American stars in choice time-spots: the comedians Milton Berle and Jackie Gleason, the contemporary singers Dinah Shore and Perry Como, a relaxed Garry Moore and the beloved clown Red Skelton, or singalong leader Mitch Miller and the unpredictable Jack Paar. Obviously the Canadian viewer had easy access to the delights of the showbiz scene shaped by New York and Hollywood.[11]

That viewer could also sample quite a range of home-grown shows, especially on the Anglo schedule, because CBC-Toronto devoted much more of its production time to variety than did its Montreal counterpart. It was, of course, very tempting to try to emulate Ed Sullivan. Right away, CBC-Toronto launched 'The Big Revue' (Fall '52 to Summer '54), which, at a cost of $10,000 a week, was one of the most expensive shows around. It offered up comedy, dancing, and assorted singing, only to evoke criticism from viewers and critics because it seemed so amateurish by comparison with American hits. CBC-Toronto also allowed Alex Barris ('Barris Beat,' Summer '56 to Summer '58) to try to import the informal style of hosting, talk, and comedy developed by Steve Allen, though Barris was always kept on a low budget. Much more successful were 'Showtime' (Fall '53 to Summer '59), which featured music, song and dance, and comedy, and later 'Parade' (Summer '59 to Summer '64), which devoted a half-hour to everything from one star, to a kind of song, to a musical comedy.[12]

The only successful rival to Ed Sullivan was a Montreal creation, 'Music Hall,' born in Fall '55 to compete with 'The Ed Sullivan Show' on Sunday night. It lasted seven years, hosted by such television personalities as Michelle Tisseyre and later the comedian Jacques Normand, and was briefly revived in Fall '65. 'Music Hall' showcased both Canadian stars, such as Denyse Filiatrault and Monique Leyrac, and international (normally French) talent, such as Maurice Chevalier, Edith Piaf, Charles Aznavour, and Georges Guétary. It was, by Canadian standards, a lavish spectacle, at one point boasting an orchestra of twenty-seven musicians, and offering everything from operetta and musical comedy to popular songs or ballads, to acrobats and ventriloquists. Its longevity resulted from the fact that Quebec had a dual allegiance to the 'showbiz' worlds of both Paris and America.[13]

Although there was a certain amount of comedy in many shows, home-grown comedy-variety didn't do very well on any Canadian network, with the outstanding exception of Wayne and Shuster. cbc-Toronto tried out a few shows of this ilk: 'After Hours' (Spring '53 to Summer '53), which was important because it introduced John Aylesworth and Frank Peppiatt who would go on to much greater things, 'Ad Lib' (Summer '54) with Larry Mann, and Jack Duffy as well as Larry Mann on 'Here's Duffy' (Summer '58 to Summer '59). But more often than not comic acts on other variety shows depended on guest appearances by Americans. cbc-Montreal had slightly more success with the one-time radio staple 'Quelles nouvelles' (Spring '56 to Summer '59), in which Jean Duceppe and Marjolaine Hébert offered two sketches in fifteen minutes about the small aspects of life. The episode of 'Quelles nouvelles' of 31 August 1957, for example, featured a girl in a hospital bed and the visit of a social worker to the home of an unemployed man. ctv's only foray was the short-lived 'The Jerry Lester Show' (Fall '63), which tried to resurrect an old American comedian whose style harked back to early Milton Berle.

Where both cbc-Toronto and cbc-Montreal put most of their energy was in the realm of musical variety. The result was a host of programs that catered to some specialized taste in what was fast becoming a very fragmented market for music: contemporary and traditional pop ('Cross-Canada Hit Parade,' 'Chansons-vedettes,' or 'Juliette'); easy listening ('Rollande et Robert' or 'The Denny Vaughan Show'); jazz ('Jazz with Jackson' and 'Feu de joie'); big-band music ('The Jack Kane Show');

country ('Holiday Ranch') and western ('Red River Jamboree'); old-time folk ('Les Collegiens Troubadours' or 'Dans tous les cantons'), international folk ('Lolly Too Dum'), and eventually 1960s folk (CTV's 'Let's Sing Out'); even a bit of rock (CTV's 'A Go-Go '66/It's Happening'). Here were signs of a Canadian PopCult.

Variety did indeed bring a collection of different performances. A show featuring a lot of soft pop, 'The Jackie Rae Show' (7 December 1955), for example, not only offered some romantic ballads and some jazz by guest Dizzy Gillespie but an up-tempo dance number plus a comedy skit by Frank Peppiatt. A test of audience responses to that episode learned that teenagers preferred both the dance and the skit to the rest of the show. The comedy sketches in 'The Wayne and Shuster Hour' (11 March 1962) were separated by song, dance, and a 'Pop Bottle Symphony,' a cleverly edited film of the production line in a Canada Dry plant set to music. This so-called film fantasy was only one in a very long list of novelties tried out on an unsuspecting public: innumerable animal acts (even on Ed Sullivan), magicians, puppet shows, jugglers, and the like.[14]

Yet there was a sameness to many of the variety shows, American as well as Canadian. They were so terribly 'nice.' Most telling were the adjectives people applied to the shows: pleasant, agreeable, casual, sincere, natural, light, gay, cheerful. One early venture of CBC-Montreal, 'Café des artistes,' the counterpart to the 'The Big Revue,' was set in a bistro to convey a friendly and intimate atmosphere of people at play. The finale to a 'Milton Berle Show' (5 June 1956) offered up the whole cast in a rendition of 'The Poor People of Paris,' which suggested fun and joy. The style of dialogue in 'Chansons canadiennes' (20 March 1959) was informal and relaxed, full of jokes and laughter, emulating a discussion among friends who just happened to be at a rehearsal. The performers on 'Holiday Ranch' sported an assortment of friendly nicknames: 'Bouncing Billy' Richards, the fiddler; 'Flying Fingers' Ralph Fraser; 'Dapper Don' McFarlane on the mandolin. A full episode of 'Music Hall' (6 March 1966) was devoted to a send-off for Michel Conte, a song-writer now leaving the show to return to his native France. It was full of the language and gestures of friendship.[15]

Naturally the emcees were cast in a similar mould. A story in the CBC Times said that Billy O'Connor, then the host of his own show, was 'a man you'd like to get to know.' Hugh Garner thought another host, Bud Knapp, was clearly 'a nice guy,' who tried a bit too hard to suggest informality. One test audience found Alex Barris 'likeable, easygoing, natural, and friendly.' An admiring Dennis Braithwaite noted the 'naturalness' of Perry Como.

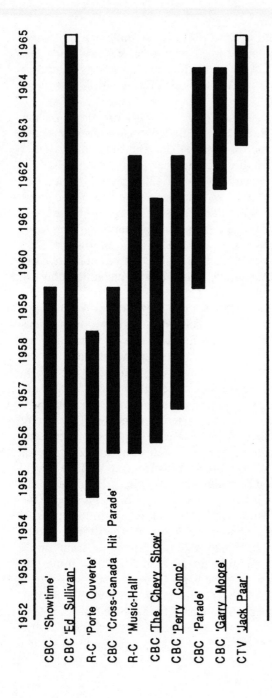

Chart 6.2 Some examples of 'showbiz' variety

Note: The dates are approximate, indicating the season (Spring, Summer, or Fall) in which a show commenced or ended on the schedule of one of the Canadian networks. Shows which continued beyond the end of 1964 are indicated by an unfilled block. The American imports have been underlined. These often ran for a longer period of time on their parent American networks.

A telephone survey of the public's response to 'En habit du dimanche,' a short-lived program in the music-hall tradition, found rave reviews for the ever-personable host Jacques Normand.[16]

Early on, Miriam Waddington, the television critic of *Canadian Forum*, pondered why variety should adopt this particular style. She argued correctly that it was deemed necessary by producers to please the viewer: the potential audience was so huge and so diverse, made up of all kinds of people, that this seemed the only way to build a sense of community between a show and its public. But did these producers ever ask themselves how all the 'goodness and gaiety' they purveyed was accepted by an audience, 'maybe with curlers-in-hair, or victims of sharp arthritic pains, or worriers about the problems of earning a living'? That, however, was the question of the sophisticate and the snob. What Waddington failed to realize was that viewers wanted exactly the kind of escape into a dream world offered by these apparently superficial and syrupy shows.[17]

The 'Showbiz' World: Pop Music

The most successful variety shows fell into two distinct camps, each of which manufactured a special realm of fantasy to capture the imagination of the viewer. The first and most common brand I term 'showbiz' because it dealt in a world of glamour and glitter, handsome and beautiful people, much hype and much clever talk (see chart 6.2). This was the abode of the city-slicker. The most striking feature of 'Music Hall' (6 March 1966), for example, was its trendiness, what with its go-go girls, miniskirts, loud ties, abstract decorations, and the like. The whole show shouted its devotion to fashion.

That was very common. Much earlier, 'Cross-Canada Hit Parade' had always tried to present itself as an extravaganza of what was most up to date in the 'showbiz' world. Its gimmick was the visual presentation of the top songs of the week. The announcer was constantly telling the viewer how the upcoming song was from the number-one album or a smash hit. Special care was obviously taken with background sets. The troupe spent a considerable amount of time planning out just how to present the tune. That could be very difficult at times: in the 1956/7 season the 'Hit Parade' crew had to find a different way of staging 'Green Door' over a period of nineteen weeks! The camera work was often imaginative and sophisticated. Dance numbers were subtle, complicated examples of synchronized movement in the best traditions of modern dance.

How did all this work? One of the songs featured in the 10 November

1958 episode was Frank Sinatra's 'It's a Lonesome Old Town.' The scene opened with the camera zooming down a dark, empty city street to focus on the male co-star, Wally Koster, leaning against a post near the entrance to a club called the Blue Hole. Dressed in a fedora and suit, a cigarette in his left hand, he imitated the mannerisms and voice of Sinatra. When he changed to an upbeat song, the street suddenly became bright, people appeared, and Koster broke into enthusiastic song and dance in a simulation of new-found joy. It was very much a land of make-believe.

An episode of 'Showtime' (4 March 1956) supplies an even more intriguing commentary on the 'showbiz' world. The show was 'all about magic,' said its star Shirley Harmer. The mythology of magic allows one to escape from reality, to renounce the assorted constraints that bind people in their day-to-day lives. The presentation of this 'escape' provided much room for an innovative, experimental use of the camera to win the eye of the viewer. During the show Shirley seemed to float in the air; she made a hat appear with a snap of her fingers; a group of tiny men came out of the hat to dance on its brim; a genie appeared out of a lamp; a dance routine featured a split screen showing the top half of three men performing with the bottom half of three women; and so on. The camera shot certain scenes on an angle, from below to suggest floating or flying through the air and from above to create a sense of the miniature. The sets were elaborate, the costumes striking, and the songs underlined the mood of fantasy. One of the key scenes occurred in a harem, complete with a sultan and the requisite bevy of females reclining on rugs. What wizardry, what a demonstration of the technological marvels of television.

The world of 'showbiz' was the home of the celebrity, a place of extravagance and ostentation that contrasted dramatically with the world of ordinary folk. In fact 'showbiz' variety rose and fell by trading in celebrity: these shows discovered celebrity ('Here's a new star!'), they championed it ('Sure to impress you with his talent!'), they stroked it ('A singer who always pleases'). That wasn't to everyone's taste: Ira Dilworth, then a CBC director of program evaluation, complained bitterly about how Jack Kane engaged in 'a demonstration of quite unpardonable "boot licking" ' in his treatment of a guest, the song composer Arthur Schwartz, on one episode of 'Music '60.' But most viewers were a lot more tolerant. Ed Sullivan was a master of the art of making and hyping celebrity, which was the chief reason he excelled as an emcee and became such a power in the land of entertainment. Here too lies the explanation as to why CBC-Toronto imported even second-rate American stars to feature on their variety shows, and Radio-Canada did much the same with French stars – their very appearance bestowed legitimacy on the programs.[18]

'Showbiz' variety typically cast men and women in contrasting roles. Men came in many different shapes and sizes. Ed Sullivan or Milton Berle or Alex Barris was definitely ordinary. However, Bob Goulet of 'Showtime' was exceptionally handsome, even glamorous. All were on display, of course. Miriam Waddington talked about the 'irresistible, darling, boyish energy' of Jackie Rae and 'the clean-cut winsomeness' of Bob Goulet. But the treatment of the male figure was discreet. The previously mentioned episode of 'Showtime' featured three male dancers in balloon pants, short vests, and turbans, while their female counterparts appeared in revealing costumes.[19]

What in fact was 'on display' most of the time was not the male physique but male authority. Nearly all of the emcees were male, and in charge of events. Pierre Paquette, the host of 'Chansons canadiennes' (20 March 1959), walked around the set of the supposed rehearsal in a sports coat and tie (while others were in casual clothes), carrying a stack of index cards as his symbol of authority. The oft-expressed dissatisfaction with Alex Barris as an emcee was rooted in the fact that he didn't conform to the macho image dominant at the time – Waddington, for example, considered him 'spineless.' Likewise the female host of CBC's 'The Joan Fairfax Show' was criticized by a program-evaluation committee because she seemed to lack the personality and the voice to emcee the show: indeed, her voice was described as 'strident, harsh and thin.' The mantle of authority was normally worn by a man even where he received only equal billing as a star: Wally Koster was definitely the dominant figure on 'Cross-Canada Hit Parade.' And on that episode of 'Showtime' which featured the magical journey of Shirley Harmer, a male played the role of the magician, able to command people and things to obey his will. This species of variety confirmed, albeit in a subtle fashion, the prevailing wisdom about the naturalness of patriarchy in nearly all dimensions of life.[20]

The portrayal of women, of course, was equally stereotyped. Witness that one episode of 'Hit Parade' (10 November 1958). The opening routine of Joyce Hahn, the show's co-star, found her on a set made up of a collection of highway signs warning Danger, No Right Turn, Caution, etc. She moved around them blithely, singing her song 'Cockeyed Optimist.' It was all a neat statement on the lot of the well-endowed woman in a male world. Later on, the program offered four distinct images of women in a number featuring a western setting based on music from the Broadway hit *The*

Music Man. Out of a stage-coach came first the 'whore,' in this case a saloon girl, introduced with bump-and-grind music; then the typical 'girl-next-door,' shy and virginal; the 'prude,' a school-marm or preacher's wife, looking severe; and finally the 'tomboy' who flexed her muscles and acted tough. All, by the way, got into a fight, were pulled apart by the men, and soon succumbed to male charms.

Women were first and foremost sex objects. But that didn't necessarily mean any vulgar display of the female body. Rather the opposite. The women, especially on Canadian television, were supposed to be attractive and wholesome. The key, as Waddington pointed out, was to introduce sex in 'an acceptable, yet titillating way,' to be both revealing and delicate. That's why Shirley Harmer appeared on 'Showtime' (4 March 1956) as a beautiful woman on a pedestal, treated with respect by all, including a raunchy sultan. Her coolness came across to viewers: one test audience, for example, found her 'beautiful, talented, charming, natural, poised,' but less frequently 'vivacious' and hardly sultry. A *Toronto Daily Star* article referred to the 'potent if non-inflammatory sensuality' of Sylvia Murphy, then a regular on one of Jack Kane's shows. The next season, on an episode of 'The Wayne and Shuster Hour,' she looked like a doll in a white filmy outfit, with white-blonde hair, and a very white face, her mouth and eyes highlighted by black shading – pretty yes, but not at all threatening. Elaine Bedard, the young, attractive host of 'Music Hall' (6 March 1966), appeared in a fashionable hair-do and a revealing black dress, cut above the knee and plunging down at the top, the very epitome of the modern female. Her position ensured that she wasn't made the butt of any overt sexual interest, though.[21]

Yet the sexual innuendo could become quite obvious. The female dancers on 'Showtime' (4 March 1956) were clad in halter tops and transparent harem pants, made all the more intriguing because the dim lights accented their legs. An attractive Debra Paget, the dancer featured on 'The Milton Berle Show' (5 June 1956), was dressed in a brief costume that highlighted her figure. When she danced, the camera followed the contortions of her body carefully, and ended up with an angle shot that focused on her breasts. Joyce Hahn of 'Hit Parade' (10 November 1958) appeared in the first routine dressed in a spangled short-sleeved dress and a knee-length skirt with crinolines underneath. The whole costume gave her an hour-glass figure, and particularly exaggerated her breasts. (But in the actual number the camera did make an awkward switch to avoid showing too much of her leg.) Later in the show Phyllis Marshall sang a Spanish tune that translates as 'Come Closer to Me.' She wore a low-cut dress, baring her arms and shoulders and with a full frilly skirt. Throughout she wore a 'Come Hither' expression on her face, and made inviting, suggestive gestures to emphasize her availability. Such displays disclosed a world of glamorous sex inhabited by attractive women – at the very least, these catered to the male voyeurs in the audience.

The theme of much of 'showbiz' variety was the mystique of romance. Falling in love was presented as the key to fulfilment, to personal happiness. That was a reflection of the courtship mores of the times, and it locked the sexes in a peculiar kind of embrace. Both were typecast as pawns of the game of romance. Men and women, so it seemed, were always searching for romance. The women might appear to have a greater control, since it was they who doled out the sex. Shirley Harmer played the role of such a woman in the episode of 'Showtime,' forcing the men to strive to impress her. Denyse Filiatrault in 'Chansons canadiennes' flirted with one Jacques Laurin, then in the stands, beckoning him down onto the stage to dance. Wally Koster ended his Sinatra rendition on 'Hit Parade' with 'I've Got the World on a String,' once he was joined by his woman. But women could also be the victims of love, should their men walk away, a plight sentimentalized by Sylvia Murphy's verson of 'Stardust' on 'The Wayne and Shuster Hour.'

Both 'Showtime' and 'Hit Parade,' by the way, employed dance to symbolize the complicated rhythms of romance. 'Showtime' offered three women and three men in a routine that initially suggested the age-old battle of the sexes, each group separately competing for attention, only to end with one of the men and one of the women dancing as a couple. The dance on 'Hit Parade' began with couples lying down in shadows; their movements were initially stiff and slow; when the tempo of the music increased, their movements became sensual and erotic; after this peak, the music slowed again and the dancers returned to their former prone positions. It was all part of the message of happiness and sadness played out time and again on the little screen for the pleasure of viewers.

The popularity of the made-in-Canada shows was never as great as the CBC had hoped. Elliott-Haynes ratings surveys in February 1957 and February 1962, for example, showed that French Canadians didn't really fancy variety all that much. 'Music Hall' could manage only to place somewhere around fifteenth in the top twenty. An extended Radio-Canada investigation in 1959 showed that the entertainment programming its audience least valued was the variety shows. Similarly, the Elliott-Haynes surveys showed that the most popular 'showbiz' variety in English Canada was 'The Ed Sullivan Show,' followed by 'The Perry Como Show' in 1957 and 'The Garry Moore Show' in 1962. Ed Sullivan's appeal was so great that in January 1961 he captured a quarter of the francophone audience in Montreal, even in the face of competition from 'Music Hall.' In 1957 'Showtime' did rank ninth on CBMT-Montreal's schedule, but only nineteenth on CBLT-Toronto's roster. In the spring season of 1962, 'Parade' averaged seventeenth in the ratings across the country. Overall, the appeal of 'showbiz' variety was greater in urban, notably medium-sized cities, than in small towns and on the farms: in November 1961, for example, 'The Danny Kaye Show' reached roughly a third of the homes in medium and big cities, though fewer than one-fifth of the farm homes. That was only further evidence of how these shows were designed for the city-slicker at heart.[22]

A lot of blame, as usual, was laid at the door of the CBC for the fact its shows rarely hit the top of the ratings. Over the years people charged that the CBC didn't understand the mass taste, that there wasn't sufficient money or proper studio facilities, that there was never enough rehearsal time, or that there was too much copying of American originals. The arrival of videotape and the passing of live television was blamed for the lack of vitality in existing shows, because performers no longer had to put out that extra bit of energy to ensure the quality of their programs. Barris would later argue that the CBC followed a no-star policy, perhaps to keep down costs, certainly to prevent the rise of a series of prima donnas. Unfortunately the policy also prevented the hyping of talent so necessary to effective variety because the audience was given little chance to identify with a personality. Witness the succession of bland titles over the years: 'Swing Easy,' 'Swing Gently,' and even 'Swing Ding'; 'While We're Young'; 'Music Makers'; 'Front and Centre'; 'Bras dessus, bras dessous'; 'Copain, copain'; 'En habit du dimanche'; or 'Mon pays, mes chansons.' Of course, even when stars did emerge, many of them hopped off to the United States: Winnipeg's Gisele MacKenzie, Ottawa's Paul Anka, Shirley Harmer and, later, Bob Goulet of 'Showtime' fame, a bilingual Québécoise such as Denyse Angé. The truth was that the United States remained the big time, for 'showbiz' variety anyway. Canada was on the periphery of the entertainment world without sufficient money, an adequate pool of talent, or enough stars to compete, even if it might sometimes mimic styles or borrow talent from the American centre.[23]

In the Land of the 'Squares': Country-and-Western Music

Turning to the second brand, 'old-fashioned' variety, represents a swift descent into the land of the 'squares.' Consider a small exercise in myth-making: an article by Cathy Perkins in *Liberty* in 1963 about the Hames Sisters, who had been country-and-western singers on the very popular 'Country Hoedown' for seven years. Her concern was neither with their artistry nor even with their status, which might well have troubled a later generation, but with their television personalities. On the screen the trio had nourished a special appeal as 'the girls next door,' noted for their 'warm simplicity.' They sang traditional songs, dressed in plain clothes, wore their hair in the same style. They even seemed to enjoy the tunes they were singing. Was this just another instance of 'TV hokum'? No, said Perkins: they really were all sweetness and light. Success hadn't spoiled this wholesome trio. They had no vices and many virtues – they didn't smoke, drink, swear, or gossip; they spent little on clothes, went to church regularly, and valued home life; the two married sisters looked after their kids, refusing extra help except when the need was extreme; and they all saw each other and their parents often. 'If you've ever thought the Hames sisters off-camera would be the same sincere, home-loving, affectionate folks you watch on *Country Hoedown*,' she concluded, 'why, shucks, you're absolutely right.'[24]

There was never a lot of 'old-fashioned' variety on the network schedules (see chart 6.3). One of the main ingredients, country-and-western music, had only begun to advance across North America in any significant fashion after the war. 'Old-fashioned' variety wasn't especially big in the United States, although ABC did launch Lawrence Welk and 'Ozark Jubilee' (under various titles) in the mid-1950s, and NBC gave air time to Mitch Miller's peculiar renaissance of the old favourites in music via his sing-along hour a bit later. Over the years Radio-Canada mounted a couple of programs to showcase the folk tunes of Quebec, notably the summer series 'Dans tous les cantons' which used local, often amateur, talent to feature the songs and dances of the various regions of the province. But the chief source was CBC-Toronto, which sponsored four long-running country-and-western shows plus the traditional 'Juliette.' That was almost by accident, since programmers and producers were clearly much more interested in 'showbiz' variety. 'Don Messer's Jubilee,' for example, began locally in Halifax in 1957 and came to network television as a summer replacement (for 'Country Hoedown'); it so surprised the programmers by winning a mass following that they had to give it a place on the winter schedule. CTV

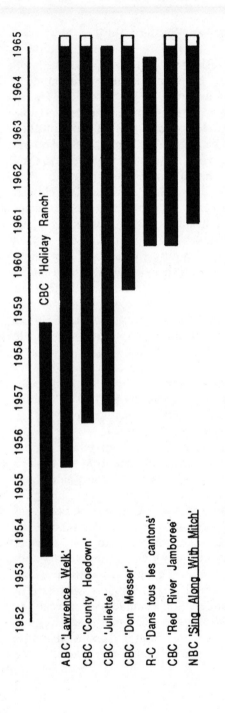

Chart 6.3 Some examples of 'old-fashioned' variety

Note: The dates are approximate, indicating the season (Spring, Summer, or Fall) in which a show commenced or ended on the schedule of one of the Canadian or American networks. Shows which continued beyond the end of 1964 are indicated by an unfilled block. The American programs have been underlined.

merely followed in the Corporation's footsteps, with a series of short-lived clones sporting fiddlers, guitar players, ballad singers, and square dancers.[25]

The style of these shows contrasted sharply with 'showbiz' variety. The male stars were neither fashionable nor debonair. Cliff McKay was a jolly fat man, dressed up in a formal suit and string tie, which gave him the appearance of a happy penguin. Lawrence Welk was an old man with a funny accent. Don Messer was also old, but so retiring that he rarely spoke and seemed to disappear into the background. The women were usually ordinary, not at all sexy. The costumes of the Hames Sisters always sported high necklines. Marg Osburne of 'Don Messer's Jubilee' was a plump, cheerful woman who struck observers more as a housewife than as a television celebrity. Juliette tried to portray the image of the wholesome blonde, a bit flirty but really very proper, dressed in nice though not revealing clothes and full of romantic banalities and cheerful smiles.

A second crucial difference was that all the made-in-Canada shows were very low budget. The cost of 'Holiday Ranch' in 1956 was under $5,000 a week, of 'Dans tous les cantons' in 1961 around $6,000 to $7,000, of 'Don Messer's Jubilee' in 1968 a mere $8,000, or roughly one-quarter of the average for CBC Toronto's variety shows. The production values weren't very high. 'Holiday Ranch' had a sort of nitty-gritty appearance, which was fitting because it was supposed to take place on a Canadian dude ranch; 'Dans tous les cantons' employed very primitive settings because it was filmed in a special tent on location in small towns; and 'Country Hoedown' made do with a stage decked out as a barn.[26]

As a rule content changed very little. 'People expect our show to be more or less the same every week,' claimed Loyd Brydon, the producer of 'Holiday Ranch,' 'and we don't disappoint them.' McKay actually bragged about how the show was put together as if it was determined by a mathematical formula, offering something for seniors and something for teens each week. Usually the tunes played were anything but modern: fiddle music, old ballads and hymns, folk favourites, very conventional pop. Neither Juliette nor her musical director, Bill Isbister, Barris argued, had anything but conventional instincts, which led them to distrust novelty. 'Dans tous les cantons' (27 July 1960) opened with a lively square dance and followed this up with a jig, a traditional dance from France, and folk songs, including a spirited song about St Jean, the locale of this broadcast. One celebration of Don Messer emphasized that some of his tunes were two hundred or three hundred years old. Occasionally, though, some recent material did creep into the repertoire. Cliff McKay, for instance, allowed a few new ballads, though only those that were clearly of a traditional character. At least one viewer took umbrage at such innovation, and demanded that Cliff and his group remove their western clothes before further defiling them by playing rock 'n' roll.[27]

That brings me to the extraordinary range of responses all this 'old-fashioned' music and dance provoked. The assorted critics in the print media found the popularity of these shows incredible. How could anything so homespun work so well? 'Holiday Ranch' was often the number-one Canadian show in its first three years. No wonder that in 1956 Dorothy Sangster thought 'Holiday Ranch' was 'the most baffling show' on the CBC. 'Country Hoedown' consistently outscored rival 'showbiz' programs made by CBC-Toronto. When Norma Hames's baby was born, cards, letters, and even gifts were sent in by devout fans – 'a hand-knit sweater,' 'a bunting bag,' 'two sets of jackets and bonnets, with matching booties,' 'a pair of beaded moccasins.' Although never a big winner, Juliette benefited from her show's placement, right after the Saturday-evening hockey broadcast, and she did manage to retain a fair portion of this massive audience. But the real phenomenon was 'Don Messer's Jubilee.' It rose so high in the ratings that at one point, in November 1961, it was the most popular show throughout Canada, ahead of hockey and Ed Sullivan. The jump in the sales of Pillsbury cake mixes and Massey-Ferguson farm implements that year was partly ascribed to the enormous success of the show they sponsored. Although the show couldn't maintain this level of popularity, it remained very high on both the made-in-Canada and the national viewing lists right to the end. So, in 1968 Tom Alderman could still puzzle about why a 'lousy TV program' such as 'Don Messer's Jubilee' could draw three million viewers.[28]

It shouldn't surprise that the appeal of these shows was skewed towards the Maritimes, the West, and rural Canada. The Hames Sisters, for instance, admitted that their style really didn't go over very well in Toronto. But when they went on a personal tour to the Maritimes, the source of most of their fan mail, they were treated like stars. At its high point, 'Don Messer's Jubilee' was reaching over half of farm homes, though only a quarter of big-city homes. Something over a year later, Elliott-Haynes claimed the show was capturing almost 96 per cent of the potential audience in the Maritimes.[29]

Cynics were always ready to throw sticks and stones. One such person found the key to Don Messer's success in 'a sick-making sincerity – you know, all the homely virtues cooked up in one sweetly indigestible batch of fudge.' Indeed the show was variously damned as 'amateurish,' 'a third rate revival of Floradora,' 'a national laughing stock.' Dennis Braithwaite thought 'Juliette' was marred by 'an unexciting format, uninspired production, bad writing, unglamorous costuming and a drab image of wholesomeness.'[30]

But in fact what appealed about these shows was their apparent sincerity and ordinariness, as Don Messer himself once reflected, such a striking contrast to the unreality of the 'showbiz' world. Early on, the Vancouver columnist Jack Scott pointed out that 'Don Messer's Jubilee' was about real people 'like you and me,' who didn't claim the perfection of most of the celebrities of television-land. As well, the made-in-Canada shows seemed to be exuberantly patriotic, quite unlike the ersatz 'showbiz' brand that tried to emulate things American. So 'Holiday Ranch,' according to its producer, was 100 per cent Canadian, with no U.S. jokes or guns or jewelled holsters, and not a single drawl among the performers. And 'Don Messer's Jubilee,' according to its memorialist Lester Sellick, was unashamedly Canadian in its love of the land, the people, and their traditional melodies. Above all, these programs harked back to an older Canada, when things were presumably less complicated and the old ways of behaving cherished. Thus Braithwaite found in 'Don Messer's Jubilee' 'an echo of our country and people as they used to be in simpler days.' That came through in the celebration of the Hames Sisters. It was also present in Sellick's account of Don Messer as a great family man and neighbour, a sort of small-town boy unspoiled by big-city living. It doesn't take much digging to discover an element of rebellion here, a rebellion against the flash and glitter of high living, against the insidious ways of the United States, against the headlong rush into the future.[31]

There were good reasons why these shows might seem quaint. The message of 'old-fashioned' variety was one of timelessness and togetherness. You couldn't have asked for more friendly shows. 'Holiday Ranch' (28 September 1957) opened with the whole group doing a rendition of 'Tell Us Where the Good Times Are.' Cliff McKay then told viewers the good times were right here, at his Saturday-evening party, and invited them 'to step right in and make yourselves to home.' 'Country Hoedown' (8 September 1962) began with four couples singing 'Come Right In. It's Country Hoedown Time.' Gordie Tapp, the emcee, then welcomed the audience with 'Hi there, friends and neighbours'; the phrase 'friends and neighbours' he repeated constantly throughout the half-hour. The language was colloquial, folksy, down to earth. Juliette was famous for delivering such homilies as 'Hi, honey,' 'C'mon, fellas,' and 'Good night, Mom,' all the while acting in a warm and cheery manner. Both 'Holiday Ranch' and 'Country Hoedown' were filled with banter and much kidding around.

Their square dances were simple celebrations of harmony and fun, unlike the complicated and subtle routines of modern dancing. The old-time morality was always around to inform or uplift. McKay peppered his show with little comments on what was right and proper: he noted how one ballad underlined the virtues of love and satisfaction, he told adults to reflect on the merits of a kid's safety song, he urged support for the United Appeal, and he closed the show with a 'Thought for Tomorrow,' the hymn 'Abide with Me.' Juliette made very clear that all her romantic gestures and the like were in fun, that she was very much a wife, married to a man who played in her orchestra. 'Country Hoedown' closed off its show with the whole gang singing and dancing 'Love is the Only Thing.' Tommy Hunter, a graduate of 'Country Hoedown,' would end his show, first on radio and then on television, with the words 'Be the Good Lord willing.' And so it went. 'Old-fashioned' variety celebrated a way of life that cherished the ideals of home, family, and neighbourhood.[32]

The tunes and songs might also seem corny to the sophisticated ears of the citified viewer. Not to a fan of country-and-western music, though. It was music that touched the soul, in the words of Tommy Hunter, music that embodied the simple ways of times past, the joys and the hardships and the anguish of ordinary people. There were songs about railroad life ('I'm Moving On'), about love and its troubles ('Your Cheatin' Heart'), about loneliness ('I'm So Lonesome I Could Cry'), about man and God ('May the Good Lord Bless and Keep You'), and on and on, each a small, sincere story about life, at least to the true believer. He and his wife, and their sons and daughters as well, could find in country-and-western music a moral tale, a little anecdote, to explain, to warn, to celebrate just about everything that might happen to a person in the daily course of living.[33]

English Canada's Comedians

Johnny Wayne and Frank Shuster were two stars of Canadian variety who seemed to have an almost universal appeal across the country. By the mid-1960s they had become 'an institution, as familiar, as well-liked and as durable as the monarchy,' remarked Dennis Braithwaite. They should be 'designated our National Comedians, by default if not by act of Parliament.' That kind of accolade was especially striking, given the fact that native comedy simply had not flourished on Canadian television. And their achievement seems all the more remarkable when one realizes what had happened in the United States, where comedy-variety was once an extraordinarily popular form. Some big-time American comics of the 1950s, such as Milton Berle, Sid Caesar, and Imogene Coca, had virtually disappeared from sight, and the predominant kind of comedy had become the sitcom, a special type of storytelling. Why did these Canadian masters of comedy-variety prove so successful and so lasting?[34]

Part of the answer lies in the nature and purpose of this genre. Comedy-variety was nearly always contemporary and topical: it could take the shape of ridicule, satire, irony, or farce, and each of these could be directed at people, institutions, conventions, or ideas. The comedy served to demystify by highlighting the absurd, pointing to contradictions, spoofing the accepted ways, deflating pomposity and authority. It contained elements of confrontation and iconoclasm since, however mildly or gently, it challenged those very myths and conventions that conditioned the lives of viewers. That suggests its appeal as well as its effects. Good comedy relaxed the viewer, reduced the strains and stresses caused by everyday life, simply by poking fun at aspects of that life. Whatever its particular message, whether serious or playful, comedy humanized an often rough, impersonal, and unfair society.[35]

Wayne and Shuster had slowly developed a special style that encompassed a wide range of the techniques and targets available to the comic. They'd begun in school before the war, graduated to entertaining the troops at home and abroad, moved into radio in 1946, and more cautiously entered television in 1954, two years after its debut in Canada. Tests in the mid-1950s indicated that they appealed 'pretty much to "middlebrow" tastes.' Their great success, though, didn't come until they performed 'Rinse the Blood Off My Toga,' a long comedy sketch based on a blend of Shakespeare's *Julius Caesar* and Dashiell Hammett's style of hard-boiled detective tales, on 'The Ed Sullivan Show' in May 1958. It was a sudden smash hit, a major event of the entertainment season: what Sullivan said he found so welcome was that the two Canadians offered his audience 'a fresh, satirical approach,' a 'literate' style of comedy – no doubt he was even more pleased that their act did boost his ratings. Their enormous popularity with American audiences, it's been claimed, helped 'save Sullivan's ass': they would appear sixty-seven times on his show before its demise in 1971, a record that no other comedians could claim.[36]

More to the point, their American success salvaged their own careers in Canada, since the CBC was planning to can their own show at the end of the season. The New York triumph made the duo the grand stars of variety in Canada. Morris Wolfe recalled in *Jolts* how excited everyone was, how *The Toronto Daily Star* put the story of their triumph on the front page. A shame-faced CBC reopened negotiations with the two comedians for the next season, although now management found it was dealing with American stars whom it had to pay and treat accordingly. One result was that Wayne and Shuster were allowed much more control over the design of their show than was common in Canadian television. The whole business was ironic proof of the oft-repeated complaint that native talent was never truly appreciated in Canada until applauded by outsiders.[37]

The comic style of Wayne and Shuster baffled contemporaries a bit because of its versatility. Dennis Braithwaite managed to find echoes of Jack Benny, Sid Caesar, Phil Silvers, Fred Allen, and Weber and Fields. Borrowing the devices of other masters wasn't at all unusual in the annals of comedy. The more important truth is that Wayne and Shuster had fashioned a unique brand of literate farce, a mixing of witty or high-toned satire with low comedy and slapstick, giving their acts an astonishingly broad appeal well-suited to the needs of television. It was a Briton, writing in the BBC's *Radio Times* (2 September 1965), who best sketched the genius of these 'thinking man's comedians.' While their style harked back to 'the traditional music-hall formula of straight man and stooge,' wrote Tony Aspler, they were emphatically 'television comedians' who were very aware of the special demands of TV. Their arsenal was full of comedy techniques: 'corn,' 'acid,' madness, sophistication, 'humour and pathos.' 'Irony is the secret weapon of Wayne and Shuster's comedy, and intelligence their touchstone,' he concluded. 'Their particular quality is their ability to drop the cudgel and take up the rapier when the mood demands.'[38]

The comedy of Wayne and Shuster expressed the talents and wisdom of equal partners. The stage personae of the two men were different. Usually Frank Shuster was more subtle, better able to play-act a serious mood such as earnestness, while Johnny Wayne was bouncy and rough, once described as 'a fervent leprechaun.' That was why Shuster was often the straight-man, Wayne the madcap character. Yet both men could clown around, if the occasion demanded it, and neither was locked into a single type of role. In one comedy sketch, Shuster suddenly dropped his pose of a pompous German aristocrat to take on the guise of an almost manic Mitch Miller, leading the whole troupe in a comic sing-along.

A good part of their success was the result of very hard work before the actual performance. 'Show business can be a lot like a prize-fight,' Shuster claimed. 'You've got to have a punch but it's the training and planning that cinch the knockouts.' Unlike many other comedians, they wrote nearly all their own material from scratch. They had an aversion to ad-libbing, which struck them as just a lazy way to juice up a weak routine. No wonder, then, that much of their energy went into preparing a script. They designed their comedy together, one writing or typing and the other pacing around. Getting the idea may have been the hardest part, though sometimes a lot of dog work was necessary to turn it into a finished product. So, for a skit on the conquest of the Himalayas, they read widely about past attempts as well as mountain climbing in general to ensure no one would snicker over some inadvertent silliness. Rehearsals were no less important, even if the stage persona of each of the stars had been honed by years of practice. According to one report, they spent about twenty-five hours rehearsing for their first appearance on 'The Ed Sullivan Show.' Rehearsal was very much a part of the creative process where changes could be made in jokes, in acting, or in staging. Indeed that was the place to indulge in improvisation *à la* Stanislavski (one of the team's mentors), where actors try out an exchange in their own words to get a feeling for their roles, so that they could inject a greater realism into their actual performance.[39]

Increasingly they came to worry about production values, employing an assortment of special effects to embellish their performance. Wayne claimed that at the time he watched a lot of American variety (but rarely Canadian shows) to discover what the opposition was doing. That concern carried the show far away from the first days and ways of live television. By 1962, 'Wayne and Shuster' was produced on videotape in the CBC's largest studio, chock full of equipment, using the same technical crew of 125 people who worked on the prestige shows in the realm of drama and music. The quality of the camera work was good, as it had to be to capture the nuances of gesture and expression: considerable use was made of angle shots, of close-ups, and of fast cuts to highlight the humour. Sound was used to supplement what the camera showed or the script said: short pieces of music, in particular, served to set or underline a mood. Then there were the various kinds of technical wizardry such as pre-recorded songs or the split screen or special camera lenses to make the performance more professional. On one occasion, for example, producer Don Hudson shot the opening number in a series of tiny bits that, pieced together, gave the impression the two stars were descending 'an endless flight of stairs.' Hudson was an ex-magician, said Wayne, who loved to try to baffle the audience. All this effort made 'Wayne and Shuster' a highly polished show by Canadian standards.[40]

None of this effort would have mattered very much, of course, if their humour hadn't been so fine. Wayne and Shuster claimed that they were always on the look-out for inspiration. Just about anything – an incident in a restaurant, an exchange on a bus, people watching a ball game – was grist for their joke mill. Often they peppered their repartee with allusions to things Canadian, indeed to the life of Toronto, such as the arrival of private television, the Ontario Motor League, empty stores on Queen Street. They would pile one gag on top of another, using wit and costumes and props, to keep the audience in a state of nearly constant laughter. They loved to exploit the absurdity of an incongruous situation: thus Shuster and another actor played two graduates of a school of optometry at the University of Lowdelberg who greeted each other by singing the school's song with one eye covered, a song that ended in a rousing rendition of 'PKUROGUXU 20–20. Yay, Optometry, Yow!' Both men were masters of the exaggerated expression: if Wayne could make his eyes roll in astonishment, then Shuster could open his mouth wide to mimic horror. And, of course, they had a near perfect sense of timing, an ability to recognize when to deliver the gag, when to pause, when to come right back with another joke. All it took, they once suggested, was a little bit of 'insanity' to transform just about anything into humour.[41]

It also took a lot of learning. They turned to things that were in the 'common experience,' to use Wayne's phrase, of most everyone: to Shakespearean drama and the arts generally, to current television, to history and sports and the fads of the day. Here they discovered the raw material for their sketches. One of their most famous characters was Wayne's Professor Waynegartner, looking a bit like Einstein, a self-appointed 'authority on almost everything,' who played out the role of the expert and who might be an African explorer or an Egyptologist or a hockey coach or a famous artist interviewed by Shuster-as-Reporter for the edification of the television audience. Then there were the parodies of the great works of literature, such as 'The Brown Pumpernickel' in 1958 and 'The Americanization of Scheherazade, or, A Hard Day's Arabian Night' in 1965. Of equal merit were the sketches based on the hits of current movie or television drama, whether 'The Quiet Stranger,' about westerns, in 1956, or 'The Man from M.O.T.H.E.R.,' about the spy craze, in 1965. By the early 1960s, as well, Wayne and Shuster had added mime to their repertoire, a natural choice for a visual medium such as television since they had been trained in physical projection and emphatic movement as stage actors. They selected situations that allowed a humorous expression of people's emotions: the reactions of two new fathers to the sight of their babies, a duel between 'the fearless Count François de la Formidable' (Shuster) and 'the chicken-livered Count Jean de la Phinque' (Wayne), or a bank robbery in which two incompetent criminals find they're under surveillance by a camera.

Note that most of these sketches contained a substantial element of drama – 'Our skits are plays with a comic edge,' Wayne admitted. While that approach had its pitfalls because it could lead to too much emphasis on the plot or the characters, it gave to their comedy a kind of structure that worked much better on television than did the simple monologue or the typical variety sketch.[42]

The satire that characterized 'Wayne and Shuster' satire was by and large gentle. Yes, they would occasionally have a go at a person or a profession. In one sketch, for instance, a research doctor (Shuster) raises his eyes from his microscope to declare solemnly that he has proved 'a definite link between cigarettes and tobacco.' Now he would advance on 'the Number One Enemy: socialized medicine.' Dennis Braithwaite added that they had been known 'to lob spitballs' at the 'monuments' of national life, for example, Stratford, the home of Shakespearean drama and a self-conscious haven of Culture. What they'd never been noted for, however, was 'savagery.' Rarely did they draw upon politics or religion or race. Their satire was meant to be funny, not disturbing. Early on, they told an interviewer that it was simply 'mean' to injure 'people's feelings'; later, they added that because the show was going into living-rooms across the land, they didn't want 'to hurt anybody' or to offend against 'good taste.' The intent was to produce 'innocent merriment,' in Wayne's words, suitable to a Lester Pearson as well as to his grandson (two of Wayne and Shuster's greatest fans).[43]

That attitude highlighted the respect Wayne and Shuster had for ordinary folk. They played to the cameras, to the audience at home, rather than to whomever was in the studio or to the critics in the press. 'Wayne and Shuster' avoided inside jokes, simply because any material that was too esoteric or obscure wasn't going to be very funny. Their language was colloquial, their style of expression conversational. Their sketches assumed the viewer had a lively mind plus a fair amount of knowledge about life, about the great classics of literature, and of course about television itself. What especially annoyed them were charges that this comedy was above the heads of the audience. 'The retort to this is: Who is the audience, your sister?' said Johnny Wayne. 'Anyone who thinks the public is a moron, is a moron.'[44]

In fact Wayne and Shuster had made their comedy the instrument of the 'ordinary joe' in his never-ending struggle with the powers that be. So much of their material was at bottom an attack on the phoniness and pretensions of intellectuals, snobs, experts, and petty officials who were forever putting down the people. One famous mime, the airplane skit based upon Wayne's own experiences flying back from Copenhagen, revolved around what a guy flying economy class in tawdry circumstances, surrounded by bums, thinks is happening with the privileged beings in the first-class section. He learns at the end, poor soul, that the economy passengers are to be dropped off before the plane lands, leaving the first-class passengers eight more minutes of undisturbed pleasure until they are disembarked. It was such a superb spoof of the whole situation that an airline (Pan Am) bought the skit to show to its stewardesses as a training film.

There's an element of catharsis here. 'Isn't comedy really a sort of kick in the behind of anything that gets a little irritating?' said Wayne. 'It's a harmless way of playing Robin Hood.' One could claim that 'playing Robin Hood' was really an effort to pander to the prejudices of the masses out there in TV-land, by stroking their collective ego and ridiculing their betters. It's more appropriate, though, to see this as an attempt to express in comic form the mythology of democracy, to celebrate the common sense of the people by laying bare the foibles and sins of the self-declared élite as well as the absurdities of modern life. Whatever the answer, it all served very nicely to cement that sense of community between performer and viewer that was so essential to effective variety.[45]

Wayne and Shuster had reached the top of their profession by the early 1960s. One sign of that was their yearly income: *The Toronto Daily Star* (23 March 1963) estimated this at $70,000 a piece, making them the highest-paid performers on Canadian television, ahead of such other stars as Pierre Berton and Gordon Sinclair (at $60,000), Juliette ($50,000), and Kate Reid ($30,000). Another sign was the acclaim they received at home and abroad. Their shows on CBC-TV amounted to specials, better yet comedy spectaculars, cherished by hundreds of thousands of viewers as highlights of a season. In the 1964/5 season they did six episodes of the 'Show of the Week,' each entitled 'An Affectionate Look at ...,' which treated the styles of different comedians such as George Burns, Jack Benny, Abbott and Costello, and the Marx Brothers, a collection later sold to CBS. That was hardly unexpected. Late in 1962, the *CBC Times* had noted that Wayne and Shuster were under contract to CBC, Ed Sullivan, and the BBC, and that their show had appeared on Australian television. During 1965 they finally achieved what the BBC's *Radio Times* called 'a long-overdue triumph in Europe': the Silver Rose award at the Montreux Television Festival for the world's best variety show, because of a special bilingual program that featured their version of *Cyrano de Bergerac*. Even so, the proof of international fame didn't draw the two men away to richer pastures elsewhere. Their roots, so they said, were in Canada. 'We're really homebodies at heart,' mused Wayne, 'and as long as we can keep working in Toronto we'll make our homes here.' What could be more natural than that these very Canadian comics would become part of the grand patriotic build-up to the country's forthcoming centennial celebrations in 1967?[46]

On the Wane

By now it should be clear that something important is missing from this account: rock 'n' roll. Primetime television paid only slight homage to the new musical explosion, and even less to the spirit of iconoclasm among youth that the popularity of rock evidenced as well as encouraged. During the late 1950s the sudden eruption of rock 'n' roll had created a generation gap of its own: youth found its own kind of music geared to such singers as Elvis Presley and Buddy Holly, while adults stuck with traditional pop singers, such as Perry Como and Dinah Shore. Rock 'n' roll stars did perform on evening TV, of course: Elvis made his debut in January 1956 on 'Stage Show,' appeared in June on 'The Milton Berle Show,' complete with a bevy of screaming teenage girls, and conquered America on 'The Ed Sullivan Show' in September. Years later an appearance on the same show would lead to a similar conquest, this time by the Beatles. But, on the whole, the networks opted to stick with the adult audience, at least most of the time, in part because that was the audience important to advertisers – though also because few of the programmers and producers had much liking for the new music.

Some rock did creep into made-in-Canada variety. 'Cross-Canada Hit Parade' could hardly avoid catering to the new teen craze. On 29 February 1956, for example, Bill Haley and His Comets performed both 'Rock around the Clock' and 'See You Later, Alligator,' to rave reviews from the teen audience – but at the cost of turning off adults. Little wonder that in September 1957 the two co-producers, Drew Crossan and Stan Harris, emphasized that the show wouldn't become 'a rock 'n' roll runaway.' And they added that Elvis's numbers were very hard to handle because they didn't lend themselves to a visual presentation. All that twitching and groaning and swaying just didn't look right.[47]

In fact variety producers seemed to become increasingly hostile to any presentation of rock 'n' roll. There appeared to be a war on: television variety might offer a cleaned-up version of teen hits but it would neglect the hard-core rock. The rebellious world of youth was one realm of fantasy primetime television wasn't going to highlight. In 1958 Len Casey of 'Show-time' emphasized that his show would only present familiar music, and 'in a dignified way.' In 1960 Norm Sedawie of 'Hit Parade' told the CBC *Times* that he'd cut down on rock, and was frankly surprised (and it seems pleased) that there were so few complaints. According to the critic Jon Ruddy, 'The Tommy Ambrose Show' (Fall '61 to Summer '63) failed in part because Ambrose couldn't overcome the generation gap: his cleaned-up youth music didn't produce 'many squeals from the squirm set' but his 'finger-snapping, twitchy delivery' upset some adults. As late as 1965 Maurice Dubois, producer of the new 'Lucille Dumont,' emphasized that the show would offer only the best in popular music, meaning some songs made famous by teen idols but no 'yé-yé' music. Even CTV's 'A Go-Go '66' was led by a house band, Robbie Lane and His Disciples, who were featured in jackets and ties, with neat hair. Lane supposedly had a style 'which bridges [the] rock 'n' roll and crooner eras.'[48]

The failure to deliver a brand of variety appealing to youth and adults was a sign of more serious troubles with these genres. Critics, sponsors, the CBC, and even viewers were becoming disenchanted with variety by the early 1960s. It wasn't just that ratings were beginning to lag. New talent, new ideas, to renew the appeal of variety were getting scarce.[49]

Variety by no means disappeared from the primetime schedule. The pool of talent was sufficiently large in the United States to produce a new generation of hit variety shows, although not on the scale of times past. The American networks retired such antiques as Jackie Gleason (1970), Ed Sullivan (1971), and Red Skelton (1971), whose appeal was more and more skewed to an aging section of the populace. But they had already or would come up with such replacements as Dean Martin, briefly the Smothers Brothers, the pop-country singer Glen Campbell, Dan Rowan and Dick Martin, Carol Burnett, Flip Wilson, eventually Sonny and Cher Bono. Some of these newcomers turned up on English-Canadian television. In the 1969/70 season, for example, CTV was offering Carol Burnett, Glen Campbell, Tom Jones, Dean Martin, and Andy Williams; CBC gave us Rowan and Martin, in addition to old-timers Red Skelton and Ed Sullivan.

The picture was much more grim for made-in-Canada variety, though. Radio-Canada had nearly given up: a breakdown of the Spring '68 schedule found that the network had programmed only a little over one hour of 'variety and music hall' and about four hours of 'popular and dance music' a week (and this last would shortly drop away when 'Jeunesse oblige' disappeared from the schedule). At that time, all the CTV network offered was 'Country Music Hall,' 'It's Happening,' and the new English folk-song program 'Pig & Whistle' – two years later only 'Pig & Whistle' survived. That left CBC's English service, the source of so many efforts to sponsor a home-grown PopCult.[50]

By the mid-1960s CBC Toronto was engaged in a general kind of house-cleaning to retire or spruce up or replace existing shows and stars. 'Showbiz' variety was the first to suffer. In August 1963, just prior to the new season, *Maclean's* (24 August 1963) published a funny little cartoon of five once big-name stars of variety – Sylvia Murphy, Wally Koster, Joyce Sullivan, Tommy Ambrose, and Joyce Hahn – all in rags, lining up outside a soup kitchen. Apparently Hahn was confined to club work, Murphy hadn't done any TV in a year and a half, Sullivan was fast forgetting what the camera looked like, and Koster had become philosophical about his loss of fame and income. The next spring, *The Toronto Daily Star* (13 May 1964) commented on the death of 'Parade,' apparently part of the cut-back in variety, and noted that its producer Norman Sedawie was off to the United States.

Efforts to rehabilitate two of the staples of 'old-fashioned' variety weren't any more happy. The slipping appeal of 'Country Hoedown' wasn't slowed by the addition of better sets and sophisticated sketches, both of which made the regulars uneasy because the innovations ill-suited the show's temper. What replaced it in Fall '65 was 'The Tommy Hunter Show,' a more youthful style of program that producers (to the horror of the star) would strive to push in the direction of 'showbiz.' Then there was 'Juliette': in 1965/6 the CBC finally put up more money, and Juliette began to dress a bit more daringly, to make the show seem trendy and swinging. The results didn't satisfy because the CBC's own 'enjoyment index' indicated that 'Juliette' had lost its excitement. What replaced it, very briefly, in Fall '66 was 'A World of Music,' an international folk-song showcase starring two newcomers, Joso Spraljia and Malka Himel. This show was a disaster. The audience inherited from hockey didn't understand or like all the foreign songs. The producer and Barris, one of the creators of the show, desperately struggled to anglicize and to jazz up the showcase, with Irish or English songs, more dancing, once go-go girls. To no avail. The thirteen-week contract for 'A World of Music' wasn't renewed. Ironically, the very search for sophistication and novelty, in a word, trendiness, was bound to upset traditional-minded audiences who preferred shows that were simple, sincere, and familiar.[51]

That lesson hit home when CBC management had the temerity to cancel 'Don Messer's Jubilee' in mid-April 1969. Although still high up in the rankings of CBC shows, it was retired to give air time to something fresher, a program offering 'a younger look and a younger orientation,' which turned out to be 'Singalong Jubilee.' Well, that provoked a public explosion comparable to the furore caused by the cancellation of 'This Hour Has Seven Days' a few years earlier, although this time the alienated constituency was 'square' Canada. There were angry letters to the editor, special newspaper ads, denunciations sent off to MPs and the CBC, demonstrations (one with fiddlers and square dancers) on Parliament Hill, comment in the House of Commons and the New Brunswick legislature. By the end of May, the CBC itself had received nearly 1,500 protest calls, over 8,000 upset letters and petitions, and around 13,000 additional pieces of mail, mostly a large collection of protest coupons that had been published in the newspapers.

Editors and columnists across the nation had a field-day with the issue (nothing like seeing a rival squirm), though newspapers in the Maritimes in particular were very angry at the CBC. John Diefenbaker spoke out in the Commons, wondering why Don Messer was canned when 'the Black Panthers and the like apparently have an inside track with the CBC.' A protest coupon in the Sudbury *Star* (3 May 1969) carried the suggestion that the whole affair was part of a general plot to replace the old ways, the Canadian ways, with 'sex and violence.' Letters made clear that irate fans saw the cancellation as a slap in the face: a victory for the long-haired, immoral, trendy types whose style of life seemed so alien, if not obscene. Just as in the case of 'Seven Days,' however, CBC management refused to budge, an understandable decision, even though the cancellation had been a serious mistake in judgment. Knowlton Nash recalled much later that programmer Doug Nixon had announced grimly that he was 'determined to "kill the geriatric fiddlers." ' The final irony was that Don Messer did return to the airwaves in the fall via the independent Hamilton station, CHCH-TV.[52]

All the upset CBC-Toronto caused was hardly justified by later events. 'Singalong Jubilee,' once praised for its 'sunny simplicity,' may have been popular but it never approached the importance of Don Messer. The only solid hit was 'The Tommy Hunter Show,' which was eventually expanded to an hour and lasted into the 1980s. Most other ventures were short-lived, and hardly memorable.[53]

But it's hard to lay much of the blame at the feet of the CBC. The trouble with variety was rooted in the nature of television entertainment. Weekly appearances often exhausted both the talent and the viewer. More serious was what amounts to radio's revenge: private radio had become the champion of all the various brands of popular music in a way in which television could not. The very success of radio further fragmented musical tastes, and that made it increasingly difficult to craft a TV show that would have any chance of reaching everyman and everywoman. Besides the fact that the genres of variety lacked something – a problem, conflict, the suspense of drama that could hold viewer attention – hurt in the end. Audience tests had shown that viewers liked their variety to have some sort of a story or a theme. The lack of drama may not have mattered very much during the 1950s when the audience was still attuned to the ways of radio. It did matter later when programmers and viewers had discovered just how appealing storytelling, and especially series drama, really was. Display alone just wasn't sufficient any more.[54]

Focus: The Wayne and Shuster Hour

The camera opens on a stage occupied by a small, well-dressed man. He sports a brief, neat moustache, wears a suit with vest and tails and a bow-tie, and stands with his hands behind his back. While the orchestra plays some stirring introductory music, the man waits patiently until the clapping of the audience dies down. He raises his head slightly. His whole appearance and his jaunty manner suggest a man in command of the situation. That impression is confirmed by how he speaks: he announces, using a cultivated English accent, each word clearly enunciated, 'Ladies and Gentlemen, we proudly present the stars of our show: Mr Wayne and Mr Shuster.'

All the signs indicated that the announcer is a man of some quality. While he talks, the camera slowly moves in for a close-up of his face. You have the feeling that something will happen after this kind of a build-up. And it does. Just as he finishes, someone off-stage flings a pie at his head, which splatters the top portion of his face plus his nose. That's the gimmick, designed to grab the attention of the viewer. The studio audience, of course, bursts into laughter. The orchestra plays a little melody, which sounds a bit like laughter as well. The camera lingers on the face of the poor man, who now looks mildly disgusted, unable to do anything about his plight except raise his eyes towards heaven. How conventional: the pie-in-the-face was a cliché of slapstick, often used to ridicule the pompous. It still worked to provoke mirth, though. The little number nicely set the tone for the next hour of entertainment on 'The Wayne and Shuster Hour' of 11 March 1962.

The mockery of pretension was common to the three comedy sketches presented by the two comedians. It was most pronounced in the opening routine, which spoofed the high arts and praised the common taste.

Situation

A bare stage with a back-drop of a brick wall and two doors. Most of the action occurs on the stage, often with people moving on and off. Once the camera swings away to another scene before returning to the main stage. Wayne and Shuster sing the song, at times in unison, at times individually. The focus of attention is definitely upon the people in front of the camera.

Video

— **Wayne** and **Shuster** come out on to the stage dressed in tails with top hats, white gloves, and walking-sticks, in short looking very elegant.
— **Wayne** and **Shuster** shuffle and dance a comedy duet.
— **Wayne** takes off a white glove that is extra long.

— Camera switches to a scene portraying two Shakespearean actors engaged in a love scene, reminiscent of Romeo and Juliet,

Audio

[music and song]
They should erect a statue to the
  guy,
Who first thought of hitting
  someone with a pie.
Call it hokum, hoke, or what you
  will
It sure got a laugh and I'm
  laughing still.
And nothing sounds quite as
  glorious
As a laugh that's real uproarious.
[Laughter mixed with musical whirl-
ing sound]
Give them brilliant displays of
Shakespearean plays,
You'll get notices but you'll go
  broke.

the man kneeling and kissing the woman's hand, then taking her into his arms – at which point she bends backwards, her blonde wig falls off. Camera shifts to Shuster, upon whose head falls the wig.

...

– Camera focuses on two operatic singers who swiftly move from their song (in mime) to squirting each other with soda.

Give them something funny,
You'll be in the money.
You've got to give the people hoke!
[Laughter]

...

Throw away that toga [Laughter]
Belt them with a soda.
That would be a master stroke.

On it went into something called 'Cross-Canada Hoke Parade' (a play on the title of the late 'Cross-Canada Hit Parade'), which was a series of mime acts, full of exaggerated motions reminiscent of slapstick, portraying a chicken-hearted bullfighter, a graduating ceremony at a wrestling school, a bungled execution, at the end of which both Wayne and Shuster are hit in the face with pies. The routine concluded with Wayne and Shuster, backed by a company of dancers and singers, telling everyone, 'You gotta give the people, the ticket-buying people, you gotta give the people hoke,' (see frame 6.1).

The butt of this good-natured humour was not Shakespeare et al. but the snobbery of the artsy few. Convention might decree that only the High Arts deserved display. But what really counted was serving up something ordinary people could enjoy. That was the route to success.

The next sketch, 'The Story of a Dedicated Garage Mechanic,' took on a much more popular target, namely the hit doctor's saga 'Ben Casey,' which had premièred during the 1961/2 season. 'Ben Casey' was a solemn exercise in hero-worship, idealizing the doctor as an intense professional almost totally committed to the war against disease. That was the target of Wayne and Shuster. They were taking to task the grand myth of the expert-as-hero, the man (for it was rarely a woman) whose training and ethics and devotion made him the new-found leader of modern society.

Instead of a hospital though, all the action took place in a garage, a most incongruous location given the reputation of mechanics for fast dealing. Mr Zorber (Shuster) was the veteran owner of the garage, ever ready to spout some sort of wisdom, while Sam Casey (Wayne) was the youthful, dedicated mechanic who could perform 'miracles.'

Frame 6.1 The highbrows

Well, he was called upon to perform a miracle: in a scene reeking of the sexism that characterized this genre, a Mrs Hannigan pleaded successfully (complete with tears) for the quick repair of a beaten-up car (else how will she face her husband?) that actually required four days' work (see frame 6.2). The stage was set for the car doctors to go to work.

Situation

The inside of a cluttered garage with a car waiting to be repaired. Wayne and Shuster appear as the experts in white smocks.

Video	Audio
– **Wayne** and **Shuster** in discussion.	**Zorber**: How many times have I told you never to become involved with a customer? **Casey**: Mr Zorber.

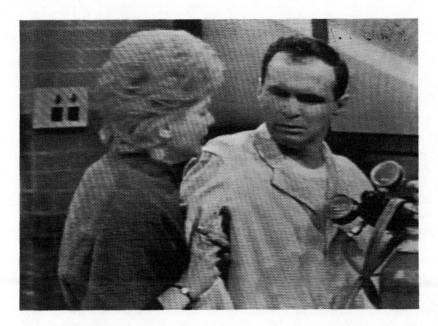

Frame 6.2 Pleading for help

— Mocking the doctors: **Wayne** and **Shuster** wash their hands at a sink in preparation for the operation to come.

Zorber: You know it'll take four days.
Casey: I think by working all out, all out [emphasized], I can have that car ready tomorrow afternoon.
Zorber: And what if you fail Sam Casey, what if you fail? [heavily exaggerated]
Casey: If I fail? Well, like we used to say at the Edsel factory, you can't win them all. [Laughter] Shall we go?
Zorber: You're a strange young man, Sam Casey, a strange young man. Some day I'd like to find out what makes you tick.
Casey: I wish you would. The noise is driving me crazy

[laughter], just like cabbage. Well, will you assist me?

Zorber: I will.

Casey: Thank you.

Zorber: All right.

Casey: I'm all set.

Zorber: Good.

– At this point the camera swings to the car's engine and the garage turns into an operating room. **Wayne** wears rubber gloves, a side table bearing an assortment of tools is wheeled over, and a special machine arrives with dials (presumably to check the car's condition?).

Casey: Gus, Charley. Let's go. I want lots of distilled water and plenty of paper towels.

Voice: All right, Sam. [Uplifting music and laughter]

Casey: I'm going to start by removing the carburetor.

The experts do their job, completing the repairs on time. But then fate intervenes: Mrs Hannigan crashes the car into the garage door – and poor Mr Zorber. Sam Casey closes off by making a telephone call to Ben Casey!

The final and longest sketch, entitled 'The Gypsy Student,' was based on the famous operetta *The Student Prince*. The satire told the story of how young Prince Rudolph (Wayne) was called away by Baron Fritz Von Holstein (Shuster) from his carefree life at the University of Lowdelberg to take over the small kingdom of Dipsomania after the assassination of his grandfather by terrorists. What confused the plot was a case of mistaken identity – at one point Rudolph was thought to be a gipsy rather than a true heir. The plot allowed Wayne and Shuster to satirize romantic notions of Old Europe and university life, to play around with such weighty problems as the responsibilities of birth and the demands of duty, to poke fun at the stereotypes of gipsies and aristocrats. The ending, though, mocked Hollywood's version of history in which the hero so often seemed to emerge as the champion of democracy American-style (see frame 6.3).

Frame 6.3 Welcoming a golden future

Situation

The stage has become a court filled with people in costume. At the back on a raised platform is the throne.

Video	**Audio**
– **Wayne** stands forth, having removed his crown, to deliver a speech.	**Rudolph**: I hereby abdicate and declare this a gipsy republic. **Voice**: What? [Now begins some inspiring music] **Rudolph**: There are new winds of freedom blowing through Europe, and this country will be a neutral, non-committed nation, and we shall all be rich and never have to work again. **Baron**: But where are we going to get our money?

> **Rudolph**: Where do all the neutral,
> uncommitted nations get their
> money, booby? FROM AMERICA!
> **Group**: Yeah! [Laughter]
> [Music and theme song]
> Hail Dipsomania, we think you're
> grand.

Was there any message here? The whole skit made the point that all of the various characters, whatever their roles or airs, were no more than ordinary folks with the normal set of prejudices and hopes and weaknesses. Human nature, it seemed, was a constant even in the Old World.

It's tempting to find something very Canadian about the comedy of Wayne and Shuster. Their satire was good-natured, not biting or controversial as in the case of Britain's 'That Was the Week That Was' or America's 'Smothers Brothers,' because a sunny disposition seemed to suit a land like Canada where the problems were more mundane, the social climate more calm. The particular targets Wayne and Shuster selected were all products of imported culture, whether from the High Arts or Hollywood – was that an expression of the hidden resentments of a rather satisfied colony? The underlying theme, the mockery of pretension, suited one perception of the national character that portrayed Canadians as a retiring, practical, unassuming people whom geography had forced to live next to the arrogant Americans.

But there was another intriguing attribute of Wayne and Shuster's style, an attribute that was both more particular and more universal than any Canadian flavour. Jerry Goodis, a Canadian advertising executive, talked in his reminiscences about what he called 'Yiddish humour,' characterized by 'a bittersweet ring, a quality of world-weariness and self-denigration,' a sensitivity to 'locale' and 'atmosphere,' and 'a sense of social realism,' which grew out of the peculiar Jewish experience in the Old and the New worlds. He was trying to describe his own brand of advertising, of course. But he could just as easily have been referring to Wayne and Shuster's brand of comedy. Their parody, their repartee, had about it a faintly cynical quality, a self-deprecating tone, a respect for learning and for human weakness, a sensitivity to detail that gave their skits an authenticity no matter what they spoofed. This Jewishness may well have been one of the major reasons that Wayne and Shuster played so well in the United States.[55]

7

In Gameland

The winters of my childhood were long, long seasons. We lived in three places – the school, the church and the skating-rink. Real battles were won on the skating-rink. Real strength appeared on the skating-rink. The real leaders showed themselves on the skating-rink. School was a sort of punishment ... As for church, we found there the tranquility of God: there we forgot school and dreamed about the next hockey game.

Roch Carrier, 'The Hockey Sweater'[1]

One brand of made-in-Canada entertainment really worked. The public's fascination with games, quizzes, and sports was probably greater in Canada than in the United States. Certainly the Canadian networks offered more of this fare in peak viewing times than did their American counterparts (see chart 7.1). One of the CBC's first panel shows, 'Fighting Words,' a game of wit and words for highbrows, lasted throughout the 1950s. The less erudite 'Front Page Challenge,' born in the Summer '57, would make new stars out of such regulars as Gordon Sinclair, Pierre Berton, and Fred Davis – and it would survive into the 1980s. For its part Radio-Canada manufactured a series of game shows for the masses. One such, 'La poule aux oeufs d'or,' so captured the fancy of viewers with its speedy quizzes and award of a huge egg to winners that it took first place in the ratings a few months after its arrival. Then there was the world of sports. A report in 1957 claimed that the women of Quebec were in love with 'La lutte,' the Wednesday-night wrestling show. But nothing could compare with the astounding pull of Saturday's 'Hockey Night in Canada/La soirée du

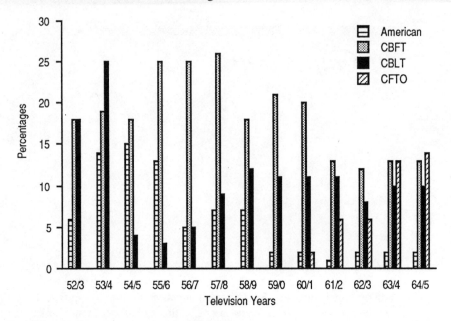

Chart 7.1 Mid-evening contests, 1952–65
Note: The chart incorporates data from the fall schedules of the American
networks as well as the full-year schedules of the Canadian networks. Mid-
evening refers to peak-time viewing, from 8:00 to 10:00 PM.

hockey,' which often ended up near the top of the rankings in the winter
months. Not only was hockey consistently more popular than any other
made-in-Canada show; it was also the one offering that could on occasion
beat out the American imports in English Canada. Perhaps Roch Carrier's
reminiscences of his boyhood expressed a much wider truth about the
culture of the land.[2]

The Contest

The contest involves a test, if not a conflict, in which individuals or teams
seek to best each other, whether in guessing answers, running and passing,
skating and shooting, or whatever, thereby demonstrating superiority.
Uncertainties are exploited and resolved, cleanly, in a fashion usually
impossible in other areas of life. On television, at least, the contest nearly
always contains attributes of the other kinds of play. The football match
or the quiz, for instance, is a display: the personalities, the talents, often

even the looks, of the participants are all part of the spectacle. Sportscasts, it has been argued, are one of the few legitimate ways in which the male body can be publicly displayed. Similarly, the spectacle may take on the shape of drama, complete with a beginning, a middle, and an end, and an assortment of heroes, villains, and victims. What gives the contest its special character, though, is the fact that it occurs in a particular site (be that the studio or the stadium) and consumes a set span of time (be that four minutes or a half-hour or three periods), that it is regulated by rules and by a moderator or referees, and above all that it has a clear-cut purpose: winning.

Part of the appeal lies in the unpredictability and the excitement of the contest, the fact that it seems unscripted, spontaneous, real. Hence the feeling of betrayal when viewers learned during the quiz scandals of the late 1950s that such popular American shows as 'Twenty-One' and 'The $64,000 Question' were fixed. The outrage also reflected the fact that viewers had identified with the people who'd won big prizes, supposedly through their easy command of some kind of knowledge. Indeed this process of identification appears crucial to the success of the contest. That may amount to a kind of 'vicarious participation' in which the viewer 'becomes' one of the players on the basis of race, language, age, a shared college or locale, looks, etc. Young people are particularly prone to identify with one or another star in their favourite sport. But much more common is the conversion of a contestant or a team into the representative of a much wider group of people. Charles Van Doren, when he was the unsullied hero of 'Twenty-One,' captured the fancy of viewers as an ideal example of American youth at its intellectual best. The victory of an individual or a team in some kind of international meet, say the Olympics, honours the nation represented as well. Winning proves the virtue of the fans and the athletes.[3]

The games people enjoy tell us something about their ways and their values. 'Games are situations contrived to permit simultaneous participation of many people in some significant pattern of their own corporate lives,' Marshall McLuhan quipped. That may explain why legions of social critics have zealously studied bullfighting, baseball, wrestling, or popular radio and television quizzes. They search for the special meaning of these contests, what they show about the culture of the place and the time. Obviously the contest embodies that spirit of competition considered well-nigh universal among human societies. But often it also embodies the spirit of co-operation, a group acting in concert to achieve a common goal. The usual confusion of life, as Roger Callois has pointed out, is replaced by a near-perfect situation in which the merit of the contestants is given equal opportunity to show its stuff. Presumably that satisfies a yearning for an ideal world in which fame is the result of skill rather than birth, class, race, or sex. The avid interest of fans in the statistics of winning – what is the batting average of this or that baseball player? – is seen by John Fiske and John Hartley as evidence of the modern fascination with ranking people according to some sort of hierarchy of skill. Beyond that, a contest can be taken as a symbolic representation of such assorted aspects of normal life as personal and family rivalries, sometimes of capitalism, and even of war itself. A disgruntled Bill Lewis, for instance, has argued that the game shows on British television confirm the (misleading?) myth that ordinary folks could win in Britain's competitive democracy. Louis Zurcher and Arnold Meadow found in bullfighting and baseball a reflection of the different kinds of tensions generated within the Mexican and American families. Michael Real discovered that American football, and notably the Super Bowl, was really about winning property. Michael Novak, by contrast, baldly declared that American football was his 'moral equivalent of war.' In short there's a lot of room for speculation in this 'game' of pinning down the meaning of a contest.[4]

Games and Quizzes

In retrospect the success with games and quizzes might seem surprising, given the disdain for this brand of programming common within the CBC. 'Regarded purely as time-killers there will no doubt always be an audience for them,' noted D.C. McArthur, the chairman of an appraisal panel in Ottawa, in 1958, 'provided that they are lively and have some degree of originality.' In fact that most original of shows, 'Fighting Words,' was repeatedly threatened with death during a run of nearly ten years, only to be saved by the outcry of viewers. Even then the show was bounced around the schedule a lot, once out of primetime, to make way for better-favoured programs. That treatment proved, to the satisfaction of the *Telegram*'s critic, Ron Poulton, that there were times 'when the CBC and the average viewer are no closer than this revolving clinker is to Mars.'[5]

All networks, the CBC included, offered games and quizzes because they were cheap, easy to design and to produce, and quick to prove their popularity (or lack thereof). This was radiovision. Visuals didn't matter that much. The key was to find the right gimmick – and the right mix of personalities. There were plenty of failures, of course. 'Face the Music' (Fall '57) didn't work, even though Wayne and Shuster were on the panel.

'QED' (Spring–Summer '61), an independent effort to fashion an updated 'Fighting Words' for CFTO-Toronto, couldn't replicate the magic of the original. Even something so apparently imaginative, so right for the times, as 'The Superior Sex' (Summer '61) flopped. It had tried to exploit the battle of the sexes by setting a team of four men against four women in tests of knowledge and skill. The Toronto critics panned the show because it showed too many people engaged in too much activity. Management agreed, though Alphonse Ouimet admitted he rather liked the idea behind the program. No gimmick could guarantee success.[6]

The standard CBC offering was the panel quiz that tested contestants' knowledge about something or other (see chart 7.2). In a way the genre celebrated the value of information, and to a lesser extent intelligence, in modern life. Paradoxically, it often also trivialized the importance of information. The quiz-show format was even reminiscent of the classroom, as Bob Hodge and David Tripp, two Australian semioticians, have pointed out, what with a teacher (the quiz-master) and pupils (the contestants), various assignments (questions or riddles), and the awarding of grades (points and prizes for guessing right). Unlike other genres, the panel shows were especially wholesome, good viewing for adults if not the whole family. There might be humour, there certainly had to be some entertainment, but nobody acted weirdly, prizes were modest, the purpose almost serious. And the expenses of getting together a group of talking heads were minimal: panelists on 'Cléopatrie,' for example, received $50 in March 1956. That was a crucial concern for cost-conscious managers.[7]

The grandfather of this genre was the long-time American favourite 'What's My Line' (1950–75), which occasionally turned up on Canadian networks, where a panel attempted to guess the occupation of a guest challenger. It allowed viewers to share in 'the gay nightlife of New York,' mused *Saturday Night*'s Mary Ross who was most interested in the characters of the regular panelists. 'Cléopâtre' (at first 'Le nez de Cléopâtre') was based on the old parlour game 'twenty questions,' where a panel was required to guess a person or object from a riddle plus assorted hints and answers. 'Chacun son métier' was Radio-Canada's version of 'What's My Line.' 'Fighting Words' tested the ability of a guest panel to identify the author of a famous quotation and then to argue over its substance – it was all reminiscent of the after-dinner discussion among a group of intellectuals. 'Front Page Challenge' had the panel guess a major newspaper story of the past, represented by a guest challenger (sometimes hidden from the panel) who was questioned about the story, his or her life, whatever pleased the panelists. Toronto critic Dennis Braithwaite thought that 'FPC' pre-

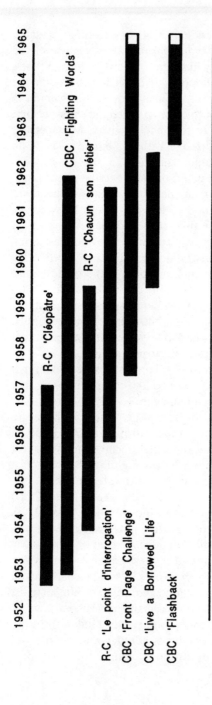

Chart 7.2 A sample of made-in-Canada panel shows
Note: The dates are approximate, indicating the season (Spring, Summer, or Fall) in which a show commenced or ended on the schedule of one of the Canadian networks. Shows which continued beyond the end of 1964 are indicated by an unfilled block.

sented 'the image of a sharp, sophisticated, tough, knowing, and terribly modern Johnny Canuck, who still manages to be a nice guy.' Viewers enjoyed the hard questioning of celebrities, especially the big names from New York and Hollywood, because it boosted our collective egos, proved we weren't just hicks, showed the clay feet of our idols. Much the same format was used on 'Live a Borrowed Life,' which had a guest challenger assume the identity of a well-known figure (such as Richard III, the boxer Sugar Ray Robinson, or Brahms). Likewise 'Flashback,' called 'Back Page Challenge' by one wit, which focused on fads and people and objects from the past. Or one of the failures, CTV's 'Nicknames of Fame' (Summer '61), though its panel had to identify phrases and events as well, using nicknames as a guide. 'Front Page Challenge' had given birth to a series of children.[8]

The actual importance of the game element seems to vary considerably. Nearly all panel shows contained some of the paraphernalia of the game: a time-limit on the guessing, hints (at first 'Fighting Words' gave three cartoon clues per quotation), a game bell, rules of conduct (the panelists on 'Front Page Challenge' weren't supposed to look at a mystery challenger), a moderator to ensure every panelist had a fair chance to get the answer. None of the panel shows was scripted (a rule eventually enshrined in broadcasting regulations), although guest panelists might be coached on how to perform or assisted with prepared questions. People were encouraged to send in suggestions regarding topics, questions, quotations, or challengers, earning a modest prize if the suggestion was selected and sometimes a bit more if the panel was stumped, which encouraged the illusion of audience participation. The emphasis in 'Cléopâtre' was clearly on game-playing where the host Roger Duhamel moved the panel rapidly through its paces. In contrast the short-lived 'One of a Kind' (Summer '58 to Summer '59) relied heavily on the by-play among host Alex Barris and his panelists. The more interesting aspect of 'Fighting Words' and eventually 'Front Page Challenge' was clearly the post-game discussion or interview. Indeed, in the fall of 1959 'Fighting Words' experimented with an occasional 'conversation in depth,' a one-on-one discussion between host Nathan Cohen and a famous guest to explore a viewpoint or an idea. Many people tuned in to see who would guess the answer, whether someone would make a gaff, just who was the better wordsmith or wit that night. At its best, for example, 'Fighting Words' promised 'a verbal explosion,' a heated exchange of views to enliven an evening's viewing. There was a competitive angle to any debate, at least from the viewer's perspective.[9]

Most of the panel shows dealt only, or usually, in the trivial. Two of the riddles put to the panel on an early 'Le nez de Cléopâtre' were about the arrival of springtime and Gulliver's travels. A panel of experts on 'Le point d'interrogation' tried to guess the name of a city from a photograph. Paul Soles, the moderator of 'Flashback,' told a reporter that what his show aimed to create was 'a pleasant sense of nostalgia.'[10]

Even so, in English Canada at least, the shows could be billed as a learning experience. What set 'Fighting Words' apart from the rest of entertainment was that it tackled weighty issues of ethics and morality, politics, or the arts. In 1960, Len Starmer, then a supervising producer of light entertainment, suggested that a viewer could salve a guilty conscience about slacking off by watching 'Live a Borrowed Life' – it was educational. Five years later, Bob Blackburn termed 'Front Page Challenge' 'the most successful of all attempts to combine a modicum of information and social stimulation with entertainment.'[11]

A good part of the appeal of any panel quiz, though, lay in the personalities it featured. The choice of moderator was of crucial importance in setting the tone of the show. That person was always a 'he': once more, male authority was on display. The ideal moderator needed a commanding presence, an unobtrusive manner, and a quick wit, quite a collection of virtues that only a male (given the times) might claim. He had to sanction the worth of the game and of the contestants, ensure that the game appeared fair, try to keep the pace going and the action stimulating, handle the unexpected, charm guests and viewers – but never dominate the game or the discussion. A tall order indeed, and only a few moderators ever seemed adequate. Much of the success of 'Fighting Words' was credited to the 'Buddha-like presence' of moderator Nathan Cohen, also a drama critic and entertainment editor at The Toronto Daily Star, who had a marvellous knack of asking just the right question to fan the flames of argument and of knowing just when a discussion had exhausted its potential. Although his persona wasn't so crucial to the success of 'Front Page Challenge,' Fred Davis (sometimes called 'Mr Nice Guy') had a 'class' image – he was handsome, mature, urbane, charming, and oh so proper – not only a contrast to some of the other males on the panel, but a man able to command the respect of the assortment of participants. By contrast Alex Barris, host of 'One of a Kind,' came in for much blame from CBC appraisers because he lacked both intellectual and personal substance: he failed to control the panel, he hogged air time, he was too coy, too trivial, too gushing, and so on. And while a more forceful moderator, Charles Templeton of 'Live a Borrowed Life' was initially criticized as too wooden by one critic and too glib and unctious by one appraiser. It was hard to please some people.[12]

The choice of panelists was no less important. Ordinary folks wouldn't do. The need was to find personalities who were both interesting and entertaining. The panelists for a light show such as 'One of a Kind' were selected not because they were bright or good guessers, but because they were charming, witty, and attractive. The particular style of 'Fighting Words' required a panel of talkative, opinionated intellectuals who were drawn from the ranks of professionals, journalists and critics, and artists. Although this highbrow show never had a permanent panel, it did boast a number of regulars: among others, the over-confident Dr William E. Blatz, head of the Institute of Child Study; the fiesty author Morley Callaghan; the ever-poised Arnold Edinborough; and the articulate Rabbi Abraham Feinberg (complete with eye-patch). Gérard Pelletier, who turned up on many panels as a guest, was once described as fulfilling the necessary role of the logician. The two key personalities on the regular panel of 'Front Page Challenge' were the journalists Gordon Sinclair and Pierre Berton. Sinclair played out the role of the curmudgeon, 'the perpetual Peck's bad boy,' claimed Montreal critic Pat Pearce, who was expected to inject vitality into a show with his loud manners and eccentric views. He could be very controversial: once he asked swimmer Elaine Tanner whether she swam while menstruating, a question that provoked a flurry of complaints and even elicited an apology from CBC president George Davidson. Berton was the aloof inquisitor, the very epitome of a hard-nosed reporter, who tracked down a story and grilled a victim with a cold zeal. What such people offered was a well-defined persona that could capture the fancy of the viewer, even the viewer who might find the particular individual unpleasant.[13]

Producers apparently had a special difficulty finding women who would fill the bill. Frank Tumpane claimed that 'Fighting Words' carried on a 'futile search for a woman, versatile enough, articulate enough and charming enough to burst into the inner circle of regulars.' Perhaps he was too harsh: other observers did note that the eccentric and candid Charlotte Whitton (sometime mayor of Ottawa) was an effective panelist. 'Front Page Challenge' avoided the problem by going for beauty not brains: the bubbly actress Toby Robins looked very good on television, adding a touch of glamour to the regular panel, though her grasp of the news, past or present, was slight. When 'One of a Kind' tried a similar tactic with actress Kathi McNeil, however, CBC appraisers found her too coy, too fluffy. Robins's replacement, Betty Kennedy, was very much the 'nice lady,' well-dressed, polite, courteous, friendly, an embodiment of a different kind of female charm. Women were needed to balance the panels: how else could a show hope to win over female viewers? Usually circumstances didn't require that these women demonstrate quite the same intellectual skills as their male partners. Their presence signified the crucial but supplementary role of women in the world of work. Women were there for decoration, for variety, for contrast; men, as the masters of fact and argument.[14]

Selecting the right guest was one of the best ways to inject a bit of novelty into any of these quizzes. That, too, wasn't always easy. Apparently 'Fighting Words' avoided most newspaper and showbiz people, as well as professors in the social sciences. The regular panelists on 'Front Page Challenge' had difficulties handling comedians (a fear of mockery?) and sports stars (in whom they had little interest). The producer of 'Flashback' decided older people weren't suitable: 'They just couldn't be light and frothy ... and this is a fun show.' Jim Guthrie, producer of 'Live a Borrowed Life,' got into hot water because he invited George Rolland, a known exponent of white supremacy, to impersonate Abraham Lincoln, 'to add a touch of controversy.' 'Fighting Words' sometimes invited a bunch of newcomers whose talents at debate were unknown; at other times, the show went after celebrities in politics, the arts, and the sciences. Early on, 'Front Page Challenge' made a point of bringing in big-name Americans: journalists such as David Brinkley, Drew Pearson, and Mike Wallace served on the panel, while celebrities such as Eleanor Roosevelt, Don Ameche, and Boris Karloff were challengers. Their appearance gave the quiz publicity and heightened viewer expectations about who might be on that night. In short the quiz was plugged into those worlds of journalism, showbiz, and celebrity that so enthralled the audience.[15]

Radio-Canada's forté was the novelty or fun show. This brand could take the innocuous shape of a word game ('Au carrefour des mots,' Fall '52 to Fall '53), charades ('La clef des champs,' Fall '55 to Fall '59, and 'Au voleur,' Summer '63), a jigsaw puzzle ('Casse-tête,' Summer '62), or a dance contest ('Le club des autographes,' Fall '57 to Summer '62). 'Le millionaire,' one imaginative summer show in 1965, gave a person $2,500 and twenty minutes to convince a merchant in a small town to deliver goods to a hotel. 'La clef des champs' was as much comedy-variety as a game show, since the antics of the competing teams of actors were supposed to provoke laughter. Similarly 'Le club des autographes' mixed instruction, song and dance, celebrity, and games, all in a night-club setting, to win the viewer's fancy. At times it was difficult to tell that any contest was involved.[16]

Then there were the shows where contestants played the fool for the pleasure of viewers, usually meaning that an ordinary person tried to test his or her skill at a silly game of some sort. Such a show teetered on the edge of bad taste. There was every chance that the contest would become an exercise in humiliation. This genre had its origin on American radio in the 1940s. One of the first of these shows on television was CBS's 'Beat the Clock' (Spring '50 to Spring '58), which had contestants try to complete some strange stunt (involving anything from fishing poles and weiners to custard pies and balloons) before a large clock had counted off the time-limit. NBC's 'You Bet Your Life' (Fall '50 to Summer '61) featured comedian Groucho Marx, who carried out interviews and asked nonsense questions, usually with the purpose of ridiculing the contestants. 'Truth or Consequences' (first CBS, later NBC, intermittently from Fall '50 to Summer '58 in the evening time-slot) victimized contestants who had failed to answer a question by making them perform a stunt, often both funny and embarrassing. The most extraordinary example of this genre never reached evening television: 'Queen for a Day' (Spring '56 to Fall '64) required a contestant to evoke the sympathy of a studio audience with a sob story in order to win merchandise. By and large these shows didn't make it onto Canadian television (though CFTO-Toronto did run 'The Best of Groucho' in 1963/4). But the shows were watched by viewers close to the border ('You Bet Your Life' garnered 20 per cent of the Toronto audience on 16 March 1960, for example).[17]

There were a few Canadian examples of this genre, however. The first, called 'La rigolade' (Summer '55 to Fall '58), came from Radio-Canada and advertised itself as 'the least serious broadcast on the air.' Contestants often dressed up in assorted costumes and disguises to add to the fun and frolic of the occasion. The games they played were usually silly. Both winners and losers were awarded merchandise prizes. Witness the routine of one episode, apparently in the 1956/7 season: the emcee, Denis Drouin, assisted by an attractive Hélène Bédard, worked every scene for its laughs, complete with the occasional risqué joke. The first contest involved four married couples, a sexy blonde, and cameras: the wives were supposed to take pictures of the husbands embracing the blonde. The most enthusiastic embrace would win the couple a new television set. A second contest required the wives to guide their husbands via pulleys over plates of strawberries and plates of cream – the husbands were supposed to use their teeth to transfer the strawberries to the other plate. The third contest had two fully clothed men in tubs who were expected to scrub themselves clean. That was impossible because the water contained a substance that turned black when it foamed. In the excitement an assistant producer got himself into a tub. The audience howled. Viewers loved it all: an Elliott-Haynes survey of February 1957 found that 'La rigolade' was the top-ranked show on CBFT-Montreal and CHLT-Sherbrooke, reaching roughly three-quarters of the available audience. But critics thought it a very sad spectacle indeed, 'un sujet de scandale,' in the words of a writer in *Le Devoir*. That may well be one reason why the sponsor, Molson's Brewery, dropped the show after its third season.[18]

CBC-Toronto disdained the genre. Not so CTV, though: in the Fall '64, the private network introduced 'It's Your Move' and 'Double Your Money' to its primetime schedule. The first show was based on charades, involving two teams (husbands and wives played on opposing teams), simple phrases that were to be acted out ('See the plump lady indicate "girdle" '), and some kissing of the opposite spouse to add a bit of spice. That was milder than 'Double Your Money,' a successful British show imported complete with emcee Hughie Green. Modest sums of money, plus a trip to Europe, could be won by correctly answering easy questions. The quiz wasn't demanding. 'We're not intellectual,' claimed Green. 'We're not interested in brains or long-hairs and we ask simple, ordinary questions. If we can get a few giggles, we're happy.' He got the 'giggles' by using Groucho Marx's technique: an interview with contestants chosen from the studio audience to be used as foils for his barbs. Green even leered and rolled his eyes *à la* Marx.[19]

What explains the popularity of this genre? People could justify watching these shows by saying it was all in fun. But this brand of 'fun and games' was no longer really a contest. Its 'victims' were simply on display. They had volunteered to accept ridicule or to behave stupidly. Who could identify with them? Playing the fool was usually to be avoided, not emulated. The contestant became something of an exhibitionist, the viewer something of a voyeur. 'La rigolade' and its ilk exploited a fascination with one of the little perils of modern life: embarrassment. We routinely spend most of our time every day obeying social convention, doing things the right way, behaving properly, so that we will not look awkward or feel ashamed in the company of our fellows. The 'fun and games' show turned that on its head. It offered relief from the discipline of convention. We could tune in to see people embarrassed, to see them squirm, even to enjoy their humiliation. Above all, we could mock them, feel smug because the fool's plight confirmed our own superiority.

The give-away show also offered viewers something of an escape from the workday world. The first and greatest of the genre was unquestionably CBS's 'The $64,000 Question' (Summer '55 to Fall '58) where 'ordinary people' expert in some kind of knowledge (be it Shakespeare, the Bible, or boxing) could win tens of thousands of dollars over a period of weeks.

At first the appeal of the show was extraordinary (where it was available, that is, since the CBC networks didn't carry it): in the first week in October 1957, CBC statistics revealed that the show had attracted over three-quarters of the viewing audience in the Toronto area. Even in Quebec, noted the critic Jacques Keable later on, the show's popularity left behind the expression 'Ça, c'est la question de $64,000' to describe any really difficult problem. First overexposure (success fostered imitation, of course, and the schedules were soon full of big-money quizzes) and then the quiz scandals killed these shows in the United States.[20]

Once again, CBC-Toronto would have nothing to do with the genre. Less troubled by moral qualms, Radio-Canada launched the first made-in-Canada give-away when 'La poule aux oeufs d'or' debuted in the Fall '58 as a replacement for the slightly scandalous 'La rigolade.' In the Fall '63 'La poule' was joined by 'Tous pour un,' which allowed a single contestant to win up to $5,000 in three weeks. Well before then, the independent francophone station CFTM-TV had come up with some of its own give-aways: 'Quiz-O,' 'Télé-poker,' 'Jouez double,' and 'Tentez votre chance.' None of these quizzes offered really big prizes, as had the American shows in their heyday. 'Quiz-O' once advertised a 1962 Mercury-Meteor plus 500 gallons of White Rose gasoline, and 'Jouez double' a grand prize of $10,000. 'Télé-poker' gave out around $40,000 worth of prizes in its first seven months on Channel 10. But all the suspense was there. And some shows, such as 'Tous pour un,' allowed viewers to help out a contestant via the telephone. No one could doubt their appeal. As late as Spring '63, 'La poule aux oeufs d'or' was the second-ranked show among Radio-Canada's offerings, still picking up an 80 share. BBM's February 1965 survey demonstrated that 'Tous pour un' was the most popular Tuesday-night offering in Montreal.[21]

What CBC-Toronto wouldn't do, CTV would. Its first success was 'Take a Chance,' launched in the Fall '61, a fast-paced give-away, designed by the self-styled 'King of Quizz' Roy Ward Dickson, that offered freezers, fur coats, even cars, as well as booby prizes. The program shot to early popularity, reaching the second spot among Canadian shows (behind hockey) in the network's ranking. By February 1963 the top afternoon game show on CTV stations was 'Line 'Em Up,' designed by the American game-master Dan Enright (whose reputation had suffered in the quiz scandals) and produced by Screen Gems: it was 'a giant version of the type of slot-machine called a one-armed bandit,' where players tried to line up sets of matching pictures to earn prizes and points, sometimes winning as much as $2,000. A bit later, in the Spring '65, came the joint English-French 'Musical Showcase,' known as 'Le grand prix musicale' in Quebec. Studio contestants were queried about their knowledge of the popular music scene, such as the number of gold records Elvis Presley could claim. Guessing right won a prize for a home contestant as well. This big production show was also billed as a variety extravaganza, music provided by Denny Vaughan's orchestra and featuring such guest stars as Denyse Angé and Joyce Hahn. But what really set 'Musical Showcase' apart was the value of the prizes, much higher than ever before: there was one prize of $50,000 in gold and the possibility existed of reaching $120,000 in money and merchandise if a contestant lasted a couple of months. Though critics panned the strange hybrid, at first the very novelty fostered a lot of interest among viewers. That interest waned, however: roughly a year later 'Musical Showcase' was ranked only twentieth among CTV offerings, well behind hockey, 'The Littlest Hobo,' 'Take a Chance,' and 'Let's Sing Out.'[22]

The give-away quiz had come in for its share of lumps from the critics. In 1963 Shirley Mair and Peter Gzowski, two *Maclean's* writers, decided these were the epitome of 'junk television.' Once again the underlying reason was moral: the genre seemed to pander to the darker side of human nature. Toronto *Telegram* columnist Jon Ruddy had nothing but contempt for the give-away. He once talked to a friend, conveniently 'an MA in psychology,' to find why he and so many others were hooked by the 'trivial, shallow and silly' 'Take a Chance.' The answer lay in the show's exploitation of our immaturity, the way it appealed to the grasping child still resident in our souls. 'Children are forever trying to get something for nothing,' concluded Ruddy. The analysis of Jacques Keable, *La Presse*'s critic, carried the argument a step farther. You could 'read' the give-away as an assault on the world of work. Keable was struck by the way in which all of these shows surrounded themselves with an aura of 'easy money': the cash prizes or the merchandise seemed to flow so freely that the 'rythme des dollars' created a kind of frenzy among members of the audience. The fact that ordinary people could win prizes with little effort, and take home the prizes immediately, highlighted the subversive appeal of the give-away. No delayed gratification here. The quizzes displayed another path than the drudgery of labour and the discipline of thrift to reach the wealth and comfort so valued by the consumer society of the age. So the give-away wasn't only a celebration of crass materialism or an exercise in greed; it was also a promise that the good life could be taken by the lucky and the skilful. Couldn't almost everybody cherish such an illusion?[23]

Hockey and the Male Ethos

Sports is a lot like religion. That's the starting-point of a marvellous book by Michael Novak entitled *The Joy of Sports*. Look at the language of sports: the agony of defeat and the ecstasy of victory, the devotion of the athlete, the striving for immortality. Look at the places where games are played: the hockey arenas, the baseball and football stadia, are akin to huge temples built to cater to the enthusiasms of fans. The sports world can be a haven, an escape from the troubles of work or family. It's a world full of passion and pageantry, icons and rituals, traditions and superstitions. Every year it captivates millions, though most especially men. Games can quickly arouse the emotions of anxiety, hope, and excitement among spectators. The little doings of football or hockey serve as a common source of discussion that can bridge the gap between strangers, parents and children, bosses and employees. Some find personal and public meanings in the games they see played out every season. Sports can teach the willing about perseverance, self-discipline, and courage; the harmony of body and mind and the emotions; how to handle defeat and victory; the search for excellence; ideals of perfection. Novak had no doubt that sports was the 'chief civilizing agent' and the 'most universal art form' (some might have given that accolade to the commercial) in an America where modernity had undone so much in the way of tradition. That last designation might be too rich for the blood of readers. But there's no denying the special prominence of sports in North America.[24]

Television didn't create sports madness. That it inherited from the press and radio. But just about any sport, even something so slow-moving as baseball, was more enjoyable with pictures. Two of the early staples of evening programming were wrestling and boxing, in part because it was easy for the cumbersome cameras of the day to cover the action in the restricted ring. Although the popularity of these two sports waned during the 1950s, in the case of boxing because its brutality offended many viewers, television's coverage of the sports world actually increased throughout the broadcast day. A survey of CBC network broadcasts in one week in February 1958 found that nearly 10 per cent of the schedule was given over to sports. Late in 1961 CBC's board of directors was told how its two networks had expanded (or would expand) their sports coverage to include curling, soccer, world ice hockey, bowling, skiing, swimming, figure skating, and golf. That was hardly the result of much direction from on high, since CBC management wasn't all that interested in sports. Alphonse Ouimet admitted later that the real pressure came from the sports fans who demonstrated an apparently insatiable hunger for more and more sports, especially on the weekend.[25]

The arrival of independent TV only improved the situation for sports fans. CTV secured the rights to Big Four football telecasts, and began to offer evening games during the late summer and early fall; then the CBC began to carry NFL Sunday football in retaliation. The CBC had made viewing of hockey on Saturday night a winter ritual, and CTV and the independent French-Canadian Channel 10 in Montreal responded with Wednesday-night hockey. Wrestling disappeared from Radio-Canada's evening schedule but re-emerged on Channel 10's. Note that sports survived in primetime in Canada, while in the United States, once boxing disappeared from the schedules, regular coverage of the sports world was generally confined to Saturday and Sunday afternoons. All this attention paid off. Television had become the medium of choice for sports events and sports news across Canada. And there's a good deal of circumstantial evidence to suggest that TV created the boom in popularity of Canadian football in the late 1950s, that it furthered the new enthusiasm for curling in the 1960s, and that it helped (as in the United States) to turn class sports such as golf and, later, tennis into the pastimes of the many.[26]

No matter what other sport might be on the air, though, the most important offering remained NHL hockey. Ironically Clarence Campbell, the president of the league, had put on record in 1949 his suspicion that television coverage would hurt hockey by keeping fans at home. Later he would call television 'the greatest menace of the entertainment world.' That didn't prevent American club owners from selling the broadcasting rights to local television stations. Nor did it prevent hockey interests and the CBC from coming to an agreement to simulcast its Saturday games on television and radio in the first winter season, 1952/3. Television covered the Montreal and Toronto teams: one week the Montreal game would go coast-to-coast, the next week Toronto's, the other game shown on a local or regional basis. There was no black-out of local markets when the home team was playing, a technique employed by owners of football clubs. Instead the telecast of games began after roughly a third of the action had passed by, this to ensure that ticket-holders got something more than was available on the tube. Much the same arrangement applied when CTV started its series of Wednesday-night games in 1961.[27]

Hockey on television was an actuality broadcast. The broadcasters adjusted to the rhythms and routines of the game itself. There has been much talk about the way television has reshaped the sports world by imposing upon games an entertainment ethic or by emphasizing the element of display. Whatever the general merit of such comments, there's little evidence that television in the 1950s or 1960s seriously altered the nature of hockey. There don't appear to have been any significant rule changes that could be ascribed to television's presence. The imposition of commercials caused a few problems: fans at the game got upset over what seemed to be needless delays to allow commercials. Eventually compromises were worked out to avoid the problem: the broadcast of the game of 15 April 1962, for instance, had brief ten-second ads, overlaid on the screen, that didn't require a break in, or a break away from, the action. Up to the 1970s television coverage may well have encouraged a decline in the severity of the violence that had been so much a part of hockey in times past, simply because such displays disturbed many viewers. The pressure was on to deliver a cleaned-up version of what had often been a brutal sport to make it suitable for a living-room audience of men, women, and children – though the decline in brutality probably had even more to do with a growing dislike for violence in society generally.[28]

Watching the game on television, of course, was not the same as going to the arena. One could go on about how the TV fan was and is caught up in a private act, unable to feel the mood of the crowd, unable to gain an overall appreciation of what is happening. But the experience wasn't all that different from being in the arena. And viewing was far better than listening on the radio, the only other alternative for most Canadians. Broadcasters took care to ensure the viewer understood and thus enjoyed the game. The camera's role was to focus always on the puck, providing close-ups around the nets or when the action got heavy and personal, say, on the boards or in the corners. The first producer of hockey was Sydney Newman, who hadn't any real experience with the sport. After watching a game, he told two old pros that it would be easy to cover – it was really like ballet! The pros looked at him strangely. Was this guy a nut? But Newman was correct. The camera had to capture the movement, the grace of the players who, however briefly, had the puck and so held centre-stage.[29].

No one then thought that the camera alone could do the job. The play-by-play announcers proved to be a very talkative lot. Silence, dead air, was a sin. The style owed much to Foster Hewitt, who had pioneered hockey broadcasts on radio and who continued as a radio and television announcer into the 1960s. The practice of simulcasting games on radio and television in the 1950s ensured its survival even as television attained dominance. Besides, the style was inherited by Danny Gallivan in Montreal and Foster's son Bill Hewitt in Toronto, eventually the two chief play-by-play announcers on the Anglo network. The language used was readily understandable, if one was initiated to the jargon of the game – face-offs, high-sticking, clearing the puck, bumping and jamming, etc. The keys were accuracy, immediacy, and brevity: the idea was to sketch a picture with words that highlighted the puck-handlers and the action. The announcers had to avoid showing any obvious favouritism towards one team or the other in a national broadcast. But they weren't just mechanical or unemotional talkers: they allowed a note of excitement to tinge their patter whenever the pace of action picked up. Gallivan was especially animated.[30].

That style didn't please everyone, of course. It amounted to 'a play-by-play radio account, a wearisome and completely unnecessary footnote,' complained Trent Frayne, a Toronto sportswriter. Nor was he any happier that Gallivan and Hewitt delivered 'their cliché-ridden litanies in a shrill and unvarying style of pseudo-excitement – if not downright frenzy.' Frayne's observations were too severe. The pace of hockey required that the announcers provide a framework of words that enabled the viewer to understand what was happening. Otherwise, no matter how effective the camera work, the viewer would quickly get lost.[31]

Broadcasters were always boosters of the games they covered. Play-by-play announcers constantly honoured the event and its players. Rarely was a game boring: it might be 'gruelling' or 'hard fought.' Likewise the tone of commentators and interviewers was usually upbeat. In 1959 the CBC began to phase out the famous Hot Stove League in hockey telecasts – between-period chats among assorted experts – in order to offer interviews and film features that focused on personalities. The master of these interviews, Ward Cornell, saw that his task was to stay in the background and ask questions, often naïve questions, that would elicit something of interest to the ordinary viewer about the game, the person, or hockey. Cornell assumed questions that interested him would interest the viewer as well. He didn't consciously seek out controversy. The approach produced a lot of personal reflection and opinion, the occasional anecdote, and a certain amount of hype about the skills of one or another player, the mood of a team, or how great the game of hockey really was. During the telecast of the game between the Toronto Maple Leafs and the Chicago Black Hawks, 15 April 1962, Cornell interviewed Punch Imlach (the Leaf's coach), a couple of ex-players, the general managers of the Detroit Red Wings and the Chicago team, a visitor from baseball, a team doctor, and a player from the Boston Bruins, all of whom paid allegiance in one way or another to the mystique of hockey as a rough, aggressive contest of skill. Those who adopted a more critical approach, as did Montreal columnist Red Fisher and Toronto columnist Scott Young, ran the risk of provoking the displeasure of the hockey owners and managers, which could be fatal to a television career. In his memoirs Dick Irvin, who became a colour commentator and later an announcer after the mid-1960s, pointed out that the Montreal Canadiens had 'the right' to ask that he be removed from 'Hockey Night in Canada.' Newspapers were the home of sports journalism, such as it was; television treated hockey as a type of entertainment.[32]

The arrangement worked very well indeed. The CBC found it had a real winner in the ratings sweepstakes. Ticket sales soon recovered after the effects of the novelty of watching the game at home had worn off. The hockey owners discovered a new and increasingly lucrative source of revenue. Imperial Oil, the sponsor, was pleased because it was so closely identified with a top Canadian show. But happiest of all were the viewers: the audience for hockey grew to about 3.5 million English Canadians and around 2 million French Canadians (see chart 7.3). Many people experienced hockey only via the television set or the radio: Ken Dryden, the Montréal Canadiens' famous goalie of the late 1970s, recalled that when as a child he played out the part of a Gordie Howe or a Frank Mahovlich, the glorious fantasy only worked when he heard the voice of the announcer in his head. The success of hockey telecasts, first on CBC and later on CTV, had no counterpart in the United States, until the birth of ABC's 'Monday Night Football' in 1970.[33]

Perhaps not everyone was satisfied, however. The ratings suggested time and again that hockey brought more men than women to the television set. The import of this was all the greater because normally more women than men were watching TV. Look at the findings of the February–March 1963 survey of McDonald Research Ltd, which analysed one week's viewing in the three markets of Montreal, Toronto, and Vancouver. Purportedly Saturday-night hockey at 9:00 won an audience of 274,000 men and 218,000 women on CBFT-Montreal, at 9:30 an audience of 339,000 men and 296,000 women on CBLT-Toronto, and at 6:30 122,000 men and 89,000 women on CBUT-Vancouver. No other show attracted so many males in any of these cities, except for CFTO-Toronto's Wednesday-night hockey. By contrast four other programs, including the quiz 'La poule aux oeufs d'or' in Montreal, and five others in Vancouver, attracted more women. (In Toronto the market was so fragmented that no other show could overcome its opposition in a fashion sufficient to capture such a large number of women.) Many of the women watching hockey, moveover, were captive viewers, compelled to view the game or suffer the fate of being 'hockey widows.' Very few homes had two television sets in 1963. Eventually, in 1976, the

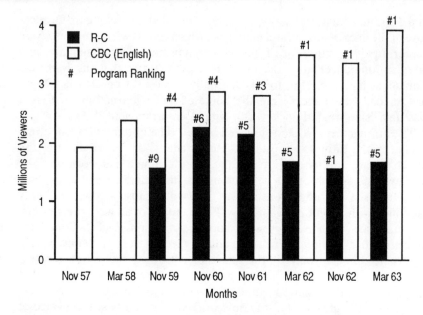

Chart 7.3 Estimated audiences for CBC network hockey telecasts
Note: The information is taken from three different sources. The November
1957 and March 1958 figures are from an Audience Research Division, CBC,
report entitled *English Television Network Program Ratings June 1957–May 1958*,
whose initial figures were derived from International Surveys Ltd. data; the
November 1959, 1960, 1961 figures come from ISL TV network reports for those
months; the March 1962, November 1962, and March 1963 figures are listed in
Elliott-Haynes *Teleratings* for those months. These figures should be treated as
estimates, which are not wholly comparable because of the different systems
used by ISL and E-H to produce their ratings. The program ratings are those
given by the ratings agencies themselves: ISL simply ranked on the basis of the
number of homes viewing the program; E-H had a more complicated system in
which the number of sets in use was multiplied by the percentage of the total
audience viewing the program. Neither ranked on the basis of the absolute
popularity (total number of viewers) of a program.

fact that hockey was much less appealing to women would be used by
Imperial Oil to explain why it withdrew as the program's major sponsor.[34]
    What explains the popularity of hockey, and the way the popularity of
the sport was skewed towards men? Part of the answer, of course, lies in
the nature of hockey. Hockey is a fast, changeable sport. Ken Dryden has

called hockey 'a *transition* game' because it is a collection of fragments of action: a team moves from offence to defence, back and forth, losing possession, regrouping, regaining possession, and the moment at which a switch in the action occurs is often the moment of vunerability, when the opportunist can strike hard. Surprises are common. George Plimpton, that professional 'amateur,' has correctly pointed to the many attributes that make hockey fun to play and to watch: the fact everyone gets a chance to handle the puck, the instinctive and imaginative style of play, the hard contact, of course, and the manoeuvrability and speed possible on ice. And, as is not the case in football or even baseball, the fans in the arena are very much a part of the broadcast. Perhaps because they are fewer in number, certainly because they are in a confined enclosed arena close to the rink, their emotion and mood is accentuated – and communicated to the home audience. All of these features made hockey a lively spectacle for the viewer.[35]

The league then was smaller, more intimate, made up of the two Canadian teams (Montreal Canadiens and Toronto Maple Leafs) and four American teams (New York Rangers, Boston Bruins, Detroit Red Wings, and Chicago Black Hawks). It was easy for a fan to know something about each team. These teams played each other often, which fostered distinct likes and dislikes among fans, and that worked to fuel sports enthusiasm. Best of all, the hockey telecasts focused on the career of the two Canadian teams, reaching one climax when the Canadiens faced the Leafs (the other climax came with the play-offs, of course). There's little doubt that the Canadiens were Quebec's 'national team': full of French Canadians, noted for a passionate style of play, usually the best team in the league, and fiercely supported by their fans. (The Canadiens won eight of fifteen Stanley Cup contests between 1952/3 and 1966/7.) Although the Leafs weren't quite so famous (picking up four Stanley Cups), they were a focus of Anglo loyalties. So hockey mirrored, albeit imperfectly, the rivalry of Canadians and Americans, French and English.[36]

Nor should we discount nostalgia. Many native-born and some immigrant boys were touched in one way or another by hockey as they grew up in post-war Canada. Hockey was a very common winter sport then, not especially troubled by competition from basketball or skiing. Roch Carrier spoke of the extraordinary infatuation in his short story 'The Hockey Sweater.' Peter Gzowski has talked about the same infatuation in his youth in southwestern Ontario. He would later imagine, so he recalled, one big game played out by youngsters on rinks, ponds and rivers, and backyards across Canada. I can remember persuading my parents to buy me, a kid from Britain who could only skate on his ankles, a completely new Canadiens outfit to show off at the local rink. Gzowski claims we all dreamed of hockey stardom. Well, that's an allowable exaggeration. But the memory of what was and what might have been remained long after the adult had hung up his skates.[37]

That brings me to the special mystique of hockey. Hockey liked to present itself as a rough, tough game of speed and skill. It was *the* Canadian game because we had created it, our players dominated the sport, and we remained 'the world's best' (remember this was before the Canada-Russia series demonstrated just how good were the Russian players). 'We're rough, rugged guys from the north,' mused a half-serious Ward Cornell, expressing here the reason why hockey had won its way into our hearts. It suited a land in which the winter always loomed so large. Even more, the game fitted an image of Canadian manhood. Hockey was, in Gordie Howe's words, very much 'a man's game.' It demanded intensity, effort, commitment, endurance – players, particularly the goalie, who must stop the hard-driven puck with his own body, had to expect pain and labour on in the face of injury. The meanings of hockey, then, are very much a part of the male ethos of the times.[38]

The adjective that best describes hockey is 'juvenile.' Embedded in the style and mystique of the game are some of the attributes of male adolescence. That's not simply because most of the players were young, since in fact many of the stars of the day, such as Rocket Richard and Gordie Howe, were veterans. Instead it reflects the fact that the spirit of the hockey team was akin to that of the teenage gang. New players had to undergo an initiation to become full members of the team, and in later years at least that often involved having various portions of their body shaved. Teammates played practical jokes on one another, which according to Ken Dryden meant ketchup in shoes or shaving cream on someone's head. There was much more of a spirit of brotherhood among players than in some other team sports: there was little of that sense of difference between offensive and defensive players true of football or between the pitching staff and the batters in baseball, for instance. A team might take on a single mood, sombre after a loss or buoyant after a win, which seemed to influence the behavior of each team member, whatever his record of achievement. Likewise, an indignity inflicted on one player by an opponent was taken as an affront to the whole team.[39]

That also highlights the emotionalism of the game. Players might be professionals at work but they were also big boys having fun, enjoying themselves. Don Cherry referred to his players at practice as 'a big kindergarten.' When a goal was scored, players slapped and hugged each other in celebration. The fans also got into the act: they wouldn't just cheer or boo, they would throw all kinds of debris on the ice. The most peculiar of these objects was unquestionably the octopus, which apparently made its debut in the 1952 play-offs in Detroit. Chicago fans were notorious because they hurled chairs onto the rink. More often, as in the case of the game of 15 April 1962, it was paper and other kinds of litter that covered the ice.[40]

Mood also affected the style of play. Punch Imlach spoke in his interview with Cornell of the great importance of the will to win. There was a psychological tempo to many a hockey game. Every coach hoped somehow that his team would capture that elusive quality of 'momentum.' When the mood was upbeat, there would be great bursts of energy by the players; when the mood turned down, the players would falter, their attack and even the defence becoming lacklustre. The game was like a concert, said Rod Gilbert (a hockey player), with its periods of pianissimo and allegro. All of which sounds reminiscent of adolescent males at play. They are noted for their energy, their intensity, and their lack of persistence: they have difficulty maintaining concerted action for very long. They lose steam, they rest, they are improperly disciplined. All that energy appears not wasted but misused.[41]

Most striking was the rowdy conduct of the players on the ice. Hockey, then as always, was a game of dominance in which a team tried to overwhelm its opponent. The legendary King Clancy, coach of the Leafs in the mid-1950s, worried more about encouraging a 'boisterous' spirit than concocting a winning strategy. This was no game for 'candy-asses,' Plimpton was told. A player had to go out and protect his 'rights,' demand 'respect,' by playing aggressively, checking hard, mixing it up on the boards. So Scott Young, the expert commentator on the play-off game, told viewers that Chicago was ahead 2–0 at the end of the second period because it was 'out-bumping' the Leafs, 'beating them to the puck.' And Tommy Iven, the Chicago general manager, put his team's success down to the fact it was 'playing a little rougher' than in the previous game which Toronto had won. What was at stake on the ice was a team's pride in itself. Hockey was almost as much a game of honour and dishonour as it was a struggle to see who would win. The result was that players sometimes became bullies.[42]

It was this attribute, of course, that led to fights. Hockey was the only major team sport in which the referees were trained in how to deal with a fight. There was much ambivalence even then about this kind of violence. Lester Pearson, a great hockey fan, once turned off a televised Leaf game in disgust because a general mêlée had broken out on the ice. A Catholic bishop wrote Alphonse Ouimet, denouncing him as personally responsible for teaching violence because of the fights in hockey. President Clarence Campbell did defend the man-to-man brawls as a 'safety valve' that let off tensions. There was more to violence than that, though. Gilbert talked about the 'jungle' rule, Don Cherry about 'the code,' which required that a player never back down from a fight. Suddenly, in the heat of action, a player would be overcome with rage, start grabbing or punching, perhaps later unable to explain what had caused the rage. It sounded very much like an overgrown boy having a temper tantrum.[43]

But few wanted fighting to go too far. The *bagarre général*, a clearing of the benches when all players got into a fight, was definitely out. So too was really vicious fighting, or an attack on a referee. Thus Campbell suspended superstar Rocket Richard, then the leading scorer, in March 1955 for the remainder of the season and the play-offs as a result of a fight he had with one of the Bruins and a swing he took at a referee. That set off the most famous brawl of them all, the infamous Richard riot in Montreal: during the next home game the fans threw eggs and tomatoes at Campbell, the Forum emptied, and people went on a rampage, breaking windows, attacking cars, even looting stores.[44]

The referees played a particularly crucial role in the game, a role analogous in some respects to that of the archetypical parent. Their authority was supposedly absolute. They could affect the tempo of a game, even determine who would win by the way in which they called penalties. If they were too quick, too severe, then they would stifle a team or a game; if they were too lax, then the game might dissolve into chaos. In theory only the captain of the team was allowed to debate a call. In practice other players might be visibly upset when a penalty, unfair or otherwise, was declared against a team-mate. And the fans would come down hard on a referee who made decisions that ran counter to the success of the home team. 'Abusing the ref' was one of the minor rituals of hockey.

It was a ritual that pointed to the spirit of rebellion that was part and parcel of hockey in the arena and on the screen. Adolescence was not a time of life much honoured in Canada. Rather it was considered a time of troubles and tensions when the child displayed unfortunate habits as he struggled towards maturity. But on the ice adolescent behavior was not just allowed, it was almost expected. The arena really was a special place, set off by memory and legend. There was an important element of catharsis involved in the appeal of hockey. The male fan could escape momentarily from the restraints of adulthood, the civilizing influence of women, to enjoy a way of life that was apparently freer, more emotional, more natural. This kind of vicarious release shouldn't be sneered at. It was a valuable safety valve in a society characterized by an excessive devotion to rules and convention, to the right way of behaving. Perhaps one reason the appeal of hockey telecasts peaked in the early 1960s was that rigidity began to disappear rapidly thereafter, so reducing the need for a spectacle such as hockey provided.

Juvenility wasn't celebrated by the apologists of hockey. Artistry was. There was a beauty to the break-away or the goalie's save. Artistry could be a team attribute, such as when the awesome Canadiens set up a power play and peppered the enemy's net with shot after shot. But, more often, it was an attribute of the individual. What was on display here was the skill and verve of the player – his accomplishments and his style, I hasten to add; not, as some analysts would argue, his physique. Hockey struck journalists as unusually, intensely competitive. We are faced again by another manifestation of that pervasive mythology of individualism. Television's focus on the puck-handler was bound to accentuate the notion that the individual was central to the action. So too did the penchant of announcers and commentators for the assorted statistics of achievement: the numbers of goals a player scored, shots on the net and the goalie's saves, penalties exacted against an aggressive player. The end-game ritual of the three-star selection only confirmed the spotlight placed on the man, however ridiculous the actual choice might seem. In that Chicago–Toronto play-off game, Gump Worsley, himself a goalie, picked the two goalies as his first and second stars (even though Toronto lost 3–0).[45]

Is it any wonder that hockey players acquired a kind of public persona? They came to represent a type or a way or an emotion that was believed to be common or widespread. Talk was about fighters (and later goons), team-players, innovators, pests, intense or moody souls. Rocket Richard was thought to boast the classic Gallic temperament: passionate, roistering, tough. Gordie Howe, sometimes called the best player of his era, was known for his ferocity on the ice and his humility off it – he had an appealing shyness, an ordinariness that belied his formidable talents. Jacques Plante, who introduced the goalie's mask to NHL hockey, was famed as an innovator and an eccentric, a colourful character not quite in tune with his fellows. The latecomer Bobby Orr emerged as the great revolutionary, a new man for new times, who managed to change the style of hockey by showing that a defenceman could also play an aggressive, offensive style of hockey and so score lots of goals.[46]

Such superstars became heroes, an uncommon status in Canada, a country that couldn't seem to find in its own past or present many people on whom to lavish worship. Richard was unquestionably the national hero of Quebec. Fans would raise funds to pay off his fines. They even booed his team-mate Boom-Boom Geoffrion when he moved ahead in the scoring race after Campbell's suspension of Richard in 1955. Kids, wrote Roch Carrier, would all play at being Maurice Richard: lace their skates like him, wear their hair like him, shoot like him, and so on. But others came in for their share of devotion too. A CTV poll in the mid-1960s found that Gordie Howe was one of the most famous men in Canada, better known that the governor general or the premier of Quebec. He was able to parlay that fame into endorsements for various commercial enterprises. Glenn Hall, Terry Sawchuk, Jacques Plante, all goalies, were Ken Dryden's special heroes whose bravery and skill was unmatched by any others. Dryden would later rail against his own image as the cool-minded intellectual, an image that he thought was a concoction of the media. But Gzowski had no doubt that Bobby Hull, the Golden Jet, was a genuine hero with whom many, many males of Gzowski's generation had identified when Hull swept down the ice. Hockey, in short, was a source of genuine Canadian celebrities who personified assorted virtues and acted as role models for men.[47]

The final meaning of hockey was also linked to a mythology, this time about modernity. It spoke about the increasing organization and structure of life, the rise of a bureaucratic Canada. That may sound absurd if the reader interprets the comment as a suggestion that hockey was somehow consciously a symbol of the new dominance of the big state and the corporate enterprise. Rather what was happening, and happening slowly, was an attempt to transform the haphazard game of hockey into more of a science where a particular action would produce a predictable result, a process that ran counter to the first two dimensions of the game I've mentioned. It reflected the kind of changes going on in work life as men, in particular, found their conduct more and more circumscribed by impersonal rules and institutional authority. Ironically in 1965 Gzowski commented on how hockey was losing its joy and colour because of the rise of a new 'grim, calculated, determination to win.'[48]

The key personality here was the coach, who, whether portrayed as a general or a manager, was supposed to have a philosophy, to know what his resources were and how to use them, to design a game plan flexible enough to win under whatever circumstances. On television the coach was treated with respect, deference, as a fount of hockey wisdom; in print, by contrast, a coach whose team lost too often found himself the target of blame.[49]

One of the chief tools of the coach was the specialist, someone trained to do a particular kind of job. The most important specialist was the goalie, and goalies have sometimes been considered a breed apart on the team. But there were also defencemen and forwards, scorers and policemen (the latter being tough guys who were supposed to punish the enemy). Very often the coach would assemble three players into a special 'line,' often one whose speciality was scoring – considered among the best, for example, was the line of Gordie Howe, Sid Abel, and Ted Lindsay for the Detroit Red Wings. The wise coach made use of substitutions, removing tired players or putting in a different set of specialists, every minute and half or two minutes, to test the strength of the opponent. What was clearly important here was team-work. The players had become parts of a machine, rather than a collection of artists.[50]

The other tool was a particular set of tactics designed to meet a special situation. The most famous of these was the power play, which came when one team was left short-handed by a penalty. The privileged coach often sent out four forwards, and only one defenceman, who concentrated on keeping the puck near the enemy's net and setting up one shot after another until the goalie was beaten. The hapless coach might respond with a box formation, two forwards and two defencemen, who formed a square in their end, each covering a particular zone of ice, and tried to block shots or get the puck out of their end. This was structured play: here a mechanism had been imposed upon the otherwise poorly disciplined game. It's worth noting that both the successful power play and the successful defence won praise from broadcasters.[51]

Hockey was right for the times. Its mystique meshed well with male concerns and moods. So television's exposure had boomed the popularity of the sport. But television also set the stage for its decline. Television had created the prospect of making really big pots of money for the NHL owners. It wasn't so much that yearly television revenues were all that spectacular: one estimate in the early 1970s had the Montreal and Toronto teams receiving about $1 million a piece from broadcasting rights, no mean sum to be sure. But they were more likely to earn three times that amount from gate receipts and extra dollops of cash from concessionaires and advertisers. What looked so good was the opportunity to expand the NHL across the continent and to use television, just as the NFL and the AFL had in the United States, to pull in extraordinary revenues. In 1967 the league took the plunge, expanding to twelve teams by selling franchises for some $2 million a piece to six American cities. Vancouver and Buffalo were left out of the deal because neither the Leafs nor the Canadiens wanted to share television revenues or face market competition from teams in these cities. In the next expansion a few years later, though, Vancouver and Buffalo were let in, at a cost of $6 million a piece. CBS did pick up network rights for Sunday-afternoon hockey in 1968 January through May, which generated about $1 million a season. Late in 1971 came a new competitor, the World Hockey Association, which thought there was room for a further series of teams to exploit the much-touted hockey boom. Meanwhile Alan Eagleson's Players Association found expansion created an ideal situation to demand higher and higher salaries from all teams, new and old, which were desperate for any kind of talent. There's no question that a lot of people got wealthy out of this craze.[52]

But hockey didn't become the sport of the 1970s. It had been oversold. American audiences found the game confusing, scores too low, the play too violent – or not violent enough. The nostalgia factor didn't apply in much of the United States: there wasn't a tradition of playing hockey to build upon. What was more serious, audiences at home in Canada soon complained that expansion had robbed the game of its quality. There were too many teams, too few good players, and too much trading of players from one team to another. The excitement of the Canada-Russia series in 1972 made the ordinary style of play of the NHL look like a travesty. The goons were taking over in professional hockey, a victory symbolized by the Stanley Cup success of the Philadelphia Flyers a.k.a. the 'Broad Street Bullies' in 1974. And the awesome power of the Russian teams shattered the illusion the Canada could any longer claim superiority at its own national game.

I was one of those alienated fans who had slipped away long before the league bottomed out. Expansion had destroyed my love affair with hockey, as it had that of other viewers. American ratings were miserable. CBS dropped the game after the 1971/2 season (the long-running anthology 'CBS Sports Spectacular' replaced it), although hockey broadcasts lingered on for three more years on NBC. CTV ended its Wednesday-night hockey after the 1974/5 season. By 1976 BBM ratings showed that the audience for 'Hockey Night in Canada' had fallen to 2.8 million. Hockey was no longer the darling of television, or even of Canada, although it would undergo a renaissance at the end of the decade.[53]

What happened to hockey highlights the futility of either praising or blaming television for the course of events. Hockey had come to prominence in the age of radio. The game and the audience television inherited. Television did have an effect, of course: it magnified the significance of hockey as an expression of Canada's way of life. It set the stage for what seemed hockey's conquest of North America. The fact that never came off, indeed that it was ever tried, may better be blamed on the greed of owners and players, though a search for higher profits and higher wages was natural. Television alone couldn't make hockey a best-seller in the United States. Nor could it stave off a decline when the character of the game and of the league altered so drastically. Instead television offered alienated fans alternatives such as golf, tennis, basketball, baseball, more football, and sports anthologies. One survey of the mid-1970s estimated that there was between thirty and thirty-five hours of sports televised per week in Edmonton during the winter months. Television still served the religion of sports well.[54]

Focus 'Front Page Challenge'

First a darkened screen. Then drumbeats, slow like a heartbeat or a pulse. It turns out the sound represents the rhythm of a city, which we learn much later is San Francisco. A series of film-clips of city scenes where nothing is happening. The partial information on the screen is explained by an announcer speaking in such a way as to generate suspense.

Video	Audio
– Opens on an empty city street. A shot of another street, with a collection of men off in the distance. A third street, largely empty. Finally an empty gas station, a sign saying 'no gas.'	The bustle and commerce of a thriving seaport is suddenly stilled. The huge city ceases to breathe. Martial law brings militia troops into the streets and the population cowers indoors.

That was the teaser: sound and images to capture the eye of the wayward viewer, to put him or her in the right mood of expectation. Superimposed on the film-clips appears the title 'FRONT PAGE CHAL-

LENGE.' The announcer continues, 'This story and others, tonight on "Front Page Challenge." ' Then the background sound becomes music and, however incongruous it might seem, the announcer tells the audience that the program is 'brought to you by the makers of du Maurier, the cigarette of good taste ...' So began the edition of 16 January 1962.

'Front Page Challenge' celebrated the journalistic enterprise. It strove to present itself as an authentic representation of what the news process was all about. The show dealt in hard-news stories from the past few decades, stories that had made the front pages of Canadian daily newspapers. The key to the show's success, however, was the panel, which played out the role of a group of inquiring reporters in search of fact and sensation.

'Front Page Challenge' was an excellent example of radiovision. The show did employ film inserts, graphics, and music to good effect at various key points during the half-hour. First the story, and later, after the story was guessed, the challengers were introduced by an abbreviated pictorial description or biography. These scripts, by the way, were written more in an essay style, reminiscent of the news writing of *Time* magazine, than in that of the much more objective and bland reports common in the daily newspaper. But what the screen normally showed was a collection of talking heads. That night, Fred Davis was the moderator, Gordon Sinclair and Pierre Berton the two regular panelists, Jack Webster, a British Columbian journalist, and Marie Torre, an American journalist, the guest panelists. Torre also gave the panel the necessary female face. There were two stories, represented by mystery challengers, from quite different worlds of experience. The first was a sports story, the breaking of Babe Ruth's home-run record by the challenger Roger Maris, the new king of swat. The second was a piece of labour history, the general walk-out on the American west coast in May 1934 provoked by a long-shoremen's strike. The challenger was none other than Harry Bridges, the long-shoremen's leader then and still a power in trade-union ranks.

The element of display was apparent throughout. Davis adopted the mode of direct address in his dealings with the home audience. He gave thanks to a Mrs Underhill who had suggested the baseball story (and told her to expect a cheque shortly from du Maurier). He referred to the viewer as 'you' whenever it was appropriate to explain to the unseen audience what was happening. ('Now we'd like to move on to round two after *you*'ve had a chance to look at this next headline.') That contrasted strikingly with the lack of attention paid to the studio audience, which played almost no part in the production. There was a definite attempt to create a pleasant atmosphere on the show, and so a pleasant impression in the living-rooms of the nation. Davis followed up the introduction of the panel by talking with the two guest panelists, which served to put them at ease and to identify them to viewers as well as to provide a bit of humour and anecdote. He engaged Webster, a sort of professional Scotsman, in a discussion over the propriety of using such words as 'kilts' and 'Scottish.' During the rest of the show, Davis stayed in the background, except when an explanation, a clarification, or a transition was necessary – and he was invariably polite. The stage was set for that night's performers, the panelists and the challengers, to do their thing.

The introduction of the panel, and of Davis himself, made abundantly clear that people were about to watch journalists in action. The accolades were delivered by an unseen announcer (emphasis added):

Video

– Camera focuses on the panel of four and then moves along the line for a close-up of each in turn.

– Sinclair smiles at the compliment.

– Torre has a friendly face, but she looks uneasy not glamorous.

– Webster starts with a stern face but smiles in the end.

– Berton's eyes hooded as he looks down, but then he smiles and shakes his head – a very appealing smile.

Audio

– Now let's meet our panel of **enquiring reporters** on 'Front Page Challenge.'
In chair number 1, a **hard-hitting newspaperman** with one of **the best known** by-lines in Canada, Gordon Sinclair. [Applause]
–And next a **glamorous** New York **newspaper-woman** with one of **the best known** by-lines in the United States, Marie Torre. [Applause]
–Guest number 2 this evening is the **provocative writer and commentator**, Jack Webster. [Applause]
– And finally the **columnist** whose by-line **gives comfort** to the downtrodden and **strikes fear** into the hearts of the blackguard, Pierre Berton. [Applause]
– And now here's the man who is

Frame 7.1 The panel

– Camera moves to Davis, who smiles – he looks very debonair, handsome, and charming.

ringmaster of **this stable of journalistic talent** and **editor-in-chief** on 'Front Page Challenge,' Fred Davis. [Applause]

Swiftly, easily, the announcer had managed to type-cast all of the performers: 'hard-hitting' Sinclair and 'glamorous' Torre (could a woman journalist be dowdy?) were famous, Webster was provocative, and Berton – well, he was the tribune of the public (see frame 7.1). There was even the bestowal of a little conceit on Davis, much more a 'ringmaster' than he was an 'editor-in-chief.'

The panel's actions were bound up in the conventions of the contest. The show implicitly promised the viewer both suspense and unpredictability. The first part amounted to a guessing game, in which each of the panel members in turn questioned the hidden challenger to determine what the story was. The audience, of course, knew what the stories were from the beginning. Davis gave the panel a clue – the west-coast walk-out was called 'an international story' – and a time limit – four minutes for that story. The panelists were allowed to ask only questions that could be answered with a 'yes' or a 'no.' Davis occasionally stepped in to help the guest panelists, either to clarify some answer of a challenger or to offer an explanation. The panelists worked in alliance, not in competition, each trying to find a piece of information before turning over the questioning to another. Not surprisingly the two regular panelists eventually guessed the right answers: Berton got the baseball story and Sinclair the labour story. The whole process was mildly interesting, though the level of suspense was pretty low, most especially since there was no attempt to pump up any excitement through the use of a clock, the sound of a bell, or warnings about the passage of time.

The panelists lived up to the expectations people had of how the journalist performed. Their style of questioning was punchy, concrete, no-nonsense. Sinclair and Berton were particularly impressive in the hunt for the story. When Berton started the questioning of Roger Maris, for instance, little had been established beyond the fact that this story was about a recent event that had occurred in New York. Berton took command. He had a firm, strong, demanding voice. His questions were short and specific. He quickly identified the fact that the story lay in the realm of sports, a team sport, baseball. After briefly going down the wrong path, he identified the challenger first as a baseball player, then as a player for the New York Yankees. It could only be Mickey Mantle or Roger Maris. Maris it was. So the story had to be Maris breaking Babe Ruth's record – or maybe he didn't Berton suggested, since everything depended on the set of statistics used. Davis covered up this potential dispute by noting that the headline carried by the papers was 'Surpasses Ruth's Record in Final Game of Schedule.' What Berton had demonstrated so well was the cool, calculating mind of the reporter at work (see frame 7.2).

Much more interesting was the second stage, the interview game: in fact the panelists were clearly more animated and more involved when the focus became querying the challenger rather than guessing the story. Why call this a 'game,' though? Because the process amounted to a struggle for dominance between the challenger and the panelists. Each panelist sought to structure the interview so as to elicit truths about the individual. Indeed the hope was that the guest would bare his soul. The panelist, especially a regular panelist who was experienced in this matter, had the advantage of asking the questions. The individual sought to answer, or rather respond, in a fashion that protected his privacy, reputation, and interests. He had the advan-

Frame 7.2 The inquisitor

tage of determining just what, and how much, information he would release. At stake were honour and dishonour, as is so often the case in the news process. The interview was reminiscent of the talk show, but with a twist, an edge, because the purpose was not just to stroke the guest but to quiz that person. The viewer waited expectantly to see if there were any sensations, any fireworks, who might win this struggle. Davis was there to ensure everything remained polite. There wasn't any formal winner, of course. But the interview engendered more suspense than the guessing-game had.

Underlying each interview was that pervasive mythology of individualism again. Maris and Bridges were portrayed as people who counted: they could command their own fate and affect the fate of others. Were they legitimate heroes, though? Maris was youthful, white, handsome, and big – he looked good on television. He was also well-spoken, but unreflective and modest if not a bit shy, and apparently uncomplicated – did that make him a model athlete? Certainly the story description and later the film biography celebrated both baseball and Maris. Just prior to his dramatic home run, he was the slugger 'on the threshhold of immortality,' he 'made history' with his 'fateful swing,' and 'the fans yowled themselves hoarse.'

The panel treated Maris gently. One line of questioning probed the psychology and the skills of the athlete. Berton wondered whether Maris got a bit rattled as the pressure mounted towards the end of the schedule. The answer was yes. Sinclair asked one of those classic 'How do you feel ... ?' questions: what was Maris's response when the fans in the bleachers began to needle or heckle him on a slow day? He didn't like it. After quizzing him about acting in movies, Torre probed Maris's commitment to baseball: 'Is baseball an ideal career?' Maris's response was nicely understated: 'Well, I don't know if it's ideal, but that's the profession I picked.' Webster tried to find out if Maris played golf well. He played it better than Webster did, we learn. What the journalists were doing was exploring the human dimension of the sports hero.

The other and more critical line of questioning probed the morality of sports and the sports hero. This Berton took up. He began by asking how much the home-run record might be worth to Maris and then moved on to question him about his involvement in advertising. Did he give testimonials, endorse products that he had never tried? Berton's query was at bottom an attempt to chip away at the moral standing of the athlete, to find a flaw in a man honoured by society. Maris, a trifle nervous at this point, argued that no star could accept an offer unless he really did use a product, though he allowed as to how this was a recent policy. Berton, who clearly didn't really believe the claim, let Maris off the hook at this point, with the snide comment that this must be an instance of 'the new morality in advertising.'

Bridges had a much rougher time. The Australian-born Harry Bridges was elderly, a small and dapper man who appeared well-dressed, though by no means flashy (see frame 7.3). He soon revealed himself as forceful and earthy, and a good deal more complicated than Maris. The film story and the bio made a lot of the bitterness of the confrontation in San Francisco and the fact that Bridges was a battler, leaving the favourable impression of the man as a brave and heroic leader who had fought successfully for his comrades' rights. The panel didn't bother exploring the story itself, or even Bridges's role in the affair. Rather it concentrated on questioning the man about his reputation and his beliefs, an approach that turned nasty when the aggressive Jack Webster took over. The irony was that Bridges handled all this

Frame 7.3 The feisty guest

well, revealing that he was indeed the kind of fighter his bio had celebrated.

Because he'd correctly identified the story, Sinclair started the questioning off. He was intrigued about the unsavoury reputation of Harry Bridges ('Have they stopped trying to deport you?') and the view Harry Bridges had of the growing respectability of the labour movement ('All of us sitting on this panel are union-card–carrying men'). Implicit was Sinclair's presumption that labour had attained success and gained status by accommodating itself to the business world.

Bridges wasn't willing to see the taming of labour as an improvement. Rather he wished labour 'would go more places in a bigger hurry.' What places? Torre wanted to know. Why, labour should be in the forefront of social change and world peace, came back the answer. Perhaps it was that response that led Webster to try to label Bridges. Wasn't he 'a British-type trade-union leader; aren't you a left-wing socialist'? Didn't he want recognition of Red China? Bridges said yes to both queries. More out of habit than any apparent animosity, Berton went for the jugular: he questioned Bridges about his view of communism, still an issue of some delicacy in the United States in the early

1960s. Bridges allowed that he didn't have 'enough courage' to actually belong to the Communist party. Then Berton asked, 'What do you think of Jimmy Hoffa as a unionist?' – Hoffa was already a kind of bogeyman, a shady type of labour leader, in the minds of many people. A firm believer in solidarity, Bridges replied that he admired Hoffa as 'one of the great trade-union leaders.' That was like waving a red flag in front of a bull: Webster couldn't resist jumping back in, but at this point Davis put an end to the interview. The fact was that Webster and Berton had managed to demonstrate Bridges wasn't just unusual, he was un-American, a kind of political animal rare in the labour movement whose ideas were strange, if not a bit subversive.

Where Bridges shone was in his defence of labour militancy. He refused to accept the construction the panelists put on events. He used the occasion to put forward his own views about the marketplace, the economy, and labour's cause. Torre had opened up these issues by asking whether there wasn't 'a point of diminishing returns' to the constant union demand for better wages. Not a bit, scoffed Bridges: the price of a commodity was affected much more by the search for profit, so labour demands were never going to hurt the economy. Webster took up the cudgels later, suggesting that the success of the long-shoremen's union had damaged the efficiency of the San Francisco docks. 'Up until recently that was true,' Bridges responded. Then came the surprise. 'That was what we're in business for. We're not interested in turning around the ships fast, we're interested in getting work.' An aghast Webster followed up by asking whether that included 'feather-bedding,' then widely considered a burden on productivity fostered by unions. An unregenerate Bridges admitted success in encouraging feather-bedding, and went on to make abundantly clear that he didn't accept the imperative of profit: 'We're working people. We work for a living. We are not in [the] business of making a profit. That's the headache of the other side.' His job, he emphasized, was 'seeing that people are protected.'

What's so intriguing about the interview is how the panel and the guest played the game. The panel took up a common position, though neither Sinclair nor Torre was as aggressive as Webster and Berton. None of the reporters employed the stereotypes of an exploited labour and a cruel business implicit in the filmed description and bio. Rather the panel had pushed a mainstream view of economic progress in which the trade union figured as something of a necessary evil, because its ability to increase labour's share of the wealth usually resulted in a decline in productivity. Bridges was cast in the role of an anti-hero because he wouldn't accept the priority of productivity. Bridges would have none of this. He read the panel a lesson on labour economics, from his own left-wing standpoint. What Bridges articulated was an oppositional view of social progress in which the trade union acted as an essential instrument of economic justice on behalf of the ordinary man.

Viewers had got a treat: 'FPC' had delivered on its promise of entertainment and education. The performers were articulate and engaging, the conversation fast-paced and interesting, all of which made for a nice mix of fun and news. People could indeed see how journalists performed. Yes, the show was superficial, if judged by the standards of public-affairs programming. Still a surprising amount of information and opinion was conveyed during the half-hour. The audience was allowed a glance into the two quite different worlds of sports and labour. A wideawake or a perceptive viewer would have been aware of the clash of opinions in the Bridges interview. How a viewer would have absorbed this 'education' depended, of course, on the person's presumptions. But investing a half-hour in watching the show was certainly worthwhile.

8

Culture on the Small Screen

> I sometimes think that television, like plastic, is one of the most horrible inventions of the 20th century. But at other times I find it so engrossing, and even satisfying, that I can't escape the conclusion that television is an art.
>
> David Greene, 1954[1]

Recall that David Greene, a sometime actor on the English stage and on Broadway, was one of the first of Toronto's drama producers. He believed that television could stimulate the imagination and the mind of the viewer, taking over the role of the live theatre. It was a charming, if naïve dream. And it wasn't unusual: there were moments when the CBC's producers and programmers seemed to be seized by a quixotic urge to deny the logic of mass communications. Public television didn't always try to serve the great audience. The two CBC networks persisted, at great cost and for many years, to mount a series of quality shows that paid homage to the demands of Culture. How ironic that such efforts not only annoyed many ordinary viewers but, all too often, failed to please the very highbrows for whom these shows were intended.

On Art

Was television a form of art?

Ask a highbrow and more than likely the answer would have been a resounding 'No!' Before long, TV-bashing had become a common sport among North America's intellectuals. Academics and literary types, the fans of classical music, and art lovers were notorious for their disdain for television. Many claimed not to watch the idiot box. It was a mark of intellectual purity for the austere highbrow to refuse to have a television set in his home.

There was good cause for all this animosity, beyond a mere snobbish desire to stand out from the crowd. The hopes that television would sponsor a new renaissance of High Culture just hadn't panned out, in Canada or anywhere else. Early in 1957 *Saturday Night* published an article entitled 'Television's March to Nowhere' by Harry Rasky that talked about the disillusionment of that first group of pioneers in Toronto who had thought they could create 'the best of all possible television worlds.' Some had moved on to the practical world of advertising, some to the big time in the United States or Great Britain, some to office jobs in the Corporation's bureaucracy, and some had said 'to hell with it,' escaping into happier pursuits outside television. The few remaining in production worked ceaselessly to manufacture shows, 'quickly forgetting what has gone before.' Two years later *Canadian Literature* carried a piece in a similar vein by George Robertson that argued sadly that writers 'felt defeated and frustrated by the medium.' The professions of a past faith, the talk of television as 'exciting' and a 'challenge,' could be heard only in the boardrooms of the CBC.[2]

By contrast the suspicions and fears about television evident in the late 1940s and the early 1950s had been confirmed by the end of that decade. Many a local highbrow would have applauded Frank Lloyd Wright's description of television as 'chewing gum for the eyes.' After a holiday spent watching Canadian television in 1956, Beverly Baxter (an Englishman of traditional tastes who wrote for *Maclean's*) declared that TV was usually a 'medium for averageness,' by which he meant second-rate drama and music, only rarely for any kind of excellence, by which he meant artistic expression. Indeed he was positive that television was actually leading the assault of mass culture against the individuality and genius that fostered art. Writing in *Canadian Art* some years later, Dore Ashton from New York warned that the best anyone could expect of television were 'doctored and devalued versions of culture.' North American TV really was the enemy, a parody of true art and at worst a sort of anti-art, a classic case of the bad driving out the good.[3]

The view reflected a particular conception of what constituted art that had been appropriated from the realms of painting and sculpture, music and dance, plays and literature. This very traditional brand of aesthetics was rarely articulated outright, simply because it was so widely accepted by highbrows. 'Art' should be, according to the common usage of the term, original or innovative, personal if not eccentric, enduring as well as demanding, and of course engaging. A look at the general body of television programming in North America from this perspective could serve only to justify the gloom of the highbrow.[4]

Pity the sensitive television critic, mused a half-serious Sidney Lamb, who sometimes fulfilled that role for *Canadian Art*. In 1962 he wrote a playlet that featured a dialogue between himself, supposedly in the midst of a nervous breakdown, and a psychiatrist, who resembled the famous Dr Zorba of 'Ben Casey' fame. The disconsolate patient had a recurring nightmare in which he was located in the bottom row of seats in a giant amphitheatre full of critics. Ranked above him were the 'real' critics, beginning, one row up, with the specialists in film and moving up through drama, music, to ballet, those at the top. What set him apart from his supposed fellows was their ability to deal with art in some form or other. 'Up there [*vague gesture above his head*] they have standards, and a medium, and a language to criticize it with.' But the lowly TV critic, his mind undone by watching too many episodes of 'Gunsmoke,' 'What's My Line,' or 'Route 66,' couldn't do much more than parrot the jargon all too familiar on television itself. ('If *Macbeth* were performed tomorrow for the first time, on television, I'd review it like this: "The CBC's *Swan of Avon* series has come up this week with something new in the historical thriller line, a welcome change from the earnest social comment that has been filling our screens of late. While your reviewer found Mr. Shakespeare's dialogue a mite on the complicated side ...' " etc.) He had nothing but the Fowler Report to guide him, which told him that good things were Canadian and bad things were American, especially their quality productions – a Leonard Bernstein or a Sir Laurence Olivier in performance – since these seriously imperilled the expression of the Canadian identity. Lamb left us with the image of an increasingly disturbed patient struggling on his knees towards the television set to watch a panel discussion on the Canadian identity, Robert Goulet in song, and a University of Toronto professor talking about 'Sophocles, Shakespeare, and the Canadian Experience.' Too much viewing had obviously brought on a severe personality disorder.[5]

Ridicule (better than madness, after all) was the last refuge of the highbrow who tried to take television seriously.

The Quality Shows

Even if television itself was a species of anti-art, though, the networks did cater to the arts. Remember Hilary and Bertram, those two Toronto highbrows introduced in Ralph Allen's novel *The Chartered Libertine*, compelled to go off to a baseball game to seek diversion? Well, if they'd decided to watch Toronto television in the third week of October 1954, they would have found quite a selection of goodies (in addition to 'I Love Lucy' and 'I Married Joan') to please their cultivated tastes. Channel 4, Buffalo's CBS outlet, had 'Omnibus' late on Sunday afternoon, from 5:00 to 6:30, where an ever-changing feast of plays, concerts, and documentaries enticed the discriminating viewer. The city's CBC station, then Channel 9, boasted a regular concert hour running from 8:30 to 9:30 on Thursday night. The NBC affiliate in Buffalo, Channel 2, featured a two-hour dance spectacular with Jeanmarie on Saturday, from 9:00 to 11:00. The same station, plus CBLT and Hamilton's Channel 11 (simulcasting was a problem for viewers even then), had scheduled Ginger Rogers, starring in a special one and a half hour show of three separate playlets on Monday at 8:00 to 9:30. But, best of all, at least if Hilary and Bertram were fans of live drama, were the range of teleplay series, mostly an hour long and generally offered after 9:00 for adult viewing: Channel 2 aired the 'Goodyear/Philco Television Playhouse' on Sunday evening; Monday had CBS's famed 'Studio One' (also on CBC) as well as NBC's 'Robert Montgomery Presents'; on Tuesday there was the CBC's own 'General Motors Theatre' plus NBC's half-hour anthologies, 'Fireside Theatre' and 'Armstrong Circle Theatre'; on Wednesday NBC carried 'Kraft Television Theatre,' which also played on stations in Toronto and Hamilton the next night, along with NBC's half-hour 'Ford Theatre' and CBS's 'Climax' on the Buffalo channels; finally, on Saturday, the CBC presented its own half-hour anthology, 'On Camera.' It would seem that 'the march of Culture' had captured some places on the schedule, amidst Milton Berle, Jack Webb, boxing, and all the other 'junk.'

The commitment of American television began to wane soon after the mid-1950s as the game shows and then the westerns spread through prime-time, although a few teleplay series lasted into the 1960s. Private television in Canada never tried to do more than the occasional special (for example, CTV's 'Inside the Canadian Opera,' 'A Gift of Music' featuring the Toronto Symphony, or 'Inside the National Ballet of Canada' in the winter of 1964/5). But the Corporation's networks laboured on with regular series until the end of the 1960s, even though, according to Ouimet, only 5 per cent of the total audience was really interested in symphonies, rising to 10 per cent for opera, ballet, and the great plays. The institutional commitment to Culture was signified by the large amount of time the program committee of the board of directors devoted to discussions of these series throughout the 1960s. It was abundantly clear that the prestige of the CBC was at stake: the success of its quality shows was taken as proof of the Corporation's devotion to that special gospel of public service, setting it apart from other North American broadcasters.[6]

Although the CBC did program arts features over the years to educate the viewer about books, painting, and the like, the corporation's greatest achievements lay in the realm of the performing arts – music, ballet, opera, and above all drama – which were showcased in a number of high-profile anthologies (see chart 8.1). The anthology format served best because it allowed the producer, at least in theory, to offer each week the choicest of selections from among these arts. The idea was to attract the discerning viewer with a promise of excellence.

The thrust of Radio-Canada's programming was slightly more traditional and highbrow than that of its anglophone compatriot. The first of its most outstanding anthologies was 'L'heure du concert' (1954–66), which also ran on the anglophone network as 'Concert Hour' (1954–8). At first 'L'heure du concert' offered viewers a mix of excerpts from concerts, opera, and ballet, although by 1958 (when it ran on alternate weeks) the show often concentrated on only one production, purportedly to allow the producer to devote more attention to the 'visual values' of the performance. The second grand anthology was 'Le téléthéâtre de Radio-Canada' (1953–66), a drama showcase of one and a half or two hours, usually devoted to plays of weight and significance (joined occasionally, beginning in the Fall '62, by performances on 'Soirée au théâtre Alcan'). It proved impossible to maintain the show as a weekly or even bi-weekly regular: during the 1960s 'Le téléthéâtre' appeared less and less frequently because of the expense of mounting a full-scale production. Its offerings were supplemented by a succession of one-hour teleplay series under different titles that were supposed to reach out to a wider audience: 'Le théâtre populaire' (Summer '56 to Summer '58), 'En première' and later 'Première' in the next two years, and then in the 1960s 'Théâtre du dimanche', 'Jeudi-théâtre,' and 'Théâtre d'une heure.'[7]

As time passed Radio-Canada came to concentrate more and more of its Culture on one evening during the week. So, in Fall '60, Thursday evening between 9:30 and 11:00 (some shows might end later, though) was the time-slot for 'L'heure du concert' and 'Le téléthéâtre de Radio-

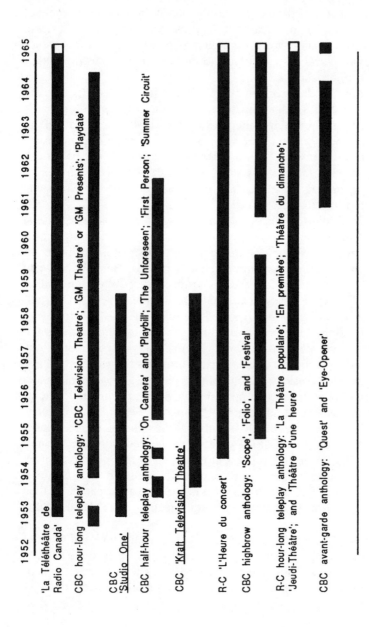

Chart 8.1 Main culture anthologies

Note: The dates are approximate, indicating the season (Spring, Summer, or Fall) in which a show commenced or ended on the schedule of one of the Canadian networks. Shows which continued beyond the end of 1964 are indicated with an unfilled block (except 'Eye-Opener' which had a brief Spring run). The two American imports are underlined.

Canada.' Four years later these anthologies had moved to Sunday at 9:00 (running either to 10:00 or to 10:30), where they shared the spotlight with 'Théâtre d'une heure' and some specials. Finally, in the 1966/7 season, Radio-Canada consolidated its dramatic and musical spectaculars in one anthology, 'Les beaux dimanches,' which was scheduled from 8:00 to 10:00.

The situation in English Canada was more complicated. For a time, in the mid-1950s, Toronto did originate some summer concerts, under the title 'Promenade Concert' (which also appeared on CBFT-Montreal). But the CBC eventually moved towards establishing a showcase for classical music, opera, ballet, and drama first with 'Scope' (Spring '55), then 'Folio' (Fall '55 to Summer '59), and finally with the much-praised anthology 'Festival' (1960–9). At least in 1961 the promotion people were apparently pushing this show, and rightly so, as 'a prestige series of quality entertainment for connoisseurs,' the most snobbish of the programs the CBC offered the discriminating Canadian. Occasionally Toronto programmed specials or short-lived series of a similar kind, such as 'Music Canada' (Fall '66 to Spring '67), a collection of eight sixty- or ninety-minute musical extravaganzas that covered folk music and opera, Percy Faith and Wagner.[8]

The dramatic anthologies were clearly aimed at a much wider audience. Some were American, including the notable imports 'Studio One' and 'Kraft Television Theatre' or much later 'Bob Hope Theatre' (Fall '65 to Summer '67), which mixed variety and drama. But Toronto strove to deliver its own brand of top-notch drama regularly in the winter, sometimes in the summer months as well. Some of that came in the shape of half-hour teleplay series: first there was 'On Camera' and 'Playbill' (which concluded in Summer '59), then came two years of a suspense anthology entitled 'The Unforeseen' (Fall '58 to Spring '60), and finally an eclectic series called 'First Person' (Summer '60 to Spring '61). Even more effort was devoted to a much-promoted television theatre, offering one-hour teleplays (in the early years, ninety minutes) that ran continuously (usually not in the summer, though) from 1953 to 1964 under such titles as 'CBC Television Theatre,' 'General Motors Theatre,' 'General Motors Presents,' and in the last three years 'Playdate.' At least when General Motors sponsored the anthology, it was common practice to invite foreign stars to host an hour – for example, Nicholas Monsarrat, Sir Cedric Hardwicke, and once Ronald Reagan – to add a bit of class. The common hope of all the various supervisors involved in planning and producing the anthology was to make it the home of both 'distinguished' and 'popular' drama, which required a balancing act, a choice of different kinds of fare, that didn't always work very well.[9]

Half-hour drama was also featured, among other items, on the avant-garde 'Q for Quest,' later 'Quest' (Spring '61 to Spring '64), another creation of Ross McLean, who'd planned a producer's workshop (hosted by Andrew Allan). In fact the anthology won fame only after producer Daryl Duke took command, in Fall '61: Duke strove to find subjects that were contemporary and to treat them in an unusual, if not controversial fashion, to excite the passions of the viewers. It always seemed a trifle pretentious, and it sometimes struck critics as 'way-out,' but it furnished a mix of jazz, plays, satire, and documentaries that was often striking in its originality. After Duke left Toronto for Hollywood, a parting that wasn't altogether friendly, the experienced drama producer Mario Prizek was given the task of organizing another experimental anthology of drama, satire, and so on, which appeared in the Spring '65 under the title 'Eye-Opener.' That too ran afoul of the authorities, and disappeared in a little flurry of controversy. The avant-garde anthology just wasn't the sort of experiment that even the CBC could sponsor for long, at least not by the mid-1960s.[10]

The CBC sold the anthologies to the public as Culture. Television eagerly appropriated what Raymond Williams has called 'the signals of art.' Sometimes that was explicit in the title, hence the 'théâtres' and the 'concert' hour, sometimes it was more subtle as in the case of a 'festival' of assorted riches. The signal might be embodied in the very structure of the broadcast: the teleplays, for example, were divided into various acts, in the manner of stage plays in a live theatre. The announcers and hosts took care to underline the dignity and quality of the performance. The host of 'L'heure du concert' (25 March 1954), for example, welcomed the audience to the show (weren't they special people?), identified the various celebrities who were performing (including the conductor of the Toronto Symphony Orchestra), and outlined the show's excerpts from Chopin, Tchaikovsky's Swan Lake, and Borodin's Prince Igor. The announcer told viewers of 'General Motors Presents' (27 September 1959) that they should be prepared for an hour of 'distinguished television drama,' a ritual that none the less identified the fact that the viewer had crossed over the boundary from ordinary fare into the realm of art. Individual performances of concerts, operas, or plays were prominently featured in the CBC Times and La Semaine à Radio-Canada and promoted on television in the days preceding a broadcast as if they were special, worthy occasions. The producers of the anthologies became passionate champions of the artistic virtues of their shows in the press. Esse Ljungh of 'General Motors Presents' (1958/9 season) talked at length to Toronto journalists about the importance of quality in plays. Daryl Duke of 'Quest' fame was ever ready with a couple of sentences for a reporter about how different, how exotic, this showcase of the avant-garde really was. It was all a deadly serious game of packaging, intent on attracting viewer interest and bestowing legitimacy and status on this kind of programming.[11]

All these anthologies were of considerable significance to the flowering of the cultural scene that occurred in Canada during the 1950s and 1960s. The CBC provided lots of employment and training for people in the performing arts, albeit mostly in the Toronto and Montreal regions (which was a source of criticism from people in the hinterland, notably in Vancouver). The Fowler Committee found that in 1963 the CBC paid out some $9.2 million for Canadian talent, over three times the payments made by all private stations combined. According to Nathan Cohen, 'L'heure du concert' in 1957 supplied enough work to allow Les Grands Ballets Canadiens 'to function exclusively as a television ballet organization.' Drama critic Robert Russel observed in 1962 that CBC drama employed 'more writers, directors and actors than all other forms of professional theatre in the country put together.' Marce Munro recalled that the CBC arranged with the local cultural groups plus the University of British Columbia to bring to Vancouver international musicians who might never have come otherwise. Mary Jane Miller has noted that a check of Stratford casts in the early 1960s shows that Frances Hyland, Douglas Rain, Hugh Webster, Eric House, William Hutt, John Colicos, and other members of the company appeared on CBC productions, which may well have allowed them to remain in the country between the short seasons of the first years of Stratford. Jeremy Wilkin, a prominent TV actor in 1960, admitted sadly that it would be impossible for him to survive in Canada without all his television work, even though he clearly preferred to act on the live stage. A lot of different people from all walks of life wrote or adapted plays that eventually appeared on one of the two networks: a count in a Radio-Canada listing of writers indicated that Marcel Dubé, one of the two chief playwrights in Quebec at the time (the other was Gratien Gélinas who also had a few television credits to his name), was involved in writing or adapting thirty-two separate teleplays between 1952 and 1963.[12]

But jobs for the boys, and a few girls, was not the chief purpose of all these anthologies. Besides, any credit the CBC might claim as a sponsor of the arts had to be shared with the Canada Council and private donors. What the CBC aspired to become was a sort of national stage and a national theatre, the place where a whole country could view the best in the performing arts.

Celebrating the Classics

The production of concerts, opera, ballet, Elizabethan drama, and the like required that television submit itself to conventions derived from the ways of the stage. Oh yes, some allowance was made for the technical characteristics of the medium. But there was a proper way of doing this kind of material. Fans of *Carmen* or *Swan Lake* were, by and large, a conservative lot. They weren't likely to accept with glee any television production that clashed with their expectations. That meant television had somehow to restrain itself: the purpose of broadcasting the classics was not to reshape a beloved performance but to reproduce as accurately as possible that performance. Over the years the CBC's two networks broadcast an astonishing range of material from the classical repertoire, although there was an understandable preference for the artists and the works that would be familiar to audiences. The names of Beethoven, Strauss, Bach, Wagner, Mozart, Moussorgsky, Stravinsky, and Ravel kept cropping up in the list of favoured composers. Along with productions, in whole or part, of *Swan Lake* and *The Nutcracker*, there were performances of more recent pieces, such as the Igor Stravinsky and Alexandre Benois's ballet *Petrouchka* ('L'heure du concert,' December 1957), or a contemporary ballet, such as Ray Powell's *One in Five* ('Festival,' April 1964). As one might expect, Shakespeare received his due with performances of *Macbeth, Othello*, and *Hamlet*, but 'Téléthéâtre' also gave its viewers an adaptation of Diderot's comedy *Est-il bon? Est-il méchant?* (25 October 1956) and 'Folio' offered its version of the medieval mystery play *The Nativity Play* (19 December 1956). Yet it was in the realm of opera and operetta that Toronto and Montreal really put forward the most extraordinary efforts: *The Barber of Seville* (1953/4), *The Rake's Progress* (1954/5), *La Bohème* (1955/6), *Carmen* (1956/7), *Madame Butterfly* (1957/8), *Eugene Onegin* and *The Merry Widow* (1958/9), HMS *Pinafore* and *Elektra* (1960/1), *Othello* and *The Gondoliers* (1962/3), and *Rigoletto* (1964/5).

The ambitions, and at times the arrogance, of CBC producers were amazing. They seemed to believe that the small screen could handle just about any kind of classic. Pierre Mercure, an early producer of 'L'heure du concert,' told a CBC *Times* reporter that 'TV can be an ideal concert-stage medium.': 'Pictorially, he says, it is many jumps ahead of the stage. In opera and ballet on TV the camera can spread the action without interruption over several sets. It can follow singers or dancers up one street and down the next. It can blot out inactive characters who often appear awkward and unreal on the operatic stage. It can catch close-ups of singers, show facial expressions, and focus attention on different objects important to the action.' Franz Kraemer, one of his counterparts in Toronto, agreed: he could provide the attentive viewer of any concert 'with camera shots and cuts which will not detract from and will possibly enhance the performance.' Kraemer also believed that whatever changes television required in, say, an opera resulted in a performance that was equally as effective as on the stage: 'In the opera house, Kraemer argues, the order of importance is (1) orchestra and singing line; (2) the picture, of cast and set; (3) the intelligibility of the words. But in TV the order becomes (1) the picture; (2) singing line and intelligibility; (3) orchestra. These factors – which seem to embrace the intimacy mentioned by [others] – make an opera successful on television.'

Kraemer's enthusiasm was exemplified in an exchange between a colleague, Norman Campbell, and the Stratford director Tyrone Guthrie over the planned television adaptation of HMS *Pinafore*. Guthrie claimed that the adaptation would require certain changes in emphasis, a couple of cuts, to adjust to the fact that the camera focused attention on a few actors and couldn't handle fantasy well. Campbell felt otherwise: television could do fantasy. It was his purpose 'to retain the essential qualities of the Guthrie production,' 'to capture the theatre experience,' and he had no doubt it could be achieved. Running through the commentary of each of these producers was the presumption that the television camera was an almost magical tool of presentation.[13]

Producers were not keen about suggestions they simply broadcast stage productions of the classics. There were occasions when this did happen, of course. The earliest mention I've come across was in a brief CBC *Times* (13–19 January 1957) note of a performance of Sophocles's *Oedipus Rex*, a film of the drama 'as presented at Stratford,' for 'Folio.' In March 1964 'Festival' did bring viewers a much-delayed recording of the Montreal Symphony's inaugural performance at Montreal's Place des Arts. But there were severe technical difficulties: it was hard to get the sound and the lighting right to produce a recording that was up to broadcast standards. And TV producers much preferred to work in the studio where they could control all of the elements that went into the performance.[14]

There's no doubt that the CBCers went to great pains to design a top-notch production. Witness all the effort lavished on Franz Kraemer's presentation of an English-language version of Bizet's *Carmen*, which was scheduled to conclude the 'Folio' season on 1 May 1957. He had a cast of eighty people, including the American star Gloria Lane as Carmen, eleven soloists, five dancers, and fourteen-voice children's chorus. The costumes

were described as 'modern Spanish dress.' Although trimming the production from three hours to two meant some cuts, the public was promised
that 'none of the familiar arias and choruses will be missing.' Indeed 'some
pantomime sections' had been added. The actual rehearsals had involved
three weeks of heavy work. Kraemer planned the use of six cameras and
two studios. The CBC Orchestra, stationed in a studio half a mile from
the TV studio, would play and their music would be piped in through
loudspeakers to the singers, the whole mix of sight and sound co-ordinated
by the conductor working in front of a TV monitor. Is it any wonder that
broadcasts of the classics were among the most expensive productions the
CBC did at that time? An estimate in 1961 suggested that a Gilbert and
Sullivan production would run to about $60,000, the National Ballet about
the same, and a 'Festival' drama $45,000.[15]

Even though individual productions earned praise, the fact remains that
many highbrows just weren't satisfied with the overall results. Consider the
criticism of the performance of Richard Strauss's *Elektra*, broadcast on
'Festival' 23 January 1961, from 9:30 to 11:15. This was a most ambitious
production, indeed the North American television première of the opera.
Strauss's tragedy is an extended nightmare of betrayal, degradation, hate,
murder, and madness, set in ancient Greece just after the Trojan War. The
music was equally wild and powerful. Franz Kraemer, the producer, had
decided on one long act, running 105 minutes! The opera was introduced
by Lister Sinclair, an experienced announcer (among much else), who
delivered a brief prologue to explain to viewers just what was about to
happen. Elektra was performed by the American soprano Virginia Gordoni, who was backed by an assortment of Canadian and American singers.
The music was provided by the Toronto Symphony Orchestra, increased
to eighty-seven players for the performance, and conducted by Walter
Susskind. Special sets had been designed to portray 'the courtyard of
King Agamemnon's palace at Mycene' and special 'ancient Greek – styled
costumes' produced, both to convey authenticity. Kraemer blithely told a
CBC Times reporter that *Electra* was 'ideally suited to the intimacy of
television' – 'it has a smallish cast, a simple but powerful story, and it's in
one act.'[16]

He was wrong. The panel of internal reviewers who sent in their comments to Ottawa headquarters in the days after the broadcast made that
abundantly clear.

Despite attraction of producing opera never done before on TV in American [*sic*],
and one which is historical milestone at that – despite distinguished presentation,

is all this enough to justify very expensive production too big and overpowering for the small screen and living room, and too strident and emotionally too high pitched through 105 minutes [?]

... We must confess the lack of action and our inability to catch words, even though they were in English gave us impression of over-long and draggy production.

While the opera was purported[ly] sung in English in what was probably a top-notch translation only an occasional English word from male singers was discernible.

Sat faithfully thru Elektra. I couldn't understand a word of what was sung. The music was unfamiliar to me and perhaps for that reason not very enjoyable. I hadn't the foggiest idea of what was going on. This being the case I was reduced to observing from various angles during her gesticulations the breasts of Virginia Gordoni the lead, and speculating on whether they were real. (I reached no firm conclusion[.]) This I believe was the first North American production on TV of Elektra and I feel it might very well be the last[.]

The point is that these comments, though a bit extreme, were only variations on a series of complaints that were made time and again about television's versions of the classics.[17]

So many of the classics had about them an air of grandeur that could rarely be conveyed by television. Ansten Anstensen, head of the Department of German at the University of Saskatchewan, thought that the mediocre quality of the television image plus the lack of colour worked against any effort to handle spectacles. 'A really large ballet ensemble or an extended chorus line,' he mused, 'will invariably present the dancers' legs as a lot of wriggling, stunted carrots which can afford the viewers no pleasure whatever.' The poor sound quality of the television set didn't help either, especially in a composition where music played an important role. In private even CBC officials admitted that no really satisfactory technique for televising classical music had been devised.[18]

The underlying problem, however, was the very intimacy of television. 'The TV audience does not undergo the kind of psychological suppression of their everyday selves possible in the modern auditorium,' mused Sidney Lamb. 'A television studio is not a stage,' noted Roy Shields, 'nor is the living-room screen a front-row seat in an opera house.' The small screen was ill-suited to grand opera or great drama. 'The gestures are too wide,' claimed Mary Lowrey Ross in a discussion of drama, 'and the emotional tone is too lofty and sustained for the necessary compressions of time and space on television.' All too often the result was parody, Lamb complained, as in the case of a 'Hallmark Hall of Fame' performance of Shakespeare's *The Tempest*, in which 'Roddy McDowall's Ariel leaped about in the background wearing some sort of strange antenna, for all the world like a Martian on a trampoline.' Likewise Strowan Robertson's exasperation over the treatment of *Swan Lake*, where producer Norman Campbell had purportedly emphasized the ballet's narrative. 'Since the narrative of Swan Lake is dated, childish and implausible, our experience was no more enhanced than if we had read a *précis* of Hamlet.' None of the ritual so much a part of the ballet had been brought out. What worked best was, say, opera with a strong narrative, for example, *Peter Grimes*; drama employing simple and uncluttered sets; dances and ballet involving only a few performers; concerts where attention could be focused on a Leonard Bernstein or a Sir Thomas Beecham.[19]

The trouble was that television persisted in trying to shape classics into a form that was unsuitable to their purpose. Especially disturbing to purists was the way television producers compacted or altered texts, necessary perhaps to render the classic understandable or to avoid boring viewers, but also likely to change the performance itself. 'TV can take a classic and empty it out,' wrote a despairing Robert Fulford, 'leaving only the plot and a few of the funnier lines.' A testy Sidney Lamb complained that the 'Festival' producers had mutilated Webster's *The Duchess of Malfi* by cutting out scenes and emphasizing some characters in order to make sense of the story: the result was that one character became 'a kind of dyspeptic Jacobean private eye' and a crucial moment of psychological torture was 'reduced to a confused shouting outside the door, rather like an unruly Hallowe'en night.' But the chief culprit seemed to be the television camera, 'that tool of the producer's bias,' in the words of Strowan Robertson, which too easily perverted a classic. There were innumerable complaints about the use of the camera in the broadcast of concerts. The cutting from one section of an orchestra to another, or from one instrument to another, could not but distract attention from the music itself. Even close-ups of one person could be distressing. That was the criticism of Frank Hawort about a broadcast of Glenn Gould, marred by the camera's attention to his 'swaying body, twitching lips and occasional essays in subdued vocalism' – it was better to shut your eyes and listen with the ears only to enjoy the music. Little wonder that W.L. Morton, a historian and highbrow who also happened to be a CBC director, concluded that further presentations of serious music were fine 'as long as visual elements were not played up to distract the viewer.'[20]

The long and the short of all this commentary was that television hadn't, indeed couldn't, take the place of the live stage.

The TV Plays

'It may seem foolish to say, but television, the scorned stepchild of drama, may well be the basic theatre of our century.' That comment by Paddy Chayefsky in 1955 should be put down to the enthusiasm of the moment. The young Chayefsky had just about completed his highly successful debut as a dramatist, and he'd done so by writing plays for 'Philco Television Playhouse,' the most famous of which was *Marty*, broadcast on 24 May 1953 with then-unknown Rod Steiger in the starring role. Chayefsky was only one among a new group of famous television playwrights in the United States: Reginald Rose, Rod Serling, Tad Mosel, Robert Alan Aurthur, Horton Foote, and Gore Vidal were some of the other big names. Nick-named 'the video boys,' these writers had been skilful, and perhaps lucky enough to seize an unexpected opportunity. During the early 1950s the disdain and rivalry of Hollywood had deprived American television of the kind of movie material the networks would have liked to use to fill some portion of their evening schedules. So CBS, NBC, and even ABC had mounted a collection of teleplay anthologies that offered viewers adaptations of existing works as well as original, made-for-TV plays.[21]

Chayefsky, Rose, and Serling were widely acclaimed as the founders of a new kind of drama. But they couldn't have succeeded without the direction of such inspired producers as Fred Coe, who looked after the 'Philco' and 'Goodyear' playhouses. These men had embraced the new medium, made a virtue of its limitations, and produced a style of drama that, in Chayefsky's words, explored 'the marvelous world of the ordinary,' the lives of typical Americans, rather than the glamorous world of the Hollywood movie. What was variously called 'personal drama' (Tad Mosel), 'psycho-drama' (Jack Gould, a *New York Times* critic), 'the drama of introspection' (Chayefsky), 'kitchen-sink' or 'keyhole' drama exploited the supposed intimacy of television by 'eavesdropping' on individuals and families caught up in some sort of crisis. The fact that it was live added to the illusion of reality. We could see ourselves in these plays – it was drama for our times, and discriminating viewers as well as many critics seemed very impressed. The rage for this new art, for that's what its practitioners thought they had pioneered, achieved an apparent permanence with the publication of Chayefsky's own *Television Plays* in 1955; Mosel's *Other People's Houses*, Vidal's *Visit to a Small Planet and Other Television Plays*, and Rose's *Six*

Television Plays the next year; and finally Serling's *Patterns* in 1957. (Canadian Arthur Hailey added his plays to the series with *Close-Up: On Writing for Television* in 1960 – after he'd achieved some fame as a playwright for American television.) Their plays even invaded the other realms of drama: Chayefsky's *Marty* became an Academy Award–winning movie and Vidal's *Visit to a Small Planet*, a Broadway production.

This bright moment in the history of American television drama didn't last long. Advertisers had grown increasingly wary of the controversial nature of the 'psycho-dramas' that undercut the cheery messages of their commercials. Programmers discovered that telefilms, especially sitcoms, westerns, and crime drama, were much more popular with the masses. Some of the 'video boys' moved on: Chayefsky himself abandoned television drama after 1955. The dramatic anthologies dropped live drama for live-to-videotape and film production, carried out in Hollywood, that ensured the teleplay would become closer in style and content to the movies. Indeed the dramatic anthology as a type of program became an increasingly rare bird, especially after 1963, although teleplays would linger on in some series that offered an assortment of specials. What did last, though, was the memory of past glories, a kind of nostalgia that proved very useful to critics who liked to condemn the cultural wasteland that American television had become. Looking back, Chayefsky would recall this was when television really had been a writers' medium – 'That was an era when writers could be writers.' The teleplay appeared unique in the annals of television: a work of art that conformed to the standards embodied in traditional aesthetics.[22]

The bright moment had inspired TV people outside the United States. New York's triumph could be Toronto's as well. In Montreal, too, producers were familiar with the experience south of the border – but their ambitions were limited by the need to fill so much of the schedule with home-grown material. Simply because Toronto could ride piggyback on the riches of American television, so freeing time and resources for other things, its masters had more reason to dream of creating a national theatre that would showcase modern classics, popular plays, and a made-in-Canada drama. The psychic investment in this dream was greater than any made in other brands of entertainment, including the struggle to fashion Canadian variety. For success in drama would demonstrate beyond a shadow of a doubt the utility of CBC-TV as an instrument of Culture. The story of what happened, the rise and the fall of the teleplay, consequently, tells us a lot about art on television.

The radio legacy seemed to furnish a solid foundation for success.

Toronto had justly won much acclaim for its plays during the 1940s and early 1950s, notably those aired on the 'Stage' series, under the direction of that extraordinary genius of radio drama Andrew Allan, and 'Wednesday Night,' where Esse Ljungh, J. Frank Willis, and Rupert Caplan were the chief forces. Management's initial policy of separating the radio and television services, however, kept the old pros out of the field of television drama in the first few crucial years of experimentation.[23]

So the task fell to new men, especially to the ex-NFB producer Sydney Newman, who became the executive producer of 'General Motors Theatre' and a supervisor of drama. More than anyone else he came to fulfil the role of the drama impresario with the vision to push people to develop a high-quality and popular style of drama. Perhaps because of his past experience in documentary films, Newman was a great champion of both realistic and Canadian drama: 'He felt it had to deal with real people and real things,' Mavor Moore claimed much later. Paul Almond, then a youthful producer, credited Newman with bringing him down to earth, making him realize the need 'to do the simple sort of homey show.' Newman's choice of the proper format for this drama was the commercial one-hour teleplay featured on 'General Motors Theatre,' much like the product of Fred Coe and the other New York producers of the early 1950s. (Florent Forget, who became the directeur des téléthéâtres in Montreal, apparently had a similar aim of creating a popular, commercial one-hour teleplay series with the launching of 'Le théâtre populaire' in the summer of 1956.)[24]

The key to success, Newman assumed, was to build a stable of Canadian playwrights. That would ensure a sufficient body of made-in-Canada plays and adaptations to tickle the fancy of audiences. 'Canadians seeing themselves in dramatic situations always seemed to me the best way to get them to watch my programmes.' He was particularly interested in getting new playwrights who would write original stories for television, plays that suited the attributes of the medium. That's why he imported from the United States the idea of hiring a special story editor whose task it was to scour the country, looking into newspaper offices and university classes for promising talent. He turned this job over to Nathan Cohen, the experienced drama critic: 'My mission, as I construed my mandate from Sidney, was to get original, preferably indigenous, plays and to create a standard to make that series talked about in the sense that people would tune in and say, "Well, we don't know what's going to be on, but we know it'll be interesting. It's going to have something to give us in good entertainment and maybe tell us something about ourselves, maybe." ' But the hidden agenda was best articulated by a successor, Hugh Kemp (whom Cohen had coaxed to write plays for TV), when he became national script supervisor in 1959. 'The network's hunger is for that small core of brilliant playwrights who can do for Canadian television what people like Chayefsky, Reginald Rose, and Rod Serling did for U.S. television in its brief period of dramatic excellence.'[25]

All this effort produced results. *Canadian Telescreen* (2 August 1956) carried a story that three-quarters of the scripts used by 'General Motors Theatre' in 1955/6 were Canadian originals or adaptations. One of the originals by first-time playwright Arthur Hailey, a thriller entitled *Flight into Danger*, aired on 3 April 1956, became the smash hit of the season. The play was later performed on NBC and a kinescope was shown by the BBC, again eliciting applause from viewers that convinced the British to buy eleven more Canadian plays. The sensational success of *Flight into Danger* seemed proof that Toronto drama was finally world-class fare. Next year's CBC Annual Report claimed 'General Motors Theatre' aired ten Canadian originals and two adaptations out of eighteen plays, 'Folio' six originals out of twelve productions, the special 'First Performance' offered four originals, and fully twenty-three of the twenty-nine half-hour dramas of 'On Camera' were Canadian originals. (Similarly, in French Canada, Montreal offered twenty originals in 1955 and again in 1957, reaching a high point of forty-three in 1958 out of a total production of seventy-three plays.) Further recognition came in the fall of 1958 when, briefly, some of the teleplays of 'General Motors Theatre' were broadcast live on the ABC network under the title 'Encounter.' An American critic, Louise Bresky, commented on how lucky Canadians were to enjoy such 'high quality' drama, and how pleased she was that it was being exported to the United States, where live television theatre was in decline. Toronto might not have reached the pinnacles of fame once occupied by New York. But the Toronto product was a lot more novel and exciting than what was being produced in England. And as Hollywood won out over New York, perhaps Toronto would be left as the only main centre of live drama for anglophone audiences in North America.[26]

All this activity fostered the birth of two groups of television dramatists, one in French Canada and the other in English Canada (there was very little crossing-over), some of whom came from radio, and some of whom were newcomers. In French Canada, after five years of broadcasting, the leading contributors were Marcel Dubé, author of *Zone* (the first original that could be counted a hit, broadcast in Quebec on 16 May 1953) and nine other plays; Felix LeClerc, Jean Desprez, and Yves Thériault, all at six scripts; and Eugène Cloutier (at five) and Guy Dufresne (at four).

Turning to English Canada, Dean Walker writing in *Saturday Night* in 1959 identified a series of 'top men' who could be listed as professionals: Len Peterson, Bernard Slade, Donald Jack, Mac Shoub, Joseph Schull, John Whelan, Byron Riggan, Mavor Moore, Lister Sinclair, Rita Allen, George Salverson, and Ron Hambleton.[27]

Things weren't quite so rosy for Canadian playwrights as one might expect, though. Walker pointed out that the public didn't know the names of many of the professionals. Arthur Hailey was an exception, of course. Likewise veterans such as Len Peterson, Joseph Schull, and Lister Sinclair and prominent dramatists such as Mavor Moore and Marcel Dubé clearly did have a 'name' in literary circles. But how many people knew about, say, Stanley Mann, who had three plays produced on 'General Motors Theatre' in the 1955/6 season (apparently he had left for England soon after)?

Nor was it easy to earn a living writing for television. By 1956 the rates for a half-hour script ran up to $500 and for an hour script $1,000. Hailey's reported take of $50,000 for the *Flight into Danger* project was unique: the script had been broadcast, and rebroadcast, in three countries, turned into a Hollywood movie, and eventually written up as a novel. Esse Ljungh told the CBC directors that a television playwright would usually have to find outside work. That may explain why Lister Sinclair was a regular host and announcer on CBC radio and television and George Salverson was at one point a CBC editor on 'On Camera.'[28]

Still, if playwrighting had never been a particularly lucrative occupation for most of its practitioners, it did, at least, have the reputation as an art, a way in which the individual could express his or her own special genius. Was that true in broadcasting? 'Neither radio nor television give to the writer that feeling, so necessary and terrible to his ego, that he is wrestling alone with his subject; that if the victory is his, it is his alone,' lamented George Robertson, a playwright and producer. At least in the radio age, if we are to believe such producers as Andrew Allan and such dramatists as Len Peterson, much effort was spent translating the work of the play-wright as faithfully as possible. Not so, or not so much, in the case of television, however. The whole ethos of television ran counter to dreams of unsullied individual expression: 'really stimulating TV drama,' declared the producer Michael Sadlier, 'calls for team-work, not a one-man job.' He added that the dramatist 'who sends in a play all ready for the air doesn't exist.' At times it seemed as though the writer was expendable.[29]

All kinds of people, from script editors to admen, not to mention the actual director, had a hand in the final product. 'No work of art, in my estimation,' feared Andrew Allan, 'with the possible exception of the King

James version [of the Bible], was ever created by a committee.' Len Peterson railed against the committee system where everyone 'put in his own little cautiousness,' which could only turn a script into 'standardized mush.' One Dr Murphy, a first-time writer, had his play completely rewritten twice, then received a 4,000-word critique, and didn't win acceptance for 'his work' until a couple more revisions were done. Even an experienced playwright had to suffer such problems: Mavor Moore's *The Man Who Caught Bullets* supposedly took a year to bring to fruition. Salverson's *The Almighty Voice* shown on 'On Camera' was a bowdlerized version of his radio play *Blasphemy*, about an athiest who challenged heaven, the references to the Christian God dropped so as not to offend. There were many taboos to worry about: J. Frank Willis warned against 'profanity' and plumped for 'good taste' and Alice Frick, an editor in the CBC's script department, bluntly told writers to avoid 'political party disputes, sectarian religion, and the use of "hells" and "damns" outside the realm of good taste.'[30]

Producers were the chief sinners, mind you. Peterson felt that producers were 'terrified of taking a gamble' on anything unusual or controversial. Nathan Cohen later recounted the story of how a half-hour script by Hugh Garner dealing with a Hydro lineman was turned down by five different producers. 'Finally, one of them said to me, "What do we know about working people? You can't expect us to do plays about people we don't understand." ' Even when a script was accepted, producers had no compunctions about altering it. According to Peterson, Newman himself couldn't 'keep his hands off other people's work.' Lesser lights could be much, much worse. 'There have been producers who have been immature, arrogant, insensitive jerks, who have nothing but contempt for the writer, with or without justification,' recalled Hugh Gauntlett, then an assistant program director. 'They would treat him, at best, as an amateur storyteller.' Such men were firm believers in the producer-as-artist: they thought 'that the producer made the television play out of raw materials, which, like Michelangelo, he molded. The script was merely something handed him like sets and lights, and he would operate on, what was, to the writer, living flesh.'[31]

What was the result? How good were the teleplays? Were they works of art? In retrospect, the range of modern drama offered Canadians during the 1950s was considerable. True in 1955 Forget had claimed that 'un immense théâtre est condamné par ses sujets scabreux, par ses théories subversives, par son nihilisme ou son immoralisme.' Yet a survey of the plays produced by Radio-Canada shows a willingness to offer popular as

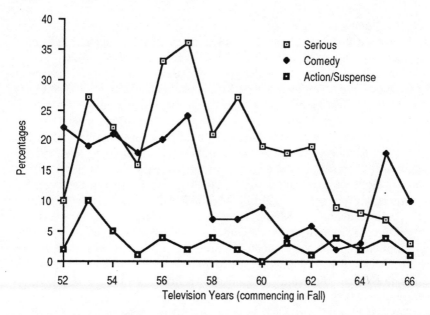

Chart 8.2 Quebec teleplays, 1952–67.
Note: This chart is based on the labels attached to the assorted plays listed in La Société Radio-Canada, *Vingt-cinq ans de dramatiques à la télévision de Radio-Canada 1952–77* (Montreal 1978)

well as difficult drama, tragedy and comedy, a bit of farce, the occasional thriller, as well as a lot of meaty, even controversial fare (see chart 8.2). These riches included works by Ibsen (*Les piliers de la société*, December 1953), Wilde (*L'éventail de Lady Windermere*, January 1955), Pirandello (*La volupte de l'honneur*, March 1958), Gogol (*Le manteau*, July 1958), and Chekhov (*L'Oncle Vania*, December 1958). Not to be outdone Toronto offered Galsworthy's *Justice*, Arthur Miller's *Death of a Salesman*, Maugham's *The Land of Promise*, and lots of Ibsen (*The Wild Duck, A Doll's House, An Enemy of the People*, and *Hedda Gabbler*). On occasion Toronto aired some American originals as well: Richard Levinson and William Link, two Americans who later became famous producers in Hollywood, got their start in television writing two plays that were broadcast on 'General Motors Presents.' But most of the play material was in some measure Canadian, either an original or an adaptation: of 435 plays aired on Radio-Canada between 1952 and 1960, 42 per cent (or 183) were Canadian originals and 49 per cent (or 212) Canadian adaptations. More fragmentary data suggest that the figures in English Canada were comparable, although not as high. The fact was that any stage play, novel, or short story selected had to be adapted to the particular regime of live, studio drama.[32]

(The following analysis of the genre is based, in part, upon a series of close readings: a British teleplay *No Fixed Abode*, Granada's 'Television Playhouse,' 30 January 1959, about one night in a flophouse; *First Born*, 'Ford Theatre,' 10 September 1953, about a child's response to a step-mother, a performance that starred Ronald Reagan in his first television role; Rod Serling's *The Arena,* 'Studio One,' 9 April 1956, which explored the moral dilemma of a young u.s. senator; *The Return of the Hero*, 'Alfred Hitchcock Presents,' 2 March 1958, on the anguish of a crippled war veteran unknowingly rejected by his family; Marcel Dubé's *Florence*, 'Le téléthéâtre de Radio-Canada,' 14 March 1957, about a young woman's quest for freedom; André Laurendeau's comedy *La vertu des chattes*, 'Le théâtre populaire,' 30 June 1957, which featured an attempt at seduction; Pierre Perrault's study in loneliness, *Au coeur de la rose*, 'En première,' 22 March 1959 [although *Vingt-cinq ans* ... lists the first date of broadcast as 30 November 1958]; Wolf Menkowitz, *The Overcoat*, 'Playbill,' 29 June 1954, a play based on Gogol's story about injustice; Pushkin's *The Queen of Spades*, 'cbc Television Theatre,' 28 October 1956, on man's search for power and wealth; Robert Louis Stevenson's *Markheim*, 'On Camera,' 14 January 1957, about murder, the devil, and man's soul; *The Ikon of Elijah*, 'The Unforeseen,' 23 October 1958, which looked at the wages of greed; C.P. Snow's *The New Men*, 'General Motors Presents,' 27 September 1959, on science and morality in the atomic age; and Sean O'Casey's *Juno and the Paycock*, 'Festival,' 15 December 1965, a play full of Ireland's tragedies. A larger than usual sample of this genre seemed necessary to evaluate the claim that the teleplay was a work of art.)

Drama was still caught in what Ed Moser, an executive producer of 'General Motors Presents,' called 'the age of the Ibsen hangover,' meaning audiences demanded a believable representation of events and characters. And television drama, in particular, suffered from an obsession with realism because both producers and viewers deemed it a photographic medium. That ruled out certain kinds of drama: just as Chayefsky felt that you really couldn't handle spectacles or 'impressionistic and lyrical dramas' on the small screen, so Hailey warned that television was not 'a place for the introspective essay.' But television was well-suited to historical drama (thus the discovery of insulin, a moment in the life of Joe Howe, John A. Macdonald and Confederation, James Whelan's assassination of D'Arcy McGee, and Louis Riel were all celebrated in Canadian plays), the works of Ibsen or Shaw (which were studies in character), and incidents drawn from real life (Hailey's *Flight into Danger* came from the author's musings while taking an air trip and *Time Lock* from a visit to a bank). Snow's *The New Men* worked well because its message that scientists, like all men, were responsible for their actions was cast in the mould of a conflict of wills. 'You can use TV drama to discuss world problems or prove the existence of God,' asserted producer Mel Breen, 'but you must have a story line.' Typically, the teleplay was a condensed slice-of-life involving a few characters that conveyed a relatively simple story, no matter how complex the meaning.[33]

A lot of the hype popular at the time was rooted in assumptions about the importance of the camera. The camera, so it seemed, allowed drama to escape the theatricality of the live stage, where actors were forced to project whatever they uttered, and the blindness of radio, where so much had to be spoken to carry the action. Much was said about the need to cut down on words and to emphasize the power of the camera to depict exactly what was happening. (That could be a boon to a writer: Brian Swarbrick told an interviewer that he could earn $600 for a sixty-page radio play – 'When I take the same play, cut its wordage in half and let the camera do the work for me, I'm paid $1,250 by the CBC.') The fact was that a viewer could only have enjoyed such plays as *Markheim* or even the simpler *The Ikon of Elijah*, to name but two cases, if he or she paid close attention to what was said – the teleplay wasn't really an assault on the importance of verbal language. Still the ability to cut from one actor to another, to use alternate long-shots and close-ups, gave producers a certain freedom. You could control time and place by shifting cameras, just as you could rely upon body language to tell the story by moving in for a close-up. The excitement of *Flight into Danger*, said Miriam Waddington, owed much 'to the many shifts of the camera from air to ground, from engine room to passenger section.'[34]

Everyone recognized that the television camera wasn't quite like the film camera: one couldn't handle the panoramic scenes or the large casts of movies. But television could capitalize on the virtues of the small screen in a way that movies could not. That's why the little story seemed best suited to the new medium. 'The key to TV drama was intimacy,' asserted Rod Serling, 'and the facial study on the small screen carried with it a meaning and power far beyond its usage in the motion picture.' Much of the action in *Markheim* consisted of images of facial expressions, gestures, and mannerisms to suggest emotions and reactions. The TV focus was on the personalities portrayed. Laurendeau's comedy *La vertu des chattes* got by with only three characters, Jerome and Sylvie whose talk carried the play and a brief visit by a beggar. 'Television is, or ought to be, superb at conveying certain kinds of intellectual and emotional stress,' mused George Robertson: 'again, it is the substance of what is happening between people at their most intimate and revealing which is of paramount importance, and it is this that television, well-used, can so triumphantly achieve.' The combination of a superb script, skilled direction, and effective acting made both *No Fixed Abode* and *Florence* excellent examples of this maxim.[35]

One of the chief claims to fame of the teleplay was that it amounted to a more compelling mix of drama and documentary than was common – or even likely – in other media. That was true in Britain and the United States, not just in Canada: there's no evidence to support the pleasing notion that Canada was *the* home of the documentary tradition, in drama or anything else. The makers of teleplays spent a lot of time on getting the details right – worrying about the accuracy of costumes, settings, props, and the like. A scene set in a monastery in *The Ikon of Elijah* featured the background sound of the chanting of monks to fix the context in the minds of viewers. In *The New Men* the scientists were identified by their lab coats while their rivals, the officials and the politicians, appeared in business suits. Pierre Perrault located his sombre study *Au coeur de la rose* on a barren island in a lighthouse, cut off from society, and complete with the sounds of a storm, seagulls, and the occasional foghorn. Dubé's *Florence* spoke to a generation in French Canada caught between a traditional and impoverished past and an affluent but alien future: he conveyed that theme, in part, with images of life at home in a modest, even tawdry apartment, at work in a modern advertising office, and at play in a fashionable bar.

Such touches were minor compared to all the bits of authenticity put into Arthur Hailey's *Flight into Danger*. The teleplay dealt with the ordeal of an ex–fighter pilot required to land a passenger aircraft when the flying crew was struck down by a case of food poisoning. Hailey's script called for a series of film inserts (unusual at that time) of planes in flight, an air strip, and planes landing. The final climax of the teleplay occurred in the actual cockpit of a North Star, which was towed from Trenton to Toronto. The dialogue was strewn with the language of flying: 'fore-and-aft control,' 'air speed,' 'trim,' 'crosswind,' 'more throttle,' and on and on. This kind of attention to detail became a Hailey trademark. In *Time Lock* the producer had to get air hammers and acetylene torches, plus build a set using concrete blocks, all to make the efforts of rescuers to free a boy from a bank vault look convincing. One commentator, Alan Thomas, thought such touches made for 'an almost perfect type of television documentary' – it all created a 'breathtaking appearance of reality.'[36]

What was most interesting about the teleplay, however, was not its effort to imitate the documentary but its exploration of man's mind and soul. In 1961 Martin Dworkin wrote a retrospective on a decade of teleplays entitled 'Much in Little,' which appeared in *Canadian Commentator*. Dworkin argued that the most significant attribute of television drama was the way in which it embodied 'the topical verities' and 'the case approach' of modern social science, particularly psychology. He was quite correct about Chayefsky who was captivated by the fad of psychoanalysis: people had turned inwards, thought Chayefsky, searching for meaning and happiness in their lives, which had made 'the jargon of introspection' a kind of 'everyday conversation.' He wasn't alone in this belief, so it seemed. The teleplays were full of characters troubled by self-doubts, inner turmoil, an unruly subconscious. Dubé's Florence was a modern gal in spirit, struggling to secure her independence in the face of family and social pressures. A British import entitled *The Kidders* and shown on CBC's 'Playhouse U.K.' in the summer of 1959 probed the psychology of a group of corporate types who were full of bonhomie on the surface but filled with jealousy and fear underneath. Robert Fulford, for a time the television critic of *Canadian Forum*, detected a taste for psycho-babble in the play *Here Today* ..., which had been aired on 'General Motors Presents': a debonair Robert Goulet confessed to a deep insecurity that infected his treatment of people and a troubled Kate Reid admitted to a terrible relationship with her father, which had coloured her dealings with men. There was some truth to Dworkin's claim that the television playwrights were really the children of Freud, and that their works amounted to propaganda for the new creed of psychology.[37]

But these playwrights were even more the heirs to generations of moralists, from Savonarola to Sartre. For what captivated them were issues of conduct, the problems of responsibility and duty, questions of right and wrong, the struggle between good and evil – in short, the whole domain of modern ethics. We lived in corrupted times, times afflicted by too much science and affluence, by human greed, by bigotry, by the decline of old verities, when people of a delicate moral sensibility were confronted by the need to make decisions.

The characters in the teleplays were forever being tested. Serling's freshman senator in *The Arena* finally chose the cause of decency rather than to blacken unfairly another's name, even though that decision is taken at the expense of his father who had demanded revenge against the man who injured him. The protagonist in *Markheim* first probed to see whether his intended victim, a grasping merchant, had any redeeming qualities – the man didn't, and so he died; then the protagonist is tempted by the devil with promises of safety and wealth, if only he would commit a second murder – he didn't, and so he saves his soul. The young girl in *Au coeur de la rose* had to choose between loyalty to her family, which meant continued entrapment in a life of gloom and despair on an isolated island, and love for a young sailor, which meant fulfilment in marriage and escape to the mainland – she sacrificed her happiness to stay at home where her parents needed her. In Menkowitz's version of *The Overcoat* the two main characters, Fender the old Jewish worker and Maury the Jewish tailor, talked and talked about the injustices of life that eventually and naturally led to the justice of stealing a coat from the company owned by the heartless Ranting. The scientists in *The New Men* battled with their consciences: they had to decide whether the pursuit of knowledge and the goal of professional success were worth the moral cost of remaining silent while the politicians were left free to play with the atomic bomb – the scientists spoke out. In nearly all of these teleplays morality triumphed at the end. Things might not be rosy: life didn't have happy conclusions (except in the teleplays of a writer such as Arthur Hailey). But what had been affirmed was the cause of righteousness.

In retrospect it may seem a bit surprising that all these plays didn't win wider applause, at least from highbrows. But critics, by and large, deemed the teleplay a lesser form of art, not up to the standard of stage plays and not even as worthwhile as the radio plays. One reason lay in something Dworkin highlighted, 'the deliberate simplification of theses and treatments' required to make any performance acceptable on television. Efforts to dramatize novels had never worked, Hugh Garner claimed, because too much had to go to keep the story intact. Adapted stage plays seemed to loose force or content in translation. Most of the character portraits in the original teleplays were little more than 'stereotypes,' in the words of critic Gerald Weales, 'that allow the author to indicate who and what they are by means of familiar, even stock, analyses.'[38]

There were other complaints about style and quality that had little to do with television's penchant for reducing everything to essentials. 'I would try to encourage Canadian playwrights in comedy,' argued J.B. McGeachy: 'they are now too devoted to the lugubrious.' Miriam Waddington grew tired of studio drama with its 'dead inert leaves,' 'artificial flowers,' the 'fake street,' 'an imitation wall,' and its actors playing such types as the 'warm, simple, Jewish mother,' all sins which she put down to the legacy of live theatre. Robert Russel thought that too little rehearsal time had 'often resulted in superficial, over-busy productions, unfair to audience, actor, playwright, the CBC.' Robert Fulford lambasted made-in-Canada plays because they lacked a sense of place (the business executive or the farmer could come from Anywhere, North America), they were too full of bourgeois pieties about Canada (which emerged as 'a quietly prosperous country, complacently middle-class and materially well fixed, politically sound'), and they avoided any investigation of the social dimension of life (unlike American plays). He yearned for plays about poverty, corruption, the rise of millionaires, or the import of European immigration that would reveal 'the Canada which actually exists behind the newspaper stories.'[39]

The most telling criticism, though, is rooted in what television hadn't done. TV didn't give birth to a novel brand of drama. The teleplay wasn't a break with the past. 'TV will not successfully present drama so long as it continues to ape the values and shape of stage drama,' warned Herbert Whittaker, the drama critic of *The Globe and Mail*. 'Television must discover its own technique, perhaps a fragmentary, enquiring technique because its strength is in the you-were-there, reportorial style.' Whatever the talk about the import of the camera, producers never really explored the potential of the new technology. Studio drama was simply not as visual as the movies. The experiments with overlapping images and film inserts, for example, were little more than gimmicks that strengthened the naturalistic imperative of television drama. Producers strove to create a harmonious whole, not to juxtapose different elements, conflicting images that might jar and so stimulate the viewer. Nor did playwrights create either originals or adaptations that differed markedly from what was available, and usually better, in stage drama. There wasn't much of an attempt to experiment with mine, symbolism, epic theatre, Brechtian drama, and all the other assorted alternatives to the mainstream. Indeed the true founders of television drama weren't Chayefsky and the boys but tough-minded realists such as Tennessee Williams and Arthur Miller, whose triumphs such as *The Glass Menagerie* or *Death of a Salesmen* embodied the lessons of psychology and the fascination with morality that characterized so many teleplays. Ironically the teleplay remained more derivative in style and content than the much-despised series drama. Why? Well, part of the explanation lies in the purposes of the producers and playwrights: they were struggling to achieve legitimacy, to create art, not to challenge the status quo. The rest of the explanation lies in the expectations of the audience: most viewers wanted entertainment, the familiar, not something really novel or unusual.[40]

In truth the day of Canadian originals, even of the teleplay itself, was already beginning to pass away. Sydney Newman had been tempted away by independent television in Britain in 1958, where he was better able to realize his dreams of a topical and national drama. The job he left behind was too big to be filled by his successors. Esse Ljungh, of radio fame, got caught up in the rat-race during his brief tenure as a supervising producer of 'General Motors Presents' in 1958/9. 'The editorial policy of "GM Presents" is to find a script for the next week,' he told a colleague who wondered just what the purpose of the anthology was. Neither Michael Sadlier nor Ed Moser, who followed Ljungh, had the will or the power to sponsor new playwrights, or even much Canadian drama, relying instead upon proved writers and material to bestow a mark of quality on their product. There was a definite feeling that Canadian writers couldn't be depended upon to produce a sufficient number of pleasing scripts to meet the demand. A sign of the times was a passing comment made by Michael Sadlier in September 1959 that 'General Motors Presents' would redo some of the plays of 'the Golden Age of television drama,' including one by Reginald Rose. According to Bill Davidson, a CBC producer, Moser went back 'to older writers from eight to ten years ago' and filled in the gaps 'with scripts from American agencies.' So while there had been nineteen scripts by Canadians on 'General Motors Presents' in 1960/1, there were only nine in the last full season of its successor 'Playdate' in 1963/4. Robert Allen over at 'Festival' was, according to contemporaries, much more interested in finding 'the best,' and putting that on the air, than on making 'new things' work. 'Festival' averaged only about three productions of made-in-Canada plays a year.[41]

The early 1960s weren't bereft of innovation, of course. Writers and producers, at least in English Canada, did experiment with avant-garde drama that broke with the previous emphasis on personal and private stories and even challenged the prevailing values or views of society. There were some new playwrights: George Ryga, for instance, wrote *Indian* (1962) and *Two Soldiers* (1963), each with a social message, for 'Quest.' Established writers appeared with novel offerings. Len Peterson adapted his famous radio play *Burlap Bags* about man's alienation in a world of corruption and sleaze, also for 'Quest.' Charles Israel updated the Easter story in *The Open Grave* by writing a fictional documentary of the last days of a Canadian peace leader, tried on false charges and executed to suit the powers that be, for the feature series 'Horizon.' The anthologies occasionally aired avant-garde drama written by Americans and Britishers. 'Festival' carried Edward Albee's controversial play *The Zoo Story* in 1961 and the next year two anti-war dramas, Marghanita Laski's *The Off-Shore Island* and John Arden's *Sergeant Musgrave's Dance*. Also in 1962, 'Quest' offered Jules Feiffer's *Crawling Arnold*, a peculiar play which dealt with a disturbed businessman who crawled around the floor, the efforts of the lady psychiatrist to cure him, and ended with what appeared to be a seduction scene. Such provocative offerings, though, weren't sufficient to save the teleplay. They may even have contributed to its demise.

The root problem was in the environment. Once the teleplay declined in the United States, its fate in Canada became uncertain. Could the dramatic anthologies continue to justify their place on the schedule? Did enough of the audience want to watch these shows? The competition for viewers became fiercer once the second stations and CTV went on the air in 1961. General Motors ended its sponsorship of the hour-long anthology reportedly because it didn't care for 'the general quality of the plays' and because it felt 'the promotional value' of the program had gone once the CBC's monopoly was undone. Little wonder that Hugh Gauntlett, speaking in 1964, noted how important it had become 'to put quality before a national label due to the intensifying competition from the commercial stations in Canada and stations across the border.'[42]

He might have added, though, that CBC management was less and less happy with the tone of the teleplays. Particularly after 1959, when a public controversy blew up in Quebec over the broadcast of *La Plus Belle de Caens*, a dramatization of the life of Marguerite d'Youville, founder of the Grey Nuns, CBC officials learned to their cost the dangers of broadcasting drama that might offend – in this case the angry 'viewers' were the bishops who thought the slightly risqué drama was a mockery of Christian faith. A few years later, in 1961, Alphonse Ouimet had to write a letter of explanation to the chairman of the Board of Broadcast Governors, Dr Andrew Stewart, justifying *The Zoo Story* as a legitimate piece of art in the face of charges of needless obscenity. The report went out a bit later from Robert Fulford's pen that the whole affair had provoked 'a new wave of puritanism' to ensure the CBC wasn't again hauled onto the carpet. The assorted outcries in public and even in Parliament about the kind of satire and drama that was a 'Quest' speciality continued to worry CBC managers. Finally, in January 1965, Toronto columnists began to talk about a clamp-down in Toronto: the installation of new men (mentioned were Robert McGall, an assistant general manager, and Marcel Munro, director of television), the demotion of others (Doug Nixon was cited as an example), plus the creation of a special review committee to oversee what was being planned. The first victim was apparently the series 'The Eye-Opener,' some of whose intended shows were cancelled or revised. The clear implication was that CBC-Toronto was no longer a home for provocative drama.[43]

Last but never least was the problem of funds. This fact program director Doug Nixon cited in mid-1965 as the chief cause for the dwindling 'output' in drama. There just wasn't sufficient revenue, from government or advertising, to continue doing everything in the realm of programming. Something had to be sacrificed. Hence the cut-back in drama, as well as variety, where expenses were so high. The money could be stretched farther in public affairs and documentary programming that would fulfil the essential quota of Canadian content. What was left for drama went more and more into popular storytelling, the téléromans in Montreal and such experiments as 'The Serial' mini-series, 'Seaway,' and eventually 'Quentin Durgens' and 'Wojeck' in Toronto. Only twelve plays were produced in Montreal during 1965.[44]

'There was no golden age of TV drama for us,' commented Nathan Cohen in 1966. 'We never produced a group of recognized authors identified with a specific program, such as the Paddy Chayefskys and Horton Footes and Robert Alan Aurthur of "Philco Playhouse." ' The trouble was there were never enough playwrights: indeed only a small group of television writers (he mentioned Israel, McFarlane, Salverson, Robertson, Schull, and Max Cohen) had elected to stay in Canada. Besides, the death of anthology drama wasn't really 'the betrayal of a great heritage, either in Canada or the United States,' he added. 'Here, even more so than there, it was rarely first-class, and seldom indigenous.'[45]

The teleplay had come nowhere near to realizing the dreams of a Chayefsky, never mind a Newman. The lack of artistic significance of the whole experiment was well-illustrated by the lack of interest, often the disdain, of literary types. 'Many creative writers, and even many CBC people,' wrote Dean Walker in 1959, 'still suspect that in the community of the arts, television represents the wrong side of the tracks.' A few years later, Leslie MacFarlane and M. Charles Cohen both complained about 'the lack of intelligent criticism' their work, and presumably that of other television playwrights, received from supposed compatriots. Nor was the academic community much impressed: the only entry on TV drama in William New's *Dramatists in Canada*, published in 1972, was a reprint of George Robertson's lament, 'Drama on the Air,' which concluded that broadcast drama in general had failed to realize its promise.[46]

Responses

The final verdict on CBC Culture must depend on some understanding of its impact upon the audience. That isn't easy to assess. The appreciation of even a lesser art is all to often a matter of individual taste. Let me provide some personal evidence of what I mean. I recall as a child being thoroughly bored by the one concert I saw performed on television: it seemed to be totally lacking in anything to capture the eye of the viewer. By contrast Stephen Baker, one of my researchers in Montreal, found the camera work and the sound quality of an early episode of 'L'heure du concert' (25 March 1954) sophisticated and enjoyable. Steve Strople, one of my researchers in Toronto, was much impressed by the 'Festival' performance of Sean O'Casey's *Juno and the Paycock*: it was, in his words, 'a powerful and gripping drama that absorbs the viewer.' But I felt this same play was so clichéd, the acting so overdone, that it became steadily more ridiculous as the acts dragged on.

Successful art is unfamiliar, exhilarating, distressing – it's successful because it has an effect on the viewer. People were brought up to assume that art appeared in special places: the art gallery, the theatre, bookstores and libraries, maybe the movie-house. Going to one of these places was, by and large, an act of volition; you prepared yourself to be stimulated. But broadcast art invaded the private circle of the home, and that could be very troubling. It might well evoke memories or foster ideas that had hitherto been repressed or neglected. It might use language or show scenes that were forbidden in that circle. Many viewers would be willing to accept a classical piece, whether a concert or a tragedy, allowing a certain poetic licence because the work of art or the author was esteemed. That wasn't always the case with modern plays, though: people didn't know what to expect, a fact which made this genre very different from most of the programming, including series drama. They might settle in for a half-hour or hour of entertainment, only to find themselves surprised, even shocked, by a phrase, an image, or a message that was unfamiliar, if not unwanted. (I remember how the performance of Laski's *The Off-shore Island* unsettled me with its anti-American message and its bleak portrayal of life in Britain after a nuclear exchange.) The teleplays became the most contentious, as well as the most pleasing, items on the Culture menu.[47]

It's possible to find anecdotes that illustrate the positive impact of a teleplay. There are the stories surrounding the excitement caused by what *Variety* called 'Hailey's Comet,' namely *Flight into Danger*. 'It was the right script at the right time,' recalled Don MacPherson: more and more people were flying at the time, and they were nervous about it. Right after the performance, the CBC stations were swamped with calls, expressing surprise and pleasure, and these were followed up with a flood of letters. 'This is my first attempt to thank anyone for producing a play on TV, one reason being that most plays produced by the CBC are not worth thanking anyone for,' wrote in a viewer. 'They are a little above our heads, but we thought Flight into Danger was superb.' It was, mused Cohen much later, the one time CBC plays had 'seized the public imagination.' That didn't deny the fact that on other occasions some of these plays won public favour: my parents were great fans of CBC comedies (most of which, though, were authored by non-Canadians.) In November 1960 'General Motors Presents' reached 1.8 million Canadians, enough to get it ranked seventeenth among network shows. Similarly 'Le télééthéâtre' was ranked twentieth on Radio-Canada, reaching a respectable 1.4 million viewers, in February 1962.[48]

Highbrows could get worked up too. Robert Russel, for instance, enthused about a 'Festival' production of Montherlant's *Queen after Death*, produced by Mario Prizek. 'In transferring this play to television, he had sharpened it,' wrote Russel, 'and thus deepened it, and expressed it in some of the most incredibly beautiful shots of actors-in-meaningful-relation that I had ever seen in TV' (whatever that meant). Russel's sheer pleasure in the spectacle was probably sharpened by the fact that he had studied various Parisian productions of Montherlant's work. But he admitted that nothing had prepared him for 'the depth, beauty and power' of the teleplay.[49]

In another vein, there's Michel Tremblay's reminiscences about how he became enamoured with the idea of writing drama. Only ten years old when Montreal went on the air, he swiftly became 'obsessed with TV. You might say I grew up in front of the television screen.' And it was the teleplays that captured his heart and mind. 'In that decade between my tenth and twentieth birthdays I must have seen about one thousand plays!' Is it any wonder that when he began to write plays they were copies of TV drama? He was to become famous during the 1970s, though, as the author of plays that used joual, criticized traditional values, and parodied the revered stereotypes of Quebec life. That he didn't learn from television. So much for early influences.[50]

But Culture was more likely to provoke protest, not bouquets, from the mass audience and its spokesmen. In 1957, after a production of *Swan Lake* on 'Folio,' one parliamentarian got up to denounce the spending of tax monies on 'long underwear boys cavorting about.' In 1959 Catholic Quebec was outraged by the scenes of a youthful Marguerite d'Youville (in the process of becoming a saint) romping around with her lover in *La Plus Belle de Caens*, most especially because priests had suggested viewing the play, girls had been allowed to stay up late, and convents had rented or borrowed sets for the occasion. Kate Aitken's survey of anglophone and middle-class opinion in 1959 turned up a feeling that there was 'too much emphasis on the sordid side of life and not enough emphasis on normal living' in CBC drama.[51]

The experiments with avant-garde and radical drama during the 1960s in English Canada disturbed old-fashioned viewers, notably in rural Ontario and on the prairies. All too often CBC-Toronto seemed to be running well ahead of its audience, or so Marce Munro recalled. Complaints targeted on excessive drinking, filthy language, the exposure of flesh, and unpatriotic or immoral sentiments. M. Charles Cohen's *The Hostage*, broadcast on 'Folio,' upset anglophiles because it portrayed terrorists struggling against a brutal force of occupying soldiers, who were played by actors with English accents, a fact that suggested the Cyprus mess of the time. 'Quest' was undoubtedly the worst offender because of its penchant for the unconventional (one critic called this show the Canadian version of the famous British series 'That Was the Week That Was,' just because it was so shocking). In 1962, E.W. Brunsden, a Conservative MP from Medicine Hat, denounced the 'Quest' *Crawling Arnold* as 'depraved ... disgusting ... garbage ... and a rank violation of the sanctity of the Canadian home.' But 'Festival' also came in for a share of the lumps. A twelve-year-old wrote in to the CBC *Times* (7–13 July 1962) to request it be taken off the air: 'It is an awful bad influence on Canada's youth, for all they learn is to swear, drink and get into trouble.' In January 1969 its taste for the exotic again brought 'Festival' into the public eye. A couple of hundred viewers were sufficiently exercised by a lengthy bedroom scene in a Harold Pinter play to phone or write into protest. A few weeks later management pulled Charles Israel's *Noises of Paradise* from the line-up because it featured another bedroom scene: the camera shot the back of an actress clad only in a bathrobe, which a husband removes, before the two fall into bed (at least a portion of the scene had been aired in the CBC's promotion spots). All of this negative feed-back was none the less evidence of impact: the teleplays were pushing some people across the boundary of what was acceptable and respectable. They responded angrily.[52]

The fact was, however, that many viewers found CBC's Culture unsuitable simply because watching the shows was more like work than play. The success of a play required 'a sense of occasion,' just as in live theatre, and that couldn't last when television became commonplace in the home. The one-shot play demanded of the audience a willingness to concentrate, especially in the opening sequences, to understand who the characters were, what their plight was, and how the plot would unfold. The CBC's own survey of public opinion in 1962 found that what really troubled critics of CBC drama was its 'heaviness': too many of the plays were thought 'too difficult to understand, too serious in tone, too morbid, without any "sense" or "purpose", they do not have a comprehensible ending, are too highbrow, and so on.' The airing of *Waiting for Godot* provoked one poor soul who lived in Rivers Camp, Manitoba, to write in to the Toronto *Telegram* (12 December 1964) denouncing Culture because she was 'bored to death' by it all, and had only one channel to choose from. She wondered if 'the cultural group' really could enjoy such a play – indeed whether they had watched it. The mass hunger for drama was far more readily satisfied by storytelling in the shape of series drama than by most kinds of teleplays.[53]

It's clear that many Canadians didn't watch Culture, especially if something else was available. People in Winnipeg and other captive markets were known to turn off their sets when faced by the prospect of viewing 'Concert Hour.' Even in Quebec, 'L'heure du concert' couldn't garner much of an audience: a November 1959 survey found it only reached 525,000 people, a very small number. Nor could a programmer expect that such a heavily promoted and popular playwright as Arthur Hailey would be a sure winner: his *Course for Collision* (broadcast in April 1957) bombed in Toronto, winning only 13 per cent of the audience, as compared to 79 per cent for 'What's My Line' and 'The $64,000 Challenge' on WBEN. The priorities of the typical Toronto viewer weren't ever in doubt: sports fans were incensed in 1959 when the running of a 'Folio' musical prevented CBLT from showing the first game of the NHL play-offs. (Two years later the 'Quest' spot was pre-empted by hockey – had the CBC learned something?) An Elliott-Haynes report in 1963 of the ratings for a performance of *The Mikado* highlighted that the show only did well in captive markets, notably in the Maritimes where its share was 72 per cent from 9:30 to 10:00 and 86 per cent from 10:30 to 11:00. But in the cities, it was well behind 'Dr. Kildare,' 'Hennessey,' 'Gunsmoke,' 'Danny Kaye,' and so on. The waning of the CBC monopoly across Canada could only spell a further loss of audience share for CBC Culture.[54]

The anthology didn't disappear. Movies took the place of plays. By the end of the 1950s, the CBC was able to secure movies from Britain, Europe, and increasingly from Hollywood where studios had begun to unload their feature-film backlogs as early as 1955. In the Summer '57 CBC-Toronto launched 'Great Movies,' initially as a replacement for Saturday-night hockey, an initiative that soon won viewer approval. The producers' strike in Montreal in early 1959 proved movies were just as popular in Quebec: researchers learned this from surveying the viewer response to the movies that Radio-Canada had been forced to slot into the schedule to replace the lost series. So one, and sometimes two, primetime movie anthologies had already debuted on the two Canadian networks before NBC launched its 'Saturday Night at the Movies' in the Fall '61. That was made possible by the new availability of recent Hollywood product. The Canadian independents that went on the air in the early 1960s relied heavily on movies to fill out their schedule, and to compete with CBC offerings. The success of NBC's move led ABC to begin offering feature films on Sunday in 1962, NBC to try another success with Monday-night and later Wednesday-night films, and eventually CBS to launch its 'Thursday Night Movie' in Fall '65. By the mid-1960s movies were commonplace across the schedule.

The ratings showed why. In the July 1961 sweepstakes, 'Great Movies' secured fourth in the rankings, well ahead of 'General Motors Presents,' which was thirteenth. The same survey of February 1962 that ranked 'Le téléthéâtre' twentieth on Radio-Canada, ranked 'Cinéma international' seventh. Movies promised viewers stars, familiar kinds of stories, superior production values, and a bit of variety from week to week. They were, in short, much better suited to entertaining the masses than plays. Besides, movies were a cheap, safe, and profitable fare for the networks. They didn't require the collection of playwrights, producers, actors, designers, and so on, needed by plays. They could be easily edited for television, either to remove scenes that might offend or to insert commercials – or to fit the specified length of the program. The good ones were already pre-sold: that is, their prior theatrical release had created a memory that would lead viewers to watch the show. What could be more convenient?[55]

It would be absurd to pronounce the experiment of CBC Culture a failure. It was a valiant effort that, for a brief time, gave substance to the dream of making the networks a national stage and a national theatre. 'Perhaps ten times as many Canadians watched "Madame Butterfly" as had ever seen it before,' bragged the CBC *Annual Report 1957/58*, 'and more than would have seen it if it had run at Toronto's Royal Alexandra Theatre for six months.' Common sense alone would suggest that the CBC's programming did help to foster the increasing interest among Canadians in the arts. But television couldn't take the place of the live performance. It matured as a medium of entertainment and information, not of art. In the new era of competition that had come about in the 1960s, neither the francophone nor the anglophone network of the CBC could maintain its initial commitment to this brand of quality television because Culture had proved too expensive and too unappetizing for the mass audience.

Focus: The Queen of Spades

The first picture we see is the Six of Hearts, followed by the Queen of Spades, laid on top. How fitting – the images of playing-cards would haunt the whole drama. The camera jumps to a close-up of the Queen of Spades. Then it cuts to the face of a man in pain: his face is wild, his eyes mad, his breathing heavy. He makes mewling noises, born of fear. The man rushes away from the table, crashing against a wall. Suddenly, feeling trapped, he tries to escape, to push aside the wall. An attendant clasps him gently: 'Where are you going, Ernst? Ah, calm down now.' The attendant turns, and the camera pans right, to a woman in a veil, dressed in black. 'It's no use, I'm afraid, today. It's hopeless.' Screen darkens.

A back-drop of a starry night, a fanfare of music; a frontal shot of a TV camera moves forward from the centre of the picture; suddenly one of the four lenses fills the screen and the graphic 'CBC Television Theatre' is superimposed on this image. The announcer, Rex Loring, declares that it is the time 'for suspense, for comedy, for dramatic entertainment at its best ...' This time he was right. *The Queen of Spades* proved to be 'dramatic entertainment at its best.'

The hour-long teleplay, broadcast on 28 October 1956, was an example of live, studio drama. It was based on a story written by the Russian author Alexander Pushkin and adapted for television by Leo Orenstein. The producer was Paul Almond, one of Newman's boys (Newman, of course, was listed as the supervising producer), and the set designer was Rudi Dorn, widely regarded at the time as one of the true masters of his craft. Cast in the starring roles were Lloyd Bochner as Ernst Hermann, an amoral adventurer; Mary Savidge as the aged

Countess Anna, who held the secret of the cards; and Kate Reid as her lovelorn charge, Lisa.

Orenstein had kept Pushkin's basic story. 'The Queen of Spades' told how Hermann strove to overcome chance by securing a magical secret of winning at cards from the countess. He romanced Lisa in a vain attempt to win a welcome to the countess; failing that, he tried force and only frightened the countess to death. Although her ghost gave him the secret, Hermann was foiled at the gambling table by the playing of the Queen of Spades (symbolizing the old woman) and ended the story and the play in an insane asylum. Throughout story and play there was an air of fantasy, a feeling that unseen powers were interfering with human lives.[56]

Still a lot had been changed in the translation of the text from the short story to television. Pushkin had written a powerful but subtle story that could be variously described as a tragedy, a social comment, a warning of things to come. The key figure was the mysterious Hermann, 'homme sans moeurs et sans religion,' who, like Napoleon (whom he resembled), would stop at nothing to achieve his selfish ends. His quest for wealth was set in the Russian high society of the early 1830s, a milieu Pushkin characterized as full of fatuity, insensitivity, and amorality. Gambling was only one of the pursuits (gossiping, going to parties and balls, attending concerts were others) that consumed the life and times of the aristocracy and its hangers-on. But gambling did seem the way that a relatively poor newcomer such as Hermann could achieve the wealth that was the key to social significance.

Orenstein had to condense and simplify the story to make it work on television. He made the story a flashback, told to a hospital attendant by Lisa, the woman in black in the opening sequence. He divided the play into three acts: Act I contained four scenes and ended with Ernst (Orenstein's play used the man's first name almost exclusively) gloating to Paul (the countess's grandson) because he had made contact with Lisa; Act II had eight scenes, and concluded with the death of the countess; Act III had six scenes, the last a return to the hospital where we are left with a sympathetic attendant, a saddened Lisa, and a mad Ernst. Orenstein moved the location to Monte Carlo, itself a symbol of gambling passion, and brought the action into the twentieth century. He made the source of the secret of the cards a long-ago gipsy lover of the countess (rather than a fellow aristocrat as in Pushkin's version), presumably because gipsies had the reputation of a closer affinity with the supernatural. He strengthened the love interest in the play by devoting much more time to what happened between Lisa and Ernst, and to Lisa's dreams and fears, both of which would increase the appeal among female viewers. He heightened the element of suspense in the climactic scene at the casino, where on each of three nights a faro dealer dealt out the cards slowly to the delight of an increasingly confident Ernst and an expectant audience. Orenstein, perhaps Almond as well, had clearly reworked the substance of the story to suit the medium.

The teleplay was very much in the tradition of the theatre, not the movies, although the particular technology of television gave the performance a special quality that would have been difficult to imitate on the stage. The production values were superb, proof of just how well Toronto had mastered the ways of live, studio drama after only four years' experience at this sort of thing. There were some of the minor problems that often plagued a live broadcast: at one point the hospital attendant and Lisa spoke at the same time (the opening sequence); Paul made a slight slip of the tongue, as did Lisa; the shadow of a person briefly masked the countess. The legacy of the stage did hurt one performance: Kate Reid overplayed her part as Lisa, too ready to project her emotions with exaggerated looks and gestures, which didn't carry conviction on the small screen. But, overall, the acting was very good, indeed in the case of Lloyd Bochner superb because his role demanded he convey arrogance and obsession, show both smugness and anxiety, feign love, and descend into madness.

Almond used nine different sets: the hospital room, actually more like a cell (the shadow of bars appeared on the wall); the elaborate casino, complete with a gaming table, a bar, a raised floor, and an ornate staircase; the countess's bedroom, which was full of richly decorated furnishings; the hall outside that bedroom; a bare street set, facing the countess's house, and the balcony of the countess's window; a garden surrounded by flowering trees; Ernst's austere quarters; and some fantasy sets, made up of playing-cards.

The costumes, as well as the make-up, were suited to the locale and the characters. At the casino, the chief players (all male, of course) were dressed in formal clothes and the audience of women in gowns. Outside, Ernst wore a black, full-length cloak, which suggested his wicked ways. The wrinkled face of the countess, complete with a crooked nose, gave her the appearance of a witch. Lisa's plain, high-collared dress, buttoned tight in the front, flairing at the waist, and reaching to the floor, connoted her limited, repressed existence.

Sound and music was used to give cues to the viewers. The noises of children laughing at play in the sunshine in Act I, Scene 3 (where Lisa discovered Ernst outside the house), signified joy. The waltz music at the casino suggested the mood of gaiety. An eerie melody was used to alert viewers to some fantasy scene, sometimes characterized by wild, tumultuous music that connoted madness. When Ernst learned at the end of Act II that the countess had died, his final words 'She's dead!' are echoed and re-echoed to underline his anguish (not because she had died but because he hadn't got the secret of the cards).

The most interesting dimension, though, was the camera work. The camera didn't cut rapidly from one frame to another. Act I, Scene 2, where Orenstein introduces Ernst and sets up the plot, ran to slightly over five and a half minutes. It had only eight distinct cuts: the shortest sequence was nine seconds, the longest, ninety-eight seconds. In the longer sequences the camera dwelt on a face or a group, moved only slowly, sometimes to a close-up of a face, sometimes backing off for a two-shot or a group-shot, sometimes panning across a scene. It was a very languid pace. It didn't strain the eye or distract the mind, allowing the viewer to listen to the rich dialogue of the players. But it did enable the producer to focus attention on the actions, the appearance, or the gestures of the key player(s) so that he could effectively explore character. The camera, in short, conveyed the illusion of intimacy.

That said, the teleplay did boast some imaginative special effects, albeit primitive by later standards, designed to hold attention and encapsulate meaning. Double-images: the flashback in Act I, Scene 2, began with the face of Ernst superimposed on that of Lisa. Angle shots: the camera shot Ernst from above, as he stared down at a table where the cards were laid out (in the nine-second sequence in Act I, Scene 2), which highlighted his isolation. Visual clichés: the picture of a clock and a spinning roulette wheel to signify the passage of time, a rose to signify love (a rose that turns into a playing-card in Ernst's hands), or the close-up of a gun to signify violence. Horrific images: the enormous face of the now-dead countess that greeted Ernst when he opened his door in Act III, Scene 1, or Ernst's hallucination of giant cards everywhere in Act III, Scene 4. Light and shadow: in Act II, Scene 7, Ernst's room suddenly became darker as a fantasy of success took command of his mind – his stark white face, emphasized by the black background, conveyed his abiding obsession.

The best illustrations of these techniques were, naturally, in the fantasy sequences. In Act ii, Scene 8, for example, Ernst was asleep in the countess's bedroom, awaiting her return from the concert. After panning across the room, the camera moved to focus on the sharp planes of Ernst's face when he was awakened by a woman's laugh in the street. His pursed lips suggested his determination. The camera moved slowly into a close-up of his open eyes, upon which were superimposed his imaginings. The only sound was the loud clicking of a clock. The screen showed a half-body shot of the countess, bent over with age; she turned to face the camera; a hand, holding a gun, menaced her; she submitted, her head nodding, giving Ernst the secret of the cards. A new image then appeared, superimposed on the face of the countess before it dominated the screen: a series of playing-cards, suspended in mid-air, moved towards Ernst, promising the wealth and power that he craved. The sequence ended when the clock chimed 1:00 AM.

The performance worked so effectively because of the harmony of script, acting, sound, and picture. Nothing jarred. The story unfolded swiftly and effectively. The teleplay was a procession of carefully crafted sequences, mostly conversations, each packed with meaning and suffused with a sense of impending doom. It wasn't subtle: the playwright and producer used overlapping signs to drive the message home. The garden scene (Act ii, Scene 3), for example, witnessed a happy but anxious Lisa, in search of love, talking to the false, conniving Ernst, intent on meeting the countess. Lisa's quest was signified by the romantic music, the sounds of birds, her affectionate glances at the handsome Ernst, and her words of happiness. Ernst's quest was signified by his dark clothes, his sugary words, his fake smiles, and his effort to get Lisa to introduce him to the countess. The fact that he was a perfect cad was underlined by some small slips of the tongue that suggested his purpose, though of course Lisa didn't capture their meaning. Any ordinary viewer would, however. Orenstein and Almond had packaged their meaning in such a fashion that all kinds of people could readily and immediately understand what was happening. This scene, indeed this kind of scene, was absent from Pushkin's story.

The tension in *The Queen of Spades* derived from a three-way struggle: Ernst's search for power, the desperate effort of the countess to protect her house and her charge, and Lisa's quest for love. The assumption underlying and regulating these struggles was that the world existed in a balance between heart and mind, emotion and reason, good and evil, and woe-betide the pour souls such as Ernst (whose mind ruled all), or the countess (tainted by past evil), or Lisa (whose heart overcame her mind) who broke the rules of the game of life. Resolution, better yet revenge, came with the death of the countess, Ernst's madness, and Lisa's loss.

The countess recognized Ernst's type: early on, Lisa noted that the countess thought Ernst had 'come from the devil' (Act I, Scene 1). 'His personality seems to choke me, to penetrate me and chill my spirit,' she warned Lisa (Act II, Scene 1). He was a 'sorcerer' whose intentions could only be evil. Ernst saw himself as an unusual man, better than the rest, not bound by normal convention or normal morality, bent on winning at all costs. 'Did you think I would ruin my life on chance?' he bragged to fellow gamblers (Act III, Scene 5). 'The brain is meant to be used, gentlemen. It has power that weaklings never realize.' Pride cometh before a fall. His rebellion against Fate and Chance couldn't work. Shortly thereafter this villain, like nearly all deviants in television drama, was punished (see frame 8.1).

The countess was a more ambivalent character. She was described by Paul, her grandson, as 'inhuman,' 'an impenetrable fortress,' with 'a heart like a block of ice' (Act I, Scene 2). She could be insensitive, even cruel in her treatment of Lisa, hectoring her about her manners and her ways. 'She has no beauty, no money,' the countess said to Paul, in Lisa's presence (Act II, Scene 2). But, unlike Pushkin's countess, Orenstein's had a definite affection for Lisa: 'Lisa is almost like a daughter to me. I don't want to lose her to some scoundrel' (Act II, Scene 2). She was wont to denounce the materialism of her times. 'Sasha was right,' she told Paul (Act II, Scene 2). 'Money and possessions are the curse of life.' But, as Paul responded, she had money and possessions, the result of using her secret many, many years ago. The countess wished to preserve what she had against the intrusions of a corrupted world. 'There isn't anyone around these days who has a brain,' she declared (Act I, Scene 3). 'People have no minds anymore, no souls. The world is inhabited by imbeciles and vampires.' The trouble was that no one could keep the world at bay forever (see frame 8.2).

Lisa was one of those typical victims that inhabit so many dramas. She was a pawn of fate, caught up in a clash of wills of two powerful

Frame 8.1 The gambler

Frame 8.2 The witch

Frame 8.3 The romantic

individuals. She was used, by the countess and by Ernst. She couldn't take command of her own destiny. She didn't even renounce her foolish love at the end. She told the attendant why she visited Ernst in the final words of the teleplay: 'Someday, when he recovers, he'll need me.' Pushkin's Lisa, by the way, married 'a pleasant young man,' 'in the civil service somewhere and has a good income.' But Orenstein's Lisa embodied the stereotype of the always-suffering woman (see frame 8.3).

That brings me to the issue of myth. The central mythology was a variant of the old notion of the two natures, male and female. The women, in different ways, were emotional, even irrational beings. 'Our feelings are the only true things to go in a world that's false,' the countess told Lisa (Act II, Scene 6). Women were the keepers of the human soul, the fount of virtue and of love. Note that the countess was forever falling into the role of the wise old woman, spouting little homilies about life and the world. Note that Lisa was the one person consumed by romance.

Men, however, were instrumental, arrogant, caught up in the pursuit of knowledge and power. The grandson, Paul, was a gambler who sought the secret of the cards as well. He had little affection for the countess or Lisa. And Ernst, rebel though he may have been, none the less symbolized the rational man who believed that all things were possible. 'We give in too easily to fate and chance. I believe that man has power he hasn't yet realized. It's possible for me to take the uncertainty out of luck, the suspense out of gambling. Someday I'll be able to play the cards and know that every time I play, I'll win – and win until I break the bank' (Act I, Scene 2). It's ironic that Ernst decided to count upon magic (which is science turned on its head) to bring him success. His amorality blinded him to the fact that instead of mastering fate, he had in fact committed his fortune to chance, to unknown powers.

The Orenstein/Almond teleplay had transformed Pushkin's story into a character study of people in conflict as well as an investigation of obsession and madness. The focus on good and evil, the theme of balance, the emphasis upon resolution made this version of *The Queen of Spades* a moral tragedy at the end. Thus the adaptation embodied the twin fascinations with psychology and ethics that were common among the television playwrights and producers of the 1950s. It was an instance of sophisticated television. But it was also more comprehensible and more clichéd, less imaginative and less subtle, than the original short story. Pushkin's 'The Queen of Spades' was a work of art. Television's *The Queen of Spades* was a work of entertainment.

9

'And Now a Word from Our Sponsor'

This year, it seems to me, there are more memorable commercials and more forgettable programs than ever before. Good commercials are becoming a highly sophisticated form of pop art, worth at least as much attention as the shows they interrupt. I'm still waiting for the day when an entertainment columnist offers a regular review of the best commercials ...

Janice Tyrwhitt, 1966[1]

If Culture had faltered on television by the early 1960s, Commerce had thrived. Even on the CBC, never mind the upstart CTV network and the new independent stations, there were commercials galore, especially in primetime, touting the virtues of a whole host of consumer goods. And these commercials seemed to have gained a stature equal to the rest of television's offerings. Fowler I had officially accorded advertising a place on the schedule, along with information, interpretation, and entertainment. The law apparently agreed: that's why, in March 1965, CKVR-TV Barrie won a case before magistrate's court against the Board of Broadcast Governors over a purported infringement of the 55 per cent Canadian-content regulation – CKVR argued that the station's commercials and promotional announcements (mostly made in Canada) should have been included, which would have raised their level some 5 per cent, boosting them slightly above the magic minimum figure. Also in 1965 Fowler II reflected on the 'strange paradox' that led 'many of the most brilliant television producers' to look upon commercials 'as the most rewarding outlet for their creative abilities.' A few years later Martin Goldfarb Consultants found that seven in ten Canadians thought advertising really was an art-form, and one-third admitted that the commercials sometimes were more interesting than the programs themselves. Obviously the advertising industry had produced a type of message well-suited to the new medium.[2]

Advertising

There is much to admire in the artistry of some of the hucksters, say Jerry Goodis in the 1960s who strove to produce ads for such products as Hush Puppies and such services as Speedy Muffler that were entertaining, imaginative, humorous, and occasionally arresting. I've enjoyed (and still enjoy) a few commercials, notably the Ban deodorant ads of the early 1970s, which were clever and poignant statements on the human condition, its aspirations as well as its absurdities. Sad to say, the claim that the quality of the commercials (for example, the fun-and-games ads of the beer companies) is at times far better than that of the programs they pay for is all too often true. Any aging group of North Americans is likely to recall with a certain nostalgia a catchy jingle such as 'You'll wonder where the yellow went ...' (Pepsodent) and other bits of advertising trivia. Advertising is, as Marshall McLuhan pointed out, part of the 'folklore of industrial man,' an art-form especially representative of our economic abundance, our ways of life, the dreams of an affluent society. Its brand of art might best be called, in Michael Schudson's words, 'Capitalist Realism,' which, like the socialist counterpart, 'simplifies and typifies' life around us. Advertising strikes a cord in our minds, even if its purpose might repel.[3]

At bottom national, brand-name advertising (classified and retail ads are more akin to commercial news) is a special, indeed privileged, form of discourse about the virtues of purchasable commodities and services. But it is a lot more than that. Advertising is also 'an ideology of efficacious answers,' as Roland Marchand has argued. 'No problem lacks an adequate answer. Unresolvable problems may exist in the society, but they are nonexistent in the world glimpsed through advertisements.' Advertising highlights a consumption ethic, emphasizing personal indulgence, over the production ethic, with its utilitarian bias, although this is done in terms of individual goods rather than as part of a general crusade. Likewise it seeks to manufacture a vague sense of discontent with life as it is, in order that the consumer might look to the product to assuage the discontent. Its apologists have thought advertising was a lot more than just a way to move goods: it promised to nurture economic progress and human invention, to reconcile 'social harmony with personal freedom of choice,' by offering an otherwise confused if not ignorant public guides to modern living. Scholars have agreed, though their findings might be a lot less optimistic: according to William Leiss, Stephen Kline, and Sut Jhally, for example, advertising explores the human soul, commenting upon 'the interplay between persons and objects' and supplying consumers with 'social cues' that guide their behaviour. Nearly all ads, then, carry with them a heavy freight of symbolism. They are as much the tools of our culture as they are the tools of marketing.[4]

Understanding what this means requires some brief exploration of the consumer society, as well as the marketplace that bolsters that society. There's always been a lot of loose talk about the unholy materialism of modern times, whether that's taken to signify that the acquisition of goods has become an end in itself or that commodities are valued as the means to secure respect, love, and status. The fact is, of course, that the attribute that sets the consumer society apart is the abundance of goods, not the zeal to acquire or consume, which seems well-nigh universal. Goods are 'simultaneously *communicators* (about social ideas and power) and *satisfiers* (of human needs),' asserts Sut Jhally. Nearly every commodity has always had a meaning that goes beyond its mere use: the foods people eat, the clothes they wear, the gifts they give tell tales about their personalities and their social settings. That's why Mary Douglas and Baron Isherwood have called goods 'ritual adjuncts' and talked about consumption as 'a ritual process whose primary function is to make sense of the inchoate flow of events.'[5]

Advertising has become a key method of applying meanings to goods in Canada as elsewhere. Allow me a small example of how this has worked, the case of La Québecquoise, a new cigarette first marketed in the winter of 1962/3. This made-in-Quebec cigarette, manufactured by a French-Canadian enterprise, was clearly designed to exploit the new wave of nationalism then so much a part of the 'Quiet Revolution' in the province. One television advertisement bluntly identified the firm with the whole cause of *maître chez nous*, the liberation of Quebec from its thraldom to anglophone masters. Smoking La Québecquoise was an act of patriotism ('Fumez canadienne-française, fumez la Québecquoise'). Initially the cigarette was quite a hit, not the least because of all the free publicity it received in the press. But the demand proved insufficient and the cigarette disappeared after a few years. Apparently there wasn't much beyond its ethnic meaning to make the cigarette a successful newcomer in the established market.[6]

The example also points to one of the major marketing problems of the consumer society, namely the fact that so many competing products, whether cigarettes or cars, are very much alike. This fact presents the manufacturer with a serious dilemma: how does he get the consumer to buy his product? Why, by selling a particular image, not the product itself. 'You [can] buy today three brands of refrigerator and pay about the same amount of money for them,' Dr Ernest Dichter, one of the chief apologists of motivational research, told *Marketing* magazine, the self-styled weekly for Canada's sales and advertising executives. 'You get about the same type of refrigerator as far as technological perfection is concerned. The advertiser sees himself forced therefore to sell the aura, the personality, the image of his brand rather than the nut and bolt story.' You searched for that group of consumers who would buy your particular meaning, which might be a masculine smoke such as a Marlboro or a daring shirt such as a Hathaway or a prestige car such as a Cadillac. For years Chanel used Catherine Deneuve, a French actress, to associate their mass-marketed perfume with personal glamour: buy Chanel No. 5, and you buy class, distinction, and maybe sexiness as well. It was this gospel of market segmentation that led advertisers and agencies to seek the proper 'demographics,' the magazine or program that promised to deliver the special bloc of consumers – whether women twenty-five to sixty-four or beer-guzzling men – who were likely to buy the product.[7]

The central institution in the whole process of national advertising was and is the advertising agency, hired by the manufacturer to develop a marketing strategy, design ads, and place these ads in the relevant media. The agency was usually paid by these media a 15 per cent commission on the business generated, although the notion of a client payment for services rendered won increasing favour after 1960. The advertising agency really acted as a bridge between producers and consumers, informing each how to operate in the marketplace, which also made the agency the chief pillar of that supposed democracy of goods so fundamental to the emergence of the affluent lifestyle (see figure 9.1). Jerry Goodis's memoirs *Have I Ever Lied to You Before*? were a celebration of the creative role of the agency, filled with anecdotes about how to sell ideas to clients as well as to consumers. The agency might actually play a role before manufacture, as in the case of Quaker Oats's Tintin, a sweetened cereal introduced in 1966, where market tests were employed to determine questions about taste and texture and colour prior to launching the product onto the francophone market. But the chief purpose of the agency was to produce advertising that triggered a desire in the heart of consumers to buy a particular brand – whatever the rhetoric about advertising as art, an agency's reputation

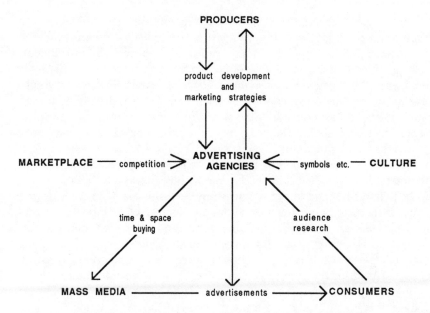

Figure 9.1 The advertising process

depended usually on a client's sales, not the ad campaign's aesthetic standards. Ironically neither admen nor their clients could be altogether sure whether any campaign would generate, or had sponsored, a boom in sales. 'Advertising is still an inexact speculation,' admitted David Ogilvy, one of New York's leading admen. He, like others, quoted with approval the old lament of a client, 'Half the money I spend on advertising is wasted, and the trouble is I don't know which half.'[8]

The industry was full of all sorts of unproved and disputed lore and riven by distinct, often opposed, schools of thought. The name of American adman Rosser Reeves was closely associated with the notion of reasoned advertising, which stressed the import of finding a 'unique selling proposition,' a particular product attribute that must be drummed into the head of the consumer. David Ogilvy, by contrast, was the 'guru' of the 'brand image' school, which tried to craft 'a riveting, emotionally powerful image for a product.' Then, rising fast in the 1960s, there was the 'visibility school,' which thought the adman must use wit, assorted bizarrerie, and striking visuals, all to grab the consumer's attention. That new wave received some hard raps in Hank Seiden's *Advertising Pure and Simple*, a memoir plus handbook of an American adman, full of dos and don'ts and of criticism of the styles of colleagues who didn't agree with his maxims. There was even dispute in the profession over just how intelligent or perceptive the consumer really was: Goodis railed against ads sporting white tornadoes, lady plumbers, the Man from Glad, and so on, which (he thought) demeaned the consumer, and so the industry, with their 'tasteless or offensive or patronizing or cynical or insultingly silly' approach; and he touted the Volkswagen 'Lemon' ads or the Avis 'We're number two, we try harder' style, which appealed to the consumer as a human being with some sense of humour and wit. Some admen swore by the virtues of motivational research and market surveys, while others put a good deal more faith in their own hunches. Even the field of media buying was a lot less scientific in fact than in appearance. A CBC study of ratings in 1960 came to the conclusion that for all the talk about the import of ratings, the actual decision-making about what air time to buy and where to buy it was left 'in the hands of people who did not appreciate the limitations of the rating system,' or who used ratings to justify decisions taken because of costs, personal tastes, even dinner conversations. 'We were informed that the sponsorship of the Plouffe family was continued by Colgate mainly because the vice-president of Colgate himself liked the show very much.'[9]

All this confusion, however, shouldn't mask the fact that the ad is a distinct form of communication. The ad is an extraordinarily compact message that can't easily be characterized as either fact or fiction. Its most striking characteristics are 'the "condensing" of ideas, the skilful combination of language and imagery, the breadth of its thematic and social references, and its accessibility to and acceptance by wide audiences that may even cross linguistic and cultural barriers.' It might focus on the product itself, although more often it was user-centred; it did inform the consumer, although in broadcasting at least it could entertain as well; it was able to use fear and humour, hard sell or soft sell, images and words, to get across its ideas. One of the more obvious developments of the post-war period was the increasing importance of the art director in the process of ad creation, usurping the role of the copywriter, which indicated how the first appeal of so many ads was to the eye rather than to reason. The effective ad is always attuned to social mores and aspirations – 'Advertising doesn't always mirror how people are acting, but how they're dreaming,' mused Goodis. That's why, as Erving Goffman discovered, ads are a marvellous source of information about the ways in which the two sexes present themselves: his survey of magazine ads noted how women caress rather than hold objects, often recline or stand with a 'bashful knee bend' or a slight 'cant' of the head, appear a bit withdrawn from events or sometimes out of control, or indulge in 'body clowning,' all signs of subordination if not submission to male authority. And the ad shows an amazing ability to appropriate nearly any symbol or phenomenon in society, even such things as the rediscovery of Nature and the women's movement, which implicitly critiques the society served by the ad, what has been called a 'recuperative capacity' that infuriates radicals. One need only call to mind the many ads for hair shampoos that boast of their natural ingredients or the Virginia Slims campaign to win women smokers. In sum there's a certain truth to the argument that advertising is 'the quintessential communications form of the modern era.'[10]

Neither affluence nor advertising was quite so advanced in Canada as in the United States during the 1950s and 1960s. According to one estimate, American income per capita in 1964 stood at $2, 248 U.S. while Canadian was only $1,643 CAN. The same year the net advertising expenditures per capita were $33.51 in Canada but more than double that figure in America, $72.77, although it should be recognized that such figures didn't take account of the overflow into Canada of made-in-America ads via magazines and television. It was an article of faith with many commentators, including Dr Dichter, that Canadians were a more cautious lot, less easy with prosperity. The Canadian economist O.J. Firestone believed the American consumer was 'advertising prone,' 'receptive to new ideas and to new products,' while the Canadian consumer was 'more conservative,' likely to follow the lead of big brother when the product 'found acceptance in the United States.' One W.H. Mahatoo, a motivational researcher, published a survey in *The Financial Post* (24 May 1969) that claimed that the Canadian consumer was in greater need of reassurance and so happier with existing brand names, more suspicious of ads and so needing more believable ads, insistent on 'good quality and durability' (whereas the American consumer was more interested in variety and adventure). Market-research studies also pointed to the more fragmented character of the Canadian marketplace: francophone consumers 'bought relatively more packaged soups, instant coffee, wine, cosmetics, ale type beer' and 'relatively less frozen foods, canned fish and meats, chocolate chips' than their anglophone counterparts. Whether this was the result of distinct ethnic preferences or a lower standard of living wasn't clear.[11]

Even so, advertising expenditures in Canada had topped a billion dollars by 1968, and had produced a number of leading agencies nearly as sophisticated and imaginative as their American counterparts. The top five in 1968, all Canadian, were MacLaren Advertising ($45 million gross billings); Cockfield, Brown & Co. ($32 million); Foster Advertising ($26 million);

Vickers & Benson ($26 million); and McKim/Benton & Bowles ($23 million). Goodis, Goldberg, Soren, tied for fifteenth place at $8.5 million, had registered the most spectacular five-year growth rate (254 per cent!) by pursuing its special approach of witty and entertaining advertising for accounts as diverse as Salada-Shirriff foods and Crown Zellerbach building materials. One of the more intriguing developments in the industry during the 1960s was the French-Canadian take-over of francophone advertising, hitherto largely a translation of English copy, as well as the birth of new, modern French-Canadian agencies that promised a specialized understanding of Quebec's 'unique' ways to clients interested in winning greater custom in the province. This brand of separatism paralleled what happened in other fields where French Canadians cut links with assorted Canadian (read, anglophone-run) organizations to sponsor their own enterprises and become *maître chez nous*.[12]

The one cloud on the horizon was the very rapid spread of American-owned agencies into Canada, including that world leader J. Walter Thompson and the aggressive if eccentric Ogilvy & Mather, which had achieved the second highest rate of growth in the five years preceding 1968. According to one nationalist brief to an Ontario legislative committee, 'the share of billings of foreign-controlled agencies among the top fifteen agencies more than doubled over the ten-year period from 1959 to 1969.' The thirteen American members of the Institute of Canadian Advertising (previously the Canadian Association of Advertising Agencies) did $112 million worth of business in 1968, or 27 per cent of the total gross billings of the fifty-three ICA members. The Yankees benefited enormously not only from the prestige of Madison Avenue as the centre of superlative advertising (supposedly the Bank of Montreal moved its $2 million account from Vickers & Benson to an American agency), but also from the understandable tendency of American multinationals to go with the branch agency of the firm that handled their main account in the United States (that was admitted to *Marketing* in 1966 by the managing director of the Schick account). The Kates, Peat, Marwick & Co. study for the Ontario legislature discovered that among the country's top seventy advertisers, foreign corporations (mostly American) gave only $40 million in billings to Canadian agencies while fully two-thirds of their accounts, or $85 million, went to foreign agencies. It was all a part of the story of the supposed American take-over of the Canadian economy that worried many a nationalist in the late 1960s and early 1970s.[13]

Goodis was one adman who did get upset since the take-over threatened to close off the options for Canada. In particular he wanted to 'stop copying

American advertising ... to find our own Canadian style of advertising.' Perhaps what's most interesting about the plea was the implicit admission that Toronto's advertising was just Madison Avenue writ small. Even Goodis was 'at fault,' if that's the correct phrase: his firm's advertising was reminiscent of the work of the more imaginative New York agencies such as Doyle, Dane, Bernbach (the makers of the famous Volkswagen 'beetle' ads), whose creative personnel became Goodis's own 'heroes.' 'Every week we screen a reel of the latest commercials from some studio in New York or London or Berlin,' claimed Goodis, just 'to spur on' the creative staff. None of which is very surprising, given the fact that made-in-America advertising was so prevalent in the country because of the viewing of American television, the circulation of American magazines, and the common practice of importing or modifying American ads for Canadian media. Certainly the Canadian consumer, whether French- or English-speaking, could rarely tell whether an advertisement in a magazine or on television had its origin in Montreal, Toronto, or New York. And why would she (for the chief consumers were women) care very much? Maybe she was more conservative or cautious, but, overall, her tastes in goods and services differed little from those of her cousins in the south. Advertising's American flavour simply fitted the pattern common to the popular culture of Canada by the late 1960s.[14]

The Great Salesman

The official response of the advertising industry to the arrival of Canadian television in 1952 might best be summed up as cautious. On 5 July 1952, *The Financial Post* carried a lengthy story about the conclusions of *Television as an Advertising Medium for Canadian Advertisers*, a report authored by a joint working committee of the Association of Canadian Advertisers and the Canadian Association of Advertising Agencies. The big warning: television 'is not a magic device which works well for all who use it.' Some manufacturers might be better advised to avoid television altogether. Even those who could benefit from the new exposure ought not to take their ad money away from proved media. The fundamental problem was cost. The CBC intended at this time to charge sponsors $1,600 for a one-hour show in Toronto and $500 in Montreal, a price that included not just station time but a minimal production crew as well. One of the ways the industry estimated costs was on the basis of cost-per-thousand households, or cpm (later rate-per-thousand individuals). Judged this way, the 'guestimate' was that Toronto's TV cpm amounted to $27, falling perhaps to $13 a year later, whereas the radio cpm at that moment was a mere $0.50! Being a pioneer on TV did indeed seem to be a risky and expensive business. This report might be cited as a further proof of the conservative and cautious side of the Canadian character; but, in fact, it was an example of the natural tendency of an established industry to avoid upsetting a profitable status quo.

The official response wasn't the final word, though. There were already some Canadian industries that had experimented with advertising on American stations: John Labatt apparently paid $3,864.40 to WXYZ-TV Detroit for ads during a three-week period in December 1951, and Labatt as well as Canadian Breweries had actually sponsored shows on WBEN-TV, aimed at the Toronto-Hamilton market, which is partly explained by Ontario's liquor-advertising regulations. By October 1952, one month after Toronto went on the air, there were quite a lot of big-name companies who'd taken the plunge and bought time on CBLT-TV: Canadian Westinghouse, Ford of Canada, Campbell's Soup, and B.A. Oil, all were sponsors; Bulova Watch, Consumers Gas, Imperial Tobacco, and Salada Tea were spot advertisers. The most aggressive agency was MacLaren, which soon boasted television accounts for Imperial Oil ('NHL Hockey'), Canadian General Electric ('Showtime'), Buick ('Milton Berle'), General Motors ('General Motors Theatre'), Chevrolet ('Dinah Shore'), and Pontiac ('Dave Garroway') plus flash and spot advertising for Bulova Watch and Buckingham cigarettes.[15]

These advertisers, many of them branches of American companies, were simply jumping on a bandwagon. The mystique of television had already taken hold of advertisers and agencies down south. Tales were making the rounds of companies that had leapt into television early and reaped huge benefits, such as Hazel Bishop lipsticks whose sales shot from $50,000 a year in 1950 to $4.5 million in 1952.[16]

The fact is that more and more advertisers believed the television commercial was a surrogate for the actual salesman. Back in March 1949, after surveying what was happening in the United States, an enthusiastic Joseph Compton told Canadian businessmen what was 'inevitable': television 'will become a show window for a variety of goods and services' because it offered advertisers the extraordinary advantage of displaying their wares in customers' homes. 'Eventually it may prove to have no equal in the merchandising field.' By the middle of the 1950s, Oliver Tryeze, president of the TV Bureau of Advertising in New York, was telling Canadians that TV could replicate 'the personalized approach,' bringing back 'face-to-face selling aimed at the young housewife' who was so important to mass sales.

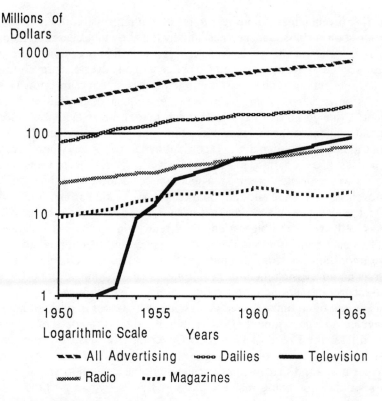

Millions of
Dollars

Logarithmic Scale   Years

- ◼◼◼ All Advertising ◦◦◦◦ Dailies ━━ Television
- ✕✕✕ Radio •••• Magazines

Chart 9.1 Media and advertising revenues
Note: Information from Hopkins, Hedlin Ltd, *Words, Music, and Dollars: A Study of the Economics of Publishing and Broadcasting*, for the Special Senate Committee on Mass Media, v. 2 of *Report* (Ottawa: Queen's Printer 1970) 121, 192, and 191, plus O.J. Firestone, *Broadcast Advertising in Canada: Past and Future Growth* (Ottawa: University of Ottawa Press 1966)[130]

A bit later A.M. Lawrence, ad manager for Nestlé Canada, which had just completed a successful television campaign, argued that TV was 'the closest possible thing to personal sell,' especially for the instant products his company marketed.[17]

By this time, of course, advertising on television had taken off, following in the wake of the rapid expansion of TV services and of the boom in sales of TV sets across the country (see chart 9.1). Television's share of advertising revenue may not appear to be all that impressive, though. Yes, television soon surpassed magazines, and by the early 1960s eased in front of radio as well. But this explosive rate of growth didn't continue during the next decade. In 1961 TV secured 9.6 per cent of all advertising revenues, radio 8.8 per cent, and daily newspapers 30.8 per cent; ten years later, TV's total was only 12.2 per cent, radio's 11.1 per cent, and the dailies' 29.0 per cent, although all had experienced substantial dollar increases since advertising expenditures in general had multiplied by 75 per cent. Television in Canada did not match the record in the United States where, even in 1961, TV's share was 14.3 per cent of advertising revenues. Canadian television was especially weak as a medium of local advertising, which includes classifieds, retail and supermarket ads, real-estate promotions and the like, the most lucrative source of funds for newspapers and increasingly radio as well. By far the biggest chunk of television revenue, on average four-fifths each year by the mid-1960s, was generated by national ads.[18]

Two important constraints, time and money, had shaped television's career as an advertising medium. Print media could simply expand their size to incorporate an increased volume of ads. Television couldn't. The actual amount of ad time allowed in an hour or half-hour of programming was regulated by government agencies, initially the CBC's board of governors and later the Board of Broadcast Governors. In 1964, for example, the BBG reduced the maximum number of ad minutes from sixteen to twelve per hour (and sixteen commercial units); the regulation was slightly more restrictive for non-Canadian sponsored shows where ad time was limited to four minutes and fifteen seconds in a half-hour program. The CBC was even stricter with itself. Its network news and public-affairs shows simply were not available to advertisers. Its 1968 rules allowed only four minutes of commercial time on other types of programming in each half-hour period, although that was supplemented by some further time during network breaks. The one way of accommodating more advertising was to reduce the actual length of the commercial. Right from the beginning, advertisers had been offered ten- and twenty-second 'flashes,' thirty- or sixty-second spots, and a few two-minute periods to showcase a variety of products. During the 1960s there was an increasing tendency to move away from the sixty-second standard to thirty-second commercials: on Thursday evening, 24 February 1966, for instance, CFTM-Montreal (the independent francophone station) aired eighty-three ads, thirty-eight running 60 seconds, twenty-six 30 seconds, and the final nineteen for periods ranging from 10 to 120 seconds. Even so, there was generally more demand for primetime spots on popular programs, notably American imports, than the networks could fill, a situation that naturally raised the value of this scarce resource.[19]

Advertisers were forever grumbling about costs, especially when they compared their plight with what was common below the border. The initial investment came in the making of the commercial itself. The early days of live and, therefore, reasonably cheap commercials soon gave way to much more costly filmed and videotape commercials. Sut Jhally has argued convincingly that these commercials should be seen as 'capital goods': they aren't meant to be consumed but rather to manufacture sales; they are made for repeated showings over a short period of time, unlike the programs themselves; and they are tax-deductible, much like machinery purchased for factories. That explains why so much time and money was devoted to ensuring their quality – traditionally more care and expense has always been lavished on capital than on consumer goods. In 1966 Janice Tyrwhitt estimated that a top-flight commercial could involve one hundred people, take twenty hours to complete, and cost more than $50,000. An average figure, according to Keats, Peat, and Marwick, was around $20,000. The overall cost of the commercial minutes could easily be much higher than the cost of the program that carried the advertisers' messages.[20]

At first, roughly in the mid and late 1950s, most commercial dollars (85 per cent according to one estimate) were spent in New York. It was a lot cheaper for a multinational to import an existing, tested commercial that had proved its worth in the United States. Even if a new commercial had to be made, New York seemed a logical choice: the facilities and personnel there were the best in the world, an important consideration if the advertiser wished to employ animation or sophisticated camera techniques. Besides the temptation to go down and enjoy the pleasures of New York's night-life was considered a marvellous perk for the ad managers of Canadian companies, or so comments in *Marketing* suggest. A 1968 survey by the Institute of Canadian Advertising found that roughly a quarter of the commercial messages aired on anglophone television were imports.[21]

By contrast 61 per cent of the commercials were produced in Canada, and another 10 per cent modified in Canada, a slightly more impressive level than was true for the actual programs. The private film industry had made a determined bid to win more and more of the business away from New York, even persuading Ottawa to slap a special duty on imported productions. In 1962 Dean Walker estimated that the cost of buying a $10,000 American-made commercial for Canadian use was, what with taxes and the exchange rate, around $16,855. Much was also made of the advantages of using Canadian talent, which, presumably, had a better grasp of the national character. Some messages had to be tailored to the Canadian market, which might require a certain amount of adaptation (translation into French, a new sound-track, an additional cut). Restrictions on commercial language were much tighter in Canada than in the United States: such expressions as 'bad breath,' 'rich and creamy,' '99 per cent fat-free,' and 'natural' were on the list of no-no's generated by government agencies and the CBC. But I suspect that advertisers cut loose from New York more because local film-makers had improved their facilities, especially in the area of videotape production where costs were once estimated at 50 per cent to 100 per cent higher in New York than in Toronto. The centre of production became Toronto: three-quarters of the 2,822 Canadian-made or modified commercials in 1970 were produced in Ontario, and fully 740 of these were in French (either original or adapted).[22]

But the costs of making a commercial were modest compared to the expense of buying time. In 1956 an advertisers' brief to the Fowler Commission claimed that the cost-per-thousand homes in the United States ran from $2.50 to $3.00, whereas in English Canada the cpm ranged from $5.00 to $8.50 and in French Canada from $7.00 to $15.00. One C.O. Hurly of Chrysler Canada decided that advertisers had 'spoiled' broadcasting in their zeal to reach the home, thus creating a kind of 'monster.' While the cpm soon improved because television coverage increased so rapidly, the dollar value of time also grew. In 1959, according to a report in *Marketing*, Ford Canada alone signed an agreement for $2.5 million with the CBC to sponsor what became 'Startime,' two French-language shows, local news and sports, a co-sponsored Hollywood western, and 'The Tennessee Ernie Ford Show.' Between 1964 and 1969, for example, the cost of a sixty-second, primetime spot on CFTO rose from $335 to $500, on CBLT from $325 to $450, on CFCF from $300 to $475, and on the booming CFTM from $340 to a whopping $700. Rates, admittedly, were much lower in smaller markets, such as Winnipeg, where a CBWT spot went for $230 in 1968, or Vancouver, where CHAN charged $265. There at least local advertisers could afford to buy air time on a regular basis. Elsewhere the big advertisers dominated primetime.[23]

It was the increasing cost of air time that weaned advertisers from the notion of exclusive sponsorship. The assumption had been that a sponsor benefited directly from the association with a quality or a popular program. For years General Motors sponsored CBC teleplays because of the supposed prestige attached to this genre of programming. O'Keefe sponsored 'En haute de la pente douce,' a téléroman about upper-middle-class life in Quebec City, because it hoped 'to upgrade the social image of its beer.'

But the extra payment seemed less and less worthwhile, especially when advertisers discovered their messages might reach a broader audience, at a cheaper cost, through a careful selection of spot advertisements on a number of different programs. This 'magazine' concept of advertising attracted television managers because it freed their programming from direct sponsor involvement and enabled them actually to produce more value from commercial time by selling to a wider range of clients. The CBC did stay with the technique of sponsorship, although most of its so-called sponsored shows had two or more advertisers. CTV didn't allow for any sponsorship, selling only spots, or what it called 'participation,' to advertisers. The most famous of the commercial broadcasts, 'NHL Hockey,' managed by MacLaren, which produced the package and bought time on Radio-Canada, the CBC English network, and CTV, was actually supported by Imperial Oil, Ford of Canada, and Molson's Brewery. The definition of the terms 'sponsorship' and 'participation' was, under these circumstances, blurred by the reality of a number of different commercial messages.[24]

That had already begun to cause some upset among advertisers and agencies. Late in 1963 *Marketing* carried a number of comments on the new peril of ad clutter on primetime TV, or 'overloading the burro' in the colourful phrase of writer Jeff Holmes. The fear was that the stacking up of multiple spots and sometimes network or station promotions could only irritate the viewer and undo the impact of any one message. But given the fact that primetime was a finite 'resource,' there wasn't too much that advertisers could do but whine about the problem – and try to exact lower rates.[25]

Even the biggest advertisers often supplemented their television time with space-buying in the print media and time purchases on radio. An enthusiastic believer in the 'visual appeal of television,' ad manager J. Edgar of Texaco none the less admitted that his firm bought radio time 'to obtain greater reach and frequency' and to back up the television campaign. When Goodis's agency mounted its television campaign to push Shirriff Instant Potatoes in 1963, which was 'an extended parody on the over-popular television taste-test,' it employed 'straight-face newspaper ads' to announce the tests and later the 'awful truth' – that the instant potatoes tasted good, but not 'like the real thing.' A survey of the habits of heavy spenders in 1971 found that while the drugs and cosmetics industry devoted 73 per cent of its $49.1 million budget to television commercials, food and food products only expended 44.1 per cent (of $60.3 million), the automotive sector 37.9 per cent (of $42.9 million), and financial and insurance services 34.4 per cent (of $19.4 million). It just didn't seem wise to most advertisers to put all their eggs in one basket, especially when they had to pay so much for the privilege.[26]

None the less the power of television to work miracles in a highly competitive market-place appeared so great – to introduce new products, to create a brand image, to incite a buying enthusiasm, to counter rival claims – that most of the major companies in the business of selling consumer goods put more and more of their dollars into video. 'The return from investment in television advertising, although not quantifiable, is believed to be the highest for many products,' intoned the Hopkins, Hedlin report to the Davey Committee on the mass media. The suggestion that some noble agency lead the crusade against ad clutter by pulling its clients off a station was greeted with the comment that its rivals would be right 'there five minutes later buying up the time – whether we'd agreed on a boycott or not.' Could companies afford not to invest? (Some did, of course: during the mid-1960s Goodis, Goldberg, Soren kept Westinghouse out of television for roughly four years, apart from a few special commercials, because its $650,000 budget seemed too slight 'to make a notable splash on TV.') Before long television in Canada had jumped ahead of all the other media as the chief vehicle of national advertising. In 1963, for example, TV received $55.1 million from national advertisers, radio $24.9 million, and dailies $51.1 million. The gap increased in later years until, by 1972, almost half of all dollars spent by national advertisers in the three media went to television. The result was that a larger and larger percentage of the business done by advertising agencies was made up of television accounts (see chart 9.2). The age-old hegemony of the daily newspaper as the grand spokesman of commerce had finally given way. The dominance of television in the field of national advertising signified that it had now become the most important instrument of the 'ideology' of advertising in Canada.[27]

Commercials and Life

It's worth starting with a couple of axioms. Although hardly part of the general programming of television, commercials were a distinct instance of the video arts that like, say, newscasts or sitcoms, broke away from the legacy of radio to become a highly visual brand of advertising through a process of trial and error. Of course the hucksters borrowed models and techniques from the other offerings of television as well as from the field of advertising – commercials were an extremely eclectic genre. Yet the difficulties imposed on the adman were greater than any that might trouble ordinary producers. Recall that the fundamental purpose of the commer-

Percentages

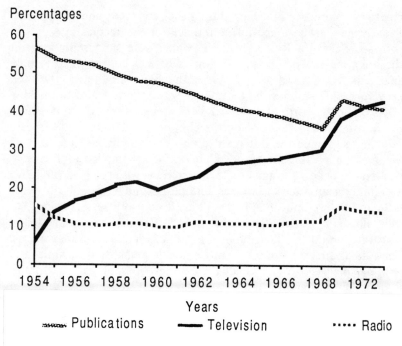

Chart 9.2 Advertising agencies: distribution of billings by media
Note: The nature of the statistics altered slightly after 1968, following which the chart tracks changes every two years. Data taken from *The Canada Year Book*

cial was to create in the mind of the viewer a favourable attitude towards the institution, service, or product being advertised, which would eventually trigger some sort of purchase in the marketplace. What was, and of course remains, outstanding about the commercial was the fact it was so compact: its message had to be delivered in a very short span of sixty or thirty seconds. Nor was the rigorous constraint on time the only factor shaping the commercial. Just as important was the need to reach viewers who were usually inattentive captives compelled by their situation to watch the screen. The commercial had to have some sort of impact to break through their lack of interest.

These axioms underlay the lists of rules about making commercials that

Marketing was forever publishing during the late 1950s and early 1960s. The magazine showed a special preference for the recipes of the New York–based Schwerin Research Corp., which were supposedly a result of the scientific analysis of the responses of test audiences to sample commercials. The key was to break out of the mode of radiovision. All too many commercials emphasized the spoken word, showing mostly a talking head, where, in the words of Ray Byrnes of Lever Brothers, the 'only action takes place between the nose and the chin of the announcer.' Schwerin urged readers to understand that video must do 'the primary job,' leaving audio only a supporting role: indeed, pictures alone should tell the whole story. Another list of 'dos and don'ts' directed the wise producer to 'strive for extremely clear visuals' as well as 'for unusual and memorable graphics at all times,' to 'use optical and electronic effects,' to 'stress close-ups,' to provide all kinds of identifying signs, and to 'let the camera show and demonstrate products.' That alone wasn't sufficient to ensure success, though. The commercial, according to Schwerin, ought to be 'simple' and orderly, moving easily from one idea to another, boasting only 'one dominant mood,' either emotional or logical, so that it would leave 'a unified impression' in the viewer's mind. And the commercial must 'involve' the consumer, 'speak the viewer's own language,' and show what the product 'will do for him.' This applied whether the commercial ran for thirty or sixty seconds: the only distinction was that the shorter spot was actually harder to make because the huckster had to pare his script down to the bone. None of the other genres of television had evolved so complete a statement of what needed to be done. The rules weren't always obeyed, of course.[28]

The chief focus of a commercial might be on the institution (for example, Westinghouse [CBS 1956] or General Motors [CBC 1959] where the purpose was to generate goodwill for the two corporations), a product or a service (Parker Pens [ABC 1958] or Imperial Esso service [CBC 1962] where the characteristics of the goods were featured), or a user (Jell-O Instant Pudding [CBC 1958] or American Motors' Ambassador [R-C 1966] where the effects of using the goods were highlighted). I say 'chief' focus because virtually all ads contained elements of the three orientations. The Westinghouse commercial tried to inform viewers of the many kinds of products, from nuclear submarines to power stations, to kitchen appliances, to elevators, in which the company's expertise was employed to their benefit. The Imperial Esso commercials sought to demonstrate how Esso was a good corporate citizen because its gas stations offered a range of services to

The pioneer of the téléromans: Roger Lemelin, creator of 'La famille Plouffe/ The Plouffe Family' (CBC Collection, MISA, National Archives of Canada: 14658)

Above, left: The creator of drama: Marcel Dubé (1958), one of the most prominent of Radio-Canada's writers during the 1950s and 1960s, producing both teleplays and téléromans (Jac-Guy Studio/National Archives of Canada/ PA-100946)

Above, right: The highbrow as producer: Mavor Moore, Toronto's chief producer in the early years (Robert C. Ragsdale Limited, CBC Collection, MISA, National Archives of Canada: 14666)

The drama impressario: Sydney Newman, the most famous of Toronto's teleplay producers in the 1950s, although this photograph is from his days as production supervisor of 'Graphic' (Ken Bell, CBC Collection, MISA, National Archives of Canada: 14669)

Bottom, facing: Culture on the airwaves: Norman Welsh, Toby Robins, and James Douglas in *The Slave of Truth* on 'Festival,' 1963 (Roy Martin, CBC Collection, MISA, National Archives of Canada: 14663)

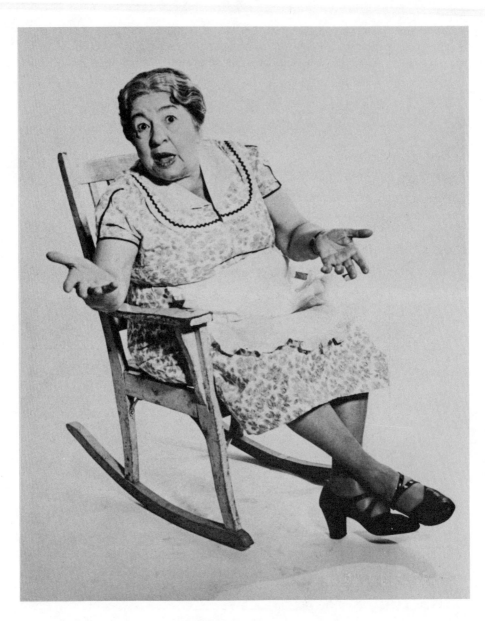

A most famous mother: Amanda Alarie of 'La famille Plouffe/The Plouffe Family' (David Bier Studios, CBC Collection, MISA, National Archives of Canada: 13641)

One of our exports: Lorne Green as Ben Cartwright, the star of 'Bonanza' (CBC Collection, MISA, National Archives of Canada: 7685)

The star journalist: René Lévesque (1953), prominent Radio-Canada journalist in the 1950s, especially as the master of the public affairs hit 'Point de mire' (Jac-Guy Studio/National Archives of Canada/PA-118733)

The thoughtful interviewer: Blair Fraser with Pierre Mendes-France on 'Close-Up' (Robert C. Ragsdale Limited, CBC Collection, MISA, National Archives of Canada: 12642).

The Ottawa reporter: Norman DePoe covering the Liberal Leadership Convention in Ottawa, 1968 (Murray Mosher, CBC Collection, MISA, National Archives of Canada: 14656)

The journalist on location: Beryl Fox, a master of the new documentary, presumably during the making of her *The Mills of the Gods* (CBC Collection, MISA, National Archives of Canada: 13991)

Fans up in arms: Picketing the CBC over the planned cancellation of 'This Hour Has Seven Days' (CBC Collection, MISA, National Archives of Canada: 12441)

meet the needs of a motorist. The Jell-O people showed just how easy it was to make their instant pudding to please the whole family.[29]

Most commercials used the forms of the report, the display, or the story to convey their messages (the contest, say a comparative test of two products, was largely absent in the 1950s and 1960s). The report endeavoured to supply as much information as possible. So a mini-documentary for Renault 8 (R-C 1965) carried the viewer through a description of the car's characteristics, providing a load of facts about its nature and operation, and ended with mention of an award the import had received from a Canadian automobile association. The much more common display tried to show viewers the virtues of a particular product. This often took the shape of a demonstration: a Kool Shake ad (R-C 1957) featured a middle-aged man who swiftly mixed up a milkshake for the kids, while an ad for Off (CBC 1967) showed how a lab man's arm was saved from attack by hungry mosquitoes with just one spray of the repellent. That approach, of course, very much fitted the analogy of the salesman that had so appealed to the early enthusiasts of television advertising. But hucksters also used testimonials, sometimes celebrities – for example, Georgia Gibbs for Instant Maxwell House Coffee (CBC 1957) or Robert Goulet for duMaurier cigarettes (CBC 1962) – who were themselves on display. Then there were the vignette commercials, a collection of assorted shots of a product, its uses, or even of problems as in the case of Lux Liquid Detergent (CBC 1962) where the ad opened with a series of images of female hands doing an assortment of tasks – to underline the slogan, 'Hands that need help, need Lux.' Lastly there were the mini-dramas, entertainment with a lesson, that didn't always bother to seek authenticity but tried to involve the viewer by bringing him or her into a happy story. A second ad for Instant Maxwell House Coffee (CBC 1957), for instance, showed how the cartoon hero Instant Max saved poor Miss Sweet from further abuse by her tyrannical boss, and won her a raise in pay.

By the mid-1960s the industry was in the midst of a debate over the tone appropriate to commercials, a debate that normally revolved around the question of whether a commercial that entertained viewers could really be successful. Convention had usually favoured a serious approach to the consumer and frowned on humour or wit. Schwerin warned that humour must be secondary to the product story. David Ogilvy argued that the commercials that people liked or that won awards didn't always produce results. But other admen realized that a humorous approach was an excellent way of catching the viewers' eye. That explained the cartoon craze of the late 1950s – Cherrios (ABC 1958), for instance, used an abbreviated cartoon drama of a kid sheriff who captures the bad man to get the attention of child viewers watching the western 'Wyatt Earp.' Some years later, Tyrwhitt talked about commercials that spoofed some of TV's hits, such as Alka-Seltzer's 'The Offenders' or 'The Girl from Fabulash.' Goodis referred to the popularity of the ongoing serial drama his firm created for Speedy Muffler, where the over-enthusiastic mechanics strove to prove 'At Speedy You're a Somebody.' Both writers praised an award-winning ad for Rose Brand Pickles, where a woman confesses, 'Whenever I think of roses, I think of pickles,' only to end with the twist: 'Remember: Pickle Brand Roses.' Nor was humour the only method of entertaining. Two little docu-dramas for Ford cars (R-C 1963) were whimsical in tone, one a fantasy of escape (complete with mellow music) in which a female passenger gets away from the pressures of life, the other featuring a family driving around in their new station-wagon, who end up at a farm where happy kids pour out of the car to play with a bunch of puppies.

Whatever the form or style, however, commercials could draw upon a large repertoire of techniques to enhance their messages. Look first at the language of the commercials. In nearly all ads the announcer used a direct mode of address, speaking to universal 'you,' which convention declared gave the commercial a personal touch. The audio of a Timex ad (CBC 1962) contained such phrases as 'You're watching ... ,' 'You see ... ,' 'You know ... ,' 'What do you think ... ?' 'Your Timex ... ,' as if the announcer were some kind of acquaintance. The language used was normally collo-quial, though announcers might employ the diction and the vocabulary of a family counsellor, a journalist, a father figure, or the ubiquitous salesman, depending on the requirements of the moment. So Murray Westgate in one Imperial Esso ad (CBC 1962), dressed up in the garb of an Esso serviceman, played the role of a reassuring, slightly paternal friend explain-ing in simple English just how the firm served all kinds of drivers: looking back, Westgate recalled that some people he met actually believed that he really was a garageman, not an actor. In addition, the huckster liked to play with words, particularly to use puns, which might etch his meaning into a viewer's mind. That was exemplified by duMaurier's slogan, 'the cigarette of good taste,' which conveyed the information that the cigarette did have a rich flavour and that it was smoked by people of quality.[30]

Even more impressive were the visual attributes of the commercials. Witness two quite different ads that appeared on 'The Wayne and Shuster Hour' (11 March 1962). A vignette commercial for Max Factor's Cream Puff, make-up in a compact, was a dazzling display of the huckster's art meant to seduce the women of the house. The opening image was of a glossy, silver material with a rich look and a black-opal inset (gilded by silver) on which would later appear words and pictures. After a flash of the graphic 'A Fabulous NEW discovery,' the camera cut to a moving collage of women's faces. Then back to the opal, where the face of a glamorous woman appeared, soon to be succeeded by two other faces. And so it went, all to convey an impression of glamour and beauty and taste. By contrast Eveready Batteries offered viewers, emphatically male viewers, a demonstration of the slogan 'POWER TO SPARE.' It opened with the slogan flashing on the screen, written in jagged letters to suggest lightning, and superimposed on a bright sun. Then it showed a man dressed in the white clothes of the lab scientist holding up two batteries, his assistant putting these into an electromagnet, and four weight-lifters raising a car that was 'caught' by the huge electromagnet. When the batteries were removed, of course, the car fell with a loud crash! Wasn't that 'power to spare'?

Franklin Russell once commented in *Marketing* on how all this effort to ensure a visual effect led hucksters to fake it. One broadcast manager admitted to using 'double-strength ingredients' in pudding commercials to withstand the harsh conditions of the studio. Another commercial producer said he had to add some black ink to the ketchup 'to restore its rich appearance,' else it came out 'pure white.' Two makers of an automobile commercial found they could make their car 'look longer by lowering the camera lens to floor level. They improved its lines by using telescopic lens at a distance. They pasted pieces of light-coloured paper to the car top, making it lower and leaner.' Janice Tyrwhitt pointed out how Hertz actually dropped 'you' in the driver's seat: 'they photograph you being yanked (by hidden wires) *out* of a stationary car, then run the film backward (to put you *into* the car) and superimpose this film on separately shot footage of moving scenery to give the effect of a car' going down the highway. It is hard to see how this was any more, or less, fakery than the hoked-up demonstration of Eveready's 'power to spare.'[31]

The hucksters were careful to use words and pictures to associate their message with the right meanings. A Lysol ad (CBC 1967) demonstrating just how the cleanser could be used in the household showed, at one point, a beautiful toddler – flashing this kind of icon was thought to be one sure way of catching Mommy's eye. A Yuban commercial (R-C 1965) was set in aristocratic surroundings: a servant, wearing white gloves, carried the coffee on a silver tray into an elegant living-room, classical music playing in the background; the camera shifts to focus on famous paintings of people eating; and the announcer makes explicit the connection between these masterpieces and Yuban's instant coffee. During the 1960s admen increasingly tried to give Quebec commercials a *visage français* to suit the nationalistic mood of the province. More and more of the products shown on television had French labels. Labatt's created Monsieur Cinquante out of the stock figure of the French-Canadian lumberjack to testify to the quality of their new Bière 50. Molson's ads had a group of singers visiting places throughout Quebec. Xerox made sure it featured images of French-Canadian progress, whether 'the Manic dam complex' or 'CAE Industries.' Jell-O made sure that its Chinese characters who delivered the spiel spoke appropriate French even if with a Chinese accent.[32]

Commercials were normally blatant. Subtlety wasn't an admired virtue here. That could undo the purpose of a commercial: the viewer might misunderstand what he or she was being told. The priority was to make the task of decoding an ad as simple as possible. So commercials were full of repetition, of overlapping signs. The sixty-second ad for Klear (CBC 1967), a floor wax from Johnson's Wax, endeavoured to associate the product with beauty and distinction. The purpose required that viewers accept Klear had the same quality of 'invisibility' as fine glass. The ad opened with what was soon revealed as a through-the-window shot of a garden. 'What a beautiful view!' gushed the well-dressed woman who narrated the commercial. 'Did you know you were looking through glass?' The camera panned to a long-shot of a living-room, a designer's dream of neatness and fashion. 'And what a beautiful floor.' The camera shifted to give a different view of the wood surface, which naturally glistened. 'Did you know you were looking through Klear?' – at the mention of the product, bingo it appeared superimposed on one side of the screen. 'Klear is the wax that dries clear as glass and never yellows.' Yellow was the great enemy: the woman held up a panel of glass, looked through the tinted section, and shook her head to emphasize the negative. 'And just think how important that is with today's light colorful floors.' She told viewers that Klear 'never yellows' asphalt tile, linoleum, or vinyl tile, on each occasion the camera showing the appropriate image. Back to the analogy of glass: the camera provided a close-up of a piece of floor, a dark strip on white – then an unseen hand lifted up a pane of glass that had been lying on that floor. 'Klear lets the true beauty of a floor shine through just as though you were looking through glass.' Altogether, she mentioned the word 'Klear' eight times. The ad concluded with the picture of Klear superimposed on the screen, along with a Johnson's Wax graphic.

As Janice Tyrwhitt pointed out, the makers of commercials had proved much more willing to experiment with camera techniques, musical forms, and script than had the ordinary producers. 'With commercials you can try anything,' mused Richard Lester, a director who, according to Tyrwhitt, had turned out eighty commercials a year before he won fame with the Beatles movies. She added that 'the photographic experiments employed in such movies as *Help!*, *Tom Jones*, and *Mary Poppins* were first used in commercials.' TV programming in the 1960s was even more affected, of course. Dennis Braithwaite argued that the spy thriller cum spoof 'The Man from U.N.C.L.E.' wasn't just a beneficiary of the techniques, notably snappy language and fast cuts, first employed by the makers of commercials; it was also one, long extended commercial for its sponsor, an auto manufacturer. It stimulated 'in the viewer an other-worldly and slightly slap-happy mood that corresponds to the unreality that TV automobile commercials generally strive for.' Its replacement in the NBC line-up early in 1968 was 'Rowan and Martin's Laugh-In,' a super-hit of the comedy-variety genre that relied heavily on all manner of techniques drawn from commercials to dazzle audiences. The most famous imitator came a year later, though: 'Sesame Street' used the visual and audio grammar of commercials to bring basic education to North American children, often through what were identified as commercials 'sponsored' by various letters of the alphabet or by assorted numbers.[33]

The representation of life in commercials was definitely peculiar. Some things were missing because their presence might offend or disturb a viewer. Ban (ABC 1962) couldn't actually show someone using the deodorant under an arm; instead a pretty young woman delicately rubbed the deodorant on her wrist to sniff its fragrance. The Ford ad (R-C 1963) lacked any engine noise that might detract from the mood of escape. But the distortion of life went well beyond these euphemisms and absences. Scholars have tried to puzzle out what happens, and sometimes have fallen into the traps of semantic confusion as a result. Commercials portray an ideal version of life, 'more real than the "real," ' according to Martin Esslin, 'which is manifested in this degraded world only in imperfect representations of the ideal, eternal, archetypal reality.' Erving Goffman has coined the term 'hyper-ritualization' to describe the process of 'standardization, exaggeration, and simplification' whereby 'scenes from actual life,' or more properly its 'social ideals,' are transformed into the stuff of commercial life. The adman selects elements from the ordinary world, asserted Judith Williamson, and rearranges or alters these in terms of the product, all to create 'the world of the advertisement.' What is clear is that the adman deals in stereotype, archetype, and myth, in a much more direct fashion than the makers of programs.[34]

Ordinary people didn't really appear in commercials. Rather the people portrayed were actually public or collective figures. Nearly all of the men and women, by the way, were white: minorities just weren't visible in the world of commercials, except for the occasional exotic such as the Chinese baby eating Jell-O with chopsticks in one series of Jell-O ads. The live ad for Nabisco Shredded Wheat (CBC 1957) was done by the star of 'Holiday Ranch,' Cliff McKay, who traded on his reputation as a champion of the old-fashioned values to explain the great family virtues of the cereal. The Robert Goulet and Gisele MacKenzie of the duMaurier ads (CBC 1962) were their public personae as stars of that genre of showbiz variety that itself expressed the myth of glamour. Similarly Timex (CBC 1962) employed a famed skater to carry out one of its 'torture tests' to prove the watch shared the toughness of the man, just as Super Shell (R-C 1965) used a celebrity racing-car driver, both in action and later speaking, to demonstrate the high-performance qualities of its gasoline. The super-mum who made Jell-O (CBC 1958) for the family in the middle of the night was a stereotype of the ideal mother everywhere and any time. The ersatz professor in an ad for Philishave Speed Shaver (CBC 1958) was there to lend credence to the potted history of rotary action, that fundamentally important principle of science that had apparently reached its apogee in the manufacture of this electric shaver. The stylish woman who extolled the virtues of Klear (CBC 1967) was a representation of the affluent housewife at her very best. These people weren't just cardboard figures, they were walking and talking signs, placards bestowing credibility on the commercial's message by their very presence.

Perhaps the most important messages these signs delivered, albeit by implication, were about sex roles in modern life. Consider first who were the voices of authority in the commercials. One might well understand why Eveready Batteries used a male announcer. But why did Instant Maxwell House Coffee, Jell-O Instant Pudding, Max Factor Cream Puff, Lux Liquid Detergent, and Lysol as well? These products were aimed chiefly at women. The fact is that men were normally considered the most authoritative spokesmen for the virtues of products of all kinds. (I say normally because, for example, 'Wendy' in the Revlon ads [CBS 1955] and Betty Furness in the Westinghouse Laundromat ad [CBS 1956] were two announcers who adopted the tactic of one woman talking to another.) Whether they spoke in soft tones, as a friendly counsellor, or in short, fact-filled sentences, as the reporter, the men represented experience, expertise, and reassurance.

Commercials highlighted two dimensions of women's existence, namely the pursuit of beauty and the cult of domesticity. Understand that the huckster didn't directly advocate either of these; instead he assumed they were natural, something everywoman (and everyman as well) would accept without question. Women in ads were nearly always on display as objects of beauty: that was one of the purposes of the young, attractive, fashionably dressed female who played the relaxing passenger in a Ford ad (R-C 1963), and she was in a long, long tradition of good-looking blondes and brunettes used to sell the automobile. Even where there wasn't any overt sexual angle, the woman added grace and style to an ad: the perfect homemaker in the Klear ad (CBC 1967) was both an expert on beauty and an expression of beauty. The pursuit of beauty, of course, was integral to the ads for cosmetics and the like. The Lux Soap ad (CBC 1958) promised women a 'rich, satin smooth lather,' a 'soft lingering fragrance,' a 'fresh new radiance' for their skin. Lady Sunbeam (ABC 1962) talked of 'feminine petiteness,' 'exquisite styling,' a product that was 'smooth, sleak, and feminine.' Max Factor Nail Polish (CBC 1962) told women, 'Now you can have the elegant look of slender hands and long graceful fingertips ...' Richard Hudnut (R-C 1965) showed just how easy it was to have perfectly curled and shiny hair. Women, one might conclude, were excessively vain and delicate creatures, forever seeking the newest method of enhancing their looks.

They were also domestic drudges. First as mother the woman had to ensure that the children were fed correctly, that they ate a nourishing breakfast (feed them Nabisco Shredded Wheat). Then as homemaker she had to strive to supply products that would keep the whole family happy (make convenient and rich-tasting Jell-O Instant Pudding). As hostess she must ensure a warm welcome for all their friends (offer them Instant Maxwell House Coffee). But, above all, as housekeeper she had to do the family wash (the Westinghouse Laundromat was a mighty assist here), get the dishes amazingly clean (with Lux Liquid), cleanse the house from top to bottom (Lysol, the universal solvent), and keep the home sparkling (Klear made your home a show-piece). Each of these products told women how they might realize their dreams of being the perfect mistress of the domestic environment, and do so with surprising ease.

The image of men, and of men's work, was never quite as well developed in the world of the advertisement. That said, men were depicted as instrumental, the people in command, at least outside the home. The tyrannical boss of the Instant Maxwell House Coffee ad might be an object of fun but he was, naturally, male. The laboratory technician in the Off ad, like the professor in the Philishave ad, was also male. The testers of the effectiveness of Yard Raid (CBC 1967) in 'the bug-infested jungles' of Costa Rica wielded the canister as if it were a weapon. It seemed particularly fitting that a man used Raid Weed Killer to destroy, while a woman used Rose Garden Spray to preserve, both in one sixty-second ad for these two products from Johnson's Wax (R-C 1963). The driver of the Ambassador automobile shown in the AMC ad (R-C 1966) was a businessman on the way up in the world, which was why he'd acquired the new, classy car to show his status. The admen for both Eveready Batteries and Timex crafted commercials that appealed to the macho man, eager for power (Eveready) and impressed by toughness (Timex). One might read these ads as displaying man the master, the expert, the exterminator, the aggressor, or the big boy, clichéd figures much celebrated in the literature and the lore of the times.

Nearly all of these commercials employed the affluent lifestyle as a backdrop to their images of life. The action occurred in well-appointed offices, in kitchens full of gadgets, in fashionable dining-rooms, in richly upholstered cars. The goods advertised promised convenience, dependability, security, quality, value, sometimes freedom or escape as well, in a phrase 'the good life.' Take the case of two of the ads for Instant Maxwell House Coffee (CBC 1957). It was surely one of the great consumables in this good life, a source of well-being and a means of hospitality, 'the most delicious coffee yet' that could bring satisfaction to the family and to guests alike. Then there was that other ubiquitous pleasure, the cigarette: the duMaurier ads (CBC 1962) emphasized theirs was a cigarette for 'discriminating smokers' enjoyed in happy, comfortable surroundings. Or consider the Imperial Esso ads (CBC 1962) that showcased an assortment of trivia available at the typical Esso station for the comfort and security of the nation's motorists. The affluent lifestyle displayed here was founded on abundance and on consumption. All you had to do was buy to become a citizen of the democracy of goods.

In this scheme of things the whole mythology of individualism found a special and intriguing expression. On the one hand people were asked to make a choice, to define their own sense of identity by purchasing, say, the discriminating cigarette (duMaurier) or the stylish watch (Timex) or the freedom car (Ford). Here was individuality. On the other hand consumers were continually assured that their choice was sanctified by the actions of everybody else. Didn't 'more people buy Timex than any other watch in the world'? Wasn't 'the trend today to duMaurier'? Here was conformity. A little story in one General Motors ad (CBC 1959) about scientific achievement showed just how the world worked. 'A man starts with a dream,' intoned Alan McPhee. 'He puts it on paper. It is discussed, modified, developed. But to make that dream a fact some 13,000 pieces are needed, some big, some small, all built to GM's unparalleled standards.' That was the corporate vision of human progress, where the success of the genius depended upon the efforts of the team. And so it was in the marketplace as well. According to commercials, there wasn't a conflict between the individual and the society – individualism amounted to everybody making the same choice. The adman had managed to square the circle.

So many of the promises of the good life rested upon what Sut Jhally has called 'the religion of technology,' which was a way of understanding the world that especially suited an age entranced by gadgets. Commercials as a rule supplied very little hard information about how their products were manufactured or what they were made of, or why, if at all, they were truly better than rivals. Yet, time and again, the commercials made reference to Science to legitimize their plea for the consumers' attention. Lux Liquid Detergent had 'new pink lotion formula,' duMaurier cigarettes had 'the exclusive millcell super filter,' Timex had 'sturdy v-Conic move-ment,' 'New Formula Ban' could claim special chemicals to ensure dryness, Philishave's razor was the acme of rotary action. Maxwell House had managed to stuff 'millions of flavour buds of pure coffee' into its instant brew. Imperial Esso research labs were constantly at work to product 'products that are right, right, right with the times.' Diagrams and photo-graphs showed how Raid Weed Killer (R-C 1963) went to work to destroy the pesky weeds. Both Eveready Batteries and Off mosquito repellent were tested under laboratory conditions. The irony was that these claims gave the various products a magical quality. Indeed the commercial turned its product into a kind of fetish, that is, an inanimate object with special, mysterious powers to provide, in this case, happy solutions to the everyday problems of living. You could buy glamour or satisfaction or prestige or love or security. Science was the source of miracles, technology its means, and the product was the result.[35]

Worrying about Effects

As much as seven and a half hours of commercials might enter a Canadian home in a week of viewing during the winter months by the mid-1960s. Probably the actual total was a lot less, especially in homes glued to a CBC station where the commercial minutes were fewer than on private television. Janice Tyrwhitt estimated that an average household received about five hours of ads a week, or 'three hundred one-minute plugs.'

But, whatever the exact figure, people clearly were exposed to a lot of commercials every time they watched television. What was the effect of this constant barrage on their minds?[36]

Part of the answer to that question lies in an understanding of the consumer and of marketing. Consumers aren't all of one kind. Some people, notably children, teenagers, and newlyweds, are more vulnerable because their perceptive abilities are unfinished, their sense of self undeveloped, or their situation peculiarly fluid. Ordinary adults are usually more resistant to all kinds of marketing techniques, though some will take risks, meaning they'll readily buy new products, while others are cautious, wedded to established brand preferences. Recently, researchers have claimed an ability to identify four different groups of consumers, boasting an assortment of lifestyles with such catchy names as 'belonger,' 'achiever,' 'experiential,' whose responses to a range of products vary accordingly. Many people won't be in the market for a good, no matter how heavily it's advertised. Even when they are, most will be influenced by personal experience, by word-of-mouth information, sometimes by news stories and other apparently 'objective' sources of information. Further, the buying decision will often be affected by other factors, such as the availability of the good, packaging or design, location in a retail outlet, and, above all, price. The extent of advertising in the industry is also important: the more heavily advertised the product is, say cigarettes or cars, the more difficult it is for one firm to use advertising to get across its particular message. The fact is that any kind of advertising, print or broadcast, operates in particular context where other kinds of influences have considerable impact upon the market decisions of the individual consumer.[37]

No less significant was the attitude of Canadians towards advertising and commercials. Advertising wasn't something foisted on Canadians. Goldfarb found that fully 84 per cent of respondents to his poll thought advertising had a positive role to play in Canadian society. 'If these things weren't advertised we wouldn't know about them,' said one person – that was a typical response. The best-liked ads were either humorous, and so entertaining, or strictly factual, a kind of marketplace news. A CBC survey back in 1962 had found that three-quarters of Canadians accepted commercials: they would rather have commercials than pay anything extra, even as little as $15 a year, to receive a television service free of ads. A third survey for the advertising industry found that people rated television better than other media as a source of information about new products (43 per cent), of 'cute and clever' ads (73 per cent), and of clear product descriptions (40 per cent). They even concluded, albeit by a bare margin (31 per cent), that television talked to the consumer 'as a real person' more than did newspapers and the rest. Well over a third of Canadians in the Goldfarb poll admitted they were influenced either 'a great deal' or 'somewhat' by ads. Four in ten respondents believed advertising was more influential than the school system. Most Canadians accorded commercials the first place as the most influential brand of advertising, because of television's visual appeal and its glamorous style. Every time he saw a smoking ad on TV, one respondent admitted, 'I light one up – darn it.'[38]

Even so, Canadians worried a lot about the ill effects of advertising. The salesman was always something of an ambivalent figure in North America because selling seemed to require a certain amount of hype, of puffery. The worst things advertising could and did do, Goldfarb found, were to mislead, to insult, to bore, and to force people to buy what they shouldn't. The last comment reflected both a puritanical distrust of conspicuous consumption and a deep-seated fear of manipulation. Charles Templeton expressed the distrust when he asked Dr Dichter, 'Is it right to exploit human frailities [sic] to make a fast buck?' The chief peril, he suggested, was that the admen would push the county 'into a mood of self-indulgence.' 'Doesn't history show that when nations become self-indulgent they go down?' Northrop Frye expressed the fear when he charged that 'the technique of advertising and propaganda is to stun and demoralize the critical consciousness with statements too absurd or extreme to be dealt with seriously by it.' Apparently, advertising snuck past conscious defences and established a bridgehead in people's minds. He thought it was, like other forms of irony, given a kind of poetic licence, allowed to say 'what it does not wholly mean.' 'Hence it creates an illusion of detachment and mental superiority even when one is obeying its exhortations.' The prevalence of such notions undermined the legitimacy of advertising, setting up a barrier to the effects of commercials – the right-thinking person, so it seemed, was honour-bound to resist the persuasions of the adman.[39]

Little wonder people could be very critical of commercials. A Gallup report in 1965 found that two-thirds of the public thought there was just 'too much advertising' in broadcasting, leaving a third who believed the amount was 'necessary' to have 'good programs.' The CBC survey had learned that just over 60 per cent, and over 80 per cent of francophones, found commercials interfered with the enjoyment of the network's programs. Ross McLean, then a critic, described what a destructive effect an ad could have upon the mood created by a drama: an episode of 'Dr. Kildare' dealing with a young girl who died of a blood sickness ended with a familiar message from 'the man who bottles the stuff that copes with tired blood.' Similarly Ira Dilworth, a CBC official, expressed indignation over one commercial delivered in mock Shakespearean style by Lloyd Bochner and another selling drugs given by Joan Fairfax in the midst of a show celebrating Christmas. But people were most exercised about the number of ads. 'It gets to the point that you don't want to continue watching,' bemoaned one of the anonymous respondents to the Goldfarb poll. 'It's just too extreme – too many ads.' Dr Stewart, chairman of the Board of Broadcast Governors, warned advertisers that their messages weren't getting through because people either avoided watching commercials altogether or swiftly forgot what they'd seen: in fact, in the United States, the rate of ad recall was estimated in 1965 (albeit in a study commissioned by newspapers) at a mere 18 per cent, meaning only a small portion of adult viewers could remember the product named in the last commercial they witnessed. And Canadians were insulted, as the CBC had discovered, by the absurdity or dishonesty of some of the claims. 'Waxes don't shine the way they say,' argued an unhappy viewer. 'Soap doesn't suds and suds and suds like the way they say.' Indeed, turning once again to Gallup, over two-thirds of Canadians believed commercials did make use of untruthful statements. They'd recognized, in short, the fraudulence of commercials.[40]

So much for the attitudes of Canadians. How did they react in the marketplace? *Marketing* carried a number of television success stories that deserve notice. Take the case of Lowney's ice cream in Montreal during the mid-1950s. Lowney's sales rose high in summer but sagged in winter. Jack Hewitt, a manager, set out to remedy the imbalance by persuading mothers that ice cream was a delicious and convenient wintertime dessert. Lowney's agency, Hayhurst, selected the English station CBMT, because it could reach more families more cheaply, and the sitcom 'Amos 'n' Andy,' because its 'light-hearted, fast-moving humour' had a general appeal. The campaign employed two basic approachs, emphasizing the 'prestige' of the Lowney's name as a maker of fine ice cream and the ease and convenience of ice-cream desserts: the commercials explained how Lowney's used the best ingredients and demonstrated just what kinds of delights, from banana splits to baked Alaskas, a homemaker could whip up (and consumers could write in for a booklet of recipes). Between October 1954 and May 1955, sales of Lowney's ice cream jumped up 25 per cent, and the next winter much the same campaign increased sales 37 per cent over the preceding year. A lot of Montreal mothers had apparently bought the commercial message.[41]

Television could work wonders for national brands as well. In November

1957 A.M. Lawrence, ad manager for Nestlé (Canada) Ltd, told happy broadcasters that the rush of makers of instant coffee into spot radio and especially TV had resulted in an extraordinary growth of sales: up 47 per cent in 1954, 25 per cent in 1955, and 51 per cent in 1956. Nestlé itself had recently benefited as a result of a massive blitz making heavy use of television during its Nestlé week, which saw its share of the instant-coffee market zoom from 19 per cent to 81 per cent, before falling back to about double the pre-blitz figure. Television alone, more properly the commercials carried on the 'Kit Carson' show broadcast by Radio-Canada, had worked a sudden change in the acceptance of Quik, the instant chocolate-milk mix, in the Lac St Jean area where sales had previously been slow. Only a few weeks after the broadcasts had begun, 'all the stores and wholesalers ... were completely sold out of Quik.' That had happened without any deals, special prices, or other advertising changes by Nestlé and its competitors, but for the ad placement in 'Kit Carson.' 'It was the perfect success story for TV,' Lawrence concluded, 'and Quik has been growing steadily there ever since.'[42]

Tests showed as well that television could have a much greater impact on sales than could print. Jerry Goodis recounted one such test his agency carried out in 1960 for Hush Puppies, a new brand of casual shoes. A commercial was run twice a week for six weeks in Kitchener and Winnipeg and a print ad was used in London and Kitchener. Sales in London weren't especially exciting. But in Kitchener and Winnipeg sales quadrupled. Thereafter television remained the main advertising medium, although it was supplemented by print ads. By 1966, apparently, Canada had 'the highest per capita sales rate of Hush Puppies (one pair per sixteen persons) in the world.'[43]

All of these examples suggest that television could make a great splash in the marketplace, especially for new products. Commercials might, as well, have broader effects upon the fate of a company, product, or industry. Time and time again, surveys indicated that association with popular programs did pay off in terms of sponsor identification. Elliott-Haynes ratings for October 1961, for example, were based on the percentage of people able to name the product or advertiser on a program: Molson's got a 94.3 for its association with the hit game show 'La poule aux oeufs d'or,' Molson's and Imperial Esso a 90.3 for hockey in French, Imperial Esso 74.3 for hockey in English, and Massey-Ferguson and Pillsbury 62.2 for 'Don Messer.' Presumably that did translate into goodwill for these sponsors generous enough to bring entertainment to the masses. Or take the case of commercials and children. One study correlated the amount of television viewing at home, attitudes towards commercials, and children's attempts to determine what Mother bought in the supermarket. The finding: not only did watching commercial television make children more aggressive in their demands, but almost half of the children's requests brought success, which commonly meant the purchase of a sugared cereal. Then there was the case of smoking. Cigarette manufacturers used commercials throughout the 1960s to combat the effects of medical research that linked smoking and cancer, an effort that eventually led to their disappearance from the CBC first and eventually television in general to protect the health of viewers.[44]

But success wasn't guaranteed – although it's much harder to find information about failures than about successes. Schwerin told the story of one commercial for an unspecified product that produced exactly the wrong switch – away from a product. Apparently the story showed a woman nagging hubby about his appearance. 'Women didn't want to be shrewish; men wouldn't identify with a "lazy bum." ' Late in 1964 Rothmans made heavy use of television to introduce its new charcoal-filter cigarette Riggio, which certainly brought it some immediate attention, though after a few years the brand was removed from the market. Goodis noted one of his failures involving an effort to make Ovaltine (a declining instant drink threatened by the arrival of the sweeter mixes) more popular with young people: he used a collection of ten-second commercials plus Reader's Digest and streetcar and bus cards for Ovaltine, which caused a lot of talk (perhaps because of the slogan 'You Can Get to Sleep with Me Tonight') but few extra sales – his agency soon lost the account. He also cited the case of Carling Breweries, which employed a very imaginative television campaign (complete with a hundred-piece band and a lot of marchers) to push its beer, until sales figures proved it wasn't delivering results. The fact that consumers noted, even liked, your commercials didn't mean they would change their existing brand preferences or stay with a new product they'd tried should the product fail to satisfy. Television's power couldn't overcome the limits consumers and the marketplace put upon the role of advertising generally.[45]

Even so, commercials were usually the most effective kind of advertising available to the makers of mass-consumption items. Moving pictures had a special ability to say things that would seem strange in print and to show products in a way that could easily involve the people. Commercials could be accepted by consumers as if they were daydreams, albeit manufactured by outsiders: he or she engaged in a sort of directed make-believe, witnessing the product in use or exploring the lifestyle presented or enjoying the situation depicted. A catchy tune or a jingle, a striking image, a slogan, and the emotions these evoked, all lingered on. The ad amounted to a 'package of stimuli,' in the words of adman Tony Schwartz, which 'resonates with information already stored within an individual.' That's why statistics about ad recall were a bit misleading. As Frye recognized, the commercial could fix elements of its messages in the viewer's mind, unbeknownst to that viewer, that would trigger an act of purchase later on. That seemed especially true in the case of so-called low-involvement products (a term that might mean candy bars to one person and headache remedies to another) where buying was often an impulsive act rather than a rational decision. It applied less to goods that the individual might value highly, and so was likely to consider carefully before purchasing.[46]

The ability of commercials to leave an imprint on the mind of consumers lay at the root of their cultural import. Janice Tyrwhitt noted just how common this had become by the mid-1960s:

Day after day we're engulfed by a tide of commercial imagery, and some of it washes right into our reflexes. We catch ourselves whistling, or at least recognizing, 'Things go better with Coca-Cola,' and 'Come alive! You're in the Pepsi generation!' Some mornings the rhythms of, 'I can spell with Alpha-Bits,' or, 'the only breakfast cereal that comes in the shape of animals,' go round and round in my head. For me, 'Look, Mom, no cavities!' will always summon up Earl Cameron interlocking his fingers to show how Crest melds with tooth enamel. I've watched that Hertz customer who plungers into the driver's seat, providing gag fodder for Jackie Gleason, Wayne and Shuster, and Ursula Andress in *What's New Pussycat?* and I wasn't even surprised to read in a Toronto newspaper that the first words an elderly woman spoke when she reached hospital after a motorcycle accident were, 'You meet the nicest people on a Honda.' After fifteen years of television we've developed some immunity to the hard sell, but we're still susceptible to the pitch that stirs our emotions. The good ones do it well, sometimes too well. An acquaintance of mine once figured as a happy drinker at a beach party in a beer advertisement. Months later, driving to the airport, the taxi driver insisted that they'd met at a barbecue. The cabbie swore he could remember a fire, hot dogs and songs (but no beer).

'We had a ball that night, didn't we?' he said wistfully. 'Let's do it again sometime.'

The bits and pieces of commercials were now part of the popular culture, the subject of jokes on television and elsewhere as well as the stuff of ordinary conversation. And like the other trivia of this culture, most of these bits and pieces didn't last beyond a year or two, especially when the particular commercial passed away, to be replaced by whatever new jingle or slogan or image had for whatever reason captured the public's fancy.[47]

Even before the end of the 1960s, commercials had emerged as a wide-spread, persuasive art-form that spoke about the character and place of goods in modern Canada and about the affluent lifestyle that rested upon conspicuous consumption. First of all, they supplied meanings for particular products and for assorted classes of goods. Thus the James Bond–type commercials for Mark Ten gave that cigarette the aura of a macho smoke. Similarly the 'think young' campaigns of Pepsi and the like, as well as the happy-times commercials of beer companies, helped to affirm the role of these drinks as the accoutrements of fun and pleasure in all manner of social gatherings. And the innumerable automobile commercials served to confirm the symbol of the car as the grand instrument of individualism and personal mastery in North America. Second, commercials took experiences from ordinary life – from breakfast time to doing the household wash, to driving a car – as the stuff out of which they moulded images of persuasion. They told people about ways to behave and what to expect in a range of settings, from the family circle to the neighbourhood bank. They reassured people that, at bottom, all was right – or at least all the problems of life could be remedied. (It's worth noting here that some people do use ads to reassure themselves that their purchase of a particular good was a wise choice.) Theirs was a story of ongoing, easy progress, of the happy marriage of industry and technology that brought people a cornucopia of marvellous goods. Naturally they helped to shape public thought, to reaffirm social clichés, although here their influence blended into the wider effects of advertising, television, and the other media.[48]

None of this was especially sinister. People weren't required to obey, to accept the advertised meaning of goods or the guides to proper living. The advertising agency amounted to only one among a number of social authorities (that included, for instance, the church, school, the profession or the union, the news media), and advertising on TV or in print was and remains a type of discourse often discredited or satirized by all kinds of people. No doubt it was a voice of capitalism, an obstacle to other ways of understanding the world or to criticizing the consequences of affluence and abundance. But it was hardly the only mainstay of capitalism. It had a limited, if at times spectacular, role in the marketplace and a wider, though more diffuse, role in the popular culture. As Michael Schudson has stated, perhaps a bit tongue-in-cheek, advertising may best be seen as 'capitalism's way of saying "I love you" to itself'![49]

Focus: Aspirin* 1967

The Aspirin ad was the first commercial in the summer rerun of the 'Wojeck' episode 'The Last Man in the World.' The sixty-second mini-drama was a 'slice-of-life' story revolving around the businessman's trip home from work in the evening rush-hour in what could have been any big city in North America. In reality the city was probably Toronto, where most made-in-Canada commercials were produced. Full understanding required that the viewer fill in the gaps, that he or she supply the information missing from the condensed story. That process, of course, would involve the viewer in a kind of directed make-believe, which is one reason why advertisers in print as well as on television often employed 'absences' to hook the consumer.[50]

The viewer was simply dropped into the midst of the story. The opening image was of an overhead traffic light, rocking slightly because of the gusts of wind from a storm that poured down rain upon a line of cars. That image was supported by an assortment of sounds of cars and horns. The camera moved back to reveal the street scene – shot from above and on an angle – where a person in an overcoat ran across the street in front of the cars, trying to protect himself from the elements (see frame 9.1). A car stopped sharply, with an appropriate squeal of tires, as the distressed driver tried to avoid hitting the stationary vehicle in front of him. Then the camera moved to pan the stopped cars, showing the windshield wipers briskly sweeping away the rain, only to blur into a close-up of the profile of one driver, who later is identified as our hapless businessman. The camera switched back to the traffic light, which changed to allow the cars to go.

The opening sequence had taken about ten seconds to set the scene: we were witness to a typical, ordinary adventure of modern urban life, the drive home, made a bit nastier than usual by a storm. It amply demonstrated just how the makers of commercials could use a cascade of overlapping signs to swiftly sketch, in this case, a scene

* Reg. Trade Mark

Frame 9.1 The drive home

that just about any city person would recognize. The commercial, I suspect, would evoke in many a viewer that feeling of fatigue, if not mild horror, that is all too often attendant on the ritual of the drive home.

It was at this point that the commercial became more personal. The camera now gave us a behind-the-head shot of the driver, moving in to focus on the rear-view mirror to show his eyes looking at what was behind. The focus suddenly shifted dramatically: the camera offered an angle shot, from on high again, of a moving car, the businessman's car. Very briefly that image was overlaid by a blurred picture of lights and cars. The businessman's car, a standard North American vehicle of the times, was driven over to the curb of the street to park. This image dissolved into a picture of the interior of the car, which showed the man rubbing his eyes. A voice-over, presumably speaking the man's thoughts, lamented, 'Oh brother [a sigh] ... what a headache,' said with feeling and frustration. The man turned to look out the window, the camera very quickly shifted to show once more the street scene of busyness, cars, and rain – and a loud horn sounded in the background. The problem had been defined: our businessman had

Frame 9.2 The recovery

an affliction that prevented him from continuing 'the battle of the streets.'

The third sequence was marked by an abrupt change of pace, sounds, and images, and dominated by the words of the voice-over announcer. A happy, bouncy tune began to play. We were treated to an image of a café, the businessman sitting down at a counter and taking out of his inside jacket pocket the little tin container of Bayer Aspirin. A waiter brought him some water, which he drank, presumably with an Aspirin tablet. The camera dwelt briefly on a picture of the Aspirin container, which the waiter moved to allow room for a piece of pie. There followed assorted shots of normal behaviour (see frame 9.2) – our businessman (whom we then saw was reasonably handsome, dressed in a dark suit and tie, and looking well-cared-for) putting sugar into his coffee, drinking his coffee, and talking with the waiter (who also wears a tie). At the same time, the announcer was intoning the virtues of Aspirin: 'With Aspirin there's no waiting for relief. Each tablet you take is ready to go to work instantly ... so that minutes later you feel better.' Meanwhile the camera offered a long-shot of the café, the man in the foreground, which displayed two

Frame 9.3 The source of relief

people leaving, one of them a young, attractive woman wearing a short skirt. Back to our businessman who was still looking, presumably at the woman, a nice little touch of authenticity. Our businessman looked noticeably better, proof of the miraculous effects of Aspirin (and perhaps the pie and coffee?). The announcer hasn't stopped during this tiny vignette: 'For fast pain relief,' he told us, 'Aspirin is used by millions more people than any other brand of pain reliever.' With this final sentence, our businessman rose, picked up the Aspirin container (on which the camera again dwelt briefly), put it in his pocket, and exchanged goodbyes with the friendly waiter (see frame 9.3).

The final sequence returned us to 'the battle of the streets.' Our businessman drove back into the traffic, sufficiently refreshed, we must presume, to face all the trials and hazards ahead. The announcer declared, 'If you have never taken Aspirin for a headache, try it.' Against the background of street and car lights appeared the icon of the saviour, the package of Aspirin plus the little tin container. 'Aspirin brings you the relief you want and does it in minutes.' The screen switched to dark grey with a large image of the actual pill smack in the centre, an image that highlighted the famous Bayer cross. 'Get genuine Aspirin with the Bayer cross on every tablet.' That concluded the commercial.

Remember Roland Marchand's description of advertising as an 'ideology of efficacious answers'? That was certainly the promise of the Aspirin ad: what began as an adventure story became a quest, a quest for relief, which ended, as always, happily. Marchand also argues that advertising is full of parables, which draw 'practical moral lessons' out of 'the incidents of everyday life,' even if these incidents are often simplified or exaggerated. The Aspirin ad falls into the realm of 'the Parable of Civilization Redeemed,' a parable that explained how mankind suffered in the era of rampant progress from one or another version of 'Nature's curses.' The headache, we would know from experience, was a result of pressure, of the daily struggle for a living topped off by the hassle of getting home. But the fact was that Civilization had already discovered products that could overcome the ill effects of Nature's curse. Aspirin was one of these: it couldn't cure the weather or the traffic but it could cure the headache. The Aspirin commercial was just further proof, then, that 'Civilization had become its own redeemer.' The commercial offered comfort, reassurance, the conviction that things would work out if only everyman and everywoman would accept the wisdom of the adman.[51]

10

Storytelling

One recent Friday evening in Montreal, a seven-year-old youngster burst into the kitchen crying. 'Mommie! Mommie!' she wailed. 'Onesime has been run over by a truck. He's dead! He's dead.'

The mother started to cry, too. She dropped her dish towel and dashed to the parlor where all members of the family soon gathered to pay tribute to Onesime. Strangely enough, the mourning took place in front of a television screen.

As it turned out, Onesime wasn't dead after all. He had, it is true, been scraped by a truck and was in hospital, but by the time the weekly half-hour visit with "The Plouffe Family" ended, this crisis had come and gone.

Lloyd Lockhart, 1956[1]

Telling stories was what North American television did best of all. These stories came in the shape of sitcoms and westerns, crime and adventure shows, téléromans and soap operas, historical romances, mysteries, thrillers, science fiction, professional sagas, and the like. 'The Plouffe Family' was only unusual because it was made in Canada: this live drama was broadcast twice each week, first in French and then in English. So popular were its heroes, 'Les Plouffes,' that they became for a brief time the quintessential French-Canadian family in the eyes of a lot of viewers. The memory of this success lingered on: in the 1981/2 season the CBC aired an independent production that offered nostalgic viewers in English Canada a return to the life and times of 'Les Plouffes.' Sadly 'La famille Plouffe' and 'The Plouffe Family' didn't have any successors: never again would the CBC produce a hit dramatic series that captivated people in both Canadas. Instead the CBC developed very different kinds of stories for Francophone and anglophone viewers. Ironically what stories they did have in common came from outside, from the United States.

Theatre of the Air

Television speaks to us mostly in the language of drama. The force of that observation can easily be exaggerated: the other forms of information, display, and contest, all persisted on television, and dramatic programming often borrowed techniques and gimmicks from these rivals. It's not difficult to find dramas that are preachy, where the actors, the settings, or the special effects are on display, in which the plot treats characters as players in some game of life. Yet, the fact remains that the most prominent form on North American television by the end of the 1950s was unquestionably drama of one kind or another. And the particular language of drama imposed itself on other brands of programming, from news and sports to advertising and even variety. Recall that Wayne and Shuster's brand of comedy relied heavily on dramatic sketches to supply the structure for their farce and satire. Roland Barthes, among others, made much of the fact that wrestling was a staged drama, a fight between good and evil. In 1963 Reuven Frank, then executive producer of NBC's evening news, declared that each and every news story ought to be designed in the manner of a drama.[2]

Explaining exactly why this is so could lead us down quite a number of paths. A large part of the answer lies in the nearly universal appeal of drama. Drama, in the words of Martin Esslin, amounts to 'a mimetic reproduction of the world.' It's not exactly reality, of course: real life has been abbreviated, rearranged, simplified, interpreted, cut to suit the occasion. But it bears some resemblance to the kinds of people and situations that we may confront in our daily lives. What the dramatist does is impose a particular structure upon the slice of life he or she has decided to highlight. At a minimum this structure involves an introduction, a problem and conflict, periods of rising and falling action, a climax, and a resolution or dénouement. The focus of attention, of course, is on personality. Nearly all dramas require a 'driver,' a hero or villain, whose activities push forward the action. Many of the themes of drama, serious or comic, boil down to a case of 'obstructed will.' People in conflict – against each other, against their situation – supplies the tension and the suspense deemed necessary to drama. The audience experiences reality, then, through the medium of personality.[3]

Of course, television soon imposed its own style upon the form of drama. Producers had learned by the end of the 1950s that series drama, rather than the play anthology, was the most effective way of telling stories to the masses. Series (which include all shows involving a degree of continuity from week to week) meant fewer surprises for everyone involved in television, albeit at the expense of innovation. The essential act of creation occurred at the beginning, when the author established the features of the leading characters and the overall design of the plots. Thereafter writers could follow the formula for each separate episode, introducing only that small element of novelty necessary to hold the attention of viewers. Actors could easily master an established role, growing into their character, so to speak. Viewers might expect that any program would be much the same from week to week. Programmers and admen had greater assurance of continued success, that their thriller or sitcom would exploit the proved viewer interest in a given set of characters or plot structure. In short, series drama offered people a repeatable experience. It was a drama submitted to the discipline of mass production.[4]

The stories employed narrative structures and literary devices that had been common long before the advent of television. They spoke to viewers in a way that was familiar, and they dealt with a subject-matter that was also familiar. Writers and producers ransacked the worlds of plays, literature, and the movies, radio's past and present, as well as the news to find material to please the millions. That's why these stories were steeped in the mythology of the times: they embodied the icons, the clichés, the concerns, and the myths that were present in the mainstream of society. Overall, TV's production houses manufactured shows that fitted into four broad categories of drama: comedy (a tamed version that explored life's little embarrassments, banalities, and absurdities: the sitcom); action/adventure (where the hero was in jeopardy: westerns, scifi, war, and so on); suspense or mystery (where the focus was on investigation and problem-solving: particularly the professional sagas about doctors, lawyers, and the like); and social melodrama (where the subject-matter was personal relationships, especially romance and marriage, friendship and animosity: the soap opera or the téléromans). In the United States only the first three types of drama were well-represented in the evening schedules (see chart 10.1). In Canada, by the early 1960s, that was also true of the line-up on the two anglophone networks, which wasn't surprising since so much of

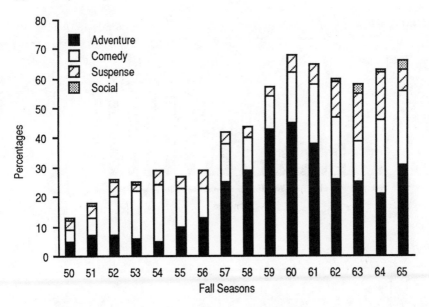

Chart 10.1 Dramatic genres, United States, 1950–65, 7:00 to 11:00
Note: This chart pertains to the network offerings of ABC, CBS, and NBC.
Sources are Tim Brooks and Earle Marsh, *The Complete Directory to Prime Time Network TV Shows 1946–Present*, 2nd ed. (New York: Ballantine 1981); Alex McNeil, *Total Television: A Comprehensive Guide to Programming from 1948 to 1980* (New York: Penguin 1980); and Harry Castleman and Walter J. Podrazik, *Watching TV: Four Decades of American Television* (New York: McGraw-Hill 1982).

their drama was American in origin. Only Radio-Canada diverged because it offered a certain amount of home-grown, and some French, social melodrama (see chart 10.2).

What Hollywood Did

In the beginning American television drama was mostly done live and in New York. That didn't last. Largely as a result of the astonishing success of the telefilm 'I Love Lucy' (1951–7) in 1951/2, the number of filmed series (not all drama, admittedly) nearly doubled, to forty-six in the next winter season, many of these produced by upstart Hollywood companies such as that founded by Lucille Ball and Desi Arnaz. At first the Hollywood majors

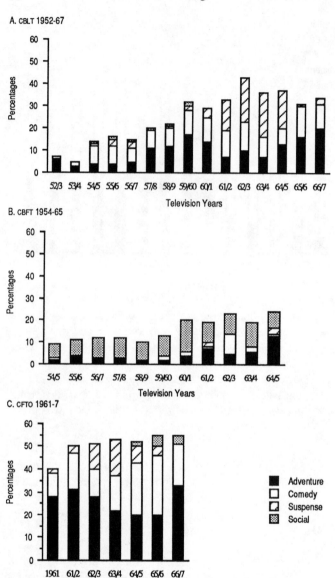

Chart 10.2 Dramatic genres, Canada, 7:00 to 11:00
Source: Based on TV listings in the *CBC Times, La Semaine à Radio-Canada*, and the *Toronto Daily Star*

stayed away from television, almost as if they hoped this booming rival would prove to be a short-lived fad that wouldn't survive without their films. But in April 1954 ABC signed a deal with Walt Disney to air the anthology 'Disneyland.' That brought an agreement between ABC and Warner Brothers for 1955/6, out of which came the hit western 'Cheyenne.' By the end of the decade virtually all of the drama programmed by the three networks in primetime came from Hollywood studios, some of which were old movie giants such as Warner Brothers and Columbia Pictures (through Screen Gems) while others were newcomers such as Desilu and MCA. The fact is that Hollywood had proved very good at producing what, for want of a better expression, I'll call believable fantasies, full of simplified plots, boldly drawn characters, and happy endings, all dressed up in the garb of authenticity.[5]

Its production mills worked to turn out large amounts of product at low cost as rapidly as possible. Look at the output of pioneer telefilm producer Jack Webb, who masterminded the hit 'Dragnet' (1952–9): his work schedule in 1953 required making a half-hour episode in three days at a cost of about $30,000. At one point he was delivering four episodes every two weeks, then breaking off the production for planning and editing in the rest of the month. The ABC/Warner Brothers deal was slightly more generous: Warner Brothers was to make forty one-hour shows for $75,000 each. Even that sum was considered modest, especially when low-budget movies cost $300,000 or more. The 'Cheyenne' episodes were shot in five days, using lots of footage of crowds and battles and stampedes from old movies to save time and money.[6]

The result was that the Hollywood system took on all the characteristics of a factory. The dominant motive was making money, not making quality. William Dozier, head of Screen Gems production in 1963, made this bluntly clear to an interviewer. The worthy series was the one that could be sold – shows weren't any good if they appealed only to your family. He had a couple of questions he raised whenever evaluating an idea for a series. First, you asked whether it had some problem that might limit its appeal or prevent an advertiser from sponsoring or buying time. Was it possible to find an existing star for the top role? Did it have 'any presale value'? (He cited the sitcoms 'Dennis the Menace' and 'Hazel' as examples, since the characters were familiar from cartoons.) Then you had to worry about what the competition was doing, whether they had a similar idea in the works. And, naturally, you had to consider just how novel it was – the idea had to be slightly different, a bit fresh. So Dozier mused about the merits of a humorous war drama, a series about a small-town attorney, and the virtues of a Dr Kildare–type character put in a church setting.[7]

The series was ruled by its design, its budget, and the constraints of time. The key person was the producer, sometimes a producer-writer, who often had thought up or acquired the original idea for the series. He had the task of hiring writers and directors, casting actors, supervising the shooting schedule and budget, editing and scoring the result. He might be helped by an assistant and a story editor, who met with writers. Writers were expected to produce scripts that fitted into the design of the series: they were provided with ready-made characters, a format, and sometimes a plot outline, which left them only the task of filling in the details. The writing team of Richard Levinson and William Link, who arrived in Hollywood in mid-1959, later complained that producers seemed most interested in plot (rather than in characters), especially in the amount of 'jeopardy' and 'conflict' in action/adventure scripts. Sterling Silliphant, the chief writer for 'Route 66' (1960–4), talked over a script with the producer before he sat down at the typewriter. He wrote fast: he took from two to five days to bang out an hour-long episode. The directors worked quickly, taking a week to prepare a show, and roughly the same amount of time to shoot it, before going on to the next job. The lead and supporting actors stayed on from week to week, of course, although only a few stars were allowed much say in the way they played their roles. Series drama, in short, was the result of a detailed, and fairly rigid, division of labour.[8]

Shows did change, especially in the early months of a run, as the production staff became aware of problems and reactions. Warner Brothers' 'Maverick' (1957–62) began life as a standard western, but soon became a bit of a spoof, with James Garner playing his character as a 'wisecracking ladies' man,' a semi-humorous role that suited his personal style. During the 1960s the renowned 'Gunsmoke' (1955–75), now expanded to an hour, became something of an anthology, each play depending upon a guest star, sometimes tackling versions of the social issues of the day, though the regular characters, and, above all, Matt Dillon, remained to ensure continuity. In time nearly every show suffered from creative fatigue because its idea was exhausted or its actors tired. Very occasionally a show's masters would take it off the air before it fell victim to the disease: no new episodes of 'I Love Lucy' were produced after the 1956/7 season, even though it had ended up at the top of the ratings. Sometimes the producer would apply a bit of surgery to save the show: 'Burke's Law' (1963–6), a crime drama, became a secret-agent thriller in its last season, though the air of glamour and sophistication that had been one of its trademarks remained. But usually the show would last until a network executive decided it had lost appeal or that its time-slot was needed for a new product. 'Gunsmoke' finally disappeared because its audience appeared too old and too rural in the new era when good demographics (meaning a youthful, urban market) had become a key measure of success.[9]

Nearly all Hollywood drama adhered to the conventions of what has been called naturalism, which means that the stories claimed to portray or represent reality 'like it is.' Television endeavoured to mask the fact that all was pretense, and cast the viewer in the role of an eyewitness who watched the unfolding of a plausible narrative. Settings were vitally important: the authenticity of the doctor's saga 'Dr. Kildare' (1961–6) was certified by the use of well-appointed doctor's offices and well-equipped operating rooms. The camera worked to focus attention upon the action and dialogue through a series of alternating two-shots and close-ups. The close-up of a face served to show a character's reaction to some comment or event. The camera was particularly active, even nervous, in the premier episode of 'The Life and Legend of Wyatt Earp' (6 September 1955), one of the first of the wave of so-called adult westerns: it moved rapidly from one face to another, during conversations and especially at moments of tension, creating an illusion of intimacy. No less important were the conventions ruling dialogue and sound. Background noise was kept to a minimum, except in, say, a crowd scene, to ensure it didn't take attention away from what the main characters were saying. Music was used to cover transitions and to suggest an emotion, a preferred way of reading the meaning of a scene. Both anguish and joy were highlighted by the music in the first episode of 'Ben Casey' (2 October 1961). Television characters were almost always articulate: they spoke clearly and concisely, usually to the point, to ensure that the audience wasn't confused. An episode of the famous crime drama 'The Untouchables' (20 November 1962) featured short, sharp dialogue, full of questions and answers, to create the impression of hectic urgency. Or a producer could induce a mood of excitement through careful editing: the spy story 'The Man from U.N.C.L.E.' (1964–8) was among the first series to use very fast cutting from scene to scene to keep viewers on the edge of their seats. Above all, it was crucial to hide the fact of mediation, that this was really a play, by covering over the joints, disguising camera changes, and so on, that might distract and so make the viewer aware this was all a construction.[10]

Producers went to great pains to ensure that their series would remain constantly attractive to the general audience. A much-favoured technique was the use of visual clichés. The previously mentioned episode of 'The

Untouchables' opened with a derailment of a sophisticated toy train, owned by crime king Charlie Rodick, to portend upset and destruction. That episode also included a close-up of Rodick's mad eyes (the killer instinct), images of a child and her doll (innocence), a lingering shot of a dark, misty pier (impending doom). Another ploy was the special effect: Joseph Stefano, the writer-producer of the scifi anthology 'The Outer Limits' (1963–5), claimed that each episode contained 'one splendid, staggering, shuddering effect that induces awe or wonder or tolerable terror.' All these images and impressions were backed up with sound. In an episode of 'I Love Lucy' (20 May 1955) the chatter of Lucy and her friend Ethel signified silly women, while Lucy's whining voice in an exchange with husband Ricky suggested spoiledness.[11]

In retrospect, however, what is especially striking is the great care producers took to make the actual stories appear realistic, even if that meant only living up to the expectations viewers had about a genre. Jack Webb presented his 'Dragnet' as a docudrama: stories were drawn from police files, scripts were checked with the police for accuracy, attention was focused on the details of police work, Sgt Joe Friday (Webb himself) delivered a voice-over narration, and the cops spoke in a laconic style, using bits of jargon. Typically each episode concluded with the criminal arrested, and an announcer would briefly spell out the results of the trial and the nature of the sentence. A few years later Quinn Martin for Desilu would do something similar with the ultra-violent crime show 'The Untouchables' (1959–63), which claimed to be a fictionalized portrayal of the battle between government men and the Al Capone mob in the last days of Prohibition in the 1930s. 'Medic' (1954–6) dramatized actual case histories from the Los Angeles medical association, shooting episodes in a hospital, at times using actual doctors and nurses, and often tried to educate viewers about some health problem or another. It got into trouble as a result of public protest over a planned episode featuring a Caesarean section. 'The Defenders' (1961–5), a courtroom drama, specialized in dealing with such controversial issues as abortion and civil disobedience. On occasion the law firm of Preston & Preston actually lost a case.[12]

Even many of the sitcoms played a similar kind of game, presenting themselves as slightly idealized representations of normal (meaning middle-class) suburban life. 'The Adventures of Ozzie and Harriet' (1952–66) was about a 'real' family, whose members 'played' themselves in a variety of supposedly common situations. Other sitcoms, including 'Father Knows Best' (1954–63), 'Dennis the Menace' (1959–63), 'Leave It to Beaver' (1957–63), and 'My Three Sons' (1960–72), expended a lot of time worrying about parents' raising children and kids growing up, a reflection of the family problems of that era of the baby boom. Bizarre sitcoms, such as 'My Favorite Martian' (1963–6), about an alien visitor, 'Bewitched' (1964–72), about a witch, and the two horror spoofs 'The Addams Family' and 'The Munsters' (1964–6), located their characters in a domestic setting where the troubles of ordinary life could easily be given a humorous twist.

The Hollywood producers also tried to make their characters, if not altogether believable, then at least interesting. One of the first adult western heroes, Matt Dillon (of 'Gunsmoke'), was supposedly kept human, made subject to doubts, so that he wouldn't become a cardboard figure. The Andersons in 'Father Knows Best' were presented as intelligent adults and parents. The teenager was given an intriguing, if exaggerated treatment in '77 Sunset Strip' (1958–64): Kookie, the parking-lot attendant, was a fast-talking brash youth, ever ready with a bit of slang. Dick Van Dyke played a very natural role as a comedy writer for a TV show in the sitcom 'The Dick Van Dyke Show' (1961–6). The two doctors, an angry and brusque Ben Casey and a more refined Dr Kildare, were depicted as men of conscience, at odds with those around them and sometimes with themselves. Then there was the ambiguous or contrary character. One of the first was Sgt Bilko in 'The Phil Silvers Show' (1955–9), who played a con man in a military camp, constantly at war with the authorities. Paladin, the hero of 'Have Gun Will Travel' (1957–63), lived a decadent life in San Francisco, replete with wine and women, sallying out into the wild west only to earn money as a hired gun. He even dressed in black, still a sign of villainy, which made him all the more intimidating. Or consider the role of Dr Kimble in 'The Fugitive' (1963–7): he was an outlaw, something of a loser, who was always escaping from the law – at the same time that he tried to help others and clear his name.[13]

The result was that you could 'read' the meanings of Hollywood drama in a number of different ways. Many a western could be portrayed as expressing a romantic view of the civilizing of the west and, alternately, as an unhealthy desire to celebrate the triumph of brute violence. Italian-Americans took issue with the implicit, if unintended, message embodied in 'The Untouchables' that criminals were largely of Italian origin. The realism of the crime drama 'The Naked City' (1958–63) conveyed the impression of New York, and, therefore, the big city, as a place of seaminess, decay, and violence. Dennis Braithwaite found in 'The Lucy Show' (1962–74) a subversive view of life, a woman's fantasy that challenged the officially sanctioned portrayal of the way things were: he argued that it celebrated a home without kids but with house-broken and handsome men, far from suburbia, full of fun. In contrast 'I Dream of Jeannie' (1965–70), a sitcom about a bachelor with a beautiful female genie, embodied a very sexist image of women as man's playthings – Capt. Tony Nelson was the master, Jeannie his slave, though of course the show only titillated, never acting out the male fantasy of dominance. Paul Hennings's sitcom 'The Beverly Hillbillies' (1962–71) was a sharp critique of the ways and values of the affluent lifestyle: the rich hillbilly Clampetts, especially Jed, represented the wisdom and decency of a rural past, while their banker, Milburn Drysdale, and his secretary, Jane Hathaway, appeared pretentious, grasping, and foolish. The rural sitcoms such as 'The Andy Griffith Show' (1960–8) and 'Petticoat Junction' (1963–70) exploited the nostalgia for a lost world, doing honour to the peace and quiet, the homeliness and the simplicity of the small town. But a spy drama such as 'The Man from U.N.C.L.E.' or a scifi series such as 'Star Trek' (1966–9) exploited the fascination with technology, celebrating the marvellous machines that gave man command over his environment.[14]

At bottom, though, much of Hollywood drama amounted to an extended exploration of the individual and his place in society. The premier episode of 'Wyatt Earp' (1955–61) chronicled how Earp became a reluctant hero: he refused to take on the task of policing the 'hoodlum cowtown' of Ellsworth, Kansas, until his old friend Sheriff Whitney was gunned down – Earp submitted to the dictates of honour and necessity, to his sense of social duty. The hero Matt Dillon and the villain Dan Grat in the premier episode of 'Gunsmoke' were both solitary figures: what set them apart was that Dillon affirmed the values of society, became its protector, whereas Grat rebelled against the same society, pursued his own selfish will. Crimefighters such as Joe Friday in 'Dragnet' and Eliot Ness in 'The Untouchables' were humourless instruments of justice who had devoted themselves to the war against corruption. The criminals were rebels and deviants, social threats, who had to be eliminated. Medical magicians such as Ben Casey and Dr Kildare were no less instruments of justice, engaged in a never-ending fight against disease, ignorance, and bureaucracy to ensure the health of their patients.

The sitcom carried out a similar exploration on a less lofty plane. One episode of 'The Dick Van Dyke Show' placed Dick in the terrible dilemma of choosing between the demands of the army (read, society) and the demands of his marriage: he was almost forced to go AWOL to celebrate his honeymoon, until the captain granted a three-day pass. Similarly an episode of 'Leave It to Beaver' portrayed Beaver's individualism as a brand of mischief; inevitably the source of trouble, Beaver was saved (because children were almost always 'saved') from the full consequences of his actions by an understanding Dad.

Time and again Hollywood emphasized that man was a social animal, that he was subject to the discipline of family, profession, community, and society. It honoured those individuals who accepted this discipline: they were the pillars of the community. And it discredited the people who didn't: rebellion, even alienation, was a social sin, the attribute of the villain and the victim.

The purpose of television's stories was escapist, to divert and entertain rather than to educate. People recognized this. On one level viewers were well-aware that the stories offered them were fiction, that the characters were no more than the slaves of a script, that 'Gunsmoke' and 'I Love Lucy' were ruled by conventions. On another, perhaps deeper level, though, these stories also appeared to be authentic and the recurring characters, real to life. That gave them a peculiar, even frightening impact on the minds of a few viewers. Witness the case of the syndicated thriller 'I Led Three Lives' (produced from 1953 to 1956), an adventure series about the fight against domestic communism in the United States. According to Virginia Stefan, the female star, people actually wrote in to ask the cast to investigate suspected communists in their neighborhood (the letters were passed on to the Federal Bureau of Investigation). Similarly Eve Arden, star of the sitcom 'Our Miss Brooks' (1952–6), was so closely identified with her role as a high-school teacher that she was invited to speak to parents and educators, and actually received offers to teach English in a dozen high schools.[15]

John Cawelti has argued that popular fiction serves to confirm existing views (about the family, for instance), to resolve tensions (such as between man and society), to explore the disreputable or forbidden (such as violence), and to recognize new meanings in life. So does popular drama on television. Our artistic experiences, again repeating Cawelti, work to shape our imaginations and our lives, although the degree of influence depends upon the individual. Perhaps they do give us a stock of archetypes to help explain and guide conduct. In any case, television drama did teach: viewers picked up appropriate visions of life now and before, where they were going, who their fellow citizens were, what was proper and what wasn't.[16]

No wonder the presence of the Hollywood product in Canadian homes caused a lot of gnashing of teeth. Hollywood's image of Canada rarely pleased people: Dennis Braithwaite denounced writer Sterling Silliphant because in the episode of 'Route 66' set in Toronto he'd featured an English actor to evoke in viewers' minds the tired stereotype that Canadians spoke with an English accent. More important, the shocks, violence, and action of westerns and crime dramas offended the moral sense of many a Canadian adult. The opinion survey collected by Kate Aitken in the heyday of the westerns produced a number of complaints about this genre: 'noisy and illiterate,' 'they glorify vice,' 'they entirely misrepresent our mode of living.' Even the CBC's president Alphonse Ouimet, in June 1962, lamented the fact that economics plus competition had forced Radio-Canada to include more and more American imports in its schedule, for 'there was nothing further away from the cultural temperament of the French-speaking Canadians.' But the most vociferous criticism came from Anglo critics. Early on Hugh Garner took the family sitcoms to task because they embodied a feminine dream-world in which women were always clever, men were spineless, and children were precocious. Mary Lowrey Ross found the private eye an equally unrealistic male ideal: a man of glamour and style and affluence, boasting a beautiful secretary and a marvellous car, who lived a life of high adventure and great success. The chief characters in Hollywood series, lamented Jeremy Brown, were fantastic: they didn't age, get married, give birth, fall sick, become bored – they weren't human.[17]

That was all beside the point. There wasn't any doubt that Hollywood drama was very popular with Canadian audiences, especially in English Canada (see table 10.1). Canadians seemed to like roughly the same things as did Americans. So many Canadians shared with their brethren down south such myths as the Old West, the Big City, the Cold War, and the Middle-Class Home that their need for escapism was easily satisfied by an imported drama that exploited this material. There may have been a more marked preference for the sitcom here than in the United States, although this certainly had something to do with the fact that the CBC preferred importing comedy to crime. But there were also lots of fans for violence of all kinds, as the independent stations recognized: during the mid-1960s, for instance, the private French-language station CFTM-Montreal used 'Le Virginien,' 'Les Incorruptibles,' and 'Le Saint' to challenge CBFT's hold on the mid-evening time-slot. The fact a nationalist or a moralist or a highbrow might decry Hollywood's invasion didn't faze the mass of Canadian viewers: they had clearly welcomed this marvellous entertainment as one of the blessings of television.

Radio-Canada's Téléromans

Radio-Canada broadcast comparatively little series drama, even by the mid-1960s. There wasn't much mystery about why this was so. There was a dearth of francophone telefilms in the world-wide marketplace, largely because France was very slow off the mark in developing a popular, full-fledged television service. Radio-Canada aired many more primetime movies than any other North American network simply to fill this gap. CBC-Montreal was compelled by necessity to make its own stories, at least for the first decade or so, if there was to be more than a smidgen of popular drama each day. These, the famous téléromans, scheduled during peak viewing times on weekdays at 8:00 or 8:30, proved a real winner with the French-Canadian public.

Montreal couldn't play Hollywood North, however. It could never offer more than eight, usually five or six, in any one season. As a rule the winter téléromans were given a rest in the summer season, though the network did sometimes schedule some mini-serials to take their place. There just wasn't enough money to do much more, given the fact that Montreal had to produce most of its own entertainment programming as well as news, views, and sports: Fowler II learned that in 1963/4 the francophone network spent a mere $2.6 million for live and videotaped drama, or 15 per cent of a total production budget of $17.6 million. A few years later CBC directors were told Montreal couldn't afford to produce a major film series such as Toronto's 'Wojeck.' Yet more money wouldn't really have solved the problem. Studio facilities were already strained to the limit by the volume of production demanded by television's hungry appetite. One consequence was less rehearsal time for Montreal's productions than was common for Toronto's. All in all, it was amazing that Montreal had been able to achieve so much with so little.[18]

The téléromans began slowly. There was already a tradition of popular drama in place. Radio serials had been very popular on Radio-Canada during the 1940s: the great hit was 'Un homme et son péché,' which had at times captured around 80 per cent of its potential audience. Yet, strange as it may seem, the CBFT schedule of that first season of television, 1952/3, boasted not one francophone serial. Guy Parent recalled that there was some prejudice against serials in the higher echelons of CBC-Montreal. Whoever was the architect of the téléromans, it appears that a key player was an adman, one Wilfred Charland, vice-president and director of McKim Advertising Ltd, which had experience sponsoring musical and dramatic entertainment on radio. He had read Roger Lemelin's novel *La famille Plouffe*, and he persuaded the author to try first radio and then television. Charland went all the way up to Davidson Dunton, again according to Parent, to get approval to put the show on television.[19]

The téléroman premiered in November 1953 (the English version was

TABLE 10.1
The popularity of American drama

(i) Network program ratings, 3–9 March 1963 (in millions of homes)

CBC network (English Canada)		CTV network (9 areas)		Radio-Canada	
#2 'Beverly Hillbillies'	1.27 (sitcom)	#1 'Lucy Show'	0.61 (sitcom)	#5 'Papa à raison'	0.53 (sitcom)
#3 'Bonanza'	1.24 (western)	#4 'Sam Benedict'	0.52 (lawyer)	#10 'Robin des bois'	0.48 (history)
#5 'Hazel'	1.14 (sitcom)	#7 'Eleventh Hour'	0.51 (doctor)		
#6 'Ben Casey'	1.12 (doctor)	#9 'Andy Griffith'	0.48 (sitcom)		
#7 'Perry Mason'	1.11 (lawyer)	#10 'Dr. Kildare'	0.48 (doctor)		
#8 'The Defenders'	1.10 (lawyer)				
#10 'Danny Thomas'	1.07 (sitcom)				

(ii) A Sunday night in Toronto, February 1965 (thousands of households for each time and show)

7:00 (371.3)			7:30 (459.8)		
CBLT 'Patty Duke'	AMN sitcom	96.5	CBLT 'Flashback'		129.6***
CFTO 'Walt Disney'	AMN child	147.4***	CFTO 'Mr Novak'	AMN teacher	87.1
WBEN 'Lassie'	AMN adventure	64.6	WBEN 'My Fav. Martian'	AMN sitcom	109.3
WGR 'Pro. in Courage'	AMN docudrama	26.9	WGR 'Walt Disney'	AMN child	81.2
WKBW Movie	?	35.9	WKBW 'Wagon Train'	AMN western	52.6

8:00 (495.5)			8:30 (516.3)		
CBLT 'Ed Sullivan'		175.3***	CBLT 'Ed Sullivan'		194.3***
CFTO 'Mr Novak'	AMN teacher	82.0	CFTO 'Man fm UNCLE'	AMN spy	104.3
WBEN 'Ed Sullivan'		111.9***	WBEN 'Ed Sullivan'		106.2***
WGR 'Walt Disney'	AMN child	76.9	WGR 'Branded'	AMN western	57.9
WKBW 'Wagon Train'	AMN western	49.4	WKBW 'Braodside'	AMN sitcom	53.6

9:00 (513.7)

CBLT 'Bonanza'	AMN western	193.5***
CFTO 'Man fm UNCLE'	AMN spy	103.3
WBEN 'For the People'	AMN lawyer	52.1
WGR 'Bonanza'	AMN western	87.1***
WKBW Movie	?	77.7

10:00 (488.5)

CBLT 'Seven Days'		169.6***
CFTO 'Hourglass'	BRI miniseries	29.1
WBEN 'Candid Camera'		108.4
WGR 'The Rogues'	AMN adventure	99.4
WKBW Movie	?	82.0

9:30 (487.1)

CBLT 'Bonanza'	AMN western	194.1***
CFTO 'Peyton Place'	AMN social	61.8
CFTO 'For the People'	AMN lawyer	53.8
WGR 'Bonanza'	AMN western	91.8***
WKBW Movie	?	85.6

10:30 (490.3)

CBLT 'Seven Days'		169.4***
CFTO 'Hourglass'	BRI miniseries	27.5
WBEN 'What's My Line'		117.9
WGR 'The Rogues'	AMN adventure	94.3
WKBW Movie	?	81.2

*** the leading show

Source: for (i) Elliott-Haynes *Teleratings*, March 1963; for (ii) BBM, *Television Station Report*, February 1965

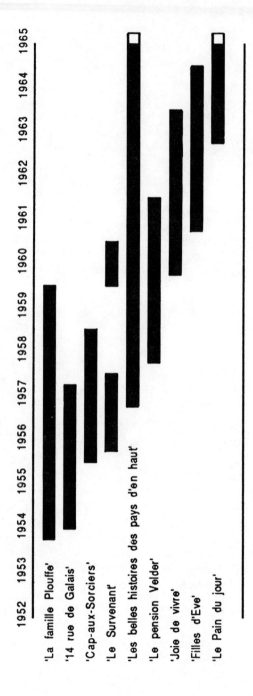

Chart 10.3 A sample of téléromans

Note: The dates are approximate, indicating the season (Spring, Summer, or Fall) in which a show commenced or ended on the schedule of one of the Canadian networks. Shows which continued beyond the end of 1964 are indicated by an unfilled block.

out a year later). The public's response was phenomenal: viewers were excited by the novelty of actually seeing a typical Quebec family on the air week after week. In the two big cities of Montreal and Quebec City the numbers of people using buses and trams noticeably slackened on a Wednesday between 8:30 and 9:00, when the show was broadcast. In the smaller towns, travelling salesmen found they couldn't make any deals on a Wednesday evening. Theatre owners everywhere complained that their attendance fell off. Hockey officials rescheduled games till later in the evening or for another night. Legions of fans wrote in to Radio-Canada to praise, advise, and to get photographs of the show's stars. An enterprising firm prepared 140,000 copies of a Plouffe family jigsaw puzzle, which sold out within a month.

The success of 'La famille Plouffe' ensured Radio-Canada would try to keep audiences pleased with a constant supply of téléromans (see chart 10.3). The Corporation was fortunate that it could rely upon the services of local writers, some already experienced in radio. Lemelin was not unique. Quebec had a small but active community of novelists and playwrights who'd turned their energies to explaining the past and present of their people's lives. Claude-Henri Grignon's 'Un homme et son péché' eventually came to television as 'Les belles histoires des pays d'en haut' (1956–70), where its longevity demonstrated that it was as popular on television as it had been on radio. A number of novels were converted into television properties: thus Robert Choquette's *Les Velders* (1941), once a radioroman, became 'La pension Velder,' and Germaine Guèvremont's *Le Survenant* (1945) and *Marie-Didace* (1947) reached television under the same titles. The famous playwright Marcel Dubé was the author of two hit téléromans of the 1960s, 'Côte de sable' and later 'De 9 à 5.'[20]

Writing téléromans was an attractive proposition for these authors. No doubt the money was welcome: supposedly a writer earned $600 per half-hour episode, though Lemelin reportedly receive $1,100 because he had to prepare French and English scripts. This could be far more lucrative than writing a one-shot play. The serial format allowed writers the freedom to deal with a range of different characters, to investigate changing circumstances, in a way that was often impossible in a stage play or a teleplay. What pleased Lemelin was that he could show the 'common denominators of human behaviour,' that people were neither all good nor all bad, that frustrations and happiness, heartaches and joys, were the lot of people in Quebec as in Saskatchewan. Françoise Loranger told *La Semaine à Radio-Canada* that her very adult téléroman 'Sous le signe du lion' (1961, repeated 1963/4) enabled her to explore in depth the ambiguous morality of men and women in real life. Perhaps best of all, the screenplay was the responsibility of the author, quite unlike the situation in Hollywood where writers had very little control over their product. This on occasion exhausted a writer who had to prepare a winter's set of scripts alone. But it meant the result seemed much more like art, not hack work, something a writer could take real pride in.[21]

The power of the author was a bit of a problem for the CBC. A producer couldn't do very much if an author of a hit téléroman decided he or she had had enough: the show would end when the season was over. More troubling was the fact that the Corporation didn't have full control over the character of the téléromans. Most writers were like Marcel Dubé, who explained that he only wrote scripts a couple of weeks ahead of time for 'De 9 à 5.' No wonder that Marcel Ouimet (the general manager, French networks) spoke favourably of Françoise Loranger who had submitted all the scripts of 'Sous le signe du lion' before any shows were broadcast. In the 1962/3 season a special problem arose over Roger Lemelin's mini-series 'Le petit monde du Père Gédéon,' a return to the world of 'La famille Plouffe.' Directors and executives found the language used in a couple of episodes just too vulgar for their tastes – not, ironically, for the sponsors who apparently didn't feel anything was wrong. The CBC's program committee was told that Lemelin wouldn't take 'direction' easily, that he wanted to be 'progressive,' in short that he was acting like an artist. The decision was made to cancel one episode and delay production of two more until Lemelin's scripts were submitted and approved.[22]

The téléromans were by and large studio dramas. Action was usually confined to indoor settings: a kitchen or living-room, a hospital room, a work-place, and so on. Nearly all of this action involved conversation. The rapid pace of, say, 'La famille Plouffe' called for some deft camera work, none-the-less. On one occasion, noted journalist Ken Johnstone, the location of the action changed forty-seven times, which meant the camera and the sound-boom had to move, roughly, once every half-minute. Later improvements in production techniques and facilities allowed directors some leeway in where and how they worked. One report in 1963 indicated that parts of 'Les belles histoires' were filmed in the Laurentians and that 'Filles d'Eve' was produced in a couple of places in Montreal. But the production values of Montreal's drama could never match those of Hollywood.[23]

Time and again the claim was made that the téléromans were a window on the ordinary life of Québécois. Much was made of the authenticity of the setting, the language, the characters, and their conflicts. Lemelin apparently took over the task of writing the English scripts for 'The Plouffe Family' to ensure they had the requisite 'French flavour.' 'Le Survenant' might be a poetic rendition of rural life at the beginning of the century, but audiences were assured that the characters were certainly real. Lise Lavallée, the author of the adolescent téléromans 'Le mors aux dents' (1961/2), admitted to using a simple form of 'canadien,' complete with some teenage slang, though she avoided 'joual' even if this might seem fitting for a serial that dealt with working-class youth. The historical drama 'Kanawio' (or 'Kahnawiio,' 1961/2) was presented as a conscious effort to handle honestly the life and culture of the Iroquois. Guy Dufresne, author of the hospital drama 'Septiéme Nord' (1963–7), went to great pains to make sure the show was realistic, that it had the touch of a documentary – the scripts were studied by a doctor to ensure authenticity. Likewise Dubé's De 9 á 5' (1963–6), set in a financial office, was about 'the daily tragedy of the white collar workers.'[24]

These claims should be taken with a grain of salt. Ordinary life was never so extraordinary. Authors filled their téléromans with little tragedies, personal upsets, family upheavals, and the like to keep up the excitement. Misfortune could strike suddenly: a highly emotional episode of '14 rue de Galais' (4 June 1956) had Louis Delisle, the victim of a car accident, stumbling around his hospital room, gauze bandages on his eyes, full of despair at the thought he was blind. Often 'La famille Plouffe' managed to encompass a lot of drama in a half-hour: the English episode of 30 December 1955 had Papa Théophile suffer a seizure and then recover to bless his family, while other members of the cast had assorted adventures in Cincinnati. Jean Filiatrault's 'La Balsamine' (1962/3) posited a well-off widow, Louise Villeneuve, who disturbed the equilibrium of her family of four children by asking them how she should divide up her fortune: that led to a complicated plot full of personal disturbances for each of the children. Yet, no matter how many tragedies piled up, most problems were resolved happily, at least for the main characters. The téléroman was at bottom an optimistic portrayal of 'ordinary life.'[25]

It shouldn't surprise us that the family was central to nearly all of these dramas. Hadn't generations of nationalists and clerics proclaimed that the family was the key institution in French-Canadian society? At first there was usually only one main family: the Plouffes, of course; the Delisles in '14 rue de Galais' (1954–7); the Paradis in 'Côte de Sable' (1960–2). By the spring of 1963, though, 'Le pain du jour' (1962–5) boasted the Deguires, the Mathons, the Allards, and the Denoyers, four families complete with children, which made for some mighty complicated plots. Other téléromans employed the metaphor of the family to explain what was going on. The action in 'La pension Velder' (1957–61) occurred within a boarding-house where the landlady and the residents behaved as though they were members of the same family. Marcel Dubé referred to his office workers in 'De 9 à 5' as an 'artificial family.' Guy Dufresne, the writer of 'Kanawio,' imposed a similar structure on the Iroquois: he focused on the lives of three families around 1640 – this was a French-Canadian tribe in another setting.

The families came in many shapes and sizes. Les Plouffes were an extended family: the two old parents, Josephine and Théophile, plus their four grown-up children, Ovide, Napoléon, Guillaume, and Cécile, some of whom got married during the course of the series. The short-lived 'À moitié sages' (Summer 1957) featured the three daughters of Madam Germain staying at a summer resort. The Martels of 'Filles d'Eve' (1960–4), early in 1963, were newlyweds without kids. The Turgeaus, inhabitants of the same téléromans, became a broken family when the mother died suddenly, leaving Jean Turgeau with Pierre and Odette, his two maturing children. The Turgeaus, like the Delisles in '14 rue de Galais' or the Mathons of 'Le pain du jour,' were clearly bourgeois – Jos Mathon, for instance, was a prosperous small-businessman. Charles and Monique Mathieu in 'La Balsamine' were struggling on his salary as a shoe merchant. Les Plouffes were really part of the working class (Théophile was a plumber), as were the Deguires of 'Le pain du jour.' By contrast Jérémie Martin in 'Sous le signe du lion' was a self-made millionaire, and as a result his family was among the wealthiest in the land.

Usually missing from this world were the very young and the very poor. Presumably the miseries of the poor didn't excite the writers and consumers of entertainment. But the absence of babies and kids isn't so easy to explain. There were still plenty of young children in the Quebec family. Yet the four families of the complicated 'Le pain du jour' (in the Spring '63 episodes) featured characters ranging in years from adolescence to late middle age. Was there a shortage of child actors? Or were the trials and tribulations of raising kids just too mundane to inspire much interest? I suspect the latter. In fact the téléromans were bent on exploring the life of people who were supposed to be active able to take command of their fate, or at least to aspire to such autonomy. This sense of purpose didn't quite suit babies or the poor.

One of the most striking attributes of the téléromans, as was true of so much on the small screen, was their sexism. They affirmed what now seems a very traditional view of the two spheres and the two natures that had its roots in the Victorian ethos of generations past. The depiction of the female way and of the feminine character was exceptionally clear-cut, sufficient that it seems the dominant mythology in most téléromans. Women lived in a fundamentally domestic culture, defined by such realities as friendship, love, marriage, and motherhood. Thus Laura Deguire and Chantel Mathon, two of the young women in 'Le pain du jour,' were led to change their lives and their behaviour by love for the same man. Young, unmarried women might occasionally work outside the home, in secretarial or nursing or other service jobs; married they usually stayed at home, housewives and mothers first. The premier episode of 'The Plouffe Family' had Josephine in the kitchen, the women's room of the 1950s, baking pies, one of the classic tasks of the homemaker that would be depicted time and again in succeeding téléromans. The opening scene in an episode of 'Le pain du jour' of October 1963 showed two housewives, obviously friends, doing the laundry and talking over personal problems of marriage and family finances. Women were portrayed as expressive and emotional creatures: in '14 rue de Galais' (4 June 1956) it was the women who were overwrought about Louis's blindness – an aged aunt broke down and cried (offering to donate her eyes) and his fiancée Renée pledged her undying love and devotion. They could be wilful: Rita Toulouse in 'The Plouffe Family' (14 October 1954) was the seductress, flirting with Napoléon and Ovide Plouffe. They could also be very manipulative: Josephine Plouffe in one episode (15 May 1957) tells Jeanne, Napoléon's future wife, 'Pretend to listen to what he says and do what you feel is best. He will follow.' No wonder wise fathers warned their sons to beware of female wiles, not to become infatuated with and therefore enslaved by one woman (that warning occurred twice in the episode of 'Le pain du jour' mentioned previously).

Man's nature as a more rational and logical being was not so carefully detailed. That was because most téléromans concentrated on the family setting, whereas the world of men was really outside the home. Certainly men did appear as the providers and protectors, nominally the heads of the households, who were supposed to supply the money to keep the family comfortable, although that didn't always make them the bosses. Look at the male characters in 'The Plouffe Family' (14 October 1954). Théophile was the bread-winner, a simple and proud man who lacked the personality to play effectively the role of the family patriarch. One sign of his incompetence was his inability to handle his own bicycle properly now, even though he had once been a provincial champion cyclist. Ovide was the intellectual, dressed in a business suit and a tie, a man of affairs with a manner and style of speech that suggested his greater sophistication. Guillaume was the overgrown boy, in training for a career as a hockey star in the NHL. Napoléon had taken on the role of protector of Ovide's girl-friend, Rita – as well as the task of preparing Guillaume for future glory. Onésime Menard, the suitor of Cécile Plouffe, arrived as the triumphant provider, having saved the $9,000 that Cécile had demanded as a condition of marriage; he left hurt and confused when she none-the-less declined his proposal. Logic was not a sovereign remedy for women's ways.

Characters were boldly drawn, sometimes to the point of caricature. The one outstanding villain was Séraphin Poudrier of 'Les belles histoires,' a land agent and money-lender, who exploited the weak and the powerless and lusted after the beautiful post-mistress Donalda Laloge. Georgette Dubuc in 'La pension Velder' (15 January 1958) was a stereotype of the bossy, jealous woman who tried to master her timid boy-friend, Frederick Gagnon. Henri Delisle in '14 rue de Galais' (4 June 1956) played out the role of the dominant father, cool and collected, who explained to Louis the seriousness of his condition and the need to confront his fate. By contrast Mama Plouffe was the matriarch, a woman of real power, who calmed upsets, counselled her charges, manipulated a situation, all to keep the family together as a unit and to set her children on the right course. The teenage Jeannette Allard in 'Le pain du jour,' during spring 1963, was a tomboy, an unnatural female, loud and aggressive, interested in sports and odd jobs rather than cooking or studies. Ovide Plouffe, claimed Ken Johnstone, began life as a parody of the self-conscious and conceited intellectual, a French-Canadian type, though he soon became a more sympathetic character. Abbé Gravel of 'Absolvo te' (summer 1962) was the new kind of Catholic priest, dynamic and full of fire, eager to serve his community. The list of types could go on and on: a shrewish and avaricious wife (Léontine Villeneuve of 'La Balsiminé'), a tyrannical father (Jérémie Martin in 'Sous le signe du lion'), a loyal family maid (Andréa in 'La Balsamine'), a lovesick girl (Julie Paradis in 'Côte de Sable'), a youthful adventurer in the big city (the country-born poet of 'Nérée Tousignant' who came to live in the Boudreau pension in Montreal). The point is that the téléromans featured recognizable personalities from the past and present of Quebec's society.

And the difficulties they faced were equally recognizable. By and large the plots were cast in the form of quests, whether for love, advancement, security, or identity. At first Cécile Plouffe was caught between her desire for independence and for love, fearful that she would remain an old maid should she reject Onésime and worried lest she lose her freedom if she submitted to his request for marriage. The three daughters of 'À moitié sages' were on the look-out for wealthy husbands, hoping to find likely prospects in the summer resort. Etienne Paradis of 'Côte de Sable,' which was set in Quebec just after the Second World War, was a soldier faced by the problems of readjusting to civilian life. Jacqueline Villeneuve of 'La Balsamine,' haunted by the memory of an aloof father, had to come to terms with her past before she could hope to find happiness with a man. This theme of entrapment was played out time and again. During the winter season of 1960/1, Brigitte in 'Filles d'Eve' was caught in an unhappy marriage with an alcoholic, who had been responsible for the death of their child and was interned in a psychiatric hospital. The white-collar workers of 'De 9 à 5' were enmeshed in the routine of their office. The priest-hero of 'Absolvo te' was stifled by the atmosphere of his wealthy parish, which was ruled by an old-fashioned priest. Echoes of a wider world, of a community's struggle for autonomy (as in the case of Quebec itself), might be found in some of the téléromans, such as 'Cap-aux-sorciers' and 'Les belles histoires.' But, on the surface at least, these dramas dealt first and foremost with personal problems.[26]

The plots normally had happy endings – resolution came through accident, outside help, self-discovery, sometimes submission, usually in a way that conformed to the dictates of a rigid and traditional moral code. Cécile marries Onésime, accepting the fate that society dictated was a woman's lot. Brigitte's husband conveniently dies, leaving her free to pursue her love interest and marry Lambert. Jacqueline Villeneuve learns that her hated father actually had an affair with his secretary, making his memory more human, which leads to her reconciliation with the past and even to plans for a marriage. The eighteen-year-old Odette Turgeau of 'Filles d'Eve' is cured of her 'nymphomania' by going to work and thus redirecting her energies. Laura Deguire in 'Le pain du jour,' an unwed mother, decides to keep her baby and work to support its needs. Carmen Denoyer, a fellow victim in that same téléroman, escapes from a marriage with a brutal man through the assistance of Charles Deguire and goes to work in a factory. And Jeanette Allard, the tomboy, is transformed into a proper young lady by her affection for Louis Deguire. Abbé Gravel is 'saved' by the arrival of a mystery – a strange penitent who is spirited away from the confessional leads him into an absorbing investigation of why. Pépé of 'Le feu sacré,' a failed actor, manages to feed his appetite for the stage by opening a restaurant/little theatre. Conformity, acceptance of the demands of the work ethic or marriage, surrender to love and to duty, these were the paths to happiness.

Radio-Canada did occasionally try to offer a different brand of popular drama. Both 'Anne-Marie' (1954/5) and 'Grand'Ville P.Q.' (April–May 1956) contained sufficient humour to suit the genre of situation comedy rather than téléroman. Much later, in the Fall '65, the independent CFTM would launch 'Cré Basile,' a series about a plumber and his wife that was modelled on the Hollywood style of sitcoms. Children's shows such as 'Kimo' and 'CF-RCK,' which often ran outside primetime, were adventure stories. One imaginative experiment was the evening serial 'Monsieur Lecoq' (1965/6), a mystery focusing on a Paris policemen in the first half of the nineteenth century and based upon the detective stories of Emile Gaboreau. Apparently it payed much attention to young Lecoq's dealings with his associates and superiors, which meant that it contained an important element of social melodrama. The show wasn't a success, though: BBM learned that it was less popular than the rival offerings on the independent stations CFTM and the Anglo CFCF. Montreal's product only worked well when it belonged to the genre of téléromans.[27]

The ratings spelled out this fact year after year. Radio-Canada's own research discovered that what women most regretted losing as a result of the producers' strike of 1959 were the téléromans. Of course the enormous appeal of 'La famille Plouffe' eventually waned. But it was replaced in popular favour by other serials, notably 'Les belles histoires.' The BBM survey in March 1963 showed that four of the top five network programs on Radio-Canada were téléromans: 'Les belles histoires' (number 1), 'Filles d'Eve' (number 3), 'Joie de vivre' (number 4), and 'Le pain du jour' (number 5). McDonald Research found that in the Montreal market the winners had audience shares, respectively, of 53 per cent, 45 per cent, 46 per cent, and 40 per cent, which was impressive given the fact that there were now two francophone stations and two anglophone stations plus a weak American station (WCAX) competing for attention.[28]

It's easy to explain why the téléromans were so popular. The genre capitalized on the parochialism of the French-Canadian population. The settings were in Quebec, the language was in the vernacular, the people and their problems were believable. Madam Velder's *pension* was typical of many a boarding-house in Montreal. Many people knew someone like the kindly and caring Josephine Plouffe or the talkative Père Gédéon of Roger Lemelin. Adéle Lauzon, a writer for *Le Magazine Maclean*, decided that Père Gédéon was pure Quebec: 'ses tics, ses manies, son histoire, son apparence physique, son accent' were all familiar. The villainy of Séraphin Poudrier in 'Les belles histoires' was so striking that for a time the term 'Séraphin' entered the language as a description of stingy characters. Nicole

Charest, another writer for *Le Magazine Maclean*, tried to pinpoint the appeal of 'Le pain du jour': why a waitress, for example, would claim that nothing would lead her to leave the house at the time of the show. Charest found that a worker claimed that he could see himself on the screen, as did a woman of forty. An employee at Radio-Canada had decided that Laura Deguire resembled her. Teenagers watched the show because it delved into the relationship of parents and children. Here was a brand of drama, then, that spoke to the common experience of a huge number of viewers. They could identify with the characters, the plots, and the settings. Indeed the themes of entrapment and survival so evident in the téléromans fitted well the message of the new nationalism that was raising the consciousness of the Québécois in the late 1950s and the early 1960s.[29]

The Anglo Series

The track record of Toronto was nowhere near as impressive as that of Montreal. CBC-Toronto was guided, though perhaps misguided is a better word, by conflicting assumptions. A series had to have mass appeal, which meant that it should be a winner in the ratings game. One apparently easy way to get an audience was to emulate whatever had succeeded in the United States. But those axioms often ran counter to the effect of the last two priorities, patriotism and economics. The CBC wanted its drama to reflect, in some fashion or another, the Canadian experience. Recall that popular drama, especially when the telefilm became the norm, was one of the most expensive kinds of programming around. The CBC simply couldn't afford to spend large sums of money producing a lot of series, else it would starve the departments that produced the rest of its made-in-Canada programming. Whatever drama series it did produce had to earn back revenues, either in the shape of advertising or through foreign sales.[30]

For all the hype the Anglo version of 'Les Plouffes' proved to be 'strangers in a strange land.' The only change in the English version was to clean-up the language a bit by dropping any profanity and cutting out any overt remarks about sex, so as not to offend the somewhat more puritanical Anglos. Otherwise it was the same family, although in memory some Anglos in the Ottawa area who got both shows would claim the French version was better. Of course 'The Plouffe Family' did have an audience in the rest of Canada. The ratings in spring 1955 showed that in captive markets, such as London and Winnipeg, viewing figures were high. But in competitive markets things weren't so rosy: in Vancouver 'The Plouffe Family' captured a third of the audience and in Toronto under one-fifth. Buffalo's WBEN-TV secured some 50 percent of the Toronto audience with the sitcom 'Topper.'[31]

The CBC commissioned the Schwerin Research Corp. to carry out a number of audience tests, in Toronto and Winnipeg, to identify just what was wrong and right with the serial. Roger Lemelin had told an English interviewer that he hoped to show the 'people in Saskatchewan or Nova Scotia' that Quebeckers were 'like themselves.' Things hadn't worked out that way: roughly one-half of the audience in one test didn't know how representative the show was of the life of a working-class family in French Canada. Most of a Toronto audience decided there just wasn't enough action in the episodes they watched. The bulk of those who identified themselves as non-viewers had trouble understanding the show, because of its fast pace and the French accent. Ironically the fans of 'Les Plouffes' usually preferred the accents, because it made the show seem more real. Very few additional people were won over to the idea of regular viewing as a result of the test. The fact was that 'The Plouffe Family' couldn't bridge the gap of ignorance that divided most Anglos from their counterparts in French Canada. Les Plouffes would always seem to most English Canadians a collection of exotics.[32]

Its successor in the winter of 1959/60, 'The Town Above' ('En haute de la pente douce' on the Radio-Canada network), also written by Roger Lemelin, was even less successful. This téléroman dealt with the struggles of the middle-class Chevalier family to maintain its status and affluence. Part of the problem may have been with the scheduling: in Toronto it aired late on a Monday night. Two Toronto critics, Dennis Braithwaite and Ron Poulton, were savage in their commentary. Braithwaite asked pointedly whether viewers couldn't have a picture of family life in Ontario or the West. Privately CBC managers weren't thrilled either: indeed Alphonse Ouimet decided that other kinds of performance (once he actually cited an episode of 'L'heure du concert') would offer Anglos 'a better picture of French Canada.' The experiment of English-language téléromans had run its course.[33]

Meanwhile the CBC had tried its hand at some adventure series for kids. The first of these was 'Tales of Adventure' in the Fall '52 which carried adaptations of Jules Verne's *20,000 Leagues under the Sea* and Wilkie Collins's *The Moonstone*. A bit later Murray Chercover produced 'Space Command' (March 1953 to May 1954), a scifi serial reminiscent of the DuMont network's low-budget hit 'Captain Video' (1949–55). Except for a few special effects, the show was shot live in a tiny studio that allowed for only a few actors and a few sets. Futuristic uniforms, control panels, bits of equipment, and frequent pictures of the spaceship were used to establish its 'authenticity.' The show was long on talk and weak on visuals. Most of the 'action' was suggested by dialogue and gesture, backed up by dramatic music, engine noise, and rocket bursts, and on occasion the shaking of the camera (to signify sudden motion in a scene). All in all, 'Space Command' was a credible effort, showing what a skilled producer could do even if constrained by a lack of money, staff, and equipment. But 'Space Command' really didn't have the production values necessary to turn a scifi thriller into a success.[34]

The CBC's next major effort in the realm of kidvid came with the big budget serial 'Radisson' (February 1957 to January 1958), a historical adventure otherwise known as 'Radishes' in the trade. It was scheduled in primetime on the weekend to win adult as well as child viewers: CBLT ran it 7:00 to 7:30 on Saturday. The series seems to have been the Corporation's first extended experiment with filmed drama. The show was inspired by the Davy Crockett craze among North America's children, which 'Disneyland' had fostered back in 1955. Parents had wondered aloud why the CBC couldn't offer their children a similar Canadian version of the past. Pierre Radisson qualified as the Canadian Davy Crockett: he and his brother-in-law Sieur de Groseilliers were adventurers and explorers active (on behalf of the French and English crowns) in the North American wilderness, especially around Hudson Bay, during the late seventeenth century. Radisson had the added advantage of a bilingual appeal, important because the show would be broadcast in both languages.[35]

'Radisson' was written by John Lucarotti, a young English writer, and translated by Jean Duprez. The two main characters were francophone actors. Filming was done outdoors and in studios by Omega Productions Ltd of Montreal, under CBC direction. Much later Hugh Gauntlett, an assistant program director, noted that the Corporation had been reluctant to get into the film business because that meant competing with private film companies. ('For a government subsidized Corporation, this can become a bit sticky.') Presumably the CBC also thought it wiser to rely on the experience of outsiders in this new field of telefilms. In fact the filming of the first set of episodes in the fall of 1957 was bedevilled with difficulties, some a result of bad weather conditions. The result was that production costs went way over budget, from a planned $7,000 to some $25,000 an episode.[36]

Much was said beforehand about the show's mix of excitement and authenticity – the scripts were supposed to be based on Radisson's own journals as well as actual records of the time. Monica Clare, then organizer of children's programs and credited with being the brain behind the show, made abundantly clear in an interview for the CBC *Times* that the purpose of the show was to produce a true Canadian hero. 'Radisson' would prove once and for all that we didn't have to import our heroes. It would demonstrate that Canadian history wasn't dull, and it would promote pride in the country. Success would obviously lead to a series of imitations glorifying other heroes in Canada's past. And Lucarotti's agents were already planning to make a killing from the expected Radisson craze: they were negotiating with companies to make Radisson rifles, knives, music boxes, dolls, and such like.[37]

All the pre–air-time promotion had an effect. People tuned in just to see what a Canadian Davy Crockett might be like. A special report by Elliott-Haynes on one broadcast at the end of February found 'Radisson' had pretty good ratings: the show even outdrew the American competition in Toronto and Vancouver. That popularity didn't last, though. The show just couldn't offer the sort of production values necessary to maintain the initial interest. Monica Clare complained privately about botched editing, the result of sticking in commercials, which destroyed continuity and pacing, sometimes putting the climax of an episode off to the succeeding week. A CBC survey of the response of middle-class kids in Ottawa learned that older children often found the show too slow or too awkward, and the characters phony. 'They've been paddling in the same stretch of river all the way from Lake Nipissing to Montreal,' complained one youngster. A story went the rounds that in one episode a jet plane actually turned up on the horizon. That gaffe came to symbolize what was wrong with 'Radisson': it lacked the polish of the Hollywood product. The show was dropped after the conclusion of the second set of episodes, roughly a year after its birth. An internal CBC memo in 1959 noted that 'Radisson' had cost $1.04 million, earning back in domestic and foreign sales $146,200, which left a whopping net loss of just under $900,000.[38]

None the less some made-in-Canada telefilms did turn up on the CBC network during the next few years. These series were produced by commercial outfits, often with American money and American talent, who hoped to cash in on the popularity of action/adventure drama and sitcoms in the North American market. Normandie Productions of Toronto, for example, brought to air 'The Last of the Mohicans' (Fall '57 to Summer '58), starring John Hart as the white hero Hawkeye and Lon Chaney, Jr., as his Indian side-kick Chingachgook, another buckskin drama based loosely on the work of James Fenimore Cooper. The same company produced the sitcom 'Tugboat Annie' (Fall '57 to Summer '58), which used stars, directors, and scripts from Hollywood, although some Canadians appeared in visiting or minor roles (for example, John Vernon). The next year Robert Maxwell Associates, an American company that had won its spurs producing 'Lassie' and 'Superman' episodes, filmed an adventure series about the life of truckers on the road and at home entitled 'Cannonball' (Fall '58 to Summer '61). The Toronto area, according to a report in the Toronto *Telegram*, had the requisite number of hills, rivers, highways, country roads, railways, small towns, and the like to make for a variety of settings. The series was consciously designed to incorporate the 'outdoors excitement' of the crime show 'Highway Patrol' and the 'family appeal' of 'Father Knows Best.' Peter Frank, the associate producer, told the *Telegram* reporter that the show celebrated the existence of the average guy: the ordinary man, in this case the trucker, was the hero, just the kind of person Frank thought the bulk of viewers could identify with. He expected success would breed similar kinds of shows, say about a forest ranger. Indeed a report in *Marketing* in March 1959 indicated that plans had been announced for series with titles such as 'Forest Ranger,' 'Bush Pilot,' 'Trouble Shooters,' and 'Hudson's Bay.' But it all proved a flash in the pan. 'The Last of the Mohicans,' 'Tugboat Annie,' and 'Cannonball' did run in syndication in the United States, although much later *The Financial Post* noted that none was very profitable. Apparently when the CBC refused to extend automatic support to the new ventures, the Americans decided it wasn't worth their time and money, and the studios readied for the expected boom were left empty.[39]

Meanwhile the CBC had got itself into a joint venture to produce another action telefilm in English and French. This was the crime drama 'RCMP' (October 1959 to October 1960), or 'Gendarmerie royale' in French Canada. Here was an attempt to exploit the legend of the Mounties as a world-renowned instrument of justice that had previously been popularized by Hollywood movies. According to a report in *The Toronto Daily Star* (10 September 1959), expenses were shared at the rate of 20 per cent by the CBC (for the Canadian rights), 20 per cent by the BBC (the British rights), and 60 per cent by Crawley-McConnell Ltd. The last was an alliance of Crawley Films, which had the expertise, and the wealthy capitalist John R. McConnell, who put up a reported half a million dollars. The costs of filming were estimated at $1,365,000 for thirty-nine episodes, or $35,000 for each half-hour program, which made it the most ambitious project to date in Canada. It's obvious that the participants expected to make big money through foreign sales, especially in the United States, where they hoped to secure a network contract.

'RCMP' dealt with the modern adventures of a three-man Mountie detachment in the fictitious town of Shamattawa, in northern Saskatchewan. The star of the show was Gilles Pelletier, a French-Canadian actor who played the role of the ever-efficient and always friendly Corporal Jacques Gagnier. He was backed up by the American John Perkins as Constable Frank Scott and the Canadian Don Francks as Constable Bill Mitchell. They were the great protectors, of the law and of Shamattawa, who not only fought crime but also helped out when some trouble afflicted the community. Budge Crawley planned to give the show that quality of 'Hollywood believable' which was essential for American sales: the company hired a retired RCMP officer to give advice on the force's customs and procedures and a couple of veteran television directors from the United States. The stories were purportedly based on actual RCMP files, though scripts were prepared by a team of writers. Filming was done in the Gatineau, to simulate a rugged environment, and a studio was constructed in the district for the indoor shots. Much effort was spent on special effects and outdoor scenes of forests and snow to convey the flavour of the North: Crawley Films, for example, used the remnants of an old airplane as a wind machine, as well as snow-blowers, to simulate blizzards. A group of twenty huskies were kept on call for whenever the script demanded dog-sleds. The film cameras were winterized with special heaters to ensure they could operate in the below-zero temperatures. It was this kind of paraphernalia that impressed reporters as proof that the filming of 'RCMP' was an example of 'Hollywood-scale production.'[40]

All of the effort was, in the end, to little avail. Once again the pre-airing hype set the stage for disappointment. Although one of the CBC's directors claimed she'd discovered 'the reaction of people in smaller towns is that the series is true to life,' neither the critics nor the mass of viewers were much impressed by the final product. Ron Poulton of the Toronto *Telegram*, for instance, found the program imitative and silly. A comparison of one episode of 'RCMP' and of 'The Untouchables' shows why. The American drama had a complicated plot, a fast pace, clever camera work, punchy dialogue, strong characters: it was full of suspense and pathos, it appeared true to life, and it contained enough jolts to grab the attention of even the most casual viewer. The Canadian drama just couldn't match this quality, though the technical side of the production was certainly competent. The episode was very slow, especially at the beginning, too much time was given to talking heads, and the final gunfight was clichéd, unexciting. The hero Gagnier lacked conviction: he was more akin to Andy Taylor, the small-town sheriff in Hollywood's hit sitcom 'The Andy Griffith Show,' than to a hard-nosed crime fighter. The talk was too polite and the action too routine to foster suspense. In a word, the 'RCMP' episode was mediocre.[41]

The program was not renewed for a second season, although it did air in Britain and in Australia. It was apparently shown on some American stations, though none of the networks picked it up. According to *The Toronto Daily Star* (16 August 1964), the world-wide distributor Freemantle International sold it in quite a number of places, including West Germany, Uruguay, and Hong Kong. Some of the French and English episodes were rebroadcast by CBC stations in 1965, and reruns appeared on CBLT as late as 1983. 'RCMP' couldn't be counted a flop, as could 'Radisson.' But it wasn't a success either.

During the mid-1960s the CBC tried one more time to sponsor a prime-time adventure show that was Canadian in content but American in design. The result was 'Seaway' (Fall '65 to Summer '66), the first filmed hour-long drama series in Canada, produced by an outsider Seaway Films Ltd of Toronto (although the producer was the ex-CBCer Michael Sadlier). As the title suggested, the stuff of the drama were the adventures, intrigues, conflicts, and romances that grew out of the lives of people in some way or another tied into the St Lawrence Seaway. The program offered viewers a team of two heroes: the Canadian 'Foxy' (Admiral Henry Victor Leslie Fox, played by Austin Willis), a veteran of clandestine operations in the Second World War, now a department of transport man, experienced and principled, who personified the authority and wisdom of age; and the American 'Nicky' (Nicholas King, played by Stephen Young), a young ex-pilot of the U.S. air force, now a trouble-shooter for the Associated Owners and Shippers, who personified the enthusiasm, recklessness, and toughness of youth. But again viewers preferred the Hollywood original to the Toronto imitation. 'Seaway' died after one season.[42]

Even before this effort, though, the CBC itself had tried out a new format, the mini-series, to capture popular favour. The results of the first few mini-series, aired in summer seasons, had been mixed: a well-regarded if technically primitive Vancouver production entitled 'Cariboo Country,' in 1960; a slow-paced adaptation of W.O. Mitchell's tales, 'Jake and the Kid' (which gave one critic 'yawnin' heartburn' and mightily upset Mitchell himself), in 1961; and a British-style mystery series, 'The Other Man,' also too slow for the tastes of some ('Fairly frequently, something didn't happen,' claimed one critic), in 1963. None the less producer Ron Weyman was able to persuade the powers that be to finance 'The Serial' (Fall '63 to Spring '66), of which he became executive producer, as a common vehicle for a number of mini-series. For the mini-series offered considerable advantages over the regular serial or series. It could be written as an extended play, then cut up for weekly scheduling, or as a limited collection of related episodes, in either case by one person. According to Hugh Gauntlett, the new approach avoided the problem of forcing Canadian writers to conform to a single story line, *à la* Hollywood, something that required 'a whole battery of skilled writers' that just didn't exist in Canada. Canadian writers were 'individualists,' so it seemed. Now the producer could approach a writer to do an original or an adaptation, allowing him the freedom to develop interesting characters. Besides the format limited the Corporation's investment of money and enabled it to experiment with different genres.[43]

Weyman had great things in mind for 'The Serial.' There was 'quite a hunger for identity' among Canadians that couldn't be satisfied by imports, he assumed. 'The Serial' was to showcase Canadian stories that otherwise wouldn't make it to television. He had secured approval to use 16-mm film on location for roughly one-third of every episode, the rest videotaped in the studio. Outdoor filming would make episodes much more realistic, more exciting than was possible with studio drama. For 'Convoy,' a war serial, he went through thousands of feet of film footage on file in Ottawa to find material that would make the mini-series authentic. And he filmed new scenes of a machine-gunning of survivors caught in the water in the Toronto harbour. Best of all, the filmed segments could be used to highlight Canadian settings. He could actually show people the bald-headed prairie or the Laurentians in Quebec or a court-house in Liverpool, Nova Scotia. 'It gives you a feeling of being there,' he enthused. Viewers 'appreciate seeing their own country, and being able to identify with the characters in the stories.' He even argued that letter-writers were 'relieved by the absence of u.s. slickness' in the mini-series.[44]

Undeniably 'The Serial' did offer viewers quite a range of Canadian stories and settings, and in a variety of genres, over the course of its three-season run. There was lots of social drama, of course. The first mini-series was an adaptation of Thomas B. Costain's *Son of a Hundred Kings*, which dealt with the troubles of an English orphan at the turn of the century in a town in western Ontario. That was followed immediately by an adaptation of Thomas Raddall's *The Wings of Night*, which was billed as 'a drama of love and ambition in a declining lumber town in the Maritimes.' But there was also suspense, crime drama, a historical romance, comedy, even a professional saga. Phyllis Lee Peterson was the author of the mystery drama 'Strangers in Ste. Angèle' in six episodes, prepared especially for 'The Serial' (although she had previously used the fictional Ste Angèle for teleplays). An adaptation of Morley Callaghan's novel *More Joy in Heaven* (which had been suggested by the life of the notorious Red Ryan, a Toronto bank robber of the Depression era) explored the problems, and eventually the tragedy, of a famous bank robber who tried to reform himself. George Salverson constructed a four-part drama, 'The Road,' that focused on the days when blacks escaped slavery in the United States by fleeing north into Ontario. Leslie McFarlane wrote 'McGonigle Skates Again,' a comedy about the wild life of a hockey scout. George Robertson created that idealistic politician Quentin Durgens, MP, for 'Mr Member of Parliament' to give people a better appreciation of just what did happen up in Ottawa. That last mini-series was an example of a drama consciously designed to meet a particular purpose.[45]

In retrospect the best of these mini-series was probably the revival of Paul St Pierre's 'Cariboo Country,' which dealt with the life and the people of the fictional community of Namko in the interior of British Columbia. It was, in many ways, a unique product. While it laid claim to authenticity, as a sort of docudrama, a reflection of some part of British Columbia, it was in the words of CBCer Len Lauk 'a bit of a fraud,' because it amounted to an exercise in mythology not a study in fact. Billed as a series, it none the less focused on a number of different characters, caught up each week in quite different situations, and so took on the attributes of an anthology. Although a bit like a western, featuring ranchers and Indians, it was set in the present and avoided the passion for good men and bad men, for gunfights and brawls, for law and order, that characterized the Hollywood brand. Uppermost was the element of social drama, since the episodes often concentrated upon the personal lives of individuals, although it would be stretching things to call 'Cariboo Country' either a Canadian soap opera or an Anglo téléroman.[46]

Consider the episode 'Sara's Copper,' which aired in spring 1966, in the last season of 'The Serial.' The plot revolved around two reservation Indians, Sara and her husband, Johnny, who desperately need money immediately to pay off a debt arising from a car accident and launch them on a new life. Sara decided to sell her 'copper,' an old relic of considerable importance in Indian custom. They approached antique dealers, one of whom explained its significance to them, before reaching an agreement with a private collector who treated the 'copper' as just one more trophy to display – he was very concerned about its authenticity, and the fact Sara and Johnny were genuine Indians from a reserve. But, at the last moment, Sara broke her 'copper' in front of the collector, replaying an age-old ritual of rejection directed both at the man and at his culture. The story touched upon issues of poverty and pride, the Indian heritage and modern ways, the white man's disdain for the native people, above all the soullessness of modern life. It celebrated alienation, a most unusual action in the context of Hollywood drama where the alienated character was normally portrayed as a victim not a hero. And the ending wasn't so much a happy resolution of the problem, for it meant Johnny would lose his truck, as a triumphant assertion of personal integrity and ethnic pride. It was, of course, the subtlety and the ambiguity of the whole drama that set it apart from the run-of-the-mill stories normally on the small screen.

Robert Reguly, a *Toronto Daily Star* reporter, argued that 'The Serial' was after 'a middle-brow mass audience,' something the CBC hadn't had much success attracting in times past. For a brief moment it seemed that Weyman had captured the attention of at least some of that audience. In its first two seasons the show was scheduled on a Thursday night, from 7:30 to 8:00, when adults and children were watching. Letters from viewers, in which the Corporation put a lot of faith, indicated people were pleased with the adaptations of the Costain and Raddall novels. Doris Gauntlett, an editor for the highbrow 'Festival,' was amazed by the number of families who wrote in to offer to take Costain's orphan, apparently not fully realizing this was a play. The Nielsen ratings of January 1964 ranked 'The Serial' higher than any of the rest of CBC dramas, giving it a reach of some 580,000 homes. But the ratings slipped in the second season, and 'The Serial' began to have sponsor trouble. The final season, lacking a sponsor, it was dropped from the full network schedule and exiled to the 10:30 time-slot on Thursday night. The Nielsen ratings of January 1966 found it was carried on only twelve stations and reached a mere 172,000 homes.[47]

Two offshoots of 'The Serial,' the filmed series 'Wojeck' (13 September to 22 November 1966) and the taped series 'Quentin Durgens, M.P.' (6 December 1966 to 7 February 1967), went on to win considerable fame in the 1966/7 season. Both were hour-long professional sagas, aired on Tuesday at 9:00 – and Ron Weyman figured as the executive producer in each case. 'Quentin Durgens, M.P.,' an update of the previous mini-series, in the words of a CBC press release, 'brought to life the conflicts and controversies, the public and private struggles, and the individual human emotions that lie beneath the surface of the political scene in our nation's capital.' 'Durgens' also brought its chief actor Gordon Pinsent into the national limelight. Yet the much more interesting show was 'Wojeck,' written by Philip Hersch, about the struggle for justice waged by Toronto's chief coroner. However unlikely that topic, the show was the best popular drama CBC-Toronto had ever produced. Hersch had written a message drama, not preachy but certainly laden with meaning: he used the saga to dramatize such public issues as the generation gap, the profit motive, and the new morality to disturb comfortable views and awaken the public conscience to the wrongs around them. But this message was nicely packaged in a gripping drama about an embattled professional. The technical quality of the production was, for once, superb. The leading player, John Vernon, became CBC-Toronto's first star of popular drama. Late in October CBC directors were told that in one survey the show had reached 2.5 million viewers and secured an enjoyment index of 77, higher than many American imports. According to a magazine article, the mini-series received even higher ratings when it was rebroadcast in the summer of 1967.[48]

CBC-Toronto may have won one battle but it had definitely lost the war. 'Quentin Durgens' and 'Wojeck' lasted only two seasons. John Vernon soon went off to Hollywood, in search, presumably, of greener pastures. Indeed Weyman recalled that Norman Jewison's agent came up from Hollywood to suck off, 'like a vacuum cleaner,' much of the talent that had brought the CBC such great success. Weyman and others struggled on with some new professional sagas such as 'Corwin' (1969–71), 'McQueen' (1969/70), and 'The Manipulators' (1970/1), none of which made a great splash. The appointment in 1970 of the first actual head of TV drama, Fletcher Markle, brought with it new layers of bureaucracy that worked against initiative and innovation. A number of experienced producers, such as Daryl Duke and Paul Almond and Eric Till, left the Corporation. According to Weyman, the channelling of funds into film meant that studio drama had withered away. Indeed lots of money was wasted making what proved to be an embarrassing flop, 'The Whiteoaks of Jalna' (1972), a mini-series that was an attempt to emulate the justly famous British import 'The Forsyte Saga.' The five years or so after 'Wojeck' turned out to be the nadir for the CBC's Drama department.[49]

Something had been achieved, of course. There's an assumption around that the anglophone CBC did in fact fashion a particular brand of popular drama, quite unlike the Hollywood genres because it was based upon a documentary tradition that went back to John Grierson and the early days of the National Film Board. So Ron Weyman argued that writers and producers in the early days were imbued with a sense of mission, as artists and teachers, to deal with 'real-life situations,' albeit in a way that was at times more earnest than entertaining. The critic Morris Wolfe in *Jolts* has made the claim that 'the tradition of telling it like it is' lies at the core of made-in-Canada films, whether for television or the cinema. Drama historian Mary Jane Miller has cited, in *Turn Up the Contrast*, an impressive list of attributes that set CBC drama apart from the American product: the anthology imprint, a taste for 'irony,' 'open narratives or unresolved emotional conflicts,' lots of 'subtext,' 'literate dialogue,' 'allusions to the actual society,' and a kind of gritty realism that grew out of the techniques of making documentaries.[50]

You can find examples of all this in 1960s drama by looking at 'Cariboo Country,' 'Quentin Durgens,' and above all 'Wojeck.' But there are problems with the thesis. It's hard to make a strong case for a distinctive tradition of drama when there are so few examples that fit the mould. A documentary thrust may seem typical simply because so little of other kinds, notably the more emotion-laden action/adventure or social melodrama, was produced by the CBC. It's quite possible, as Mary Jane Miller admits, to find American series, such as 'The Naked City' or 'The Defenders,' never mind British productions such as the renowned police show 'Z-Cars,' that might also be counted as instances of a documentary drama. Indeed the range of series drama Americans and Britons produced during the 1950s and 1960s was so great that one can find examples of all the various attributes that have been ascribed to the efforts of CBC-Toronto and CBC-Vancouver: sparkling dialogue ('The Honeymooners' 1955/6); anthology ('The Alfred Hitchcock Hour' 1962–5); continuing conflict ('Peyton Place' 1964–9); a social conscience ('Mr. Novak' 1963–5); irony ('The Man from U.N.C.L.E.') or satire ('The Flintstones' 1960–6); even ambiguity and incongruity ('The Avengers'). Besides, so much of the made-in-Canada drama the CBC aired then, even 'Wojeck,' shared Hollywood's fascination with believable stereotypes, simplified conflict, wise and powerful males, and the like. I'm left with the conviction that TV's artists in English Canada hadn't really found a distinctive voice, not even in these years an effective voice, unlike their compatriots in French Canada.[51]

In part that failure, if such it can be labelled, came about because there was no real call from the public for such a drama. CBC-Toronto did not enjoy the same 'advantage' of isolation as its Montreal counterpart. The anglophone audience was attuned to the Hollywood product. Many a Canadian viewer might say that he or she wanted more drama dealing with Canada: back in the mid-1950s, Schwerin Research found roughly two-thirds to three-quarters of the people asked in one program test liked series that dealt with 'Canadian home situations.' Yet in 1963 the Corporation's own survey of public opinion learned that English Canadians were least satisfied with its dramatic offerings. For the viewer also expected that the Canadian product adopt the same standards as was normal in Hollywood telefilms. Hugh Gauntlett, for example, noted that a plan for a simple, videotaped medical series based on a Toronto hospital was killed because Hollywood came out with 'Ben Casey' and 'Dr. Kildare,' both of which were carried by the CBC. Doug Nixon mused that he would dearly like to see a Canadian sitcom: the problem was that the program would have to be very well-written and well-done to compete. The Anglo audience, in short, was both spoiled and satisfied by what was already available from the United States.[52]

The rest of the explanation lies in the mood and the situation of the CBC itself. There seemed to be no one in high places in the Corporation eager to make popular drama a top priority. Looking back, Eric Till observed that there was a good deal of distaste for Hollywood's sitcoms and crime shows, and so an unwillingness to really try to emulate American successes. The minutes of a director's program committee meeting in 1961 recorded the observation by then chairman, C.B. Lumsden, that there wasn't 'any point sacrificing American productions for any mediocre Canadian program that would not compete favourably.' A drama critic, Nathan Cohen, lamented the fact that there was no leader, a person with vision who had charge of the drama Department. According to the television writer Charles Israel, the CBC had 'failed to develop a group of top television writers' who might churn out interesting, saleable drama. The program director in 1965, Doug Nixon, told an interviewer that tight money had forced the CBC to cut back on its 'most expensive productions, variety shows and drama,' to maintain the existing level of Canadian output. The little popular drama it did produce during the decade usually occupied only a half-hour or an hour in the weekly evening schedule. That was never enough to wean Canadian audiences from their loyalty to Hollywood, even if this was a realistic goal.[53]

What happened and didn't happen to storytelling in Canada showed that the dream of turning television into an instrument of Canadianization was only a mirage. It was all evidence of the inability of television to overcome existing cultural realities: in Quebec where there remained a lively tradition of the popular arts, television was the vehicle for a brand of drama that did express something local, but in English Canada where the tradition was feeble at best, television couldn't work any miracles. The few efforts to create series that appealed to both language groups, other than 'Les Plouffes' (and even here there were limits), foundered because audiences just didn't share sufficient myths or memories as Canadians to make the experiments compelling. By contrast the Hollywood imports, as had been true of American products for generations, were equally accessible to both audiences who did share a common experience as North Americans.

Focus: 'Wojeck'

The screen brightens to display hectic confusion: a street at night, outside Toronto's Silver Dollar tavern, a man shouting and fighting, a crowd watching, people yelling. Camera moves swiftly from close-ups of faces, action shots of the fight, group shots of the crowd, and back to close-ups. The shouting man, it becomes clear, is an Indian (later identified as Joe Smith) who is besting one of Toronto's finest – he lands one blow that sends a policeman to the street, then suddenly moves forward and kicks his victim. The very picture of defiance, he yells 'Yah!' and menaces any and all comers (see frame 10.1). The sound of sirens. Police cars arrive. Out rush reinforcements. Two policemen subdue the Indian, dragging him with great difficulty into the back seat of one of the cars. The police car speeds away. An anonymous voice in the crowd yells, 'Farewell, Sitting Bull.'

Switch to a much calmer scene – in the receiving room of a police station. Mrs Costler, an old woman, kindly, a pleading expression on her face, asks an officer, one Sergeant Fred Keeler, for a favour: to see her drunken husband. Sarge kindly consents. Terry, a policeman, goes off to collect Pete Costler. Then Terry returns in a hurry. 'Remember that Indian. He's hung himself!' Sarge: 'Oh God' – a look of shocked disbelief on his face. The sergeant and Terry rush off to the jail block. Black-out.

Screen brightens to a picture of a street at night, taken from a moving car. The loud background music has a fast drum beat and a jazzy quality. Car lights flash by. Then, zooming out from a picture of a darkened cityscape, comes the word 'Wojeck,' written in white. Picture shifts to a mature, self-confident man walking down a night-

Frame 10.1 The defiant Indian

lit busy sidewalk, looking around – the man is Wojeck, soon identified with a white graphic that reads 'starring JOHN VERNON as DR. STEVE WOJECK – Coroner.' That's followed by images of the other stars in different settings: Marty, Wojeck's wife; Bateman, the crown attorney; Sergeant Byron James, Wojeck's assistant; and Joe Smith, shirt front open, drinking a bottle of beer and reading.[54]

That was the opening of an award-winning episode of the CBC's 'Wojeck' entitled 'The Last Man in the World,' written by Philip Hersch and directed by Ron Kelly, which aired first on 13 September 1966. 'The Last Man in the World' was Joe Smith, an Indian from Moosonee, who had come to Toronto in search of a new life. He didn't succeed in finding his fortune, though. Instead he hanged himself with a belt borrowed from a fellow inmate in his jail cell. That suicide took place in full view of a group of men locked up in the drunk tank opposite his cell. We learn that it took ten minutes for a man to strangle to death. Coroner Wojeck entered the picture to discover how and why this suicide came about, and he soon realized that Smith was the victim of a heartless society. The show was an exploration of 'Canada's shame,' namely its treatment of its native people.[55]

This episode of 'Wojeck' was a fine example of popular drama – it seemed authentic and it was gripping. It had those qualities of polish and excitement all too often lacking in earlier CBC series. The complex script offered viewers a clear story line, interesting characters, and novelty, set in the conventions of the professional saga. The broadcast displayed some exceptionally skilful camera work, excellent acting and directing, and first-class editing to create an effective mix of sounds and images. What stands out, though, is the variety of techniques employed by the writer and the director to hold attention. The show itself was made up of twenty-six different scenes (not counting the series introduction and commercial breaks), of which twelve were flashbacks devoted to what had happened to Smith from the time he arrived in Toronto. These flashbacks alternated with scenes of the 'present,' which chronicled the course of Wojeck's investigation. The pace of the drama varied according to the substance of a scene, sometimes fast, sometimes leisurely. One scene might be full of talk, while another relied much more on the eye than the ear. A forlorn little melody was used now and then to underline a particularly crucial moment in the action. Sometimes the camera work was fairly standard, a series of reaction shots and two-shots; other times the director used angle shots, distance shots, a slow pan or abrupt cuts, even blurred images to underline a mood.

Note, for example, two related scenes in the last third of the episode, each of which reflected the hopes and fears of the players. The first was a flashback, in which Joe had a brief chat with the city-wise Indian Charlie. The scene opened with a picture of some leaves in the sunshine, part of a tree in a park. The camera slowly panned downward to a half-body shot of Joe, lying on the ground, singing a song. Then the shot moved through the branches of the trees, sun streaming in. Peace was disturbed when an unseen Charlie said 'Hi.' The conversation that followed saw Joe recount his hopes for a love affair with Lucy, a white woman he'd met, and Charlie respond first with surprise at his acquaintance's naïvety ('You're just a farmer ...') and then with bitterness against white society. The point is, though, that the scene occurred outdoors in a pastoral setting, and was marked by a mood of calm (except at the end), fitting the clichés of Indian life.

The next scene, by contrast, opened with the image of a man pumping his legs fast on a cycling machine, complete with a loud, abrasive noise. It moved swiftly to a group shot of older white men in exercise clothes trying to shed those unwanted pounds. Their discussion was about the coroner's investigation, more particularly whether the police were to blame for the suicide. Bateman tried to explain why a cover-up was impossible. One of his colleagues found the whole business an unwarranted embarrassment threatening the good name of the police. The camera cut from person to person. Each of the individuals was busy exercising. The language was harsh, abrupt: the angry colleague even cursed. We were in a different world, a place of power, inhabited by middle-aged whites who did their reflecting in the midst of furious activity and discordant noise.

'The Last Man in the World' was really a hybrid, mixing three different kinds of tales: adventure, tragedy, and the quest for justice (see figure 10.1). Aside from Joe Smith, none of the other characters figured significantly in all three tales, and even Joe's role changed depending on the perspective. Each scene amounted to a separate playlet, linked directly to one or the other of the tales. That said, a viewer could readily find in each of these tales messages that served to underline the basic theme of 'Canada's shame.'

On one level 'The Last Man' was a tale of adventure, reminiscent of the story of the 'country mouse' (Joe Smith) and the 'city mouse' (Charlie). Joe was a stranger in a strange land, escaping from a miserable life on the reservation to find happiness in the unknown setting of the big city. On one occasion (in Scene #12), Joe explained to his new friend Lucy, in the longest monologue he uttered during the drama (see frame 10.2), just how different was his past life of deprivation and what seemed her life of affluence:

Video	Audio
Lucy starts speaking looking down, but ends looking directly at **Joe**.	**Lucy**: What's it like where you come from? **Joe**: You mean where I come from?
Joe looks up and then down at the food. He ponders her words.	**Lucy**: Yeah.
Close-up of **Lucy**'s face, her lips highlighted. **Joe** ponders, still looking up and down. **Joe** looks around the kitchen.	**Joe**: Uh ... It's not as nice as this. Um ... we don't have electric lights or, or, um ... radio, or anything like that. And, urh ... we don't have

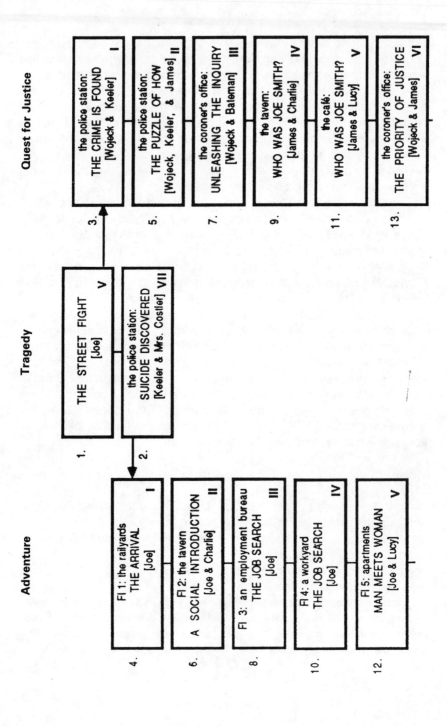

Adventure

Tragedy

Quest for Justice

FI 1: the railyards
THE ARRIVAL
[Joe] **I**
4.

FI 2: the tavern
A SOCIAL INTRODUCTION
[Joe & Charlie] **II**
6.

FI 3: an employment bureau
THE JOB SEARCH
[Joe] **III**
8.

FI 4: a workyard
THE JOB SEARCH
[Joe] **IV**
10.

FI 5: apartments
MAN MEETS WOMAN
[Joe & Lucy] **V**
12.

THE STREET FIGHT
[Joe] **V**
1.

the police station:
SUICIDE DISCOVERED
[Keeler & Mrs. Costler] **VII**
2.

the police station:
THE CRIME IS FOUND
[Wojeck & Keeler] **I**
3.

the police station:
THE PUZZLE OF HOW
[Wojeck, Keeler, & James] **II**
5.

the coroner's office:
UNLEASHING THE INQUIRY
[Wojeck & Bateman] **III**
7.

the tavern:
WHO WAS JOE SMITH?
[James & Charlie] **IV**
9.

the café:
WHO WAS JOE SMITH?
[James & Lucy] **V**
11.

the coroner's office:
THE PRIORITY OF JUSTICE
[Wojeck & James] **VI**
13.

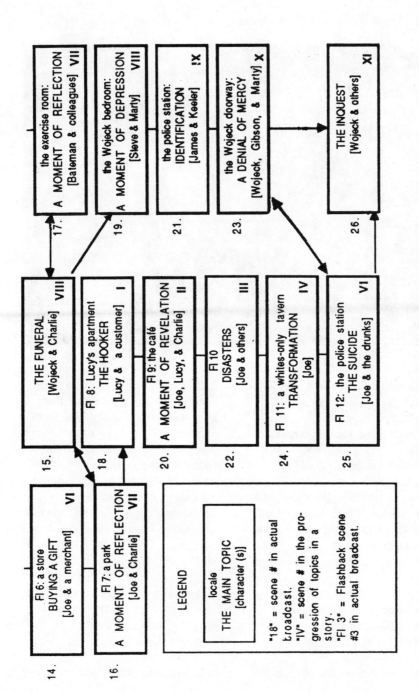

Figure 10.1 The sequence of scenes in 'The Last Man in the World'

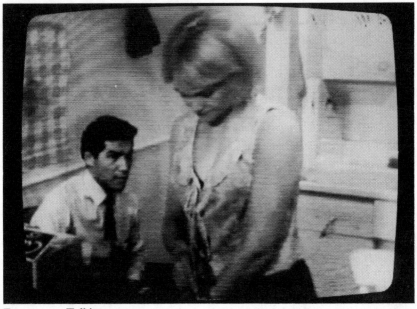

Frame 10.2 Talking

Camera switches to a close-up of **Lucy**'s face, filled with an expression of wonder.

Back to **Joe**, looking directly at **Lucy**.

Flash back to **Lucy**, eating, catching her with a look of surprise in her response to the news. Then back to **Joe**, still looking around. Flash back to **Lucy**'s face, now a bit horrified.

Alternate close-ups of **Joe** and **Lucy**.

Flash to **Lucy** eating, watching **Joe**, absorption on her face. **Joe**, looking down, looks up and shakes his head.

indoor bathrooms you have to go outside ... It's really cold up there. Don't have heating. Um, you have to keep trying to keep the stove going ... If it goes out, it's pretty cold. I know a couple of kids that froze to death. Um ... Life's an old man there killing rats for something to eat. We don't eat this kind of food either. Have rabbit and, um ... oh it's nice in the springtime. When you're a kid and going swimming and that ... we pick blueberries, go canoeing ... it's nice but ... um ... in the wintertime, it's pretty bad up there. It's pretty awful up there.

We could readily sympathize with his friendly, rather shy manner, his eagerness, his earnest goodwill. Nor did it hurt that he was reasonably good-looking. He went through various rituals of exploration and discovery: he arrived on a freight car, and had to escape a train official; he met fellow Indians in a bar; he tried to get a job at a government employment office, later at a line-up outside a factory; he met a white girl, the hooker Lucy, who invited him to supper; he wandered the streets during the day and night, looking in store windows.

Joe hoped somehow to enjoy the good life, and the key to that became his relationship with Lucy. In the park (Scene #16), he asked Charlie, 'Do you think it can happen? Me Indian and she's white. She likes me.' But Charlie 'knew' that Joe's hopes were doomed to disappointment. He had experienced disappointment, we must assume, and so became very bitter. 'Go back with the farmers in Moosonee,' he told Joe. 'They'll [the whites] steal from us and they'll starve our kids. And when we fight back, some white cop will bash your head in.' Smith's naive response said it all: 'What are you getting so mad about?'

On another level, 'The Last Man' was clearly a tragedy. There was an inevitability to Joe's suicide. His kind of wide-eyed innocence marked him as a victim. He didn't have any of the skills necessary to thrive in the big city. ('Can I get a job here? I'll do anything. I'm strong worker,' Joe told an uninterested employer.) Above all, he was an alien, unwanted by white society, and the assorted citizens of that society made very clear time and again that they didn't want him around. We met along the way a conniving pimp who tried to exploit Joe's naïvety, a snobbish Indian counsellor who treated Joe like a mental deficient, the hooker Lucy (another victim) who saw Joe as an exotic and so a source of novelty, a couple of policemen who assumed Joe was a criminal, and on and on. But the fundamental message of indifference and intolerance was spelled out time and again in what various whites had to say:

An *old, unemployed white* to Joe, (Scene #10): 'Don't worry chief, you can always go back to the reservation.'
Bateman's colleague (Scene #17): 'Yeah, but damn it I don't understand why everybody wants to make a martyr out of a drunken Indian.'
White driver, after his car struck Joe a glancing blow (Scene #22): 'You bloody savage, why don't you go back to the reservation ...?'
Lucy to Joe (Scene #22): 'I wouldn't make it with you if you were the last man in the world.'

Waiter to Joe (Scene #24): 'Listen buddy, why don't you go down the street where you belong, alright?'

The constant rejection, the casual racism, Joe's powerlessness, we must assume, led to his transformation into an alienated and angry rebel. He was driven to drink by a clash with the police, a blow from a car, and the brutal rejection by Lucy – even a white hooker didn't want him (all in Scene #22). The final straw came when the waiters in a 'whites-only' tavern refused to serve him. He exploded, attacking the waiters and smashing up the place, a fight that spread out onto the street when the police arrived. Not even in jail could he find any peace, though. Joe was placed in the same cell as the sleeping Pete Costler. He was ridiculed by the inmates of a drunk tank, who made fun of him, asked for some 'squaws,' and generally whooped it up 'Indian-style.' Escape was impossible. Death was the only release. So Joe Smith used Costler's belt (a belt Sgt Keeler should have ensured was removed) to take his own life, while his fellow cellmates watched in horrified silence.

Finally, 'The Last Man' was a quest for justice, which was after all the *raison d'être* of the series itself, an attribute that was central to all professional sagas. Joe here was cast in the role of object – a victim, especially a dead victim, can't be much more. Here too there were a series of rituals: the discovery of the crime in the jail, the inquiry carried out largely by Sgt James who identified the chief actors, the attempted obstruction by people who wished to hide their involvement, and the inquest where the facts would be revealed. The key player in the quest was Dr Steve Wojeck.

Now Wojeck was neither handsome nor tall, in the classic Hollywood style, but he was impressive. The skin of his face seemed mottled, perhaps by childhood acne; he had a high forehead; his eyes were set deep in a ridge of bone; he had a prominent nose and cheekbones; small lips, often pursed; a strong chin, often pushed forward (see frame 10.3). It was an angular face, a face of planes, that shouted the fact that Wojeck was a tough, driven man. He spoke little, and when he did, often in a clipped or sardonic or harsh style and always to the point. He moved decisively, and when he walked other characters stepped aside or followed. For Wojeck personified justice, a justice full of moral indignation. He fully recognized that he lived in a corrupt and hypocritical society. He didn't trust the police or the

Frame 10.3 The man of justice

bureaucracy. ('One of these days, Byron, one of these days this country's going to hang itself with red tape.') But that didn't stop this man.
Wojeck was determined to get to the bottom of the whole affair, no
matter who was hurt.

There was a superb scene (#23) near the end of the drama, set in
the doorway of Wojeck's home, that amply demonstrated his appeal –
and how merciless justice could be. One player, outside the door, was
Ed Gibson, an aging businessman who sold church supplies, who just
happened to be in the drunk tank the night Joe Smith committed
suicide. He believed the publicity of an appearance at the inquest
meant ruin. Nervous, eventually anguished, he pleaded with Wojeck
to tear up the summons. The stance, the tone of voice, the words, all
announced he was a supplicant, the uncaring Mr Middle Class whose
callous indifference in the jail allowed Joe's death. Shot slightly from
below, Wojeck stood tall in the doorway, the entrance frame and the
light behind his head emphasizing his presence and power. He looked
down on the sinner, his expression impassive. He refused the plea,
of course. But he couldn't resist making Gibson squirm:

Video	Audio
Cut to **Wojeck**'s hard face.	**Wojeck**: There's only one way you can get out of appearing at the inquest.
Cut to **Gibson**, waiting for deliverance.	
Cut back to **Wojeck**, a calculating expression on his face.	You wear a belt?
Cut to **Gibson**, a close-up of a face on which understanding suddenly dawns.	

It would be hard for any large number of people to empathize with a hero who was always so cold-blooded, however. Thus, just like his Hollywood counterparts, a Dr Kildare or a Dr Casey, Wojeck had a human side that was revealed on two occasions. The first (in Scene #15) found him paying for the funeral of Joe Smith, greeting and even smiling (it was a bit like granite cracking) at Charlie who actually shook the hand of *this* white man. The second (in Scene #19) occurred in Wojeck's bedroom where, caught up in a funk, he defiantly, almost like a little boy, told his wife Marty that he was going to quit the job. She'd obviously heard it all before. Initially she tried to talk him out of his depression. When that didn't work well, she put on a face of allure and invited him back to bed. His lack of response disgusted her. But, almost immediately he reconsidered, and moved slowly out of his seat by the window, almost like an animal on the hunt, towards his wife in the bed. We were left to assume that sex worked its magic cure. This last scene, of course, was another expression of the supportive role that woman as helpmate played in the life of the harried male hero.

The show put a high value on the punitive force of publicity. We are led to believe that Wojeck could right wrongs, and bring the culprits to justice, simply by disclosing their sins. Bateman's colleague in the exercise room (Scene #17) was disturbed that the hue and cry might damage the request of the police department for a 15 percent increase in its capital budget. Sgt Keeler declared his fear that his pension, certainly his record, would be endangered by a full inquest (Scene #21). Ed Gibson tried to hide his face from the public eye during the brief, final inquest scene (#26). The last image on the screen was a close-up of Charlie, the embittered Indian, who was seated in the audience to see justice done to the whites who had so mistreated his lost friend. The point is that 'Wojeck,' for all its apparent novelty, was at bottom an optimistic show: the preferred meaning of 'The Last Man in the World,' like all its ilk, was that the forces of good could and did win out in the end.[56]

11

Versions of Reality

Television is the most important medium we've got. It can involve millions of people in an immediate and total way, in a communal national experience. People watch a program, and they get up and talk about it next day, over breakfast, at the office, in Parliament, in magazines. Television means people [have] to think, and the national consciousness moves forward because of it.

Allan King, 1967[1]

Allan King wasn't saying anything very new when he trumpeted the virtues of television journalism. Far from it. He was merely repeating a cliché that had become a bit tired by the end of the 1960s. All kinds of people, and not just McLuhanites, had ascribed to television magical powers to work a revolution in the public life of the country. They were wrong. There's no doubt that television journalism fostered a lot of controversy, most especially in the halls of the CBC, largely because it did give voice to the so-called spirit of the 1960s. There's no doubt that television itself did become one of the master forces in politics, and so altered the way in which politicians played their games. But the power of television was swiftly tamed by what was called, in the jargon of the day, 'the Establishment,' really an assortment of élites, from politicos to intellectuals, nearly all of whom were city folk. The proof of that last fact was the astonishingly rapid rise to power in 1968 of Pierre Elliott Trudeau, Canada's certified 'new man,' the embodiment of modernity.

'The Distemper of Our Times'

Such was the title of Peter Newman's book about Canadian politics during the so-called Pearson years, from the downfall of John Diefenbaker in February 1963 to the arrival of Pierre Trudeau in April 1968. Newman had been a political reporter throughout the period, first as the Ottawa editor of *Maclean's* and later as the syndicated columnist of *The Toronto Daily Star*. His purpose was to chronicle 'the alienation between the politicians and the people' that had disturbed public life and made the country seem 'ungovernable' – or 'governed by fools.'[2]

In fact the term 'distemper' was applicable to the whole of the decade, which commenced with the Diefenbaker upheaval of 1957/8. His victory had not only closed twenty-two years of Liberal rule; it had returned excitement, passion, and upset to a national scene where such colourless leaders as Mackenzie King and Louis St Laurent had once presided over a time of quiet politics. The decade witnessed the collapse of Dief's huge majority government, the succession of a series of Conservative and then Liberal minority governments, and finally the Trudeau victory: Canadians went to the polls in 1957, 1958, 1962, 1963, 1965, and 1968. What added to the political confusion was the birth of two new political forces, the New Democratic party, which endeavoured to reintroduce a brand of class politics into Canadian life, and the Créditistes, who represented a right-wing populist revolt in Quebec. So much seemed to be happening to disturb the calm of governors and governed alike: Quebec's Quiet Revolution and the rise of separatism, the resurgence of provincial ambitions and of Canadian nationalism, labour troubles, the expansion of the welfare state, America's Vietnam War, ferocious feuding in Conservative ranks over Dief's leadership, acrimonious debates over a new flag and the integration of the armed forces, a collection of Liberal scandals, even the belated discovery of a sex scandal in the Diefenbaker years (the Munsinger affair). The excitement produced in 'right-thinking old Liberals' a certain nostalgia, reported Douglas Fisher in the Toronto *Telegram* (26 April 1966): 'Why can't we get back to the good old days when we ran the country efficiently and in relative quiet?' went the refrain.

It was obvious that the people weren't exactly thrilled by this excitement either. Indeed Canadians were becoming increasingly disenchanted with politicians of every kind. Pearson was told by a friend in 1963 that, all too often, he heard from ordinary people such expressions as 'all parties are alike,' 'one is as bad as the other,' and 'just a bunch of cheap politicians.' 'I don't care which set of bastards gets in,' said one cabbie about the 1963

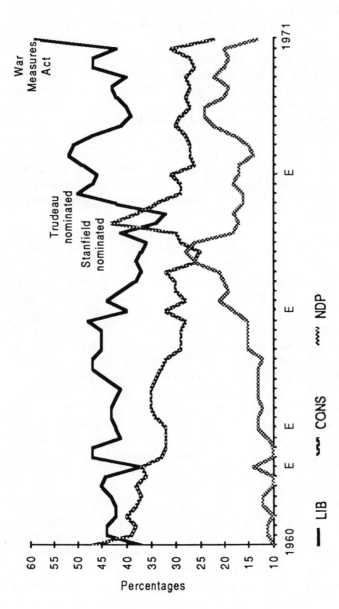

Chart II.I The uncertain public, 1960–71

Note: The statistics are derived from answers to the standard Gallup question, 'If a federal election was held today, which party's candidate do you think you would favour?' as well as the election results. The Gallup statistics only cover the people who made a positive response: the undecideds were left out. Since the chart only begins at the level of 10 per cent total occasionally fell below 10 per cent. E signifies an election.

election, 'as long as somebody gets in and leaves us alone for a few years.'
Only 34 per cent of a Gallup sample were satisfied with Diefenbaker as
prime minister in early 1963, only 41 per cent with Pearson in October
1965. Another Gallup report (14 July 1965) found that just a quarter of
respondents approved the idea of a 'son' (there was no mention of a
daughter) going into politics as 'a life's work.' Is it any wonder that electors
seemed unable to come to any clear-cut decision as to what party they
really preferred, at least prior to 1968 (see chart 11.1)? The number of
undecideds, usually around a third of the people sampled by Gallup in the
mid-1960s, reached a high of 40 per cent in the summer of 1966. A lot of
Canadians were caught up in a mood of anti-politics.[3]

Why? Well, to repeat a favourite phrase of the 1960s, the times were
changing, and changing fast. Newman wrote that the distemper was rooted
in a social, economic, and moral 'ferment' that was eating away at the
traditions of the country. He cited, among other things, 'the exodus from the
farms,' 'technological breakthroughs,' the notorious 'Pill,' even television
itself, as agents of novelty. That's correct. But the fundamental cause was
the corrosive effects of growth: massive post-war European immigration,
the baby boom (nearly 50 per cent of the population was under twenty-
four by 1966), the swelling of the cities, and above all the spread of
affluence. So many new bodies and so much extra money were bound to
cause indigestion. Existing institutions, old ways, the certitudes of the past,
all seemed under assault in that giddy decade: even Canada had become
an 'impossibility,' if one was to believe the arguments of George Grant's
Lament for a Nation, published in 1965. Those electors who looked to the
politicians to lead them through 'this maze of change,' Newman noted,
soon found the Pearson – Diefenbaker generation wanting. And no wonder:
it wasn't at all clear that the Canadian public had come to any agreement
on where it wanted to go.[4]

There were, after all, a lot of people who thought themselves more the
victims of 'future shock' than the beneficiaries of progress. It's dangerous
to generalize about who felt disturbed and who felt pleased. The cause of
Grant's lament was his belief that Canadians had surrendered their soul
to 'the homogenized culture of the American Empire,' because of their
zeal to secure the benefits of affluence. His was the most philosophical and
articulate of all dissents, at least in English Canada, and I doubt that his
views were shared, or even understood, outside of a small coterie of university and literary types. But nearly everyone must have suffered a twinge of
anxiety at the pace of change at some time or another. Many a parent
worried about the influence of rock 'n' roll, whether that of Elvis Presley

or of the Rolling Stones, on teenagers. Even so, people of a conservative temperament were more likely to be older, living outside the big cities, working in low-skill occupations or lacking much advanced education. The traditional way of doing things seemed better to these Canadians. It was the younger crowd, the affluent city-dwellers, the educated, who were excited by fads and fashions, if not eager to shed tradition for something new and modern.[5]

In each case, the crucial factor was residence: people in cities were much more likely to welcome novelty than were their town or country cousins. That split had a marked impact upon the voting habits of Canadians in 1962, 1963, and 1965: the parties of reform, Pearson's Liberals and the NDP, secured much greater support from the metropolis, whereas the parties of resistance, Diefenbaker's Tories and Social Credit, won out in the hinterland. Diefenbaker in particular had come to symbolize the traditional ways of 'Old Canada,' at least the Anglo version of that Canada, which according to Grant was the reason 'the dominant classes' were after his scalp.[6]

Diefenbaker loyalists, and at times nearly all politicians, were inclined to blame the news media for a good deal of their troubles. ('Emancipated journalists were encouraged to express their dislike of the small-town Protestant politician,' claimed Grant, 'and they knew they would be well paid by the powerful for their efforts.') That was neither unusual nor surprising: governors have always looked askance at messengers bringing bad news. There was, however, a good deal of truth to the presumption that the news media were agents of distemper.[7]

It wasn't just because the distracted mood of the electorate had enhanced the importance of publicity, although that was certainly a factor. The very structure of politics was changing: the political party was in decline as the key institution in the country's system of governance, a victim (in part) of the rise of the bureaucracy ever since the Depression. The hold of party on the minds of voters was uncertain at best – something over a third of declared partisans in 1965 had none the less proved fickle in their loyalties during the course of their political lifetimes (although it's not clear whether this was a marked increase over past times). But most important, the hallowed authority of cabinet, party, and Parliament over the political process was apparently threatened by the news media's rediscovery of the virtues of independence. The revolt of the Conservative dailies against Diefenbaker in the 1963 election campaign was a source of much comment: never before had the nation's editorial pages been so one-sided, evidence in itself of the disenchantment felt by people in the big cities, and especially the disgust of the country's élites, over Dief's brand of leadership. Still, commentators usually, and correctly, found the chief cause of the enhanced power of the media in the influence of 'the new boy on the block.' The newscasts and the public-affairs shows of television reached so many people, the influence of its images seemed so compelling, that it had altered the nature of the political game.[8]

The news media, print as well as television journalists, were bent on establishing their own brand of authority over political life. The twin notions of investigative and adversary journalism had gained increasing favour in press circles, ever since the furious pipeline debate of 1956 had converted the Press Gallery into the voice of an angered opposition. That persisted: 'I found it a stuffy and self-important place,' Harvey Kirck said of the Press Gallery in the mid-1960s, 'whose members tended to consider themselves an arm of government, albeit in opposition.' Put it down to an influx of young reporters, a new professionalism, or just the times, the journalist as party loyalist (a kind represented by the Conservative Peter Dempson or Liberal Bruce Hutchison) was fast becoming old-fashioned. Reporters and editors now seemed ready to put substance into that age-old conceit depicting the journalist as the public's watch-dog. They looked to their peers, less to political masters or cronies, for guidance. So Don Jamieson, a private broadcaster and Liberal politician, worried about the single-mindedness of CBC producers, and worried even more about their commitment to a form of social change based on a contempt for established institutions.[9]

Along with that came a greater sense of professional significance. 'To work, gentlemen,' was the sarcastic comment of Val Sears, a *Toronto Daily Star* correspondent on the Diefenbaker campaign plane in 1962. 'We have a government to overthrow.' The journalist was the chosen instrument (note self-chosen) of that mainstay of democracy, 'the public's right to know.' This could amount to a licence to disclose the misdoings of the powerful, most especially of the government. So in 1966 Peter Reilly, newly appointed executive producer of news and public affairs at CTV, casually informed a reporter that he operated 'on the theory that we should oppose the government.' The underlying assumption was that the politicians were always motivated by a personal or partisan self-interest, at odds with the public interest – the assumption proved an all too convenient way of explaining just about everything that happened in Ottawa. That kind of an attitude wasn't the only bias in news copy by any means. But the presence

and the persistence of an adversarial stance could only foster among readers and viewers a distrust of politicians, the 'them and us' syndrome, a
cynicism about how Canada was ruled.[10]

What had gained favour, wrote Ron Haggart during the furious 'Seven
Days' controversy in the spring of 1966, was a new approach to newsmaking: 'a journalism in which the journalists themselves decide what are
the issues of concern and importance, a journalism in which the issues are
established not by the politicians, but by those who watch them with
pencil and film.' Journalists were engaged in a never-ending struggle with
politicians and other notables over who set the public agenda, a struggle
that rose to a fever pitch during an election campaign. The so-called fourth
estate was given a mighty assist in its quest for power by the arrival of the
public opinion poll as the accepted indicator of the people's will, perhaps
one reason why journalists rarely questioned the legitimacy or significance
of the whole technique of sampling public opinion. The Gallup service and
its rivals not only supplied reporters or editors with headline news, making
the results 'media events in and of themselves' as John Crosbie later
regretted: the polls gave the journalist what appeared to be concrete data
that could be used to judge the performance of politicians, inside and
outside office, as well as to spark questions that apparently expressed the
public's momentary moods.[11]

During the election frenzies the politicians discovered that they had to
fit their strategies to the routines and the needs of the media – its deadlines,
its desire for 'fresh' news and 'colour,' its passion for simplicity, and so
on – if they wished to get their messages across to a public dependent on
journalists for political information. Even when an election wasn't in the
offing, the politician learned he must tailor his remarks to suit the '30- and
90-second news windows' of a television newscast. Worst of all, he no
longer seemed in command of the situation: 'I can recall, as leader,' reminisced Robert Stanfield, 'day after day being asked to comment on what a
journalist felt was interesting, or thought was important, not what I thought
was important as leader of the Opposition.' Only by appearing on television
to deliver an address, or via election commercials, could the politician hope
to escape the fact that journalists were the grand mediators in the flow of
information from governors to governed.[12]

Journalists didn't always win, of course. They couldn't altogether usurp
the power of the politician to set the agenda, especially since politicians
soon became adept at news manipulation and image politics. But journalists
were now, in a way that hadn't been true for at least a generation, news-
makers in their own right.

Toronto's Last Experiment: The Information Boom

Robert Fulford was one of the first critics to recognize that something strange was afoot in the Public Affairs department of CBC-Toronto. He told viewers, in a *Maclean's* article published during fall 1963, that they should expect a 'new wave of TV think shows' that had come about because of 'a kind of collective restlessness' among producers and supervisors, a 'dissatisfaction, really, with themselves' that had surfaced roughly a year before over the fact that their product had never won the attention of the mass audience.[13]

Understandably the 'Seven Days' phenomenon overshadows everything else that CBC-Toronto produced in the realm of informational programming. That show's notoriety creates a false impression, though. There wasn't a complete break with the past. Take the case of news. You'll recall that CBC news had become one of the major news-gatherers in the country by the end of the 1950s. But the news department, still under the leadership of William Hogg, remained wedded to the principles of objectivity and impartiality. Its weekly report 'Newsmagazine' did become a vehicle for more and more news documentaries. 'But it's always so dreadfully dull,' wrote Bob Blackburn in 1965, after a show on the Indonesian withdrawal from the United Nations. 'Thorough, yes; concientious, yes; but, by gosh, dull.' The CBC was usually able to outclass newcomer CTV in coverage of major political events, notably its campaign and election-night broadcasts, though by the time of the leadership conventions of 1967 and 1968 a feisty if understaffed CTV news team did challenge (and in some minds beat) the old master. The late-night newscasts, still read by Earl Cameron, remained carefully crafted exercises in understatement, without much sparkle or excitement. 'No matter what Earl Cameron reads,' argued Robert Fulford, 'he makes it sound less alarming than it sounds coming from anyone else.' Here too CTV did mount a challenge, modelled on NBC's enormously successful 'Huntley-Brinkley Report,' with a series of rotating teams of journalists – before the mantle of anchorman was bestowed upon Harvey Kirck, who proved in time as effective a storyteller as Cameron.[14]

There was a small collection of rebels and reformers, notably Don Cameron (executive producer of 'Newsmagazine'), Bill Cunningham (briefly executive producer of 'The National'), and Knowlton Nash (a Washington correspondent), who tried to use the 'Seven Days' crisis to realize their dreams. But their efforts to compel the Corporation to give news a much higher priority through the appointment of a news vice-president, greater expenditures on equipment and studio facilities, the hiring of specialists, the appointment of a broadcast journalist as anchor, an earlier and longer news-slot just didn't get very far. A modest revamping of the 'The National' did occur, beginning late in 1966, when Stanley Burke took over as announcer (expecting to act as a journalist as well, before the unions raised a ruckus). But management, according to Nash, wasn't about to bestow a lot more resources and greater significance upon a department it thought was full of 'sophomoric juveniles: loud, irresponsible, undisciplined, defiant of authority, and bureaucratically anarchistic.' Much later, Bill Cunningham reflected bitterly on the fact that the CBC missed a golden opportunity to establish itself as a world-class news service in the late 1960s by exploiting to the fullest its capacity to cover both sides of the Vietnam war, the Middle East muddle, and the two Chinas. No matter: CBC news was clearly delivering a service that most viewers, and many critics, found comprehensive – 'television's balanced voice of authority,' in Roy Shields's words.[15]

Likewise CBC-Toronto continued to schedule a lot of discussions, features, and documentaries designed to educate and uplift, rather than to foster controversy. One local CBLT series 'Generation' (Fall '63 to Summer '66), briefly shown on the network, tried to bridge the gap between young and old by airing all points of view about such matters as smoking, marriage, and religion. Another local show was 'Observer,' a successor to 'Tabloid,' which during the 1964/5 television year was part of a series of regionally produced, early-evening interview-cum-human-interest programs running weekdays and collected under the umbrella title 'Across Canada.' A twelve-week, half-hour series called 'Check-Up' (Summer '63), produced in association with the Canadian Medical Association, endeavoured to outline the difficulties doctors faced handling the illnesses of the public, from back-ache to cancer. Even 'Citizen's Forum' reappeared briefly under the new title 'The Sixties' (Fall '64 to Spring '66, but in the evening only during the second season). That exercise in science education 'The Nature of Things,' launched outside of primetime in Fall '60, won increasing notice as it moved away from the studio to feature nature documentaries, particularly the famous series 'Animals and Men' and the colour film *Galapagos*. The intermittent hour-long documentary 'Camera Canada,' begun in 1961, offered documentaries on such different subjects as sports ('Hockey: An Affectionate Look'), ballet ('The Looking Glass People'), views of urban life ('Tale of Three Cities'), and the immigrant experience ('The Promised Land'). In the Summer '63 'Telescope,' a sponsored half-hour essay show, was launched with much fanfare, likely because it involved two greats of the past, Fletcher Markle as host and Ross McLean as producer. According to Peter Kelly, who took over as series producer the next season, he could do anything that wasn't controversial, a freedom that allowed him to interview the cast of 'The Beverly Hillbillies,' feature a nostalgia film by Paul Almond on life in Gaspé, and cover a jazz session in New York. All of which is only a sample of the many programs, some earnest and some light, that carried on the tradition of 'information for everyone.'[16]

Even in public affairs, moreover, the work and the ideas of that past master Ross McLean continued to inspire producers. It's only a slight exaggeration to call the bevy of new offerings an extension of the 'Close-Up' experience. There, Ross McLean had trained some producers, notably Patrick Watson and Douglas Leiterman, and coached others, including Daryl Duke, Peter Kelly, George Ronald, Charles Templeton (who would head CTV's news and public affairs), and Jim Guthro (briefly McLean's successor at 'Close-Up'). The common aim was to make public affairs exciting. Watson's 'Inquiry' (Spring '61 to Summer '64), hosted first by Davidson Dunton and in its last season by Laurier LaPierre, was noted for its hard-hitting interviews, the very type of exciting contest McLean had loved. Leiterman, at first a story editor on 'Close-Up,' became a specialist in documentaries, some of which appeared in the 'Close-Up' time-slot, and moved on to supervise his own news documentary series, first 'Background/ The Critical Years' (1961/2) and later 'Document' (1962/6). He was the most public champion of the new style of *cinéma-vérité*, a type of documentary that appeared not only on his shows but on Kelly's 'Telescope,' summer specials such as 'The Living Camera/The Human Camera' and 'Compass' in 1965 and 1966, as well as Guthro's series. After 'Close-Up' disappeared, Guthro used 'Horizon' (Fall '63 to Summer '64) to offer a similar kind of eclectic mix: a docudrama such as 'The Presumption of Innocence,' which dramatized the plight of a suspect in a burglary case, filmed interviews in 'Another Canada,' which probed the life of the poor, or a study of ecological peril entitled 'And Then There Were None' about the extinction of species. His effort the next year, 'Other Voices' (Fall '64 to Summer '65), hosted by the actor Don Francks, was equally trendy, using drama, music, documentary, comment, and interviews. What was novel in the public-affairs repertoire was political satire, a result of the astonishing success of the BBC's 'TW3' ('That Was the Week That Was,' Fall '62 to Fall '63), which had secured impressive ratings and caused much excitement because of its abuse of the powerful. The CBC's first attempt to mix satire and straight reporting, 'Let's Face It' (Fall '63), produced more embarrassment than controversy, though, which is why it was canned after only a few shows.

The rub was that none of these shows, no matter how good they were, was able to capture the imagination of the mass audience.

'Seven Days' was different. It was the brain-child of Watson and Leiterman, both in their mid-thirties, both television enthusiasts and political idealists, and both proven veterans of the public-affairs game. Their backgrounds and their personalities were different, mind you. Watson was something of a charmer, urbane and unflappable: 'the immensely likable, but slightly solemn, fellow every Anglo-Saxon mother would like her son to be,' wrote Alan Edmonds. Leiterman, by contrast, was a workaholic, an aloof and driven individual with little time for the social graces: Doug Fisher decided he was 'the dangerous man, intense, almost fanatical, the iron fist beneath the velvet glove.' Watson was the more intellectual of the two: he'd embarked first on an academic career, got an English MA and started a PhD in linguistics, before joining the CBC, at first as a free-lancer, in 1955. He was particularly taken by the ideas of Marshall McLuhan: 'Television is not an analytical medium, it's a synthetic medium – it gives you an organic moment,' Watson once claimed. Leiterman wasn't much impressed by McLuhan, perhaps because he affected the pose of the hardbitten journalist: he'd worked in newspapers after university for eleven years before joining the 'Close-Up' team in 1958. Leiterman wanted public-affairs television to grow up, to adopt the techniques of investigative and advocacy journalism, which he believed newspapers and news magazines had embraced a decade or so earlier. Eventually Leiterman argued that both the dictates of journalism and the bias of television made outmoded 'the old myths of objectivity and "studious neutrality" ' still enshrined in CBC lore.[17]

None the less the two men hit it off. They'd talked about the dismal appeal of public affairs back in their 'Close-Up' days. They apparently carried on 'a non-stop telephone conversation,' while Watson was in Ottawa for 'Inquiry' during the early 1960s, about what they were doing and how they were doing it. Finally they sat down to draft a manifesto for a novel news-magazine, modelled in part on 'TW3,' meant for the Sunday at 10:00 time-spot, and consciously designed to appeal to everyone, from truck drivers to university professors. They promised 'a film report,' supplemented with 'live links' on 'the significant current affairs of the week'; 'an investigative report,' using *cinéma-vérité* to 'probe honesty and hypocrisy,' 'a kind of TV ombudsman'; 'a hot seat,' where 'a prominent guest' would be 'grilled'; and 'sound-off,' 'says you,' and 'hot line,' where viewers could air opinions, about the show if they wished. Once a month a 'Document' film would be dropped into the schedule, providing in-depth coverage of a single subject. This proposal was accepted for the autumn of 1964 as the flagship public-affairs show of the new season by a management eager to experiment. Ottawa allowed a sizeable budget for the time, something over $30,000 per show, and, in September, hyped the newcomer with a special three-city press conference and showing for the critics. The fanfare, the ballyhoo, was greater than any Doug Fisher could recall for single program.[18]

There had never been anything quite like the 'Seven Days' team assembled by Watson and Leiterman, at least not in the experience of CBC-Toronto. In the first season the two men, each with their own crews, alternated as producer and director; in the second, Watson became one of the co-hosts, and acted as producer of the 'Document' series, while Leiterman was executive producer of 'Seven Days,' assisted by Ken Lefolii (recently from *Maclean's*) and Robert Hoyt (an American journalist) as alternating producers. The program had two front men, an English and a French co-host, which advertised its intention to span the two solitudes: John Drainie, a well-known radio actor, was selected for the first season because of his stalwart image (his illness, and eventually death, from cancer brought in Watson the next year); and Laurier LaPierre, a witty and sometimes emotional man with a winning manner, who also happened to be an academic historian, was brought over from 'Inquiry' to take up the French spot (a footnote to this is that Watson approached Pierre Trudeau first, who turned the job down because, among other reasons, hosting was not to his taste). The program also required a 'beautiful doll,' a 'cover girl,' for song and satire and grace, a role filled initially by Carole Simpson but soon by Dinah Christie (however unconventional 'Seven Days' was in other areas, it didn't propose putting a woman in the key slot of host). The support staff Watson and Leiterman recruited numbered between twenty-five and forty: over the two-year span the show employed some of the most talented people in Canadian television – director David Ruskin; Roy Faibish, as Ottawa editor; the NFB film-maker Donald Brittain; Allan King, Daryl Duke, Beryl Fox, and Ross McLean for 'Document'; reporters and interviewers Larry Zolf and Warner Troyer; Peter Pearson and Alexander Ross, as story editors; even Mavor Moore, who wrote the lyrics for Christie's songs.[19]

Reports then and later stressed that working at 'Seven Days' was an experience in itself. The team became a citadel of arrogance, established in separate offices and isolated from the CBC proper by a special esprit de corps. Watson and Leiterman, especially Leiterman, demanded commitment and hard work. Each week's program was reviewed by all the staff, and people were encouraged to express their criticisms, rate each item, and propose new subjects or techniques. This wasn't a democracy: the producer's word was final – Peter Pearson noted how a film report he prepared on over-medication was constantly edited, and pared down, by his producer Ken Lefolii, who told Pearson to find 'a victim' before the report was accepted for airing. According to one estimate, only 20 per cent of the material collected was ever shown on air. Everything was carefully scripted, even the remarks of the co-hosts, although the scripts were subject to change as late as Sunday afternoon. In short the pace of activity was unbelievably hectic. It's no wonder that people suffered burn-out. Indeed, by the end of the second season, both Watson and LaPierre were getting exhausted, and LaPierre began to tell interviewers that he wasn't sure he would continue (in part because he was only a 'performer'). Watson and Leiterman could justify such a work situation because 'Seven Days' had a special mandate.[20]

You can't understand the 'Seven Days' phenomenon without some knowledge of the philosophy of its founding fathers. Even if they came at the 'truth' from different directions, Watson and Leiterman shared an awareness that television was above all a visual medium that communicated with the public in a way quite unlike print. What television did best, apparently, was 'to focus attention and impress images' (Leiterman), providing a snapshot 'of a person or an event' that captivated and involved the viewer – 'what is said is far less important than the impression conveyed' (Watson). Watson liked to cite the response of some friends to an interview with Bertrand Russell on 'Close-Up,' where what was memorable about the interview was the lasting impression of the man's intellect, not anything he'd said. Done properly, TV could propel a 'far greater emotional charge (and a correspondingly lower intellectual cargo),' working on the viewer 'largely at a nonintellectual and non-rational level,' than the messages of radio or print (Watson). The new kind of television journalism 'was stripping away sham and pretension. It was revealing people and events as only the camera eye could see them' (Leiterman). Neither man worried much about superficiality, since each assumed television conveyed a version of reality that nothing else could do so well.

The other thing that made television so extraordinarily exciting to any journalist worth his salt was the fact that it could reach across all social boundaries, 'from the Prime Minister and the Papal delegate to the university president and the pauper' (Watson). The purpose of 'Seven Days' was, first and foremost, 'generating conversation, provoking interest' (Leiterman), so that people talked and thought about the Pill or racism or separatism after the broadcast. I get the feeling that both Watson and Leiterman believed 'Seven Days' could become an catalyst for the much-touted 'participatory democracy' (Leiterman even talked later about creating 'some modern equivalent of the Greek city-state') where an excited, informed public would be able to act on major public questions. All of which meant 'Seven Days' had to attract people who'd never before watched a public-affairs show, perhaps had never read anything other than 'the comics and the sports page' (Watson). They did watch television, however, and the task was to 'lure the common man' (Leiterman) by packaging the classic substance of public affairs (Watson, for example, replied to Dennis Braithwaite, an early critic, by citing statistics that supposedly proved how standard was the content of the news-magazine) in a way that was pleasing to these types. But the priority of numbers meant showbiz; it meant 'Seven Days' would employ all of the techniques of display, contests, and storytelling to win and hold attention. There was the kicker: the type of stories 'Seven Days' selected and the way these stories were treated were determined, in part at least, by the alien standards of entertainment, rather than the normal conventions of journalism (making Watson's stats a bit specious). Put another way, the practice of showbiz opened the door to charges of sensationalism and sleaze.[21]

The fact is that 'Seven Days' did capture the imagination of the mass audience, just as Watson and Leiterman had planned. That success translated into a modest degree of public power, forcing politicians and newspapers to respond to 'Seven Days' initiatives: according to Helen Carscallen, twenty of the items featured on 'Seven Days' generated national issues. Right from the beginning, the show clearly appealed to a cross-section of viewers, whatever their educational attainments, the fans of 'Bonanza' as well as the public-affairs *aficionados*. CBC statistics indicated that by the end of the Spring '66 the program was reaching more than three million viewers a night, putting it in the same league as the hockey broadcasts. Equally amazing, the so-called index of enjoyment, in which management put great store as an indicator of impact, was running in the 80s, a phenomenal score.[22]

Watching the show was clearly a Sunday-night ritual in many anglophone homes. Viewers tuned in to see what might happen this week. Watson and LaPierre had become national stars, admired and sometimes loved by thousands (once, after a show when the hosts were taking calls that were aired to the studio audience, a woman cooed to Watson, 'You're a beautiful man, Patrick'). The show itself did provoke the very kind of Monday-morning conversations in home and office and work-site and schoolrooms that it was supposed to. People took a proprietary interest in its survival. ('I don't even have a TV,' admitted Mrs Anna Fedele, a Toronto housewife who picketed the CBC in April 1966. 'But I always go next door on Sundays to watch Seven Days. It gives you something to think about. I don't think I could do without it.') The very irreverence, the iconoclasm, that defined 'Seven Days' had touched something in the Canadian soul. 'Seven Days' had become 'a symbol,' wrote Roy Shields: 'It represents a new, rambunctious English Canada, determined to speak up, to shout and fume and fuss ...'[23]

By the end of Spring '66, however, Ottawa had become fed up. The 'Seven Days' crew refused to listen to the top brass, consistently infuriated the conservative-minded among the public and the politicians, and flouted the principles of balance and impartiality and even decency that were supposed to underlay public-affairs broadcasting. In early April the news that Ottawa intended to split up the 'Seven Days' team, removing both Watson and LaPierre, led Leiterman, Watson, and their supervisor, Reeves Haggan, to declare war on management, not only by going public but by organizing a save 'Seven Days' campaign to mobilize mass support and pressure the politicians. There followed three months of agitation: newspapers had a field-day, fans wrote letters and paraded outside CBC offices, Toronto producers threatened to strike, Pearson appointed a fact-finder, a parliamentary committee quizzed both the rebels and the managers. In the end, of course, the top brass won and the show was cancelled. But the cost was very high: in a retrospective published nearly a decade later, Martin Knelman decided that the 'Seven Days' legacy was really to inaugurate 'a scorched-earth period in CBC public affairs broadcasting.' 'People stopped talking about CBC public affairs shows,' Knelman recalled, 'and the newspapers stopped running front-page stories about them, and within a year or two many of us gave up watching them, too.' The experiment had come to an end.[24]

The Record of the 'New' TV Journalism

'The general purpose is to make the situation real, make it believable, credible, suspend disbelief,' claimed Watson. At its best, the self-styled 'new' journalism was eye-catching (the days of 'radiovision' had finally passed) as well as confrontational. That made for 'good television,' admitted a worried Don Jamieson, since the message was tailored to suit the medium. But at what cost? The fact was that the conventions and the repertoire of journalism were transformed by the new priorities. That's why many in the CBC's news service looked on public affairs as a flashy rival, especially when 'Seven Days' was in full flight, that secured too much money and fame given its dubious record. That's why a lot of print journalists, most especially in and around Toronto, had never accorded 'Seven Days' anything like the support it won from the viewers during its two seasons. So Dennis Braithwaite, the most consistently hostile, just never cared for the 'pretentiousness,' the 'juvenile frivolity,' the 'vulgarity,' the 'pandering' to 'the lowest common denominator of taste and intelligence' that made 'Seven Days,' in his words, 'a sort of intellectual *Beverly Hillbillies.*' Such comments suggested that columnists were suffering a measure of professional envy over the popular success of the program.[25]

There's no doubt that producers and reporters became a lot more adventuresome in what kinds of subjects they thought suitable for treatment, and how they went about treating them. The initiatives of 'Seven Days' became legendary. It tried to smuggle equipment into a shareholders' meeting of a controversial trust company to record the proceedings. On New Year's Eve, 1965, a 'Seven Days' crew flagged down cars outside a Toronto nightclub to show just how common was the practice of drinking and driving. Larry Zolf was sent off to interview at home Pierre Sevigny, a public figure involved in the Munsinger sex scandal, which got Zolf some blows about the head by a cane-wielding Sevigny, all recorded on camera, though the film wasn't shown on 'Seven Days' (because of an Ottawa ban). The famous interview with Fred Fawcett, an inmate of Ontario's Penetanguishine Hospital for the Criminally Insane, did get on the air, however. Although denied permission, a 'Seven Days' crew smuggled its equipment into the hospital (in picnic baskets), posing as friends of Fawcett's sister on a visit to her brother. The segment was the catalyst for a special inquiry into Fawcett's case, which resulted in his eventual release. 'Seven Days' carried an interview with Carol Doda, a topless dancer whose breasts had been enhanced by silicone injections, purportedly to highlight the spiritual emptiness of some people in an affluent society. Was any of this wrong or sensational? No. 'Sensationalism is the exploitation of appeals to the senses for base motives,' claimed Watson. 'Pornographers are sensational. They wish to excite people. Our purpose is to use sensory involvement to illuminate.'[26]

The initiative of 'Seven Days' was so great that CBC's President Ouimet could later, and justly, charge the team with setting up 'an independent news-covering organization.' The CBC's news service was understandably distressed by the reportorial thrust of the team, although the rivalry that fostered had its humorous side. 'Seven Days' staffers and regular newsmen jostled each other for preference in the press room set aside for all journalists in the lower floor of the East Block of the Parliament Buildings. Someone on staff actually stole news film from the news service, which infuriated newsmen so much that the local news union came out with a denunciation of the arrogant pilferers. Another incident, in which 'Seven Days' aired the report of de Gaulle's election before the eleven-o'clock news, may have led the newsmen to refuse 'Seven Days' a tape of the press conference held by British prime minister Harold Wilson on a Sunday afternoon; 'Seven Days' immediately contacted the rival Ottawa station CJOH for a tape they could use.[27]

Producers and hosts were also much more eager to editorialize than they'd been in the decade earlier. Recall that the CBC had always asserted, to quote from the executive minutes of 1965, 'that it is improper for the "CBC" host of a program to offer any editorial comment on the matter under discussion.' Yet 'Toronto File' won notoriety because it was willing to take a stand on issues of local import. 'We often oppose,' admitted host Ed McGibbon, 'but, we hope, in a loyal and constructive way.' Laurier LaPierre got into trouble with management, first at 'Inquiry,' because his asides and even his facial expressions seemed to convey an opinion. On one occasion at 'Seven Days,' during an interview with Créditiste leader Réal Caouette, he interjected, 'Oh, my God' after Caouette made an especially outrageous statement. But that was only symptomatic of the overall tone of the series – true, the editorial line of 'Seven Days' was never spelled out; but its approach was to abhor violence, support ordinary people, ridicule prejudice, expose hypocrisy, and even incite political action. Right after an interview with White House adviser McGeorge Bundy over Vietnam, and 'Seven Days' clearly was in the anti-war camp, Watson urged viewers to write to the prime minister if they had any views about the war. 'Seven Days' wished to be a player in the public arena, not just a conduit for the views of others.[28]

The ways in which 'Seven Days' and other shows fulfilled that ambition was usually through the use of satire, talk, and documentaries. No matter how great the fame of 'TW3,' satire wasn't very common, which was probably all too the good since management was always worried about this brand of comment. Watson's 'Inquiry' had occasionally employed a bit of humour to catch the viewer's eye: a show on how to get political action opened with a shot of the Peace Tower in Ottawa, an icon of government, and as the announcer droned a count-down, 'the tower shot out flames from its roots and, apparently, took off into the stratosphere.' But only 'Seven Days' incorporated satire as a regular, and highly successful item in its special mix, again to win viewers. 'We have to remember that many viewers come to the show just for a yuk, you know,' Leiterman told a reporter. The episode of 24 October 1965, for example, contained a little skit that purported to be a phone call between Harold Wilson and Lester Pearson, chiefly over Wilson's troubles with Rhodesia (on the verge of independence) and Pearson's worries about the forthcoming election. It was gentle and witty, a nice light touch, hardly objectionable to any but the most straight-laced viewer. A sketch a few weeks earlier, though, about a TV executive who tried to persuade the Pope (about to arrive in New York) to umpire a baseball game between the Yankees and the Cardinals caused a lot of fuss, in large part because some people read this as a satire of the Pope, when in fact it was poking fun at television. Management publicly apologized for this offence (an apology that 'Seven Days' didn't endorse). Management didn't like the linking of satire and serious items, and worried that too many people would be disturbed if their beliefs or authorities were ridiculed. In any case the fact was that most public-affairs people found their business too serious to allow much room for satire. The 'Seven Days' experience suggests that they underestimated the tolerance of the viewing public.[29]

But consider what happened to that staple of the trade, the interview. Reporters were now on the look-out for unusual or bizarre subjects to probe some hidden aspect of life. The local CBLT show 'Toronto File,' for example, featured an interview in early December 1962 with a professional burglar, kept anonymous of course, who managed to present a very favourable view of his life of crime – ease, good money, a happy family, even respectability. At the time of the 1965 election, 'Seven Days' gave a bizarre twist to the classic 'man-in-the-street' interview by sending Larry Zolf in Toronto and Jack Webster in Vancouver to talk to some of society's dropouts, the so-called bums, about their political views. Early on, 'Seven Days' had caused an enormous furore among the Jewish community by featuring an interview with Lincoln Rockwell, the American Nazi leader, dressed in full regalia and guarded by his henchmen. Leiterman defended the segment because it brought home how heinous racism was, in a way an interview with, say, a rabbi never could. Watson readily admitted that if the interview had been 'bland and dull,' then it wouldn't have been aired. The purpose was to shock the viewer.[30]

Reporters sometimes went to great pains to squeeze out every drop of emotion from an interview, even if this meant an invasion of privacy, all to convey to viewers the essence of an experience. An admiring critic in *The Toronto Daily Star* (27 June 1963) told how a 'Toronto File' crew had 'relentlessly forced' a young disabled girl 'to admit how wretchedly lonely her life was'; 'it was a cruel exposure – but it drove home the program's point' about society's neglect. A 'Seven Days' reporter pressed the surviving wife of a murdered policeman to discover how she felt, whether she had regrets, what she would do, while his camera focused on the saddened, bewildered faces of the woman and her children. Also for 'Seven Days,' Roy Faibish set out to evoke tears in an interview with Mrs Truscott, the mother of Steven, the boy who'd been convicted of the rape-murder of a schoolmate. He asked her questions about her visits to her son in prison, whether she embraced him, whether she hoped he would soon be freed, what times were the most difficult. The impact was such that Laurier LaPierre, watching the film for the first time on the air, shed a tear when delivering the afterword about capital punishment.[31]

More and more the interviewer turned into an inquisitor, at least when his victim was a prominent person in the public eye. The rationale was that anyone under pressure was more likely to reveal his true self. That could easily lead to bullying. Jack Webster, for instance, cruelly cross-examined Victor Spencer, a Vancouver postal worker and an accused spy, for 'Seven Days.' 'Spencer was the underdog,' noted Helen Carscallen, 'and we were reminded of classic examples of police interrogation: stroke them, slap them!' Similarly Doug Johnson, this time for CTV's 'W5,' badgered a Japanese ex–fighter pilot who'd been in the lead plane during the Pearl Harbor assault to secure a confession of guilt. The confused guest, unable to express himself clearly, finally got up and walked off the set, with the cameras rolling. Apparently the show's producer was very pleased – 'Great, great television,' he told Charles Templeton.[32]

'Seven Days' had a special 'hot seat,' inherited from 'Inquiry,' that was designed to make a person feel ill at ease and was reserved mostly for the politician, 'who in a sense has to account for his actions.' Wasn't it the task of the journalist to get behind the façade of a Mitchell Sharp, then minister of trade and commerce? asked Leiterman. 'The audience can see the essential worth and value of the person and the color and the texture, so that the next time you read about the minister of trade and commerce, suddenly you have an image in you mind that's not just a stick of type in a newspaper. You've seen him tested.' The guest was seated in a bare, light-coloured swivel chair, no arm rests, with a large black microphone (akin to a rifle) pointing up towards his face from a base attached to the floor. One or more interviewers, complete with clipboards and prepared material, were seated slightly to the side, also in swivel chairs, so that they could pepper the guest with tough questions. That kind of grilling led

Justice Minister Cardin to admit that Victor Spencer had been suspended from his job without sufficient evidence that would stand up in a court. The interview occurred in a 'bear pit' and the live audience was seated, ringed in tiers above the guest. The aisles were full of cameras to capture the least expression of the guest. On one famous occasion a camera close-up caught the beads of sweat on the forehead of the then minister of justice, Guy Favreau, who was having difficulty explaining the escape from justice of union leader Hal Banks. This testing was something fewer and fewer politicians, including Lester Pearson, were willing to undergo. Indeed it seemed so cavalier, so unfair, that the CBC top brass insisted in the second season that the 'hot seat' go, to be replaced by a gentler round-table format.[33]

'Seven Days' interviews, whether in the 'bear pit' or not, took on the character of a contest in these circumstances. They were carefully planned beforehand, even scripted, to produce the necessary effect. One of the more famous clashes in the first season involved an exchange between René Lévesque and Larry Zolf, with Pierre Trudeau largely in the background. At issue was separatism. Zolf, who played the heavy, was intent upon finding out where Lévesque stood: was he a closet separatist, were separatists 'off their rocker,' wasn't separatism a violent creed? Both Zolf and Lévesque got heated up in the discussion: Zolf emerged as the voice of an angered English Canada, while Lévesque spoke for a self-confident Quebec intent on deciding its own fate. Some critics thought that Zolf had been terribly offensive, and tarnished the image of English Canada, simply by his line of questioning. In fact 'Seven Days' had taped a second Lévesque interview, again with Zolf and Trudeau. Watson and Leiterman didn't run this one because 'the exciting things' in the first encounter hadn't recurred. The justification, as Watson spelled out, was that the exchange was bound to proke discussion among viewers.[34]

The most pernicious aspect of the transformed interview, though, was a result of the editing of filmed or taped discussions to ensure, again, 'good television.' In theory editing allowed a producer to summarize and even to clarify the comments of guests, an argument enshrined in CBC program policies. In practice editing could lead to distortion and superficiality, indeed could fabricate reality.[35]

Complaints about distortion were very, very common. Red Story, an NHL referee, attacked CBC's 'Question Mark' for cutting out so much of what he'd had to say that the show was woefully biased against his employers. Judy LaMarsh noted that in the case of Favreau's hot-seat appearance, 'the truncated interview condemned him, as it appeared, out of his own mouth.' Knowlton Nash charged that the 'Seven Days' edit of the interview with McGeorge Bundy had made him seem much more of a 'hawk' on Vietnam than he really was. Bundy and the White House were sufficiently upset that they released their own transcript of the interview and retaliated by cutting off all sources of information from CBC correspondents in Washington.[36]

Journalists might go beyond the simple edit to actually create a scene or a mood, using sound, images, or intercuts. Templeton freely admitted interspersing separate interviews with evangelist Billy Graham and *Playboy*'s Hugh Hefner to contrast their two philosophies for 'W5.' Jamieson talked about the poor official who discovered that when his optimistic views on the progress of public housing were aired, the screen was filled with shots of slums. Or pity the public man whose interview was played with sounds of 'derisive laughter from an unsympathetic studio audience' in the background. Metro Toronto's Planning Board was understandably disturbed when year-old film-clips of the planning commissioner were intercut by 'Toronto File' with scenes from a panel discussion, leaving the impression he'd actually been involved in the panel (in fact he'd refused). Much worse was an 'Other Voices' documentary on 'mediocracy' and tastelessness in modern life, which, according to Dennis Braithwaite, patched together interviews from unsuspecting victims to suggest the world was filled with 'tasteless lunkheads' who couldn't understand beauty even if they tripped over it. The message was underlined by false comparisons of a dowdy University of Toronto building with a college structure in Mexico City, a Toronto street and a scene from Florence. One of the victims, Gladys Taylor, felt she'd been misled into believing she would talk about the arts, only to discover she was lampooned as a 'mediocrat.' Even putting aside the unfairness of these techniques, the airing of such 'pseudo-events' amounted to a manipulation of the viewer's perception of reality since it capitalized upon the assumption that he or she was somehow watching the real thing. The edited interview was very much an instance of what Peter Trueman has called 'smoke and mirrors,' selling illusions to an often gullible public.[37]

The 'new' documentaries, as well, traded on the illusion of actuality. Indeed the possibilities for distortion were far greater here, since the raw film had to be crafted by the producer and director into a finished product. Much more film was exposed than was ever used. In one day alone, Allan King shot some 11,000 feet for his documentary *Warrendale*. Leiterman admitted to a *Toronto Daily Star* reporter that roughly twenty feet were filmed for each foot that actually appeared. The documentary couldn't be anything else but a version of reality.[38]

The crucial change over times past was that the documentary had now moved out of the studio into the streets, halls, rooms, and countryside of the nation. That was made possible by the new lightweight mobile cameras that had recently become available: back in the mid-1950s, Leiterman noted, a camera crew meant six to twelve men plus a 'two-ton pencil'; but in the mid-1960s the same crew was 'down to two men and thirty pounds.' In filming *Warrendale*, for example, Allan King used a two-man crew, a hand-held camera, a microphone, and some lighting equipment, all on location. It was the ease of the new technology that fostered the boom of *cinéma-vérité*, which, simply put, meant taking the camera to the action and filming reality supposedly as it happened. Witness this enthusiastic comment from Leiterman in 1964:

For the first time in history it is possible for picture and sound to be recorded anywhere – well, almost. We don't have to re-enact events any more. We don't bring people over into the spotlight so they can talk to the camera.

We don't have to hang microphones around their necks or slap clipboards in their faces. We don't tell them anymore to sit still, ignore the lights and speak up on cue.

We can now film it, much of the time, just as it happens. At a political convention our reporter can wander around the floor as Warner Troyer did for Inquiry, with a mike wrapped in a newspaper and a small transmitter in his breast pocket.

We can record sound, as Beryl Fox did in One More River, with a microphone disguised as a broach. In both cases the cameras were a hundred feet away but their 300 millimeter lenses could almost count the pores.

According to Beryl Fox, what she did was to 'endeavour to portray life as it is.' Well, maybe she tried, but even Leiterman admitted that the new techniques had increased the potential for 'mischief.' For, as Robert Fulford warned, if *cinéma-vérité* meant it was 'possible to capture more truth on film,' it also meant it was 'possible to create more convincing lies.'[39]

One source of mischief was that many of the film-makers didn't really just set up a camera to record action, whatever the rhetoric to the contrary. If Fox claimed she never used a script, and rarely staged events, that wasn't true of others. 'There's a real problem of developing a coherent emotional experience in a film with no script,' admitted King, 'of making what actually occurs into a shape, or pattern.' Patrick Watson himself had to admit that in his famous special on Red China, 'The 700 Million,' he'd reconstructed (without telling the viewers) what had appeared as a chance meeting between himself and an Italian, because when the event took place there wasn't a camera around. Knowlton Nash recounted two instances where producer Don Cameron staged an event for 'Newsmagazine' documentaries. In 1963, for a film on Cuba after the revolution, he directed Ché Guevera to drive a tractor slowly through a sugar-cane field, before arriving where Nash waited for the interview, presumably to underline that here was a man of the people. (Ché complied with the instructions, which is merely further evidence of just how amenable even the powerful were to the directions of a TV master.) Four years later, covering the Hemispheric Summit Conference in Uruguay, Cameron dreamed up a wild introduction: the action was located on a ranch, a musical trio was hired, cattle and gauchos were rounded up so that they could thunder by, and poor Knowlton was set on a horse to ride out to a tree off in the distance. 'It'll grab people's attention and set them up for the conference,' Cameron enthused. 'In just a couple of minutes it can set the scene beautifully, convey the problems of Latin America, and give visual excitement and vibrancy to a bloody complicated story.' A more jaundiced observer might conclude that exactly this sort of introduction confirmed the stereotypes that already cluttered Canadian minds when they thought about Latin America.[40]

It appeared as though a horde of film-makers had fanned out across the country, and even overseas, to record life in the raw. People were sometimes a bit bewildered by the results. 'The camera bounced around, in and out of focus, catching random views of various members of the quartet,' said a grumpy Jon Ruddy in a review of a 'Telescope' documentary on the Beatles, 'while a microphone picked up their voices and random background noises.' A CBC audience panel complained about 'unnecessarily prolonged close-ups of Legge-Bourke's face, mouth and moustache,' one of the politicians featured in Donald Brittain's 'The Campaigners' aired on 'Seven Days.' Alphonse Ouimet banned the broadcast of Richard Ballentine's 'Mr. Pearson' because he found it too amateurish, and the official CBC statement added that it showed 'no intellectual grasp' of the prime minister. Dennis Braithwaite got sick and tired of the stream of visual clichés foisted on the viewer: 'Quick cuts of traffic or twist parties, accompanied by loud rock-'n'-roll rhythm' or 'dizzying shots of skyscrapers' had become all too common sign-posts of urban living.[41]

Yet it's also clear that a lot of viewers found *cinéma-vérité* more convincing than other brands of documentary. Thus Frank Moritsugu, a *Toronto Daily Star* critic, decided he couldn't 'identify with the problem' in 'The

Presumption of Innocence' that aired on 'Horizon' because it was a kind of docudrama, not an authentic record of an arrest and trial. By contrast, Bob Blackburn believed that a 'Newsmagazine' treatment of the routine of Joey Smallwood was 'a most uncommonly revealing half-hour,' which would leave even a viewer otherwise ignorant of Smallwood with the feeling that 'you knew a good deal of him afterward.' Beryl Fox's famous documentary on Vietnam, 'The Mills of the Gods,' was widely acclaimed, in the United States as well as Canada, for its authenticity as a portrait of the plight of the ordinary people, American soldiers as well as the Vietnamese, in the war-torn land. 'This was the most beautiful, disturbing and moving work of art I have ever seen on television anywhere at any time,' wrote the novelist Hugh MacLennan. 'It had the indescribable beauty of absolute truth revealed in perfectly selected counterpoint.'[42]

'The Mills of the Gods' was a fine example of the fact that so many of the new documentaries amounted to personal statements by the film-makers. At times these statements were more poetic than political or confrontational. So Brian Nolan's mini-biography, for 'Seven Days,' of George Chuvalo, a Canadian boxer, was a collection of icons of the sportsman at work: the distance shot of a Chuvalo running, close-ups of his gloves hitting a punching bag, a two-shot of him sparring with a partner, all served to underline Watson's commentary about the ordeals of training and the troubles of Chuvalo's life, the anguish of a fighter who faced his last chance for real greatness. Ballantine's 'Mr. Pearson' (not aired on CBC until 1969, after Ouimet had retired) was an intimate and candid portrait of the prime minister at work and at home – according to Tom Kent, a Pearson aide, 'it emphasized the pleasant, charming, but always rather harassed and fumbling style of Mr. Pearson.' In another vein, there was 'Caroline,' produced by Clement Perron and Georges Dufaux of the NFB for the series 'Temps Present,' which conveyed the experiences of a slightly frustrated young woman living in Montreal. Braithwaite thought it was subtle, impressionistic, telling a story gracefully through 'images of Montreal' and 'bits of verse and philosophy.'[43]

Yet even this kind of story could become controversial, if it clashed with someone else's version of reality. That was the case with Ron Kelly's portrait of Toronto's Italian community, 'Ciao Maria,' which was aired in the 'Camera Canada' series in January 1963. Kelly had decided to do a social and cultural study by filming the habits of a few Italian Canadians, notably the barber Frank Nalli. He'd included bits of a wedding ceremony, a religious procession, shots of Italian women on the beaches, a couple inspecting a home, some men looking at girlie magazines, scenes of drinking and singing, and so on. He often cut from one scene to another, to juxtapose the religious procession with fun at the beach for instance. The voice-over narration was actually done by the actor Bruno Gerussi, using 'Italianese' because Nalli's pronounciations made his words too difficult to understand. 'The documentary is a cultural contribution,' Kelly announced: 'I tried to convey to the rest of Canada the warmth, the vitality, the enthusiasm of these people.'

Some of the established spokesmen for the Italian community did not agree. Reverend Emmanuel Faraone, a Franciscan father serving at Toronto's St Mary of the Angels Church, was especially offended, attacking Kelly and the CBC, through the press, for making 'it seem Italians in Toronto live like pigs.' Johnny Lombardi, the so-called Mayor of Little Italy, added the show could give viewers only 'an image of uneducated, unmusical, ill-mannered and unlikely Italian Canadians.' The irate spokesmen called not only for a CBC apology but for the right to reply through some special program on the network. What troubled such men was that the treatment clashed with the self-image of cultured, respectable, religious Italian-Canadians that they were struggling to fix in people's minds.

There was even a meeting involving Kelly, other CBCers, and the irate leaders to view the documentary and air the problems. Faraone, naturally, charged 'Ciao Maria' with deception. Kelly angrily claimed that everything happened, on location, without coaching. Truth, to repeat a cliché, is in the eye of the beholder. Although he hadn't set out to besmirch the reputation of Italian Canadians, Kelly's documentary was biased, one-sided, an expression of his view of the community. He hadn't worried about balance, or about overall accuracy, never mind the feelings of the community's leaders. It's no wonder his vision proved insulting. It certainly wasn't, as he claimed, 'most innocuous.'[44]

Of course, the most troublesome problems with balance and the most upsetting stories resulted from the alarums and the exposés, which seemed little better than propaganda to some critics. On occasion CBC management banned the broadcast of a documentary because it seemed so one-sided, a move that usually brought much criticism down on their heads. 'Cuba, Si' (1961) on 'Intertel' was doomed because it apparently favoured Castro and the Communist cause; King's *Warrendale* (1966 and 1967) was suppressed, partly because of some offensive scenes and language but also because it seemed to cheer on director John Brown's controversial approach to the treatment of disturbed children. In both cases, the action was rooted first in an awareness of the politics of the issue, the fact that many people (including politicians) would have been very excited by these broadcasts.

Certainly the CBC allowed all manner of biased documentaries that weren't likely to spark some extreme outrage from the powers that be to go on the air. So viewers were treated to a critique of the welfare state in Sweden ('The Critical Years': 'Pursuit of Happiness,' 1962), exposés of the plight of the Indians ('Inquiry': 'The Glass Cage,' 1963) and of the poor ('Horizon': 'Another Canada,' 1964), alarms about higher education ('Crisis in Higher Education,' also on 'Horizon,' 1963) or pollution ('Air of Death,' 1967), among much else.[45]

Allow me to probe one such exposé, in this case of North American television, produced by Douglas Leiterman, entitled 'Report from the Wasteland,' and aired May 1962 on the series 'The Critical Years.' The title was taken from Newton Minow's famous 1961 denunciation of American television in his address to broadcasters, a portion of which was included in the documentary. It was hosted by the urbane Alistaire Cooke, himself established as one of the more presentable men of Culture in the mass media. There were interviews with an assortment of other highbrows, such as Gore Vidal, David Susskind, and Paddy Chayefsky, a public-spirited businessman named Pete Peterson of Bell & Howell (who'd sponsored a documentary on blacks), the adman Richard Pinkham, and the Hollywood production boss Allan Millar. There were shots of a ratings board and television sets and antennae, cuts from various programs, pictures of a studio at work, along with the footage of the individuals. Altogether, it was a well-researched and well-crafted job, both clear and interesting, an evaluation with which many letter-writers and critics concurred. 'Report from the Wasteland' was exactly the kind of good television journalism that Leiterman hyped in his later public statements.[46]

But the documentary's success had a lot to do with the fact that it confirmed the unhappiness felt by the typical viewers of public-affairs shows over the quality of television entertainment. The word 'wasteland' was a clear indication of the bias of the documentary: it embodied the highbrow critique of television as a medium that had fallen from grace. Cooke gave the game away right at the beginning: 'Ladies and Gentlemen, good evening,' he said. 'If you are satisfied with television as it is, this program is not for you.' The problem, he elaborated a bit later, was to explain why television hadn't realized its marvellous promise, why 'is so much television so bland, so trivial, so boring? Why this relentless determination to avoid themes of significance or depth? Why should so much of television be a cultural barbiturate, a tranquillizer for the ills and anxieties of our age?' The answer was supplied in words and pictures – chiefly because of the triumph of the ratings and of commerce. Like so many of the products of the 1960s, the argument reeked of moralism, filled with a sense of indignation that wrong had won out at so much cost to the good of society. That was part of the reason two Toronto critics, Jon Ruddy of *The Telegram* and Jeremy Brown of the *Star*, took issue with what the first called 'venom' and the other a 'hatchet job.'

The documentary that caused the most flap was the CBC special 'Air of Death,' a study of air pollution, part of which focused on the health of the Ontario town of Dunnville, named the names of polluters, and left the impression that business didn't much care about the safety of the public in the scramble for profits. This classic exposé was produced by Larry Gosnell and hosted by Stanley Burke, an interesting choice because his role as news anchor gave him the status of an impartial authority. The show was aired for maximum effect on Sunday, 22 October 1967, at 8:00 PM, pre-empting 'Ed Sullivan.' The portrayal of Dunnville was so bleak that the Ontario government appointed a committee to investigate the show's claims. The committee decided there was no foundation for the alarm, that evidence had been suppressed, and that the CBC was at fault for airing 'unwarranted, untruthful and irresponsible statements.' Then the Canadian Radio-Television Commission got into the act, holding a public inquiry in March 1969 on the merits of the show.

The result was a forum for the champions and the victims of what was by then the not-so-new style of documentary. The line of argument pursued by the champions was especially interesting. They emphasized the virtues of accuracy over balance, the need for a point of view and even passion, and the fact that extensive research (as in the print media) was sufficient justification for an attack where the evidence warranted it. Gosnell admitted to a prior bias against pollution, though he thought his treatment was fair. Burke stated, 'I hope we did exaggerate,' although he also testified to the thoroughness of the research. Both Leiterman and Templeton suggested that objectivity was a myth that stood in the way of sound journalism. Templeton and Murray Chercover, the CTV president, noted that balance could better be realized by a mix of programs, instead of by each program trying to present all sides of a question.

Finally, in July 1970, the CRTC delivered its own balanced report, critical of some aspects and laudatory of other aspects of 'Air of Death.' It also counselled against exaggeration, favoured the labelling of opinions and of any bias, and asserted the virtues of accuracy. It was, by and large, a victory for the champions of television journalism since it admitted the right to a point of view and the primacy of solid research as the source of legitimacy. But the very fact that the CRTC had investigated at such length one program probably had a chilling effect on producers. There was much less freedom allowed the TV journalist to be wrong than was accorded his print rival, simply because of the assumed power of television.[47]

The Power of the Image

The sound and fury generated by the battles over CBC public-affairs programming masked the much bigger story of how television itself was conditioning public life. The old idea that television could strip away hypocrisy to reveal the true self of the politician – no more phonies in the new electronic age, please – and so make 'democracy workable,' remained current, to be trotted out at the appropriate occasion. That wasn't much help in explain what was happening, though. Television did have particular biases, partly a result of the medium, partly because of the conventions of the journalists who usually controlled the medium. Generally speaking, television favoured individuals over organizations, personality over policy, novelty over tradition, conflict over consensus, and sensation over subtlety. These biases didn't necessarily make Canadian democracy any more workable; but they did make it different.[48]

The fact that television was still banned from the august halls of Parliament and that election television was still hobbled by strict regulations, issues that continued to exercise some critics throughout the period, hadn't prevented television from working its way into nearly all the nooks and crannies of the political game. Its reach was just too great to be ignored by politicians, which explained why they became regulars on talk and interview shows, even if complaints about mistreatment mushroomed. Early in 1961 Peter Newman used his *Maclean's* column, 'Backstage in Ottawa,' to report on how the Conservatives were falling over themselves to use television to address the nation: 'More and more Ottawa cabinet ministers are saving explanations of important announcements for the CBC's late national news show, which has an average audience of 1,300,000 viewers. Ministers' executive assistants actively lobby with CBC reporters for air time, and some ministers pre-film interviews, if they're planning to break news in speeches at towns that have no TV facilities. One Toronto cabinet minister even manages to get himself on the French TV network by pinning a list of typed answers on the interviewer's jacket, where viewers can't see them. Then he glances down at the answers as he's asked prearranged questions.' The Liberals weren't far behind: Newman counted Paul Martin, a former minister, as 'Ottawa's most adroit television performer' because of his ability to deliver easily a speech fitted to suit TV's brief news window. 'The power of the little silver screen,' *The Financial Post* (10 March 1962) noted wryly, was 'being worshipped as never before in the ranks of the vote seekers.'[49]

If proof was needed of the impact of television, then the sudden eruption of the Créditiste movement seemed to supply that proof in spades. Social Credit had been around in Quebec since before the war, although it didn't appear to hold much appeal to voters until after 1958, when a break-away group led by Réal Caouette decided on the novel course of using television to get across their message of right-wing protest. Costs were very high, so the campaign started only with twenty-six bi-monthly broadcasts of fifteen minutes' length on a Rouyn-Noranda station, and a bit later in Jonquiére as well. The response was extraordinary: not only did the main performer, Caouette, become a star but his broadcasts drew in recruits and collected money. In the fall of 1959 the decision was made to extend the broadcasts to the Sherbrooke and Quebec City regions, and by the winter of 1961/2 a report claimed that the movement was using nine stations and had recruited 12,000 members. Television remained the key element in the Créditiste election strategy in 1962, when Caouette made a big splash as the champion of the underdog: a party that had got only about 13,000 votes in Quebec in 1958 won (in its new form) 542,000 votes and 26 seats in 1962. Of course Caouette had swum with the tide, exploiting the resentment of townspeople and farm-people over their lack of prosperity, the booming of the urban middle class, and more generally the assault on tradition. Television couldn't work its miracle alone. But what politicians and others focused on was the miracle itself. The next time round the Liberals learned their lesson, using another political street-fighter in the person of Yvon Dupuis to fight Caouette on TV and in person.[50]

The character of election campaigns, of course, was shaped by the presence of television. It reduced the significance of local candidates and local meetings, played up the importance of political stars and scheduled events and the national campaign, and fostered a particular style of appeal which highlighted the need for leadership and the effort to win the trust of the electorate. Back in his 1961 article, Newman had pointed out that the Conservatives planned to make television coverage the centre-piece of their forthcoming campaign. Liberal organizers were no less aware of television's import, apparently all having read (or heard of) Theodore White's famous *The Making of the President*: they tried to run an American-style campaign, resting heavily on American expertise and polling, to push the idea of an efficient Pearson team via television – indeed Pearson opened his campaign with a challenge to Diefenbaker to join him in a TV debate, a challenge declined probably because Dief and his advisers were well aware that the Nixon-Kennedy debate had worked to the distinct advantage of the newcomer, Kennedy. The result of such efforts to exploit television, then and in the next two elections, were TV addresses, plenty of film opportunities, special interviews, partisan commercials, and so on, all designed to reach stay-at-home voters in their living-rooms.[51]

All in all, Bob Blackburn decided, the 1965 campaign had been a dull one for TV viewers, partly because the politicians had learned the ropes and refused to experiment with television, relying on the 'safe' and 'tested' methods of persuasion. (The NDP ran afoul of CTV in one modest experiment: a campaign ad attacking misleading advertising was turned down by four independent stations who insisted that the ad itself was an instance of misleading advertising!) The damage was already done, though. Gérard Pelletier noted that the traditional campaign meetings in local constituencies in Quebec had gone 'out of style,' since people in the television age were interested only in the stars. His door-to-door canvass quickly revealed the public's indifference to the whole contest – except in one home where he was welcomed as a long-lost friend because of his past TV appearances. Pearson was more scathing about what had happened, although he blamed the whole of the media, not just television. The huge campaign meetings, once full of speeches and significance, had been turned into 'circus performances.' 'People want a show, and the competition for their attention is savage,' he lamented. 'So a show it must be, with excitement, headlines, personal attacks, and appeals to prejudice or fear or other emotions.'[52]

Pearson's bitterness was understandable, given the fact that he was one of the victims of image politics. Canadians, and particularly Canadian reporters, suffered from an overdose of the Kennedy mystique throughout the 1960s. The memoirs of two quite different journalists, Gérard Pelletier and Knowlton Nash, make abundantly clear just how attracted they and their fellows were to the candidacy of the unorthodox John Kennedy in 1960. The example of this youthful, dynamic president would haunt TV and print coverage of national politics until Canada secured its own messiah in the form of Trudeau in 1968. Leadership was the one big national issue, at least from the standpoint of television, a justification (if such was needed) for what would later be called 'horserace journalism.' Both Diefenbaker and Pearson suffered from this priority, since the focus on leadership hurt their political fortunes. How typical of the times was Richard Nielsen's theme in his treatment of the Diefenbaker-Pearson years for 'The Public

Eye' in June 1966: their bitter confrontation, it seemed, had hidden from sight 'the real issues gnawing at the roots of the nation.' There was something of a paradox here.[53]

Recall that Diefenbaker was the country's first politician to master the arts of persuasion on television. His manner and his diction seemed to convey both sincerity and passion on the little screen. And he found in television an extremely valuable tool to address the nation, to reach those ordinary folks he so often claimed to represent, particularly when the country's newspapers and eventually elements of his own party turned against him. On 13 May and again on 14 September 1964, he used TV to spread his message of 'One Canada,' menaced by the Liberal infatuation with duality and, by implication, an aggressive Quebec. On 17 February 1965 an appearance on CBC-TV gave him the opportunity to damn party rebels as tools of the sinister, unnamed interests who strove to rule Canada, part of an effort to exploit the resentment of his public who felt outside the centres of power in the big cities. The 'old magic,' in the words of Lorne Parton, writing after the 1965 election, never left him. He remained 'a thunderer, a dreamer, a spellbinder' who could perform marvels when on stage in front of the cameras.[54]

But the 'old magic' wasn't enough. For film-clips, backed up by commentary, portrayed Diefenbaker as a tired curmudgeon, out of step with his times, perhaps a bit absurd because of his antics and his attitudes. A Conservative loyalist, Chester A. Bloom of the Toronto *Telegram*, was especially critical of Leiterman's 'The Servant of All' on 'Document' in 1962 as a case study in bias. And Dief's television interviews, where his face looked so old and his hands might shake, increasingly suggested a man who was in an advanced state of decay. Television always shed a very harsh light on the politician who looked aged, something that Paul Martin discovered some years later when he ran for the Liberal leadership. Early in 1965, NDPer and columnist Doug Fisher visited his constituency to sample political opinion. He found there was a continued fascination with Diefenbaker, and a lot of hostility because people wanted him out. 'Repeatedly there comes question and comment about Mr. Diefenbaker which originates from the physical impression of his CBC television appearances,' wrote Fisher. 'There seems to be a feeling that he's very old and very shaky and very confused.' Fisher's response that you should see the fiesty old gentleman at work in Parliament brought only doubts about Fisher's 'objectivity' or 'judgment.'[55]

Pearson's image problems were of a different kind. His advisers hoped to convey the impression that Pearson could offer exactly that brand of responsible, experienced leadership lacking since Diefenbaker had taken command in 1957. Echoes of this turned up in the occasional political documentaries, where the treatment of Pearson was noticeably gentler than that of Diefenbaker, a reflection again of the reporter's bias in favour of the urban insider. Pearson did make good use of television addresses on a couple of occasions, notably in February 1968 when he bypassed Parliament by appealing for support from the public after his minority government had narrowly lost a vote on a budget resolution, normally grounds for resignation. Pearson's skilful crisis management was correctly taken as evidence of how important television had become, and how much that had hurt the import of Parliament itself. But the crucial fact was that Pearson just couldn't sell himself or his team effectively to the electorate, at least not enough to secure the kind of majority government so many people seemed to want. Particularly in 1962 and 1965 the polls showed he'd managed to snatch 'defeat from the jaws of victory' (see chart 11.1), a sure sign that his campaign style didn't work well.[56]

Why? Well a considerable part of the answer lay in the fact that Pearson just couldn't shine on television. He came across as 'a smart-aleck,' claimed Keith Davey, whether because of his famous bow-tie, his style of speaking (he suffered from a lisp), or his mannerisms (he had a tendency to smile at the wrong moment, say, when he was telling people just how bad unemployment was). He could never relax on television, even though many people found him marvellous in casual and intimate surroundings. 'He had a tremendous self-consciousness in the midst of television apparatus,' reminisced Richard O'Hagan, an adviser. 'Unlike many public men, he found it difficult to elevate himself, to motivate himself to give a spirited statement or deliver a speech with vigour sitting isolated in front of a television camera. He found it all terribly impersonal.' The result was that Pearson's advisers hired experts and produced suggestions to make his manner more easy and his image more appealing. Rarely was a leader subjected to more indignities, and rarely did a leader submit so patiently, to suit the notorious image-makers. None of this worked. Pearson just couldn't convince enough people that he was a leader with 'the right stuff.'[57]

There was a great sense of relief among reporters when, in 1967 and 1968, they could turn to the transfer of leadership. The masters of television, of course, were especially pleased with the prospect of new faces. The Conservative leadership convention of 6–9 September 1967 was carefully designed as a television spectacular, so that the party could put behind it the in-fighting of the past and hype the new leader, whoever he was. 'After all, it was live for only a few people,' noted an organizer, 'so in convention planning we decided that we were really holding it in four million living rooms.' Some 2,000 prime seats were set aside for the news media. Colours were picked that would show right in the living-room. There was close consultation with CBC and CTV people to ensure that they could cover events for maximum effect: that aim affected not only the placement of television facilities but the scheduling and timing of speeches and the like. The planners even insisted that hospitality suites be closed during plenary sessions so that no roving camera would catch a tipsy delegate, drink in hand, to show viewers at home. The planning apparently paid off. Gallup indicated late in October that 61 per cent of its sample thought the newly selected Robert Stanfield was a good choice, a finding confirmed by the party's sudden rise in polls (see chart 11.1). A later report indicated people found him responsible, experienced, dependable, exactly the sort of man to give Canada the style of leadership lost when St Laurent had fallen a decade earlier. Evidence that this favourable impression might not last, though, came with the note that 'public opinion was formed by sight of rather than knowledge of the man' – people were relying on the TV image again.[58]

The change wasn't long in coming. The Liberals thoroughly upstaged their opponents when Pierre Elliott Trudeau appeared on the scene. Trudeau was a relative unknown, until as minister of justice he grabbed media attention by introducing bills to liberalize the country's moral legislation in December 1967, just around the time Pearson announced his retirement. The year's centennial celebrations had proved an occasion for an orgy of patriotic expression, at least in English Canada, and left the impression that Canada really was a dynamic and innovative land. The lingering euphoria fitted exactly the emerging image of the intellectual-cum-swinger that Trudeau soon disported, a Canadian Kennedy who seemed quite unlike the other shop-worn contenders. Even so, Trudeau soon revealed that his philosophy suited well mainstream Liberalism, a fact that made him acceptable to delegates and power-brokers in the party.[59]

No matter: reporters spoke in awestruck tones about his abilities, his mind, his style – 'everybody was having orgasms every time he opened his mouth,' was the sour comment of Dalton Camp (then a leading Conservative) about the press. Stanfield's qualities could only pale by comparison: his apparent unease in front of the cameras, his slow and hesitant manner, his lack of fire made him seem more old-fashioned, indeed just plain old and dull. Trudeau himself told reporters they were to blame, if anybody was, for his entering the leadership race, when he finally made public his intention to run in February 1968. But that was misleading. In fact Trudeau's rise in popularity was carefully masterminded by his friends Gérard Pelletier and Jean Marchand, plus the team they built, which included assorted Montreal and Toronto insiders. Simply put, these people used the infatuated news media to sell Trudeau first to the party and eventually to the electorate.[60]

Television was crucial to their strategy. Trudeau was a TV natural, certified such by Marshall McLuhan who later talked (as usual, mysteriously) about his 'soothing' and 'cool' image that had something for every age. Now Trudeau did have an unusual face, which photographed well on TV: angular and smooth, fitted with a high forehead and expressive lips and eyes. But the real reason for Trudeau's TV skills lay in the fact he was something of a showman who had, as George Radwanski claimed, an instinctive 'sense of drama and timing that most professional actors would envy.' He knew how to appear charming or firm, how to be witty or sincere, how to seem humble or shy, whatever the occasion might demand. He had the treasured ability to make 'a personal contact' with the television audience. Little wonder Trudeau's organizers went to great pains to control access by the journalists and to exploit any film opportunities, even if that meant accommodating camera crews and not newsmen.[61]

As a matter of fact, though, Trudeau benefited much more from free or 'wild' coverage on newscasts and public-affairs programs, a privilege that had little to do with his organizers and a lot to do with the enthusiasms of the TV newsmen. He'd pretty well been designated the front-runner, even before he entered the race. His skilful handling of Premier Daniel Johnson of Quebec at the federal-provincial constitutional conference at the end of January was highlighted on newscasts. He appeared on CBC's 'Newsmagazine' on 23 January, later on 'The Public Eye,' 'The Way It Is,' and eventually CTV's 'W5.' The Sunday before the opening of the convention at Ottawa in early April, 'The Way It Is' made it official, via poll results of course, that Trudeau was the man to beat. A few days later, presumably for the edification of delegates, Ottawa's CJOH-TV ran a pre-taped interview of Trudeau by his admirer Patrick Watson, which seemed to reveal anew that here was a man of great substance and depth, of compelling honesty. The convention itself was again treated as a spectacle, cameras and reporters zooming in to pick up the most intimate conversations (notably the LaMarsh outburst when she called on Paul Hellyer to join the stop-Trudeau forces). Eight camera crews gathered around Trudeau, which made him the central attraction of the whole extravaganza. Afterwards, it was estimated that around seventeen million Canadians had viewed or heard at least a portion of the last day of the convention. Was it any wonder that newspaperman Maurice Western would call Trudeau 'the anointed of the television establishment'?[62]

The election campaign became, at times, 'more like a joyous coronation,' as crowds gathered to see, hear, and maybe touch the new 'pop star' of politics. Personalities and style dominated campaign activities and campaign coverage, even if Stanfield and Tommy Douglas (the NDP leader) tried desperately to emphasize issues and policies. Liberal organizers sent Trudeau, dubbed by one wit 'Pierre de la Plaza,' off to shopping centres, malls, town squares, and the like, to deliver simple speeches, full of hope but not of promises, for maximum television exposure. Douglas and Stanfield relied more on the traditional type of meeting, a less-exciting spectacle on TV because it lacked the colour and the pizazz of Trudeau's stops. At long last there was a so-called TV debate among the three party leaders, which, ironically, proved a bore, since there wasn't much opportunity for a clash between Trudeau and Stanfield. The most exciting moment occurred by accident right at the end of the campaign, on the evening of 24 June, at the St Jean Baptiste Day ceremonies: while Trudeau and other dignitaries watched, and the cameras recorded the events, the separatists staged a demonstration that swiftly turned ugly; the near riot drove off the others, but not Trudeau, who stayed to face the separatist anger, an image of courage that was sent into TV homes across the nation. It seemed a concrete affirmation of all things apologists had said about Trudeau as a leader for today and tomorrow. 'I just want you to know I've been a Conservative all my life,' a caller told a Trudeau organizer, after watching the event on television, 'but Trudeau's got my vote tomorrow.'[63]

Trudeau finally won the majority that Pearson had hungered for: 46 per cent of the popular vote and 155 seats. Although his charisma touched just about all kinds of Canadians, his support was skewed towards the young and the affluent, especially in the big cities, the very people who were so enamoured of novelty. A Gallup survey just before the election revealed, for example, that while 62 per cent of people between the ages of twenty-one and twenty-nine thought Trudeau a good choice as leader, only 43 per cent of those fifty and over agreed. The addition of one million first-time voters to the electoral lists no doubt helped the Liberal cause. Post-election reports indicated the party had won more than twice as many votes in the upper-middle and upper classes, measured, that is, by years of education and income. And the Liberals actually increased their lead in the big cities over the totals in 1965 – they picked up 68 per cent of the votes in communities that had more than 500,000 people and sixty-six of eighty-five constituencies available in the country's nine largest cities. Whatever

Trudeau may have said about his 'Just Society,' he had crafted a victory of the 'haves' over the 'have-nots.' The well-off city folk were the kinds of people who got caught up in that peculiar brand of mass hysteria called Trudeaumania, where normally sane individuals came to feel an emotional loyalty to the man and, so, a strong involvement with politics. I can recall, that strange spring, standing outside an Ottawa hotel with my wife and parents, and a crowd of other well-wishers, just to get a glimpse of the great man.[64]

The Trudeau phenomenon owed its life to the media and, in particular, to television. I don't mean to suggest that Trudeau was wholly the creature of the image-makers. Later events would prove beyond a shadow of a doubt that he was nobody's creature. But the fact is that he couldn't have shot to stardom without television carrying his charisma into the homes of Canadians. In the midst of the excitement, journalist John Marshall talked about 'the telescoping of time' that had seen Trudeau emerge from obscurity to reach the heights of victory within six months. That was the first indication, in Canada at least, of what Austin Ranney has called TV's 'fast-forward effect,' the way the coverage itself has the result 'of speeding up the worlds it portrays, including the world of politics.' Diefenbaker, Pearson, and Stanfield had been involved in politics for years before being blessed with leadership. Trudeau hadn't – he'd come to Ottawa only in 1965. He was able to leap all barriers, to act a bit like a political superman, because television gave him the necessary boost.[65]

Canadians experienced a striking example of the new political importance of television only a few years later, during the October Crisis of 1970. On the evening of Friday, 16 October, Prime Minister Pierre Trudeau appeared on television to justify his government's imposition of the War Measures Act. The terrorist Front de libération de Quebec had taken direct action to foster its dream of national revolution and Quebec's independence. FLQ members had seized British trade commissioner James Cross and later provincial cabinet minister Pierre Laporte (whose body would be found on 17 October). There were pro-FLQ demonstrations in Montreal. There was pressure on the provincial government to negotiate, perhaps to reconstitute itself as a coalition, with representatives from outside groups and the separatist camp. Fear of an upheaval was spreading quickly throughout Quebec. Elsewhere the public's mood was understandable tense. Trudeau gave a superb performance: he spoke of the need to resist 'crude blackmail,' to buttress the rule of law, to safeguard 'freedom and personal security,' to banish fear. These words were important. They represented an effort to call into play the well-known Canadian respect for law and order. Yet what I remember is his presence – his impeccable dress, his solemn manner, his stern expression, his cool delivery. There indeed was an icon of power. He was the man in charge, just the leader needed in a moment of crisis. It was a marvellously effective appeal to our hearts and minds. Not everyone was swayed, of course. But most people were. Trudeau's performance had set the tone for the nation's response, and polls later showed that a whopping 87 per cent of the country (here, at least, French Canadians differed little from English Canadians) endorsed the government's action.[66]

Whether television's influence had made 'democracy workable' or revealed the true face of politicians is quite another matter. The chief effect of television was to simplify the man and to fix an image in the minds of viewers. All of the leaders, Diefenbaker and Pearson, Trudeau and Stanfield, were a good deal more complex than TV suggested. The impression of Stanfield as a dodderer was very wrong, though he could never quite shake that image. The sense of political involvement evoked by Trudeaumania soon proved ephemeral, and Trudeau eventually suffered from his own image problem when he was identified as aloof and arrogant (although, even up to the end of his career, many people still ascribed to him positive attributes, if not heroic qualities). When he tried stunts similar to his speech on the October Crisis later in the 1970s, appealing for public support via television over wage and price controls and then an austerity package, the issue and the times were wrong. Not even a master of the art of mass communication can always succeed. Certainly the mood of anti-politics has persisted, and the habit of 'negative voting' (where people vote against a party or a leader) has grown more pronounced in national politics since 1970. It's really more appropriate to say that television, along with many other factors, has made governance more difficult, which may or may not be 'a good thing,' depending on one's assumptions about democracy.[67]

Focus 'This Hour Has Seven Days'

'*Seven Days* is part showbiz, part crusader, part ombudsman, part freak show, part through-the-keyhole titillation, part documentary,' wrote Alan Edmonds. A neat summary indeed, though it hides the fact that 'Seven Days' was also a very nice example of 'smoke and mirrors.' There was a lot of illusion in the mix 'Seven Days' offered its audience. Consider the show's format. Even though it was carefully scripted, the fact it was done live managed to communicate to viewers, as Peter Gzowski put it, 'some of the excitement and involvement that goes into it.' Sometimes that led to minor slip-ups: LaPierre, for instance, once faltered when giving his own name because he couldn't see the TelePrompTer. But going live conveyed the impression that viewers really were seeing the news 'as it happens.' Contrast this with the show's content. However radical the techniques employed to get the message across, 'Seven Days' dealt in the commonplace most of the time. It wasn't out to challenge the fundamentals of Canadian society. Admittedly it boasted a liberal ethos that could justify a critical appraisal of individuals and institutions. But its messages, whether the abbreviated editorials or the less obvious sub-texts, rarely strayed far from mainstream views, even if many people found the show thought-provoking and at times disturbing. The amalgam of novel packaging and standard opinions was, at bottom, the key to the show's success.[68]

The 'Seven Days' episode of 24 October 1965 was typical of the whole run of the series, except that by this time the production team had developed a sophistication missing in the first season (see figure 11.1). I'll use the episode of 6 December 1964 as well to provide some additional information.

The packaging is relatively easy to describe. The opening of the show might sport an image, a song, some comment designed to grab the attention of the viewer: so this episode opened on Dinah Christie, dressed in a black top with white collar, seated against a dark flickering

INTRODUCTION (1:30)
-sound of hoofbeats
-'Seven Days' logo
-Dinah Christie and KKK ballad
-shots of Calvin Craig and Jim Bevel from the
KKK interview
-announcer identifies Craig
-trumpet music
-each of the words of the show's title zoom
onto the screen
-close-ups and self-identification of Christie,
Watson, and LaPierre
-LaPierre welcomes audience
-Watson gives brief rundown of what's
coming up

1. THE COP STORY (4:36)
-LaPierre introduction
-policeman's picture appears behind
LaPierre
-action film of event (noise of sirens)
-interview of policeman at the scene of the
crime
-film interview in the police room
-film pan of the Sudbury landscape,
including cliché of smokestacks
-interview of policeman's family
-film report of the funeral procession (sound
of drums)
-LaPierre's gloss
(music and break to studio shot)

2. ELECTION STORIES (4:38)
-Watson introduction
-man-on-the-street interviews with a few of
society's drop outs
-L. Zolf in Toronto: daylight picture; serious
and staid interviews (2 people)
-J. Webster in Vancouver: night picture;
playful and humourous interviews (2 people)
-Watson and logo (some wry music)
-LaPierre and Watson: will the party leaders
be questioned?
-studio table, full of letters of viewers
-shot of the empty hot-seat

3. THE WILSON/PEARSON SATIRE (3:30)
-Christie introduction (photo of Wilson,
picture of southern Africa
-Wilson in easy chair, pipe in hand, on phone
-occasional changes in camera angles
-audience laughter
-cut to Christie

(music and pan to smiling LaPierre)

4. PENTHOUSE STORY (5:50)
-LaPierre introduction
-assorted images: LaPierre leafing through
magazine, a female bunny, cars, a film of female
and male mannequins
-Guccione interview
-LaPierre comment (*Penthouse* girls)
-interview of liberal and conservative critics
-brief LaPierre comment
-interview with a news-vendor
-a final film sequence as background to LaPierre
gloss
(cut to and pan of audience)

5. ORSON WELLES INTERVIEW (8:52)
-introduction: Welles photo, Watson comment,
photos of Welles in various roles
-Welles interview, on location, *Is Paris Burning?*
-camera focus on Welles, occasional changes of
angle, one cut back to Watson in studio
(cut to Christie)

6. GEORGE CHUVALO STORY (3:47)
-LaPierre introduction (promo picture of Terrell/
Chuvalo fight)
-film bio (complete with bits of Spanish music)
-Watson narration
-occasional comments by Chuvalo
-cut to studio photo of Chuvalo's face after a fight
(strident music and shot of audience)

7. THE KKK STORY (22:29)
-introduction (3:31)
-Dinah Christie comment
-satire of KKK appearance before House Un-
American Activities Committee (the pointed
head of KKK member)
-film on civil-rights activities (Watson narrates)
-interview (19:45)
        -picture of two KKK members, Craig and Sly,
        arriving on stage, then brief interview
        -later arrival of Bevel
        -Hoyt intrudes (roughly 11 minute mark)
        -Hoyt suggests 'shake hands' (at 18:35)
        -KKK members exit
-LaPierre comment (0:13)

CLOSING (1:40)
-Watson's invitation to call in
-Christie and ballad, the credits roll by
-announcer closes show

Figure II.I Outline of 'This Hour Has Seven Days,' 24 October 1965

background that suggested flames, the sound of hoofbeats in the distance, singing a ballad about the Ku Klux Klan. Then followed a short cut from the main item (the KKK story), the introductions of the hosts, and a brief run-down of some of the forthcoming highlights.

Each 'Seven Days' episode (excluding the 'Document' weeks, of course) featured a collage of items, seven in this episode (nine in the case of the episode of 6 December 1964), which included documentaries, interviews, satire, and brief comments by the hosts. Some items were light, others heavy. The first item on 6 December 1964 dealt half-seriously with the condition of Ringo Starr (who'd just had his tonsils out), followed by the Duke of Windsor reading a tribute to Winston Churchill who'd recently turned ninety. In the episode of 24 October 1965 two satirical sketches provided the necessary touch of relief, although the 'man-on-the-street' piece boasted a bit of humour as well: the Vancouver segment was playful, with Jack Webster and the interviewees trying to outdo each other. But the emphasis was on the most serious items, such as the Lévesque interview on 6 December or the KKK interview here. It wasn't always an interview, mind you, though 'Seven Days' had a preference for the drama and excitement resulting from the testing of opinions.

A couple of items might be grouped in a longer sequence. The episode of 6 December had three 'colour' stories – about a black physician in a small Canadian town; an interview with the 'jazz-loving' new president of the United Nations, who happened also to be African; and an interview with one of the Canadian nuns who'd survived the Stanleyville massacre in the Congo. The KKK story in this episode was actually made up of a satirical sketch, a very brief film report on civil-rights activities in the South, and the actual interview with the Klansmen and the black activist.

Viewers were carried forward by a constant tide of words, images, and sounds, which allowed little time for rest and reflection. A swift camera close-up, a sharp musical note, a little quip from a host, all were used to keep attention. The camera, for example, focused for a few moments on the empty hot seat while Watson noted that Pearson and Diefenbaker hadn't yet agreed to come and be interviewed (see frame 11.1). The Chuvalo story ended with an enlarged photograph of the boxer's bruised face after one of his previous bouts. By contemporary standards, 'Seven Days' was extremely fast-paced, zipping along from item to item. That did make it an exotic at the time.[69]

It requires more digging, though, to reveal the views of 'Seven

Frame II.I Telling it like it is?

Days.' I'll deal in detail only with three of the items in this episode: the cop story, the *Penthouse* story, and the KKK story. Each of these embodies some of the most common mythologies present in the series, and for that matter in the wider society. They also highlight the way in which 'Seven Days' carried out the journalist's game of honouring and dishonouring both people and ideas.

The cop story considered the death of one Sgt Larry Connell, a Sudbury policeman killed in the line of duty (trying to apprehend a mental patient), who'd left behind a family of four, including a new-born baby. On the surface it looked a bit like filler, made up of some footage from the local station plus a couple of interviews, which served as a sad commentary on the small tragedies of daily life. Another angle on the story, not pursued here, would have led 'Seven Days' to puzzle out why the police had been after a mental patient in the first place (he was apparently on leave from hospital), and why that patient opened fire.

But Connell's death was given a more substantial meaning because his story was taken as representative of all policemen, who were honoured as the servants of the community. Underlying the approach was that old staple, the mythology of individualism. The interviews with an anonymous policeman and with Connell's wife made clear that Connell was a regular joe, a good husband and provider, who took his duties seriously and meted out justice with an even hand. LaPierre's gloss at the end of the item underlined this message of celebration:

Video	Audio
Closing image of 13-year-old daughter (a lost face). Side-shot of policemen carrying a coffin. Front shot of the entourage. Distance shot of the entourage, showing spectators gathered around. Side-shot of policemen laying the coffin by the grave site.	[Sound of drumbeats – dirge.] **LaPierre**: There's nothing very sensational about Larry Connell's story. He wasn't the first Sudbury policeman to be killed on duty. There are 27,000 policemen in Canada. Most, like Larry Connell, are ordinary men, doing an ordinary job. Getting killed is sometimes part of that job.

We are face to face with one of democracy's heroes, a man who lost his life trying to defend the social order. The fact that the item honoured the police is an interesting commentary on the conservative charge that 'Seven Days' was forever undermining the country's institutions.[70]

The *Penthouse* story was in a quite different vein. Here the obvious target was the hypocrisy of the kind of soft-core pornography peddled by *Penthouse* and *Playboy*, occasioned by the fact that *Penthouse* had just entered the English market. The interview with Robert Guccione, publisher of *Penthouse*, offered an excellent portrait of the slick man, as a type of person, living in a lavish apartment, full of himself and of glib talk about how he was leading a moral revolution in England. That was balanced by an interview with two critics from the Presbyterian *British Weekly*, both individuals typecast. The liberal-minded Christian talked about 'cancerous tripe' and 'masturbatory imagery,' though he refused to see the need for censorship and touted the virtues of education; his conservative colleague, by contrast, believed the effect of *Penthouse* was to 'nibble away ... at the standards of common life,' so the result was both 'harm' and 'threat.' The next interview with a

Frame II.2 Lecturing the masses?

news-vendor simply showed that the British public was buying the magazine, whatever the moral concerns about its content. It's revealing of the times that 'Seven Days' didn't carry a single comment from a woman about these girlie magazines – I must presume it wasn't thought proper to ask a woman what she thought about such matters. In any case LaPierre made clear that the whole business of a moral revolution was a blind. The trouble with the 'formula of instant sex,' he emphasized at the end, was that it said 'nothing about liberating women' – women 'climb obediently out of their clothes, and back into their chains.' Surely that was enough to dishonour the porn-vendors?

Beneath that message, though, was a reflection on the ills of modernity, the fact that affluence had brought with it the transformation of people into objects. LaPierre, the narrator, tried to make this very clear in his opening statement (see frame 11.2), before the actual mini-doc:

Video	Audio
Camera focus on LaPierre who	**LaPierre:** ... *the Playboy/Penthouse*

uses arm and hand motions to emphasize his points.
In the background, photos of a car, then of a car with an attractive woman lying in front.

policy of [stumble] selling a fast hip world, made up of fast cars and fast girls, is, of course, very exciting. But there seems to me to be a certain flaw in the ointment. I get confused because the editors of these magazines seem to feel that objects are ... [stumble] ... have more personality than human beings. And so you begin to wonder whether the girls in maga- zines could be dummies, fantasy girls, girls without blemish ...

Then the screen filled with images of female and male mannequins, while LaPierre explained that the 'adman' had come to recognize the commercial virtues of turning women into a 'piece of merchandise' to exploit the fantasies of 'the jet-age male.' The whole story was reminiscent of the many critiques of what affluence and advertising were doing to the human spirit, critiques that were all too current in liberal circles during the prosperous 1960s. The necessary revolution, it seemed, was not to shore up outdated moral standards but to liberate men and women from the adman's grasp.

The interview with Calvin Craig and George Sly, two Ku Klux Klan leaders, revealed just how far 'Seven Days' would go to dishonour a cause the team disliked. The segment was introduced with a brief satire of the appearance of the KKK before the House UnAmerican Activities Committee in the United States, all to show how dumb and hypocritical the group was (at the end the KKK character took off his hat to reveal a pointed head). Then followed a film report in which Watson's narration plus images of the civil-rights agitation suggested that the KKK was really made up of terrorists, who incited violence in the South to defeat the just cause of the blacks. Finally, the two KKK leaders, in full dress, appeared for their interview, shortly and unexpectedly to be confronted by the arrival on stage of a Reverend Jim Bevel, a young, black, civil-rights leader (see frame 11.3). During the course of the long interview, however, things went awry: the KKK members, especially Calvin Craig, the Grand Dragon of Georgia, got the better of Bevel. So the moderator, Robert Hoyt, stepped in, and posed a series of questions designed to embarrass the KKK. At the

Frame 11.3 The strange discussion

end he suggested that Craig, Sly, and Bevel shake hands to confirm a deal to have a conference to solve racial difficulties in Georgia. There was no way the KKK guests were going to shake hands with a black. Sly left the stage. Craig, correctly, charged Hoyt with intent to shame, and then he too left. 'They told us they rather liked this "nigra fellow," ' commented LaPierre, 'but they never did shake his hand.' What great theatre. 'Seven Days' had proved its point.

Again, though, there was more to the contest than simple entertainment. It provided an opportunity to trot out all sorts of liberal verities. One obvious theme was the virtue of talk: Hoyt justified the arrival of Bevel as an opportunity to discuss matters and, later, pushed the notion of the conference to clear the air, reveal truth, or at least produce a compromise. Talk, after all, was better than violence. Second, the story enabled Watson, Hoyt, and Bevel to lament the evils of ignorance and prejudice: what made the KKK so hideous was the fact that it believed in racism and practised violence, and Hoyt kept hammering away at these points. Finally, the interview itself allowed these liberals to propose the vision of a community of free men, marching forward in harmony and progress. Hoyt, in particular, assumed the priority of the idea of brotherhood: 'one way or another,' he preached, 'we're all members of the human race.' The dramatic ending, the proposal to shake hands, was from this perspective a way of getting all parties to admit that grand fact.

Note that all three items carried with them a heavy freight of morality. That's not just a comment on the liberalism of the day; it applies to much of the journalism, on television anyway. Indignation was one of the stocks-in-trade of public affairs. 'Seven Days' very often assumed a pose of moral arrogance from which it could condemn or praise. It presumed not only that there was a 'right' and a 'wrong' way of doing things, but that social betterment was indeed a real possibility. The task was to reveal abuses, uncover hypocrisy, and educate the public. This thrust, I would suggest, fitted very well the times. A later, more cynical generation might well find 'Seven Days' and its ilk a trifle tiresome.

12
On Viewing

It makes people lazy. They don't bother to read books. Children learn a lot of bad expressions and, if they watch too much, they lose their initiative to do things themselves. It is convenient for parents to get rid of children while they do something.

An anonymous non-owner on television, 1955[1]

On 12 January 1963 *The Financial Post* printed a line graph that recorded the 'toilet flow' registered by a Toronto pumping station during the course of a day. The water pressure dropped dramatically when a television program was interrupted or ended by commercials, and the peaks and valleys were particularly obvious during the primetime hours. The nation's bathroom habits were being dictated by television's offerings. The graph was merely further incidental proof of just how extensively the habit of viewing had penetrated into the routines of Canadian life.

The Video Habit

Boredom was one of those hidden but none the less real curses of modern life. Outside of agriculture, the hours of work of the paid employee had been falling for quite some time, down from about fifty hours a week in the mid-1920s to forty hours by the mid-1950s. The arrival of labour-saving devices in the home had fostered both a higher standard of home care and a reduction in the time it took to complete many tasks. The spread of high-school education to more and more adolescents created a new 'class' of non-working dependents, who weren't always occupied by their studies. So, even if work, home care, or school remained the determining fact in the lives of most people, increasingly Canadians were faced with the need to fill spare time, to find some sort of pleasurable and fulfilling activities to wile away the hours. Leisure might mean an escape from work or an extension of work, a source of recuperation or compensation, but more and more often it was an accepted part of life. A host of industries had grown up to satisfy the increasing hunger for leisure, from that traditional source of relaxation the breweries and distilleries, to organized sports, home hobbies, tourism, and above all the mass media. Yet Peter Newman, writing in 1959, wondered whether this growth of spare time was really a boon for Canadians. After all, he mused, 'the largest portion of our off-work waking hours is spent slouched in front of the TV set.'[2]

Undeniably TV viewing was a habit that had almost immediately captured the fancy of all kinds Canadians. It wasn't at all unreasonable that an adman, interviewed by *Marketing* (27 January 1956), should categorize the few non-watchers, either the very poor or a couple of highbrows, as 'a lunatic fringe.' People picked up the habit very early in life: the survey of the TV practices of American and Canadian households in the late 1950s carried out by Wilbur Schramm and his colleagues learned that kids first discovered TV at age two and were making regular use of the set a year later, sufficient that they could shout out their favourite shows to the researcher. International Surveys Ltd reported that, in February 1957, the television was on in homes an average of 4.3 hours a day; ten years later, in March 1967, Nielsen found that the daily average was just over 6 hours. BBM's Fall Survey of 1972 noted that the normal dosage of television for every Canadian over the age of two was 22.8 hours a week.[3]

True enough, some people viewed a lot more TV than others. A CBC study of leisure in Halifax in 1958, for example, discovered that out of 422 adults, 34 per cent were light viewers (one to two hours a weekday), 44 per cent were medium viewers (two and a half to four hours), and 22 per cent were heavy viewers (four and a half to nine and more hours). On average in 1959 first-graders in Schramm's 'Teletown' (the small town of Langley, British Columbia) watched 10.5 hours a week, sixth-graders 20.5 hours, and tenth-graders 11.6 hours. A Canadian-government study of the leisure activities of nearly 50,000 people aged fourteen or over in the spring of 1972 estimated that roughly 13 per cent of the population were true fans, consuming over thirty hours a week. At the same time, an overwhelming 94 per cent of the people had watched at least one hour of television during the survey week. No other leisure activity (except listening to radio) approached this figure. According to Charles Hobart, a recreation survey in Alberta in 1967/8 involving 4,300 people aged eighteen or over reported that watching TV was among the favourite activities of slightly more than three-fifths of the respondents, well ahead of working around the house or visiting friends or playing with the kids. It shouldn't surprise anyone, then, that viewing television ranked third, behind work (or school) and sleeping, as a consumer of the time of most Canadians.[4]

The video habit grew out of early patterns of behaviour born in the radio age: in Schramm's 'Radiotown' (Quesnel, British Columbia), for example, where television wasn't available, kids read comics, listened to the radio, and went to the movies to satisfy their need for fantasy. In some measure television had only inherited the place once belonging to radio: the sets-in-use figures for radio in the evening during February 1950, for example, were comparable to roughly equivalent statistics for television a decade later. One early report in *The Financial Post* (17 December 1955) estimated that 85 per cent of the television sets went into the living-room, later the rumpus or family room, pushing out the radio (often into the kitchen). But television's status in the family did seem greater than that of its predecessor. The Goldfarb report on Canadian attitudes prepared for the Davey Committee on mass media learned that most people, and particularly young people and the less educated, would be 'most reluctant to lose' their television in any comparison with radio and newspapers. (Perhaps that choice would have been more striking if the comparison had been with the family car or pet.) The very fact that magazines and newspapers would publish features describing what it was like to give up television for a week or a month might well suggest that this was a new form of torture for the affluent generation. Not a one recommended the experiment continue indefinitely. Doing without television caused too much distress.[5]

Television-watching is akin to reading, movie-going, and above all radio-listening. In many households viewing TV retained for a couple of years some of the character of a special occasion, like going out to a play or to the cinema: so the children in one farm home were required to remove their work clothes before entering the TV room. A case could also be made for the claim that viewing carried over some of the attributes associated with a lot of work: busyness, limited initiative and effort, routine, even casual attention. Indeed one analyst, Sut Jhally, has talked about the 'labour' of viewing, and so the alienation of the TV masses, because people are compelled to spend time watching commercials to receive their daily 'wage' in the form of programs. The more optimistic Marshall McLuhan, though, described this same feature as a kind of 'paid learning' wherein people deigned to consume the ads to enjoy their favourite shows. In each case, of course, the connection was drawn between other sorts of activities, working or schooling, common in industrial society.[6]

And that by no means exhausts the analogies. The historian Peter Wood thought viewing was very similar to dreaming since television programming was so visual, highly symbolic, full of wish-fulfilment, and easily forgotten. Patricia Palmer, a social psychologist, decided that kid's viewing habits might best be seen as a form of play, both because of how they watched TV and what they did with it. Talking about adults, the TV critic Michael Arlen, a bit tongue in cheek, in his collection of essays entitled *The Camera Age* compared watching television to airplane travel, because viewing required a similar mode of passive behavior where one is carried forward by a machine through, in this case, a voyage of the mind. Another of his comparisons, this time of TV-viewing with masturbation, and thus a kind of self-abuse, was more sinister. That cast of mind was most common among critics such as Jerzy Kosinski (author of the black comedy about television, *Being There*), Jerry Mander (adman turned culture critic), and Marie Winn (the self-appointed guardian of the American family), who feared that viewing amounted to a dangerous addiction, like drug dependence, ultimately harmful to social and personal life.[7]

Usually people turned on the television set to be entertained. Yes, sometimes these same viewers might feel a duty to watch a newscast, perhaps turn on a religious broadcast or some Culture for uplift, but these were not the normal reasons. Early on in the days of Canadian television, the president of a TV Owner's Association in Toronto, A.A. Marshall, declared that what he wanted in the evening was 'relaxation, not uplift.' That was normal. 'I work long days and when I come in at night I like to watch something to take my mind off my problems for a while,' an annoyed farmer wrote to the CBC, some years later. 'If you like to come home to a discussion on world affairs or opera you either don't have any trouble or you don't work.' Whatever else may be said about changing fads or fashions, the ratings data demonstrated time and again that most viewers were almost always in search of relaxation and diversion.[8]

Yet it would be wrong to think that viewing was always the same kind of experience. The impression cultivated by all too many critics, and some journalists, that viewers were typically a collection of slack-jawed, glassy-eyed videots, caught up in some sort of a trance, just didn't fit what happened in front of the small screen. Viewing wasn't only a passive activity, or non-activity. Rather there were and would remain certain styles of viewing, reflecting the different experiences, moods, and purposes of members of the audience. That's why Patricia Palmer was able to count eleven distinct kinds of behaviour – she called them 'interactions with television' – apparent in her 'lively audience' of Australian children.[9]

When newcomers were first introduced to TV, they usually watched the set with rapt attention. According to a report in *Canadian Broadcaster & Telescreen* (18 March 1953), the sets-in-use index for the evening hours in TV households was double that in radio households. People were filled with a sense of wonder: everything seemed exciting, even the commercials if one could believe Grace Secord, an early TV owner. Alphonse Ouimet told the story of an old sports fan who got so excited watching his first telecast of a baseball game on a set of Ouimet's cottage ('His eyes were just riveted on the screen') that the poor soul suffered a heart attack in the midst of the game. Peter Morgan noted that the natural tendency of any family when they first purchased a set was 'to go on a TV binge in which the program itself is far less important than is the thrill of watching a show in one's own home.'[10]

That sort of fascination didn't necessarily disappear as television became familiar. Miriam Waddington, the television critic of *Canadian Forum*, argued forcefully that the TV set had an 'absorbing enslaving quality': she couldn't think of another activity that so completely engaged a person's senses. Enjoying a program required the viewer to surrender to the demands of the moment, be these Sid Caesar's 'imaginative comic values' or 'the homefelt delightful corniness' of 'Holiday Ranch.' One slightly distraught mother recalled how her son David became oblivious to what was around him when watching some brand of television violence. 'He once sat through The Lone Ranger with a nail sticking up in his shoe, and though it had drawn blood and was painful, he didn't notice it till the shooting and shouting was over.' Viewing could be an intense experience.[11]

What attracted some viewers, of course, repelled others. That contradiction was best illustrated by the different reactions to incidents of violence in sports or drama. Four out of ten people, and about half of the men, questioned in the Goldfarb poll admitted to a taste for 'fighting on TV,': 'This is the spice of life.' / 'It's human nature.' / 'I'm a sadist.' / 'Livens it up more.' / 'Excitement makes a show entertaining.' / 'I like action. It's stimulating.' But there were more viewers, including nearly 70 per cent of the female respondents, who found violence unpleasant, even indecent: 'Most of it is unnecessary.' / 'Uncontrolled emotions are a lack of strength of character.' / 'We see enough of it in the world today without watching it on TV.' / 'Violence upsets me.' / 'It interrupts the hockey game.'[12]

It wasn't at all unusual for people to get upset or involved in a program.

The Goldfarb poll learned that one in three Canadians admitted to talking back to their radio or television. Any disturbance in the normal schedule was bound to bring complaint, as Ernie Bushnell and Stuart Griffiths discovered to their astonishment when a flood of protest greeted their decision to drop CJOH-TV Ottawa's regular fair of variety and drama to cover the Kennedy assassination. The CBC received a constant stream of letters, full of both praise and blame. The 1958 showing of a physics series on CBLT's 'Live and Learn' brought nearly 1,500 letters to the station, only 17 critical. The broadcast of a documentary on American television, 'Report from the Wasteland,' aired on 'The Critical Years' (21 May 1962), elicited exclamations of delight and pleasure from viewers disturbed by Primetime America. Yet writers also found time to protest the fact that a woman on the panel of the quiz 'Fighting Words' had 'a cigarette dangling' from her lips; that the TV personality Joyce Davidson should be able to continue on 'Tabloid,' even though she had made certain unwelcome remarks about the Royal Family on an American talk show; or that the newsman Stanley Burke was apparently allowed to get off scot-free, after accidentally making some unspecified 'blasphemous remarks' on air involving 'our Saviour.' A good deal more poignant were the letters sent to politicians and to the CBC president in mid-1969 when the news came out that 'The Don Messer Show' was due to be axed because it lacked youth appeal. One admitted 'pair of old timers' said it was a favourite program, and they wondered why everyone in those days had 'to cater to the youth of today.'[13]

But the passage of time did make most adults much more blasé in their normal response to television's offerings. 'By the time I got my set, the novelty had worn off for both me and my friends,' wrote R.G. Lewis, editor of *Canadian Broadcaster & Telescreen* (3 February 1954), 'and I found I could look at my watch, turn on *Dragnet* or some other program of my choice, look at it, and then switch off the set to return to my book or whatever I was doing.'

In fact what American researchers soon discovered was that many supposed viewers were often distracted by other activities, if not oblivious to whatever was on the screen. As much as a third of the time, nobody was paying attention when the TV set was on in the evening hours. It wasn't just that people did a lot of talking while a show was on. Or that family members wandered in and out of the TV room. They also ate, dinners as well as snacks. Children would play around, fight, or get dressed in front of the set. Students might try to study, women to do housework. Couples even made love when the television was on. Sometimes watching television led to sleep. 'Often, if I don't turn it off,' Lewis commented, 'I doze off to waken with a start when it goes silent.' Many viewers wouldn't watch the whole of a show: a CBC profile of the audience for a performance of *H.M.S. Pinafore* on 'CBC Folio' found that only half had watched the whole thing, the others citing such reasons as the arrival of company for breaking off viewing or just coming in from a visit with friends for watching the last portion of the operetta.[14]

Besides, research indicated that the eyes of actual viewers often wandered away from the screen during the course of an evening or a program. It wasn't at all unusual for people to ignore commercials completely. This 'tuning out' was a notable problem for admen, after viewers had witnessed a powerful scene, say, in a drama or a play. The episodic character of televised sports and newscasts meant such shows were likely to lose the interest of a portion of their audience at various times during a broadcast. The tests carried out by Schwerin Research showed how individuals responded quite differently to the assorted singers and sketches, liking some segments but being bored by others, that made up the variety shows aired by the CBC. Is it any wonder that the Canadians interviewed during the course of the Goldfarb poll decided that television required much less 'concentration of energy' than newspapers (though not, of course, radio)? In short, viewing could be a casual affair, demanding little of the individual and easy to do even while other aspects of life went on merrily about him or her.[15]

Perhaps it was the very ease of watching television that made it seem like just another way of wasting time. American researchers detected a certain amount of guilt among people when they admitted just how often they turned on 'the idiot box.' Writer Hugh Garner extolled 'The Joys of a Sabbatical' one summer when for two months his set 'was on the complete blink,' which allowed him to rediscover the pleasures of reading. Vivien Kimber recalled how she felt a little thrill of pride when her husband discovered her reading a magazine rather than watching a show she had yearned to see. 'Why did I feel so smug and virtuous about it?' Even the kids in 'Teletown' said that they would be happier if their friends found them reading a book instead of watching television. The CBC's Halifax study claimed that only a few people would watch more television if they had an extra hour of 'spare time' – rated higher was going out, hobbies, sports and outdoor activities, even (slightly) working on the job. Viewing, especially a lot of viewing, clashed with the ethic of self-improvement, the stress on achievement that still bedevilled people's attitudes towards leisure. Children showed a marked preference for doing something other than just sitting in front of the TV: the survey of Calgary's children in 1976 learned that two-thirds of them 'would prefer play or talking with friends.' Watching television was stamped early on with the label 'time-wasting,' making it a peculiar kind of activity very similar to doing nothing at all.[16]

None the less the extraordinary popularity of viewing showed that it did satisfy a range of needs. It was one of the most convenient sources of both fact and fantasy. Just about anyone could go to the set to find comfort, relaxation, diversion, or release. Research soon learned that the most susceptible people, and among the heaviest viewers, were lonely kids and lonely seniors, often suffering from low esteem, who got the illusion of companionship by settling down with television. Watching TV was something of a cure for the jangled nerves of the harried housewife or the distressed office-worker: you could focus on something else, perhaps someone else's troubles, to get away from your own problems. The survey of Calgary's kids found that their chief motives for turning on the set were, in ranked order, because they were bored, feeling lonely, wanted to be alone, or were sad. But it was also a way of avoiding unpleasant or routine things: the child could delay doing homework, the mother her household chores, or the husband the paying of bills. Watching television was one of the easiest ways to escape from real life, especially from the ills of boredom.

The Mass Audience

The ways people used television fitted into existing patterns of family life and social activities. The television year saw viewing totals at their peak in January and February, when winter kept families indoors, and at their lowest in July and August, when people were off enjoying summer fun. During any typical week, viewing was higher on the weekends, especially on a Saturday when more people were free of work or school duties. During a weekday, noon and afternoon television was for the ladies of the house, late-afternoon TV (roughly 4:00 to 6:00 PM) for the kids, and the night-time for a mass of older viewers, especially so after 8:00, the children's bedtime (see chart 12.1). The evening-viewing profile invariably took the shape of a hump: audience totals grew over the first two hours (6:00 to 8:00) when families finished their suppers and gathered in front of the television set, reached a peak between 8:00 to 10:00, and then slackened off rapidly as mother and father retired to bed.[17]

Almost immediately observers began to wonder about the preferences of these viewers. What was really at issue was whether television served a mass audience, as commercial broadcasters presumed, or a series of minor-

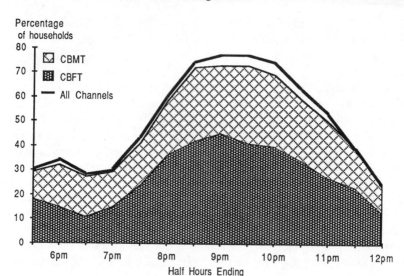

Chart 12.1 Viewing totals, Montreal, spring 1957
Source: Data from BBM, *Television Area Report Spring 1957 Survey*

ity audiences, as the CBC and the royal commissions argued. There was no doubt that people did have idiosyncratic tastes. 'My tastes run from the artier of the CBC's dramatic programs which I catch over Toronto to the bloodiest of the whodunnits, which catch me from Buffalo,' wrote R.G. Lewis in 1954. 'Music, I feel, is disillusioning when you see the artists; quiz shows and discussion panels depend on who is on them; they haven't latched onto a good news formula yet; and telecasts of sporting events are too exhausting.'[18]

Lewis was a fortunate viewer, though. Not only was he a bachelor, and so didn't have to worry about the likes and dislikes of others, but he was living in Toronto where people could get a number of different stations. Most Canadians wishing to turn on the TV set, especially during the 1950s, found themselves victims of 'enforced viewing,' either because they had only one channel available or because there was only one set in the household, which often meant the individual must submit to whatever the family willed would be the evening's pleasure. There were on average three people watching TV in each household on a Sunday evening at 8:00 PM in the 1958/9 television year, for example. Only from the early 1960s, chiefly because new private stations in the big cities eliminated many 'captive' markets and there was a slow increase in the number of homes that had a second TV, were viewers offered more and more choice in what they could see each evening. As usual, of course, people living in much of rural Canada weren't so fortunate because alternate signals just didn't reach their homes.[19]

Central to any understanding of this audience, though, remained the fact that viewing was, above all, a habit. The primetime audience was indeed a mass audience, and that underlay many of the difficulties that the CBC had to suffer as long as it tried to buck the trend. Paul Klein, once NBC's chief programmer, pointed out how the sets-in-use at any given time was ordinarily the same whatever the television schedule. The pull of television itself was so strong that most families succumbed each night unless otherwise engaged in an outing, a party, or the like. That guaranteed a larger audience for Radio-Canada's public-affairs show 'Les idées en marche' than could be expected on the basis of viewer preferences – a fair portion of the audience watched because there wasn't any other French-Canadian show available. A CBC investigation of viewing habits during the Montreal producers' strike of early 1959, moreover, disclosed that nearly half of the married persons surveyed admitted to little change in their patterns of TV-watching because of the disruption in normal programming. Gathering around the set was apparently a ritual of evening life in their homes.[20]

Klein also argued that people searched across the dial to find the 'least objectionable program,' since rarely was there any show that satisfied their particular tastes. The key, then, was not to offend, to produce a show that wouldn't grate on the nerves of any significant group of people. The most popular shows won top honours because they were scheduled at the best hours in the evening and because they did entertain people of all kinds. There was some evidence for such claims. What really drew readers of *Le Devoir* to their screens were the drama favourites 'Le gendarmerie royale' and 'La pension Velder' – in fact wrestling attracted more of these 'discriminating' viewers than did most public-affairs or Culture programs. Similarly, a greater number of women in BBM's February 1965 report of CBFT's ratings watched 'La soirée du hockey' on Saturday night than watched 'Le pain de jour' on Wednesday night.[21]

Audience levels were quite predictable over the course of a day, a week, or a month. A group of British researchers working on data from the late 1960s and early 1970s found that you could actually estimate, in Britain and the United States, the proportion of people in an audience who would watch a series in two consecutive weeks, regardless of the program. They added that the largest chunk of the audience was normally made up of heavy viewers, whose devotion to TV ensured they would watch just about anything; what made a show a hit, ironically, was that these faithful were joined by light viewers. Early on, CBC's Audience Research made clear that 'timing,' 'regularity of placing,' the appeal of that type of programming, as well as the draw of shows before and after the broadcast in question would normally have a major effect on the size of its audience, whatever the merit of its content. The concept of 'audience flow' was based on the presumption of viewer inertia: programmers assumed that a lot of viewers would stay put with the first channel they'd tuned unless something really special forced them to switch to a rival. Get them early, and the odds were you'd have a large number of them for the rest of the evening.[22]

But Klein's 'least objectionable program' theory was too cynical – and simplistic. People really weren't quite as sheep-like as some programmers assumed. Some viewers were on the look-out for glamour, action, excitement, even upset; others wanted more realism, more complexity; and still others preferred gentle or homespun programs. And surveys indicated that the individual gave his or her loyalty not so much to a channel or even a genre as to particular programs. A glance at the CBC's 'index of enjoyment' proves that most people had a pretty good idea of what they relished, and that audiences expressed satisfaction with shows of all kinds, from sitcoms to election coverage. So, on a Sunday evening in 1965, a documentary on 'This Hour Has Seven Days' had a slightly higher index (85) with its viewers than the popular western 'Bonanza' (81). (*Maclean's* ran its own version of the 'flush test' to prove that more 'Seven Days' viewers stayed put in their seats than did 'Bonanza' watchers.) At least some analysts came to believe that each individual show had its own special appeal to a particular audience: what was called 'a psychometric analysis' of the audience of a 1970 show starring the pop singer Engelbert Humperdinck concluded that the 'likers' in the audience were middle-aged, conservative-minded housewives, rather blah (lacking curiosity), very motherly, distrustful of change or ambiguity, fearful of harm, but desirous of routine and order and the esteem of others. Readers shouldn't take that kind of finding too seriously, though, since it really demonstrates how inane the hunt for viewer profiles could become.[23]

A glance at what happened in Toronto proves just how fickle the audience could be when it actually was offered a choice (figure 12.1). There, on 23 February 1963, the viewers had the luxury of five different channels to pick from. Although CBLT won the top honours that Saturday evening, the audience obviously shifted around a lot. If 60 per cent of homes viewed CBLT's imported sitcom 'The Beverly Hillbillies' at 7:00, then a half-hour later 40 per cent were watching Jackie Gleason's variety show on WBEN.

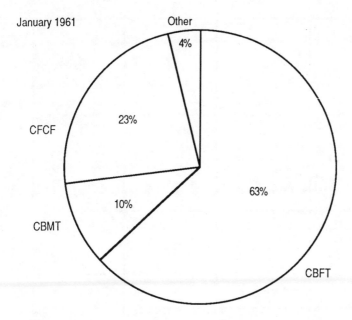

January 1961

Chart 12.2 Where did the French-Canadian audience go?
Source: Data from Elliott-Haynes Ltd, *Teleratings January 1961*

Yet not even episodes of top-ranked American dramatic series such as 'The Defenders' or 'Have Gun Will Travel' on the Buffalo station could compete with the appeal of CBC's hockey broadcast. That said, viewers could catch both series on the two Canadian channels at other times in the week. The great feature of competition was that the Toronto audience usually had two opportunities to watch the best of American entertainment in the course of any week, because both the public and private stations carried so many imported programs.

Montreal's viewers were not quite so advantaged, since they normally lacked direct access to American channels. But the bilingual public, which was largely French Canadian, could choose from among the francophone and anglophone services. A survey of the preferences of francophones in January 1961 indicated that the Anglo channels got about a third of that audience over the course of a week (chart 12.2). Their share was even greater on the weekend. The higher total of the private station, CFCF, was evidence that its emphasis on popular entertainment was paying off. What most attracted French Canadians to the Anglo channels was the imported

	CBLT	CFTO	WBEN	WGR	WKBW	total homes (000s)
7:00-7:30	'Beverly Hillbillies' AMN sitcom 60%	'Stoney Burke' AMN a/a drama 06%	'University of Buffalo' feature 11%	'Dragnet' a/a drama 05%	Movie anth. drama 18%	359
7:30-8:00	'Nurses' AMN prof. saga 27%	'Stoney Burke' AMN a/a drama 05%	'Jackie Gleason' variety 40%	'Sam Benedict' prof. saga 10%	'Gallant Men' a/a drama 17%	440
8:00-8:30	'Nurses' AMN prof. saga 29%	Movie anth. drama 08%	'Jackie Gleason' variety 34%	'Sam Benedict' prof. saga 11%	'Gallant Men' a/a drama 17%	453
8:30-9:00	'Red River Jamboree' CDN variety 37%	Movie anth. drama 10%	'The Defenders' prof. saga 18%	'Joey Bishop' sitcom 25%	'Mr. Smith' sitcom 10%	425

9:00-9:30	Hockey CDN sports 56%	Movie anth. drama 06%	'The Defenders' prof. saga 09%	Movie anth. drama 18%	'Lawrence Welk' variety 11%	578
9:30-10:00	Hockey CDN sports 61%	Movie anth. drama 05%	'Have Gun, Will Travel' a/a drama 06%	Movie anth. drama 17%	'Lawrence Welk' variety 11%	567

Figure 12.1 The Toronto audience and its choices, 1963
Note: The programs on the two Toronto channels have been identified according to origin, either 'CDN' (Canadian) or 'AMN' (American). Among the descriptions of the program genres, 'anth. drama' indicates anthology drama and 'a/a drama' action/adventure drama. The percentages in each time-slot indicate the proportion of the Toronto audience watching the show. The data taken from McDonald Research Ltd, *TPR Television February–March 1963*.

American drama, notably action/adventure series such as 'Naked City,' 'Maverick,' 'The Aquanauts,' and 'Route 66.'

The likes and dislikes of viewers reflected the social realities of Canadian life: the significance of place, language, sex, age, and to some extent class as well. Perhaps the hardest question to evaluate was the importance of place. Not only was there a dearth of comparative statistics, but the relevance of what did exist was confused by the remnants of 'enforced viewing' plus substantial differences in the degree of choice available. None the less, the amounts of viewing did vary by setting, city, and region: the country folk, at first anyway, watched a bit less than the city folk (perhaps people in the cities went to bed later?), viewers in such places as Halifax and Regina (where alternatives weren't plentiful?) were more avid than their fellows in Toronto and Vancouver (which could boast more pleasures to attract people out of the home?), and people watched more TV on the Prairies (at times almost an hour more) than in British Columbia (perhaps the west coast's famed milder weather was a cause?). Less puzzling was the fact that country-music shows such as 'Don Messer's Jubilee' and 'Country Hoedown,' in International Surveys ratings of November 1960 and 1961, proved much more popular in the Maritimes and on the Prairies and in farm and town than elsewhere in the country. But why did football and even hockey broadcasts earn more favour in the big cities – was it because such professional sports were closely identified with urban loyalties? Maybe the greater cosmopolitanism of the city audience, and its awareness of the stars of entertainment, accounts for its liking for the 'Ed Sullivan' and the 'Danny Kaye' shows. And the fact that 'Front Page Challenge' reached a higher percentage of homes in Ontario than in any other region could be put down to its highlighting of Toronto personalities.[24]

In any case the different likes and dislikes of anglophones and francophones are much easier to spot and to explain. All in all, French Canadians were more avid fans of television, and especially made-in-Canada television, than their fellow citizens. The Québécois bought TV sets more rapidly than Quebeckers or Ontarians. Francophones in Montreal watched a bit more television than did anglophones in an average week (although people in 'Winterpeg' early in 1962 recorded much higher viewing totals than people in Quebec City). The 'Top Ten' programs, the ratings winners, in the two language communities invariably showed that the francophones were much happier with their own fare (table 12.1). Poll results merely confirmed these lessons. The CBC's own survey of Canadian opinion learned that Anglos were not very satisfied with made-in-Canada variety

TABLE 12.1
The top ten, January 1964

CBC	Radio-Canada	CTV
1. 'Hockey Night'	'Poule aux oeufs d'or'	'Hockey Night
2. 'Bonanza'	'Belles Histoires'	'Walt Disney'
3. 'Ed Sullivan'	'Le pain de jour'	'Jack Paar'
4. 'Beverly Hillbillies'	'Cinéma international'	'Dr. Kildare'
5. 'Perry Mason'	'Cité sans voiles'	'The Littlest Hobo'
6. 'Ben Casey'	'Heure des quilles'	'Mr Novak'
7. 'Hazel'	'Tête d'affiche'	'Eleventh Hour'
8. 'The Lucy Show'	'Filles d'Eve	'McHales Navy'
9. 'Flashback'	'Insolences d'une caméra'	'Zero One'
10. 'Juliette'	'Adele'	'The Saint'

Note: Foreign shows underlined. Data from *Nielsen Television Index*, January 1964

and light entertainment, and above all that they were upset by the quality of local drama. French Canadians were not only pleased with their brand of song and jollity but actually enthusiastic about the primetime téléromans made in Quebec. The Goldfarb poll of 1969 learned that over two-thirds of Québéçois preferred Canadian television to its American rival, whereas only one-quarter of Ontarians were so persuaded. This francophone love affair with Canadian television may well have been, in part, the result of some visual bias on the part of French Canadians. Right from the beginnings of popular journalism, back in the 1880s and 1890s, francophones had never taken quite as eagerly as anglophones to the dominance of the newspaper – or so circulation figures suggest. But much more important was the fact that so much of Radio-Canada's programming reflected what was unique in Quebec's past and present. That's why Radio-Canada earned the nickname 'tribal medium.'[25]

The importance of sex and age is a bit hard to disentangle. The profile of the changing composition of the audience one Sunday in Vancouver shows just how the proportions and totals of grown-ups, children, and teens, as well as adult males and females, fluctuated over the course of an evening (chart 12.3). The rise and fall of the child and teen share is one striking feature – they constitute about one-third of the audience up until 7:30, and that was true on weekdays as well. Estimates by Nielsen argued that in 1966 children viewed about 15 1/2 hours a week, teenagers slightly over 21 hours, which suggests that viewing was a very important aspect of that much-touted youth subculture of adolescents in the 1950s and 1960s. The other striking feature was the number of women in front of the set,

Percentage
of viewers

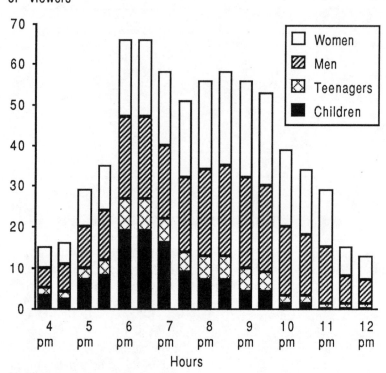

Chart 12.3 Vancouver's Sunday, 1963
Source: Data from McDonald Research Ltd, TPR *Television*
February–March 1963

which almost always was slightly greater than the number of men. That
was even clearer in profiles of the weekday audience. Nielsen's estimates
of 1966 for women were close to 29 hours a week, men close to 24 hours,
a substantial difference of 5 hours resulting in large part from the fact that
women were much more available for viewing television during the daytime.
They merely confirmed the old truism about separate spheres: men enjoyed
a wider realm of experience in the world outside, while women were still
bound more closely to the home.[26]

The sex of a viewer could be used to predict whether he or she was more
likely to prefer one type of program over another (chart 12.4). Movies

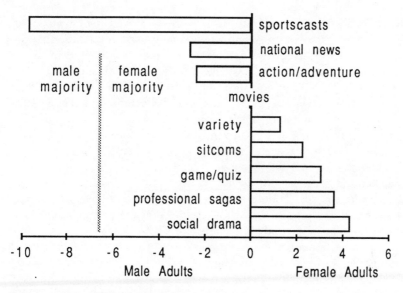

Chart 12.4 Sex and preferences, Canada, 1965
Note: Data from BBM *Television Station Reports* for February 1965, which supply
estimates of the numbers of adult males and females. The graph represents an
investigation of the characteristics of 474 separate adult-only, evening audiences
in Canada served by stations in Montreal, Toronto, Calgary, and Buffalo.
Overall there were 6.6 per cent more females than males in an audience, based
on a calculation of the actual shares for each of the forms. So what the chart
equates as preference is any divergence from the norm: more men than would
be expected produces a male preference, even though the largest share of
viewers may still be women. The dotted line indicates where women and men
had equal shares (50 per cent) of the adult audience.

appealed equally to both sexes, which suggests that the old ritual of going
to the movies, something looked forward to as a joint undertaking, had
continued, merely changing its locale from the cinema to the living-room.
Variety shows similarly had a general attraction, although certain programs
such as 'The Don Messer Show' in Calgary and 'The Red Skelton Show'
everywhere did seem to have some peculiar attraction for men. Sports were
undeniably a 'male' genre: that was the only brand of programming in
which the typical adult audience contained more men than women. This
liking carried over, by the way, into related shows such as sports round-
ups and sports news. Men had a definite taste for the action and excitement

of the playing-field and the hockey rink, a taste that was first developed in childhood by the style of upbringing then common for boys. Note that the type of contest preferred by women was the gentler competition of the game or quiz that might test knowledge rather than physical prowess. The manly taste for action, of course, explains why more males than normal turned up for westerns and crime drama. Series offering a heavy dose of jeopardy such as 'Combat' or 'The Untouchables' were especially preferred by male viewers. Men still lived in a 'macho' world. The greater attraction of newscasts also demonstrates that the pull of citizenship was a bit more compelling among men than women, though again only in terms of total viewing. This interest sometimes carried over into a liking for information about the wider world of public affairs or science: so a CBC report comparing the appeal of CBC and CTV shows found that males much preferred 'The Nation's Business' and 'The Nature of Things.'

Social drama, meaning the téléromans and American serials such as 'Peyton Place,' were clearly a 'woman's' genre (although it's worth noting that in one Radio-Canada analysis married men ranked the téléromans very high on their list of personal favourites). Such programs dealt with the wealth of problems arising from personal life, often in a domestic setting, and including romance, marriage, sickness, child-raising, the maintenance of the family, likewise a world into which early upbringing and later education put the female. Equally important, they featured women in leading roles with which female viewers could sympathize, if not identify. The liking for professional sagas reflected a preference for the more cerebral and gentler rhythm of these celebrations of doctors, nurses, lawyers, and teachers, as well as the fact that such series often incorporated elements of social melodrama by focusing upon friendship and even romance. So too the sitcoms whose setting was often the family, though here at least the appeal of comedy was such that many men would come to the screen to view a hit like 'The Beverly Hillbillies.'

Not surprisingly these sex differences occurred fairly early in childhood when viewers were especially on the look-out for role models. A CBC study of children's tastes in 1956 found that boys preferred action/adventure in which males were highlighted – 'Circus Boy,' 'The Lone Ranger,' 'I Search for Adventure,' 'Superman,' and 'Wild Bill Hickok.' By contrast girls went for social drama, comedic or gentle, where female characters played out significant roles: 'Father Knows Best,' 'I Love Lucy,' 'My Friend Flicka,' 'Oh Susanna,' and 'Annie Oakley.' 'La famille Plouffe est le programme que je préfère,' said one Jocelyne Savard, aged eleven, 'parce que cette famille représente la réalité d'après moi.' As a child grew up, whatever his or her sex, however, that child typically showed an increasing desire for more action and more realism. So a CBC report (1957) on the ill-fated historical saga 'Radisson' found that its appeal was much greater among kids in grades 5 and 6 than those in 7 and 8. A similar kind of study (1958) also indicated that older children demanded a faster pace in whatever kinds of programs they watched. My own survey of ages and audiences showed that children watched a surprising amount of news, which hinted at an effort by parents to teach them what was going on in the world.[27]

Television catered much less to teenagers as a group than, say, to children or women. Where a show did sport a teen flavour, it could win the hearts of adolescents: Schwerin Research in the mid-1950s found that teenagers liked episodes of two variety shows, 'The Jackie Rae Show' and 'Cross-Canada Hit Parade,' which featured fast numbers and rock ('Hit Parade' offered Bill Haley and His Comets, which the test audience of adults heartily disliked), a finding confirmed a decade later by the appeal of rock extravaganzas such as 'Shindig.' Teenagers didn't like news and information, plus most professional sagas, both of which explored what for many must have been a boring adult world. Otherwise, the statistics don't make clear just what suited the teen taste, perhaps an indication that this taste was still not a very distinct quantity in the Canada of the mid-1960s.

Very few Canadian studies probed the different habits or tastes fostered in adults by the very process of growing older. *A Leisure Study – Canada 1972* did indicate that American findings probably applied to Canada: the government researchers found that the oldest people (65 plus) were more likely than not to be heavy users of television. Retirement often left people with a lot of time on their hands, too much time, which given the problems of frail health or limited resources meant that they spent more hours with television than did other adults.

As to tastes, McDonald Research Ltd did break down the grown-up audience into those aged 20 to 34 and those 35 and older, presumably because advertisers were interested in reaching the young adults who were busily engaged forming families and buying lots of products (see chart 12.5). The assorted kinds of drama seemed to capture the fancy of both age groups. The younger adults, however, clearly showed a greater interest in the extraordinary, the sports contest or a movie, whereas the older adults had more of a passion for regularity, what was routine. Just as American studies demonstrated, the audience for news and information programming was skewed towards older viewers who had the time and the inclination to follow public affairs. Likewise I'm tempted to believe that the apparent preference of the 35-and-older group for variety and games indicated their

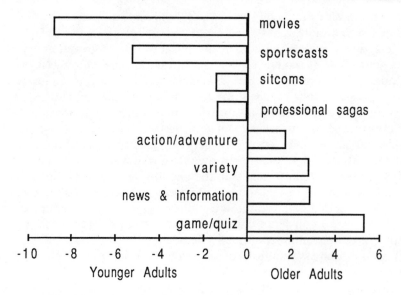

Chart 12.5 Age and preferences, Toronto, 1963
Note: Based upon an analysis of all audiences for one week's programming
from 6:00 to 11:00, inclusive, in Toronto, the data derived from McDonald
Research Ltd, *Time Period Ratings: Television February–March 1963*. Note that
there were invariably many more old adults than young adults watching shows.

liking for fun and trivia over the action and energy that highlighted the
sports contest. What the Goldfarb poll of 1969 uncovered was evidence
that people over 44 were much more impressed by Canadian shows and
Canadian television (and by Canadian magazines) than youth. This finding
bears out the presumption that the faster pace of so much of American
television was oriented towards the tastes of youth. But more important
was the fact that growing old in Canada engendered a loyalty to things
Canadian, especially when this was reinforced by greater consumption of
news about the life and affairs of the land.

The last major influence on viewing was class, better yet the social milieu
and the attitudes born of the effects of education, occupation, status, and
income. Once again, contemporary data are very sparse. Well-educated
and high-income Canadians did watch less television, as they claimed in
the Goldfarb poll, if only because their tastes and their money encouraged
a wider range of leisure activities. Perhaps, as well, many of these viewers
enjoyed more the educational and highbrow offerings on the tube. One

Radio-Canada study, for instance, found that in 1960 a larger percentage of the readers of Montreal's élite newspaper, *Le Devoir*, watched programs of this ilk, such as 'Tribune libre,' 'Pays et merveilles,' 'Concert,' 'Arts et lettres,' and 'Carrefour,' than did the readers of the city's popular dailies. Yet American reports warn against carrying the argument too far: Gary Steiner found that the so-called class viewer watched much the same kind of entertainment show as did the mass viewer, even when presented with a definite choice.[28]

What is clear, however, is that this 'class' viewer, in Canada as in the United States, was a good deal more critical of the normal television fare. Another survey by Radio-Canada, this in 1958, learned that the popularity of 'La famille Plouffe' was much less among the better educated. Similarly, a Schwerin Research report on the English version, 'The Plouffe Family,' found that 'liking' for the show declined as the income level of the audience increased. (Besides, recall that the show was about working-class or lower-middle-class life, not about the well-off.) The CBC's own poll of Canadian opinion in 1962 noted that well-educated Canadians were more disturbed by the apparent readiness of the networks to accept all kinds of commercials. But the most intriguing enquiry was published by *Le Magazine Maclean* (March 1965) based on the responses of white-collar workers, business people, and professionals when questioned about the virtues and defects of Montreal television. That brought forth a litany of complaint: the CBC was too heavy, the independent station too light, American television too banal, the famed téléromans too drawn out, the teleplays 'trop morbide,' and so on. Upscale Canadians regarded themselves as more discriminating viewers, and thus bound to find fault with what was offered. Indeed such people were likely to speak loudly about the need for worthwhile television, whether that be quality entertainment or more educational programming, even if in practice they didn't always select that programming when it was available. Hypocrisy was an all too common sin.[29]

Undeniably, some people were angered by the wealth of mass entertainment. There was 'a vast public,' according to one writer to the CBC, 'who are crying for something that is more than a waste of time in T.V. viewing.' Another expressed disgust 'to see so much time, effort, money frittered away on "garbage." ' The Goldfarb poll noted that people of strong views (and little tolerance) often attacked the favourites of others. But, time and again, polls also showed that people were reasonably satisfied with their television fare. No doubt the most gratifying finding of the CBC poll of 1962 (to its designers anyway) was that nine out of ten Canadians thought the Corporation was doing a 'good' job. Likewise a majority of Canadians (51 per cent), according to the Goldfarb poll, had decided that television gave them a greater 'sense of satisfaction' than did newspapers (27 per cent) or radio (18 per cent). They believed that TV was the 'most exciting,' 'most relaxing,' and by a slight margin the most involving of the big three. Television might not win rave reviews – but clearly it did please much of the time.[30]

Life with Television

A new authority had come into being. Canadians realized that television had swiftly acquired a lot of significance in ordinary life. Three out of five people, according to the Goldfarb poll, thought that television was unquestionably the 'most influential' of all the media. That influence resulted from its special character: television was more pervasive, 'sensational,' 'factual,' 'educational, open, and frank' than radio or print. Although a lot of people recognized that 'a television camera can distort the truth,' most still rated its credibility high because it was a visual medium that brought 'reality to life' – seeing really was believing: 'The picture tells the story and the memory lingers.' / 'More people watch TV and you can "see" it.' / 'The picture shows me. You're right there.' / 'Appeals to more people; affects all your sensory perceptions.' / 'You look at it and it makes an impression on you.' Two out of three emphasized that television had its greatest effects upon 'thought and life-style,' on people's attitudes towards 'travel, sex, love, marriage, family, political enthusiasm, clothes styles, student movements, personal habits, and profanity.'[31]

People weren't altogether pleased by this development, however. Only about half the public, according to a Gallup report in 1966, were willing to call TV 'a good influence on family life,' whereas two-thirds had been so persuaded a decade earlier. Back then, Frederick Elkin's survey of suburban parents found they were generally satisfied with the way TV had educated and entertained their children. But now the proportion of optimists was smaller among individuals aged thirty or older. About one-quarter couldn't say whether TV was good or bad. This kind of statistic was evidence of the steady growth of something I'll call TV phobia.

The roots of the fear of television were complex. Its origins go back to the early 1950s, and concerns about the dangers posed to life and values by the forthcoming video age. Television clearly hadn't realized the aims of the highbrows: it had been captured not by the fans of Culture but by Hollywood and commerce, the merchants of vulgarity. The proclamations by Marshall McLuhan about the forthcoming demise of print culture didn't give much comfort to people still wedded to the power of the Word. Among the general public, nostalgia for some past time of simple family pleasures, say when people gathered to play games or to chit-chat rather than to look at 'Ed Sullivan,' played a part in cultivating misgivings about TV. So too did that general worry about technology, and what it was doing to present-day life, which had become increasingly evident during the 1960s – television was one of the foremost of the new machines that now seemed to have a sinister purpose. There was even, towards the end of the 1960s, a scare about the radiation hazards posed by emissions from the television set. Then there was the continuing guilt about watching television: such a time-waster must have an ill effect. Right away, people worried about the consequence of watching too much TV on people's eyes, especially on kids, who were wont to snuggle up close to the television set. Indeed the kids' passion for television frightened both parents and teachers, the traditional childhood authorities, since TV seemed to establish a direct, unmediated link with the hearts and minds of their charges. What pleased parents was the notion that television might be educating their children; what fright-ened parents was that this education might result in thoughts and actions alien to the family. Nobody likes to see their authority usurped, especially not by a machine over which they have little control. It wasn't really surprising that much of the controversy swirled around this one issue of kids and television since common sense suggested that their unfinished personalities were most vulnerable to any ill effects of television.

The TV phobia was grounded in the culture of our times. It was, as Dennis Giles and Marilyn Jackson-Beeck have pointed out, a modern 're-presentation' of the age-old myth of the 'evil eye,' and such a superstition couldn't easily be banished by fact or argument. The maxim about 'seeing is believing' had its dark side, the belief that anything able to command the power of the eye could become a tyrant of men's minds and souls. Wasn't television technology's way of producing a better eye? Hadn't it invaded all manner of public and private spaces, including the home? Didn't it rule the lives of its addicts? 'It is all too easy to become lost in admiration and fall under the hypnotic sway of this magic box,' wrote Peter Morgan back in 1954. 'Hour after magical hour slips away and before very long the entire pattern of family living has changed to fit the daily schedule of the monster in the living room.' It was natural that alarmists would conclude the extent of the TV addiction represented a dangerous retreat into unreality, that moralists would argue the plethora of violent program-ming on the little screen could not but debauch the TV masses. And it was inevitable that some people would exploit the paranoia, often by turning

McLuhan on his head. So in 1977 Marie Winn published *The Plug-In Drug*, which told Americans that they must turn off their TV sets to protect their children, and themselves, from all manner of ills. A year later came Jerry Mander's *Four Arguments for the Elimination of Television*, which, as its blurb stated, found TV inimical 'to personal health and sanity, to the environment, and to democratic processes.'[32]

These and other works of alarum were able to draw upon a wide spectrum of more scholarly accounts. Academe had not been slow to exploit the TV phobia. The public's apprehensions fuelled a new growth industry in the social sciences in Great Britain and especially the United States: psychologists and sociologists began to churn out more and more research projects, some funded by government, mostly about the impact of TV violence. The first studies on kids and TV, notably *Television in the Lives of Our Children* by Wilbur Schramm's team in 1961, won a lot of attention from journalists who tried to summarize the findings for an anxious public. The book's very cautious conclusion that TV might or might not have ill or good effects, depending on circumstances, didn't satisfy troubled parents, though it did establish what became a pattern of inconclusive results. During the 1960s and 1970s, researchers alone or in teams carried out an incredible variety of tests: showing films to children who later were set loose to bash Bobo-dolls (Albert Bandura), long-range surveys of violent programming and extensive polling of heavy viewers (George Gerbner), efforts to prove a link between violent viewing and catharsis (S. Feshbach), comparisons of towns before and after television (Tannis Macbeth Williams), probes of television and fetishism (H.J. Eysenck and D.K.B. Nias), 'disprovals' of the whole laboratory approach (D. Howitt and G. Cumberbatch), and on and on. The field was littered with claims and counter-claims. Governments got into the act, of course. At the end of the 1960s the U.S. National Commission on the Causes and Prevention of Violence commissioned a number of studies on the issue, none of which seemed able to establish a convincing case for the idea of TV's banefulness. In Canada in the mid-1970s the furore led the Ontario government to sponsor the Royal Commission on Violence in the Communications Industry, complete with more research studies, and the CRTC, the Symposium on Television Violence. Neither of these enterprises had any more success uncovering the hard answers the public wanted. One can sympathize with the claim made in 1976 by André Martin, the CRTC research director, that TV remained 'an enigma.' Social science had failed. The controversy goes on even today, albeit at a less frenzied pace – ironically a new generation of researchers trained in such exotic disciplines as semiotics have begun to produce results which suggest that TV may be a friend rather than an ogre.[33]

All this earnest academic inquiry wasn't wasted, though. It did produce a wealth of information about the impact of television on ordinary life in North America from the 1950s through 1970s. (I've carried my analysis into the 1970s, in certain instances to take account of the 'legacy' of TV viewing.) Some of the attributes of television were fairly obvious; others could be surmised from all these data. The TV phobia only survived because of superstition: obviously, the dire predictions of social or cultural disaster had proved unfounded. Likewise McLuhan's prophecies of a revolutionary change in human culture were woefully exaggerated: there were definite limits to the power of TV. Television couldn't claim the influence over private behaviour routinely exercised by family, friends, or even peers. And, as a rule, real-life experience at play, at work, in the supermarket, at home was a much more important teacher than was television – a striking ad campaign might lead a person to buy a product but only her satisfaction would guarantee a second purchase. Nor, of course, could TV usually act alone: television's import depended upon the messages of the other media, the social milieu, a person's views and situation, the circumstances of the moment. Most important, TV obeyed the iron law of mass communications: as a rule, mass media have worked best to reinforce the already existing values, attitudes, and fears of the populace rather than to change them.[34]

TV, moreover, had relatively little effect where it couldn't satisfy self-evident needs. The initial fascination with television did cause observers some worries. A report in *Marketing* (10 October 1958) on the situation in a town in British Columbia talked about fewer children going out to play, less socializing among adults, even a trend towards less complicated dinners and snacking. That fascination passed, of course. Attendance at concerts or operas or plays and, at least after the first effects of television's surge had worn off, professional sports events as well wasn't damaged. One international study by UNESCO discovered that the spread of the viewing habit only resulted in a total reduction of sleep time by thirteen minutes. Schramm's survey of kids in 'Radiotown' and 'Teletown' learned that television cut play time by about a half-hour a day, bedtime was pushed back by eleven minutes, and homework lost a mere fifteen minutes a week.[35]

But television did consume much of the spare time a person or a family might have spent with other forms of passive recreation, and that remained true long after the novelty of ownership had warn off. So the spread of television was especially hard on the media that had once served up fantasy and entertainment to the masses. People found that they could secure pleasure more cheaply and more efficiently from television: Schramm reported, for instance, that TV's children took time away from radio (especially radio drama), movies, comics, and pulp magazines offering adventure and violence to watch westerns, sitcoms, and the like. The position, though not the stature, of print was slowly undermined because the reading habit began to lose its hold on the general public, though it remained strong among upscale and well-educated Canadians. And overall television forced the rival media to offer a more-specialized fare to reach particular segments of the public.

The effect on the book industry was uneven. Fiction borrowing at libraries was hurt: one analyst, Rodolphe Laplante, found that there was a modest decline in the lending of novels (though not biography or history) at a Montreal library between 1953 and 1955. Worth noting is the fact that the CBC researchers learned nearly 60 per cent of the people they interviewed in Halifax in 1958 had not read a book in the previous month. The American publishing industry, the source of so much of the reading matter consumed by Canadians, adjusted to the new times: between 1950 and 1970 the number of new titles in the realms of fantasy fell from 22 per cent to 13 per cent of trade books. But titles promising aid to the individual (the pocket-book, the body, the diet, and the mind), true stories of the past or present, exposés and reminiscences, and so on were in increasing demand. Brian Stewart, writing in the CBC Times in 1959 about children and television, detected a definite tendency towards 'non-fiction in reading.' A government leisure report in 1972 claimed that 70 per cent of the Canadian population did read in their leisure time, although the reading group included 'relatively fewer people' with a below – grade 9 education and in the blue-collar work-force of the people under twenty-five. Overall, then, television worked to limit the popularity of reading fiction, especially among people with a limited education, but not of reading fact. It should be added, as well, that television apparently didn't harm quality fiction: that brand flourished in English Canada during the 1960s and beyond.[36]

The impact of television on the movie industry was much more immediate and dramatic. One optimist, J.H. Fitzgibbons of Famous Players Canada, had predicted in a piece for *The Financial Post* (23 February 1952) that the advent of television could only benefit movies. These were 'famous last words.' Movie-going was particularly vulnerable to the spread of television because movies offered a more expensive and less convenient brand of visual entertainment. According to one report, also in *The Financial Post* (15 March 1958), movie admissions dropped by 50 per cent in Quebec City when television went on the air. In 'Teletown' both the movie-house and the drive-in theatre closed down after TV came. Overall, the number of movie theatres in Canada fell by 523 (or 25 per cent) between 1955 and 1960. Most striking, though, was the collapse in motion-picture ticket sales: dropping from 247,733,000 in 1952 (with the population about 14.5 million) to 107,705,000 in 1960 and a mere 78,918,000 in 1970 (when the population had reached 21 million). Going to the movies might remain important as a special occasion, notably among the young (nearly half of the movie audience was under 24 by 1972) where it was a part of dating and 'having fun.' It could no long claim to be a mass ritual as in the 1940s, however. What Hollywood and its associates did to stem the decline was to produce movies for special groups (such as teenagers) as well as to exploit an increasing taste for violence and explicit sex among the public that television could never dare to satisfy.[37]

By contrast the challenge of television fostered something of a transformation of radio during the 1950s. At first there were lots of people ready to predict radio's eclipse. Sales figures of radio sets did fall off, briefly. Listening totals were significantly lower in TV homes than in radio-only homes: by almost three hours a weekday in April 1957 in Vancouver and Victoria according to International Surveys Ltd. Besides much of that listening had shifted from the evening, when viewing dominated, to the daytime and especially the morning hours. National advertisers poured their monies into television. The American broadcasters stopped producing the radio shows that had been so prominent on the CBC's own networks. The situation even compelled the CBC to close down one of its two Anglo networks, the Dominion service, in 1962, although the Corporation's own stations continued to offer much the same kind of content as before to a devoted but declining audience. Money for radio productions was tight because of the insatiable demands of television. There was an exodus of radio talent to television. People at the top gave little direction, a sign of their lack of interest. The gloom and doom that afflicted the producers and fans of public radio was understandable: one of these producers, Sandy Stewart, spoke of the sense of bitterness that spread through what some unkind colleagues in television now referred to as the 'blind' service.[38]

The changed environment pointed the way to a renaissance for the rest of the industry, however. Private radio moved towards a new rolling format of nearly constant music, broken by news, sports, time and weather checks, commercials, and hosted by a special on-air personality called a disc jockey. Soon stations also began to boast a particular style of music to appeal to a segment of the audience: in the mid-1950s, for example, CHUM-Toronto became a Top-40 station, playing the popular hits to win over teenagers. Instead of the mass audience, lost to television, radio now searched for minority audiences, offering them a daytime companion and a music box tailored to their needs and tastes. The technique worked. Radio served individuals rather than the family: it was, above all, a source of background noise while people did housework, studied, drove, whatever. Radio sales had picked up even before the end of the 1950s, aided no doubt by the arrival of the transistor radio. Indeed more and more homes owned two or more receivers, plus a car radio. In 1965 Fowler II noted that since 1950 the number of radio stations had more than doubled to 321, as had the number of receivers to an estimated 10.4 million. Admen were impressed: the Hopkins, Hedlin report for the Davey Committee a few years later recorded the fact that the radio industry had greatly increased its revenues from both national and local advertising. Success had brought its welcome reward to the entrepreneur once again.[39]

Canada's 'troubled magazines' should have been so lucky. The Canadian industry had always been feeble because of the economics of culture: its own market was dominated by overflow circulation from the United States. The situation had grown worse after 1950, in part because of the rise of billboard advertising and of those American 'children,' *Time* and *Reader's Digest*, that reduced the amounts of money available to made-in-Canada magazines. But the competition of television for the advertising dollar and for readers was even more severe. The share of net advertising revenue going to Canadian consumer magazines dipped from 4.2 to 2.4 per cent between 1954 and 1968. During the 1950s, apparently for the first time, the number of magazine deaths in Canada surpassed the number of births. The actual circulation of magazines fell by over a tenth between 1959 and 1969, though the Canadian industry suffered even more, losing a quarter of its sales. By the end of the 1960s, one-time giants such as *Canadian Home Journal, Liberty, The Family Herald*, and *The Star Weekly* had disappeared from the scene. Even a survivor, such as *Maclean's*, struggled throughout the 1960s, without much success, to find a formula to woo readers and dollars sufficient to ensure prosperity. Only the specialized magazines geared increasingly to the tastes of the affluent city-dwellers had a bright future. Television was a much more effective and appealing national medium, whether for brand-name advertising or for reflection and discussion, than general-interest magazines. Little wonder Goldfarb found that by and large Canadians didn't consider magazines of much importance in the television age.[40]

The effect of television's arrival on the daily newspaper was much slower, and more insidious. Over time, television journalism worked to upset the news primacy of the press, something that even in its wartime heyday radio news had never been able to do. In 1958, for example, CBC researchers in Halifax found that more people rated the newspaper the 'greatest' and 'most reliable' news source. Yet within five years, the CBC could proudly claim that its newscast was 'more reliable and believable than news from any of the other usual sources,' noting in passing that the newscasts of private television also earned a lot of respect. And by 1969 Goldfarb stated baldly that television was 'the most believed and most important medium for international news and for Canadian news of national importance.' That survey also revealed Canadians thought television really outshone newspapers for reports on special events, for example, the American landing on the moon.[41]

One result of this shift was a decline in the quantity of foreign news appearing in daily papers. Another was a greater emphasis on coverage of the local scene where newspapers still seemed the best source to the public. A third was a renewed interest in publishing opinion, and finding appealing columnists, thus taking over some of the attributes of the magazine. What was obvious from circulation figures, though, was that these changes didn't eliminate the threat from television. In the mid-1950s, there were slightly more copies of daily newspapers around than there were Canadian households, which suggested just how central and useful the newspaper was, especially in an urban setting. But by the end of the 1960s the figure had shrunk to 82 newspapers per 100 households, which showed that a growing number of people – particularly the young and the less educated – found less and less need for a daily paper. That was especially true in French Quebec, where only two out of three individuals told Goldfarb they normally read a daily.[42]

Yet if television was both a thief and a usurper, it was also a powerful agent for the 'cause' of mass communication. Television often took the messages generated by another medium, be that popular novels or Hollywood's movies or front-page news, and distributed these to a wider audience. It was widely believed in the 1960s (and beyond) that the items the Toronto *Globe and Mail* in particular featured on its front page in the morning would be highlighted on the CBC's evening news. Subjects first noted on television would spark some people to go off to their library, read a newspaper or a magazine, in search of further information. The rise of television, moreover, coincided with an increase in the amount of time people devoted to the mass media each day. All in all, then, television moved the mass media into an even more central position in the lives of most Canadians.[43]

Television could play many roles in family life. No doubt television sometimes did schedule events, such as suppertime and the kids' bedtime. On Sunday nights, for instance, Ernie Dick, in the 1950s a farm boy living outside Leamington, Ontario, was able to get his bedtime extended to 9:30 or 10:00 to watch assorted family favourites. Parents often treated the set as a kind of electronic baby-sitter to keep children happy and quiet, especially when engaged in household duties. A CBC study of children and viewing in 1958 found that most of the sample were watching TV between 5:00 and 6:00 PM, just before supper, presumably while mother prepared the meal. John Brehl, one of those who tried to live without 'the idiot box,' rediscovered just how noisy a house with seven children could get without the calming influence of television. Television might also work to harmonize relations between the spouses and within the family. Vivien Kimber thought television 'a wonderful peacemaker': the common act of watching a show, and talking about it afterwards, eased the little tensions between her and hubby. Another housewife claimed that television kept parents at home with children, 'especially on Sunday nights,' making 'for a much nicer family relationship.' Watching Saturday-night hockey was a family ritual in the Dick house. And television supplied friends and neighbours with a reason for a social gathering – to see a show normally – or with topics of conversation, since watching was such a common experience. Indeed talking about TV was second only to 'family interests' in one survey of the substance of social chit-chat. One of the problems with giving up the set was that people lost contact with an important part of the shared reality of life.[44]

All this togetherness wasn't without a price, though. Viewing gave birth to that wretched practice of eating dinner in front of the set (done by up to 60 per cent of Wingham's households, if one can believe the statistics) as well as that sin against the palate, the infamous TV Dinner. More seriously, television seemed to reduce the amount of time devoted to conversation within the family circle, and to focus some portion of the remaining conversation on the programs and messages it carried. The kids became so wrapped up in their shows, Vivien Kimber lamented, that they didn't notice when their father came home or even speak to their parents. By the same token parents often reduced the time they might spend playing with their children. TV producer Len Lauk lamented, as had many others, that the past custom of reading nursery rhymes to children (and he could have added fairy tales and other stories) had largely disappeared. 'Children don't seem to get read to at night. TV puts them to sleep, rather than a parent reading them a story.' Television habits also worked, in some instances, to reinforce the isolation of the nuclear family: Tannis Williams's study of three British Columbia towns in the early 1970s, one of which had just got TV, indicated that the viewing habit did lessen participation in community events, notably local sports.[45]

But the most obvious consequence was that control of the television set became a new source of conflict, especially in dealing with children. Mary Jolliffe talked about the difficulty mothers had getting children pried loose from the set to do their chores. Kimber told of a battle she had forcing her daughter to go to bed (full of tears of course) and so miss a favourite sitcom, 'Father Knows Best,' which had been rescheduled to a later time at night. Frederick Elkin learned that the mothers of suburbia often had problems regulating when and what their children watched. Middle-class homes, in particular, usually had rules about how much television could be watched and when it could be watched. One family in Toronto's Forest Hill, a well-off neighbourhood, in the early 1950s, for example, had placed a total ban on TV from Monday through Thursday. Right through to the end of high school, recalled Ernie Dick, his parents allowed their children one hour of TV per weeknight between 7:00 and 9:00, later 10:00 PM. His parents, like many others, were in the end much more concerned about how much he watched rather than what he watched, even when they had doubts about the quality of a program. Seventy per cent of a group of francophone youngsters claimed that their parents never gave them any guidance, or even answered questions, about television programs. Dick recalled that he found it much easier to make a case to see a particular show than to win an extension of his allotted time.[46]

When homes were given a choice of channels, then a new kind of battle emerged over what to see. In the Dick home, the males 'invariably convinced' his mother and sisters of the virtues of watching hockey. American researchers discovered that in practice children often gained control of the family set, at least in the early evening, and could usually prevail when the parents were split about what to watch. That said, 90 per cent of the Calgary homes in one 1976 survey were the scenes of clashes between youngsters over rival choices, which were usually resolved by a parent intervening. Is it any wonder that affluent families by this time were buying extra TVs to solve the problem? Such stories leave the impression of a country full of households where there were daily skirmishes, usually very minor of course, among children and parents in a long-running war over the use of television.[47]

The most difficult question to answer satisfactorily is whether television taught its viewers anything. Understanding why, how, and most especially what requires a brief exploration of communications and learning theory. Communication is a complicated process that involves the exchange of meaning between the sender of a message and the receiver of that message. The television producer encodes his message in a fashion that will make it appealing and persuasive to as wide a range of viewers as possible. The most appealing attribute of television, of course, is that it displays visual motion: our eyes are drawn to images that are dynamic. The producer may use familiar language and images, stereotypes and clichés, jolts of violence or sex, fast cuts and mood music, a mix of close-ups and distance shots, lots of redundant and repeated information, all to capture the eyes, ears, and mind of the viewer. The viewer is hardly a helpless pawn in the hands of the producer, though. Most viewers will have what is called a negotiated response to the message, for they will bring their own perspectives to bear, decoding the message in a fashion suitable to their mentality and beliefs. When given a choice, in fact, the viewer will normally select a program that is both predictable and suitable, that fits his or her tastes and views, rather than something novel. Even then, the exchange of meaning is an imperfect process plagued by a lot of 'aberrant decoding': the message that the viewer(s) picks up isn't quite what the producer planned. That's a partial, and crude, explanation for the innumerable scrapes the CBC got into over airing programs that seemed blasphemous, immoral, left-wing, or just plain distasteful to certain viewers – they had misinterpreted the intent of the show, believing that it honoured views that they abhorred. Even more striking, though, is the fact that tests have shown viewers will sometimes actually record something in their minds that never appeared on the screen: so adolescent boys will remember a female doctor as a male, thus suiting their sexist presumptions of the way life is.[48]

The so-called learning process is no less complicated: it involves both the acquisition of knowledge and some kind of behavior conditioned by that knowledge. Acquisition depends on the viewer's frame of mind, particularly his degree of arousal, the attention he pays to what's on, his comprehension of the message, and of course his retention of this message. There are built-in problems to acquisition in the case of television. As a picture medium television has a right-brain bias: it communicates more readily with that portion of the hemisphere that stores images, sounds, smells, and emotions rather than the left hemisphere that, in most people, handles the higher thought processes. Because it must be consumed at the pace of the show itself, leaving the viewer little time to reflect and preventing a return to an earlier sequence for understanding (as in the case of a book), television can bring about a kind of 'system overload' where information tumbles down upon the individual beyond his or her capacity to retain all the bits and pieces. And given the casual nature of viewing, the fact that many people are watching television to unwind or to escape, is it any wonder that a lot of people don't pick up very much from a night's viewing? One Finnish study discovered that almost half of the viewers questioned right after a newscast couldn't recall any of its content. Still, people are more inclined to notice a message when it, or at least the setting, appears to be authentic, that is when the characters, the story, or the style seem to coincide with images of reality. People are also more inclined to comprehend and retain that message when it is repeated many times. Even then, however, acting out what has been acquired depends upon chance: the viewer must be offered or must find an opportunity to behave in the fashion directed by the message. A boy may fully understand the intent of a commercial but will often lack the money to buy the particular good; however, he may have the willpower to bug his mother to purchase the good for him. What happens should he so act, how useful the belief or action is to realizing some purpose, whether he receives praise or reward rather than retribution or punishment, will usually determine if he takes the message to heart. In short there exists a dynamic relationship among the viewer, television, and the real world about which it is difficult to generalize.[49]

The television message could have an immediate impact on some viewers, under special circumstances. Television certainly did inform the style and the content of child's play: one of the first crazes was inspired by Walt Disney's airing of the 'Davy Crockett' saga (December 1954 to February 1955), which had youngsters walking around with coonskin caps and toy rifles as pretend frontiersmen. Television offered idealized types of teenagers – of the young woman (such as Annette Funicello of 'Mickey Mouse Club' fame, a heart-throb of male teens) or of the athlete (such as Rocket Richard, the great scorer of the Montreal Canadiens). The 'Crestwood Heights' survey in the early TV years took note of the fact that TV, along with movies, had a particular impact on the peer group in upper-middle-class culture in determining role models, styles of dress, and appearance. *The Toronto Daily Star* (11 May 1961) reported that James Butler, a police magistrate in Toronto, blamed 'The Untouchables' for inspiring three kids who had burglarized a Scarborough home. The Calgary police claimed that a detailed 'how-to' story on glue-sniffing shown by 'This Hour Has Seven Days' brought on a rash of these instances in a city where previously the practice was unknown. There were occasional reports of someone imitating a television act: the 1970 showing in Montreal of *The Doomsday Flight*, a movie that highlighted an 'altitude-sensitive bomb,' sparked a telephone threat about such a bomb to a British Overseas Airways jet. In addition television could have a considerable impact on public views when the subject at issue was relatively novel to viewers: a CBC study in 1970 showed how the viewing of the documentary 'The Dying Waters' heightened the awareness of the pollution menace (although a follow-up study also indicated that this concern decayed shortly thereafter). Similarly, the films and photographs of starving children in Biafra that appeared on the screen and on the front pages of newspapers in 1968 had much to do with the sudden outpouring of public support for aid to the people of the secessionist province in Nigeria. All of this might be taken as evidence for the so-called bullet-theory of communication where the message strikes home with unerring effect, bringing an immediate response. Such cases, of course, weren't all that common.[50]

Much more important was the long-range effect of television viewing. There's mounting evidence that television did have a distinct impact upon the cognitive skills of individuals, most especially of children. It was estimated by the mid-1970s that the average child viewed about 12,000 hours of TV before the end of high school. The result was that some children, especially kids who watched a lot more TV, didn't do other things that might well have stimulated their intellectual and imaginative abilities: they were, in particular, less likely to read books, magazines, or newspapers.

Now, true enough, watching television can demand the active participation of the viewer, and so engage his or her mind, a claim put forward with a bit too much vigour by McLuhan. Understanding the television message, for example, requires a mastery of parallel processing, the ability to handle a lot of different pieces of information quickly. Furthermore, television can foster visual or spatial skills, the ability to recognize details, to integrate fragments, to interpret different perspectives. And certain kinds of slow-moving kid's programs (such as 'Maggie Muggins' or 'The Howdy Doody Show' that I recall), which were much more common on TV before the mid-1960s, can leave time for reflection as well as encourage imaginative play. But usually reading is a much more demanding intellectual exercise than watching TV, especially among experienced viewers. Reading mobilizes language skills, it requires a measure of parallel processing, it allows for reflection, it fosters day-dreaming and other mental play. Even radio is a more effective catalyst of the imagination because it requires listeners to create their own pictures. A study by Gavriel Salomon found, to his surprise, that TV-wise American kids practised a much shallower kind of viewing, meaning they invested less mental activity in processing information and retained less meaning or detail, than a comparable group of Israeli children who weren't so blasé about TV. The key element, then, is not so much the medium itself as the audience's attitude towards the medium. The viewing public commonly treats television as a source of relaxation, even a time out from thinking, which rests rather than exercises the mind.[51]

The effects of shallow viewing ran through all age groups. According to Jerome and Dorothy Singer, TV worked to hobble or supplant the imagination of pre-school children by supplying them with packaged fantasy to enjoy and act out. The relationship between a low IQ and high TV was noted in 'Teletown,' among children in the sixth and tenth grades, which didn't demonstrate that TV had 'made' its viewers less intelligent, only that such people found TV easier to use than books. Williams and her team discovered that adults in 'Notel' in 1973, the British Columbian town without television, performed better at problem-solving tasks than did those of 'Unitel' (CBC only) and 'Multitel' (four networks) – a further study completed two years after 'Notel' finally got television service suggested that here too adult skills had deteriorated. Her study, along with others, also indicated that TV viewing encouraged impatience and impulsiveness in all age groups, both of which were obstacles to effective thinking. So television, especially if used to excess, contrary to what McLuhan had suggested, could and did dull the senses. A certain amount of credit ought to go to the schools and their still fairly traditional curricula, at least until the disastrous 'reforms' of the late 1960s, for drilling so many students in the mechanics of intellectual endeavour.[52]

Did TV also dull the moral faculties? That was a more difficult question to answer. Statistics certainly showed an upward trend in crime. There was, for example, a substantial increase in the number of juveniles appearing before the courts in Canada between 1955 and 1960, the very years when television was spreading rapidly across the country. The number of adults convicted of criminal negligence, manslaughter, attempted murder, and murder doubled between 1956 (when the figure was 214) and 1968 (when it reached 438). According to police reports, the number of actual crimes of violence tripled between 1962 (44,026) and 1975 (135,424). We do know that, in certain circumstances, the viewing of violent shows can increase the level of aggression in individuals, especially among males, which can be taken as evidence that TV confirmed what was a 'natural' tendency in our society for males to use physical and verbal force to win disputes. We do know that certain people in the population, perhaps only 5 per cent but still numerically significant, are especially vulnerable to the effects of portrayals of what has come to be called 'anti-social' behaviour. Yet many factors can cause an increase in crime statistics: not just the problems of poverty and injustice or the early influences of conditions at home, but the growing number of violence-prone youth (recall this was the era of the baby boom), changes in the law and in law enforcement (the number of police officers per 1,000 people grew from 1.5 in 1957 to 2.0 by 1972), the representation of life in other media, never mind the changes that occurred in the moral temper of the times. If a lot of television programming did incidentally encourage violence, and I believe it did (and still does), then TV acted in league with a host of other agents and influences. Disentangling the particular influence of television becomes a well-nigh impossible task.[53]

There were, as well, certain crucial variables in understanding the social and moral import of television. Time and again, it's been proved that parents could play a central role in determining the effect of television programming on youngsters: by punishing a wayward child (or by rewarding that child's 'pro-social' behaviour); by explaining the meaning of a program, whether a commercial or a western; and by determining what the child watched. There's no doubt that television posed a challenge to the moral influence of the family because it breached the walls of the family, more than radio did before; there's also no doubt that many parents met and overcame that challenge, ensuring TV did little 'harm' and perhaps some 'good.' Second, the lasting impact of television was in part a function of just what the individual viewed. Too much consumption of TV's 'junk food,' especially if it wasn't countered by other kinds of intellectual nourishment, could well twist a person's view of life. The practice of heavy viewing of Hollywood's drama did lead at least some of its 'victims' to perceive life through the television lens, to see life as more violent than it really was for example, a process that George Gerbner and his associates have dubbed 'mainstreaming.' Finally, what people got out television depended very much on their own personality and experiences. Thus TV violence in the form of fantasy could reduce frustrations: it was when people took the portrayal of violence as true-to-life that imitation became much more serious. Most people learned at an early age, and certainly before they were ten, the difference between fantasy and fact on TV, which is one reason why the apparently high level of violence in kid's cartoons (where conflict was an essential ingredient) didn't much matter. Besides, Anthony

Doob and Glenn Macdonald demonstrated using data from Toronto in 1976 that the persuasiveness of TV's image of a violent society depended on whether the individual, even a heavy viewer, lived in a crime-ridden neighborhood. Or take the case of sexism: according to Bob Hodge and David Tripp, boys have tended to exaggerate TV's male-dominated portrayal of the world in their own perceptions of reality, whereas girls have tended to resist that bias. These were just two of many instances where the lessons of TV and of real life were and are intertwined.[54]

Sometimes, mind you, it did seem that TV's images of life were more persuasive than reality. Television viewing taught people of all ages about their culture. It's stories introduced children to the archetypes, the beliefs, and the mythologies of North America. Its fantasy, fact, and commercials became the most important source of a common, second-hand experience for nearly everyone by the end of the 1960s.[55]

It certainly emerged as the most powerful agent of socialization among the mass media. The Schramm team of researchers detected signs of a 'head start' among viewers in early childhood: kids of high and below-average intelligence in 'Teletown,' apparently, had a greater command of the language, and heavy viewers a much better knowledge of topical words, than did comparable children in 'Radiotown' – although this 'head start' disappeared as the kids became teens. Perhaps that was because the teachers tried to keep television's lessons at bay, imposing instead their own version of what was knowledge about life upon their pupils. Even so, TV taught youngsters about many things, from the modes of polite behaviour to the latest fashions in dress to the norms of the world of public affairs. So one study in 1972, cited by Grant Noble, discovered that children's attitude's towards Canada's native peoples reflected very much their television and movie experience: the stereotype of the 'Red Indians,' to use Noble's term, among nine-year-olds was of a primitive savage, for whom killing was a way of life. Likewise, TV's consistently sexist portrayal of men and women, and its representation of patriarchy as the norm, made it an important agent in defining the personal identities and the proper conduct of girls and boys, notably at the teenage level. Equally central, it trained children in their future role of consumers. That wasn't just through commercials, although these were clearly important in cultivating a spendthrift attitude. The television image of toys and cars and homes emphasized the tangible advantages of having things, lots of things, to define one's identity and status.[56]

On an even wider scale what television did (along with the other mass media, of course) was to enhance the spread of a 'generalized information' about life and affairs as well as to foster a shared repertoire of images and clichés. It popularized such new terms as 'atoms for peace,' 'satellite,' 'peaceful co-existence,' and 'the generation gap.' It offered up portraits of other institutions, from schools to unions, and of occupations, from housewives to professionals. It fixed stereotypes of supposed subcultures, be that teen ways or the college style, rural and small-town existence or the executive mode, that could serve as guides to behaviour. It presented impressions of rebellion and of conformity, of men and women, of Canadians and foreigners, of the class system and the democracy, of the way the law worked, that might serve to legitimate or even challenge the status quo. It allowed everyone 'to see life as others live it,' claimed a whooping 80 per cent of the people polled by Goldfarb, creating an illusion that we really could know what it was like to be poor or rich, male or female, even an African tribesman or a Chinese Communist. This mythologizing of life didn't necessarily homogenize views or behaviour across the country. Rather it created a common context, an accepted range of ideas and actions, within which the individual could locate himself and so understand what was happening around him.[57]

Ironically, the overall cultural significance of the primetime phenomenon was already on the wane by the end of the 1960s. For what gave it such an impact was the commonality of the experience, the fact that so many different kinds of people were sitting in front of their TV sets to watch the same shows during the course of an evening. Primetime TV was then very much an instance of *broad*casting. The rise of private television, the emergence of new provincial channels and of PBS in the United States and of independent stations in Canada, the purchase of two or more sets per family, the spread of cable and satellite broadcasting, and eventually the appearance of pay television and most especially VCRs in homes across the land undid that commonality. Increasingly people could watch, as individuals rather than in a family setting, programs that suited their own tastes and moods. The slow arrival of the new era of *narrow*casting might not lessen the import of television itself, but it certainly did mean that the mass sharing of the same messages once a part of the primetime experience no longer applied. 'Life with television' meant something that became more and more different for the generation of the 1970s and 1980s.

Afterword: Understanding Television

You can pin almost anything on the box. Television is destroying democracy or its propaganda for the status quo. TV breeds violence or its a numbing drug. Television is educating the world or driving it crazy. *It seems that television insists on mixing paradox with its power.*

'Television,' Granada Television, 1985[1]

All that remains is to place this study of Primetime Canada in a broader context: what happened elsewhere and what happened later.

Allow me another brief foray into mythology, classical mythology this time. Cast your mind back to the pantheon of Roman gods. You'll find there a lesser-known deity called Janus who was unique to the Italian peninsula, unlike so many of his compatriots. Even more unusual was his appearance: Janus was typically represented as a two-faced god (occasionally four-faced), one face on the front and another on the back of his head. This unique being, according to one story, had been called Chaos, and when the world took shape, he was left with two faces to signify the confusion of his original state. He was considered the father of the Roman pantheon, coming before all other gods, including Jupiter himself. Such a being laid claim to considerable powers. Janus was first and foremost the protector of doorways and archways, controlling the gates of society, whether public or private. It followed then that he was also the god of departure and return, or in modern terms of communications, and was thought to stand at the beginning and ending of all things. Eventually he was worshipped as the promoter of initiative, and placed in charge of all human enterprise.

Janus is a surprisingly appropriate symbol for modern television, at least as that medium has developed in North America and other parts of the so-called First World. Haven't we all heard a bit too much about the god-like powers of TV? Didn't it fast become the chief means of mass communication? Isn't it true that television commands access to the minds of governors and governed alike, that it does reign over human enterprise, that it can both open up and close off initiatives? But what strikes me as most fitting is the double-faced representation of the deity. For the story of television is full of confusion, studded with so many ambiguities and opposites as to defy easy explanation. That's why all too many studies of television seem unsatisfactory: they grasp just a portion of this truth. Indeed I think that television can only be understood if the observer recognizes the full significance of its contrary nature.[2]

Consider the organization of television. Right from the beginning there has existed a tension between the aims of public broadcasting and the challenge of private interests. It's fashionable nowadays to talk about the crisis of public TV. During the past twenty years, one investigation after another has charted the apparent decline of the CBC as the central broadcasting agency in Canada. The country seems much more confused now over the degree to which the airwaves are any longer a public resource, if the 1986 report of the Task Force on Broadcasting Policy is any indication. In Britain, ever since the emergence of Margaret Thatcher as a power on the political scene, the BBC has been in trouble, especially over how much it costs as well as what it broadcasts. Yet throughout the 1980s BBC and the CBC have all remained of considerable importance in the make-up of their respective television industries. Even in the United States, the dominion of private television has been challenged since 1970 by the rise of a public alternative in the shape of the PBS stations, designed to serve an upscale audience.[3]

Or look at how television programs are made. Many critics, writers, and producers have worried about the conflicting pressures of creativity and profit. Who should be served – the mass audience or large minorities? What should be served – Commerce or Art? The usual answers in Hollywood were and remain the ordinary viewer and the businessman. The growth of competition, especially after 1961, effectively doomed the CBC's efforts to deliver a wide range of highbrow programming in primetime. But even later 'quality' or 'excellence' has sometimes made it onto the screen. That may have something to do with executives such as Bill Paley, founder and long-time master of CBS, who as a man of taste thought a bit of excellence was occasionally worth the expense because of the pay-off in prestige. And the victory of quality, if such it should be called, is much more noticeable where public TV originates shows. The CBC has continued to offer its anglophone audiences major historical series such as 'The National Dream' (1974), 'Riel' (1979), and 'The King Chronicle' (1988) to explore the country's past. PBS has made its name as the instrument of 'Pervasive Albion' by distributing the best drama of British television to American highbrows.[4]

Above all, there's the issue of the place of television in modern society. Since well before television arrived, you will recall, there has been a debate over just what it will do or is doing to us. The confusion among experts and others is quite enough to exasperate a public eager to find scientific evidence to buttress its prejudices. Instead contradictions abound: twenty-five years ago Marshall McLuhan suggested that television would usher in a better time for mankind; more recently Joyce Nelson, another Canadian, has portrayed television as a death machine that has strengthened the age-old hold of patriarchy and empire over the human soul. Perhaps the best way to illustrate the confusion is simply to list an assortment of the claims that have been made about the impact of television on society, leaving to the reader to decide what is pro or con, whether that places television on the side of the angels or the devil:[5]

a source of upset	the buttress of authority
the cause of immorality	the defender of morality
a means of incitement	a source of catharsis
a stimulant (healthy or not)	a pacifier (always unhealthy)
educational	escapist
produces anxiety	desensitizes the audience
boosts family togetherness	causes individual isolation
lowers IQ	enhances general knowledge
the agent of identity	the agent of confusion
fosters cynicism and disbelief	fosters conformity/reinforcement
a liberal bias	a conservative bias
irrational	rational

Some of these differences are only a matter of appearances. Others are obviously exaggerated. Yet there is a grain of truth in nearly all of these claims. The documentary on TV's history produced by Granada Television in 1985 cited the case of Ronny Zamora, a fifteen-year-old boy convicted of murder, who may well have been influenced by watching too much violence on TV (he was a great fan of the detective series 'Kojak'), as well as the case of Tony Lara, a prisoner who earned a university degree while in jail, a man who'd been stimulated and assisted by television and its educational programming (he was a great fan of Dr Jacob Bronowski). Depending on your purpose and perspective, it's possible to find evidence to support the claim that television did this or that, in fact that it did both – even if the conclusion means TV worked as a tool of opposites.[6]

That observation about the contrary nature of television begs the question 'Why?' The crucial fact is that we are dealing with a failed revolution. There's little doubt that McLuhan and his successors were correct in identifying the extraordinary potential of television as an instrument of social and intellectual change. Television was the culmination (to this point anyway) of a new wave of communications born with the telegraph and the photograph. Like movies, TV engages two senses, sight and sound. Like radio, TV invades the home. Television conveys instant information in the form of moving images, backed up by sound, which are inherently very appealing to the public. Seeing is both pleasing and believing.

The trouble with all the apocalyptic visions of a manipulated society or a debauched populace or a wave of TV-inspired violence is that they were and are so hopelessly exaggerated. The dimensions of life don't change drastically from generation to generation, even in this age of future shock. Society can't be easily overwhelmed by any technology yet invented (barring the atom bomb). That's why the wild-eyed prophecies of the social import of cable in the early 1970s proved outlandish only a few years later. And that's why the various announcements about the assault of satellite broadcasting or the onset of an information revolution aren't likely to pan out either. Flights of fancy about one or another machine ought to be left to the science-fiction writers: I heartily recommend *TV:2000*, a collection of short stories about 'the awesome powers of television – and what it will be like in the future,' to those who want to be scared. Social commentators should be wise enough to realize that inertia alone is sufficient to slow the course of an innovation.[7]

In fact, television's potential was never fully realized because society moved immediately to tame its disruptive force. Broadcasters were long prepared for its arrival: David Sarnoff, head of RCA, directed his corporation to invest an estimated $50 million into the development of television before getting any return. The chief agents of control were the state and business, manifest in particular through the institutions of the existing media, notably radio: each had a stake in ensuring television didn't upset the applecart. That was why the early years of television were dominated by established networks, the BBC, CBC, NBC, or CBS – outsiders such as the National Film Board in Canada or the cinema interests in Great Britain, newcomers such as Allen DuMont in the United States, or novel delivery systems such as early cable or pay television were kept on the margins. Only when things had settled down did rivals such as ITV in Britain and CTV in Canada, or belatedly PBS in the United States, make an appearance.[8]

There's little doubt that politicians have kept a close watch over the behaviour or rather the misbehaviour of television. As a matter of course French authorities of all parties have attempted to control the actions and even purged the top personnel of public television. In 1968 threats by Japanese politicians not to renew the licence of a commercial station, because its reports seemed anti-American and even anti-government, led the station to get rid of its trouble-making journalists. Late in 1969 Vice-President Spiro Agnew launched a stinging attack on the news services of the three American networks, as part of a campaign to gentle their treatment of the Nixon administration. In 1971 the agitation of opposition leader Harold Wilson managed to force the BBC to cut out part of an interview with him that he found offensive. Towards the end of the 1970s the Trudeau government directed the Canadian Radio-Television and Telecommunications Commission to investigate separatism at Radio-Canada. Public TV in Canada was supposed to be a bastion of pan-Canadian unity.

Television came to act as a service agency for a wide variety of outside interests that competed for mastery of its messages. Some were very successful. Witness the power of the advertising industry. True, the agencies in the United States lost a direct say in production when the networks moved at the end of the 1950s to gain control of their programming, partly as a result of the quiz scandals. But the dependence on ad revenues of the commercial networks, and for that matter of the CBC, ensured that the adman would still be able to influence the whole tone of programming and the shape of the schedule. Other interests have had more difficulties. Women's groups in particular have taken producers and programmers to task for portraying women as sexual objects or man's helpmates rather than as persons in their own right. But whether it be spokespeople for business or labour, pro-choice or pro-life, all expect that television will act to legitimize their special causes.[9]

Likewise the public imposed limits on the new medium. The very habit of viewing, usually both casual and inattentive, ensured that the visual power of television wouldn't get out of hand. That's at least one lesson to draw from findings that about a fifth of viewers can't recall any news item within an hour of broadcast and that the average viewer only retains one-fifth of the information from a new story. There's some reason to the charge that television is really just 'moving and talking wallpaper,' in the words of the London *Times*. The rules of the game subjected television to another discipline, the tyranny of numbers: it couldn't reach too far beyond its audiences without running the risk of losing viewers. Television's programming had to reflect the prevailing myths and values and presumptions of the social mainstream. How often has television featured radical views, indulged in overt war-mongering, attacked religion, offered hard-core pornography, or experimented with the drama of a Bertolt Brecht?[10]

It is important to recognize that the practices of a literate and logical mode of thought common to producers and managers alike were imposed upon the character of programming. BBC types, for instance, have occasionally celebrated the literacy of their television as the chief reason for its great reputation. Television newscasters have often pointed out that their actual conventions and ideal standards are much the same as those of journalism in general. In 1980 one Canadian anchor, Peter Trueman, offered a variety of suggestions that would make television news even more like the daily newspaper. (Eight years later, however, he would retire from TV because he was convinced that an entertainment ethic had perverted the character of network news.) As things turned out, television wasn't only a visual and an aural medium, it was also a scripted medium where sound and images were marshalled according to well-established rules of sequence and logic.[11]

Yet all this is only half of the story. The suppression of TV's potential, in Canada as elsewhere, has only been partial. Neither the inertia of the masses nor the will of 'the powers that be' could wholly restrain television's ability to subvert. Television intruded into nearly every sphere of public life, as well as into the private domain of the family. The results weren't always predictable. Look at what's been happening in the American home. Francis Wheen, who wrote the companion volume to the previously mentioned Granada series on TV, selected a couple of letters sent to 'Dear Abbie' (Abbie Van Buren), the syndicated columnist in the United States, which serve to illustrate TV's sometimes peculiar impact. There was the complaint about how friends drop in unexpectedly when the family would much rather watch television – should the family be rude? There was the mother left tied up by a robber in the bedroom while her four-year-old boy peacefully watched television for three hours. And what about the husband who turned on the TV upon arrival at home, watched anything that was showing, ate dinner in front of the tube, refused to talk to children or wife, and stayed up till 2:00 in the morning? Or the children displayed in a public-service announcement in Cleveland who solemnly told an interviewer that they would give up talking to Dad more readily than they would give up TV?[12]

The very fact that so many men, women, and children watched so much television every day gave it a greater presence in the ordinary life of the public than most other institutions, certainly than any of the lesser sources of 'civilization' from the museum and the church to the school or the newspaper. In 1982 A.C. Nielsen estimates put family viewing per day at three to four hours in Western Europe, six and three-quarter hours in the United States, and eight and one-fifth hours in Japan. Per-capita viewing in Canada was roughly three and a quarter hours a day, or twenty-four hours a week, according to BBM data – the next year the ratings registered that the highest reported amount of viewing in a week was 121.3 hours. Millions upon millions of people have been brought to the small screen to watch the great spectacles of modern times, to share awe and joy and grief, from the Coronation of Queen Elizabeth II in 1953, through the funerals of John Kennedy and Winston Churchill and the American landing on the moon in the 1960s, to the marriage of the darling couple Prince Charles and Lady Diana Spencer in 1981, which was seen by 750 million people in seventy-four countries.[13]

'So if you don't watch, you're out of touch,' a Japanese youngster claimed in a conversation at school. Being without TV was 'like a death in the family,' asserted one anonymous viewer. Little wonder TV seems essential to many households: in 1977, 93 out of 120 families turned down an offer by the Detroit *Free Press* of $500 if they would do without television for a month. A recent survey of the life and attitudes of Canadian teenagers found watching television was the second most popular leisure activity, after listening to music: TV served as a necessary diversion from the troubles of living, including 'loneliness and boredom.' It can seem more important than just about anything else to a few poor souls: in 1983, a young, lonely, overweight Genaro Garcia in New York shot himself to death after his father banned television.[14]

Put another way, television soon occupied centre-stage in the communications system, and it superseded as well as altered the functioning of more limited institutions. Whether you wanted to sell goods, win souls, seek votes, or divert the masses, television demanded conformity to its own style. Evangelists such as Billy Graham in the United States were among the first to recognize and exploit the potential of the medium as a way of spreading their gospel and challenging the mainstream denominations. From the mid-1970s the Christian broadcaster Pat Robertson successfully employed the style of the nightly talk show in his '700 Club' to win an audience of the faithful. Just as in Canada, so in Britain leading politicians had begun by the mid-1960s to bypass Parliament for the television camera when they wished to communicate something very significant. Campaign commercials have given rise to a new, clipped style of partisan rhetoric, first in the United States and then everywhere else where political advertising has become commonplace. In a similar vein an account of Campaign '79 in Canada found that newspaper reporters and editors were intent on finding anecdote, colour, conflict, to make print news as entertaining as television news. It's no accident that the Kent Commission discovered in its study of the Canadian press in 1980/1 that regular newspaper readers were declining in numbers, since more and more people had found that they could do without a daily paper. The emergence of lengthy local news shows in American cities during the 1970s spelled disaster for many afternoon papers, which lost subscribers and then advertisers. Television had found 'a better way of packaging information,' according to the veteran journalist Val Sears ('It was more exciting, more compelling, easier to absorb'), and that feat had undone the grand old tradition of the newspaper as the chief storyteller in modern society. The little screen, especially in the evening, had become the chief vehicle for spreading common knowledge, news and views, to a wide public.[15]

Television has always operated in something of a cultural marketplace, established back in the 1920s when news, movies, and popular music became items of international export. That marketplace has hindered the efforts of governors and broadcasters outside the United States who wished to protect their own societies from infection by 'alien' messages. The so-called Canadian dilemma, the fact that Canadian audiences often preferred American programming to the home-grown variety, isn't really unique. European youth and the British working class welcomed the products of American TV as a more appealing alternative to the staid or élitist offerings of their local public TV. A world-wide survey of programming in 1970/1 found that imported shows, many of which were American, constituted a significant percentage of schedules nearly everywhere: if less than 10 per cent in Japan and France and around 13 per cent in Britain, the totals were 23 per cent and 30 per cent for the two West German channels, 35 per cent in Portugal, 39 per cent in Norway, 55 per cent in Chile, 57 per cent in Australia and Yemen, and 71 per cent in Malaysia. Over a period of roughly thirty years 'I Love Lucy' has played just about everywhere in the non-Communist world, and it still appears on the air in Toronto nowadays. By 1985 the famous primetime soap opera 'Dallas' had been seen in ninety countries. Television spread to all corners of the globe a superficial knowledge of the American way of life and, perhaps more insidious, fostered a style of home-grown programming that conformed to American norms – such as 'Château Vallon,' a French version of 'Dallas.' Even news styles have been effected: Britain's ITN was modelled on American news, Japan's News Centre 9 was designed in New York, and Soviet news bears a striking resemblance to the American standard. I recall marvelling at how similar to North American norms in tone, style, and visuals were the commercials for consumer goods (notably a sliced bread called 'Panrico') I witnessed on one of the Spanish channels in Barcelona during a visit in 1988. It's here that television appears as the instrument of an assault on particular cultures.[16]

The Canadian case would suggest that this peril can easily be exaggerated by anxious nationalists. The fears of a Davidson Dunton, or of the highbrows back in the early 1950s, that the Americanization of the airwaves would somehow undo Canada weren't realized. True enough, the accessibility plus the popularity of Hollywood entertainment made virtually impossible the survival of an indigenous and vigorous PopCult in English Canada. But this so-called colonization of the imagination didn't prevent the flowering of the arts and letters that has been so notable a feature on the cultural landscape of English Canada over the past three decades. Besides the Caplan-Sauvageau investigation of the broadcasting scene in the mid-1980s learned that Canadian audiences of both language groups still overwhelmingly preferred their own news and views (and their own sports as well) to the American alternative. That was crucial. The continuous supply of information about all things Canadian was and remains sufficient to nurture a separate national identity and a distinctive civic ethic. The impassioned free-trade debate of the fall of 1988 amply demonstrated that Canadians had no desire for a continental union, whatever they thought about the merits of the Canadian/U.S. commercial agreement. An international, even a made-in-America, PopCult featured on television isn't any more likely to destroy the foundation of nation-states in Europe or other parts of the world.[17]

However, the Canadian case could just as well be cited to demonstrate the import of television as a tool of a nationalist revival. There's one lesson to be drawn from the experience of Quebec. Radio-Canada offered to the Québécois a concrete, visible expression of their own unique places, past and present, and ways. 'Television in Quebec,' Susan Mann Trofimenkoff has observed, 'magnified the tiny world of a Laurentian village, a lower town Quebec, or a local hockey arena into a provincial possession.' Its newscasts and its public-affairs shows plus the many, many features and documentaries swiftly created a novel means of focusing attention on the activities and concerns of the province. The enormously popular téléromans sent images of life into homes every week that gave substance to the new nationalism that swept through the francophone community during the 1950s and 1960s. This drama didn't so much create as perpetuate and update a cluster of symbols that gave definition and meaning to the community. That's why one can sympathize with the nationalist purpose that has informed the CRTC's insistence in the past decade or so that Anglo-Canadian television, especially CTV, carry primetime drama that reflects the life, the people, 'the soul' of the country. Whether success would foster a similar popular nationalism, never mind an upheaval in attitudes and actions comparable to the Quiet Revolution, is very doubtful however.[18]

That said, television, whether American or otherwise, has acted as a subversive force in all kinds of societies. Ironically the fact television is plugged in to what is happening means that a week's or a month's viewing can serve to reveal as well as to mask the contradictions inherent in society. Recall how 'showbiz' variety and country and western shows, most especially the latter, exploited the distinction between urban and rural lifestyles. Contrast the way in which 'Ben Casey' glorified the professional, in this case the doctor, while Wayne and Shuster's skit 'The Story of a Dedicated Garage Mechanic,' spoofed the cult of the expert. Indeed such attempts at satire as 'That Was the Week That Was,' 'The Smothers' Brothers Comedy Hour,' 'NBC's Saturday Night Live,' or 'SCTV' have consciously undermined the messages of other brands of programming, the conventions of society, and the pretensions of the politicians. Witness the effect of the network coverage of America's Vietnam misadventure: while the focus on battlefield scenes, body counts, and 'our boys' may have buttressed the government's case, in the end the repeated scenes of death and the increasing signs of failure (notably the coverage of the Tet Offensive early in 1968) eventually undermined that case as well. There's some evidence that Walter Cronkite's eventual and public critique of the war finally convinced Lyndon Johnson that the jig was up, it was time to leave, since he'd lost 'Mr Average Citizen.' It's not surprising that later Margaret Thatcher and Ronald Reagan would take care to limit television's handling of their respective escapades in the Falklands and Grenada. Not even dissent is free from television's contradictions: TV, admittedly with the great assist of the press, played a key role 'in the making and the unmaking of the new left' in America during the 1960s.[19]

Furthermore, television isn't the same as the book or the newspaper: everyone has had to adjust to a medium of flash and glitter, especially after the introduction of colour. Radiovision didn't last in the main centres of the TV world. Whatever was borrowed from older media or the stage was soon refined to suit the technological and social requirements of video – witness the turn to drama, the showbiz imperative, and the emphasis on speed and novelty (nowadays the average shot on American network television has been estimated at 3.5 seconds long). The resulting schedules are dominated by the storytelling mode. The increasing fascination with the visual dimension of television was bound to favour some kinds of messages over others, in particular exciting entertainment in the form of action and comedy drama over slow-moving exchanges of views between talking heads. Ratings throughout the English-speaking world and beyond have shown that fact. There's some reason to think that over time viewing has had a dismal effect on the problem-solving abilities of American youth: the baby-boomers' 'embrace' of television was one reason, among others, for the steady decline between 1963 and 1979 of their average score on America's infamous Scholastic Aptitude Tests, which purport to measure the ability of the annual crop of university freshman – the score fell on the verbal test from 478 to 427 and the mathematical test from 502 to 467.[20]

More serious, the literate mode of thought was challenged by the moving camera. In a night of television the eye can't rest, the mind can't easily reflect. Icons, music, personalities became just as important as what was said. 'The power of pictures is symbolic rather than factual,' argued Reuven Frank, one-time president of NBC News. 'And it appeals to a different part of the brain.' Recall the first presidential debates of 1960 where viewers seemed much more intrigued by how Richard Nixon and John Kennedy performed than by the substance of their exchanges. Kennedy came out looking like a winner on TV, whereas Nixon apparently did better among radio listeners. In 1984 a similar contest in Canada undermined the shaky appeal of then prime minister John Turner, who appeared to be on the defensive, and enhanced the cause of challenger Brian Mulroney, who cultivated an image of vigour and confidence. Four years later, though, it was Turner who scored in the debate: his forceful attack on Mulroney's patriotism and integrity rehabilitated 'the Turner image' as a national leader and transformed the election campaign into a closely fought contest for power. And consider how leaders have employed television to mobilize a nation in a time of emergency: John Kennedy did this in 1962 over the Cuban missile crisis, Pierre Trudeau did the same in 1970 over the FLQ crisis, in each case crafting an image of himself as the embodiment of the national will. The power of the Word must share time with the power of the Image, the appeal to the mind with the appeal to the eye.[21]

But the subversive effect of television is best illustrated by its impact upon our perceptions of people and life around us, and so on how we behave at home, at work, and in public. The very existence of television altered the environment we live in: TV made accessible and visible more and more information about patterns of personal behaviour. All kinds of people of all ages and classes and nationalities and both sexes have gathered in front of the small screen to share in watching the same thing, quite a different phenomenon from the way books or even newspapers are used, where readers select different texts according to their skills and interests. That experience crosses over the physical and social distances that separate individuals. Because television news and drama open up hitherto private spaces to the public eye, they can demystify life: women see men in their special domains, children learn a lot about the adult world, citizens perceive the human face of politicians, all of which makes it increasingly difficult for men, adults, and politicians to play out their traditional roles. The overt message of a broadcast might be conservative: say, that politicians are experts in government or that justice will be achieved; the covert message might well be otherwise: that politicians and policemen are flawed males seeking their own self-interest. The formal proclamations of party virtue or civic pride or even patriotism can easily appear forced, if not false, on so intimate a medium as television, especially when we 'know' that the spokespeople have an ulterior motive. Much that we watch may also work unintentionally to subvert the official values or views society upholds.

That may help to explain some of the push behind social change in recent decades. We can't yet identify just how important television in North America has been to the booming demands for equal rights by women and gays, native peoples and blacks, the disabled and the poor, and so on. But there's sufficient 'circumstantial evidence,' to use a piece of jargon from the courtroom drama, to suggest that the images of life portrayed on television have done a lot to raise people's expectations, to enhance resentment and sometimes pride, and to bring about the dissolution of a past order. The portrayal of the anxieties and inadequacies of the typical male in sitcoms, professional sagas, and the like could well excite contempt for that person in the minds of some of the 'victims' of his authority. The celebration of success at work as the route to social esteem or the representation of so-called feminine virtues such as caring in the same kinds of programs could lead these same people to recognize there were other ways to personal satisfaction than those honoured by the mainstream. The fascination of the news eye with the novel did spread rapidly the knowledge of alternatives to a much wider audience. All of which may serve to dissolve the apparent paradox as to why feminism and gay liberation should both emerge at a time when the overt TV message was so sexist, so homophobic (though I wouldn't suggest TV caused either movement). What we think we know about others and about ourselves does indeed affect how we behave.[22]

So we're left with the analogy of Janus. Television is a medium looking backwards and forwards. It is restrained by the force of tradition; it is also an instrument of novelty. Television entertainment still encourages sexism, even if television itself may be undermining the legitimacy of traditional views of the sexes. The focus of television news privileges the leaders of society, although all the concentrated attention may deprive them of that mystery upon which authority often depends. Nobody really controls television because so many people share influence over television. What people get out of programs may be as much a result of 'aberrant decoding' as it is of any successful preaching by producers and their masters. The images of an affluent America have excited envy and provoked revulsion in the Third World: TV did contribute to the horror of things American, and so to the deep distrust of modernization, among the traditionalists in the Shah's Iran. All this ambiguity explains why TV's messages and its effects can be so contradictory. Let me close with this little story by James Reston, resurrected from *The New York Times* (7 July 1957) by the always mischievous McLuhan: 'A health director in [a] Blue Ridge Virginia county reported this week that a small mouse, which presumably had been watching television, attacked a little girl and her full-grown cat .... Both mouse and cat survived, and the incident is recorded here as a reminder that things seem to be changing. The mice in the world are no longer doing what the cats say.'[23]

Forms and Genres

There are many, many schemes of classification for television programming. Those people who set out to analyse the culture of television, whether communicators or regulators or scholars, must have a method of organizing their research and findings to avoid getting lost in a welter of titles. The trouble is that each scholar or agency designs a slightly different scheme to suit a particular purpose. I've had to do the same thing, although my brand of content analysis is based upon the work of others, particularly Raymond Williams (in *Television: Technology and Cultural Form*) and Gérard Laurence (*Le contenu des médias électroniques*). The results really provided the skeleton of the book – what I found after analysing the overall contents of television determined the ways in which I organized my arguments on genres into chapters and sections.

My scheme divides television programming into four different 'forms,' each sharing a common purpose and shape, as well as a much larger number of 'genres,' each having a distinct character and set of styles, usually a definite substance as well, that are manufactured according to a generally accepted set of conventions. The scheme was designed to deal only with regular series (that is, shows that appeared at least four times in a season), not with specials. It is by no means perfect. Television producers occasionally employ conventions from two different genres to develop a kind of hybrid, such as the musical game show or the comedy/adventure drama, where classification becomes very much an arbitrary act. One hybrid, the docudrama, was sufficiently common that it can be designated a genre in its own right. Some shows are really anthologies of different genres, which for the sake of convenience I've simply classified as omnibus.

Genres may also share a common subject-matter; thus both social drama or 'soaps' and situation comedy often use the family or a surrogate of the family as the focal point of their stories. In short my scheme is abstracted from the realities of television programming: it has a certain utility in helping the researcher and the reader to understand the overall character of the culture of television.

This appendix includes an abbreviated description of my scheme of content analysis plus two tables that survey the programming of the American networks, the two CBC flagship stations (CBLT-Toronto and CBFT-Montreal), and the CTV station in Toronto (CFTO), during the primetime hours. The American material is based on published collections of program descriptions and primetime schedules: Brooks and Marsh (1981), McNeil (1980), Castleman and Podrazik (1982 and 1984), all cited in the notes. The table on American networks only deals with what was aired in the fall schedule of a year. The Canadian material is based on surveys of the listings in the *CBC Times* and *La Semaine à Radio-Canada*, newspapers in Toronto and Montreal, occasionally *TV Guide*, and CBC program files in Toronto. The Canadian tables are based on what was supposed to be on, not what actually appeared, which means the findings are only an approximation, not the kind of definitive break-down that could only come through the use of program logs – but, for my purposes, an approximation was suitable (and working with logs was just too formidable a task to be worthwhile). The Canadian tables analyse what was on during the course of a television year. Keep in mind, when drawing any comparisons, that the American data pertain to networks and fall seasons, the Canadian data to stations and television years.

Content Analysis

A / *Information*: a form that purports to deal with reality, past or present or even future. It can lay claim to authenticity and, often, to objectivity as well. Its declared aim is to inform the viewer about something, perhaps, in addition, to educate and enlighten the viewer. In practice, though, what is often supplied is trivia, information as entertainment, which can serve to amuse or titillate the viewer. Usually some sort of mediator, whether anchor or reporter or interviewer, plays a crucial role in the broadcast.

Newscasts: a round-up of significant events drawn from the world of affairs, though the show may include human-interest stories, and often has sports and weather items as well. The typical newscast is made up of a number of different items, though where possible these items are clustered into assorted groupings around some sort of theme (Ottawa politics, foreign affairs, plane crashes, etc.). The anchor, or 'anchorman' as he then invariably was, is the person who links together the program and who gives the news a human face.

Public affairs: a genre that employs a number of different styles – the news interview/discussion ('Conference de presse' or 'Close-Up'), the news documentary ('See It Now' or 'Point de mire'), or the newsmagazine ('This Hour Has Seven Days'), which may include interviews, documentaries, and other items. All of these have a serious purpose, to educate the viewer about the world of affairs. They involve experts, news-makers, and above all broadcast journalists who comment on this world. In varying degrees they pay allegiance to such principles of journalism as accuracy, fairness, balance, and objectivity.

Features: such programs offer viewers knowledge, broadly defined, via the means of documentaries, travelogues, university lectures, personal essays, sermons or homilies, on life (Bishop Fulton J. Sheen's 'Life Is Worth Living'), nature or science, history and biography. Although the appeal of these shows was usually limited, still features have often been counted among the 'best' of television's offerings – they constitute an especially flexible genre that lent itself to innovation and quality.

Popular facts: this genre employs the conventions of news, public affairs, and features to supply trivia to amuse the viewer, or to convey information to enhance the pleasure of entertainment. Included here are talk shows (NBC's famous 'Tonight Show'), human interest ('Candid Camera'), life's review (a sports round-up), and instruction ('Mr. Fix-It').

b / *Display*: a form in which the public demonstration of talent is uppermost. Its genres usually serve to entertain or divert the viewer, though those shows that fall within the realm of Culture may also claim to uplift or enlighten.

Variety: this collection of closely related genres includes a wide range of performances and styles (song, dance, comedy, music, dramatic sketches, circus acts, skating, and so on) derived from the live stage and the tradition of vaudeville. By and large, though, such programming falls into one of the three categories of general or showcase variety ('Ed Sullivan'), comedy and comedy variety (notably 'Wayne and Shuster'), or musical variety ('Don Messer'). Almost always, variety means just that: a number of different acts during the course of the half-hour or hour. A variety show normally has one host, occasionally two, who tie the collection of items together.

Arts and music: performances of the High Arts, such as opera, ballet, and concerts. These are prestige offerings, and they presume a sophisticated, discriminating audience which finds pleasure viewing what a cultural élite has deemed worthy of notice.

c / *Contests*: a form in which the participants are contestants expected to perform in some kind of arena according to a set of rules to win a prize.

Game/quiz: these amounted to competitions staged in a studio for the pleasure of viewers, and included big-money give-away shows ('The $64,000 Question') as well as highbrow quizzes ('Fighting Words').

Sports: the telecast of any sporting event, normally an outside broadcast of an actual game such as a boxing or wrestling match, a football or a hockey contest. This genre does not include sports discussion though, which appears as one brand of 'popular facts.'

d / *Storytelling*: drama in all its main guises, whether fantastic or realistic, serious or comic, fictional or factual, the most common form on primetime television in the end. Once again the chief purpose is to entertain the viewer, although sometimes episodes of a series do hope to inform or educate as well.

Movies: long-form drama drawn from the tradition of the cinema, made in Hollywood and other production centres in Europe. By the late 1960s made-for-TV movies had begun to appear, taking the place of the earlier made-for-TV plays.

Plays: the much lauded dramatic anthologies of the 1950s (from 'Studio One' to 'GM Presents' and Radio-Canada's assorted télétheatres) were derived from the live stage and from radio. The anthologies were a mix of classics, adaptations from short stories or novels, and scripts written especially for television. They lost favour in the United States, and so in Canada, when dramatic series proved more popular with viewers and advertisers.

Action/adventure drama: the type of drama where the emphasis is on motion, not so much on character, which makes for fast-moving shows, full of jeopardy and hazard, as in westerns, crime shows, spy stories, science fiction, war drama, and adventures. This is the most violent of all the dramatic genres.

Suspense and psychological drama: a genre in which the emphasis is more upon character than motion, where there is often much attention payed to intellect and to the emotions, as in mystery series ('Alfred Hitchcock Presents') or professional sagas ('Dr. Kildare' or 'Wojeck').

Social drama: shows that concentrate on the trials and tribulations of the person, the family, or the group in managing what are purportedly day-to-day problems. Often these are serials, with unresolved conflicts carried over from episode to episode. The most important examples are the American soap operas and Radio-Canada's téléromans.

Comedy drama: this genre might best be called 'social drama with a comic thrust,' since the programs often deal with the life of a family or a surrogate of the family. The most important instances are, of course, the sitcoms, which have proved over the years the most popular genre offered by Hollywood.

Docudrama: a dramatic representation of some actual event that claims authenticity to enhance its impact on viewers. Some observers might consider the docudrama a kind of 'Information,' especially since the genre borrows from the style of the documentary, though by and large I think docudramas are fictionalized accounts that tailor the facts to suit the purposes of drama.

Basic Tables

Totals for the tables often don't add up to 100 per cent since certain series couldn't easily be classified or offered programming that can be counted in two or more forms. Recall that primetime refers to the hours between 7:00 and 11:00 PM.

TABLE A.1
Primetime forms: American networks 1950–65 (fall seasons)

	50	51	52	53	54	55	56	57	58	59	60	61	62	63	64	65
Information	11	13	18	17	14	12	09	08	08	03	08	07	07	03	04	03
Display	35	40	24	23	20	21	24	23	23	17	10	12	16	21	18	16
Contest	20	10	14	17	17	13	13	13	12	09	06	04	05	05	03	02
Drama	32	36	44	44	50	53	52	56	57	67	75	76	71	68	73	77

TABLE A.2
Primetime forms: Canadian stations 1952–67 (television years)

	52/3	53/4	54/5	55/6	56/7	57/8	58/9	59/60	60/1	61/2	62/3	63/4	64/5	65/6	66/7
CBLT-Toronto															
Information	20	21	18	20	20	20	18	20	24	27	24	29	27	24	23
Display	13	28	33	27	28	23	24	24	24	23	17	16	18	18	17
Contest	16	18	07	07	06	08	11	10	07	06	06	07	07	06	06
Drama	38	28	36	44	45	48	46	46	44	42	51	47	47	51	53
CFTO-Toronto															
Information									13	03	12	02	01	02	07
Display									08	09	11	08	13	17	16
Contest									05	12	06	09	09	08	05
Drama									73	75	70	78	74	73	73
CBFT-Montreal															
Information			31	34	32	31	30	30	35	32	35	43	43		
Display			16	16	16	18	13	11	12	19	11	13	11		
Contest			13	18	19	19	14	16	12	10	07	08	08		
Drama			32	28	29	30	37	40	40	36	36	33	37		

Viewing Analysis

Much of my information was derived from the close readings of an assortment of programs and advertisements. The decision on what to watch had to be made carefully. Using my breakdown of programming into the forms and genres of television, I tried to find samples that were representative in the holdings of CBC-Toronto and CBC-Montreal, the Museum of Broadcasting in New York, and the British Film Institute. That wasn't always easy: the records of past programs from the 1950s and 1960s are, in some instances, very sparse. I was unable to find a complete copy of the western hit 'Have Gun Will Travel' in the Museum of Broadcasting, for example. CBC-Toronto only had available a very small number of the national newscasts prior to the mid-1960s. The quality of one of the recordings of 'Point de mire' in CBC-Montreal was awful. But enough had been saved by these repositories to meet my needs (any other researcher with more specific requirements for a range of documentaries or newscasts or westerns may have much greater problems, though).

Just as crucial was the issue of how to handle these samples: what was viewed had to be analysed in detail, else the whole exercise would be largely pointless. I needed a scheme to ensure any viewing elicited answers to a common set of questions applicable to all kinds of programming. That was all the more essential since much of the viewing would be carried out by research assistants.

I turned to the discipline of semiotics to discover the tools necessary to reading a television text, and in particular to the ideas and approach outlined in *Reading Television* by John Fiske and John Hartley. Semiotics is the study of signs: all kinds of communication can be broken down into a collection of words, images, noises, smells, gestures, and so on, which are encoded by the communicator in conventional ways to convey a message and decoded by the receiver, also according to his or her knowledge of the requisite conventions, to produce specific meanings. I hasten to add that the eventual scheme is by no means an example of the advanced techniques some semioticians have employed in the fields of folk-tale or play analysis. Indeed I only paid modest attention to one of the fundamental concepts of semiotics, namely the so-called paradigmatic and syntagmatic dimensions of any system of signs where analysis focuses on the arrangement of signs into a vertical set of related units (from which one has been selected) and a horizontal chain of units (in which the one selected is connected to all the others). The true fan will no doubt find my scheme jejune.

Even so, on first reading, the scheme may appear too complex. It certainly is elaborate. Viewing analysis is something akin to peeling an onion – the task is to find the different layers of information in any broadcast. Keep in mind that the television message is itself a sophisticated result of the conjunction of the visual, oral, and literate modes of discourse. The scheme attempts to break down the broadcast into some of its smallest elements of meaning, the signs, and then use these to re-create the ever larger sets of meaning, the mythologies and ideology. The fact that at times the particular questions may seem to overlap is really the result of trying to develop effective tools of analysis that will approach the television message from every major angle.

What appears below is the scheme that was provided to my research assistants. I tested the scheme in 1983 on programs available on television at the time. With the help of Margarita Orszag, I carried out the first complete survey, using early American shows held by the Museum of Broadcasting. Two of the key research assistants were also required to carry out trials on present-day shows before setting to work on the Canadian samples. Often two researchers were used to view a single program, at least twice, to get a range of opinion. I 'read' many more times the six programs and the one advertisement selected for each 'Focus,' and I assembled for all but two a transcript which incorporated dialogue, the sequence of images and sounds, camera angles, and so on. Experience proved that all kinds of programming could be handled by the single scheme, although clearly some questions applied more to one form or genre than the others. The one exception was the commercials, where a separate scheme (based on the initial one, of course) had to be designed (that isn't included here).

i / Basic data: The title of the series and where appropriate of the episode; the date, time, and length of the broadcast; the nationality of the broadcast; the genre; the originating station/network; and whether the program was network, regional, local, or syndicated.

ii / Program synopsis: A description of what the program was about, which was often supplemented by a much more detailed abbreviation of the sequence of words and images over the course of the program.

iii / Techniques: One answer to the question of how the broadcast was organized and presented. I was interested in what, for the sake of convenience, could be called the technical side of the broadcast (a result of conventions as well as technology though).

Type of production: live, film, videotape, studio or outdoors.

Use of camera: a special concern here was whether the program was an instance of 'radiovision' or whether the program relied heavily on the visual dimension of television. Attention was paid to the use of angle and distance shots, close-ups, and the sequence of shots. In the opening episode of 'The Plouffe Family,' there were many two-shots of people constantly exchanging opinions, itself a sign of the domestic character of the drama.

Sounds: the use of music, a voice-over, modulated tones, and so on. In a test carried out on an episode of 'Cagney and Lacey' (25 July 1983), the ringing of a telephone was employed to suggest the intrusion of the outside world and a cassette recording of classical music used to convey a sense of peace.

Visuals: any symbols, graphics, stills, playback, filmed inserts. In 'CBC Television Theatre': *The Queen of Spades* (28 October 1956) a cut from one scene to another was masked by a closing shot on a gun and an opening shot on that same gun.

Mix: how effective was the integration of camera, sounds, and visuals? What was the pace of the show? Did the technical side 'work'? Stephen Strople and Brigid Higgins had this to say about the country-and-western variety 'Holiday Ranch' (28 September 1957): 'Very good. Smooth. Camera is unobtrusive but effective in capturing many of the asides that make the program authentic and rich in a folksy, down-home style.'

iv / Aesthetics: The second answer to the question 'how?' this time focusing on the actors and their performances.

Cast: who are the stars and the supporting players? What roles do they play? How do they dress? Are animals or machines used in a significant fashion? Are they any unusual features, such as the appearance of blacks (remember this applied to the 1950s)? In a 'Hockey Night in Canada' (15 April 1962), there were the hockey players themselves, some with definite specialities, the coaches, the succession of intermission experts and the interviewer, the play-by-play announcers, and the raucous Chicago crowd, all of whom contributed to the performance that appeared on the screen.

Settings: where the activities occur, particularly whether indoors or outside, the sequence of settings, and why these shifts are made. In the episode of '14 rue de Galais' (4 June 1956) Louis, the young man, hurt in a car accident, gauze bandages covering his eyes, tries on his own to survey his hospital room, hands outstretched, fumbling his way around, full of the fear he is permanently blind, which establishes the tone of anguish that runs through the drama.

Dialogue and action: the amount of talk and action, of solitary and group activity, any sex or violence. The episode of 'The Untouchables' (20 November 1962) had large amounts of both talk and action. The dialogue among the players was sharp and short, except when a child was involved, often amounting to a series of questions and answers, and in some cases the offering of threats and the response to those threats. There was a general undertone of menace throughout the program, realized in occasional jolts of violence in the form of gun-play and the like.

Quality of the performance: just how well did the performers play out their roles and did their performance suit the occasion? The feature on Cardinal Leger by 'Profile' (25 April 1955) saw the obsequious interviewer and the fatherly Leger play out their roles superbly to emphasize the 'gospel' of life according to the Catholic church. The trouble for a researcher here was escaping the standards of journalism of the 1980s: using the present-day conventions of interviewing, this feature was more an advertisement than it was a public-affairs program.

v / Codes: My concern here was the third aspect of the mode of presentation. By a 'code,' I referred to the organization of certain signs according to certain conventions to produce a system of meaning. At its simplest level, a 'system of meaning' may be no more than the parent's admonition to the child, 'Don't eat the cookies.' But I was interested in something a bit more advanced. Recall the fact that communication involves a process of negotiation to produce meaning: communicators employ various kinds of codes to bring their messages to viewers, but viewers, being ornery, decode these message according to their own experience and prejudices and knowledge. What's most interesting is how the communicators try to get around the problem of aberrant decoding.

Catalogue of codes: one of the most studied, of course, is the journalistic code, often displayed in the form of questions and answers as in the case of 'Front Page Challenge.' But among other codes are those of the expert, the criminal and the policeman, the parent and teacher, the friend, and so on. Sometimes, in comedy shows or sequences, these are parodied: Wayne and Shuster parodied television's version of the doctor's code. The point is that the viewer can recognize from the way a person speaks, the words and gestures used, his or her general stance and dress, just what kind of a person the performer is playing.

Patterns and styles of speech: a particular focus on the use of a colloquial or refined pattern of speech, on language styles (humorous, solemn, chatter, etc.), and contrasting patterns and styles and even codes. The hosts of 'Tabloid' (31 January 1958) employed quite a range of approaches, sometimes the friend, sometimes the reporter, using humour and chatter (a few jokes) to relax viewers, solemnity (the issue of heart disease) to bring home the gravity of the subject, a rapid-fire if colloquial delivery (Saltzman, the weatherman) to shoot bits of information at an audience already attuned to this mode of presentation.

Authenticity/fantasy/sensation: is the show believable? Does the communicator ever try to employ elements of fantasy or sensation to capture the viewer's fancy? The producer, director, and host of 'The $64,000 Question' (20 September 1955) were clearly determined to make their contest appear authentic, and so to build up suspense and viewer interest – the fact that these big-money shows succeeded in this endeavour made people all the more angry when they learned that their trust had been betrayed. In the case of one 'Conférence de presse' (23 September 1963), the guest Dr Marcel Chaput, a separatist, went out of his way to attack the panel of four journalists who questioned him – he was himself the sensation of the show.

Effectiveness: what amounts to enlightened speculation about how effective the codes might be in realizing the purpose of the show. Thus the hour-long 'Close-Up' (11 February 1962), 'The Psychology of the Cold War,' seemed full of long-winded talking heads, using an elaborated vocabulary to outline complex ideas, making the whole discussion seem far removed from the problems of the real world.

vi / Mood: Broadcasts generally have some sort of emotional tone, dictated in part by the codes employed. What I wanted was an account of the nature and sequence of feelings, explicit and implicit. These were often best expressed as a series of dichotomies: love/hate, anxiety/hope, altruism/ selfishness, envy/satisfaction, pride/shame, anger/celebration. There are others, of course: my researchers found another, namely anticipation/ disappointment, albeit in a parody, in one of the sketches in the variety program 'Cross-Canada Hit Parade' (10 November 1958). The purpose of these conflicting moods is to capture the attention of the viewer, which led me to ask whether the intention was to spark the curiosity of the viewer ('Dans tous les cantons' [27 July 1960] tried to do this by featuring its locale for that episode, 'the historic town of St Jean') or to involve the viewer (as 'This Hour Has Seven Days' [24 October 1965] attempted in its treatment of the death of a policeman). I did try to judge the intensity of the experience, although such a judgment was always subjective, since common sense suggested it must have varied from one person to another. Personally, I found the British play *No Fixed Abode* on Granada's 'Television Playhouse' (30 January 1959) a gripping exposé of an evening in the life of a flophouse. People at the time, though, may well have found it another dreary example of the kind of psychological drama so prevalent then. By contrast, I was simply bored by the 'Festival' performance of *Juno and the Paycock* (15 December 1965), even though one of my researchers was mightily impressed.

VII Mediator(s): A good number of television's genre involve a more or less obvious mediator (even if only a voice), a man or woman in between the activities on the screen and the viewers at home. This is especially true of nearly all kinds of information, quiz and game shows, sportscasts, much of variety, and many ads. Pure drama is less likely to boast 'a man in between,' though such a person was present in the hosted dramatic antholo- gies common during the 1950s and early 1960s – and occasionally one character would play out such a role (for example Jack Pheeny, the political pro, in *The Arena* on CBS's 'Studio One' [9 April 1956]). Mediators can play a crucial part in determining the meaning and effect of a broadcast – so the commentary of sports announcers converts a game into a trial where skill and conduct are evaluated according to non-partisan criteria.

What kind(s) of mediator: host, narrator, announcer, anchorman, com- mentator, quiz-master, etc.

Roles played: introducing, explaining, judging, etc. Any contradictions? Does the mediator have a definite point of view? The hostess of 'Théâtre populaire' (30 June 1957) who introduced André Laurendeau's *La vertu des chattes* told the expectant audience that this performance was only a light sketch, meant to entertain and to help people rediscover their youth.

Honour/dishonour: what does the mediator honour, or sometimes dishonour? Nathan Cohen, the host of 'Fighting Words' (19 January 1958), went out of his way to honour intellectualism, to encourage the exchange of opposing opinions, and to highlight the significance of Culture.

VIII / Problem-solving: Another set of television's genre (overlapping with the mediated broadcasts, of course) dealt directly or indirectly with problem-solving. This is especially true of stories, whether fact or fiction, and advertisements, but it may also appear in other forms that lack much obvious dramatic content – for example, some brands of display, notably comedy-variety. Even if broadcasts that feature problem-solving are not meant consciously to serve as guides to living, they do function as a source of information about how problems are dealt with – hence the worry about children's viewing habits or sex and violence on television.

Definition and significance: what is the problem and how central is it to the broadcast or to the item in the broadcast? How to solve the riddle is the key to winning on 'Le nez de Cléopâtre' (28 April 1954), although that was hardly a problem of much significance; what to do about the atomic bomb is absolutely central to C.P. Snow's *The New Men*, broadcast on 'General Motors Presents' (27 September 1959), which dealt with one of the most significant issues facing post-war society; the update on the nuclear-arms debate in Parliament, given top billing on the 'CBC Television News' (31 January 1963), was an excuse to inform/entertain (?) viewers with more examples of politicians railing at each other and, in this instance, the Americans. In each case, then, there was a problem, though what it meant, and how it was treated, varied very widely indeed.

Conflict: the purpose here is to identify goals, adversaries (including non-human antagonists, such as the bugs in an ad for Off), the rules of the contest (meaning its boundaries and its conventions), the moral context or structure, and the intensity of conflict. Take, for example, the conflict in 'I Love Lucy' (20 May 1955). Lucy yearned to meet the movie star Richard Widmark; husband Ricky said absolutely not. Lucy's mad desire to see the star involved a host of other characters, compelling friend and neighbour Ethel to assist her. The rules seemed fairly straightforward: a wife, especially when her goals were so unusual, should do what her husband says in the traditional family, although Ricky's initial refusal wasn't altogether fair. There was an important element of moral ambivalence here, because it wasn't clear who was right or wrong. The conflict was hardly intense, however zany Lucy might be – we were entertained by Lucy's effort to evade the rules.

Resolution: normally conflicts were in one way or another resolved, and this resolution often conveyed some sort of lesson. My chief concern was to learn whether resolution was possible, how it occurred, and what was its moral content. So Lucy eventually did get to see Richard Widmark, and acquired an autographed grapefruit to boot. She proved the efficacy of womanly wiles. Ricky wasn't really angry: he soon demonstrated his understanding of Lucy's foibles and madness and his love for a person who was his 'problem,' his burden in life. The show could be read on the surface as confirmation of patriarchy and a celebration of domestic harmony. But it might also be read in a subversive fashion, since Lucy got her way without being punished. Comedy, good comedy, often had a double meaning.

IX / Images and clichés: These terms are used for convenience to refer to symbols, stereotypes, values, and, of course, myths, the basic ingredients out of which the TV people built their broadcast. The researcher was expected to look and listen for signs that conveyed some special meaning, such as the gun (symbol of violence), the innocent child, woman as whore or helpmate, the dangerous city, and on and on. *The Nativity Play* presented on 'Folio' (19 December 1956) reeked of Christian symbolism, of course. Much more subtle was the presentation of the Devil as a businessman, and the constant emphasis on money as a source of evil, in the teleplay *Markheim* (19 January 1957) shown in the 'On Camera' series. Or consider the case of 'Wojeck' (13 September 1966), where the Indian is beaten up, exploited, confused, and rejected by one white person after another, all of which signify 'Canada's shame.'

X / Mythologies: I used the term 'mythology' to mean no more than a collection of connected images and clichés. Although I suggested researchers look for a wide assortment of mythologies, I was most interested in the representation of four such collections that run through so much of discourse in North America.

Modernity: the idea of an onrushing progress, the source of peril as well as promise. I've already pointed out, in chapter 9, how frequently the 'religion of technology' was highlighted in commercials. In the play *The New Men*, though, the emphasis was upon the perils of technology. And in *The Queen of Spades* the amoral ways of the modern, rational man were opposed to an older morality of the supernatural.

Affluence: what might be called the materialist's definition of the good life. The adaptation of Gogol's *The Overcoat* by 'Playbill' (29 June 1954) explored the gulf between affluence (meaning possessions, security, comfort) and poverty (leading to deprivation and death). The big-money quizzes and later the give-away game shows were celebrations of greed. The two performers in 'Front Page Challenge,' Roger Maris and Harry Bridges, were both intent on getting their share of the pie (though in Bridges's case that meant for his workers as well).

Community: the notion that our personal existence is defined by belonging, to all kinds of groups, from family to friendship to occupation (or class) to nationality. *First Born* on 'Ford Theatre' (10 September 1953) emphasized the virtues of domestic harmony, and the recognition that this happy resolution could only come about when every member, including the ten-year-old boy, admitted his obligations to the family. The plight of the Indian in 'Wojeck' was that he didn't belong, and rejection brought his suicide. What the CBC newscast of 31 March 1960 highlighted, from this standpoint, was first the clash of parties over the new budget and second the clash of blacks and whites in South Africa.

Individualism: the notion that the individual is the key actor in the human drama. That might seem to run contrary to the emphasis upon community. Not so. Matt Dillon in 'Gunsmoke' (10 September 1955) was the individual who found his forte in defending the community against the gunslinger who denies social and moral restraints to gratify himself. The police on the rebroadcast of 'RCMP' were definitely social protectors, who saved their small town from the predatory ways of urban outsiders. Wojeck's stature as the heroic individual rested on the fact he embodied the ideal of justice in Canada. The commercials continually told people how they could each express themselves by buying a common product.

XI / Ideology: I adopted the common definition of ideology as a world-view. The collection of all the material mentioned so far enabled the researcher to see just how the broadcast represented society. That goal presumed that television doesn't mirror social realities (though sometimes it does come close) but aspects of the cultural realities, which is why television has been described as an agency of legitimation and, even more imposing, an instrument of bourgeois hegemony. I was more interested in answers to three sets of questions.

Social dynamics: who were the social players, what were their priorities, and who were the villains and the heroes? The chief purpose is to try to understand what kinds of people are honoured or dishonoured, as well as who are objects of pity or praise or hate. In the episode of 'The Untouchables' Eliot Ness and Aggie Stewart represent the police, the first an instrument of justice and the second of decency; the crime lord Charlie

Radick represents the criminal class, although he undergoes something of a transformation from villain to victim; and most of the other players, including the lost daughter Margaret, represent the community and appear as victims.

Social engines: what are the forces that define, bind, and divide people? The most attention was paid to sex, age, ethnicity, locale (city or country), beliefs (Catholic or Protestant; liberal and conservative), and class (broadly defined to include background, occupation, status, wealth, power, and consciousness). I also worried about the ways in which these 'engines' were presented – and which of them were given priority, as well as what was missing from the social equation. It won't surprise that in all kinds of dramas the most important 'engine' was usually sex: typically men were instrumental, rational, worldly, while women were objects or helpmates, emotional, domestic. Class was dealt with sometimes, but often in terms of occupation or status or background, not in terms of consciousness, never mind conflict. Of course many shows were like 'Space Command' (probably 1953) or 'Gunsmoke' where the key individuals appear as 'classless' males. That aside, the forces of age (the respect paid to the parents in 'The Plouffe Family'), of ethnicity (the spoof of the gipsy stereotype by Wayne and Shuster), of locale ('Wyatt Earp' showed Ellsworth, Kansas, the uncivilized town that stood for the American West in legend), and beliefs (Roman Catholicism in the 'Profile' episode) were all common ingredients. A popular play such as *The Arena* on 'Studio One' explained human actions according to the limited set of sex, age, and belief; a highbrow play such as *Juno and the Paycock* on 'Festival,' though, employed the whole range of 'engines' in its explanation of the social equation. That was no criterion of quality – both shows suffered because their characters became vehicles representing particular types in their societies.

Social attitudes: people have different views towards the world around them. The purpose of this section was to see how these were dealt with by television. What kinds of attitudes towards the status quo were honoured, dishonoured, or investigated as well as what did the broadcast 'say' about the assorted social conventions that conditioned the ways in which people responded to the pressures and institutions of ordinary life? I derived my basic scheme from Fiske and Hartley (p 104) who in turn had employed the classification of 'meaning systems' orginated by F. Parkin in *Class Inequality and Political Order*.

Aspiration and deference: the character shared the values of present society. That attitude was normally honoured in most kinds of popular storytelling, especially if the broadcast was made in Hollywood. Wyatt

Earp, for example, subscribed to the 'code of the West,' which required that he establish law and order, even at the cost of his own freedom. Wojeck may have been angered by the callous indifference of whites towards the Indian, and thus by the structure and ways of society, but he none the less embodied the higher ideals of justice and equality that were supposed to inform conduct in that society.

Acquiesence and accommodation: the character accepted the values and the ways of present society, even though he/she cannot fully endorse these. The attitude was implicit in the comedy of 'The Milton Berle Show' (5 June 1956): Berle and his compatriots searched for fun and pleasure, spoofed the official values, in a world that often seemed absurd.

Opposition and revolt: the character opposed the values and ways current in society. That attitude was normally dishonoured in most action/adventure drama because it was associated with criminals and other deviants who preyed upon the community. Comics were allowed to get away with some criticism of the foibles of the status quo: witness the satires of Wayne and Shuster. Beaver, in 'Leave It to Beaver' (an unidentified rebroadcast episode from the series), was very much a deviant, whose wilfulness caused all manner of trouble – he wasn't in any way condemned for this 'opposition and revolt.' But rarely, very rarely, did a broadcast offer viewers a sober critique of life, never mind a radical alternative to that life, which would thus have cast television in a consciously subversive role.

Alienation: the character is doomed by personal failings or circumstance to unhappiness, if not death. Such poor souls often appear in the role of victims in Hollywood's drama. The alienated person is normally to be pitied. But the episode of 'Cariboo Country' entitled 'Sara's Copper' (21 April 1966) did honour alienation: the final response of Sara and Johnny, two Indians who had found that getting ahead in white society required a surrender of their heritage and integrity, was to reject the values and ways of the society, preserving their pride at the cost of their future.

'The moral of the tale': what lesson (or lessons) might a viewer derive from watching the broadcast? The lesson might or might not be intended by the producer and his staff since the viewer could have an idiosyncratic response to, for instance, the news of a riot or a comedy about marriage, depending very much on his/her experience. But all sorts of programming did have a moral. Consider the quiz shows. Stephen Strople and Brigid Higgins decided that the particular moral of the episode of 'Front Page Challenge' they analysed was that 'personal qualities are responsible for success and achievement in widely varied fields of endeavour,' in this case sports and trade unionism. The structure of the program, though,

emphasized the virtues of journalism as a method of seeking the truth in life. Likewise 'The $64,000 Question' told viewers there was a 'democracy of knowledge' (that knowing about baseball was as worthwhile as knowing about Shakespeare), in which all could share, and to their profit, simply by memorizing facts. Here again, we're face to face with the didactic quality of television programming.

Notes

CF	*Canadian Forum*
FP	*The Financial Post*
MM	*Maclean's*
QQ	*Queen's Quarterly*
SN	*Saturday Night*
BBM	Bureau of Broadcast Measurement
E-H	Elliott-Haynes
ISL	International Surveys Limited
MDL	McDonald Research Limited
Nielsen	A.C. Nielsen
Schwerin	Schwerin Research Corporation
M&S	McClelland & Stewart
OUP	Oxford University Press
UTP	University of Toronto Press

Introduction: A Personal Journey

1 Herschel Hardin, *Closed Circuits: The Sellout of Canadian Television* (Vancouver: Douglas & McIntyre 1985). Hardin lays most of the blame on the Canadian Radio-Television Commission, which in fact faced the impossible task of trying to undo the 'damage' of the past. That said, his account contains some fascinating descriptions of the process of acquiring cable

licences and the hypocrisy that surrounded the debate over Canadian television in the 1970s and into the 1980s.

2 The term 'highbrow' has been used throughout this book, in preference to, say, 'intellectual', since it better suits a cultural history. 'Highbrow' indicates a person of superior taste in cultural products, namely someone devoted to élite or high culture rather than to mass culture. An intellectual may not necessarily fall into this camp. Morris Wolfe, *Jolts: The TV Wasteland and the Canadian Oasis* (Toronto: James Lorimer & Company 1985). Much of the book deals with the period after 1970, and so considers programs outside the scope of my work. Still, Wolfe is surely one of the best television critics this country has produced – very few of his fellows have been able or willing to think deeply about television – and so it deserves close attention.

3 Marshall McLuhan, *Understanding Media: The Extensions of Man* (New York: New American Library 1964). H.A. Innis's views can be sampled in *The Bias of Communication* (Toronto: UTP 1951). The works that have most influenced my own analysis are Raymond Williams, *Television: Technology and Cultural Form* (Glasgow: Fontana/Collins 1974), and John Fiske and John Hartley, *Reading Television* (London: Methuen 1980).

4 G. Laurence, *Histoire des programmes-TV, CBFT Montréal, Septembre 1952–Septembre 1957* (CRTC Research Report 1982) and M.J. Miller, *Turn Up the Contrast: CBC Television Drama since 1952* (Vancouver: University of British Columbia Press/CBC Enterprises 1987)

5 F. Peers, *The Public Eye: Television and the Politics of Canadian Broadcasting 1952–1968* (Toronto: UTP 1979)

6 Anyone interested in the joys of researching television history can read my account, 'Researching Television History: Prime-Time Canada, 1952–1967,' *Archivaria 20*, Summer 1985, 79–93.

7 The standard, one-volume work on the history of American television remains Erik Barnouw's *Tube of Plenty: The Evolution of American Television* (New York: OUP 1975). The schedule and program data for Primetime America has already been published in a variety of extremely useful collections: Alex McNeil, *Total Television: A Comprehensive Guide to Programming from 1948 to 1980* (New York: Penguin 1980); Tim Brooks and Earle Marsh, *The Complete Directory to Prime Time Network TV Shows 1946–Present*, rev. ed. (New York: Ballantine 1981); and Harry Castleman and Walter J. Podrazik, *Watching TV: Four Decades of American Television* (New York: McGraw-Hill 1982). The best overall survey of television is the thirteen part TV series called 'Television' produced by Granada Television for ITV in Britain and supplemented by Francis Wheen, *Television: A History* (London: Century Publishing 1985). As yet, CTV has not found its own historian.

1 Expectations

1 Cited in Max Rosenfeld, 'How TV Is Changing Your Life,' *MM*, 1 December 1954, 34. Mutrie was at one point the man in charge of developing television in Toronto.

2 Peet, 'Your House of Tomorrow,' *MM*, 15 September 1943, 12ff., and 'Tomorrow's Television,' *MM*, 15 October 1943, 19ff.; the ad was in the 15 March 1945 issue of *MM*, 23.

3 Ad figures from O.J. Firestone, *Broadcast Advertising in Canada: Past and Future Growth* (Ottawa: University of Ottawa Press 1966), 29, 46–7; circulation data for the press, magazines as well as dailies, from *Canada Year Book 1952–53*, 860–3

4 On motion-picture attendance over the years, see Garth Jowett and Barry Hemmings, 'The Growth of the Mass Media in Canada,' in B.D. Singer, ed. *Communications in Canadian Society*, 2nd rev. ed. (Toronto: Copp Clark 1975), 252–3. My figures don't jibe exactly with those of Jowett and Hemmings because I've included attendance at drive-ins, taken from M.C. Urquhart and K.A.H. Buckley, *Historical Statistics of Canada* (Toronto: Cambridge/Macmillan 1965), 580.

5 Charles Siepmann, 'Aspects of Broadcasting in Canada,' Royal Commission on National Development in the Arts, Letters and Sciences [hereafter Massey Commission], *Report* (Ottawa: King's Printer 1951), Appendix vi, 454

6 The American shows were carried on the CBC networks in the 1950/1 radio year; Siepmann, 'Aspects of Broadcasting in Canada,' 469: the average refers to twenty-two of the thirty-six independent stations then on the air.

7 The march of Culture is discussed briefly in Bernard Ostry, *The Cultural Connection* (Toronto: M&S 1978); the dates of the founding of the societies are taken from the listing in Appendix xii of the Massey Report, 503–5; see chapters 3 and 4 in Massey, *On Being Canadian* (Toronto: Dent and Sons 1948), 29–65; the other members of the commission were Georges-Henri Lévesque, Norman Mackenzie, Hilda Neatby, and Arthur Surveyor (the engineer); an abbreviated, more popular version of the report was prepared by Arthur Shea, under the title *Culture in Canada*, for wider distribution.

8 La Société des Écrivains Canadiens, 'Brief,' Massey Commission, 4; F. Underhill, 'Notes on the Massey Report,' *In Search of Canadian Liberalism* (Toronto: Macmillan 1961), 209 (the article was first published in 1951 in *CF*).

9 Program Services Committee, National Council of Young Men's Christian Associations of Canada, 'Submission,' Royal Commission on Broadcasting [hereafter Fowler 1], May 1956, 4; Neatby, 'The Massey Report: A Retrospect,'

Tamarack Review, Autumn 1956, 40; Lower, 'Brief,' Fowler I, 1956, 15

10 Massey Report, 7; see Robert Ayre, 'The Press Debates the Massey Report,' *Canadian Art*, August 1951, 25ff., for a survey of responses.

11 B.K. Sandwell, 'Present Day Influences on Canadian Society,', Massey Commission, *Royal Commission Studies* (Ottawa: King's Printer 1951), 2 and 3

12 There is a brief but useful discussion of Innis theories in Daniel Czitrom, *Media and the American Mind: From Morse to McLuhan* (Chapel Hill: University of North Carolina Press 1982), 147–65. Innis's concepts of 'bias,' of 'monopolies of knowledge,' of the effects of media competition or the dominance of one medium are fruitful instruments for understanding the process of social and cultural change. But Innis didn't devote much attention to broadcasting, saying virtually nothing about television, and his ideas seem to have had only limited influence upon academe prior to the 1970s. That's why I've expended far more space in this chapter in analysing Marshall McLuhan (see pages 26–38).

13 On the American scene, see Bernard Rosenberg and David Manning White, eds., *Mass Culture: The Popular Arts in America* (Glencoe, Ill.: Free Press 1957); Underhill, 'Notes on the Massey Report,' 212–13; Michel Brunet, 'Une autre manifestation du nationalisme Canadian: le rapport Massey,' in *Canadians et Canadiens* (Montreal: Fides 1954), 47–58, first published in 1952 (note that Brunet saw the Massey solution as meant only for English Canada and not designed to satisfy French Canada's needs); Dinsdale speech in Canada, House of Commons, *Debates*, 2nd Session 1951, v. 2, 1865–9.

14 Lower, 'Brief,' 9; and Neatby, 'The Massey Report,' 45

15 Lower, 'Brief,' 20; Public Affairs Institute, 'Brief,' Massey Commission, 3

16 This view of history had some merit: see Margaret Prang, 'The Origins of Public Broadcasting in Canada,' *Canadian Historical Review* [hereafter CHR], 46, March 1965, 1–31; *Canadian Forum*'s chief spokesmen were first Carleton McNaught as 'R.B. Tolbridge' and later Allan Sangster; see comments on 'upgrading' in the Massey brief of the Public Affairs Institute, 3, and Sangster, 'On the Air,' January 1952, 230.

17 For samples of the initial discussions of television, in addition to the articles by Peet mentioned in note 2, above, see Stuart Griffiths, 'Television Tomorrow?' *Canadian Homes & Gardens*, November 1944, 78; Merrill Denison, 'What about Television?' *MM*, 15 December 1944, 17, 38–41; Joseph Crampton, 'Canada's Television Tease,' *Canadian Business*, January 1949, 38–40, 76–8; C. Walter Stone, 'Plan Now for Television,' *Food for Thought*, 9, January 1949, 5–8, 38; 'Television Session,' *Industrial Canada*, July 1949, 186–97; Pierre Berton, 'Make Way for the One-Eyed Monster,' *MM*, 1 June 1949,

8, 56–7. Stratovision involved telecasting from airplanes to receivers on the ground. Barbara Moon, 'The Next Ten Years of TV,' *MM*, 13 October 1956, 16ff.

18 L. Greene, 'Television – Medium or Tedium?' *SN*, 23 May 1950, 43; A. Ouimet, 'Television and Its Impact on Our Way of Life,' Address to the Alumnae Society of McGill University, 16 February 1953, National Archives of Canada, RG41, v. 401, file 23-1-4, pt. 1; La Fédération des Sociétés Saint-Jean-Baptiste du Québec, 'Memoire,' Fowler I, 13 April 1956, 13 and 14

19 Jean McKinley, 'Seeing Is Believing,' *Canadian Homes & Gardens*, August 1949, 11; Pelletier, 'Un défi: la télévision,' *Cité Libre*, August 1956, 9; Confédération des Travailleurs Catholiques du Canada [hereafter CTCC], 'Mémoire,' Fowler I, 5; Canadian Mental Health Association, 'Brief,' Fowler I, April 1956, 1

20 F. Mutrie, 'What Future for Television?' *Food for Thought*, 10, March 1950, 28; Ouimet, 'Television and Its Impact on Our Way of Life,' 5; N. Morrison, 'Television and the Humanities,' in 'Is Television a Threat? – A Symposium,' *QQ*, 63, Summer 1956, 267; A. Larendeau, 'Sur la television et les Canadiens français,' in ibid, 277–85; and G. Pelletier, 'Un défi: la télévision,' 4–11

21 Massey Report, 42; Mavor Moore, 'What We'll Do with TV,' *SN*, 24 May 1952, 19; CTCC, 'Mémoire,' 5; the script of the two American talks were printed in the *CBC Times* of 22–28 July 1951 and 20–26 July 1952, respectively.

22 L'Association des Professeurs de Carrière de l'Université Laval, 'Mémoire,' Fowler I, June 1956, 3; J. Tweed, 'American "Dumped" Films Can Kill Canadian Television Industry,' *SN*, 17 May 1949, 6

23 Crampton, 'Canada's Television Tease,' 38 and 78; Deakins, 'Industry Position and Trade Potentialities of Television,' *Industrial Canada*, July 1949, 196–7; Canadian Marconi Company, 'Brief,' Massey Commission, November 1949, 14 (the company owned CFCF-Montreal); Toronto Broadcasting Company, 'Brief,' Massey Commission, November 1949, 28 and 29 (the company owned CKEY-Toronto)

24 A. Lower, 'The Question of Private TV,' *QQ*, 60, Summer 1953, 174, 175, 176

25 R. Allen, *The Chartered Libertine* (Toronto: Macmillan 1954), 264

26 Eliot's comments were even published in the endnotes of the Massey Report, 413; McGeachy quoted in *FP*, 13 January 1951, 12; Don Magill, 'What TV Will Do to You,' *MM*, 1 March 1951, 22–4; Nancy Cleaver, 'TV ... Home-Breaker or Home Maker?' *SN*, 16 January 1951, 22; YMCA, 'Brief,' 6; University of Toronto, 'Educational Television in Canada: The University's Role,' Fowler I, April 1956, 1.

27 YMCA, 'Brief,' 9; Children's Section, Ontario Library Association, 'Brief,' 1; Parossiens de l'Immaculée-Conception, 'Mémoire,' 7; and the Women's Inter-Church Council of Canada, 'Brief,' 2

28 Fowler I, 6

29 Morrison, 'TV and the Humanities,' 269–75

30 Humanities, 'Brief,' 2; Moore, 'What We'll Do with TV,' 20; CTCC, 'Memoire,' 6; Saint-Jean-Baptiste, 'Memoire,' 15–16

31 YMCA, 'Brief,' 7–8; Fowler I, 6; Laurendeau, 'Sur la télévision et les Canadiens français,' 281–5; CRTL, 'Brief,' II; Lower, 'Brief,' 17

32 The term 'McLunacy' from a 1967 poem by E.F. Miller, published in John Robert Colombo, *Colombo's Little Book of Canadian Proverbs, Graffiti, Limericks, and Other Vital Matters* (Edmonton: Hurtig 1975), 85. My analysis of McLuhan's ideas and his stardom are based upon his three main books in the 1960s (*The Gutenberg Galaxy, Understanding Media*, and *The Medium is the Massage*); the edition of his letters edited by Matie Molinaro, Corinne McLuhan, and William Toye, *Letters of Marshall McLuhan* (Toronto: OUP 1987), plus an assortment of articles and interviews; the collections of book reviews, essays, and comments on McLuhan edited by Gerald E. Stearn, *McLuhan: Hot & Cool* (New York: Dial Press 1967); Raymond Rosenthal, ed. *McLuhan: Pro & Con* (Baltimore, Md: Penguin 1968); and Harry H. Crosby and George R. Bond, *The McLuhan Explosion: A Casebook on Marshall McLuhan and* Understanding Media (New York: American Book Company 1968); and the works of criticism by Sidney Finkelstein, *Sense and Nonsense of McLuhan* (New York: International Publishers 1968); Dennis Duffy, *Marshall McLuhan* (Toronto: M&S 1969); Jonathan Miller, *McLuhan* (London: Fontana/Collins 1971); Donald F. Theall, *The Medium Is the Rear View Mirror* (Montreal: McGill-Queen's University Press 1971); and Czitrom, *Media and the American Mind*. McLuhan's letters are an especially revealing source of information about the man's attitude towards himself and toward other people. Philip Marchand's fascinating biography, *Marshall McLuhan: The Medium and the Messenger* (Toronto: Random House 1989), contains a lengthy discussion of McLuhan's rise to stardom. And there's an intriguing portrait of McLuhan in Robert Fulford's *Best Seat in the House: Memoirs of a Lucky Man* (Toronto: Collins 1988), 162–84.

33 Most of the descriptions are taken from pieces in Stearn, ed., *Hot & Cool*; Rosenthal, ed., *Pro & Con*; and Crosby and Bond, *The McLuhan Explosion*. Miller's phrase closes off his book *McLuhan*. The comment by Frye is from *The Modern Century: The Whidden Lectures 1967* (Toronto: OUP 1967), 39. Dudek's description is in his address 'Technology and Culture,' *Transactions*

of the Royal Society of Canada, Series IV, v. 7 (1969), 60. The final nickname from *Newsweek*, 28 February 1966, was reprinted in Crosby, 100.

34 For McLuhan's comments on Canada, see his letters to Claude Bissell of 4 March 1965 and 28 January 1966 and to Pierre Trudeau of 16 April and 2 December 1968 in Molinaro, McLuhan, and Toye, eds., *Letters*. Theall, *The Medium Is the Rear View Mirror*, 245–51, has a brief description of the importance of Toronto itself.

35 See Theall, Ibid, and Miller, *McLuhan*, for extensive discussions of the source of McLuhan's ideas.

36 Miller was then more sympathetic to McLuhan – see his comments made on a BBC symposium on McLuhan in 1966 and reprinted in Stearn, Ed., *Hot & Cool*, 238; McLuhan's own comments on his style in an interview with Stearn (see especially pages 285, 294, and 297). McLuhan's comments on money, in *Understanding Media*, 123; his play on Shakespeare, in *The Medium Is the Massage*, 14; and on radio, in *Understanding Media*, 263.

37 Nairn's comment, in Rosenthal, ed., *Pro & Con*, 141. Nairn was a British sociologist.

38 'Talk of the Town,' *The New Yorker*, 15 May 1965, and the *Time* review, both reprinted in Crosby and Bond, *The McLuhan Explosion*, 85 and 43, respectively. The marvellous Tom Wolfe piece is reprinted in Stearn, Ed., *Hot & Cool*, 15–34. On McLuhan's TV appearances see Dennis Braithwaite's scathing criticism of his efforts on a CBC show (Toronto *Globe and Mail*, 24 June 1965) and the articles by Michael Arlen, 'Marshall McLuhan & the Technological Embrace,' reprinted in Rosenthal, ed., *Pro & Con*, 82–7, and Robert Shayon, 'Not-So-Cool Medium,' reprinted in Crosby and Bond, *The McLuhan Explosion*, 208.

39 There's a run-down of where, and how many, pieces about McLuhan were published in the period 1965 through 1967 in Crosby and Bond, 4–6. The statistic on *The New York Times* is in Molinaro, et al., eds., *Letters*, 175.

40 I don't wish to speculate as to whether all this means that McLuhan's ideas were somehow uniquely Canadian in origin. That would require a thorough investigation of just what Americans were saying about TV in the immediate post-war years to see whether there was a substantial difference in the approach or the themes of the discussion. What limited knowledge I have of the literature, though, suggests that the Canadian observers were merely echoing what other people were saying in Great Britain as well as in the United States.

2 Enter CBC-TV

1 *CBC Times*, 15–21 December 1957, 2
2 Ouimet, 'Report on Television,' *The Engineering Journal*, 83, March 1950, 173, cited in Dallas Smythe, *Dependency Road: Communications, Capitalism, Consciousness, and Canada* (Norwood, NJ: Ablex Publishing 1981), 179. Smythe, however, believes that this decision wasn't inevitable; rather it was an unfortunate surrender to the demands of North American business.
3 See Black's *Chronology of Network Broadcasting in Canada 1901–1961*, 67, NAC, RG 41, and the *Canada Year Book 1952/53*, 848. The cost of running the international service was an additional $1.5 million in 1949/50.
4 R.E. Keddy, 'Les fonctions du Bureau des Gouverneurs,' *La Semaine à Radio-Canada*, 14–20 September 1952, 4. There was, however, a small executive committee that could meet to give advice and consent to the chairman in the event of an emergency.
5 See Alan Phillips, 'They All Throw Rocks at Davey Dunton,' MM, 2 April 1955, 24–5, 37–8, 40, for a contemporary discussion of Dunton's skills.
6 On early television experiments in Canada, see Leonard Spencer, 'Birth of the TV Miracle – 1925,' *Canadian Broadcaster*, 25 April 1968, 58, 60–1; Ouimet, 'The Foothills of Unity,' *The McGill News*, Autumn 1962, 6–7, 27.
7 See Peter Stursberg, *Mr. Broadcasting: The Ernie Bushnell Story* (Toronto: Peter Martin Associates Ltd 1971).
8 Young, 'Let's Stop Monopoly Television,' MM, 1 May 1954, 76. The description of the CBC's gospel of television is taken from Dunton's piece in *Canadian Unionist*, February 1953; his 'Television and Our Way of Life,' Address to the Canadian Public Relations Society, 14 May 1953, 4 (in RG 41, v. 401, file 23-1-4, pt. 1); his 'Television and Business in Canada,' *Business Quarterly*, 20, Winter 1955; Ouimet's 'Television and Its Impact on Our Way of Life,' Address to the Alumnae Society of McGill University, 16 February, 1953; Moore, 'What We'll Do with TV,' in SN, 24 May 1952; and the CBC's 'Memorandum,' Fowler I, 29 March 1956.
9 Black, *Chronology*, 69; *Canada Year Book 1952–53*, 848
10 The coverage figure for March 1960 is a bit inflated because the CBC *Annual Report* 1959/60 (9) included homes unlikely to receive very good reception all the time. Data on loans to CBC from Peers, *The Public Eye: Television and the Politics of Canadian Broadcasting 1952–1968* (Toronto: UTP 1979), 51; data on private investment from Canada, Parliament, Committee on Broadcasting, *Report* [hereafter Fowler II] (Ottawa: Queen's Printer 1965), 392.
11 Barris, *The Pierce-Arrow Showroom Is Leaking: An Insider's View of the CBC* (Toronto: Ryerson 1969), 2–6; the Radio-Canada figures from Gérard Lau-

rence, *Histoire des programmes-TV, CBFT Montréal, Septembre 1952–Septembre 1957*, 427–32; the overall figure on staff is from Black, *Chronology*, 91.

12 Canada, Dominion Bureau of Statistics, 'Household Facilities and Equipment,' *Bulletin: 64-202*, 1959.

13 Wilbur Schramm, Jack Lyle, and Edwin B. Parker, *Television in the Lives of Our Children* (Toronto: UTP 1961), 17

14 See the briefs by Jack St John, an MLA, and Thomas Goode, an MP, to Fowler I; the statistics on antennae in ISL, *Season Listening and Viewing Habits in Canada and Its 3 Major Markets 1958–59*, 75; for a sample of views on pay television, see *FP* 20 September 1952, 14 December 1957, 21 March 1959; and in *SN*, John Creed's 'Rediffusion Hits TV,' II October 1952; Walter Dales's 'Toll TV – Threat or Promise,' 20 August 1955; Gordon Donaldson's 'Pay TV: A First for Canada?' 30 August 1958; and Dean Walker's 'Toll-TV: The Money Pipeline,' 26 November 1960.

15 Stursberg, *Mr. Broadcasting*, 173. Not that bureaucracy was something novel to the corporation: Bronwyn Drainie in *Living the Part: John Drainie and the Dilemma of Canadian Stardom* (Toronto: Macmillan of Canada 1988), 63–4, recounts some examples of where the CBC's penchant for going through channels made things difficult for Andrew Allan in Vancouver, and hopeful playwrights in Winnipeg, during 1940 as they began to lay the foundations of the golden age of radio drama.

16 Hudson story from Morris Duff, '10 Years of Toronto TV Today,' *Toronto Daily Star*, 8 September 1962; Guy Parent, *Sous le règne des bruiteurs* (Montreal: Éditions du Lys 1963)

17 Payne interview (Finlay Payne was an announcer who became in the late 1950s the editor of special projects at head office); CBC, *Annual Report* 1953/4, 34; and CBC, 'Organization, Functions and Management,' Fowler I, 36

18 Austin Weir, *The Struggle for National Broadcasting in Canada* (Toronto: M&S 1965), 410; Stursberg, *Mr. Broadcasting*, 169; Judy LaMarsh, *Memoirs of a Bird in a Gilded Cage* (Toronto: Pocket Books 1970), 252; Fraser interview (Ron Fraser was a Maritime farm broadcaster who became a director of Public Affairs, a vice-president of Corporate Affairs, and a special assistant to Ouimet)

19 Figure 2.2 based on CBC, 'Organization, Functions and Management,' Fowler I. The document, which runs to eighty-four pages plus appendices, contains a number of organizational charts as well as an extensive description of the lines of authority. Munro and Dunton interviews (Marcel Munro began as a radio announcer, served as a manager in British Columbia, and eventually became a director of television of the English network and an assistant general manager of television for the English Services division).

20 Jennings was speaking to the first meeting of the program committee of the board of directors (*Minutes*, 2). Boyle, MacPherson, and Lauk interviews: Boyle was a long-time CBC radio producer and supervisor who eventually joined the Canadian Radio-Television Commission in the 1970s; MacPherson was an accountant and manager who worked in the CBC, off and on, as well as in other institutions of Canadian television; Lauk was a CBC television producer in Vancouver who eventually moved into administration.

21 Ouimet II; 'Backstage with the CBC Strike,' *MM*, 14 March 1959, 3; Woods, 'Arbitration Report,' 20 January 1960, 7–12 (RG 41, v. 675). There is extensive comment on the strike in the interviews of Guy Parent and Ouimet II.

22 The best two accounts of the dispute, quite opposite in their approach, are by Peers, *The Public Eye*, 193–200, and by Stursberg, *Mr. Broadcasting*, 189–222. Margaret Conrad, *George Nowlan: Maritime Conservative in National Politics* (Toronto: UTP 1986), 226–7, notes that George Nowlan, the minister through whom the CBC reported to Parliament, did admit he'd occasionally mentioned to Bushnell the wisdom of avoiding too much controversial programming, but not that he'd told Bushnell to cancel 'Preview Commentary.' Bushnell overcame his drinking problems and went on to build, with others, private television in Ottawa and elsewhere during the 1960s.

23 Royal Commission on Government Organization [hereafter Glassco Commission], *Report 19: 'Canadian Broadcasting Corporation,'* v. 4: *Special Areas of Administration* (Ottawa: Queen's Printer 1963), 29, 33–40

24 Barris, *The Pierce-Arrow Showroom*, 1. Such problems are not uncommon in the history of public broadcasting, however: see K.S. Inglis, *This Is the ABC: The Australian Broadcasting Commission 1932–1982* (Melbourne: Melbourne University Press 1983), 332.

25 On Howe's outburst, see Robert Bothwell and William Kilbourne, *C.D. Howe: A Biography* (Toronto: M&S 1979), 294–5. Dunton was apparently unperturbed by this outburst, which had occurred over the phone. On a later occasion though, in 1956, during the infamous pipe-line debate, Dunton did contemplate cancelling a proposed press conference on television with the opposition leader George Drew because he feared that no Liberal would agree to come the week following – and that would break the rule of balance. But, in the end, Dunton was persuaded to let the invitation go out, and Howe himself came in the succeeding week. Dunton and Earle interviews.

26 Barney Milford, 'Exhibit "B" in the Great TV Debate,' *MM*, 15 October 1953, 30 and 80; for the comments of the first two politicians, see Canada, House of Commons, *Debates*, 2nd Session 1951, v. 2, 13 December 1951, 1890, and Session 1952/3, v. 1, 10 December 1952, 524; for the views of Jack St John, see his 'Brief' to the Fowler Commission, 1956.

27 On media monopolies, see 'Television and Freedom,' *CF*, May 1953, 27.

28 The anecdote is in Walker, 'Canada's TV Dilemma: The American Influence,' *SN*, 23 July 1960, 16.

29 CFPL data from F.O. Baldwin, 'Those Private TV Men Are Still in Business,' *Canadian Business*, May 1956, 19; CBC payments from Leslie Reed, 'Public Ownership + Private Enterprise = CBC,' *Industrial Canada*, October 1961, 38, and Fowler II, 331; ranking cited in Graham Spry, 'The Decline and Fall of Canadian Broadcasting,' *QQ*, 68, Summer 1961, 216.

30 Phillips, "They All Throw ... ,' 37

31 Starmer interview; Barris, *The Pierce-Arrow Showroom*, 124 and 28; Scott Young, 'Let's Stop Monopoly Television,' 77; on the American situation, see Erik Barnouw, *The Sponsor* (New York: OUP 1978).

32 CBC, Board of Directors, fifth meeting, 23 June 1959, 3–4 (RG 41, v. 675). A little later, Radio-Canada would employ a special evaluation committee made up of outsiders to decide whether or not an interview with Simone de Beauvoir should be broadcast – the decision was no. See the report in the *Minutes* of the 7th Program Committee. In short the principle of permanent oversight groups was wrong, not the occasional use of such groups.

33 Fowler I, 43; *Minutes*, 1st Meeting of Sub-Committee of Program Committee, 11 June 1959, 6. Thelma McCormack, in an article on Fowler I, claimed that the commission's failure to understand the import of public concern, and its determination to strengthen the position of management, were serious flaws, in the minds of many people. One worry she had about the board was that it was appointed, not elected, and so didn't seem particularly representative of popular sentiment: 'Canada's Royal Commission on Broadcasting,' *Public Opinion Quarterly*, 23, 1959, 92–100.

34 'The Future Role of the CBC,' 3–4 (RG 41, v. 675)

35 The CBC's fiscal year ended in March. The figures are taken from a number of sources: CBC Annual Reports, the *Canada Year Book*, and Fowler I. Note that the figures on television expenses do not include costs for supervision, services, and administration (initially listed on CBC balance sheets as a radio expense), which were chargeable to the CBC as an entity. The net TV cost in 1959/60 results from subtracting the ad revenues earned from what was considered the total cost of television operations (Fowler II, 330).

36 Fowler II, 331

37 CBC 'Memorandum,' Fowler I, 25

38 Pierre Berton, 'Everybody Boos the CBC,' *MM*, 1 December 1950, 7; Massey Report, 294; Roger E. Carswell, 'C.B.C. Finances,' *Canadian Tax Journal*, 4, no. 3 (May–June 1956), 201

39 The radio licence fee was also ended, and a similar excise tax imposed on

radio sets and parts, though there was a ceiling on the amount the CBC could secure from this tax because of the statutory grant. Figures on surplus or deficits from CBC Annual Reports.

40 The other commissioners were Edmond Turcotte, one-time editor of Montreal's Liberal daily *Le Canada* but lately an ambassador, and James Stewart, president of the Canadian Bank of Commerce. The Fowler proposal for statutory grants involved linking the specific sum of money to some economic indicator, such as the consumer price index.

41 Diefenbaker cited in Eric Hutton, 'What Kind of TV Will We Get This Fall?' *MM*, 3 August 1957, 11; see Peers's testimony to the parliamentary committee on broadcasting, quoted in Stursberg, *Mr. Broadcasting*, 207.

42 The estimated public cost calculated from the operating grant for 1959/60 and number of sets as of May 1959 (Canada, Dominion Bureau of Statistics, 'Household Facilities and Equipment,' *Bulletin: 64-202*, 1959, 18).

43 Statistics on commercial programming from CBC *Annual Report* 1950/1, 13, and CBC, Audience Research Division, 'Program Statistical Analysis Report: 4th Quarter, January–March 1956' (CBC Ottawa), 25; GM contract from CBC, *Minutes*, 2nd Program Committee, 4

44 Dorothy Sangster, 'The Most Baffling Show on Television,' *MM*, 9 June 1956, 87. CBC policy also discussed in the Payne interview. Fowler Commission, Appendix XII: 'Report of the Financial Advisor, Guy E. Hoult' [hereafter Hoult], *Report*, 449; Bushnell's statement in CBC, *Minutes*, eighth meeting of Program Committee, 25 January 1960, 3

3 What's on Tonight?

1 'Bloody but Unbowed, CBC Will Live,' *FP*, 25 July 1959, 7

2 For an example of a book based on this myth, see Sally Bedell, *Up the Tube: Prime-Time TV in the Silverman Years* (New York: Viking 1981), which analyses the wild career of Fred Silverman as a 'programmer' (among other things) at the three American commercial networks in the 1970s.

3 The process, if such we can call it, of misunderstanding a message is closely related to what is called, in the jargon of semiotics, 'aberrant decoding.' That ugly phrase refers to a situation where the viewers interpret a message in the light of their own special experiences, according to codes and conventions that differ from those of the communicators, with the result that the meaning of the message is not what was intended. Aberrant decoding is thought to be very normal throughout the mass media. See John Fiske and John Harley, *Reading Television* (London: Methuen 1980), 57.

4 Put another way, television contains a large element of redundancy. That

phrase comes out of information theory where redundancy refers to rule-bound messages or supplemental data that work to reduce the surprise effect upon the receiver of the message itself. For a discussion of redundancy, see Fiske, *Introduction to Communication Studies* (London: Methuen 1982), 10–17, and Campbell, *Grammatical Man: Information, Entropy, Language and Life* (Harmondsworth: Penguin 1984), 67–74.

5 My adoption of the term 'form' is based upon the approach adopted by Raymond Williams, *Television: Technology and Cultural Form* (Glasgow: FonFard/Collin, 1974), 44–77, although he identifies as much wider range of forms that 'raises' the stature of some of the groups I refer to as 'genres.' The discussion of television programming, of course, is continued in each of the chapters on a brand of programming as well as in Appendix I.

6 Fowler I, 44. The commission's conclusions rested on a detailed content analysis of one week of television, 15 to 21 January 1956, carried out by Dallas Smythe.

7 Sources for the discussion of American programming, as well as the schedules and shows of the networks, are Harry Castleman and Walter J. Podrazich, *Watching TV: Four Decades of American Television* (New York: McGraw-Hill 1982); Tim Brook and Earle Marsh, *The Complete Directory to Prime Time Network TV Shows 1946–Present*, 2nd ed. (New York: Ballantine 1981); and Alex McNeil, *Total Television: A Comprehensive Guide to Programming from 1968 to 1980* (New York: Renguis 1980). DuMont, the fourth network, was such a limited network, soon unable to program a full evening schedule and eventually dropping out of the network game in 1955, that its shows haven't been analysed.

8 Ouimet I; CBC, 'Memorandum,' Fowler I, 16; Moore, 'Canada and Television,' 9; see Dunton, 'Television and Our Way of Life' and 'Television in Canada.'

9 Berton, 'Everybody Boos the CBC,' 33

10 Smythe, *Canadian Television and Sound Radio Programmes*, 1957, Fowler I, Appendix xiv to the *Report*, 70; on the price of imports see Graham Spry, 'The Decline and Fall of Canadian Broadcasting,' 217, and Barnouw, *Tube of Plenty*, 235; Shield, *The Toronto Daily Star*, 27 September 1962.

11 CBC Audience Research, *Report of the Ratings Review Committee*, July 1960, quotations from pages 12 and 38

12 See 'How CBC Spends $125,00 to Test Listener Reaction,' *FP*, 10 September 1955, 28; and Neil Morrison, 'CBC Audience Research Division,' *Food for Thought*, 18, January 1958, 162–9, for descriptions of the early service. There is also material on the activities of the division in the Morrison and Lewis interviews.

13 Gwyn, 'The Critics,' *Canadian Art*, 9, no. 5 (September/October 1962), 344–

7. Ironically, Bob Fulford doesn't really discuss his writings on television in his memoirs, *The Best Seat in the House*, proof perhaps that even the most perceptive of critics didn't see much lasting significance to his work.

14 CBC, *Annual Report* 1957/8, 21; on the NFB'S ambitions, see Martin Knelman, *This Is Where We Came In* (Toronto: M&S 1977), 23. The comment on Mulholland's efforts mentioned in the Weyman interview.

15 On CFPL-TV see Baldwin, 'Those Private TV Men Are Still in Business,' 19; on CKNX-TV see 'Everybody's Star in Small Town TV,' *FP*, 28 June 1958, 21; Spry, 'The Decline and Fall of Canadian Broadcasting,' 215.

16 Fowler I, 66 and 76: the definition was taken from the brief of the University of British Columbia; Ouimet was quoted in *CBC Times*, 23–29 January 1960, 27.

17 Moore, 'What We'll Do with TV,' 20; CBC, 'Memorandum,' Fowler I, 8 and 15

18 Fowler I, 218 and 220; Fowler II, 59; CBC, 'Memorandum,' Fowler I, 20

19 1953 figures from 'CBC Talking Points – Commercial,' in RG 41, v. 170, file 11-15-2; Manings quoted in Frank Rasky, 'Canada's TV Season: Alive and Kicking without a Horse,' *Liberty*, February 1959, 54; Roger Lee Jackson, 'An Historial and Analytical Study of the Origin, Development and Impact of the Dramatic Programs Produced for the English Language Networks of the CBC,' unpublished PhD thesis, Wayne State University, 1966, 154–5. Jackson's thesis is an excellent source of information on the ways of CBC Toronto because it was largely a compilation of quotations from the extensive interviews he'd carried out with people associated with the production of CBC drama in the 1950s and 1960s.

20 'Qui fait la valeur d'une émission?' *Point de Vue*, April 1957, 36. Parent interview

21 Cohen quoted in Jackson, 'Dramatic Programs,' 105

22 Guy Parent, in the interview, charged that Mulholland had carried out a purge of francophone producers at the NFB, which was why so many turned up in Radio-Canada.

23 Allen interview. Hart quoted in *CBC Times*, 27 February–5 March 1955, 6; Kaplan quoted in *CBC Times*, 10–14 January 1954 11; Greene quoted in *CBC Times*, 24–30 October 1954, 3 and 11; Parent, *Sous le règne des bruiteurs*, 29–30; Roger Rolland, 'La télévision, un art populaire où CBFT fait des miracles,' *Points de Vue*, April 1956, 15–16

24 *CBC Times*, 21–27 September 1952, 5; A. Barris, *The Pierce-Arrow Showroom: An Insiders' View of The CBC* (Toronto: Ryerson 1969), 14–20. Barnes quotation cited in Jackson, 'Dramatic Programs,' 162–3

25 *La Semaine à Radio-Canada*, 3–9 July 1955, 8; Kaplan in *CBC Times*, 24–30

October 1954, 2; Weyman interview; Hull, 'Pay Attention to TV Writing Rules,' *Canadian Author and Bookman*, Summer 1960, 9

26 Kemp quotation in Jackson, 'Dramatic Programs,' 170–1, and Israel in ibid, 98–9

27 Jewison in *CBC Times*, 7–13 March 1954, 2; Newman in *CBC Times*, 24–30 October 1954, 2; Orenstein in *CBC Times*, 12–13 December 1959, 4

28 Moore, 'What We'll Do with TV,' 20

29 Canadian Association for Adult Education, 'Brief,' Fowler I, II; Ouimet and McDonald in Rasky, 'Canada's TV Season,' 52; Parent, *Sous le règne*, 102; Peter Gzowski, 'Ross McLean, the TV Star You Never See,' *MM*, 16 January 1960, 13

30 Reginald Boisvert, 'Qui veut la fin prend les moyens', *Cité Libre*, August 1956, 55–6; Willis in *CBC Times*, 23–29 January 1955, 3; on the 'Human Relations Forum,' see page 5 of the minutes of the first meeting of the Sub-Committee of the Program Committee and on the Simone de Beauvoir affair see the appendix to the minutes of the seventh meeting of the Program Committee; Hull, 'Pay Attention to TV Writing Rules,' 9

31 J.A. Ouimet, *'Canadian* TV Is Worth It!,' 6; Moon, 'How to Get on Television,' *MM*, 19 December 1959, 48; Rasky, 'Canada's TV Season,' 17; Bill Stephenson 'The Wonderful World of French-Canadian TV,' *MM*, 8 June 1957 edition; 'CBC-TV Sweeps Board at Ohio,' *CBC Times*, 23–9 May 1959, 4–5; Les Reed, 'CBC-TV 1952–62: A Decade of Achievement,' *Canadian Geographical Journal*, 55, September 1962, 88

32 In *MM*, 14 April 1956, 13–15, 108, 110, 112–119

33 Hutton, 'What Kind of TV Will We Get This Fall?' 12 and 42

34 Gauntlett in Jackson, 'Dramatic Programs,' 156; programming statistics from a document entitled 'Canadian Foreign Balance,' dated 16 February 1961, in RG 41, v. 65, file 2-3-17-6, pt. I

35 Fowler I, 69; Barnes quoted in Jackson, 'Dramatic Programs,' 163 – his feeling hadn't changed when he was interviewed in the 1980s; Rasky, 'Canada's Most Successful Export: TV Talent,' SN, 6 June 1959, 14

36 Quotation from Frank Shuster in Rasky, 'Canada's TV Season,' 53

37 Garner, 'Remember When TV Was Fun?' *Star Weekly Magazine*, 23 December 1961

38 Payne and Weyman interviews

39 On the made-up quality of modern TV, see Peter Gzowski, *The Private Voice: A Journal of Reflections* (Toronto: M&S 1988), 240–3. MacPherson, Nutt, and Weyman interviews. Israel quoted in Brian Stewart, 'TV Drama: Where Will It Go from Here?' *CBC Times*, 10–16 December 1960, 10

4 Enter CTV

1 Thomson was talking about his Scottish Television Limited, one of the program-makers licensed by Britain's Independent Television Authority. Russell Braddon, *Roy Thomson of Fleet Street* (London Collins 1965), 240
2 That was the opening line in the report, 3.
3 The Fowler II quotation has been used outside Canada, too: for example,
  E.G. Wedell, in his study of the British scene, *Broadcasting and Public Policy*
  (London: Michael Joseph 1968), started his discussion of 'institutional form
  and programme content' (p. 161) by mentioning the Fowler II maxim.
4 As was the case in chapter 2, the best single source for detail about the politics
  of broadcasting is Frank Peers's *The Public Eye: Television and the Politics
  of Canadian Broadcasting* (Toronto: UTP 1979).
5 George Nowlan, the minister of national revenue and the man through whom
  the CBC reported to Parliament, had apparently begun the task of producing
  a new act in the spring of 1958. After the election, he did try to sell the full
  'Fowler formula' to cabinet, though without success because other more
  powerful ministers were determined the CBC would be brought under control
  and that the government would appear committed to 'free television.' See
  Margaret Conrad, *George Nowlan: Maritime Conservative in National Politics*
  (Toronto: UTP 1986),
6 Canada, Broadcasting Act, *Statutes of Canada 1958*, 140 (page 4 of the act)
7 LaMarsh became secretary of state in 1965, thus responsible for broadcasting
  policy in the Pearson government. LaMarsh, *Memoirs of a Bird in a Gilded Cage*
  (Toronto: Pocket Books 1970), 255. Two very useful discussions of the career
  of the BBG are Peter Stewart Grant's lengthy investigation of its Canadian-
  content rulings (among other matters) in 'The Regulation of Program Content
  in Canadian Television,' *Canadian Public Administration*, 11, 1968, 322–91, and
  W.H.N. Hull's defence of the board in 'Captive or Victim: The Board of
  Broadcast Governors and Bernstein's Law, 1958–68,' *Canadian Public
  Administration*, 26, Winter 1983, 544–62. The CBCer Finlay Payne recalled
  that the permanent members of the BBG never went to CBC personnel to
  find out what was going on in broadcasting, to somehow overcome the members' lack of experience – Payne interview.
8 See Walker, 'Canada's TV Dilemma: The American Influence,' *SN*, 23 July
  1960, 15–17 – KVOS actually had a company registered in Canada with offices
  in Vancouver to sell time to Canadian advertisers (see Albert Shea, *Broadcasting the Canadian Way* [Montreal: Harvest House 1963], 81); Spry, 'The Costs
  of Canadian Broadcasting,' *QQ*, v. 67, Winter 1960–1, 512 and 513. Ironically,
  a year earlier, in *Marketing*, 31 July 1959, 8, Walker had decided that the

Conservative victory plus business pressure meant 'Canadian broadcasting operations will become more American in style.'

9 Fowler II, 45

10 The transcript of the 'Close-Up' interview of 19 November 1959, in RG 41, v. 63, file 2-3-17, pt. 2

11 Walker, 'Canada's TV Dilemma,' 16; see Fulford's columns in CF, May 1961, 37, and October 1961, 147–9; the Winnipeg Tribune's piece outlined in Shea, Broadcasting the Canadian Way, 35–6

12 Maggie Siggins, Bassett (Toronto: Lorimer 1979), 191–201

13 Dean Walker, 'Business Moves in on Canadian Television,' SN, 19 March 1960, 10; Marcus Van Steen, 'How CBC Will Meet the Challenge of Competition,' SN, 23 July 1960, 80

14 The arguments in this and the preceding two paragraphs based on Vantel Broadcasting Co. Ltd, Submission, October 1959, RG 41, v. 156, file 10-2-3, pt. 1; R.S. Misener and Associates, Application, October 1959, ibid, pt. 3; CFTM brief, ibid, pt. 8; Bushnell promise noted in Grant, 'The Regulation of Program Content in Canadian Television,' 361; Baton Aldred Rogers brief cited in Siggins, Bassett, 221–2; Dean Walker, 'Business Moves in on Canadian Television,' 11–13

15 LaMarsh, Memoirs of a Bird in a Gilded Cage, 252. Apparently the thought among the CBC brass was that the Conservatives would appoint their own people to head the corporation. Even Ouimet claimed he was surprised when suddenly summoned to Nowlan's office to learn he was to be president. See Payne interview and Ouimet II. It is interesting that Finlay Payne, then a colleague, and Len Lauk, then a producer and a severe critic, agreed later that Ouimet was 'one of Canada's great public servants' (Payne interview), 'one of the most brilliant broadcasters in Canada' (Lauk interview). The passage of time has apparently worked in this instance to rehabilitate the man's reputation.

16 See Andrew Stewart's 'Statement' at a meeting with the corporation's board of directors, 14 February 1962, RG 41, v. 670, file 22nd Directors' Meeting. 'Analysis by Corporate Affairs of Statement by Chairman of BBG about National Broadcasting,' RG 41, v. 670, file 23rd Directors' Meeting; the 1960 report entitled 'The Future Role of the CBC,' RG 41, v. 675; and 'Second Television Network: CBC Position,' 30 September 1960, RG 41, v. 402, file 23-1-4, pt. 6.

17 Reserved time meant the time that was contracted to the network. The quotation from the unnamed CBC official in Marketing, 30 November 1962, 34. Allen, 'The Big Heat on the CBC,' MM, 9 February 1963, 31

18 Fowler II, 114; LaMarsh, Memoirs, 255

19 Touche, Ross, Bailey, and Smart, 'Report of the Final Advisers to the Committee on Broadcasting' [hereafter, Touche, Ross]; Appendix A, Fowler II, 375; Peter Stursberg, *Mr. Broadcasting: The Ernie Bushnell Story* (Toronto: Peter Martin Associates Ltd, 1971), 238–9. The 'freeze' is discussed in Hull, 'Captive or Victim,' 554–6; E.A. Weir, *The Struggle for National Broadcasting* (Toronto: M&S 1965), 364; and Robert E. Babe, *Canadian Television Broadcasting Structure, Performance and Regulation* (Ottawa: Economic Council of Canada, Ministry of Supply and Services 1979), 23.

20 The BBG had already approved an agreement whereby Famous Players and Britain's ATV each secured 12 per cent equity in CHAN-TV. During the CFTO crisis, Graham Spry wrote a letter to Diefenbaker in which he mentioned there was some British or American involvement in eleven Canadian stations. See Peers, *The Public Eye: Television and the Policies of Canadian Broadcasting 1952–1968* (Toronto: UTP 1979), 242 and 245.

21 See, for example, John Dalrymple, 'Canada's Local TV Stations: the Exuberant Experimenters,' *Liberty*, February 1961, 20–1 and 35–6, and ' "Showmanship Awards" to Canada's TV Stations,' *Liberty*, April 1963, 16 and 29. The ACTRA complaint noted in Weir, *The Struggle for National Broadcasting*, 403; the quotation from a letter written by a manager of a private station to Graham Spry, 16 May 1963, cited in Peers, *The Public Eye*, 273; Grant, 'The Regulation of Program Content in Canadian Television,' 361. Cohen quoted in Robert Fulford, 'Notebook: Promises, Promises,' *SN*, July 1987, 6

22 The term 'personality-oriented' was Michael Hind-Smith's, quoted in the Toronto *Telegram*, 23 April 1962. The averages for the news reach calculated from figures in BBM's *Television: National Program Report, Spring 1963 Survey*.

23 Siggins, *Bassett*, 210: that's a bit of an exaggeration, though, because while Dickson did produce 'Take a Chance' and 'Try for Ten' at CFTO, Screen Gems produced 'Showdown' designed by Dan Enright, NBC Canada produced 'A Kin to Win' in Montreal, and Winnipeg's CJAY was involved with a Canadian version of an Associated-Rediffusion (Great Britain) '20 Questions.'

24 Fowler II, 234

25 Ibid, 395; Hind-Smith is quoted in Siggins, *Bassett*, 211; 'Analysis by Corporate Affairs ... ,' 26.

26 Touche, Ross (375) mentions CTV had 'an interest,' unspecified as to how great, in CJCH, and Stursberg, *Mr. Broadcasting* (238, and footnote on 242–3), discusses the attempted Ottawa take-over. See Siggins, *Bassett* (213–18), for comments on the affiliate take-over of CTV and Keeble's views.

27 Hopkins, Hedlin, 292, 344, and 322–3. The estimate of earnings from prime-

time ads in O.J. Firestone, *Broadcasting Advertising in Canada* (Ottawa: University of Ottawa Press 1966), 103.

28 Actually the comment of a witness, repeated in Special Senate Committee on Mass Media, v. 1 of *Report*, entitled *The Uncertain Mirror*, 205.

29 See Gilles Constantineau, 'Tout le monde regarde le 10,' *Le Magazine Maclean*, September 1966, 11–13, 52–3. The CBC's complaint discussed in the Draft Minutes, 48th and 49th Program Committee Meetings, 8 February 1967 and 5 and 7 April 1967.

30 'TV Station Share of Audiences in CBC-Owned Station Areas 1960–To Date [1970],' MISA, Box 56 of Ratings Data

31 Fulford, 'Notebook: Promises, Promises,' 6; see the section on private television in Canada, Task Force on Broadcasting Policy, *Report* (Ottawa: Minister of Supply and Services 1986), 415–72.

32 Caldwell cited in Roy Shields, 'The Networks' War to Woo & Wow You,' *Liberty*, April 1963, 13. In the mid-1970s, for example, the Canadian sitcom 'Excuse My French' cost around $30,000 per episode to produce and generated about $16,000, while the American sitcom 'M*A*S*H' cost roughly $2,000 per episode to buy and generated about $24,000 – cited in Stuart McFadyen, Colin Hoskins, and David Gillen, *Canadian Broadcasting: Market Structure and Economic Performance* (Montreal: The Institute for Research on Public Policy 1980), 197.

33 The Broadcasting Act of 1968 did give the CRTC explicit power to attach conditions of performance to licences. The existence of that clause, though, hasn't led to much change in the performance of private TV, although CTV was eventually compelled to program some primetime, made-in-Canada drama.

34 Ouimet's address was reproduced in the *CBC Times* over the course of three weeks, commencing in late January 1960, and constitutes one of the most complete statements the president made in public about the role and purpose of the Corporation – this comment was near the beginning of his address, published in the issue of 23–29 January, 9.

35 CBC Research, *What the Canadian Public Thinks of the CBC*, 1963

36 *The Uncertain Mirror*, 195; the unnamed senior official quoted in Allen, 'The Big Heat on the CBC,' 32

37 *What the Canadian Public Thinks of the CBC*, 32 (although people also thought that a larger percentage of CBC revenues came from advertising than was in fact the case)

38 Glassco Commission (Royal Commission on Government Organization), 'Report 19 Canadian Broadcasting Corporation,' v. 4: *Special Areas of*

Administration (Ottawa: Queen's Printer 1963), 29, 33–40; Fulford, 'Starburst at the CBC,' *CF*, September 1965, 125

39 See Blackburn's comments in the *Telegram*, 20 June 1962; for a sample of outbursts from politicians, see Wilfred Kesterton's, 'Mass Media' section in the *Canadian Annual Review* for 1964 (441, 442, 426) and for 1968 (431–2); on the petition, see *The Ottawa Journal*, 27 October 1964.

40 Vizinczey, 'Regionalism,' *Canadian Art*, 9, no. 5 (September/October 1962), 352. Fulford had made public his doubts about the CBC in his 'Television Notebook' in *CF*, May 1960, 39–40; his attack, though, was the 'Starburst at the CBC' of 1965, article mentioned above.

41 Ouimet's comments taken from the *CBC Times*, 23–29 January 1960, 27 and 30 January–5 February 1960, 9 and 21. 'The Future Role of the CBC' was a special report to the board of directors (RG 41, v. 675).

42 The CBC's request was a response to Fowler II's suggestion of $25 per television home for both capital and operating expenses (313). There were roughly 4,759,000 television homes in Canada in May 1967. The government operating grant was $112,403,000 for 1966/7. Statistics on the CBC's share of net ad revenues from Hopkins, Hedlin, 527

43 Allen, 'The Big Heat on the CBC,' 32; Hallman in Allen, 33; the problem over 'The Nature of Things' mentioned in Minutes, 26th Program Committee Meeting, 28 and 29 October 1964, 5; Hopkins, Hedlin, 149; Trotter, 'Canadian Broadcasting Act IV: Scene '67 or Double Talk and the Single System,' *QQ*, 73, Winter 1966, 474. It is, however, important to recognize that there was a lot of non-commercial programming available on the overall network schedule. The Touche, Ross report (333) noted, not with any pleasure, that the percentage of programs with advertising had actually fallen from 46.8 per cent in 1960 to 35.6 per cent in 1965, chiefly because the CBC had mounted more sustaining programming.

44 The senator's comment quoted in Toronto *Telegram*, 16 December 1966

45 Fowler II, 171 – the committee did add that the producer should stay within budget and be accountable for the quality of the product.

46 Both French Canadians presented statements to the 1966 Parliamentary Committee on Broadcasting, Film, and Assistant to the Arts, Thibault on 12 May and M. Ouimet on 19 May, available in RG 41, v. 234, file 11-25-7, pt. 13. Lord Windlesham, *Broadcasting in a Free Society* (London: Basil Blackwell 1980), 84

47 The idea of alternative service was enshrined in the CBC's 'General Coverage Policy – October, 1964,' cited in Fowler II, 79; 'The Future Role of the CBC,' 7; the business of rescheduling the news noted in the Minutes of the 15th

Program Committee Meeting, 26–28 June 1961, 12; statistics from Fowler
II, 71, and Peers, *The Public Eye*, 284; Fowler II, 81; Ouimet's comment noted
in the Toronto *Telegram*, 12 January 1966; the difficulties over the switch to
colour broadcasting are described at length in CBC, 'A History of the Development of Color Television in Canada,' 1970 (RG 41, v. 402, file 23-1-4, pt. 6) –
the CBC had estimated that partial conversion would cost at least $21 million
in 1964 and full conversion much more.

48 Ouimet's warning in Minutes, 20th Meeting of Program Committee, 16 and
19 April 1962, 9; Don Jamieson, *The Troubled Air* (Fredericton: Brunswick
Press 1966), 108

49 The statistics on television programming costs are calculated from figures in
Hopkins, Hedlin, 543.

50 The football business discussed in Minutes, 17th Meeting of the Program
Committee, 30 and 31 October 1961, 6; 'Nielsen – January 1965. Compara-
graph – Major Markets. CBC vs CTV,' MISA, Ratings Box 56; Braithwaite's
column in *The Globe and Mail*, 6 May 1964, quoted in Weir, *The Struggle for
National Broadcasting in Canada*, 382; Saltzman, 'How to Survive in the CBC
Jungle – and Other Tribal Secrets,' MM, 6 February 1965, 44.

51 Pearson, *Mike: The Memoirs of The Right Honourable Lester B. Pearson* v. 3,
1957–1968 (Toronto: UTP 1975), 189; Trotter, 'Canadian Broadcasting Act
IV,' 481

52 Ouimet's comment from an interview, 2 July 1975, quoted in Peers, *The Public
Eye*, 274

53 The Australian model was no cure-all, of course. Sandra Hall's *Supertoy: 20
Years of Australian Television* (Melbourne: Sun Books 1976) and K.C. Inglis's
This Is the ABC: The Australian Broadcasting Commission 1932–1982 (Melbourne: Melbourne University Press 1983) made abundantly clear that there
were definite problems, a fair number of which could be ascribed to a lack of
funds for the public system and the overwhelming presence of commercial
stations in Australia's television system.

54 Nash, 'From Musty Charms to Future Shock,' May 1972 (RG 41, v. 404, file
23-1-4-3, pt. 2), 1

55 Statistics generated from Hopkins, Hedlin, 572, and Dominion Bureau of
Statistics, 'Household Facilities and Equipment,' *Bulletin: 64-202*, 1967, 19

56 Statistics from Hopkins, Hedlin, 527, 539, 548; *Canada Year Book 1968*, 880

57 Hopkins, Hedlin, 572, 527; Grant, 'The Regulation of Program Content in
Canadian Television,' 384

58 Hopkins, Hedlin, 100–6 (on Southam-Selkirk)

59 CRTC, *Special Report on Broadcasting 1968–1978* [hereafter CRTC Study], v. 1

(Ottawa: Ministry of Supply and Services 1979), 7, 10, and 43 – Fowler II, 35, had a slightly different estimate for 1965 based upon the number of households, claiming 54 per cent could get American TV; Hopkins, Hedlin, 390 and 391. What happened later bore out this concern: in 1977, when cable had made extensive inroads across the country, the audience levels for CBC/R-C had fallen to 29.41 per cent and TVA to 11.12 per cent, while CTV had risen to 24.95 per cent and U.S. to 23.45: Paul Audley, *Canada's Cultural Industries: Broadcasting, Publishing, Records and Film* (Toronto: Lorimer 1983), 265.

60 The statistics on television ownership are from the yearly totals supplied by DBS, *Bulletin: 64-202.*

61 The figure on the amount of choice from the CRTC Study, 20. The new rules on Canadian content, plus the CRTC's back-down, discussed in Babe, *Canadian Television Broadcasting Structure*, 141–3. The comment on the unspecified mp cited in Herschel Hardin, *Closed Circuits: The Sellour of Canadian Television* (Vancouver: Douglas and McIntyre 1985), 33, which also contains a highly critical discussion of the CRTC's course in the whole affair. The Gallup poll, released 4 July 1970, revealed that 53 per cent of the English Canadians polled opposed the idea, 39 per cent approved; by contrast, fully 65 per cent of French Canadians were in favour of the new rule.

62 See Section Four: 'Cable Television,' in Hopkins, Hedlin, 357–417. The cost estimate from CRTC Study, 84.

63 Hull, 'Captive or Victim,' 556–7 on BBG and cable; Babe, *Canadian Television Broadcasting Structure*, 161–2, and Hardin, *Closed Circuits*, 32, on the CRTC and cable

64 Statistics on Canadian Content from CRTC Study, 48

65 Fowler II, 34

66 Nash, *Prime Time at Ten: Behind-the-Camera Battles of Canadian TV Journalism* (Toronto: M&S 1987), 209

67 1978 statistics from Audley, *Canada's Cultural Industries*, 258. By the mid-1980s the actual percentage of time anglophones spent viewing American stations had grown to just under one-third, and it was clear cable households tended to watch far less of the CBC product (18.9 per cent in cable homes compared to 31.3 per cent in non-cable): see *Report* of the Task Force on Broadcasting Policy (Ottawa: Ministry of Supply and Services 1986), 103–4.

68 This has remained true since 1970 as well, of course. The CBC has had one enormous sucess, with the adventure series 'The Beachcombers,' exporting it to countries throughout the world. And, recently, private interests have produced a run-of-the-mill police drama 'Night Heat,' which in 1987/8 showed on American as well as CTV stations. But the list of such exceptions is very short.

5 Information for Everyone

1 Trotter, 'Educational Television,' *Food for Thought*, 20, April 1960, 308
2 The META comment cited in A.F. Knowles, 'The Sight and Sound of Learning,' *Food for Thought*, 20, May/June 1960, 358. For similar kinds of comments, see Eugene Hallman, 'Educational Television and the CBC,' *Canadian Education and Research Digest*, 1, no. 3 (September 1961), and Dr Andrew Stewart, 'Some Observations on ETV in Canada,' *Canadian Education and Research Digest*, 1, no. 3 (September 1961), 23–44.
3 The appearance and activities of these agencies has been surveyed by Ron Faris in *The Passionate Educators: Voluntary Associations and the Struggle for Control of Adult Educational Broadcasting in Canada 1919–1952* (Toronto: Peter Martin Associates 1975), although he has little to say about the universities and the labour organizations. On Grierson, see Gary Evans, *John Grierson and the National Film Board: The Politics of Wartime Propaganda 1939–1945* (Toronto: UTP 1984).
4 The show ran for three winters on CBLT in the evening hours, from the Fall '53 to Spring '56, first on Monday nights at 7:30 to 8:00 and later on Sundays at 6:00 to 6:30. The anecdote from Robin Harris, 'TV and the Universities,' *QQ* 63, Summer 1956, 289–90. Harris was associated with the University of Toronto.
5 Information on 'Live and Learn,' 'Two for Physics,' and 'Speaking French' from the program files in the CBC Reference Library in Toronto
6 For instance, 'La cuisine de la bonne humeur' (Fall '54 to summer '56), 'Hans in the Kitchen' (Spring '53 to Summer '54), 'Les bricoleurs' (Fall '53 to Fall '54), 'Mr. Fix-It' (Fall '55 to Fall '64, on Saturday at 6:30–6:45, until Fall '62, when it moved to Wednesday at 7:45–8:00), 'Chambre noir' (Summer '54), 'Club de golf' (Spring and Summer '54) or 'Golf with Stan Leonard' (Summers, 1960–2), 'Small Fry Frolics' (Summer '54), 'Les travaux et les jours' (Fall '55 to [at least] Summer '65), 'Country Calendar' (Summers '55–7), 'Country-time' (Fall '60 to Summer '65). That last show promised 'the why-to-do-its and how-to-do-its of practical agriculture,' along with lots of information on innovations, marketing, and expert opinions (CBC press release, 21 September 1960, from the CBC Reference Library, Toronto). Basic information on Radio-Canada's programming 1952–7, used here and elsewhere, has been taken from Gérard Laurence's program sheets in *Histoire des programmes-TV, CBFT Montréal, Septembre 1952–Septembre 1957* (CRTC, Research Report 1982).
7 Usually, though, housewives received instructions about babies and cooking and fashion along with news and interviews, even music sometimes, on afternoon shows such as 'Open House' or 'Place aux dames.' 'C'est la loi'

(Summer '54 to Summer '55); 'A Case for the Court' (Summers, 1960–2); quotations on 'Graphic' from *CBC Times*, 26 February–3 March 1956, 3, and 21–27 October 1956, 2.

8 'The Tapp Room' (Spring '56 to Spring '58, at 11:30 on Monday); Michelle Tisseyre was on from 1953 to 1962; 'Encyclopédie sportive' (Fall '53 to Fall '55) and 'The Vic Obeck Show' (Spring '54 to Summer '56); 'The Jim Coleman Show' (Fall '55 to Summer '60); and 'The King Whyte Show' (Fall '55 to Spring '62).

9 Here is a run-down of the career of 'Tabloid': Spring '53 to Summer '54 (excluding July and August), Monday through Saturday, 7:00–7:30; Fall '54 to Spring '55, Monday through Saturday, 6:30–6:50; May and June 1955, Monday through Friday, 6:30–6:50; July 1955 to September 1962, Monday through Friday, 7:00–7:30; September 1962 to September 1963, four weekdays (missing Wednesday), 7:00–7:30. Munro interview.

10 CBC Audience Research, *English Television Network Program Ratings June 1957–May 1958*, which used ISL data for one week in every month from October 1957 to May 1958. *CBC Times*, 17–23 September, 1960, 3, an issue that also includes the Davidson quotation

11 McLean was thirty-three in 1958. Material on McLean taken from the Frank Peers interview; Brain Swarbrick, ' "Close-Up": The New Journalism,' *SN*, 2 August 1958, 10–11 and 30; Peter Gzowski, 'Ross McLean, the TV Star You Never See,' *MM*, 16 January 1960, 11–13 and 40; *CBC Times*, 24–30 January 1954, 3.

12 *CBC Times*, 6–12 June 1959, 3; 8–14 March 1953, 5; 6–12 June, 1959, 3 and 16

13 *CBC Times*, 5–11 July 1953, 3, and 7–13 August 1955, 2–3

14 Information on the case taken from a summary in Wilfred H. Kesterton, *The Law and the Press in Canada* (Toronto: M&S 1976), 222–4.

15 *CBC Times*, 5–11 July 1953, 3; Robert Olson, 'Percy Wows Them with the Weather,' *MM*, 15 May 1954, 14–15 and 86–7; Peter Allison, 'The Charm of Chatter: Television's Talking Dolls,' *MM*, 15 December 1962, 18–21 and 63; *CBC Times* 5–11 July 1953, 4; and *The Toronto Daily Star*, 14 June 1958.

16 'On the Scene' (Spring '60 to Summer '66) – the anecdote from the Toronto *Globe and Mail*, 8 October 1964; 'Here and There' (intermittently, Summer '56 to Fall '58); similar kinds of travelogues about Canada were 'Window on Canada' (Fall '53 to Spring '55, Fall '55 to Spring '56), which showed National Film Board shorts, and 'Passe-partout' (Fall '56 to Spring '57), a half-hour on Saturdays at 8:30 (though it moved later to Sunday afternoon), which offered films on Canada though also explored topics such as the history of trade unionism in French Canada, according to Laurence's program sheet; 'Four Corners' (Summer '57); 'Pays et merveilles' (Fall '52 to Summer '61); one

interesting variation was the fifteen-minute 'Pour elle' (Fall '55 to Summer '61), for women, which used French film to look into the life of Paris.

17 'Explorations' (Fall '56 to Summer '64). The description of the series in CBC *Times*, 21–27 March 1959.

18 On 'Panoramique' see *La Semaine à Radio-Canada*, 7–13 December 1957, 1; 'Le roman de la science' (Fall '57 to Spring 58); 'Je me souviens/Dateline' (Fall '55 to Spring '56), involving Associated Screen News and some historical experts; the comment on the Anglo docudramas, specifically regarding one of the shows on Lord Elgin, in *The Toronto Daily Star*, 25 May 1961; among foreign features were 'La guerre des ailes' (June–October 1955), the BBC's 'War in the Air,' and 'Time to Remember' (Fall '60 to Fall '61), a British series of historical reconstructions on CBLT.

19 The discussion of the documentary based upon a close reading; Robert Fulford, 'What's Behind the New Wave of TV Think Shows,' *MM*, 5 October 1963, 62

20 'Profile': Summer '55, Summer '56 Summer–Fall '57, a half-hour variously scheduled in the 10:00 to 11:00 slot, on Thursday, Sunday, and finally Tuesday. The discussion based on a close reading of the interview

21 The two 'Explorations' series are described in the CBC *Times*, 28 February– 6 March 1959, 3; and 9–15 January 1960, 8–9.

22 The examples of audience response to assorted educational shows are all taken from a series of articles by Brian Stewart: 'The Professor in Your Living Room,' CBC *Times*, 19–25 November 1960, 5; 'Children and Television,' CBC *Times*, 22–28 August 1959, 4; and 'Je Parle Français,' CBC *Times*, 2–8 January 1960, 7.

23 On the nature of news, see in particular John Hartley, *Understanding News* (London: Methuen 1982), and the Glasgow University Media Group, *Bad News*, v. 1 (London: Routledge & Kegan Paul 1976). Hartley describes 'discourses' as 'specialized meaning-systems' (4) or 'as the different kinds of *use* to which language is put' (6). The first quotation is from Philip Schlesinger, 'The Sociology of Knowledge' (a paper presented at the 1972 meeting of the British Sociological Association, 24 March 1972), 4, cited in Herbert Gans, *Deciding What's News: A Study of CBS Evening News, NBC Nightly News, Newsweek, and* Time (New York: Pantheon Books 1979), 81; Michael Arlen, *The View from Highway 1: Essays on Television* (New York: Ballantyne 1976), 79.

24 Eggleston, 'Report on the CBC National Television News,' June 1956 (RG 41, v. 174, file 11-17-4, pt. 3), 12, 13–14

25 Iyengar and Kinder, *News That Matters: Television and American Opinion* (Chicago: University of Chicago Press 1987)

26 Dunton interview

27 This account is based upon a series of anonymous memos, 'A Report on CBC News and Certain Recommendations,' June 1967, and its supplement 'CBC News Service,' as well as 'News Service Policy,' 1 August 1958; the minutes of the News Conference prepared by C.G. Gunning, 27 October 1960, all of which are in RG 41, v. 171, file 11-17, pts. 2 and 6; and the Earle interview. The first source identified the kinds of organizational difficulties: the news service was divided between television and radio (budgetary authority lay with the directors of those media), the chief news editor's office had only a narrow 'functional relationship' with the different newsrooms, the foreign correspondents were not responsible to the news office, and even within television news the news production unit actually reported to the network production manager not to a newsman.

28 The statements of news policy taken from 'Policy: CBC National News Service' included in a memo from Frank Peers, director of information programming, to D.R. McCarnan, corporate supervisor (see also *CBC Times*, 30 December 1955 to 6 January 1956, 2), RG 41, v. 171, file 11-17, pt. 4; draft letter, Dunton to Paul Roddick, 25 May 1956, RG 41, v. 171, file 11-17, pt. 2; *CBC Times*, 12–18 June 1955, 2, though the comment here pertained directly to radio; Hogg cited in the minutes of the News Conference of 1960, 8; and on offensive language, see Ira Dilworth, Ontario director, to general manager, 29 September 1954, RG 41, v. 171, file 11-17, pt. 2.

29 Safer quoted in George Brimmel, 'Their Cameras Cover the Globe,' Toronto *Telegram*, 16 August 1958; 'A Day Like Any Other Day,' *CBC Times*, 7–13 November 1959, 6–7 and 27; Eggleston, 'Report on the CBC National Television News,' 6–7

30 Some impression of the extent of the commitment can be gleaned from the account of the planned election coverage in *CBC Times*, 9–15 June 1957, and *La Semaine à Radio-Canada*, 29 March–4 April 1958; E-H report on 'The Opening of the Seaway'; 'L'Actualité' ran from Summer '54 to Fall '58, 'Newsmagazine' from Fall '52 to Summer '58 (in its first primetime appearance); see Michael Maclear's statement on the nature of 'Newsmagazine' in Brimmel's 'Their Cameras Cover the Globe'; 'Metro News' came in April 1959, 'Edition métropolitain' in June 1959.

31 This edition was selected simply because it was the earliest complete copy of a newscast available at CBC-Toronto. Eggleston, 'Report on the CBC National Television News,' 9–12; Cameron's nickname bestowed in: Harvey Kirck, with Wade Rowland, *Nobody Calls Me Mr. Kirck* (Toronto: Collins 1985), 151. The comment by the anonymous CBC executive cited in Knowlton Nash, *Prime Time at Ten* (Toronto: M&S 1987), 22.

32 The description of the attributes of news comes from Hartley, *Understanding News*, and Eggleston, 'Report on the CBC National News,' as well as Bernard Roshco, *Newsmaking* (Chicago: University of Chicago Press 1975) and Edward J. Epstein, *News from Nowhere: Television and the News* (New York: Vintage Books 1974).

33 The term 'unambiguous' comes from Hartley, *Understanding News*, 24; the notions of news as a fragment and the partiality towards official news-makers are developed in Arlen, *The View from Highway 1*, 26 and 85; the ideas of a 'repertory of stereotypes,' derived from the work of Walter Lippmann, and of the application of the dictum of fairness are analysed in Epstein, *News from Nowhere*, 242 and 243.

34 Lévesque story in Jean Provencher, *René Lévesque: Portrait of a Québécois* (Toronto: Gage 1975), 88

35 Lévesque quoted in *Vrai*, 15 December 1956, and the quotation cited in Provencher, *René Lévesque*, 98 – technically speaking, Lévesque was then a free-lancer on contract with the CBC for the public-affairs show 'Point de mire.' Duke quoted in *The Toronto Daily Star*, 24 February 1962 – this reference courtesy of Frank Peers.

36 Peers interview; quotations from a memo (1 December 1959) on the cancellation of the Simone de Beauvoir interview in RG 41, v. 675: the intent had been to interview her on the women's question. The principles and practices are outlined in Frank Peers, 'The CBC and Public Affairs Broadcasting,' January 1954, reprinted from *Education in Public Affairs by Radio*; and 'Some Notes on Public Affairs Broadcasting,' distributed to directors at the 7th Board Meeting, 28–30 October 1959 (RG 41, v.675); Dunton interview.

37 Jennings to director of TV network programming (Toronto), 4 September 1958 (RG 41, v. 206, file 11-18-11-69)

38 Flint to Robert Kerr, 25 October 1956 (RG 41, v. 257, file 11-40-1-6) – Flint was with the J. Walter Thompson company and Kerr was with the Broadcast Regulations department. Flint's view of what was appropriate is intriguing because it foreshadowed changes in political broadcasting that would occur in later decades: 'I have always failed to see why the dramatic presentation of political principles should be prohibited. Politics, as the "father of government", should be "sold" just the same as any other commodity. It is very unstimulating to see a speaker, often a dull one, stating facts, making promises, and so on. Why shouldn't he, or the party he represents, be able to present points in a manner that would command an audience of luke warm [*sic*] people?' Hind-Smith to D.L. Bennett (program organizer, Public Affairs, Toronto), 13 June 1957 (RG 41, v. 262 file 11-41-9); McNaught, 'The Failure of Television in Politics,' *CF*, August 1958, 104–15.

39 On the Liberal preparations, see Reg Whitaker, *The Government Party: Organizing and Financing the Liberal Party of Canada* (Toronto: UTP 1977), 249–51; Camp, *Gentlemen, Players & Politicians* (Toronto: M&S 1970), 262; CBC Audience Research, 'Report of a Study on Audiences of the 1957 Election Campaign Broadcasts,' February 1960.

40 The description of the 1957 election in this and the following paragraphs is based upon John Meisel, *The Canadian General Election of 1957* (Toronto: UTP 1962); Peter Newman, *Renegade in Power: The Diefenbaker Years* (Toronto: M&S 1963); Dale Thomson, *Louis St. Laurent: Canadian* (Toronto: Macmillan of Canada 1967); Peter Stursberg, *Diefenbaker: Leadership Gained 1965–62* (Toronto: UTP 1975); Patrick Nicholson, *Vision and Indecision* (Don Mills: Longmans 1968); Robert Bothwell and William Kilbourn, *C.D. Howe: A Biography* (Toronto: M&S 1979); Whitaker, *The Government Party*, and Camp, *Gentlemen, Players & Politicians*. The Liberal adman was H.E. Kidd of Cockfield, Brown, and he is quoted in Whitaker, 251.

41 Hind-Smith to D.L. Bennett

42 I'm using the term 'a necessary cause' as defined by Colin Seymour-Ure, *The Political Impact of the Mass Media* (London and Beverley Hills: Constable/Sage 1974), 21–2 – that is, was television necessary to the eventual result? Clearly television was not a 'sufficient' cause, able in itself to fashion the eventual result. The Toronto results cited in CBC Audience Research, 'Report of a Study on Audiences of the 1957 Election Campaign Broadcasts,' February 1960, 16, note that respondents in Halifax and Edmonton also thought the Conservatives more effective, whereas in French Montreal the impression was of a Liberal success. The comments on the feeling in southwestern Ontario come from Stursberg, *Diefenbaker: Leadership Gained 1965–62*, 53, and on Howe from Bothwell and Kilbourn, *C.D. Howe*, 327–8, and Whitaker, *The Government Party*, 251. Television's importance was much less the next year in 1958, when Diefenbaker won an enormous majority, because by this time the tide of affairs was running so strongly in his favour that he could hardly be stopped.

43 Solway's aim noted in the Toronto *Telegram*, 21 July 1959; 'Background' on Summer '59 to Fall '60.

44 CBC press release, 18 October 1955, from the Reference Library, CBC Toronto; *La Semaine à Radio-Canada*, 16–22 October 1955, 1, and program sheet in Gérard Laurence. 'Citizen's Forum' (Fall '55 to Spring '56); 'Les idées en marche' (Fall '54 to Summer '60)

45 On 'Press Conference' (Fall '52 to Summer '60), see *CBC Times*, 30 November–6 December 1952, 5; and 27 December–2 January 1958, 3; on 'Conference de presse' (Spring '53 to Summer '66) see *La Sémaine à Radio-Canada*, 18–

24 February 1956, where Landry quoted, and Laurence's program sheet, where mention made of the submission of questions in advance; Frank Peers wrote a special memo to the assistant director of programs (Ottawa), 31 March 1955, on 'Press Conference' participants in 1954/5 (RG 41, v. 208, file 11-18-11-32), which showed that Talks and Public Affairs had been careful in its selection of panelists; the excessive use of *Maclean's* men noted by Marcel Ouimet (assistant controller of broadcasting) to the director of TV network programming (Toronto), in an internal memo on 'Close-up,' 7 January 1958 (RG 41, v. 197, file 11-8-11-36, pt. 1).

46 On the troubles caused by the pipeline debate, see Peers, *The Public Eye*, 119–23.

47 Dunton interview. See also Susan Mann Trofimenkoff's chapter 'Ici Radio-Canada,' in her *The Dream of Nation: A Social and Intellectual History of Quebec* (Toronto: Gage 1983), especially 284–5, for an account of the effects of television on Quebec, and Gérard Pelletier, *Years of Impatience 1950–1960* (Toronto: Methuen 1983), 171–203, on information and television in general. As well, I've drawn examples from Laurence's very useful article 'Les affairs publiques à la télévision 1952–1957,' *Revue d'Histoire de L'Amérique Française*, 36, no. 2 September 1982), 213–39.

48 On Murrow see Alexander Kendrick, *Prime Time: The Life of Edward R. Murrow* (Boston: Little, Brown and Company 1969); 'Point de mire' (Fall '56 to Summer '59); 'Close-Up' (Fall '57 to Summer '63); 'Inquiry' (though first aired in late December 1960, a regular Spring '61 to Summer '64, with absences).

49 The account is based upon Hartley's *Understanding News*, 87–106, where he discusses 'the mode of address.'

50 One superb example of the Murrow style was the 'See It Now' episode of 1 April 1955, where Murrow interviewed J. Robert Oppenheimer: Murrow shaped the interview through a series of questions, but did not intrude on the flow of answers, and allowed Oppenheimer to express his opinions on a wide variety of topics. See Mary Lowrey Ross, 'Interview TV Technique,' *SN*, 6 July 1957, 25, and 'TV's "Interesting" Personalities,' *SN*, 26 September 1959, 34–5; 'How to Be an Interviewer,' *CBC Times*, 14–20 November 1959, 6–7, 16, and 30.

51 The list of questions derived from Hartley, *Understanding News*, 113–14; see Arlen, *The View from Highway 1*, 30–42, for an excellent discussion of 'How do you feel?'; the anecdote about the 'Close-Up' question from Miriam Waddington, 'Radio and Television,' *CF*, February 1958, 255; the 'Viewpoint' episode occurred on 28 April 1960.

52 The discussion of Lévesque based on material in Provencher, *René Lévesque*,

especially 92–103; Peter Desbarats, *René: A Canadian in Search of a Country* (Toronto: M&S 1976); and Alain Pontaut, *René Lévesque ou 'l'idéalisme pratique'* (Montreal: Les Editions Leméac 1983). Pelletier's comment appears in his memoirs *Years of Impatience*, 229.

53 Audience size cited in the CBC's *Annual Report 1958/59*, 6

54 Much of this account of 'Close-Up' rests on material available in the program files of the CBC Reference Library in Toronto. But see in particular McLean, ' "Close-Up" on an Anniversary,' *CBC Times*, 28 September–4 October 1958, 2, 6–7; Swarbrick, ' "Close-Up": The New Journalism'; and 'Toro! ...,' *CBC Times*, 16–22 July 1960, 6–7; audience size cited in the CBC's *Annual Report 1958/59*, 6.

55 Ouimet to director of TV network programming Toronto, Internal Memo on 'Close-Up,' 7 January 1958 (RG 41, v. 197, file 11-8-1136, pt. 1)

56 The source material derived from press clippings in the program file located at the CBC Reference Library, Toronto. See, in particular, Ross McLean, 'McLean Again: Postscript to the Shady Lady Case,' Toronto *Telegram*, 31 August 1963, and *Time* (Canadian edition), 17 March 1961, 10, on the Exelby affair.

57 Ronald Cohen, 'The CBC and the News,' *Canadian Commentator*, July–August 1959, 2

58 LaMarsh, *Memoirs of a Bird in a Gilded Cage*, 7–8. CBC Audience Research, 'English Television Network Program Ratings June 1957–May 1958' – though note that both 'Close-Up' and 'Newsmagazine' did quite a bit better in Vancouver; ISL, 'TV Network: Program Report. French,' 4–10 February 1962.

59 Trotter, 'Educational Television,' 308, and Knowles, 'The Sight and Sound of Learning,' 353

60 *CBC Times*, 17–23 September 1960, 3; Toronto *Telegram*, 19 September 1961 and 21 March 1962; *Toronto Daily Star*, 26 January 1962; Ralph Thomas, 'In at Birth and Death,' *Toronto Daily Star*, 28 September, 1963.

6 Variety's Heyday

1 'Why I'm out of TV,' MM, 30 April 1955, 74

2 Bell had fashioned his own group, the Leslie Bell Singers, who had proved very popular on the road and on radio. They had seemed a logical choice for television when it debuted in the fall of 1952. The ratings soon showed otherwise.

3 The subject of play has intrigued a couple of scholars over the past generation or so. The basic work remains Johan Huizinga's *Homo Ludens: A Study of the Play Element in Culture*, 1950 ed. (Boston: Beacon Press 1970), a book that

finds in play the chief source of civilization. Roger Callois's *Man, Play, and Games* (London: Thames and Hudson 1962) is a bit less grandiose, and much more precise, though he too feels that play serves a wide range of important functions in modern society. One eccentric scholar, William Stephenson, has tried to apply Huizinga's notions directly to the study of mass communication: *The Play Theory of Mass Communication* (Chicago: University of Chicago Press 1967). Recently, the analysis of play seems to have blended into the study of leisure and the sociology of sports.

4 Callois, *Man, Play, and Games* (120–5), in fact, deems this kind of identification as crucial to the survival of a democratic society. How else can the vast majority of working folk be taken away from their dismal lives, made to believe that success is possible for them or their children? A more prosaic account of such matters can be found in Percy H. Tannenbaum, 'Entertainment as Vicarious Emotional Experience,' in Tannenbaum, ed., *The Entertainment Functions of Television* (Hillsdale, NJ: Lawrence Elbaum Associates 1980), 107–31. A good survey of the rise of the professional entertainer is Robert C. Toll's *The Entertainment Machine: American Show Business in the Twentieth Century* (New York: OUP 1982). The comment on stardom and individualism is drawn out of David Lusted's 'The Glut of Personality,' in Len Masterman, ed., *Television Mythologies: Stars, Shows & Signs* (London: Comedia Publishing Group/MK Media Press 1984), 73.

5 For a discussion of the spectator and the viewer, see Sebastien de Grazia, *Of Time, Work, and Leisure* (New York: Anchor Books 1962), 320; Gregor T. Goethals, *The TV Ritual: Worship at the Video Altar* (Boston: Beacon Press 1981); Stuart M. Kaminsky, with Jeffrey H. Mahan, *American Television Genres* (Chicago: Nelson-Hall 1985), 26 and 31; and Margaret Morse, 'Sport on Television: Replay and Display,' in E. Ann Kaplan, ed., *Regarding Television: Critical Approaches – An Anthology* (Frederick, Md.: University Publications of America 1983), 47–8. De Grazia, for example, seems disgusted by the fact that television turns spectators into the position of cats and dogs, while Goethals is excited about the way in which television involves viewers in the rituals of American life.

6 See Lusted, 'The Glut of Personality,' 76. On talk shows and hospitality, see Michael Arlen's 'Hosts and Guests,' in his *The Camera Age: Essays on Television* (Harmondsworth: Penguin Books 1982), 307–19. The ways of display apply as well to the forms of informational programming, notably the newscasts where the anchorman was so important a fixture – but here the journalist reworks the theme of teaching rather than hospitality. It has also been suggested that the 'eye-to-eye' contact establishes the authenticity of the experience, underlining the illusion that TV is unmediated and so more

truthful – Dennis Giles and Marilyn Jackson-Beeck, 'Television, the Evil Eye,' in Kaminsky and Mahan, *American Television Genres*, 199.

7 The source material on this show comes from press clippings in the 'Network' Programme File, CBC Reference Library, Toronto. The most important stories were in the Toronto *Telegram*, 8 August 1962 and 12 January 1963.

8 L. Starmer, in Minutes, 17th Meeting of the Programme Committee, CBC Board of Directors, 30 and 31 October 1961, 19. On vaudeville and its meaning see Albert F. McLean Jr, *American Vaudeville as Ritual* (Lexington: University of Kentucky Press 1965).

9 On Bonheur see *La Semaine à Radio-Canada*, 18–21 September 1956, 8; Moon, 'How to Get on Television,' MM, 19 December 1959, 15; on success stories, see *Liberty*, October 1956, 60 and Alex Barris, *The Pierce-Arrow Showroom: An Insider's View of One CBC* (Toronto: Ryerson 1969), 99. Barris' book is a mine of information about variety programming in the 1950s and 1960s at CBC-Toronto.

10 Barris, *The Pierce-Arrow Showroom*, 121 and 123. Barris was the emcee of a number of variety and game shows, as well as a writer (sometimes on other shows), and a noted Toronto columnist who dealt with television.

11 This does not exhaust a list that includes such people as Guy Lombardo, Liberace, Patti Page, Lawrence Welk, and Danny Kaye, who had scheduled shows on Canadian television.

12 On the criticism of 'The Big Revue,' see Hugh Garner's comments in *SN*, 6 February 1954, 6; Barris, *The Pierce-Arrow Showroom*, 11; Lloyd Lockhart, 'New TV Showtime Is Seeking Prestige,' *Toronto Daily Star*, 11 January 1958, 28–9.

13 See Bill Stephenson, 'The Wonderful World of French-Canadian TV,' MM, 8 June 1957, 82; the program sheet on 'Music-Hall' in Gérard Laurence, *Histoire des programmes-TV, CBFT Montréal, Septembre 1952–Septembre 1957* (CRTC Research Repair 1982); *La Semaine à Radio-Canada*, 29 October–4 November 1955, 1; 16–22 November 1957, 8; 12–18 April 1958, 3; 30 September–6 October, 1961, 5.

14 Comments on the former from Schwerin Research Corporation, *Report C-CBC-56-6: Comparison of Teenage & Adult Audiences: 'Cross-Canada Hit Parade' and 'The Jackie Rae Show'*, 6.

15 The nicknames of the Holiday Ranchers from Dorothy Sangster, 'The Most Baffling Show on Television,' OOMM, 9 June 1956. '84; the comment on Music-Hall' is based on a close reading.

16 *CBC Times*, 8–14 August 1954, 6–7; Garner in *SN*, 6 February 1954, 9; Schwerin *Report C-CBC-57-3: 'Barris Beat,'* 18; Braithwaite in *Toronto Daily Star*, 8 October 1959; ISL, *Telephone Survey*, October 1962, 7; reference was made in

the CBC's Program Committee to another survey that found that Normand received a 98.4 per cent rating for acceptability – Minutes, 25th Meeting of Program Committee, 3 February 1963, 6.

17 'Radio and Television,' CF, July 1957, 83–4

18 Dilworth's comment mentioned in a letter to D. Nixon, 5 January 1960, RG 41, v. 277, file 11-53-11; on Sullivan see Jerry Bowles, *A Thousand Sundays: The Story of* The Ed Sullivan Show (New York: G.P. Putnam's Sons 1980).

19 Waddington, 'Radio and Television,' 84

20 See program evaluation in RG 41, v. 277, file 11-43-12. There were, however, some female emcees, notably Dinah Shore who headed 'The Chevy Show' throughout most of its run.

21 Waddington, 'Radio and Television,' 84; Millard Research Associates, *A Research Study of* Showtime, January 1958, 35; *Toronto Daily Star*, 27 July 1961; the comment on Murphy based on a close reading of 'The Wayne and Shuster Hour' of 11 March 1962.

22 Additional ratings data taken from E-H *National Teleratings* for January 1963 and an ISL report for November 1961 cited in Lester Sellick, *Canada's Don Messer* (Kentville, NS: Kentville Publishing 1969), 72. The Radio-Canada survey came from the Service des Recherches et Sondages, entitled *Emissions Régulières ou Longs Metrages*, April 1959, 44–7.

23 See Bell, 'Why I'm out of TV,' 72; Blair Fraser, 'If I Ran the CBC ...,' OOMM, 14 April 1956, especially 15 and 117; Frank Rasky, 'CBC's Flirtation with Profit-Making Sponsors,' SN, 14 September 1957, 10–11, 37; Barris, *The Pierce-Arrow Showroom*, 91–102.

24 Perkins, 'Hames Sisters: TV's Calico Combo,' *Liberty*, February 1963, 20–1

25 Country music was most closely associated with the American South, where it had its origins in the British folk music brought over at the time of initial settlement and since changed by a couple of centuries of experience – see Tony Palmer, *All You Need Is Love: The Story of Popular Music* (Harmondsworth: Penguin 1977), 173–93. An earlier Radio-Canada offering, 'Les Collegiens Troubadours' (Fall '56 to Fall '58), seems to have been along the same lines. 'Dans tous les cantons,' by the way, had an educational purpose, namely to give viewers a better understanding of their cultural heritage. CTV's offerings were 'King Ganam' (Spring–Summer '61), 'Country Style' (Spring '61 to Fall '62), 'Barn Dance' (Fall '61 to Spring '62), and Country Music Hall' (beginning Fall '64).

26 Cost figures from respectively Sangster, 'The Most Baffling Show on Television,' 26; Minutes, 16th Meeting of Program Committee, Board of Directors, 18 and 19 September 1961, 3; and Tom Alderman, "What Lousy TV Program Draws 3,000,000?' *The Canadian*, 29 November 1968. The descriptions of

the staging come from three close readings: 'Holiday Ranch' (28 September 1957); 'Dans tous les cantons' (27 July 1960); and 'Country Hoedown' (8 September 1962).

27 Brydon quoted in Sangster, 'The Most Baffling Show on Television,' 84; Barris, *The Pierce-Arrow Showroom*, 50 (Barris was a writer on the show). Sellick, *Canada's Don Messer*, 61; Sangster, 'The Most Baffling Show on Television,' 85; apparently Tommy Common on 'Country Hoedown' would do pop with a western flavour, and Tommy Hunter would even try a bit of rock 'n' roll.

28 Ranking of 'Holiday Ranch' from Sangster, 'The Most Baffling Show on Television,' 26; the Toronto *Telegram*, 10 January 1958, reported that both 'Holiday Ranch' and 'Country Hoedown' were reaching 2.5 million viewers a week; on Don Messer's victory, see Sellick, *Canada's Don Messer*, 72; the anecdote re Messer's sponsors in Christina McCall Newman, 'What Makes the Don Messer Show Go?' *Chatelaine*, January 1961, 21.

29 Perkins, 'Hames Sisters,' 21; Sellick, *Canada's Don Messer*, 72; E-H *National Teleratings*, January 1963

30 Cynic's quotation in Newman, 'What Makes the Don Messer Show Go?' 56; assorted condemnations and Messer's comment found in an essay by Pat Johnson in the program file, CBC Reference Library; Braithwaite in Toronto *Globe and Mail*, 16 April 1965

31 Scott (from *Vancouver Sun*, 11 October 1960) cited in Sellick, *Canada's Don Messer*, 61; Sangster, 'The Most Baffling Show on Television,' 84

32 The comments on Juliette taken from *The Toronto Daily Star*, 11 June 1966, and Barris, *The Pierce-Arrow Showroom*, 47–55

33 Tommy Hunter with Liane Heller, *My Story* (Toronto: Methuen 1985), especially 34–62. This biography, by the way, is an excellent expression of the ethos and style of the country and music scene.

34 Toronto *Globe and Mail*, 26 October 1966 and 10 February 1965

35 This discussion of television comedy is based upon Paul E. McGhee, 'Toward the Integration of Entertainment and Educational Functions of Television: The Role of Humor,' in Tannebaum, *The Entertainment Functions of Television*; Hal Himmelstein, *Television Myth and the American Mind* (New York: Praeger 1984); Albert Hunt, ' "She Laughed at Me with My Own Teeth": Tommy Cooper – Television Anti-Hero,' Masterman, *Television Mythologies*, 67–72; A.F. Wertheim, 'The Rise and Fall of Milton Berle' and Bert Spector, 'A Clash of Cultures: The Smothers Brothers vs. CBS Television,' in John E. O'Connor, *American History/American Television: Interpreting the Video Past* (New York: Frederick Ungar 1983), 55–78 and 159–83. It is the oppositional bias of comedy that has made it one of the few forms of television that wins

some praise from radical critics of the medium such as Himmelstein and Hunt.

36 Biographical data from Walter Harris, 'TV Triumph on the Bigtime,' SN, 24 May 1958, 11 and 43, and J.G., 'How Johnny and Frank Became "Wayne and Shuster" ' CBC Times, 13–19 April 1952, 2. For the early response of the Canadian audience, see Schwerin (and Canadian Facts, Limited), *Report CBC-57-4 'The Wayne and Shuster Show'* and E-H, *A Survey on Audience Reaction to the Wayne & Shuster Show*, February 1958. Sullivan's opinion on the duo cited in Harris, 10; the two comics had apparently been offered $176,000 for twenty-six appearances (Harris, 10), although in the end they agreed to do only sixteen to eighteen according to Johnny Wayne (interview, 22 July 1986). They did, however, have one flop in the United States a few years later: in 1961 they starred in a sitcom called 'Holiday Lodge,' a summer replacement for Jack Benny, which proved a failure and a mistake. Later on, though, they were ready and able to make fun of their mistake in other shows.

37 Morris Wolfe, *Jolts: The TV Wasteland and the Canadian Oasin* (Toronto: James Lorimer and Company 1985) 99

38 Braithwaite's comment in the Toronto *Globe and Mail*, 10 February 1965; the CBC Times, 20–26 October 1962, 12, referred to their comedy as 'a blend of highly literate sophistication and broad slapstick.'

39 Quotation from J.A.G., 'Many TV Talents Combine When Wayne and Shuster Plan a Knockout,' CBC Times, 22–8 November 1958, 2. The other material taken from 'It's No Joke Being Funny,' CBC Times, 21–27 November 1954, 3; Harris, 'TV Triumph on the Bigtime,' 10.

40 See the story by Blaik Kirby in The *Toronto Daily Star*, 28 April 1962, about the technical side of the show. Len Starmer has also talked about Hudson and his team as a major force in variety programming, introducing a collection of innovations to enhance 'the look' of variety programming in the late 1950s and early 1960s – Starmer interview.

41 Quotation about 'life' from 'It's No Joke Being Funny,' 3; examples from 'The Wayne and Shuster Hour,' 11 March 1962

42 Quotation about 'plays' from Brian Stewart, 'Wayne & Shuster,' CBC Times, 3–9 December 1960, 10

43 Stewart, 'Wayne & Shuster,' 10; Toronto *Globe and Mail*, 10 February 1965; 'It's No Joke Being Funny,' 2 and Stewart, 'Wayne & Shuster,' 9 and 10. That approach, by the way, upset some critics right from the beginning: Miriam Waddington, for example, took them to task for failing to deal with the serious issues of life facing men and women and the place of the individual in society – 'Radio and Television,' CF, November 1956, 183. In the next decade some critics came to lament the lack of a tradition of hard-hitting satire:

Dennis Braithwaite (Toronto *Globe and Mail*, 29 April 1963), for example, praised American comedian Jack Carter for offering up political jokes about Canada of a sort rarely found on Canadian television. Carter had appeared on 'The Ed Sullivan Show' when it was produced from Toronto in April 1963. J. Brown (*Toronto Daily Star*, 10 April 1962) complained that 'Parade' had recently deleted two satires about the prime minister, which suggested it would always steer away from 'biting satire.' Bob Blackburn (Toronto *Telegram*, 15 July 1961) was upset that Canada hadn't produced any satire that was angry and trendy, whereas, of course, the Americans had.

44 See comments on television and the audience in 'It's No Joke Being Funny,' 2 and 3; quotation from Harris, 'TV Triumph on the Bigtime,' 11. One anecdote (from Bowles, *A Thousand Sundays*, 150) has it that Pierre Berton once warned them against doing a skit about the troubles of the Stratford baseball team *à la* Shakespeare on 'The Ed Sullivan Show,' because he thought the Americans would never get the joke. They did the skit anyway, once more to the acclaim of the audience. Afterwards an American journalist expressed surprise that Canadians had also understood and enjoyed the same performance.

45 Wayne interview

46 These figures are only estimates, though – the key fact is not the actual sum, but the differentials between 'Wayne and Shuster' and the rest. The sale noted in CBC Press Release 316, 28 April 1966, 1, a part of the program file of 'Wayne and Shuster' in the CBC Reference Library in Toronto. *CBC Times*, 20–26 October 1962; *Radio Times*, 2 September 1965, and CBC Press Release 347, 10 May 1965, 1 and 2; quotation in *CBC Times*, 20–26 October 1962, 3. The Silver Rose award was a second prize.

47 The episode of 'Hit Parade' (29 February 1956) was evaluated by Schwerin, *Report C-CBC-56: Comparison of Teenage & Adult Audiences: 'Cross-Canada Hit Parade' and 'The Jackie Rae Show'*; CBC Press Release in 'Hit Parade' program file, CBC Reference Library, and see also 'Backstage at "Cross-Canada Hit Parade," ' *CBC Times*, 16–22 May 1959, 7.

48 Casey quoted in Lockhart, 'New TV Showtime Is Seeking Prestige,' 28; *CBC Times*, 12–18 March 1960, 6; Toronto *Telegram*, 9 May 1963; *La Semaine à Radio-Canada*, 5–11 June 1965, 8; Toronto *Telegram*, 9 September 1965. Teenage shows were offered in the late afternoon, such as CBLT's 'Club Six' and CBFT's 'Jeunesse oblige.' Neither appears to have been especially 'rebellious.'

49 As early as 1960, one CBC executive told the directors that there was a lack of interest, even from sponsors, in weekly variety programes in the United States – Minutes, 12th Meeting of Program Committee, 5 December 1960, 2.

A bit later one of the directors, W.L. Morton, wondered whether it wouldn't make more sense, at least in terms of money, to buy more American variety. The answer was yes, though management felt that would hurt Canadian performers (Minutes, 17th Meeting of Program Committee, 30 and 31 October 1961, 18–19). The exchange was of interest because it showed there was little pressure from the directors, the supposed representatives of the public, to improve CBC variety.

50 R-C data from CBC, French Television Network, 'Analysis and Comparison of Fourth Quarter Schedules 1967/68 and 1968/69,' in *Normal Weekly Schedule – French Programming 1968–69*, 19, courtesy of CBC Ottawa.

51 Hunter and Heller, *My Story*, 217, 229–56 (on Hunter's own show); Roy Shields in *The Toronto Daily Star*, 11 June 1966; Barris, *The Pierce-Arrow Showroom*, 80–90

52 The basic source for this account is Sellick's *Canada's Don Messer*, though of course it is totally biased in favour of Messer. The program file at the CBC Reference Library, CBC-Toronto, contains a large amount of newspaper comment about the whole affair, as well as the show in general. Diefenbaker's statement taken from the Toronto *Telegram*, 1 May 1969. Nash, *Prime Time at Ten* (Toronto: M&S 1987), 132

53 *MM*, 7 August 1965, 46

54 By 1967, the Canadian Radio-Television Commission found a series of rock or Top 40 stations, pop-oriented stations, middle-of-the-road and easy listening, and some country across Canada – cited in Paul Audley, *Canada's Cultural Industries: Broadcasting, Publishing, Records and Film* (Toronto: Lorimer 1983), 199. It should be noted that towards the end of the 1970s variety virtually disappeared from the primetime schedules of the American networks.

55 Goodis, *Have I Ever Lied to You Before?* (Toronto: M&S 1972), 30–1

7 In Gameland

1 In Carrier, *The Hockey Sweater and Other Stories*, translated by Sheila Fischman (Toronto: Anansi 1979), 77

2 The success of 'La poule aux oeufs d'or' noted in *Marketing*, 16 January 1959, 12. The comment on the preferences of Quebec's women taken from Bill Stephenson, 'The Wonderful World of French-Canadian TV,' *MM*, 8 June 1957, 84

3 The term 'vicarious participation' taken from Michael Real, 'The Super Bowl: Mythic Spectacle,' in Horace Newcomb, ed., *Television: The Critical View*, 2nd ed. (New York: OUP 1979), 179. During the weeks he strove to answer ques-

tions and earn monies, Van Doren was featured on the cover of *Time* and even offered a movie contract – Harry Castleman and Walter J. Podrazik, *Watching TV: Four Decades of American Television* (New York: McGraw-Hill 1982), 115

4 McLuhan, *Understanding Media* 2nd ed. (New York: New American Library 1964), 216. Callois, *Man, Play, and Games* (London: Thames and Hudson 1962), 19; Fiske and Hartley, *Reading Television* (London: Methuen 1980), 130; Lewis, 'TV Games: People as Performers,' in Len Masterman, ed., *Television Mythologies* (London: Comedia 1984), 44; Zurcher and Meadow, 'On Bullfights and Baseball: An Example of Social Institutions,' in Eric Dunning, ed., *Sport: Readings from a Sociological Perspective* (Toronto: UTP 1972), 175–97; Real, 'The Super Bowl,' 188; Novak, *The Joy of Sports* (New York: Basic Books 1976), xv

5 McArthur cited in appraisal of 12 September 1958 episode of 'One of a Kind,' in RG 41, v. 277, file 11-43-16; Toronto *Telegram*, 28 October 1955

6 Re 'The Superior Sex' see CBC Programme File in CBC Reference Library, Toronto, and Minutes, 16th Meeting of Program Committee, 18 and 19 September 1961, 1.

7 Bob Hodge and David Tripp, *Children and Television: A Semiotic Approach* (Stanford: Stanford University Press 1986), 181. 'Cléopâtre' expenses mentioned in the program sheet in Gérard Laurence, *Histoire des programmes-TV, CBFT Montréal, September 1952–September 1957* (CRTC Research Report 1982).

8 *SN*, 16 March 1957, 18; Braithwaite in *The Toronto Daily Star*, 22 June 1960; nickname for 'Flashback' mentioned in Bob Blackburn's column, Toronto *Telegram*, 17 October 1962

9 By 1959, for example, people sending in quotations to 'Fighting Words' received two records and a book, and, if the panel was stumped, an encyclopedia as well. The comment on 'Le nez de Cléopâtre' based on a viewing analysis of the 28 April 1954 edition. The comment on 'One of a Kind' based on an extensive series of program evaluations in RG 41, v. 277, file 11-43-16. The comments on 'Fighting Words' and 'Front Page Challenge' based on viewing analyses of the respective episodes of 19 January 1958 and 16 January 1962 and information in the program files of the CBC Reference Library in Toronto. The *CBC Times*, 16–22 May 1959, 3, decided the unpredictability of the discussion on 'Fighting Words' was a key explanation for the success of the show.

10 Soles quoted in Toronto *Telegram*, 24 September 1962

11 Frank Peers noted in a letter to the director for Ontario and English Networks, 8 October 1958 (RG 41, v. 206, file 11-18-11-69) that in the past three years

the show had tackled racial discimination, divorce laws, religion and reason, socialism, conscription, and so on; Starmer quoted in *The Toronto Daily Star*, 2 July 1960; Blackburn in the Toronto *Telegram*, 19 May 1965.

12 The description of Cohen taken from Frank Tumpane, 'Sincerely Yours,' Toronto *Telegram*, 17 July 1962; on Davis, see Alex Barris, *Front Page Challenge: The 25th Anniversary* (Toronto: CBC 1981), 16–20; Barris 'sins' outlined in the previously mentioned CBC program evaluation files; and Templeton's failings noted by Braithwaite (*Toronto Daily Star*, 2 July 1959) and Ira Dilworth in the evaluation of the 30 September 1959 episode (RG 41, v. 277, file 11-43-13).

13 Stuart M. Kaminsky has noted how the panelists is similar American quizzes played the roles of gods or heroes, masters of data and by implication of intellect. In fact he has a complicated scheme for the analysis of all game shows based on the approach of Northrop Frye in his *Anatomy of Criticism*, wherein the crucial variable is the 'power' of the participant vis-à-vis the viewer – is it greater, the same, or less? The scheme makes for an interesting exploration of this genre, though in the end the scheme is a bit too rigid to fit all the realities of game/quiz format. See Stuart M. Kaminsky with Jeffrey H. Mahan, *American Television Genres* (Chicago: Nelson-Hall 1985), 43–8. The comment on 'One of a Kind' from Alex Barris, *The Pierce-Arrow Showroom Is Leaking* (Toronto: Ryerson 1969), 32; the regulars of 'Fighting Words' described in a story in *The Toronto Daily Star's TV Week*, 20 June 1970, 4–5; the description of Pelletier in *La Semaine à Radio-Canada*, 23–29 August 1953; there are some good descriptions of Sinclair and Berton in the program file of 'Front Page Challenge,' CBC Reference Library, Toronto, as well as in Barris, *The Pierce-Arrow Showroom* and *Front Page Challenge* (on 74–5 he talks about the Tanner incident).

14 The Tumpane retrospective, 'Sincerely Yours' – Charlotte Whitton and Hilda Neatby were exceptions according to other sources such as the CBC *Times*, 16–22 May 1959, 3, and the *Star's TV Week* story; on Robins and Kennedy, see Barris's two books, mentioned in note 13, above.

15 Barris, *Front Page Challenge*, 72; 'Flashback' producer quoted in *The Toronto Daily Star*, 27 October 1962; on the Rolland story see *The Toronto Daily Star*, 10 September and 15 September 1959, and Toronto *Globe and Mail*, 11 September 1959 – the CBC apologized and Guthrie was suspended for two weeks. Cohen notes the 'Fighting Words' policy in his farewell to the show, *The Toronto Daily Star*, 14 July, 1962.

16 The description of 'Le club des autographes' based on a viewing analysis of the episode of 24 October 1959

17 The descriptions of these American shows taken from Tim Brooks and Earle

Marsh, *The Complete Directory to Prime Time Network TV Shows 1946– Present*, 2nd ed. (New York: Ballantine 1981), 69–70, 841, 779–80, and Alex McNeil, *Total Television* (New York: Penguin 1980), 79, 790, 736, 575–76. The rating from E-H *Teleratings*, March 1960, 19.

18 The description of 'La rigolade' taken from Bill Stephenson, 'The Wonderful World of French-Canadian TV,' 82–3; viewing statistics in RG 41, v. 211, file 11-19-6, pt. 2; *Le Devoir*, 22 October 1955, cited in Laurence's program description; on Molson's decision, see *Marketing*, 16 January 1959, 12.

19 Quotations from *MM*, 17 April 1965, and the Toronto *Telegram*, 16 September 1964.

20 CBC Audience Research, *English Television Network: Program Ratings: June 1957 to May 1958*, 36, a document derived from ISL data. The show appeared on WBEN-TV – at the time CBLT-Toronto and CHCH-Hamilton ran 'Close-Up,' which secured a mere 9 per cent of the audience. *La Presse*, 8 June 1963 – Keable wrote the regular column 'Radio-télévision.'

21 Keable, ' "Tous pour un": le savoir et les gros sous!' *La Presse*, 16 January 1965, 11; advertisements in *La Presse*, 16 January and 21 July 1962; E-H *Teleratings*, March 1963; BBM, *Television Station Report*, February 1965 – according to this survey, 'Tous pour un' captured 192,700 homes at 8:30– 9:00 on Tuesday, while 'La poule aux oeufs d'or' got only 148,888 homes at 8:30–9:00 on Thursday.

22 Comment on success of 'Take a Chance' from *TV Guide*, 20 October 1963, and on Dickson's nickname from *The Toronto Daily Star*, 11 September 1961. The description of 'Line 'Em Up' from Shirley Mair and Peter Gzowski, 'The Carnies on the Picture Tube,' *MM*, 23 February 1963, 17. (Mair and Gzowski also comment on just how prevalent this kind of show was on daytime television: an eastern Canadian favourite such as 'Domino,' for example, was cheap to produce, costing only $10,000 a week in some cities; Canadian, so it filled up the Canadian-content quota; and very appealing to housewives.) The material on 'Musical Showcase' from Pat Pearce in the Montreal *Star*, 29 March 1965, and Bob Blackburn, Toronto *Telegram*, 5 April and 20 September 1965. The ranking from *Nielsen Television Index: Report for January 1966*, 45.

23 Mair and Gzowski, 'The Carnies on the Picture Tube,' 16. 'Game shows where the winners go "Ooh" and "Aah" when confronted by big bundles of cash or shiny new items are worthy of unmitigated contempt,' declared Jon Ruddy in the Toronto *Telegram* (24 September 1962). Ruddy's comments on the psychological roots of the viewing passion in *Telegram*, 28 November 1961. Keable's comments in *La Presse*, 8 June and 28 October 1963.

24 See especially chapter 2, 'The Natural Religion,' pp 18–34. Novak is an

academic, an American philosopher, and above all a devoted sports fan. His book was very much a defence of sports, against those indifferent to its appeal or critical of its existence. The fact that a lot of people in North America don't share Novak's enthusiasm for sports puts his conclusion in doubt. It doesn't, however, undermine the analogy with religion – most religions have had to suffer the existence of agnostics and athiests. See also Garry J. Smith and Cynthia Blackman, *Sport in the Mass Media*, Cahper Sociology of Sport Monograph Series (Calgary: University of Calgary, n.d.), 2–4, and Gregor Goethals, *The TV Ritual* (Boston: Beacon Press 1981), especially chapter I, 'Ritual: Ceremony and Super-Sunday,' 5–31.

25 CBC *Annual Report 1957–58*, 18; Minutes, 17th Meeting of Program Committee, 30 and 31 October 1961, 15 and 17; Big Four football refers to the professional league in central Canada, and NFL football to the major American league; Ouimet I.

26 Smith and Blackman, *Sport in the Mass Media*, for example, cite a study in Edmonton (1974) conducted by one of the authors that showed the obvious, namely that TV was most often mentioned by respondents as the medium of choice. Bob Moir talked about the impact of CBC-TV on sports in Canada, especially football, in his interview.

27 Campbell's 1949 comment noted in Scott Young, *Hello Canada: The Life and Times of Foster Hewitt* (Toronto: Seal Books 1985), 114; the Campbell quotation cited in Brian McFarlane, *50 Years of Hockey: An Intimate History of the National Hockey League* (Toronto: Pagurian Press 1970), 119. McFarlane notes that in the first season of telecasts there was some cause for alarm because of the low turn-out for one visit of the Detroit Red Wings to play the Toronto Maple Leafs.

28 Novak, *The Joy of Sports*, 249–56, for example, charged television with cheapening and degrading sports by distancing fans from the game, personalizing team sports, filling the air with banality, and such like sins. Hal Himmelstein, in a highly critical, and often absurd, book entitled *Television Myth and the American Mind* (New York: Praeger 1984) claims television has changed the tempo of games (239). Margaret Morse, 'Sport on Television: Replay and Display,' in E. Ann Kaplan, ed., *Regarding Television: Critical Approaches – An Anthology* (Frederich, Md.: University Publications of America 1983), 44–5, argues that sports on television is, among other things, a means of displaying the male body (44–5). Fiske and Hartley, *Reading Television*, maintain that British television has transformed soccer, taking it out of a working-class context and putting it into a bourgeois context (145). Richard J. Harmond finds that television has fostered some rule changes, focused extra attention on sports stars, declassed certain kinds of sports, and ushered in the era of

big money sports – 'Sugar Daddy or Ogre? The Impact of Commercial Television on Professional Sports,' in Frank J. Coppa, ed., *Screen and Society: The
Impact of Television upon Aspects of Contemporary Civilization* (Chicago: Nelson-Hall 1979), 81–105.

29 The anecdote about Newman told in Young, *Hello Canada*, 118

30 Comments on the style of announcing based upon a viewing analysis of
'Hockey Night in Canada,' 15 April 1962. Local announcers, by contrast,
were often paid by or approved by the club they covered, and so they were
expected to be partisan – see Gerald Eskenazi, *A Thinking Man's Guide to Pro
Hockey* (New York: E.P. Dutton & Co. 1972), 151–2. See Dick Irvin, *Now
Back to You, Dick: Two Lifetimes in Hockey* (Toronto: M&S 1988), 100–6, for
some comment on Gallivan and his style of announcing.

31 Frayne in *MM*, 7 January 1961, 88; Bob Blackburn in *The Toronto Daily Star*
(17 April 1961) also complained about simulcasting, which left listeners and
viewers confused because the words and images didn't always deal with the
same thing.

32 Interview with Ward Cornell – Cornell had announced Big Four games in the
mid-1950s and joined 'Hockey Night in Canada' in the fall of 1959 for the
CBC's intermission shows. According to Eskenazi, *A Thinking Man's Guide*,
Fisher became a "non-person" on TV and Young lost a pre-game show, each
because he offended the powers in the industry (152–3). See also Jack Batten,
'Hello Canada and Hockey Fans in the United States and Newfoundland,'
SN, 24 April 1976, 22, on the Young case. Cornell, by the way, claimed that
he never faced any sort of pressure from the industry to alter or influence
his performance. Only once did an ad-agency man suggest a change, and that
was with regard to his appearance. Irvin, *Now Back to You, Dick*, 123.

33 A survey in April 1963 discovered that it had by far the highest recognition
rate among viewers in English (74.0) and French Canada (88.2, shared with co-
sponsor Molson's) quizzed about the sponsorship of leading programs – E-H
Teleratings April 1962. Ken Dryden, *The Game* (Toronto: Totem Books
1984), 56. Dryden's book is a superb and fascinating account of the nature of
hockey. Mahovlich and Howe, by the way, played for the Toronto Maple
Leafs and the Detroit Red Wings, respectively.

34 McDonald, *TPR February–March 1963* – CFTO's hockey at 9:30 got 346,000
men and 251,000 women. On Imperial Oil's decision, see Toronto *Globe
and Mail*, 3 March 1976, and *The Toronto Star*, 26 and 27 February 1976 – one
estimate had it that by this time (when there were more households with
multiple sets) the audience was two-thirds male. By 1976 Imperial Oil was
contributing more than $3 million in advertising support for a program costing
some $12 million to produce.

35 Dryden, *The Game*, 226–7; George Plimpton, *Open Net: The Professional Amateur in the World of Big-Time Hockey* (New York: W.W. Norton 1985), 60. Plimpton has an interesting perspective because he has investigated and 'played' in a number of sports.

36 Dierdre Clayton notes in *Eagle: The Life and Times of R. Alan Eagleson* (Toronto: Lester & Orpen Dennys 1982), 45, that in the early 1960s many English-Canadian players hoped to end up with the Leafs. Not that one should carry this theme of national rivalries too far. I doubt that all fans were aware of it, or that it was usually uppermost in the minds of viewers. Ward Cornell, for instance, didn't recall the rivalry of Toronto and Montreal as in any way a reflection of the French/English division.

37 See Gzowski, *The Game of Our Lives* (Toronto: M&S 1981), 79–84. Gzowski's book is a superb account of the game, centred upon the career and the personnel of the Edmonton Oilers in the 1980/1 season. Along with the books by Dryden and Plimpton, it is invaluable to anyone trying to understand the game of hockey.

38 Cornell interview; Novak, *The Joy of Sports*, 93–4, thought hockey expressed the exuberance, the struggle for survival, the emphasis on endurance that he associated with the north; Howe quoted in Rod Gilbert, with Stan Fischler and Hal Bock, *Goal: My Life on Ice* (New York: Hawthorn Books 1968), 64; Plimpton, *Open Net*, 44, noted the comment of the Boston Bruin's coach, Don Cherry, that there was no such thing as ' "painless" goal-tending.' Plimpton, *Open Net*, 219, also felt that hockey was more 'male-oriented' than other sports, pointing out how the wives of hockey players had almost no place in or at the game, unlike, say, baseball. Note that I'm talking about perceptions: other sports, notably football, might make similar claims to 'manliness.'

39 See Gzowski, *The Game of Our Lives*, 54–5; Plimpton, *Open Net*, 70, 71, 76; and Dryden, *The Game*, 33, on initiations and practical jokes and the sense of brotherhood.

40 Cherry quoted in Plimpton, *Open Net*, 59

41 Gilbert, *Goal*, 79

42 Note on King Clancy from Eskenazi, *A Thinking Man's Guide*, 90; Plimpton, *Open Net*, 28

43 The Pearson anecdote from Keith Davey, *The Rainmaker: A Passion for Politics* (Toronto: Stoddart 1986), 92; Ouimet 1; Campbell's comment from Eskenazi, *A Thinking Man's Guide*, 112; Gilbert, *Goal*, 64, and Plimpton, *Open Net*, 154; Novak, *The Joy of Sports*, 94, uses the phrase 'hot temper tantrums' to described one of the aspects of hockey.

44 The term *bagarre général* mentioned in Plimpton, *Open Net*, 208; description of the Richard Riot taken from Eskenazi, *A Thinking Man's Guide*, 38

45 The idea that individualism is a great characteristic of the Canadian style of play has been around for some time – see, for example, Clayton, *Eagle*, 49. See also Plimpton, *Open Net*, 242, on the competitive spirit. Once the Russians began beating NHL stars, though, there emerged a counter-argument that individualism was a sin, that central to good hockey was the interplay of teammates.

46 On Richard see Stan Fishler, 'A History and Critique of the Canadiens,' and Richard, 'My Life with the Canadiens,' in Maurice Richard and Stan Fischler, *The Flying Frenchmen* (New York: Hawthorn Books 1971), and on Howe see Jim Vipond, *Gordie Howe Number 9* (Toronto: McGraw-Hill Ryerson 1968).

47 The anecdote about fans paying Richard's fines from Gregory Stone, 'American Sports: Play and Display,' in Eric Dunning, ed., *Sport*, 60; the anecdote about Howe in Gzowski, *The Game of Our Lives*, 156; Dryden, *The Game*, 73, 159–60; Gzowski, 82–3.

48 Gzowski, 'Epilogue: The Changing Styles of Watching and Playing,' in Trent Frayne and Peter Gzowski, *Great Canadian Sports Stories: A Century of Competition* (Toronto: Canadian Centennial Library 1965), 124. The process had already swept over American football with its inflated coaching staffs, highly specialized players, defensive and offensive units, set plays, and so on.

49 Mind you, the degree of sophistication varied considerably with each coach. Don Cherry told Plimpton, *Open Net*, 50, and this was in the late 1970s, that it took him five minutes and one napkin to explain to a newcomer all the Bruins' plays.

50 In his description of the Edmonton Oilers, Gzowski, *The Game of Our Lives*, 93–4, noted that this process had gone much farther with all the skills of players rated and fed into a computer to identify individual strengths and weaknesses.

51 On the power play and the defence, see Eskenazi, *A Thinking Man's Guide*, 55, and Gilbert, *Goal*, 131.

52 The estimates of money from Eskenazi, *A Thinking Man's Guide*, 92, 159–60. There had been an earlier CBS experiment with Saturday-afternoon hockey telecasts from 1957 through 1959 – noted in Harry Castleman and Walter J. Podrazik, *The TV Schedule Book*.

53 BBM ratings noted in *The Toronto Star*, 20 March 1976, story on Imperial Oil's leave-taking. It is only fair to note that after the mid-1970s things began to improve. The Montreal Canadiens again fielded a superb team, of which Dryden was a major part. The World Hockey Association came to an end, some of its healthier franchises (including Quebec City, Winnipeg, and Edmonton) joining the NHL. A new superstar came along in the shape of

Wayne Gretzky. And the style of play steadily improved with better training, better players, and new techniques.

54 The Edmonton statistic from Smith and Blackman, *Sport in the Mass Media*, 22

8 Culture on the Small Screen

1 Quoted in *CBC Times*, 24–30 October, 1954, 2

2 *SN*, 5 January 1957, 8; 'Drama on the Air,' *Canadian Literature*, no. 2, Autumn 1959, 60. Thus, at one of the meetings of the CBC's Program Committee a high official talked about 'the challenge' before television to design suitable techniques to broadcast classical music – see Minutes, 12th Program Committee Meeting, 5 December 1960, 8.

3 'My Holiday at the TV Set: Beverly Baxter in Canada,' *MM*, 18 February 1956, 67; 'Letter from New York,' *Canadian Art*, 20, no. 4 (July/August 1963), 245

4 For a discussion of this traditional aesthetics and television, see Robert C. Allen's 'Soap Operas in Aesthetic Discourse,' in *Speaking of Soap Operas* (Chapel Hill: The University of North Carolina Press 1985), 11–18. Need I add that these presumptions continue to bedevil the analysis and appreciation of television today?

5 'A Dialogue,' *Canadian Art*, v. 9, no. 5 (September/October 1962), 348–9

6 Ouimet 1

7 There were, of course, many other short-lived series or collections of specials that provide ballet or operetta, folk music, assorted dances, and on and on. In 1954/5 Radio-Canada attempted an anthology devoted to experimental broadcasts – mime, ballet, drama – under the title 'Trente secondes.' More important, the network did attempt some half-hour drama, notably with 'Quator' (Fall '55 to Summer '58), which featured mini-series roughly four episodes long. And there were various summer collections, some under the unimaginative title 'Théâtre d'été,' purportedly a vehicle for Canadian plays. Interested readers may consult a survey of the early teleplay experience by Gérard Laurence, 'La rencontre du théâtre et de la télévision au Québec (1952–1957),' *Etudes littéraires*, August 1981, 215–49. In 1961 the minutes of the seventeenth meeting of the Program Committee record the comment by Marcel Ouimet that Radio-Canada scheduled about two avant-garde plays a year.

8 Note that there was a brief hiatus in the scheduling of a highbrow anthology, namely the television year 1959/60. That was filled by the peculiar hybrid 'Startime,' a sixty- to ninety-minute series that carried a mix of NBC spectacu-

lars (drama, variety, and musicals) and CBC productions (mostly drama, though at least one ballet). Although the series ran in the United States, the Canadian productions were only aired over the CBC network. Clearly the show had a more middlebrow than highbrow tone. The quotation on 'Festival' from a column by Bob Blackburn in *The Toronto Daily Star*, 23 March 1961. Blackburn took issue with the approach, since he regarded the show as very good, not just highbrow.

9 Note that in the early years the CBC also scheduled a lot of much less famous half-hour anthologies from the United States, with titles such as 'Celebrity Playhouse,' 'Douglas Fairbanks Theatre,' 'Errol Flynn Theatre,' 'Regal Theatre,' 'Royal Theatre. There were, of course, other made-in-Canada series, such as the three brief runs of 'First Performance' (in the Fall of 1956, 1957, and 1958), regional theatre such as Montreal's 'Dorchester Theatre' (Summer '57) and Vancouver's 'Studio Pacific' (Summer–Fall '59), and 'Summer Circuit' (Summer '61) which offered new material and rebroadcasts of plays from earlier series. Interested readers may find a lot of further information about the Canadian anthologies in Mary Jane Miller, 'Canadian Television Drama 1952–1970: Canada's National Theatre,' *Theatre History in Canada*, 5, no. 1 (Spring 1984), 51–71, and in her book *Turn Up the Contrast: CBC Television Drama since 1952* (Vancouver: University of British Columbia Press/ CBC Enterprises 1987), 187–226.

10 During the last half of the 1950s CBLT had offered a late-night American omnibus, at times delving into the avant-garde, entitled 'Camera Three.' The program files in the CBC Reference Library contain a lot of material on 'Quest' and 'Eye-Opener' taken from the *CBC Times* as well as from the Toronto press. For 'Quest' see in particular Nathan Cohen's retrospective in *SN*, March 1964, 10; *CBC Times*, 31 December 1960–6 January 1961, 4; and *The Toronto Daily Star*, 26 September 1962. For 'Eye-Opener' see *CBC Times*, 5 January 1965, 8–viii; the Toronto *Telegram*, 19 January 1965; and the Montreal *Star*, 20 February 1965.

11 Williams, *Culture* (Glasgow: Fontana 1981), 130. Williams explores the sociology of culture in this book. He provides some very interesting analysis of art and society, as well as artists and institutions.

12 Fowler II, 44 – note, however, that this figure pertains to payments made in all fields of entertainment, not just Culture; Cohen, 'TV Dance in Canada,' *CBC Times*, 1–7 September 1957, 2; Russel, 'Drama,' *Canadian Art*, 9, no. 5 (September/October 1962), 360; Munro interview; Miller, 'Canadian Television Drama 1952–1970,' 53; see the *CBC Times* story on Wilkin, 13–19 August 1960, 4–5 and 20–1; the count of Dubé's plays or adaptations from La Société

Radio-Canada, *Vingt-cinq ans de Dramatiques à la télévision de Radio-Canada 1952–77* (Montreal 1978).

13 Mercure interview in CBC *Times*, 10–16 April 1955, 2; Kraemer interview in Brian Stewart, 'Music on Television,' CBC *Times*, 23–29 January 1960, 6–7, 21 – Stewart was also talking to Walter Susskind, conductor of the Toronto Symphony, and Ron Poulton, the TV critic; the Campbell-Guthrie exchange in CBC Press Release 506B, 28 September 1960, from the program files of 'Festival' in the CBC Reference Library, Toronto.

14 See the comment on broadcasting live-theatre productions in the draft minutes of the forty-eighth meeting of the Program Committee, Board of Directors, 8 February 1967, 5.

15 The description of this production of *Carmen* taken from the CBC *Times*, 28 April–4 May 1957, 2; estimates cited in the minutes of the eighteenth meeting of the Program Committee, Board of Directors, 13 December 1961, 9. Eric Koch in *Inside Seven days* (Scarborough: Prentice-Hall 1986), 66, claimed that the direct cost of putting on *Rigoletto* on 'Festival,' 3 February 1965 was $97,200.

16 CBC *Times*, 21–27 January 1961, 11 and 31

17 The evaluations can be found in RG 41, v. 277, file 11-4-3.

18 Anstensen, 'Ibsen on Television,' CBC *Times*, 18–24 June 1960, 11. Ralph Thomas in *The Toronto Daily Star*, 20 February 1964, for example, criticized one 'Festival' performance because 'the recording of her performance [a young pianist] was one unending distortion.' On the sound quality of TV and the problems of televising music, see the comments by Eugene Hallman, J.R. Royal (Montreal's supervisor of music), and Alphonse Ouiment, in the minutes of the Program Committee, both the ninth meeting and the twelfth meeting, 19–21 April 1960 and 5 December 1960.

19 Lamb, 'Television,' *Canadian Art*, 19, May/June 1962, 233; *The Toronto Daily Star*, 1 April 1965; Ross, 'Quality Shows: A Re-Examination,' SN, 6 August 1960, 35; Robertson, 'Dance,' *Canadian Art*, 19, no. 5 (September/October 1962), 359

20 Fulford, 'Television Notebook,' CF, July 1960, 91 – Fulford's special concern was with the adaptation of classic literature; Lamb, 'Television,' 233–4; Robertson, 'Dance,' 359; Hawort in Toronto *Globe and Mail*, 4 June 1964; Morton in minutes of twelfth meeting of the Program Committee, 9

21 Chayefsky, *Television Plays* (New York: Simon & Schuster 1955), 132. Chayefsky's collection, like those of the other television playwrights, contains notes and comments that are invaluable to understanding the conventions and purposes of the live teleplay. For discussions of this era, see Erik Barnouw, *The

Tube of Plenty: The Evolution of American Television (New York: OUP 1975),
154–67; the highly critical chapter 'The Video Boys,' in Gerald Weales,
American Drama since World War II (New York: Harcourt, Brace & World
1962), 57–75; the very sympathetic chapter 'The Bard of the Small Screen'
by John M. Clum, in *Paddy Chayefsky* (Boston: Twayne Publishers 1976), 29–
57; and Kenneth Hey, '*Marty*: Aesthetics vs. Medium in Early Television
Drama,' in John E. O'Connor, *American History/American Television* (New
York: Frederick Ungar 1983), 95–133.

22 On American teleplays in the 1960s, see Richard Averson and David Manning
White, 'Preface,' *Electronic Drama: Television Plays in the Sixties* (Boston:
Beacon Press 1971), xi–xxvi; Chayefsky cited in Max Wilk, *The Golden Age of
Television: Notes from the Survivors* (New York: Delta 1976), 137; the notion
of teleplay as art, of course, has had much more currency in Great Britain
where the genre thrived for a much longer period of time: see David Self,
Television Drama: An Introduction (London: Macmillan 1984), 2–9, and
George W. Brandt, ed., *British Television Drama* (Cambridge: Cambridge
University Press 1981), which deals at length with a number of television
playwrights.

23 On radio drama, see the special issue 'Radio: Canada's Dramatic Voice' of
Canadian Theatre Review, 36, Fall 1982, in particular Howard Fink's 'Cana-
dian Radio Drama and the Radio Drama Project,' 12–22; and Andrew Allan,
A Self-Portrait (Toronto: Macmillan of Canada 1974).

24 Moore and Almond quoted in Roger Lee Jackson, 'An Historical and Analytical Study of the Origins, Development and Impact of the Dramatic Programs
Produced for the English Language Networks of the CBC,' unpublished PhD
thesis, Wayne State University, 1966, 121 and 117. Jackson's thesis is largely
a compilation of interviews completed in the mid-1960s with assorted Toronto
types who were or had been in the television-drama field. It was an invaluable
source of information for my account. See Laurence, 'La rencontre du théâtre
et de la télévision au Québec (1952–1957),' 217: he notes that Forget emphasized the adoption of the American model plus the aim of reaching out to 'la
gros public' as well as 'la classe plus cultivée.' Forget apparently was also
convinced of the need for more original scripts from, in his case, Quebec
authors.

25 Newman and Cohen quoted in Jackson, 'Dramatic Programs,' 121, 122 – see
also the interview with Newman in 'What They Say: CBC-TV Drama Producers,' *CBC Times*, 24–30 October 1954, 2; Kemp quoted in Dean Walker, 'CBC's
Search for $1000 Manuscripts,' *SN*, 18 July 1959, 42.

26 CBC, *Annual Report 1956/57*, 10. The reception of Hailey's thriller is described
in Janice Tyrwhitt, 'Arthur Hailey Slays 'Em with Suspense,' *MM*, 27 April

1957, 20. The statistics on Radio-Canada's output are from *Vingt-cinq ans de dramatiques à la télévision de Radio-Canada 1952–77*, xvii – note, however, that these data refer to calendar rather than television years and incorporate four-part plays written for 'Quator.' Bresky's comments repeated in a 'Comment' column in *CBC Times*, 15–21 November 1958, 15.

27 The French-Canadian playwrights taken from Laurence's count, 'La rencontre du théâtre et de la télévision au Québec (1952–1957),' 238–9, and the English-Canadian list from Walker, 'CBC's Search for $1000 Manuscripts,' 42. Not included here was Robert Choquette, who apparently wrote fifty-six half-hour scripts for 'Quator.'

28 Wages cited in Frank Rasky, 'Canada's TV Writers: Timid but Slick,' *SN*, 27 October 1956, 10; on Hailey's profits, see Walker, 'CBC's Search for $1000 Manuscripts,' 42; Ljungh's comments made at the seventeenth meeting of the Program Committee on 30 and 31 December 1961.

29 Robertson, 'Drama on the Air,' *Canadian Literature*, no. 2, Autumn 1959, 61; Sadlier quoted in *CBC Times*, 9–15 May 1959, 3. Veteran radio actors also found television a difficult and unsatisfying medium, or so Bronwyn Drainie's *Living the Part: John Drainie and the Dilemma of Canadian Stardom* (Toronto: Macmillan of Canada 1988), 182–229, suggests.

30 Allan quoted in *CBC Times*, 24–30 August 1958, 3; Peterson cited in Rasky, 'Canada's TV Writers: Timid but Slick,' 12; Willis in *CBC Times*, 23–29 January 1955; Frick quoted in Rasky, 'Canada's TV Writers,' 11

31 Petersen comment in Rasky, 'Canada's TV Writers,' 12; Cohen quoted in Wayne E. Edmonstone, *Nathan Cohen: The Making of a Critic* (Toronto: Lester & Orpen 1977), 236; Peterson and Gauntlett quotations from Jackson, 'Dramatic Programs,' 118 and 166

32 Forget cited in Laurence, 'La rencontre du théâtre et de la télévision au Québec (1952–1957),' 229. The count of the authorship of Radio-Canada plays from *Vingt-cinq ans de dramatiques à la télévision de Radio-Canada 1952–77*, xvii – note, however, that this includes all manner of productions, a Shakespeare as well as a Dubé, so that it is not specific only to modern drama. Richard Levinson and William Link, *Stay Tuned: An Inside Look at the Making of Prime-Time Television* (New York: St. Martin's Press 1981), 12–13

33 Moser quoted in Brian Steward, 'TV Drama: Where Will It Go from Here?' *CBC Times*, 10–16 December 1960, 13; Chayefsky, *Television Plays*, 127; Hailey's comment in June Graham, 'How to Make a Mint in Television Drama,' *CBC Times*, 9–15 April 1960, 8; Breen quoted in Steward, 9. My comments here and later on realism owe much to the account in John Ellis, *Visible Fictions: Cinema, Television, Video* (London: Routledge & Kegan Paul 1982), 6–10.

34 Swarbrick quoted in Jackson, 'Dramatic Programs,' 93; Waddington, 'Radio and Television,' *CF*, September 1957, 135

35 Serling, *Patterns* (New York: Simon & Schuster 1957), 10; Robertson, 'Drama on the Air,' 63

36 The description of the making of *Flight into Danger* and *Time Lock* taken from Tyrwhitt, 'Arthur Hailey Slays 'Em with Suspense,' 56; Thomas, 'Television,' *Food for Thought*, 18, September/October 1957, 40

37 Dworkin, 'Much in Little,' *Canadian Commentator*, 5, no. 2 (February 1961), 15–18; Chayefsky, *Television Plays*, 132; *The Kidders* was by the American Donald Ogden Stewart – the teleplay mentioned in *CBC Times*, 25–31 July 1959, 5; Fulford, 'Television Notebook.' *CF*, February 1960, 254

38 Dworkin, 'Much in Little,' 15; Garner's comment from his television column in *SN*, 6 August 1955, 18; Weales, 'The Video Boys,' 59

39 McGeachy quoted in 'If I Ran the CBC ...,' *MM*, 14 April 1956, 108; Waddington, 'Radio and Television,' *CF*, September 1957, 135; Russel, 'Drama,' 361; Fulford, 'Television Notebook,' *CF*, June 1960, 49–50

40 Whittaker quoted in Steward, 'TV Drama: Where Will It Go from Here?' 9. In that same series of interviews, George McCowan, a free-lance TV producer, said, 'I feel TV must find new conventions, a new format – though I can't say exactly what.' One investigator, though, has found the teleplays much more diverse than I've suggested: Miller in *Turn Up the Contrast*, especially 195, has claimed that English-Canadian teleplays employed 'a wider variety of styles,' including 'fantasy and surrealism,' 'dramatized documentary,' 'absurdist drama,' and so on, than was true of American television, at least after the first surge of dramatic anthologies.

41 Newman had been increasingly frustrated by the bureaucracy of the CBC. 'His ideas had to be cleared by a chain of command that extended around the Arctic Circle,' reminisced Nathan Cohen. 'It was simply an impossibility for him to do things the way he wanted to do them' (Jackson, *Dramatic Programs,*' 125). Ljungh's comment to Hugh Kemp quoted in Jackson, 128; Sadlier's comment cited in a story in the *CBC Times*, 26 September–2 October 1959, 9; Davidson quotation in Jackson, 131–2; the description of Allen's style also drawn from interviews in Jackson, 107–8, 110 (where Kemp gives the particular description from which the brief quotations are drawn), and 114.

42 The reasons for the General Motors withdrawal mentioned in *The Toronto Daily Star*, 17 July 1961; Gauntlett in Jackson, 'Dramatic Programs,' 176

43 The denunciation by the Episcopal Assembly of Quebec province and the CBC's abject apology, plus the results of an internal investigation, are contained in RG 41, v. 211, file 11-19-5; Ouimet's letter in the same collection, v. 677, file 16th Directors' Meeting; Fulford, 'TV Notebook,' *CF*, May 1961, 36.

The Toronto clamp-down was aired in stories by Jeremy Brown in *The Toronto Daily Star*, 19 January 1965; Dennis Braithwaite in the *Globe and Mail*, 19 and 20 January 1965; and Bob Blackburn in the Toronto *Telegram*, 20 January 1965.

44 Nixon's comments in Jackson, 'Dramatic Programs,' 179–81. The figure of twelve plays in 1965 comes from *Vingt-cinq ans ...*, xvii. The next year, by the way, the figure went up to thirty-two, but in 1967 it fell to seventeen. Pierre Pagé and Renée Legris in *Répertoire de dramatiques québécoises à la télévision 1952–1977* (Montreal: Fides 1977), 130, count four original plays in 1964/5, eight in 1965/6, and five in 1966/7.

45 Cohen's article appeared in *The Toronto Daily Star*, 21 May 1966: it marked what he thought was the final passing of anthology drama on 'The Show of the Week' (which, in fact, did continue). Cohen also believed that the production values of CBC drama weren't equivalent to those of American anthologies. That comment is open to question – I didn't note any such difference in my own research. But witness the comment of Len Lauk, a CBC producer, made during an interview: 'When you look at old kines, they were pretty miserable, so you can call them golden age for the process, but I wouldn't call them golden age for the result. A lot of it was trash.' Of course the production values of studio drama of Canada or the United States were inferior to those in the Hollywood series. I must note that Cohen's views weren't necessarily shared by contemporaries. Russel's 1962 article on drama was much more impressed by the achievement. Likewise Herbert Whittaker, in 1961, praised the CBC for the quality of its plays: 'In the field of drama, its taste has been high, its approach both serious and creative.' Whittaker quoted in E. Austin Weir, *The Struggle for National Broadcasting* (Toronto: M&S 1965), 395. Furthermore, Mary Jane Miller, in her article 'Canadian Television Drama 1952–1970,' clearly disagrees with Cohen's view (63), and the whole tenor of her argument runs counter to the thesis that has been put forward here. Yet Bronwyn Drainie, in *Living the Part*, her biography of her father, John, claims there were only around 'two dozen extraordinary plays and productions' (228) during the first fifteen years of television drama. In short the final judgment of this whole enterprise hasn't yet been delivered.

46 Walker, 'CBC's Search for $1000 Manuscripts,' 14; the two writers mentioned in Russel, 'Drama,' 361. Miller, *Turn Up the Contrast*, 192, notes with regret that even the CBC had, by the 1980s, forgotten its 'remarkable record' as a producer of plays before 1968.

47 This argument reflects some thoughts in Self, *Television Drama*, 3 and 147–8.

48 MacPherson interview; Tyrwhitt, 'Arthur Hailey Slays 'Em with Suspense,' 20 and 58; Cohen in *The Toronto Daily Star*, 21 May 1966; the ratings are

taken from the ISL, *TV Network Program Report English*, 6–12 November 1960, and *TV Network Program Report French*, 4–10 February 1962.

49 Russel, 'Drama,' 361

50 Tremblay's thoughts in Geraldine Anthony, ed. *Stage Voices: Twelve Canadian Playwrights Talk about Their Lives and Work* (Toronto: Doubleday 1978), 279

51 Comment on *Swan Lake* cited in *The Toronto Daily Star*, 23 May 1959; *Survey Report on CBC Programs*, Appendix 1, 3 (RG 41, v. 675, folder 4th Directors' Meeting)

52 Munro interview; 'The Hostage' story noted in *The Toronto Daily Star*, 23 May 1959; the critic was Herbert Gardiner in the Toronto *Globe and Mail*, 10 May 1963; Brunsden was supposedly quoting from the letters of constituents – cited in Toronto *Telegram*, 15 February 1962; on troubles with 'Festival' see *The Toronto Daily Star* and *The Globe and Mail*, 30 January 1969.

53 CBC Research, *What the Canadian Public Thinks of the CBC* (published in 1963 using 1962 data), 67

54 'L'heure du concert' ratings from ISL, *TV Network Program Report French*, 1–7 November 1959; Hailey's rating in E-H, *Television Audience Trends during the CBC Television Theatre Programme*, 7 April 1957; on scheduling see *The Toronto Daily Star*, 23 May 1959, and Toronto *Telegram*, 7 April 1961; on *The Mikado*, see the E-H report, *National Television Audience Tuned to the* Mikado *Broadcast*.

55 The Anglo statistics from E-H *National Teleratings Report*

56 The version of the short story I've used is from Alexander Pushkin, *The Queen of Spades and Other Stories* (Harmondsworth: Penguin Books, 1982 reprint), 151–83.

9 'And Now a Word from Our Sponsor'

1 Tyrwhitt, 'What Do You Mean You Don't Like Television Commercials,' *MM*, 1 January 1966, 21

2 CKVR case mentioned in Peter Stewart Grant, 'The Regulation of Program Content in Canadian Television: An Introduction,' *Canadian Public Administration*, II, 1968, 339; Fowler II, 213; Martin Goldfarb Consultants, 'The Media and the People' [hereafter Goldfarb], in Special Senate Committee on Mass Media, *Report*, v. 3: *Good, Bad, or Simply Inevitable?* (Ottawa: Queen's Printer 1970), 32 and 33.

3 Goodis's memoirs are fascinating reading: *Have I Ever Lied to You Before?* (Toronto: M&S 1972). See also the memoirs of American creative genius David Ogilvy: *Confessions of an Advertising Man* (New York: Atheneum 1963), who admitted to a deep distaste for commercials, even if he thought televi-

sion 'the most potent advertising medium ever devised' (163). The McLuhan phrase, of course, was the subtitle of *The Mechanical Bride*, and Schudson's description of 'Capitalist Realism' can be found in chapter 7 of his *Advertising, The Uneasy Persuasion: Its Dubious Impact on American Society* (New York: Basic Books 1984), 209–33. Schudson's book is an excellent analysis of the advertising industry and of the nature of advertising, although personally I think his main thesis underestimates the import of ads.

4 Roland Marchand, *Advertising the American Dream: Making Way for Modernity, 1920–1940* (Berkeley: University of California Press 1985), 227 – Marchand's work is one of the few first-rate historical discussions of advertising, which shows just how sophisticated and pervasive advertising was long before the era of television, a point that needs emphasis because of the tendency to think that modern advertising reached maturity and the pinnacle of its influence with television. The comment on the apologists of advertising taken, in part, from Daniel Pope, *The Making of Modern Advertising* (New York: Basic Books 1983), 259. Leiss, Kline, and Jhally, *Social Communication in Advertising: Persons, Objects, & Images of Well-Being* (Toronto: Methuen 1986), 47.

5 Sut Jhally, *The Codes of Advertising: Fetishism and the Political Economy of Meaning in the Consumer Society* (New York: Francis Pinter 1987), 9; Mary Douglas and Baron Isherwood, *The World of Goods: Towards an Anthropology of Consumption* (London: Allen Lane 1978), 65. The paragraph is not meant to be a justification of the consumer society, though: I admit that the extraordinary level of consumption in affluent countries is a legitimate source of worry given the waste of resources that entails.

6 The example is told in Frederick Elkin, *Rebels and Colleagues: Advertising and Social Change in French Canada* (Montreal: McGill-Queen's University Press 1973), 175–8.

7 *Marketing*, 10 October 1958, 49; on Chanel, see Janice Williamson, *Decoding Advertisements: Ideology and Meaning in Advertising* (London: Marion Boyars 1978), 25.

8 The Tintin example from Elkin, *Rebels and Colleagues*, 164; Ogilvy, *Confessions*, 59

9 Schudson, *Advertising*, 74; Hank Seiden, *Advertising Pure and Simple* (New York: Amacom 1976); Goodis, *Have I Ever Lied to You Before?* 124; CBC, Audience Research, *Report of the Ratings Review Committee*, July 1960, 54

10 Leiss et al., *Social Communication in Advertising*, 72; Goodis quoted in Toronto *Globe and Mail*, 16 April 1983, cited in Jhally, *The Codes of Advertising*, 129; Erving Goffman, *Gender Advertisements* (New York: Turner and Row 1979);

on 'recuperative capacity' see Williamson, *Decoding Advertisements*, 170, and Torben Vestergaard and Kim Schrøder, *The Language of Advertising* (London: Basil Blackwell 1985), 8–9; Leiss et al., 72.

11 Statistics taken from O.J. Firestone, *Broadcast Advertising in Canada: Past and Future Growth* (Ottawa: University of Ottawa Press 1966), 37 (footnote 32), 29, and 32; apparently Dichter had once written that Canadians were 'more puritanical and straight-laced' – *Marketing*, 10 October 1958, 50; Mahatoo's study cited in Kates, Peat, Marwick & Co., *Foreign Ownership and the Advertising Industry* [hereafter KPM & Co.], for Ontario, Legislative Assembly, Select Committee on Economic and Cultural Nationalism, June 1973, 126–7; Elkin, *Rebels and Colleagues*, 73.

12 Figures from Hopkins, Hedlin Limited, *Report*, v. 2: *Words, Music, and Dollars: A Study of the Economics of Publishing and Broadcasting* [hereafter Hopkins, Hedlin], for the Special Senate Committee on Mass Media (Ottawa: Queen's Printer 1970), 123 and 138; the 'rebellion' of French-Canadian admen is documented in Elkin's *Rebels and Colleagues*.

13 The brief's findings cited in KPM & Co., 59; Hopkins, Hedlin, 137; Bank of Montreal account mentioned in Goodis, *Have I Ever Lied to You Before?* 112, and Schick account in Elkin, *Rebels and Colleagues*, 23; KPM & Co., 72.

14 Goodis, *Have I Ever Lied to You Before?* 151, 36, 78

15 *FP*, 5 July 1952, 3; and 11 October 1952, 2; MacLaren advertisement in 'Canadian Retail Sales Index, 1953–1954,' published by *Canadian Broadcaster*.

16 Erik Barnouw, *The Sponsor: Notes on a Modern Potentate* (New York: OUP 1978), 46.

17 Compton, 'The Advertiser Looks at Video,' *Canadian Business*, March 1949, 50; Tryeze quoted in *Marketing*, 27 January 1956, 4; Lawrence quoted in *Marketing*, 1 November 1957, 4

18 Statistics on the media shares, 1961 and 1971, from KPM & Co., 50; Firestone, *Broadcast Advertising in Canada*, 32 and 153; Hopkins, Hedlin, 277.

19 Firestone, *Broadcast Advertising in Canada*, 68–70; Grant, 'The Regulation of Program Content in Canadian Television,' *Canadian Public Administration*, 11 (1968), 345–6 – Canadian shows were allowed an extra minute; Hopkins, Hedlin, 277; CFTM ad breakdown from Elliott Research, *National and Local Advertisers using CFTM-TV–Montreal, 19 February–4 March 1966*.

20 Jhally, *The Codes of Advertising*, 111; Tyrwhitt, 'What Do You Mean You Don't Like Television Commercials,' 21; and KPM & Co., 128.

21 Franklin Russell, 'How TV Commercials Conversion Saves Money for Cdn Advertisers,' *Marketing*, 31 March 1961, 18; on the advantages of going down to New York, see, for example, Franklin Russell, 'Why Buy Our TV Commer-

cials in U.S.?' *Marketing*, 17 March 1961, 44; ICA survey noted in KPM & Co., 118.

22 Walker, 'In Sight,' *Marketing*, 3 August 1962, 11; regarding prohibitions see KPM & Co., 124; on videotape, see Walker, 'In Sight,' *Marketing*, 26 July 1963, 20. See also Walker's 'When 60 Seconds Can Cost $15,000.00,' *Industrial Canada*, February 1962, 19–24.

23 Firestone, *Broadcast Advertising in Canada*, 117, footnote 86; Hurly quoted in *Marketing*, 28 June 1957, 8; *Marketing*, 18 September 1959, 2; Hopkins, Hedlin, 280 – the equivalent rate for radio station CFRB in Toronto was $150 (275).

24 The O'Keefe story in *Marketing*, 23 October 1959, 6; on MacLaren and hockey, see Hopkins, Hedlin, 148.

25 See the issue of 29 November, 1963, 20–1 and 34–5.

26 Edgar's views noted in *Marketing*, 30 November 1962, 64; Goodis, *Have I Ever Lied to You Before?* 99 and 101; KPM & Co., 48.

27 Hopkins, Hedlin, 121; *Marketing*, 29 November 1963, 35; Goodis, *Have I Ever Lied to You Before?* 68 – when Foster took over the account, it brought Westinghouse back to TV; statistics on national advertising from Hopkins, Hedlin, 127, and calculated from data in KPM & Co., 47.

28 Byrnes cited in *Marketing*, 29 November 1963, 72. See the Schwerin recipes in *Marketing*, 18 July 1958, 37; 9 October 1959, 32; and 14 December 1962, 8 and 10. 'Do's and Don'ts' in *Marketing*, 27 April 1962, 76.

29 Most of the specific examples of ads mentioned in this section are drawn from a pool of fifty commercials that received close readings by Stephen Baker and Phillipe Landreville (francophone), Steve Strople and in some cases Brigid Higgins (anglophone), Margarita Orszag and myself (American). I also analysed in depth fourteen of the anglophone commercials. The commercials will be identified by the network on which they appeared, CBC referring to the English service and R-C to Radio-Canada, as well as the year of the broadcast.

30 Westgate interview. The intimate style wasn't a television innovation; Roland Marchand has pointed out that this style became very common on American radio prior to the Second World War.

31 Russell, 'How Far Should We Lean in the Making of Faked Commercials?' *Marketing*, 3 March 1961, 26; Tyrwhitt, 'What Do You Mean You Don't Like Television Commercials,' 21 and 38.

32 On the *visage français* campaign, see Elkin, *Rebels and Colleagues*, 49, 144–6, 150–2, 164–5.

33 Tyrwhitt, 'What Do You Mean You Don't Like Television Commercials,' 38; Braithwaite in *The Globe and Mail*, 22 October 1964

34 Martin Esslin, *The Age of Television* (San Francisco: W.H. Freeman 1982), 53;

Goffman, *Gender Advertisements*, 84; Williamson, *Decoding Advertisements*, 23

35 Jhally, *The Codes of Advertising*, 198–9 – see also Williamson, *Decoding Advertisements*, 103–20.

36 The figure 'seven and a half hours' is based upon weekly household viewing of thirty-eight hours and twelve minutes of commercials in an hour. Tyrwhitt, 'What Do You Mean You Don't Like Television Commercials,' 21

37 Life-style research, and especially the VALS scheme, is dealt with in Benjamin D. Singer, *Advertising & Society* (Don Mills: Addison-Wesley 1986), 71–4. There's an excellent discussion of the consumer and marketing in Schudson's chapter 'The Consumer's Information Environment,' 90–128.

38 Goldfarb, 30, 95, and 99; CBC Research, *What the Canadian Public Thinks of the CBC*, 1963, Table 34 – almost exactly the same percentage of the American public felt commercials were a fair price to pay for entertainment (Gary A. Steiner, *The People Look at Television: A Study of Audience Attitudes* [New York: Knopf 1963], 218); 'CARF Four-Ad-Media Study Leaves Much to Be Answered,' *Canadian Sponsor*, 19 August 1963, 6; Goldfarb, 63 and 97

39 'Is Motivation Research a Science?' *Marketing*, 10 October 1958, 50; Frye, *The Modern Century: The Whidden Lectures 1967* (Toronto: OUP 1967), 26

40 Gallup Report, 28 April 1965; *What the Canadian Public Thinks of the CBC*, Table 20; Goldfarb, 97; McLean in *The Toronto Daily Star*, 14 October 1961; Dilworth's comments in RG 41, v. 277, file 11-43-16 and file 11-43-12 – the latter comments were actually made by a program-evaluation committee with which Dilworth agreed; Stewart's comments cited in Firestone, *Broadcast Advertising in Canada*, 123 – Stewart was speaking to the Association of Canadian Advertisers in 1961; the ad-recall rate mentioned in Schudson, *Advertising*, 107; *What the Canadian Public Thinks of the CBC*, 27; Goldfarb, 31 and 97; Gallup Report, 30 September 1969

41 'He Put Winter Sales on Sunny Side,' *Marketing*, 30 March 1956, 12–13

42 'Radio, TV Boost Nestlé Instant Sales,' *Marketing*, 1 November, 1957, 1 and 4

43 Goodis, *Have I Ever Lied to You Before?* 56–7

44 E-H ratings cited in *Marketing*, 24 November 1961, 37; the children's study carried out by Joan Paley Galst and Mary Alice White, cited in Singer, *Advertising & Society*, 91

45 The Schwerin example noted in *Marketing*, 14 December 1962, 10; 'Broadcasting Launches That Riggio,' *Canadian Sponsor*, October 1964, 6; Goodis, *Have I Ever Lied to You Before?* 88 and 118

46 On the analogy of the daydream, see Vestergaard and Schrøder, *The Language of Advertising*, 117–18, and Goffman, *Gender Advertisements*, 15; Schwartz

quotation as cited in Pope, *The Making of Modern Advertising*, 292, from
Schwartz, *The Responsive Cord* (New York: Anchor Books 1974), 24–5; on
'low-involvement products,' see Raymond A. Bauer and Stephen A. Greyser,
Advertising in America: The Consumer View (Cambridge, Mass.: Harvard
University Press 1968), 359, which draws upon the work of Herbert Krugman.
47 Tyrwhitt, 'What Do You Mean You Don't Like Television Commercials,' 21
48 Jhally has argued that the 'real' role of advertising in general 'is not to create
demand, to affect market share or even to dispense ideology – it is to give
us meaning' (*The Codes of Advertising*, 197).
49 Schudson, *Advertising*, 232
50 See Williamson on the question of absences: 'you are invited to slip into it
[the advertisement], to enter *its* space, drawn in to participate in a "discovery"
of meaning' (*Decoding Advertisements*, 77).
51 Marchand, *Advertising the American Dream*, 227, 206–7, and 223. Marchand
also talks about the parables of 'the First Impression,' 'the Democracy of
Goods,' and 'the Captivated Child.'

10 Storytelling

1 Lockhart, 'Trials and Tribulations of TV's "First Family," ' *Star Weekly*, 3
March 1956
2 The observation about television and the language of drama is most closely
associated with Martin Esslin, *The Age of Television* (San Francisco: W.H.
Freeman 1982); see also his 'The Language of Drama: Drama as a Language,'
Stratford Shakespearean Festival, Celebrity Lecture Series, 14 August 1983.
Esslin was the long-time head of BBC radio drama and a well-known writer
on theatre and playwrights before becoming a professor of drama. See
Barthes's essay 'The World of Wrestling,' in *Mythologies* (London: Granada
1973), 15–25, and Gregory P. Stone, 'Wrestling: The Great American Pas-
sion Play,' in Eric Dunning, ed. *Sport: Readings From a Sociological Perspective*
(Toronto: UTP 1972) 301–35. Frank's memorandum quoted in Edward Jay
Epstein, *News from Nowhere: Television and the News* (New York: Vintage
Bodas 1974), 4–5
3 Esslin, *The Age of Television*, 19. Stuart Griffiths, *How Plays Are Made: The
Fundamental Elements of Play Construction* (Englewood Cliffs, NJ: Prentice-Hall
1982), 10 and 11
4 As used here, then, series drama includes shows with continuing characters
from week to week, shows with continuing theme or specialized anthologies.
For a discussion of series drama, see Bob Millington and Robin Nelson, *'Boys
from the Blackstuff': The Making of TV Drama* (London: Comedia 1986),

which is an extended analysis of the creation of one British mini-series; and Robert C. Allen, *Speaking of Soap Operas* (Chapel Hill: University of North Carolina Press 1985), 45–60.

5 For a discussion of American drama programming, see Harry Castleman and Walter J. Podrazik, *Watching TV* (New York: McGraw-Hill 1982); Erik Barnouw, *Tube of Plenty* (New York: OUP 1975); David Marc, *Demographic Vistas: Television in American Culture* (Philadelphia: University of Pennsylvania 1984), which selects various kinds of shows for a close analysis. The memoirs of two Hollywood producers, Richard Levinson and William Link (*Stay Tuned* [New York: St. Martin's Press 1981]), provide a fascinating insight into the ways Hollywood operates. See also their *On Camera: Conversations with the Makers of Prime-Time Television* (New York: New American Library 1986).

6 'Dragnet,' in Jay S. Harris, ed., *TV Guide: The First 25 Years* (New York: New American Library 1980), 20–1; Barnouw, *Tube of Plenty*, 194

7 Richard Gehman, 'What Is a Screen Gem?' *MM*, 4 May 1963, 55, and 'Screen Gems' TV Tastemaking Machine,' *MM*, 18 May 1963, 21

8 Levinson and Link, *Stay Tuned*, 14–they have a chapter devoted to making a series, 'Columbo,' 66–101, which is a very interesting account of the whole process.

9 Brooks and Marsh, *The Complete Directory* ..., 480 ('Maverick') and 307 ('Gunsmoke'). There were, however, some hour-long specials that dealt with Lucy, Ricki, and their friends in later years. The cancellation of 'Gunsmoke' noted in Erik Barnouw, *The Sponsor*, 73.

10 Based on analyses of 'Wyatt Earp,' 'The Untouchables,' and 'Ben Casey.' The issues of realism and naturalism are discussed at some length in Millington and Nelson, *'Boys from the Blackstuff*,' 7–17, and John Fiske and John Hartley, *Reading Television*, 160–5. Both books make the point that some forms of drama or literature, associated with Bertolt Brecht or James Joyce, try to demystify by breaking below the surface, making the reader/viewer aware the text is a construction of reality, challenging preconceptions, and so on.

11 Stefano quoted in *TV Guide*, 4 February 1964, 28. See Morris Wolfe, *Jolts* (Toronto: Lorimer 1985), for a slightly different discussion of how Hollywood's TV (since the late 1960s, though) uses assorted shocks and hooks to capture the attention of the viewer.

12 The troubles of 'Medic' mentioned in Robert S. Alley, *Television: Ethics for Hire?* (Nashville: Abingdon 1977), 58–9

13 Dwight Whitney, 'Why "Gunsmoke" Keeps Blazing Away,' in Harris, ed., *TV Guide: The First 25 Years*, 42–3; the Dr Kimble character discussed in Castleman and Podrazik, *Watching TV*, 166; John Cawelti, *Adventure, Mystery,*

and Romance: Formula Stories as Art and Popular Culture (Chicago: University of Chicago Press 1976), 11–12, discusses what he calls 'stereotype vitalization,' by which he means invigorating a role by adding contrary qualities to a character and/or by giving the individual some complexity.

14 Braithwaite in Toronto *Globe and Mail*, 13 October 1965; on 'The Beverly Hillbillies' see David Marc, *Demographic Vistas*, 39–63, and Castleman and Podrazik, *Watching TV*, 161–2.

15 The two anecdotes from Brooks and Marsh, *The Complete Directory* ..., 923–7, 351, and 570

16 Cawelti, *Adventure, Mystery, and Romance*, 24 and 35–6. This book is an excellent and pioneering study of the nature of popular literature.

17 Braithwaite in Toronto *Globe and Mail*, 5 December 1963; complaints from Appendix I, *Survey Report on CBC Programs* (1959) in RG 41, v. 675, folder 4th meeting, Board of Directors; Minutes, 21st Program Committee Meeting, 25 June 1962, 10; Garner in *SN*, 26 March 1955; Ross in *SN*, 9 July 1960; Brown in *The Toronto Daily Star*, 3 September 1961

18 See Appendix A, 'Report of the Advisors,' Fowler II, 335; Montreal's troubles discussed in Minutes, 48th Program Committee Meeting, 8 February 1967, 1 and 9

19 E. Austin Weir, *The Struggle for National Broadcasting in Canada* (Toronto: MRS 1965), 279; Ken Johnstone, 'Meet Quebec's Most Famous Family,' *MM*, 1 February 1955, 56. Parent interview

20 Information on the lives of individual writers taken from R. Hamel, J. Hare, and P. Wyczynski, *Dictionnaire pratique des auteurs québécoises* (Montreal: Fides 1976)

21 Wages cited in Bill Stephenson, 'The Wonderful World of French-Canadian TV,' *MM*, 8 June 1957, 84; Lemelin's comment in Lloyd Lockhart, 'Trials and Tribulations of TV's "First Family" '; *La Semaine à Radio-Canada*, 13–19 May 1961

22 James Bamber, 'De 9 à 5: Marcel Dubé raconte à la télé la tragédie quotidienne du colle-blanc,' *Le Magazine Maclean*, March 1964, 50; Ouimet's comments in Minutes, 15th Program Committee Meeting, 26–28 June 1961, 3–4; Lemelin affair discussed in Minutes, 24th Program Committee Meeting, 3 December 1962, 3 and 25th Program Committee Meeting, 4 February 1963, 4–5

23 Johnstone, 'Meet Quebec's Most Famous Family,' 56; 'French Drama Serials: Sponsors Still Strong after Decade,' *Canadian Sponsor*, 2 September 1963, 7

24 Johnstone, 'Meet Quebec's Most Famous Family,' 18; *La Semaine à Radio-Canada*, 4–10 November 1961, 9; *La Semaine à Radio-Canada*, 13–19 Octo-

ber 1956, 1; *La Semaine à Radio-Canada*, 14–20 October 1961, 3; Louis Martin, 'Septième Nord,' *Le Magazine Maclean*, February 1965, 10–12

25 Viewing analysis of '14 rue de Galais'; Schwerin Report C-CBC-56-8, 'Pick the Stars' and 'Plouffe Family,' Toronto and Winnipeg, 5; Line Ross and Hélène Tardif, *Le Téléroman québécoise, 1960–1971: Une analyse de contenu*, Cahier 12, Laboratoire de recherches sociologiques, Université Laval, 1975, 405–7–this analysis of a series of shows is an invaluable survey of the ingredients that went into the making of the téléroman.

26 Renée Legris, 'Les fonctions de destinateur et de sujet dans les téléromans québécois, 1953–1963,' in Annie Méar, *Recherches québécois sur la télévision* (Lavol: Albert Saint-Martin 1980), 29–45, contains an extended discussion of the assorted plots of a number of téléromans, and notes these 'echoes of a wider world.'

27 On 'Cré Basile' see *La Presse*, 16 September 1965; 'Monsieur Lecoq' discussed in *La Semaine à Radio-Canada*, 5–11 September 1964, 6; BBM, *Television Station Report*, February 1965 survey

28 The Radio-Canada report was *Emissions régulieres ou longs métrages*, April 1959; BBM, *Television National Program Report (Network and Selective Shows)*, Spring 1963 survey; MDL, *TPR Television*, February–March 1963.

29 'French Drama Serials,' 6–7; Lauzon, 'Le Professeur Lussier a cédé la place au Pére Gédéon,' *Le Magazine Maclean*, April 1962, 19; Charest, 'Le Pain du jour: Réginald Boisvert décrit la grisaille d'une petite ville ouvrière,' *Le Magazine Maclean*, March 1964, 20–1

30 The English service also had some experience with radio stories (although, at the time of my writing, there is very little published on this topic). Among the most memorable of the efforts was the weekly social drama about a farm family called 'The Craigs' in Ontario and 'The Jacksons' out west, which apparently lasted twenty-five years. During the war Canadians could listen to topical drama in the shape of such series as " 'L" for Lanky,' 'Fighting Navy,' and 'Soldier's Wife.' After the war there was an early evening sitcom called 'John and Judy' and a Canadian soap opera about the life and affairs of a small community entitled 'Newbridge.' The *CBC Annual Report* of 1950/1 noted two humorous series, 'Jake and the Kid' and 'My Uncle Louis,' a weekly story about an amateur drama group called 'The Footlighters,' plus an assortment of mini-series such as 'It's Murder' (eleven episodes) and 'The Count of Monte Cristo' (ten episodes). The information is taken from brief notes in Weir, *The Struggle for National Broadcasting in Canada*, 281; Roger Lee Jackson, 'Dramatic Programs,' 61 and 79–80; and Sandy Stewart, *A Pictorial History of Radio in Canada* (Toronto: Gage 1975). The basic reference work on CBC's English-language television drama is Mary Jane Miller's

fine work, *Turn Up the Contrast*: this monograph is essential reading for anyone wanting additional information on Anglo story-telling, and indeed drama of all kinds on the CBC English-language network.

31 On changes, see Johnstone, 'Meet Quebec's Most Famous Family,' 18; CBC Audience Research, *Report on Audience Size for the Weekly English Network TV Programme: The Plouffe Family, January–May, Inclusive, 1955*, 3 – using statistics from E-H *Teleratings*.

32 The reports I consulted were C-CBC-55-5, C-CBC-56-7, and C-CBC-56-8; quoted in Lockhart, 'Trials and Tribulations of TV's "First Family," '3.

33 See *The Toronto Daily Star*, 20 October 1959, and Toronto *Telegram*, 14 October 1959 and 27 April 1960; a comment by Eugene Hallman and two statements by Ouimet in Minutes, 10th Program Committee Meeting, 21–23 June 1960, 2, and Minutes, 11th Program Committee Meeting, 24 October 1960, 5

34 Based on a reading of an unspecified episode of 'Space Command' viewed from the 'Rear View Mirror' rebroadcast series

35 The nickname of 'Radisson' noted in Sandy Stewart, *Here's Looking at Us: A Personal History of Television in Canada* (Toronto: CBC Enterprises 1986), 245

36 Barbara Moon, 'How They're Making a Hero of Pierre Radisson,' MM 19 January 1957, 57; Gauntlett (interview 30 September 1964) cited in Jackson, 'Dramatic Programs,' 156

37 Moon, 'How They're Making a Hero of Pierre Radisson," 14; CBC *Times*, 3–9 February 1957, 1; CBC *Times*, 27 October–2 November 1957, 3

38 E-H, *Television Audience Trends, before, during and after the Radisson Programme of Feb. 23rd and Feb. 24th,* February 1957; CBC Audience Research, *A Preliminary Bulletin: The Radisson Series on Television: Some Children's Reactions and General Audience Size Trends,* 6 June 1957; memo in RG 41, v. 211, file 11-19-6

39 Information on the three series from CBC *Times*, 22–28 September 1957 and 13–19 October 1957 as well as the *Telegram*, 13 September 1958; *Marketing*, 6 March 1959, 14; FP, 7 March 1964

40 This description is based on stories in *The Toronto Daily Star*, 25 February 1959 and 10 September 1959; *The New York Times*, 5 March 1959; *TV Guide*, 18–24 March 1961; Toronto *Telegram*, 23 May 1959

41 Alixe Carter at the eighth meeting of the Program Committee, 25 January 1960, in the minutes, 9. Toronto *Telegram*, 8 January 1960; undated 'RCMP episode rebroadcast by CBLT on Saturday, 3 September 1983, at 11:00 AM; reference to the previously cited 'The Untouchables' episode of 20 November 1962

42 *CBC Times*, 11–17 September 1965, 14–15; Stephen Young was actually a Canadian.

43 On 'Jake and the Kid,' see the Toronto *Telegram*, 6 July 1961; on 'The Other Man' see the *Telegram*, 1 May 1963, and the *Globe and Mail*, 8 May 1963; Gauntlett interview of 30 September 1964, in Jackson, 'Dramatic Programs,' 140.

44 Weyman's comments from interviews in *Globe and Mail*, 16 April 1964; *CBC Times*, 6–12 June 1964, 8-i; Jackson, 'Dramatic Programs,' 141 (interview on 26 October 1964); and an undated newspaper cutting from a story by Robert Reguly of *The Toronto Daily Star* contained in the CBC Programme Files

45 Sources for this survey of contents are the CBC Programme Files (Toronto) for 'The Serial' and 'Cariboo Country'; on the purpose of 'Mr Member,' see Minutes, 42nd Program Committee Meeting, 8 and 10 December 1965, 2.

46 Lauk interview. Information on the series taken from the program file at CBC Toronto. Mary Jane Miller has dealt with this series extensively in 'Cariboo Country: A Canadian Response to American Television Westerns,' *American Review of Canadian Studies*, xiv, no. 3 (1984), 322–32, and *Turn Up the Contrast*, 68–85.

47 Gauntlett interview (23 November 1964) in Jackson, 'Dramatic Programs,' 142; not everyone was pleased with the show, of course – Jon Ruddy of the Toronto *Telegram*, 15 April 1964, called 'The Serial' 'a cut-rate, low-aiming excuse for TV drama.'

48 CBC Information Services, no. 778, 'Quentin Durgens MP Begins in Tuesday Night Wojeck Spot,' 25 November 1966; Rolf Kalman, 'The $300,000,000 Question,' *The Performing Arts in Canada 1967*, 5, no. 2, 4–6; Minutes, 46th Program Committee Meeting, 27 and 28 October 1966, 1

49 This account is based on material in the Weyman interview and Miller's *Turn Up the Contrast*, especially 227–8.

50 Weyman interview; Wolfe, *Jolts*, 80; Miller, *Turn Up the Contrast*, especially 24, 48, 49, 81, 374–9. It's only fair to note that both Wolfe and Miller carry their accounts well beyond 1967, and so are able to cite a much larger range of examples of the 'distinctive' tradition of Canadian drama. They recognize as well that much of what they count as particularly Canadian drama has often failed to please the mass audience, which remained happy, thank you very much, with the Hollywood product.

51 In a similar vein – Brian Clemens, one of the makers of 'The Avengers,' admitted that he and his colleagues used incongruity to capture viewer interest: the very masculine Steed fought 'like a woman' with whatever might be available, from an umbrella to a jar of honey, while his very female partner Emma Peel was an expert in the martial arts and proved very capable

with a gun as well. Clemens comments in a press clipping from the London *Observer*, 7 October 1965, found in the CBC-Toronto Programme Files.

52 *C-CBC-56-8: "Pick the Stars" & Plouffe "Family,"* Toronto and Winnipeg, Suppematory Material, 3–4; Gauntlett and Nixon cited in Jackson, 'Dramatic Programs,' 139 and 158. CBC Research, *What the Canadian Public Thinks of the CBC* (1963), 63 – note, however, that 50 percent thought it was doing a good job here; only 10 percent thought it was doing a poor job.

53 Till's views cited in Miller, *Turn Up the Contrast*, 27. Minutes, 16th Program Committee Meeting, 18 and 19 September 1961, 8; Cohen, Israel, and Nixon cited in Jackson, 'Dramatic Programs,' 187, 171, and 179

54 Marty was played by Patricia Collins, Bateman by Ted Fellows, James by Carl Banas, and Smith by Johnny Yesno. For a somewhat different interpretation of the episode, see Mary Jane Miller, *Turn Up the Contrast*, 50–3 – both of us do agree it was a powerful drama, though she points out that according to the CBC's own index of enjoyment the episode didn't rate very high with the audience.

55 The episode won the Wilderness Award (Canada) and the Golden Nymph Award (Monte Carlo). The episode used for this viewing analysis was actually reproduced in the summer rerun series in 1967 of 'Wojeck,' a fact made clear by the character of the ads, notably the promotion for Canada's centennial celebrations.

56 I use the term 'preferred meaning' because, whatever the intention of the writer and producer, it was possible to read the show in quite another fashion, to suggest that whatever might happen in this particular case, the plight of the Indian in a white Canada was insoluble in the near future.

11 Versions of Reality

1 Cited in Jean Bruce, 'Warrendale,' The Performing Arts in Canada 1967, 5, no. 2, 19. King was one among a new breed of documentary producers; his study of disturbed children, *Warrendale*, was provoking a lot of comment at the time.

2 Newman's book, subtitled 'Canadian Politics in Transition: 1963–1968,' was published by McClelland and Stewart in 1968. It was in part a continuation of the story he had begun with his earlier best-seller, *Renegade in Power* (Toronto: MRS 1963).

3 The letter to Pearson quoted in L.B. Pearson, *Mike: The Memoirs of the Rt. Hon. Lester B. Pearson*, v. 3: *1957–68* (Toronto: UTP 1975), 79; the Toronto cabbie quoted in the *Canadian Annual Review* [hereafter CAR] for 1963, edited by John Saywell (Toronto: UTP 1964), 16

4 The quotations from Newman, *Distemper*, xiii. Canada's population stood at
around 14 million people in 1951: over the next decade it increased by a
whopping 4.2 million, and in the 1960s by another 3.3 million. Roughly three-
quarters of the 7.5 million new bodies was the consequence of a baby boom;
the effects of the baby boom have received an interesting treatment, albeit
somewhat alarmist and exaggerated, in John Kettle, *The Big Generation*
(Toronto: M&S 1980). The rest of the increase came from a tide of immigrants,
mostly from Europe (immigration reached a post-war annual peak of 282,000
in 1957), which was sufficient to alter the ethnic mix of the Canadian population, increasing the significance of the 'third force' (neither Anglo-Irish nor
French) in the community. A lot of the newcomers ended up in Canada's big
cities: for example, Greater Montreal grew from 1.83 million in 1956 to 2.57
million a decade later and Metro Toronto from 1.57 million to 2.29 million –
by 1966 the total farm population had fallen under 2 million. Finally, on
average, ordinary Canadians were getting steadily better off, enjoying higher
living standards, even if the fruits of abundance weren't shared equally: the
index of average wage rates for major industries, based on 1949 figures, had
risen to 175.5 by 1960. The assorted statistics on growth are taken from M.C.
Urquhart and K.A.H. Buckley, *Historical Statistics of Canada* (Toronto: Macmillan 1965), 16 and 84; Robert Bothwell, Ian Drummond, and John English,
Canada since 1945: Power, Politics, and Provincialism (Toronto: UTP 1981), 32;
and Jack Granatstein, *Canada 1957–1967: The Years of Uncertainty and
Innovation* (Toronto: M&S 1986), 2–3 and 8.

5 Grant, *Lament for a Nation: The Defeat of Canadian Nationalism* (Toronto:
M&S 1965), 5

6 According to one contemporary account, in the 1962 election the Liberals
and the NDP took 62 percent of the urban constituencies (or 64 of 104) while
the Conservatives and Social Credit captured 71 percent of the rural constituencies (or 86 of 121). The next year a Gallup poll survey discovered that the
two reform parties had garnered six out of ten votes in communities of over
100,000 while their opposition took roughly the same percentage of the rural
vote. That trend continued into 1965: in the twenty-five constituencies of the
Toronto-Hamilton region the Liberals won 42.6 percent of the popular vote,
the Conservatives 29.1 percent, and the NDP 27.8 percent. The NDP was
threatening to become the second party in urban Canada (it already was in
Winnipeg and Vancouver). One survey found that the Liberals captured fully
three-fifths of the popular vote in metropolitan centres (over 500,000 people), leaving the NDP and the Conservatives tied at about a fifth each; by
contrast the Conservatives got 47 percent of the rural vote, the Liberals 41
percent, and the NDP 9 percent. The figures are taken from the *CAR* for 1962

(23), *CAR* for 1963 (37), *CAR* for 1965 (111), and Harold D. Clarke, Jane Jenson, Lawrence LeDuc, and Jon H. Pammett, *Political Choice in Canada* (Toronto: McGraw-Hill Ryerson 1979), 123. Two caveats to all this. In 1965 the Conservatives secured a slight plurality of votes in Winnipeg. In 1965, as always, the most outstanding correlations were between voting behaviour and religious affilation: while 65 per cent of Catholics voted Liberal, 44 per cent of Anglicans, Presbyterians, and United Church members voted Conservative (36 per cent voted Liberal) – Clarke et al., *Political Choice*, 101. Grant argued that Canada had undergone a process of 'Finlandization' (my word, not his) which commenced during the Second World War, with the hearty support of most Liberal politicians, bureaucrats, businessmen, and intellectuals. He saw Diefenbaker as one of the last hold-outs of the ideal of an un-American Canada, whose instinctive opposition to American imperialism, as represented by his resistance to the arming of the Bomarc missiles in 1962–3, infuriated these 'dominant classes.' Grant did admit that Diefenbaker was a flawed instrument of the older, pro-British nationalism, though, unable to realize how Canada had changed and what could be done to revitalize the forces of tradition.

7 Grant, *Lament*, 1
8 See John Meisel, 'The Decline of Party in Canada,' in Hugh G. Thorburn, ed., *Party Politics in Canada*, 5th ed. (Toronto: Prentice-Hall 1985), 98–114: Meisel identifies a whole series of causes, including the rise of the bureaucratic state, that contributed to the decline of party. The statistic on the strength of party affiliation comes from Clarke et al., *Political Choice*, 146; there is an extensive discussion of 'flexible partisanship' in the authors' successor volume, *Absent Mandate: The Politics of Discontent in Canada* (Toronto: Gage 1984), 55–76 – there the argument is made that 63 per cent of the electorate in 1980 was made up of flexible partisans. J.M. Beck, *Pendulum of Power: Canada's Federal Elections* (Toronto: Prentice-Hall 1968), 357, notes that the Conservatives received support only from the Ottawa *Journal*, the Winnipeg *Tribune*, the Vancouver *Province*, and the Fredericton *Gleaner*. Beck also argues that an equal one-sidedness existed in the infamous wartime election of 1917, although my reading suggests that then at least the Laurier Liberals won support from the French-Canadian dailies whereas the Union government won the anglophone papers. For a contemporary account of voting patterns and party loyalty, see Peter Regenstreif's classic, *The Diefenbaker Interlude: Parties and Voting in Canada* (Don Mills: Longmans 1965) – Regenstrief also observed that party was not as important 'a reference affiliation' for the public in Canada as it was in Great Britain and the United States (6).

9 The 'rebellion' of the Press Gallery has been discussed in J. Callwood, 'The Truth about Parliament,' *MM*, 17 April 1965, 9–11, 42–6, and 45–50. Harvey Kirck with Wade Rowland, *Nobody Calls Me Mr. Kirck* (Toronto: Collins 1985), 138. See these memoirs for an insight into the views and habits of an older generation of partisan reporters: Peter Dempson, *Assignment Ottawa: Seventeen Years in the Press Gallery* (Toronto: General Publishing 1968) and Bruce Hutchinson, *The Far Side of the Street* (Toronto: Macmillan 1976). Jamieson's concerns were expressed in his book, *The Troubled Air* (Fredericton: Brunswick Press 1966), 163–4 and 171.

10 Sears quoted in Newman, *Renegade*, 246, and Reilly in the Toronto *Telegram*, 27 August 1966

11 Haggart in *The Toronto Daily Star*, 30 May 1966. The Crosbie gloss from his speech published in *Politics and the Media: An Examination of the Issues Raised by the Quebec Referendum and the 1979 and 1980 Federal Elections* (Toronto: Reader's Digest Foundation of Canada and Erindale College, University of Toronto, 1981). This book is an edited transcript of the proceedings of a symposium that brought together politicians, organizers, journalists, and academics: the result was a very interesting exchange of opinion on a whole variety of questions relating to the news media and politics. John Crosbie, by the way, was a leading Conservative politician, who had been minister of finance in the Joe Clark government that had gone down to defeat in Parliament in 1979, a decision confirmed by the voters in the election of early 1980.

12 Quotations from Desmond Morton on newscasts and from Stanfield in *Politics and the Media*, 44 and 118. Stanfield was leader of the Conservative party from 1967 through 1976.

13 Fulford, 'What's Behind the New Wave of TV Think Shows,' *MM*, 5 October 1963, 25–7, 59–62. The now aged 'Close-Up' had finally been retired (the even older 'Explorations' disappeared in the following summer). The successful Ottawa-based program 'Inquiry' had had its budget increased by 25 per cent, which presumably would allow it to expand the scope of its probes. Sunday night at ten had been given over to the hour-long documentary series 'Horizon,' which would alternate every other week with the more light-hearted 'Let's Face It,' featuring French and English talent, and the interview show 'Question Mark,' which promised some stern questioning of guests. The result? Longer, better-crafted documentaries; the expression of more, possibly stronger opinions; attempts at political satire; and an effort to make all offerings 'more entertaining and more involving than they have been in the past.'

14 Blackburn in Toronto *Telegram*, 7 January 1965 – his added comment, 'they can't make the picture tube throb the way White Paper or CBS Reports

does.' Fulford's comment from his 'Television Notebook,' *Canadian Forum*, March 1963, 276. Re the calming effect of Cameron's news style: a close reading of the newscast of 27 July 1965, which featured a report on a nation-wide postal strike, was a very balanced appraisal of the chances for a peaceful settlement of the dispute. For an anecdotal survey of CTV's efforts, see Kirck, *Nobody Calls Me Mr. Kirck*, 133–56, and some comments on convention coverage in Charles Templeton, *An Anecdotal Memoir* (Toronto: M&S 1983), 125–54.

15 The story goes that Burke ran afoul of a dispute between the announcers' union and the reporters' union over what kind of persons should be involved in news-reading and news-gathering (Wilfred Kesteron, 'Mass Media,' CAR for 1966, 432); but an unsigned memo suggests that at least one of the supervisors believed Burke wasn't yet fitted to realize 'the Cronkite concept' of editing the news ('A Report on CBC News and Certain Recommenda-tions,' June 1967, RG 41, v. 171, file 11–17, pt 6.). Nash, *Prime Time at Ten* (Toronto: M&S 1987), 43, and this issue of management's 'low regard' for news also comes up in his interview with Ross Eamon. Cunningham interview. Shields comment in *The Toronto Daily Star*, 6 November 1965. For further discussions of CBC news see Knowlton Nash's earlier book, *History on the Run: The Trenchcoat Memoirs of a Foreign Correspondent* (Toronto: M&S 1984) and Peter Trueman, *Smoke and Mirrors: The Inside Story of Television News in Canada* (Toronto: M&S 1980), although neither deal in any detail with the news service in the early and mid 1960s. Trueman's memoirs cover the strug-gles in the late 1960s and early 1970s to reform the service. (See, as well, the previously mentioned 'A Report on CBC News ...'). He casts himself in the role of one of the reformers. Although I can't attest to the accuracy of his chronicle, it seems apparent that CBC news was in something of an upheaval during this period. Nash's *Prime Time at Ten* gives another, similar if less critical, account of this story. In his interview, though, Cunningham blames Nash for 'selling out' to management and thus betraying the purposes of the reformers.

16 Markle had wowed the public in the early 1940s with his radio dramas for CBC, before moving on to the United States – in New York he became the master force of CBS's 'Studio One.' Later efforts in Hollywood, in movies and television, didn't work well, so in 1963 he returned to Toronto.

17 Edmonds, 'Pain in the Network,' MM, 5 March 1966, 26; Fisher in Toronto *Telegram*, 26 April 1966; Watson quoted in Fulford, 'TV Think Shows,' 61; Leiterman drew the analogy between TV and newspapers in an undated draft entitled 'Television Journalism,' excerpts of which appeared in the Ottawa *Citizen*, 20 May 1966 (RG 41, v.234, file 11-25-7, pt. 13).

18 This from Koch, *Inside Seven Days* (Scarborough: Prentice-Hall 1986), 36–8.
Koch's book is, of course, a major source of information for this and other
discussions of the personnel, purpose, and style of the program. Koch notes
that around the same time 'Telescope,' a half-hour program, had a show budget
of $13,660 and 'The Public Eye' $18,000 (66). For the second season, the
'Seven Days' budget was up to roughly $35,000; a break-down of costs for
the year ending 31 March 1966 charged 'Seven Days' (exclusive of the 'Document' weeks) with total costs of $895,672 (account sheet in RG 41, v. 232,
file 11-25-7, pt. 1). The promises in the manifesto are taken from Helen
Carscallen, 'Nine Years and Seven Days Later,' *Content*, 54, August 1975,
3. On the opening fanfare see, for instance, Jeremy Brown and Douglas Fisher
in the Toronto *Telegram*, 26 September 1964 and 10 October 1964.

19 Koch has a two-page list of 'the team,' what they did then and where they
ended up (262–3). Dennis Braithwaite described (*Globe and Mail*, 14
December 1965) the blonde Christie in this fashion: 'The show's permanent,
approved and certified feminine image is Dinah Christie, a lass as square
and as sturdily Canadian as one could wish for. Her counterpart, in dress,
hairdo, manner and deportment, could be found in any small-town public
library in the land.' Maybe so, although Christie also happened to be both
attractive and talented, which suited the needs of 'Seven Days' as much as
her 'Canadian-ness.'

20 On the routine of 'Seven Days,' see Edmonds, 'Pain in the Network'; Peter
Gzowski, 'Seven Days Gets Ready for Its Hour,' *Canadian*, 19 February
1966, 2–5 and 7–8; Kathy Brooks, 'Up in the Air with the Junior Birdsmen,'
in the Toronto *Telegram's TV Weekly*, 4–11 February 1966, 3; as well as
Carscallen, 'Nine Years and Seven Days Later,' and Koch, *Inside Seven Days*.

21 The quotations are taken from an assortment of sources: Watson's comments
in Fulford, 'TV Think Shows'; an interview with Leiterman in 1981, portions
of which appear in Koch, *Inside Seven Days*; Leiterman, 'Television Journalism' and a piece he wrote for the Toronto *Globe and Mail*, 25 June 1964;
Watson's comments in Carscallen, 'Nine Years and Seven Days Later,' 2–9;
and an interview by Percy Saltzman of the two men, 'How to Survive in the
CBC Jungle – and Other Tribal Secrets,' *MM*, 6 February 1965, 12–13 and 39–
44. Watson's response to Braithwaite appeared in a letter to the *Globe and
Mail*, 17 December 1964.

22 Carscallen, 'Nine Years and Seven Days Later,' 5; the CBC statistics from a
summary report of weekly panel findings on 'Seven Days' in its second
season (RG 41, v. 232, file 11-25-7, pt. 1)

23 The Watson anecdote in Edmonds, 'Pain in the Network,' 26; Mrs Fedele
quoted in Toronto *Telegram*, 18 April 1966; Shields in *Toronto Daily Star*,
23 April 1966

24 The details of the dispute have been dealt with at length by Frank Peers in
The Public Eye, 327–51 and in Koch's *Inside Seven Days*. Knelman, 'The
Ghost of Seven Days Still Mocks the CBC,' *SN*, October 1975, 48. Knelman's
article heralded the possibility that a new public-affairs show called '5th
Estate' might rekindle the old excitement. It didn't.

25 Watson quoted in Carscallen, 'Nine Years and Seven Days Later,' 4; Jamieson,
The Troubled Air (Fredericton: Brunswick Press 1966), 170–1; Braithwaite quotations from *Globe and Mail*, 20 October 1964 and 18 December 1964, as well
as Edmonds, 'Pain in the Network,' 25. See also Fulford in *The Toronto
Daily Star*, 12 December 1964; Ron Haggart in *The Daily Toronto Star*, 26
October 1964; Nathan Cohen in *SN*, March 1965, n.p. (CBC Program Refer-
ence files); and Gzowski in *MM*, 1 November 1965, 71. On the issue of
professional rivalry, see the comments in Edmonds, 'Pain in the Network,' 25;
Ron Haggart in Toronto *Telegram*, 22 April 1966; and Roy Shields in *The
Toronto Daily Star*, 23 April 1966.

26 Watson quoted in the Montreal *Star*, 30 November 1965

27 Ouimet's comment taken from his first statement to the Commons broadcasting committee, 6 May 1966 (CBC Reference Library, Toronto), 10; the Parliament story from Wilfred Kesteron, 'Mass Media,' *CAR* for 1965, 484; the other
stories noted in Braithwaite's column in the Toronto *Globe and Mail*, 10 December 1964; Edmonds, 'Pain in the Network,' 10; and Blackburn's column in the
Toronto *Telegram*, 22 December 1965

28 The meeting was held on 15 February 1965 (RG 41, v. 232, file 11-25-7, pt. 1);
McGibbon quoted in *CBC Times*, 26 September–2 October 1964; LaPierre
interjection mentioned in Koch, *Inside Seven Days*, 102.

29 The description of 'Inquiry' taken from a review by Peter Gzowski, *MM*, 9
March 1963, 64; Leiterman quoted in Brooks, 'Up in the Air with the Junior
Birdsmen,' 4.

30 A year later, though, the producer Glen Sarty (to the distress of the host Ed
McGibbon) finally rejected an interview with a supposed teenage rape
victim, one 'Jackie,' partly because he found her tale lurid, partly because he
doubted whether she had been raped. I and my assistants have carried out
close readings of two episodes of 'Seven Days,' 6 December 1964 and 24
October 1965. The 'drop-out' interviews were in the second of these shows.
The Leiterman and Watson comments on the Lincoln Rockwell interview
from Saltzman, 'How to Survive in the CBC Jungle,' 40. For a brief description
of the Rockwell interview, see Sandy Stewart, *Here's Looking at Us: A Personal
History of Television in Canada* (Montreal: CBC Enterprises 1986), 161.

31 The interview with the policeman's wife in 'Seven Days,' 24 October 1965

32 Carscallen, 'Nine Years and Seven Days Later,' 4; Templeton, *An Anecdotal
Memoir*, 128. Templeton was the director of news and public affairs.

33 Watson and Leiterman comments from Saltzman, 'How to Survive in the CBC Jungle,' 40 and 43; description of the hot seat taken from the image of that seat as presented on 'Seven Days,' 24 October 1965, and from Stewart, *Here's Looking at Us*, 160; Hal Banks was a union leader who had skipped to the United States to avoid a prison term, and charges were aired that past donations to the Liberal cause made the government reluctant to secure his return.

34 The Lévesque interview was aired in the 6 December 1964 episode. See Leiterman's comments in Saltzman, 'How to Survive in the CBC Jungle,' 41, and Watson's in Carscallen, 'Nine Years and Seven Days Later,' 4.

35 On CBC policy, see the quotation from CBC Program Policy No. 65–3, 'The Recorded Statement or Interview,' Ottawa, 18 June 1965, reprinted in the Canada, Parliament, *Report of the Committee on Election Expenses* (Ottawa: Queen's Printer 1966), 375.

36 Storey's complaint in *Globe and Mail*, 7 February 1964; LaMarsh, *Memoirs of a Bird in a Gilded Cage*, 262; Nash, *History on the Run*, 259. There's some dispute over the accuracy of the charge of unfair treatment in the case of Bundy: Warner Troyer in his *The Sound and the Fury: An Anecdotal History of Canadian Broadcasting* (Toronto: John Wiley 1980), 159–60, claims that the White House transcript was itself doctored, and that the edited interview was eminently fair.

37 Templeton, *An Anecdotal Memoir*, 132; Jamieson, *The Troubled Air*, 168; 'Toronto File' story in *The Toronto Daily Star*, 11 March 1965; 'Other Voices' story taken from *The Toronto Daily Star*, 30 December 1964, *Globe and Mail*, 31 December 1964, and Taylor's 'Dissent,' in Toronto *Telegram*, 5 January 1965; my reference of course is to Trueman's memoirs, although there he assigns the origin of the phrase to Bill Cunningham, at the time Global's vice-president of news. My criticism of editing reflects, as well, a reading of Gary Gumpert's *Talking Tombstones and Other Tales of the Media Age* (New York: OUP 1987), 48–53.

38 Bruce, 'Warrendale,' 15; *The Toronto Daily Star*, 3 May 1966

39 Leiterman's comments on the tools of the trade in his drafted piece entitled 'Television Journalism,' 8 – the author of the phrase 'two-ton pencil' was the American Fred Friendly; the long quotation from Leiterman's *Globe and Mail* essay of 1964; Fox's comment appeared in *The Toronto Daily Star*, 3 May 1966. She'd described a series she produced called 'The Living Camera' in *CBC Times*, 22–28 May 1965, in much the same terms: 'The Living Camera is another word for being there when it happens. The camera disappears into the action, and becomes an instrument to record events as they occur, to observe life as it is lived.' Fulford's worries recorded in Wilfred Kesterton, 'Mass Media,' *CAR* for 1964, 440

40 King quoted in Bruce, 'Warrendale,' 13; Watson's so-called deception noted in Toronto *Telegram*, 16 November 1964; Nash, *History on the Run*, 166 and 183–4

41 Ruddy in Toronto *Telegram*, 25 February 1964; CBC Research, National Panel Survey, *Audience Reactions to 'This Hour Has Seven Days*,' broadcast 1 November 1964 – but note that Frank Moritsugu in *The Toronto Daily Star*, 2 November 1964, was very impressed with the documentary that focused on the campaigns of a British and an American politician to win office; on the 'Mr Pearson' affair, see Koch, *Inside Seven Days*, 21–3, and Kesterton, 'Mass Media,' CAR for 1964, 438–40; Braithwaite in *Globe and Mail*, 10 June 1964 (see also his comments on a 'Telescope' documentary about the National Theatre School, 6 March 1965).

42 *The Toronto Daily Star*, 15 October 1963; Blackburn in *Telegram*, 10 February 1965; MacLennan to Leiterman, quoted in Koch, *Inside Seven Days*, 101

43 Chuvalo biography on 'Seven Days,' 24 October 1965; Kent quoted in Peter Stursberg, *Lester Pearson and the Dream of Unity* (Toronto: Doubleday 1978), 179 – a description of the film in Koch, *Inside Seven Days*, 21–3, as well; 'Caroline' described in *Globe and Mail*, 10 June 1964, by a very pleased Dennis Braithwaite, and *The Toronto Daily Star*, 9 June 1964

44 The 'Ciao Maria' dispute was covered in all three Toronto dailies, from whence come the various comments of the participants. Note that not all Italian-Canadian leaders felt offended: Dan Iannuzzi, publisher of *Corriere Canadese*, for instance, defended the show.

45 The 'Cuba, Si' affair discussed in *The Toronto Daily Star*, 3 and 13 October 1961; as to *Warrendale*, aside from Bruce's article, there's mention of the difficulty in the Draft Minutes, 49th Program Meeting, 5 and 7 August 1967, 9

46 The discussion of 'Report from the Wasteland' based on a script and a collection of letters as well as reviews (RG 41, v. 206, file 11-18-11-71)

47 The discussion of 'Air of Death' is based on accounts in Wilfrid Kesterton's articles on 'Mass Media' in the CAR for 1968 and 1969, plus the account in Stewart, *Here's Looking at Us*, 130–1.

48 The quotation re television and democracy from Roy Shields, cited in Newman, *Distemper*, 69. Although experience with television has made journalists and politicians a lot more critical of the effects of television, indeed I think a bit too critical, the old myth still occasionally surfaces: see, for example, the 'Epilogue' to Warner Troyer's *The Sound and the Fury*. The most complete analysis of the role of television, and the media generally, in recent elections is Walter Soderlund, Walter Romanow, E. Donald Biggs, and Ronald Wagenberg, *Media and Elections in Canada* (Toronto: Holt, Rinehart &

Winston 1984), though readers may also benefit from Arthur Siegel's *Politics and the Media in Canada* (Toronto: McGraw-Hill Ryerson 1983) and the anecdotal account of election reporting by Clive Cocking, *Following the Leaders: A Media Watcher's Diary of Campaign '79* (Toronto: Doubleday 1980). My understanding of the import of the television image has been much influenced by a provocative little book on the American scene by Austin Ranney, entitled *Channels of Power: The Impact of Television on American Politics* (New York: Basic Books 1983). While I think he exaggerates that impact, and obviously what he has to say can only be applied cautiously to Canada in the 1960s, none the less his speculations are both imaginative and well-informed.

49 Fulford, for instance, was a champion of televising Parliament ('Television Notebook,' *CF*, March 1963, 275); see also the account in John Bird, *FP*, I May 1965, 12. Newman in *MM*, 25 February 1961, 54

50 The description of the Créditiste phenomenon is drawn from M. Pinard, *The Rise of a Third Party: A Study in Crisis Politics* (Toronto: Prentice-Hall 1971) and Michael Stein, *The Dynamics of Right-Wing Protest: A Political Analysis of Social Credit in Quebec* (Toronto: UTP 1973). Actually, the Liberals had tried to ward off the Créditiste menace in the dying days of the 1962, when it seemed that indeed disaster might be on the way, by using René Lévesque on television in a last-ditch effort to make Quebec Liberal – noted in John Saywell, 'Parliament and Politics,' *CAR* for 1962, 19.

51 In the 1963 election, though, a lack of money may well have accounted for a certain decline in the use of television, and according to John Saywell the import of television (see his 'Parliament and Politics,' *CAR* for 1963, 16–17). Diefenbaker also consciously avoided the routines of the modern campaign and endeavoured to whistle-stop across the country to meet the people so that he might re-create the excitement of the 1958 campaign. He would do the same thing in 1965. Of course that didn't prevent television from covering the campaign anyway. On Liberal strategy and the like in 1962 see Walter Gordon, *A Political Memoir* (Toronto: M&S 1977), 97–104. The standard treatment of each of the election campaigns is in J.M. Beck's *Pendulum of Power*, 329–8. The first television debate between leaders actually occurred in Quebec in the 1962 provincial campaign. Gilles Carle, commenting in *Le Magazine Maclean*, January 1963, 49, was much impressed by how the debate cut through the masks of the politicians. But Dale Thompson in *Jean Lesage and the Quiet Revolution* (Toronto: Macmillan 1984), 121–2, points out that Lesage was trained for the event by advisers who secured the most up-to-date American advice, so that he could (and indeed did) shine in front of the television camera.

52 Blackburn in Toronto *Telegram*, 6 November 1965; NDP story noted in Wilfrid
   Kesterton, 'Mass Media,' CAR for 1965, 482 – Kesterton (484) also notes
   that in December the CBC cancelled an NDP free-time provincial-affairs broadcast in Ontario because it included satire, which seemed to violate the rule
   against dramatization; Pelletier, *Years of Choice 1960–68* (Toronto: Methuen
   1987), 186–8; Lester Pearson, *Mike: The Memoirs of the Right Honourable
   Lester B. Pearson*, v. 3: *1957–1968* (Toronto: UTP 1975), 205 – Pearson's anger
   resulted from the experience of the 1965 election.
53 See Pelletier's *Years of Choice 1960–1968* and Nash's *History on the Run*. The
   comment on the Nielsen show by Roy Shields in *The Toronto Daily Star*, 8
   June 1966
54 Parton quotations from an article on the 1965 election coverage taken from
   files in the CBC Reference Library in Toronto
55 Bloom in the *Telegram*, 19 September 1962; Fisher in the *Telegram*, 5 January
   1965
56 On Pearson and the February crisis, see the reports in the CAR for 1968, 9
   and 433. One should remember, in this context, that Pearson's record in
   government was so full of stumbles and mishaps that selling his leadership
   wasn't the easiest task in 1965. The quotation from 'The Four-Way Stretch',
   The Economist, 6 April 1962, 27, cited in Beck, *Pendulum of Power*, 362
57 Davey and O'Hagan quoted in Stursberg, *Lester Pearson and the Dream of
   Unity*, 71–3. On the remoulding of Pearson, see also Newman, *Distemper*,
   69, and Keith Davey, *The Rainmaker: A Passion for Politics* (Toronto: Stoddart
   1986), 67
58 Convention quotation in Martin Sullivan, *Mandate '68* (Toronto: M&S 1983),
   185 – the description of the convention is taken from this source. Gallup reports
   of 28 October and 1 November
59 The changes related to divorce, homosexuality, and abortion.
60 Camp quoted in Geoffrey Stevens, *Stanfield* (Toronto: M&S 1973), 213
61 McLuhan's comment noted in John C. Courtney, *The Selection of National
   Party Leaders in Canada* (Toronto: Macmillan 1973), 166; Radwanski, *Trudeau* (Toronto: Macmillan 1978), 103; Toronto *Globe and Mail*, 12 February
   1968, cited in Paul Sevens and John Saywell, 'Parliament and Politics,' CAR
   for 1968, 19
62 Estimate of viewers and listeners from Stevens and Saywell, CAR for 1968, 39;
   Newman, *Distemper*, 459; Western in *Winnipeg Free Press*, 4 April 1968,
   quoted in Rick Butler and Jean-Guy Carrier, *The Trudeau Decade* (Toronto:
   Doubleday 1979), 13
63 Radwanski, *Trudeau*, 106. On the TV debate, see Kesterton, 'Mass Media,'
   CAR for 1968, 433–4, and Sullivan, *Mandate '68*, 403–4; Gallup found that

Tommy Douglas was the winner, though most people thought the overall show was poor – the trouble was that it was really a panel show with newsmen putting questions to the leaders. The anecdote about the life-long Conservative in Sullivan, *Mandate '68*, 14

64 Gallup survey released 1 June 1968; statistics on class support from Beck, *Pendulum of Power*, 416, and Clark et al., *Political Choice in Canada*, 112 and 115; statistics on metropolitan support from Clarke et al., *Political Choice in Canada*, 123, and Stevens and Saywell, CAR for *1968*, 64; the comment on 'haves' made by Peter Regenstreif in *The Toronto Daily Star*, 26 June 1968, cited in Beck, *Pendulum of Power*, 416

65 Marshall in the Toronto *Telegram*, 4 May 1986, cited in Kesteron, 'Mass Media,' 433 – Marshall wished to show that Trudeau had won on his merits, not just because of the image-makers; Ranney, *Channels of Power*, 73

66 'Mr. Trudeau sat almost motionless at his desk, his face impassive throughout,' in the words of Denis Smith; 'but he conveyed the sense of an implacable will and a relentless anger through slight shifts of intonation and an icy stare that shot out at moments from frigid depths.' Smith, *Bleeding Hearts ... Bleeding Country: Canada and the Quebec Crisis* (Edmonton: Hurtig 1971), 53 – Smith was a severe critic of Trudeau and his handling of the crisis.

67 The survival of Trudeau's image is discussed, along with the whole question of images, and the practice of 'negative voting,' in Clarke et al., *Absent Mandate*, 100–29, 142–3.

68 Edmonds, 'Pain in the Network,' 10; Gzowski, 'Seven Days Gets Ready for Its Hour,' 8

69 Viewers two decades later, though, would find many of the individual segments much more languid than has become the norm on North American television.

70 It's worth noting that the Orson Welles interview (the artist) and the George Chuvalo story (sportsman) were similar efforts to consider the trials and tribulations of the individual.

12 On Viewing

1 Cited in F. Elkin, 'Television in Suburbia,' *Food for Thought*, 17, May/June 1957, 381

2 On the debate over the relationship between leisure and work, see Kenneth Roberts, *Leisure* (London: Longman 1981) and Stanley Parker, *Leisure and Work* (London: George Allen & Unwin 1983); Peter Newman, 'The Dilemma of Greater Leisure: Threat or Opportunity?' QQ, 66, Spring 1959, 108

3 Schramm et al., *Television in the Lives of Our Children* (Toronto: UTP 1961)

4 CBC Audience Research, *The 1958 Halifax Study of Leisure Time Activities in the Television Age: Initial Tabulations*, Table 7; Carol Kirsh, Brian Dixon, and Michael Bond, *A Leisure Study – Canada 1972* (Ottawa: Arts and Culture Branch, Department of the Secretary of State 1973), 121 and 225; Charles Hobart, 'Recreation in Alberta: Current Practices and Prospects,' in S.M.A. Hameed and D. Cullen, Eds., *Work and Leisure in Canada* (Edmonton: University of Alberta 1972), 76–95

5 A CBC study on farm families in the Wingham area of Ontario in the spring of 1958 found that 56 per cent of the sets were in the living-room, 17 per cent in the dining-room, and 27 per cent in the kitchen (compared with 84 per cent of radios) – CBC Audience Research, *Radio Listening and TV Viewing in an Ontario Farm Area*, November 1958, 9; on giving up television, see Hugh Garner, 'The Joys of a Sabbatical,' SN, 12 November 1955; Vivien Kimber, 'What Happened When We Threw Out Our TV Set,' MM, 30 March 1957; and John Brehl, 'We Turned Off the TV for a Week – and LIVED!' *Toronto Daily Star*, 22 January 1966.

6 Jhally, *The Codes of Advertising* (New York: Francis Pinter 1987), 83–5, 181; McLuhan, 'Television: Prospect,' *Canadian Art*, IX, no. 5 (September/October 1962), 366

7 Wood, 'Television as Dream,' in Horace Newcomb, ed., *Television: The Critical View*, 2nd ed. (New York: OUP 1979), 517–35; Arlen, *The Camera Age: Essays on Television* (Harmondsworth: Penguin 1982), 139–45; David Sohn Interviews Jerzy Kosinski, 'A Nation of Videots' in Newcomb, *Television: The Critical View*, 334–49; Jerry Mander, *Four Arguments for the Elimination of Television* (New York: William Morrow 1978); and Marie Winn, *The Plug-In Drug*, rev. ed. (Harmondsworth: Penguin 1985; first published in 1977)

8 Marshall quotation cited in a report dated 30 April 1953 by P.A. Meggs, entitled 'TV Owners' Association,' in RG41, v. 401, file 23-1-4; the farmer's letter in RG41, v. 206, file 11-18-11-71

9 Patricia Palmer, *The Lively Audience: A Study of Children around the TV Set* (London: Allen & Unwin 1986), 70

10 Ouimet I; Peter Morgan, 'Television and You,' CF, December 1954, 200

11 Waddington, 'Radio and Television,' CF, July 1956, 83; and Kimber, 'What Happened When We Threw Out Our TV Set,' 17

12 Martin Goldfarb Consultants, 'The Media and the People' [hereafter Goldfarb], in Special Senate Committee on Mass media, *Report*, v. 3: *Good, Bad, or Simply Inevitable* (Offower: Queen's Printer 1970), 23 and 101

13 CJOH-TV incident mentioned in Peter Stursberg, *Mr. Broadcasting: The Ernie Bushnell Story* (Toronto, Peter Martin Associates Ltd. 1971), 240–1; the 'Live and Learn' incident mentioned in Brian Stewart, 'The Professor in Your

Living Room,' *CBC Times*, 19–25 November 1960, 4; the viewer's letters cited may be found in RG 41, v. 206, files 11-18-11-69 and 11-18-11-71, as well as v. 236, file 11-25-3, pt. 8, and 11-25-12.

14 American findings, based on films of what people actually did in their living-rooms, cited in George Comstock, Stephen Chaffee, Natan Katzman, Maxwell McCombs, and Donald Roberts, *Television and Human Behaviour* (New York: Columbia University Press 1978), 141–7, and George Comstock, *Television in America* (Beverly Hills: Sage 1980), 29–30; CBC Audience Research, *Preliminary Results: H.M.S. Pinafore Telephone Recall Survey: Ottawa-Hull and Vicinity*, 9 November 1956

15 Goldfarb, 38

16 See Gary Steiner, *The People Look at Television* (New York: Alfred A. Knopf 1963), and Richard T. Bower, *Television and the Public* (New York: Holt, Rinehart & Winston 1973) for discussions of American views; Garner, 'The Joys of a Sabbatical,' 45; Kimber, 'What Happened When We Threw Out Our TV Set,' 62; Schramm et al., *Television in the Lives of Our Children*, 52–3; CBC Audience Research, *The 1958 Halifax Study*, Table 13; on the Calgary kids, see Gregory T. Fouts, 'Effects of Television on Children and Youth: A Developmental Approach,' in *Report of the Royal Commission on Violence in the Communications Industry*, v. 6: *Vulnerability to Media Effects* (Toronto: Queens's Printer n.d.), 84.

17 ISL report on viewing habits for 1956–57 found that winter viewing totals rose to 75 per cent of all television homes between 8:00 and 9:00 PM in the winter, but only to a high of 60 per cent between 9:00 and 10:00 PM in summer, for the three major markets of Montreal, Toronto–Hamilton, and Vancouver–Victoria. A.C. Nielsen, *Special Presentation to Canadian Broadcasting Company*, 1966, estimated for January the average viewing totals in the 7:00-to-midnight slot were 3:02 (weekdays), 3:06 (Sundays), and 3:18 (Saturdays).

18 In *Canadian Broadcaster & Telescreen*, 3 February 1954

19 The dreaded evil of 'enforced viewing' is discussed in a British study by G.J. Goodhardt, A.S.C. Ehrenberg, and M.A. Collins, *The Television Audience: Patterns of Viewing* (Westmead and Lexington: Susan House/Lexington Books 1975); ISL, *1958–59*, 75 and 72; the big city/farm split computed from ISL, *1959–61*.

20 Klein, 'Why You Watch What You Watch When You Watch,' in Barry Cole, *Television Today: A Close-Up View* (New York: OUP 1981), 214–17, an article first published in *TV Guide*, 24 July, 1971

21 Thus 'Tribune Libre' got 24 per cent and 'Concert' 19 per cent of the potential *Le Devoir* group while 'Le gendarmerie royale' won 46 per cent, 'La pension Velder' 56 per cent, and 'La Lutte' 29 per cent – Radio-Canada, *Rapport*

General II. *Volume 1: La Télévision d'Expression Française*, March 1961;
201,600 for the hockey (at 8:30) and 191,500 for the téléromans (at 8:00).

22 Goodhardt et al., *The Television Audience*. Scheduling comments in CBC, *An Analysis of the Relative Popularity of* Lolly-Too-Dum, 1957, 6, citing a BBC *Audience Research Reference Book*, 13

23 *A CBC Research Report* TV/65, 122, Table I; 'How the "Flush Test" Rates Your TV Habits,' *MM*, 19 June 1965, 53. See Hilde T. Himmelweit, Betty Swift, and Marianne E. Jaeger, 'The Audience as Critic: A Conceptual Analysis of Television Entertainment,' in Percy H. Tannenbaum, ed., *The Entertainment Functions of Television* (Hillsdale NJ: Laurence Erlbaum Associates 1980) for an extensive treatment of the preferences of audiences in Great Britain, and a refutation of the claim that the public didn't or couldn't make judgments.

24 According to ISL, nightly viewing in January 1957 was around 10 per cent higher in large cities than in towns or farms. E-H 'sets-in-use' ratings for January 1961 found that cities differed greatly in their weekly averages: Toronto (43 per cent), Saskatoon (45 per cent), Regina (51 per cent), Sudbury (59 per cent), and Halifax (65 per cent). A special survey by Nielsen for the CBC using January 1966 data confirmed the existence of such a range, though this time Vancouver had the weekday low of 4:52 per household and Regina the high, with 6:46. The March 1966 averages were 6:06 (Atlantic), 6:35 (Quebec), 6:06 (Ontario), 6:12 (Prairies), 5:18 (British Columbia). And Nielsen's *Canada '67* survey found that viewing totals per week for households ranged from a high of 46 1/2 hours in Quebec to a low of 36 hours and 18 minutes in British Columbia. The ISL reports are its respective *TV Network Reports* for the French and English surveys.

25 By 1960 the percentage of households with television was the same in Quebec and in Ontario (at 89 per cent), even though Ontario had once led by a substantial margin, both the lag and the catch-up explained by Québécois buying sets more rapidly than English Quebeckers – DBS, 'Household Facilities and Equipment.' Compare monthly sets-in-use figures for anglophones and *Francophones* in Montreal: October 1960 (37.8 and *41.0*), November 1960 (39.6 and *44.7*); December 1960 (39.7 and *46.6*), January 1961 (45.3 and *50.2*) – from E-H, *Teleratings January 1961*, 1 and 8.

26 Nielsen, Special Presentation – the actual hourly totals were 28:40 (women) and 23:44 (men).

27 CBC, *What Ontario Parents Think of Children's TV Programs*, July 1959 (though the data used was almost three years old); Savard quotation from *Points de Vue*, April 1957, 45; CBC, *The Radisson Series on Television*, 6 June 1957, 2–3; Audience Research Division, CBC, *Nursery School Time Study*, 1958, II

28 BBM data from 1983 shows that high-income Canadians watched less television

and preferred educational, documentary, and sports shows (BBM, *Data 1985*, 50–2); Goldfarb, 128; Radio-Canada, *La Télévision d'Expression Française*, March 1961; Steiner, *The People Look at Television*, 231–5

29 Service des Recherches et Sondages, Radio-Canada, *Les Téléspectateurs Face aux Téléromans et à la Famille Plouffe*, August 1958, 9; Schwerin, *Report C-CBC-55-5 "Plouffe Family"*, 15, and *Report C-CBC-56-7 "Plouffe Family"*, 31;CBC Audience Research, *What the Canadian Public Thinks of the CBC*, Table 30; Fernand Benoît, 'Les "classes moyennes" et la télévision,' *Le Magazine Maclean*, March 1965, 22–3, 34

30 Letters in RG41, v. 206, file 11-18-11-71; *What the Public Thinks of the CBC*, 18–19; Goldfarb, 52,122, and 36

31 Goldfarb, 18,16,9,8,10,57 (quoted opinions), 10

32 Dennis Giles and Marilyn Jackson-Beeck, 'Television, the Evil Eye,' in Stuart M. Kaminsky, *American Television Genre* (Chicago: Nelson-Hall 1985) 191–202; Morgan, 'Television and You,' 200

33 For some contemporary response to Schramm et al., see Sidney Katz's summary 'What Television Does to Children,' MM, 22 April 1961; Jacques Coulon's 'La TV peut faire autant de mal que de bien aux jeunes,' in *Le Petit Journal*, 21 May 1961; Pat Pearce's 'Researchers Warn Parents,' Montreal *Star*, 3 June 1961; and Dennis Brathwaite's 'The Influence of TV on Children's Minds,' *The Globe Magazine*, 16 December 1961. Martin in CRTC Research Branch, *Symposium on Television Violence* (Ottawa: Ministry of Supply and Services 1976), viii. For some of the findings of semiotics on the issues of television and violence as well as television and children, see in particular Fiske and Hartley, *Reading Television*, Bob Hodge and David Tripp, *Children and Television* (Stanford: Stanford University Press 1986), and Patricia Palmer, *The Lively Audience* (Sidney: Allen & Unwin 1986).

34 The iron law is most closely associated with one of the early works that located television in the context of the whole apparatus of mass communication; J. Klapper, *The Effects of Mass Communication* (Glencoe, Ill.: Free Press 1960).

35 UNESCO study cited in Comstock et al., *Television and Human Behaviour*, 154

36 Laplante, 'Lecture et télévision,' *Culture*, December 1956, 343; the American publishing statistic in Comstock, *Television in America*, 35; Brian Stewart in *CBC Times*, 22–28 August 1959, 4; *A Leisure Study – Canada 1972*, 145

37 Statistics on movie-houses and admissions from Urquhart and Buckley, *Historical Statistics of Canada* (Toronto: Macmillan of Canada 1965), 580, and Garth S. Jowett and Barry R. Hemmings, 'The Growth of the Mass Media in Canada,' in Benjamin D. Singer, ed., *Communications in Canadian Society*, 2nd ed. (Toronto: Copp Clark 1975), and footnote 252 17 on 265

38 The actual amounts of listening time were 1:42 and 4:30 hours respectively –

ISL, *1958–59*, 37; Sandy Stewart, *A Pictorial History of Radio in Canada* (Toronto: Yage 1975), 148. Finlay Payne in his interview made similar comments about the plight of CBC radio in the late 1950s and early 1960s.

39 The CHUM story in Harvey Kirck, *Nobody Calls Me Mr. Kirck* (Toronto: Collins 1985), 88–9; there was an average of 2.33 radio sets in Canadian homes in 1969 (Goldfarb, 11); Fowler II, 265; Hopkins, Hedlin, 127.

40 The term from the title of the chapter on periodicals appearing in the *Davey Report*; statistics from *ibid.*, 156–7; comment on deaths in 1950s from Dean Walker, 'Magazines in Canada,' in *Good, Bad, or Simply Inevitable?* v. 3 of Canada, Senate, Special Senate Committee on Mass Media, *Report* (Ottawa: Queen's Printer 1970), 210; Goldfarb, 9

41 CBC, *The 1958 Halifax Study*, Table 12; CBC, *What the Canadian Public Thinks of the CBC*, 44; Goldfarb, 6

42 Circulation figures from Jowett and Hemmings, 'The Growth of the Mass Media in Canada,' 249; Goldfarb, 12 – Saskatchewan, by the way, had the same ratio.

43 Comstock notes that the UNESCO study found that television increased total time with mass media by one hour – Comstock, *Television in America*, 33

44 Personal letter, Dick to Rutherford, 11 August 1987 – at the time of writing Mr Dick is Corporate Archive Liaison for the CBC; CBC, *Nursery School Time Study*, 1958, 9; Brehl, 'We Turned Off the TV ...'; Kimber, 'What Happened When We Threw Out Our TV Set,' 62; quotation from Elkin, 'Television in Suburbia,' 381; on the rise of the 'TV evening' see Mary Jolliffe, 'How TV Affects a Canadian Community,' *SN*, 8 November 1952, 19, and CBC's *The 1958 Halifax Study*, tables 3a and 3b.

45 CBC, *Radio Listening and TV Viewing in an Ontario Farm Area*, November 1958, 7 and 31; Lauk interview; Tannis Macbeth Williams, ed., *The Impact of Television: A Natural Experiment in Three Communities* (Orlando: Academic Press 1986)

46 Mary Jolliffe, 'How TV Affects a Canadian Community,' 19; John R. Seeley, R. Alexander Sim, and E.W. Loosley, *Crestwood Heights: A Study of the Culture of Suburban Life* (Toronto: UTP 1956), 198–9; Patrick Allen, 'La TV pour jeunes: cheval de Troie dans nos foyers,' *L'Action National*, 50 (June 1961), 977; Dick, review of Neil Postman's *Amusing Ourselves to Death*, in *ASCRT Bulletin*, no. 30 (July 1987), 2.

47 Comstock, *Television in America*, 134; Fouts, 'Effects of Television ...,' 83

48 See Williams, *The Impact of Television*, 286, for a summary of how more than half of the children in a test reversed the gender of a doctor and a nurse in their memory.

49 This discussion is based largely on Comstock et al., *Television and Human*

Behavior, and H.J. Eysenck and D.K.B. Nias, *Sex, Violence and the Media* (London: Paladin 1978); on the right-brain bias of TV, see Jerome L. Singer, 'The Power and Limitations of Television: A Cognitive-Affective Analysis,' in Percy H. Tannenbaum, ed., *The Entertainment Functions of Television* 31–65; the Finnish study is cited in the Glasgow University Media Group, *Bad News*, v. 1 (London: Routledge & Kegan Paul 1976), 10.

50 Seeley et al., *Crestwood Heights*; the glue-sniffing story and bomb incident cited in Stanley and Brian Riera, 'Replications of Media Violence,' Ontario, *Report of the Royal Commission on Violence in the Communications Industry*, v. 5: *Learning from the Media* (Toronto: Queen's Printer for Ontario 1976), 68 and 79–80; the pollution study taken from W. Brian Stewart, 'The Canadian Social System and the Canadian Broadcasting Audience,' in Benjamin D. Singer, ed., *Communications in Canadian Society*, 63–4. The pictures of Biafran children were in fact part of a propaganda effort on the part of the secessionists to win world opinion.

51 See Patricia Marks Greenfield, *Mind and Media: The Effects of Television, Video Games, and Computers* (Cambridge, Mass.: Harvard University Press 1984) on TV and cognition; Gavriel Salomon, *Interaction of Media, Cognition, and Learning: An Exploration of How Symbolic Forms Cultivate Mental Skills and Affect Knowledge Acquisition* (San Francisco: Jossey-Bass 1979), 212.

52 Jerome L. Singer and Dorothy G. Singer, *Television, Imagination, and Aggression: A Study of Preschoolers* (Hillsdale, NJ: Lawrence Erlbaum Associates 1981)

53 Juveniles are defined as people under sixteen: the figure on court appearances rose from 7, 186 to 14, 137 (Urquhart and Buckley, *Historical Statistics of Canada*, 653). The figures on convictions based on annual material in the *Canada Year Book*. The figures for crimes of violence and for police officers from F.H. Leacy, ed., *Historical Statistics of Canada*, 2nd ed. (Ottawa: Statistics Canada 1983), Series Z1–14 and Z63–5.

54 See George Gerbner, Larry Gross, Michael Morgan, and Nancy Signorielli, 'The "Mainstreaming" of America: Violence Profile No. 11,' *Journal of Communication*, 30, no. 3 (Summer 1980), 10–29. Anthony N. Doob and Glenn E. Macdonald, 'Television Viewing and Fear of Victimization: Is the Relationship Causal?' *Journal of Personality and Social Psychology*, 37, no. 2 (1979), 170–9. Hodge and Tripp, *Children and Television*, 93–5

55 Albert Bandura 'places television third behind family and social milieus in which a person resides as a source of influence' (Comstock, *Television in America*, 137). Comstock, himself, emphasizes that television is best thought of as a 'secondary rather than a primary influence' (ibid, 135) and 'a particu-

larly important source of vicarious influence' (Comstock et al., *Television and Human Behaviour*, 393). See Greenfield, *Mind and Media*, for comments on TV and the making of consumers (51–3).

56 Noble, *Children in Front of the Small Screen* (Beverly Hills: Sage 1975)

57 The notions of 'generalized information' and a 'shared repertoire' are discussed in the articles by Paul M. Hirsch, 'The Role of Television and Popular Culture in Contemporary Society,' and Michael Novak, 'Television Shapes the Soul,' in Newcomb, *Television: The Critical View*, 249–79 and 303–18. The other media of radio and newspapers rated very poorly on this question of seeing life: Goldfarb, 122.

Afterword: Understanding Television

1 In 'Visions of Power,' the first part of the thirteen-week Granada Television documentary on the history of TV, which was shown in Toronto by TV Ontario, on 4 October 1985. The comment was part of the narration by Ian Holm. The emphasis is mine.

2 The argument that television is a multi-faceted phenomenon, of course, is hardly much of a discovery. That has recently been charted by John O'Connor in his excellent opening essay 'Introduction: Television and the Historian,' in *American History/American Television: Interpreting the Video Past* (New York: Frederick Ungar 1983), xiii–xliii.

3 Indeed, Michael Leapman, in *The Last Days of the BEEB* (London: Allen & Unwin 1986), feels the BBC has been in trouble since the happy days of Sir Hugh Greene's renaissance of the early 1960s.

4 On the Hollywood scene, see R. Levinson and New York W. Link, *Off Camera: Conversations with the Makers of Prime-Time Television* (New York: New American Library 1986), on Paley's tastes, see David Halberstam, *The Powers That Be* (New York: Knopf 1979), 26–7; 'Pervasive Albion' in Arlen, *The View from Highway 1* (New York: Ballantine 1977), 152–63.

5 Nelson, *The Perfect Machine: TV in the Nuclear Age* (Toronto: Between the Lines 1987)

6 Zamora and Lara cases in the episode 'The Good, the Bad, and the Ugly'

7 At some length, Brian Winston has demonstrated in his description of the emergence of the telephone, television, computers, and satellites just how ahistorical and naîve is all this technological determinism. Winston, *Misunderstanding Media* (Cambridge, Mass.: Harvard University Press 1986) – Winston's debunking, unfortunately, goes a bit too far in the other extreme, leaving the impression that nothing changes; Isaac Asimov, Charles G. Waugh, and Martin Harry Greenberg, *TV :2000* (New York: Fawcett Crest 1982)

8 Comment on Sarnoff from Laurence Bergreen, *Look Now, Pay Later: The Rise of Network Broadcasting* (New York: New American Library 1980), 123

9 Indeed Erik Barnouw, in *The Sponsor: notes on a Modern Potentate* (New York: OUP 1978), concluded that sponsor power over American television was actually greater by the 1970s than before.

10 Figures cited in Postman, *Amusing Ourselves to Death: Public Discourse in the Age of Show Business* (Harmondsworth: Penguin 1985), 152; *Times* quotation from Leapman, *The Last Days of the BEEB, 278*

11 Comment on BBC self-praise in John Fiske and John Hartley, *Reading Television*, 124; Peter Trueman, *Smoke and Mirrors* (Toronto: M&S 1980); see Trueman's explanation of his move to print in the 'Yours Truly' ...' column of *Star Week* (*Toronto Star*), 1–8 October 1988, 110. The well-known American sociologist Herbert Gans concluded after lengthy observation that in truth there were many more similarities than differences between the electronic and print news media – Gans, *Deciding What's News: A Study of CBS Evening News, NBC Nightly News*, Newsweek & Time (New York: Pantheon Books 1979), xii.

12 Francis Wheen, *Television: A History* (London: Century Publishing 1985), 41; the Cleveland case mentioned in Dennis Giles and Marilyn Jackson-Beeck, 'Television, the Evil Eye,' 200

13 Nielsen date from Wheen, *Television*, 46, and BBM data from source; audience for the royal wedding from Wheen, 229

14 Japanese youngster quoted in 'Visions of Power'; anonymous comment quoted in a later episode entitled 'The Good, the Bad, and the Ugly'; *Free Press* story reported in Landon Y. Jones, *Great Expectations: America and the Baby Boom Generation* (New York: Coward, McCann & Geoghegan 1980), 125; Reginald W. Bibby and Donald C. Posterski, *The Emerging Generation: An Inside Look at Canada's Teenagers* (Toronto: Irwin 1985), 40–1; Garcia case reported in Bob Hodge and David Tripp, *Children and Television* (Stanford: Stanford University Press 1986), 133 – his suicide note claimed that he would 'take my television set with me.'

15 On the British Parliament see Colin Seymour-Ure, *The Political Impact of Mass Media* (London and Beverly Hills: Constable/Sage 1974), 144–9; Edwin Diamond and Stephen Bates, *The Spot: The Rise of Political Advertising on Television* (Cambridge, Mass.: MIT 1984); Clive Cocking, *Follow the Leaders: A Media Watcher's Diary of Campaign '79* (Toronto: Doubleday 1980); Sears, *Hello Sweetheart ... Get Me Rewrite: Remembering the Great Newspaper Wars* (Toronto: Key Porter 1988), 200.

16 See Raymond Williams, *Television: Technology and Cultural Form* (Glasgow: Fontana/Collins 1974), 132–3, on the European welcome to American TV;

statistics in Jeremy Tunstall, *The Media Are American: Anglo-American Media in the World* (London: Constable 1977), 278–9; on 'Dallas' see Wheen, *Television*, 150; comments on news from 'News Power,' part of the Granada Television documentary

17 Government of Canada, Task Force on Broadcasting Policy, Report (Ottawa: Ministry of Supply and Service, Canada 1986), especially 95. For a general discussion of the problem see Chin-Chuan Lee, *Media Imperialism Reconsidered: The Homogenizing of Television Culture* (Beverly Hills: Sage 1980).

18 Susan Mann Trofimenkoff, *The Dream of Nation: A Social and Intelligence History of Quebec* (Toronto Gage 1983), 284

19 Michael Arlen's collection of essays, *The Living Room War* (Harmondsworth: Penguin 1982); originally published in 1969), remains a fascinating collection of insights into the coverage of the Vietnam conflict. The Cronkite story cited in Halberstam, *The Powers That Be* 514. On the plight of the New Left, see Todd Gitlin, *The Whole World Is Watching* (Berkeley: University of California 1980).

20 On the SAT decline, see Jones, *Great Expectations*, 128–41.

21 Frank in 'News: The Power of Pictures,' part of the Granada Television documentary. This line of argument has been carried much further by Postman in *Amusing Ourselves to Death*, where he argues that TV has overthrown an older tradition of rational public discourse, born in the era of print, and promoted instead a kind of 'anticommunication' that abandons logic or reason or content to entertain and amuse. This, I consider, is an extreme overstatement.

22 This approach to understanding the impact of television is most closely identified with Joshua Merowitz's *No Sense of Place: The Impact of the Electronic Media on Social Behavior* (New York: OUP 1985). It is one of the most provocative and original thesis on television's effects published in this decade. All too often, though, I find the force of Meyrowitz's arguments weakened by a tendency to exaggerate the import of TV and the extent of social change.

23 Cited by McLuhan in *Understanding Media*, 19, although I've added some material from the original source.

Primary Sources

Included here are the chief primary sources that were used in the course of researching the book.

Manuscript Collections

CBC Collection, RG 41, Federal Archives, National Archives of Canada, Ottawa. This extensive collection is organized in volumes and sometimes file folders. The single most important group of records were the minutes of the Program Committee of the board of directors from 1959 to 1967, which dealt with all kinds of details about programming. At the time that I consulted this collection, the minutes were included with material relating to the actual meetings of the board of directors.

CBC Headquarters Collection, Ottawa. I gathered a wide range of material from CBC Ottawa, much of this in the shape of programming statistics, program evaluations, and ratings information.

CBC Programme Files, Reference Library, Toronto. The program files are replete with magazine and press comment on individual shows, even including some comment in the 1960s on CTV programs.

Moving Images and Sound Archives, National Archives of Canada, Ottawa. MISA has extensive holdings of information pertaining to the history of broadcasting, videotapes of many television programs, and a huge collection of CBC photographs. I consulted chiefly the files of ratings data (especially BBM to 1965) stored at MISA as well as the photographic collection. There is, in addition, a modest collection of photographs in the National Photography Collection of the National Archives of Canada.

Government Documents Section, Robarts Library, University of Toronto. One of the depositories holding the briefs submitted to the Massey and Fowler royal commissions.

Periodicals and Series

I was able to locate many magazine articles on television using the *Periodical Index*. The three Toronto dailies, *The Globe and Mail*, The *Toronto Daily Star*, and *The Telegram*, plus two Montreal dailies, *Le Devoir* and *La Presse*, were also consulted for specific program listings and descriptions. Listed below are the sources that were researched by me or my assistants.

Canadian Forum, 1952–62
CBC *Annual Reports*, 1950–67
CBC *Times*, 1950–65
The Financial Post, 1950–60
Food for Thought, 1949–60
La Semaine à Radio-Canada, 1952–65
Maclean's, 1952–67
Marketing, 1956–64
Saturday Night, 1952–62

Interviews

1. CBC Oral History Project, under the supervision of Professor Ross Eamon, the taped interviews held by Moving Image and Sound Archives, National Archives of Canada

Subject	Interviewer	Date
Allen, Robert	Ross Eamon	1982
Cunningham, Bill	Ross Eamon	1983
Dunton, Davidson	Denise McConney	1984
Earle, Tom	Paul Follis	1982
Fraser, Ron	Barry MacDonald	1981
Lauk, Len	Ross Eamon	1981
Lewis, Raymond	Nancy Gnaedinger	1983
Moir, Bob	Joan Dixon	1983
Morrison, Neil	Nancy Gnaedinger	1983
Munro, Marce	Ross Eamon	1981

Nash, Knowlton	Ross Eamon	1983
Nutt, Tom	Vic Owen	1982
Ouimet, J. Alphonse	Joan Dixon	1983 (Ouimet I)
Parent, Guy	Ross Eamon	1981
Payne, Finlay	Ross Eamon	1981
Starmer, Leonard	Ross Eamon	1983
Westgate, Murray	Eva Major-Marothy	1982
Weyman, Ronald	Ross Eamon	1981

2. Interviews by Sandy Stewart, held by Moving Image and Sound Archives, Public Archives of Canada

Barnes, John	1976
Boyle, Harry	1975
MacPherson, Don	1976
Ouimet, J. Alphonse	1976 (Ouimet II)

3. Interviews by Paul Rutherford

Cornell, Ward	1986
Peers, Frank	1986
Wayne, Johnny	1986

Program and Advertisements

Listed here are the assorted 'close readings' of programs and ads carried out by researchers and by myself.

SB: Stephen Baker
SS: Stephen Strople
PL: Phillipe Landreville
BH: Brigid Higgins
MO: Margarita Orszag
PR: Paul Rutherford

I. Radio-Canada (from CBC-Montreal)
'Chacun son métier,' August 1958, by SB
'Chansons Canadiennes,' 20 March 1959, by SB & PL
'Club des autographes,' 24 October 1959, by SB

'Conférence de presse,' 23 September 1963, by SB
'Les Couche-tard,' 1965, by SB & PL
'Dans tous les cantons,' 27 July 1960, by SB
'En première,' *Au coeur de la rose*, 22 March 1959, by SB & PL
'La famille Plouffe,' 15 May 1957, by SB & PL
'14 rue de Galais,' 4 June 1956, by SB & PL
'L'heure du concert,' 25 March 1954, by SB
'Music Hall,' 6 March 1966, by SB
'Le nez de Cléopâtre,' 28 April 1954, by SB & PL
'Le pain de jour,' October 1963, by SB
'Pays et merveilles,' February 1953, SB
Pension Velder,' 15 January 1958, by SB & PL
'Point de mire,' 3 March 1957, by SB
'Point de mire,' October 1958, by SB
'Quelles nouvelles,' 31 August 1957, by SB & PL
'Téléthéâtre de Radio-Canada' *Florence*, 14 March 1957, by SB
'Théâtre populaire,' *La vertu des chattes*, 30 June 1957, by SB
'Toi et moi,' 26 September 1957, by SB

2. CBC English (from CBC-Toronto)
'Cariboo Country,' 'Sara's Copper,' 21 April 1966, by SS & BH
'CBC National News,' 27 July 1965, by PR
'CBC National News,' 31 January 1963, by PR
'CBC National News,' 31 March 1960, by PR
'CBC Television Theatre,' *The Queen of Spades*, 28 October 1956 by SS, BH, & PR
'Close-Up,' 'The Psychology of the Cold War,' 11 February 1962, by SS & BH
'Country Hoedown,' 8 September 1962, by SS
'Cross-Canada Hit Parade,' 10 November 1958, by SS & BH
'Explorations,' 16 March 1958, by SS & PR
'Festival,' *Juno and the Paycock*, 15 December 1965, by SS, BH, & PR
'Fighting Words,' 19 January 1958, by SS
'Folio,' *The Nativity Play*, 19 December 1956, by SS & BH
'Front Page Challenge,' 16 January 1962, by SS, BH, & PR
'General Motors Presents,' *The New Men*, 27 September 1959, by SS, BH, & PR
'Graphic,' *The Face of God*, 15 April 1960, by SS
'Hockey Night in Canada,' 15 April 1962, by SS
'Holiday Ranch,' 28 September 1957, by SS, BH, & PR
'Inquiry,' 'Canadian Trade with Cuba,' 26 December 1960, by SS
'On Camera,' *Markheim*, 14 January 1957, by SS & BH

'Playbill,' *The Overcoat*, 29 June 1954 by SS & BH
'The Plouffe Family,' 14 October 1954, by SS & PR
'Press Conference,' 'Celebration at the Cape,' 23 February 1962, by SS & BH
'Profile,' 25 April 1955, by SS, BH, & PR
'Q for Quest,' 'Bob Dylan – The Times They Are a 'Changing,' 10 March 1964,
   by SS & BH
'Showtime,' 4 March 1956, by SS
'Space Command,' probably 1953, by SS, BH, & PR
'Tabloid,' 31 January 1958, by SS, BH, & PR
'The Unforeseen,' 'The lkon of Elijah,' 23 October 1958, by SS & BH
'This Hour Has Seven Days,' 6 December 1964, by SS & BH
'This Hour Has Seven Days,' 24 October 1965, by SS & PR
'Viewpoint,' 28 April 1960, by SS & BH
'The Wayne and Shuster Show,' 11 March 1962, by SS, BH, & PR
'Wojeck,' 'The Last Man in the World,' 13 September 1966, by SS & PR

In addition one action/adventure show was viewed off-air in a rerun:
'RCMP,' rebroadcast on CBLT-TV, 3 September 1983, by PR

3. American (from the Museum of Broadcasting in New York City)
'Alfred Hitchcock Presents,' CBS, 'The Return of the Hero,' 2 March 1958, by
   MO & PR
'Ben Casey,' ABC, 2 October 1961, by PR
'Ford Theatre,' NBC, 'First Born,' 10 September 1953, by MO & PR
'Gunsmoke,' CBS, 10 September 1955, MO & PR
'The Life and Legend of Wyatt Earp,' ABC, 6 September 1955, by MO & PR.
'I Love Lucy,' CBS, 20 May 1955, by MO & PR
'The Milton Berle Show,' NBC, 5 June 1956, by MO & PR
'See It Now,' CBS, 'Communism: Domestic and International,' by MO & PR
'See It Now,' CBS, 'J. Robert Oppenheimer,' 1 March 1955, by MO & PR
'The $64,000 Question,' CBS, 20 September 1955, by MO & PR
'Studio One,' CBS, *The Arena*, by MO & PR
'The Untouchables,' ABC, *Elegy*, 20 November 1962, by MO & PR

In addition two more sitcoms were viewed off-air in syndicated reruns:
'The Dick Van Dyke Show,' rebroadcast on CHCH-TV, 31 August 1983, by SB and
   PR
'Leave It to Beaver,' rebroadcast on CKVR-TV, 2 September 1983, by SB

4. British (from the British Film Institute in London)

'The Avengers,' ABC Television, 'The Little Wonders,' 11 January 1964, by MO & PR

'People in Trouble,' Rediffusion Television, 'Mixed Marriages,' 21 May 1958, by MO & PR

'Steptoe & Son,' BBC, 'The Offer,' 7 June 1962, by MO & PR

'Television Playhouse,' Granada, *No Fixed Abode*, 30 January 1959, by MO & PR

5. Commercials

'Ambassador DPL' (30 seconds), in 'Music Hall,' 6 March 1966, by SB

'Association of Fire Chiefs' (60 seconds), in 'Cariboo Country,' 21 April 1966, by SS & BH

'Ban' (60 seconds), in 'The Untouchables,' 20 November 1962, by MO & PR

'Bayer Aspirin' (60 seconds), in 'Wojeck' rerun, summer 1967, by PR

'Canadian Bible Society' (60 seconds), in 'Cariboo Country,' 21 April 1966, by SS & BH

'duMaurier Cigarettes #1 & #2' (55 seconds each), in 'Front Page Challenge,' 16 January 1962, by SS, BH, & PR

'Eveready Batteries' #1 & #2 (60 seconds each), in 'The Wayne and Shuster Hour,' 11 March 1962, SS, BH, & PR

'Ford' #1 & #2 (30 seconds each), in 'Le pain du jour,' October 1963, by SB

'General Foods' Kool Shake' (30 seconds), in 'Cap aux sorciers,' 4 June 1957, by SB

'General Mills Cheerios' (65 seconds), in 'Wyatt Earp,' 6 October 1958, by PR

'General Motors' #1 & #2 (45 seconds each), in 'GM Presents,' 27 September 1959, by SS & BH

'Imperial Esso Products & Services' #1–#4 (45, 90, 60 and 80 seconds, respectively), in 'Hockey Night in Canada,' 15 April 1962, by SS

'Instant Maxwell House Coffee' #1, #2, & #3 (60 seconds each), in 'On Camera,' 14 January 1957, by SS & BH

'Jell-O Instant Pudding' (60 seconds), in 'The Unforeseen,' 23 October 1958, SS & BH

'Klear' (60 seconds), in 'Wojeck' rerun, summer 1967, by PR

'Lady Sunbeam' (60 seconds), in 'The Untouchables,' 20 November 1962, by MO & PR

'Lux Liquid' (60 seconds), in 'The Unforeseen,' 23 October 1958, by SS & BH

'Lux Liquid Detergent' (60 seconds), in 'Front Page Challenge,' 16 January 1962, by SS & BH

'Lux Soap' (60 seconds), in *'The Unforeseen,'* 23 October 1958, by SS and BH

'Lysol' (30 seconds), in 'Wojeck' rerun, summer 1967, by PR

'Max Factor Cream Puff Compact Make-Up' (60 seconds), in 'The Wayne and Shuster Hour,' 11 March 1962, by SS, BH, & PR

'Max Factor Nail Polish' (60 seconds), in 'The Wayne and Shuster Hour,' 11 March 1962, by SS, BH, & PR

'Nabisco Shredded Wheat' (30 seconds), in 'Holiday Ranch,' 28 September 1957, by SS & BH

'Newfoundland' (120 minutes), in 'CBC Television Theatre,' 28 October 1956, by SS, BH, and PR

'Off' (30 seconds) in 'Wojeck' rerun, summer 1967, by PR

'Parker Pen' (60 seconds) in 'Wyatt Earp,' 6 October 1958, by MO

'Philishave Speed Shaver' (30 seconds), in 'Cross-Canada Hit Parade,' 10 November 1958, by SS & BH

'Raid Weed Killer & Rose Garden Spray' (60 seconds), in 'Le pain du jour,' October 1963, by SB

'Renault' (30 seconds), in 'Les Couche-tard,' 14 May 1965, by SB & PL

'Revlon' (30 seconds), in 'The $64,000 Question,' 20 September 1955, by PR

'Richard Hudnut' (30 seconds), in 'Les Couche-tard,' 14 May 1965, by SB & PL

'Super Shell Gasoline' (30 seconds), in 'Les Couche-tard,' 14 May 1965, by SB & PL

'Timex' #1 & #2 (60 seconds and 30 seconds), in 'The Wayne and Shuster Hour,' 11 March 1962, by SS, BH, & PR

'Touch & Glow Make-Up' (95 seconds), in 'The $64,000 Question,' 20 September 1955, by PR

'Vancouver & Victoria' (120 seconds), in 'CBC Television Theatre,' 28 October 1956, by SS, BH, & PR

'Westinghouse' (50 seconds), in 'Studio One,' 9 April 1956, by MO & PR

'Westinghouse Laundromat' (120 seconds), in 'Studio One,' 9 April 1956, by MO & PR

'Yard Raid' (30 seconds), in 'Wojeck' rerun, summer 1967, by PR

'Yuban' (30 seconds), in 'Les Couche-tard,' 14 May 1965, by SB & PL

Index